lonely planet

Georgia & the Carolinas

Amy C Balfour, Jade Bremner, Ashley Harrell, MaSovaida Morgan, Kevin Raub, Regis St Louis, Greg Ward

PLAN YOUR TRIP

BOB POOL/SHUTTERSTOCK ©

OKEFENOKEE SWAMP P158

ESB PROFESSIONAL/SHUTTERSTOCK ©

GEORGIA STATE CAPITOL BUILDING P49

ON THE ROAD

Contents

COVID-19

We have re-checked every business in this book before publication to ensure that it is still open after the COVID-19 outbreak. However, the economic and social impacts of COVID-19 will continue to be felt long after the outbreak has been contained, and many businesses, services and events referenced in this guide may experience ongoing restrictions. Some businesses may be temporarily closed, have changed their opening hours and services, or require bookings; some unfortunately could have closed permanently. We suggest you check with venues before visiting for the latest information.

UNDERSTAND

SURVIVAL GUIDE

SPECIAL FEATURES

Right: Newfound Gap Road, Great Smoky Mountains National Park (p315)

JIM SCHWABEL/SHUTTERSTOCK ©

WELCOME TO

Georgia & the Carolinas

Some of my fondest childhood memories involve trips to this enchanting swath of the South – shelling on Hunting Island, canoeing through cypress swamps in Congaree National Park and wide-eyed bear encounters in the Great Smoky Mountains. Years later, I find these wondrous settings have lost none of their magic. Of course nature is only one – admittedly significant – draw to this trio of states. There's also the great food scene (fresh-off-the-boat seafood in Charleston, multiethnic food markets in Atlanta), arts-loving neighborhoods, disarming southern charm, and those astonishing discoveries (pirate ghosts on Ocracoke, wild horses on Cumberland) that make for unforgettable days of travel.

@regisstlouis regisstlouis

For more about our writers, see p384

Georgia & the Carolinas

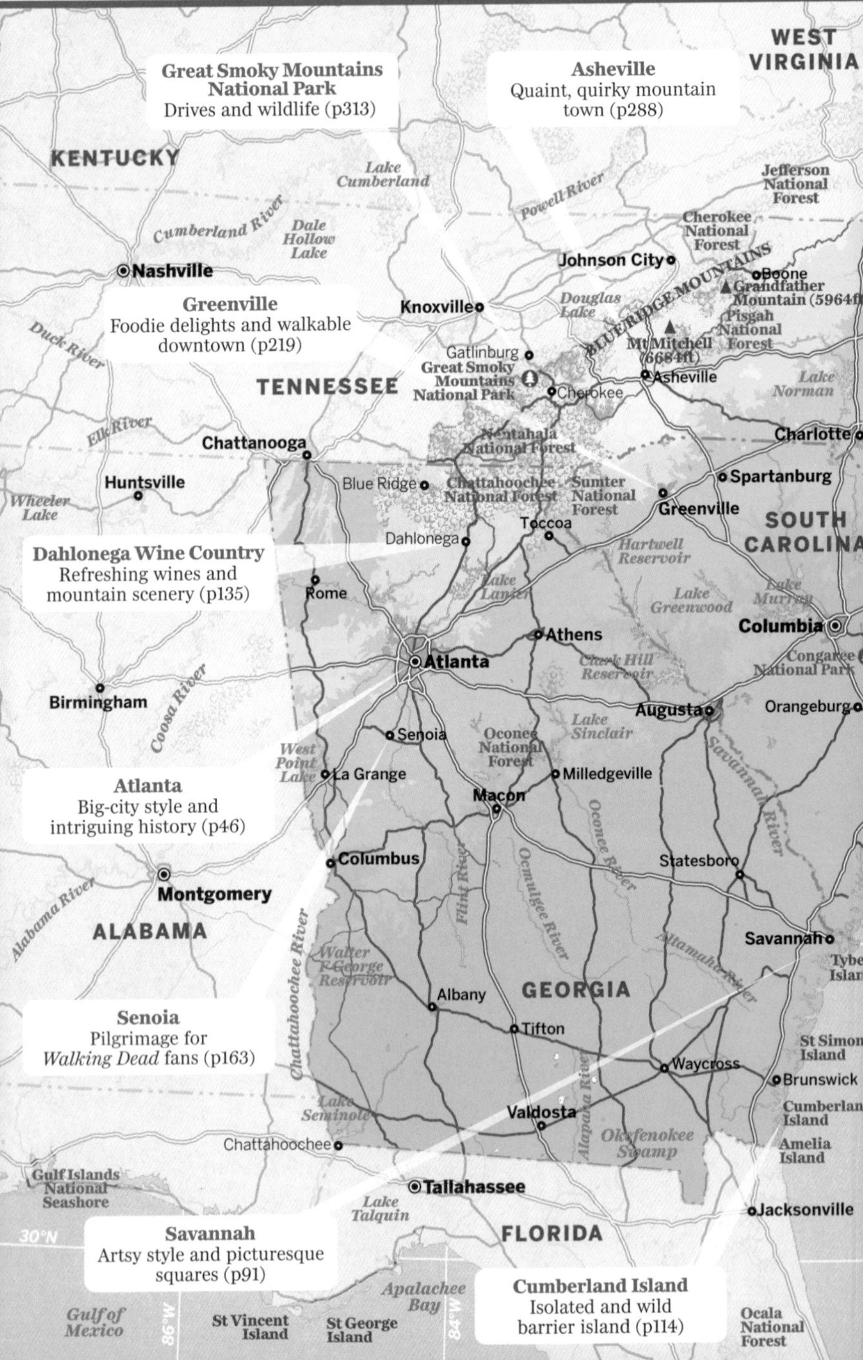

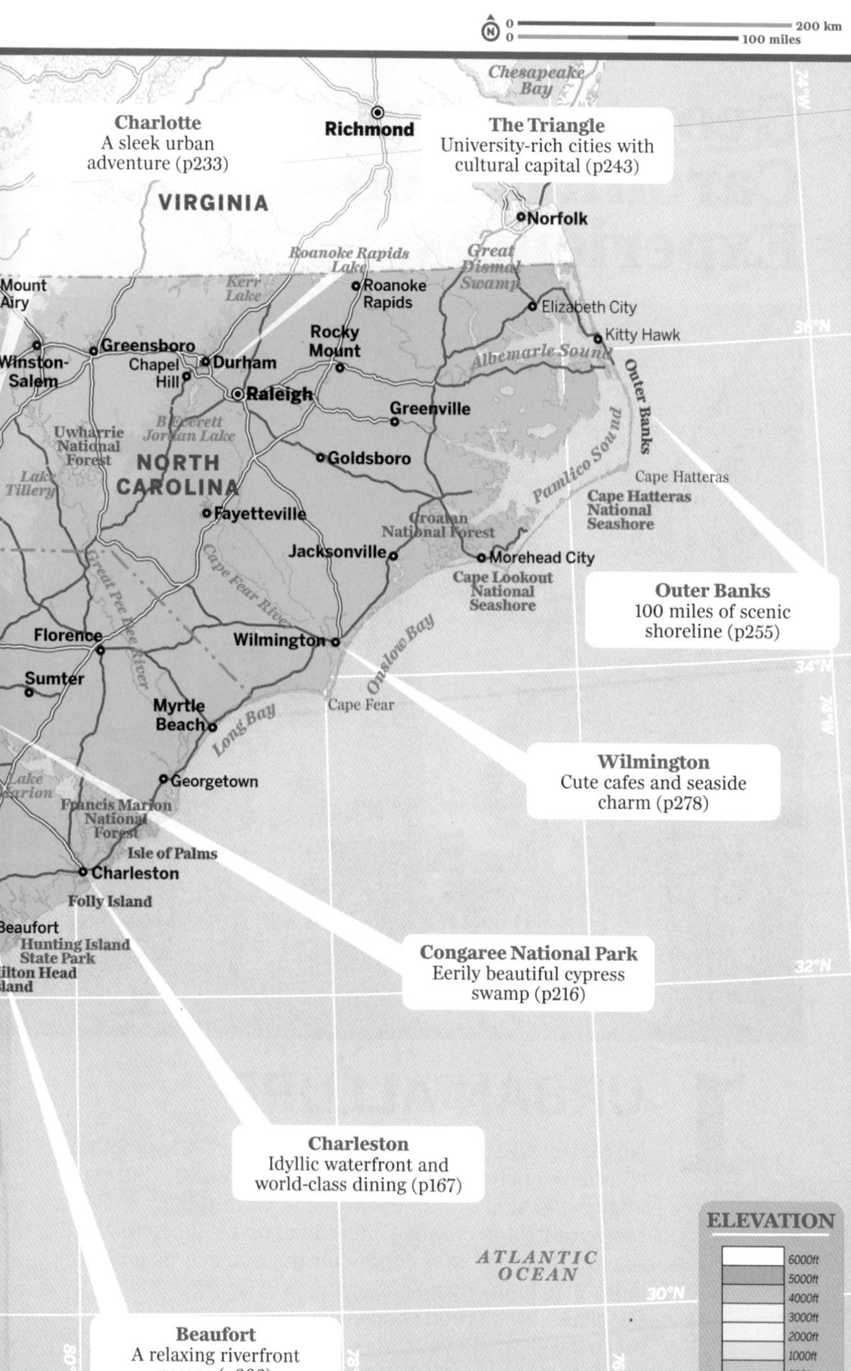

0
200 km
0
100 miles
Charlotte
A sleek urban adventure (p233)
The Triangle
University-rich cities with cultural capital (p243)
Outer Banks
100 miles of scenic shoreline (p255)
Wilmington
Cute cafes and seaside charm (p278)
Congaree National Park
Eerily beautiful cypress swamp (p216)
Charleston
Idyllic waterfront and world-class dining (p167)
Beaufort
A relaxing riverfront escape (p203)
Chesapeake Bay
Richmond
VIRGINIA
Norfolk
Roanoke Rapids Lake
Kerr Lake
Great Dismal Swamp
Mount Airy
Roanoke Rapids
Elizabeth City
Kitty Hawk
Winston-Salem
Greensboro
Chapel Hill
Durham
Rocky Mount
Albemarle Sound
Outer Banks
Raleigh
Greenville
B Everett Jordan Lake
Uwharrie National Forest
NORTH CAROLINA
Goldsboro
Pamlico Sound
Lake Tillery
Cape Hatteras
Cape Hatteras National Seashore
Fayetteville
Croatan National Forest
Jacksonville
Morehead City
Cape Lookout National Seashore
Cape Fear River
Great Pee Dee River
Florence
Wilmington
Onslow Bay
Sumter
Myrtle Beach
Long Bay
Cape Fear
Lake Marion
Georgetown
Francis Marion National Forest
Isle of Palms
Charleston
Folly Island
Beaufort
Hunting Island State Park
ilton Head
sland
ATLANTIC OCEAN
ELEVATION
6000ft
5000ft
4000ft
3000ft
2000ft
1000ft
500ft
0
36°N
34°N
32°N
30°N
74°W
76°W
78°W
80°W

Georgia & the Carolinas' Top Experiences

1 URBAN ALLURE

No matter when you travel, you're sure to find something simmering in the South's most dynamic cities. Cutting-edge art exhibitions, chef-owned farm-to-table restaurants and creative cocktail dens are just a few reasons to chart your course for the boulevards and back lanes of arts-loving neighborhoods in Georgia and the Carolinas. New green spaces and revitalized districts make it well worth your while even if you've been before.

Above: St Michael's Church (p170), Charleston

ESB PROFESSIONAL/SHUTTERSTOCK ©

Atlanta

Georgia's culturally rich and multifaceted capital illustrates the dual nature of today's South: it's a bastion of African American pride, a hip-hop hotbed, a film and tech industry upstart and LGBTIQ+ epicenter that's also steeped in Old South wealth and Fortune 500 investment. p48

EQROY/SHUTTERSTOCK ©

SEAN PAVONE/GETTY IMAGES ©

The Triangle

Made up of Raleigh, Durham and Chapel Hill, North Carolina's 'Triangle' contains three of America's most gorgeous university campuses: Duke (pictured above), the University of North Carolina and NC State. It's also a buzzing culture capital with a thriving entertainment and music scene. p243

Savannah

Georgia's oldest city boasts eye-catching architecture and thriving arts – plus an iconoclastic streak a mile long. People-watch in the live-oak-shaded squares or rifle through treasure-filled antiques shops, then fill your belly with Southern seafood dishes straight from the sea. p91

2 INTO THE WOODS

It's easy to reconnect with nature along the forested slopes of the Appalachian mountains. Fern-lined trails wind past gurgling streams and old-growth poplars up to lofty lookouts with a panoramic sweep of wilderness-covered horizon. Hiking and camping immerse you in the region's natural wonders, though you can also plot scenic drives, picnic by thundering waterfalls or just bunk for the night in a cabin, with wildlife watching right outside your door.

Great Smoky Mountains

Don't miss out on the eastern USA's most magnificent park, with its myriad cascades and jaw-dropping viewpoints, such as Clingmans Dome (pictured below; p316). Take a stunning scenic drive, soak in frontier history at Cades Cove or hike through miles of misty mountain trails while on the lookout for deer, birds and even black bears. p313

SEAN PAVONE/SHUTTERSTOCK ©

JULIE RUBACHA/SHUTTERSTOCK ©

ALI MAJDFAR/GETTY IMAGES ©

Amicalola Falls State Park

Georgia's highest waterfall (pictured above left) is also a link to the southern end of the legendary Appalachian Trail, which continues for more than nearly 2000 miles all the way to Maine. Come in the spring for mountain laurel, dogwood and azaleas, or in the fall for blazing autumn colors. p138

Providence Canyon

Explore Georgia's 'Little Grand Canyon' and wander the multihued gullies as deep as 150ft (pictured above). From the rim, you'll have views over exquisite rock formations, some of which were formed over 60 million years ago. p158

3 SOUTHERN CHARM

The best places to discover the soul of the South are in the small towns found all across Georgia and the Carolinas. In diverse communities, you'll hear the region's colorful accents, and often be left speechless at the utter politeness that locals sprinkle liberally in their interactions. Small-town pride runs deep, and you needn't limit your travels to the city to discover one-of-a-kind museums, creative craft-makers and innovative eateries.

Above: Cuthbert House Inn (p206), Beaufort

DEBORAH MCCAGUE/SHUTTERSTOCK ©

NOLICHUCKYJAKE/SHUTTERSTOCK ©

KEVIN RUCK/SHUTTERSTOCK ©

Beaufort

It's easy to lose yourself in this small, well-preserved Southern town that's fit for the silver screen. The charming streets are lined with gorgeous antebellum homes, restored 18th-century mansions and Spanish-moss-covered magnolias, and the riverfront brims with colorful cafes and shops. p203

Greenville

Stroll the Liberty Bridge over the cascades of Falls Park in Greenville (pictured above), and it's hard not to feel a crackle of good energy. The picturesque downtown and mountainous backyard are big draws, as is Greenville's celebrated local dining and drinking scene. p219

Asheville

Perhaps North Carolina's prettiest mountain town, Asheville (pictured above top) charms with its quaint and quirky 1930s downtown, established craft beer culture and easy access to some of the state's best outdoor adventures. The Biltmore Estate is a key draw with house tours, wine tasting and strolls around acres of manicured grounds. p288

4 IDYLLIC ISLANDS

Amid hundreds of miles of captivating shorelines, you'll find deserted islands, enchanting coastal towns and some of America's loveliest beaches, with a fair mix of historical attractions (including one well-known spot where two famous brothers first took flight). Wherever you roam, it's hard not to feel like you've left the modern world behind as you head out to a place where nature rules supreme in a salt-tinged realm of sea, sand and sky.

IOFOTO/SHUTTERSTOCK ©

DAVID LOUIS ECONOPOULY/SHUTTERSTOCK ©

Cumberland Island

This thoroughly wild barrier island off the coast of Georgia (pictured above top) harbors more than 36,000 acres of marshland, mud flats and tidal creeks, plus dune-swept beaches. You can pitch a tent at a forest campsite or sleep in luxury at the Greyfield Inn. p114

Outer Banks

On North Carolina's underdeveloped shoreline (pictured above left), you can spy Spanish mustangs thundering through the surf on Corolla, explore the history of flight at Kitty Hawk, and look for the ghost of Blackbeard who met his bitter end on isolated Ocracoke Island. p255

Hilton Head Island

Some call Hilton Head (pictured above) the Hamptons of the South, with its elegant waterfront homes, golf courses and high-end eateries. But it is also an eco-destination, where you can bike through woodlands, boat with resident bottlenose dolphins, and relax on 12 miles of beaches. p197

5 REMEMBERING THE PAST

SFRAMEPHOTO/GETTY IMAGES ©

ENRICO DELLA PIETRA/SHUTTERSTOCK ©

The Trail of Tears, Revolutionary War battles, Sherman's March to the Sea, the first airplane flight and the continuing struggle for Civil Rights – Georgia and the Carolinas have seen some of the country's most tragic and triumphant moments. Pay homage to heroes and delve into the complexities of the past at the region's many museums and historical sights, and ponder the way the past has influenced the present.

Martin Luther King Jr National Historic Site

A giant of the Civil Rights movement, Martin Luther King Jr was born and raised in Atlanta's Sweet Auburn neighborhood, and the places where he lived, prayed, preached, and is laid to rest (pictured left) serve as powerful inspiration to visitors from across the globe. p49

Museum of the Cherokee Indian

On the edge of the Great Smoky Mountains, this fascinating museum lets the Cherokee tell their own story, covering myths, culture and history. p302

Fort Sumter

Out on this artificial island where the first shots of the Civil War rang out (pictured left), you'll hear moving stories about America's most devastating conflict. p172

6 UNCOMMON ADVENTURES

Georgia and the Carolinas offer seemingly limitless opportunities for adventure, and not just within the region's two outstanding national parks. Rafting world-class white-water rapids, hiking the oldest mountain range in the US, shelling on pristine beaches, diving deep into rugged canyons or exploring steamy, primordial swamps – nature beckons here, and mild winters mean that many of its lures can be enjoyed year-round. The biggest challenge is deciding where to begin.

Congaree National Park

Paddle your way along the inky-black swamp surrounded by 27,000 acres of old-growth bottomland forest (the largest contiguous stretch in the US). p216

MATTMANAGED/SHUTTERSTOCK ©

PATRICK JENNINGS/SHUTTERSTOCK ©

NATURE PICTURE LIBRARY/ALAMY STOCK PHOTO ©

US National Whitewater Center

Equal parts water park and nature enclave, this 1300-acre adventure-center just outside Charlotte has kayaking, ziplining and biking (pictured above left). You might spot an Olympic athlete in training (or be inspired to become one yourself). p237

Tsali Recreation Area

Nationally celebrated for its mountain biking, this North Carolina wonderland takes you along lakefront and up steep climbs to mountain views (pictured above). p312

7 SOUTHERN DECADENCE

With culinary roots in Europe, the Caribbean and West Africa, it's no surprise that millions of people travel here just to eat. Every region has its draw from the James Beard award–winning chefs and fine-dining fusion eateries in the big city, to the seafood shacks and BBQ joints in the countryside. Wash it all down with the South's famous sweet tea, a local craft brew or a surprisingly quaffable North Georgia wine.

Athens

In the heart of Georgia, you'll find a foodie-centric college town with farm-to-table Southern haunts, intellectual coffeehouses and wildly fun breweries and bars (pictured below). p130

Lowcountry Cuisine

No trip to the South is complete without gorging on the fresh, seafood-centric, African-influenced cuisine of the coastal lowlands. Charleston is the gateway to feasting on crab, fish, shrimp and oysters. p194

Above: Steamed oysters at Bowens Island Restaurant (p202)

PinPoint

On a leafy street in Wilmington (pictured right), this dazzling farm-to-fork eatery showcases fine local produce from land and sea in a mouth-watering menu that changes by the day. p280

8 OFFBEAT LOCALES

EXETER_ACRES/SHUTTERSTOCK ©

It's fitting that the Netflix hit *Stranger Things* was filmed in Georgia. The whimsical, the frightful and the downright bizarre are all part of the cultural landscape in this region of dark swamps and moss-covered cemeteries. From wacky roadside stops (Goats on a Roof!) to museums you didn't know you were looking for (car parts turned folk art), there are many weird and wonderful sights in Georgia and the Carolinas.

Pasaquan

The surreal imagination of one self-taught artist created this bright and sprawling expanse of buildings over a span of 30 years – folk-art aficionados shouldn't miss his fusion of pre-Columbian, African and Far Eastern designs. p163

Foxfire Museum & Heritage Center

Learn weaving, blacksmithing and other old-time skills at this hands-on museum (pictured above) that celebrates the ingenuity of Appalachian people. p146

Senoia

Fans of the *Walking Dead* can indulge their inner zombie by visiting the filming sites of the HBO drama. Don't miss the Cobb Energy Performing Arts Center (aka the CDC in Atlanta). p163

Need to Know

For more information, see Survival Guide (p365)

Currency

US dollar ($)

Language

English

Visas

Visitors from Canada, the UK, Australia, New Zealand, Japan and many EU countries do not need visas for less than 90 days, with ESTA approval. For other nations, see www.travel.state.gov or www.usa.gov/visas-and-visitors.

Money

ATMs are widespread, and credit cards are accepted almost everywhere.

Tipping

A tip is expected in most cases for a job well done.

Mobile Phones

International travelers can use local SIM cards in an unlocked smartphone or buy a cheap US phone and load it up with prepaid minutes.

Time

Eastern Standard Time (GMT/UTC minus five hours)

When to Go

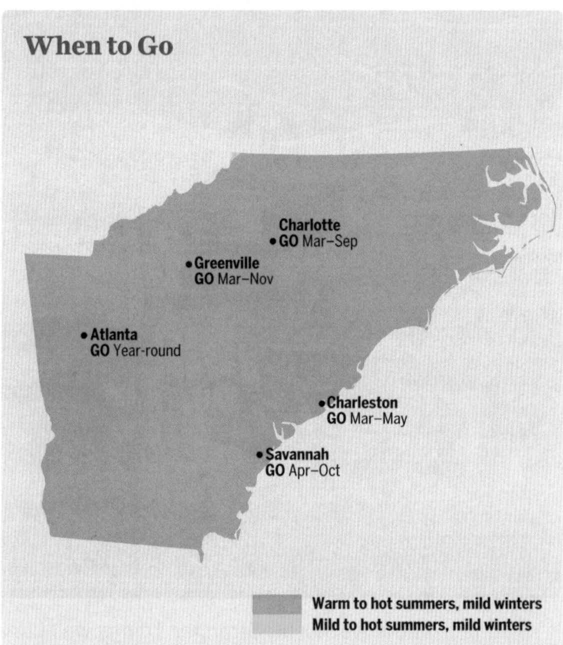

High Season

(Jun–Aug)

➡ Everyone heads to the shore or the mountains to escape the heat and humidity; expect crowds in places like Myrtle Beach and Great Smoky Mountains National Park.

Shoulder

(Mar–May & Sep–Nov)

➡ Spring is perhaps the best time to visit, with mild temperatures, beautiful blooms and fewer visitors.

➡ Fall foliage is prime time for mountain hikes and scenic drives.

Low Season

(Dec–Feb)

➡ Ice and snow can hit the mountains. Sections of the Great Smoky Mountains National Park will be closed.

Useful Websites

Lonely Planet (www.lonelyplanet.com) Destination information, hotel reviews, traveler forum and more.

Explore Georgia (www.exploregeorgia.org) Official Georgia Tourism & Travel website.

Atlanta Now (www.atlanta.net) The official bimonthly visitors guide from the Atlanta Convention & Visitors Bureau.

Visit Savannah (www.visitsavannah.com) Information on attractions, restaurants, accommodations and more.

Charleston Area Convention & Visitors Bureau (www.charlestoncvb.com) Lists hotels, dining and nightlife, itineraries, events and packages.

Important Numbers

Emergency services (fire, police, ambulance)	☎911
Local directory	☎411
Municipal offices & information	☎311

Exchange Rates

Australia	A$1	US$0.72
Canada	C$1	US$0.77
Europe	€1	US$1.16
New Zealand	NZ$1	US$0.66
UK	£1	US$1.30

For current exchange rates, see www.xe.com.

Daily Costs

Budget: Less than $100

- Campsite: $25
- Double room in budget hotel chain: $55–80
- Self-catering: $10–20
- Bicycle rentals: $25–35
- Parks and museums: $10 or less

Midrange: $100–250

- Double room in midrange hotel: $100–150
- Midrange meals: $30–50 per day
- Cheap night out: $30–60
- Car rental: $40–70

Top end: More than $250

- High-end hotel: from $200
- Top-flight meal (with tax and tip): $80 or more
- Guided tours: $30–70
- Big night out: $100 or more

Opening Hours

Standard hours are generally as follows.

Banks 9am–4pm Monday to Thursday, to 6pm Friday, some also 9am–noon Saturday

Bars 4pm–3am, from noon on Saturday

Clubs 9pm–3am

Restaurants Breakfast 6am–11am, lunch and weekend brunch 11am to around 3pm, dinner 5pm–10pm

Shops 10am to around 6pm weekdays, to around 8pm Saturday, 11am–6pm Sunday, if they're open at all

Arriving in Georgia & the Carolinas

The biggest transit hub in the region is Atlanta, though visitors may also arrive through Charlotte, Charleston or Savannah.

Hartsfield-Jackson International Airport The airport is 9.5 miles south of Downtown. You can rent a car, hop on a shared-ride van, ride the MARTA ($2.50) or take a taxi ($30) from the airport to Downtown.

Charlotte Douglas International Airport (p370) Seven miles west of Uptown, this American Airlines hub welcomes nonstop flights from Europe and the UK.

Charleston International Airport (p167) The 10-mile trip downtown is easy and fast with shuttles, taxis, buses, ridesharing and a rental-car center at your service.

Savannah/Hilton Head International Airport (p370) Rent a car, or rideshare or taxi to the Historic District for around $28. Chatham Area Transit (CAT) operates the 100X Airport Express route ($8 return) between the airport and the JMR Intermodal Transit Center.

Getting Around

Bicycle A great way to get around, especially in the flat coastal regions. Major cities have bike-share programs, and many regional tour operators and shops rent bikes.

Boat Ferries usually connect the mainland with the region's many barrier islands.

Bus Greyhound connects the region's main cities, and many of its smaller ones. Only major cities – notably Atlanta, Charlotte and Charleston – offer substative public bus transit.

Car & Motorcycle Having your own wheels is the best way to explore this expansive region. There are car-rental companies at the airports. Note that parking is often tricky in urban downtowns.

Taxi Ridesharing apps are usually cheaper and easier than taxis, although smaller towns may not have ridesharing available.

Train Amtrak connects major cities.

For much more on **getting around**, see p371

Month by Month

TOP EVENTS

Lowcountry Oyster Festival, January

Masters Tournament, April

Merlefest, April

Spoleto USA, May/June

Dragon Con, August/September

Euphoria, September

Music Midtown, September

January

Temperatures are low, especially in the mountains, where snow is possible.

Lowcountry Oyster Festival

Rain or shine, 80,000lb of bivalves will be consumed at the Lowcountry Oyster Festival at Boone Hall Plantation every January. There are also shucking and eating contests, live music, beer, local food and more beer. (p195)

Bill Murray Look-a-Like Polar Plunge

Exactly what it sounds like. On New Year's Day, some incredibly bold individuals dress like Bill Murray and jump into the freezing cold water at Folly Beach. There's also a contest for the best dressed.

February

Winter is on its way out, and temperatures start to climb (particularly in the Lowcountry). You can still find good deals on hotels, though.

Savannah Black Heritage Festival

This city-wide arts and heritage festival spans the first three weeks of Black History Month. (p100)

March

One of the wettest months of the year, but temperatures are mild and wildflowers start popping out in South Georgia and South Carolina.

National Shag Dance Championships

The longest continuously running shag dance competition in the US has been held every March in Myrtle Beach since 1984. More at www.shagnationals.com.

April

Azaleas and dogwoods are in full bloom and the climate is mild, making this month ideal for hiking, cycling, biking and golfing. Farmers markets start up in much of the region.

Masters Tournament

The sporting world focuses on golf's most prestigious professional tournament, which takes places annually at the members-only Augusta National Golf Club. (p155)

Merlefest

Set up by legendary guitarist 'Doc' Watson after his son Merle died in 1985, this four-day Wilkesboro festival (www.merlefest.org) features 'traditional plus' music across 13 stages.

Atlanta Dogwood Festival

Atlanta's native dogwood trees are admired and celebrated at the obviously named Atlanta Dogwood Festival, a full-on weekend of live music, arts and crafts, food and, of course, dogwoods. (p55)

Indie Grits Festival

Held over three days in April, the Indie Grits Festival is Columbia's answer to SXSW, celebrating art, tech, film, food, music and more around the city. (p214)

May

Everything (including prices) starts to heat up. Summer attractions such as water parks open their doors again. Bring your sun hat and bathing suit!

Atlanta Jazz Festival

For more than 40 years, the city's massive Atlanta Jazz Festival has drawn hordes to Piedmont Park over Memorial Day weekend for world-class – and free! – jazz performances from some of the genre's best known powerhouses. (p55)

Shaky Knees Music Festival

One of three music festivals under the Shaky umbrella, the Shaky Knees Music Festival draws a fiercely indie lineup to Centennial Olympic Park – think LCD Soundsystem, the XX, Band of Horses, Lumineers, Phoenix and Portugal the Man. (p55)

Gullah Festival

Held in Beaufort over Memorial Day weekend, the Gullah Festival is the states's largest celebration of the history, culture, language and accomplishments of the Lowcountry's African Americans. Expect art, music, exhibits, presentations, workshops, dance and regional cuisine. (p206)

World Famous Blue Crab Festival

Each May, the World Famous Blue Crab Festival draws 50,000 people to the Little River waterfront just north of Myrtle Beach for art, food, music and revelry. (p210)

Spoleto USA

The performing-arts extravaganza Spoleto USA takes place over 17 days in May/June in Charleston, with operas, dramas and concerts happening all over the city. It's South Carolina's largest event. (p178)

June

One of the best times to be outdoors in Georgia and the Carolinas – summer wildflowers line hiking trails and mountain river rafting waters are high.

Synchronous Fireflies

For two weeks in late May or early June each year, you can see the incredible display of Synchronous Fireflies, when thousands of fireflies blink in perfect harmony. Elkmont Campground is the best place to see it. Enter the lottery in late April to earn a spot.

July

Most of the region is a hot muggy mess in July; head for the mountains to find considerably cooler climes.

Appalachian Summer Festival

Boone owes its prestigious month-long showcase – rooted in classical music, but now extending across theater, film and the visual arts – to the presence of the dynamic Appalachian State University. (p287)

National Black Arts Festival

Considered one of the world's most important festivals celebrating art and culture of the African Diaspora, the National Black Arts Festival fills Piedmont Park to commemorate African American music, theater, literature and film. (p56)

August

August is peak tourism season, crowding cities, the beaches in the east and the mountain roads in the west. Hurricane season threatens the coast beginning this month.

Mountain Dance & Folk Festival

The oldest folk festival in the country, Asheville's three-night Mountain Dance & Folk Festival was founded by banjo and fiddle player Bascom Lamar Lansford in 1928, and remains North Carolina's premier showcase for old-time music. (p290)

BLUIZ60/SHUTTERSOCK ©

DANNY E HOOKS/SHUTTERSTOCK ©

Top Dragon Con festival parade (p55)

Bottom Masters Tournament (p155)

Decatur BBQ, Blues & Bluegrass Festival

The name says it all. What could possibly make this perfect threesome better? Brews! Decatur's big day out is a barbecue, blues and bluegrass bonanza but we're quite sure there is plenty of beer, too, making this trio of Bs boozy as well. (p55)

September

The summer heat begins a slow retreat in September, making outside festivals more pleasant, especially at higher elevations. Fall colors begin to peek out toward the end of the month.

Dragon Con

Dragon Con sees some 80,000 die-hard science-fiction, fantasy, comic-book and other fan-related fantasy-genre devotees, who take over downtown Atlanta at this internationally famous convention. (p55)

Euphoria

Euphoria is Greenville's big food and wine throw down, with four days of tastings, cooking demonstrations, wine seminars, multi-course dinners, celebrity chef sightings, live music and general revelry. (p221)

Shalom Y'all Jewish Food Festival

Jewish food and heritage festival (www.mickveisrael.org/food-fest) in Monterey Sq draws a big crowd with traditional ethnic cuisine, plus music and dancing.

Music Midtown

Atlanta's Piedmont Park is the site of yet another massive festival: Music Midtown hosts some of the biggest names in rock and pop for two days of audio overload. (p55)

October

Spectacular fall color covers the region; ospreys, falcons and other raptors migrate over the coast. It's one of the best times to get outdoors.

MOJA Arts Festival

Charleston's MOJA Arts Festival is held over the last weekend in September and a week in October, with spirited poetry readings and gospel concerts celebrating African American and Caribbean culture. (p178)

Oktoberfest

Helen's annual beer-fueled bash celebrating German music, food, drinks and dancing lures some six million attendees over weekends in September and daily in October. (p144)

Atlanta Pride Festival

An estimated 250,000 visit Piedmont Park for one of the oldest and biggest LGBTIQ+ celebrations in the USA, Atlanta Pride Festival. (p56)

November

The most budget-friendly time to visit. Cozy up in a mountain inn, or stick to shorts and a T-shirt in the South.

Greenville Craft Beer Festival

The Greenville Craft Beer Festival draws an intoxicating array of microbrewery samples from all over the South. There's also music, food and 'beer college' classes. (p228)

Telfair Art Fair

Free open-air art fair (www.telfair.org/artfair) with food trucks, music and children's activities. Preview selections at the Arty Party before the official event.

December

Things pick up again during the holidays, with a hoard of Christmas and New Year's events, and prices temporarily rise. Temperatures continue to drop.

Wrecking Bar Strong Beer Fest

Ward off the cold with high-gravity barrel-aged stouts, triple IPAs and imperial porters at the Wrecking Bar Strong Beer Fest, a small but serious beer-nerd gathering at the city's best brewpub. (p56)

Itineraries

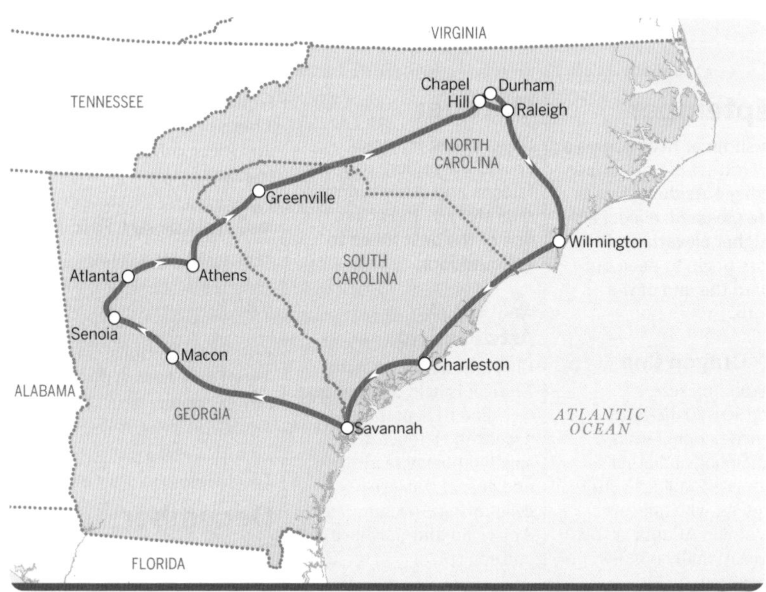

2 WEEKS Georgia & the Carolinas Highlights

You'll have to hit the ground running for this one. Start in **Atlanta** for three nights, spending two full days on the city's excellent museums and the Martin Luther King Jr National Historic Site. Take time to walk, bike or jog the Atlanta BeltLine and drink or dine along the way at spots like Krog Street Market. On day three head east through **Athens** in time for an afternoon stroll and early dinner at the outstanding Home.made from Scratch; catch some live music if you can before hopping over to **Greenville**, two hours away. Get outdoors on the Swamp Rabbit Trail or take a walk through Falls Park on the Reedy and enjoy a good meal or three before heading on to the Triangle. Pick from **Raleigh**, **Durham** or **Chapel Hill** and spend a day and night – then it's time to hit the beach. **Wilmington** is good for a relaxing day or two, or a fun night out on the riverfront. Then head south to **Charleston** for at least three days, meandering around the Historic District, visiting sights such as the Old Slave Mart Museum and the Nathaniel Russell House and, of course, hitting the city's hot dining scene. Then it's south to **Savannah** to check out the artsy vibe at places like the Jepson Center for the Arts and unwind under the Spanish moss-draped live oaks in Forsyth Park. Conclude your trip by driving back to Atlanta with a break in **Macon** or **Senoia** if time permits.

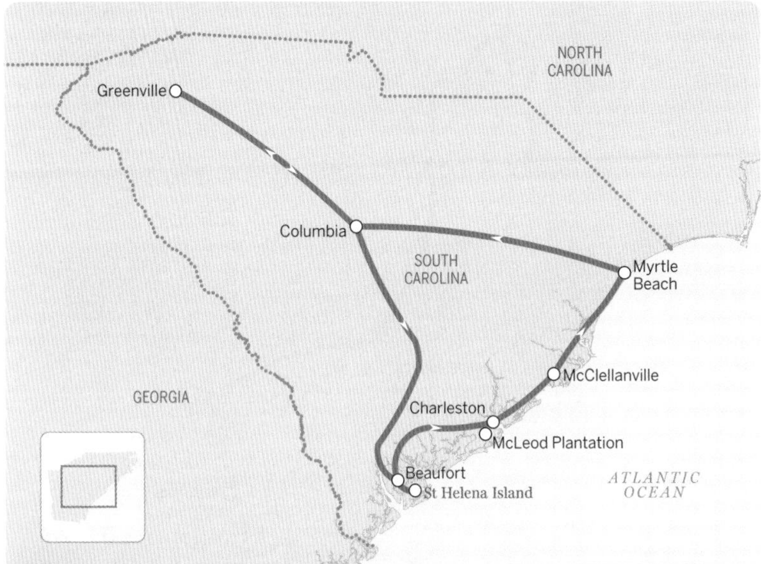

South Carolina Sampler

For those hungry for a taste of the whole dang state, including Upcountry hiking, Lowcountry adventuring, capitol crashing and even a stopover in tacky Myrtle Beach.

Begin in **Myrtle Beach**, so you can get your putt-putt and deep-fried-seafood hankerings out of the way (it only gets better from here). It's usually cheap to fly in. Base your number of nights in Myrtle on how much you love America, and continue on to the state capitol, **Columbia**, which is far more interesting than it usually gets credit for. You can tour the State House and party with college students at Five Points before continuing on to 'it city' **Greenville**.

Spend a few nights here, giving yourself time for day trips to the nearby state and national parks, which offer superb hiking. Be sure to also stroll over the stunning Liberty Bridge in Falls Park on the Reedy and take a peek at up-and-coming art galleries and locavore restaurants in West Greenville. Try a few craft beers but not so many that you can't drive back through Columbia to **Beaufort**, South Carolina's most darling little town. Spend at least two nights relaxing by the waterfront and paddleboarding out to the sandbar. On neighboring **St Helena Island**, visit the Penn Center and hop on a Gullah tour for a wonderful introduction to the Gullah people, who have fought for centuries to keep alive the customs of their enslaved ancestors brought from West Africa.

Finally, finish the trip with South Carolina's crown jewel, **Charleston**. Spend at least five days here exploring the downtown, wandering the Historic District's cobblestone and brick alleyways and admiring the meticulously preserved antebellum mansions and historic churches. Pop over to **McLeod Plantation** for an inside look at a typical Sea Island cotton plantation, which was at one time occupied by both the Confederate and Union forces, along with a federal agency that helped transition emancipated slaves.

Head back up the coast to Myrtle Beach if you've got a round-trip flight, and be sure to stop for lunch along the way at TW Graham & Co in **McClellanville** for the best fried seafood in the state.

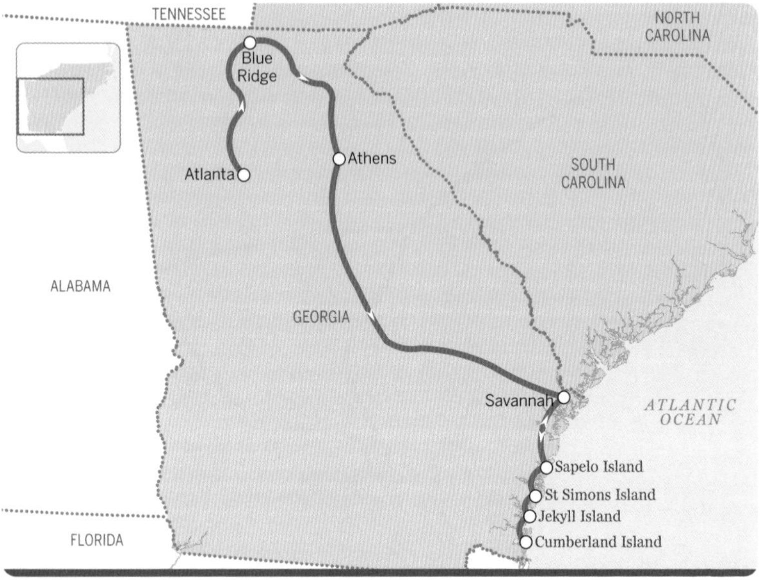

TENNESSEE
NORTH CAROLINA
Blue Ridge
Athens
Atlanta
SOUTH CAROLINA
ALABAMA
GEORGIA
Savannah
ATLANTIC OCEAN
Sapelo Island
St Simons Island
Jekyll Island
Cumberland Island
FLORIDA

The Best of Georgia

From cosmopolitan Atlanta and artsy Athens in the north to historic Savannah and the barrier islands of its pretty and protected southeastern coast – Georgia is chock-full of diverse geography and storied history. This long Atlanta to Atlanta loop will hook y'all with city, sand and Southern hospitality.

Land at the world's busiest airport in **Atlanta** and spend a few days putting a little South in your mouth in the city's top restaurants. Immerse yourself in all things MLK at the Martin Luther King Jr National Historic Site and visit the world-class museums. At night, take a stroll along the Atlanta BeltLine Eastside Trail, drinking and eating your way through its good-time breweries and restaurants. Head north from the city to the Blue Ridge Mountains and the appropriately named **Blue Ridge**, North Georgia's most charming mountain town – consider a ride on its scenic railway. You're in Appalachia, so woodland warriors might want to delay their departure to explore many of the hikes in the surrounding area.

Heading southeast, spend a day in **Athens** enjoying its bustling and bohemian downtown – take in a University of Georgia football game if you can – then make a break for the coast. First stop: **Savannah**. Wander its moss-draped public squares taking in historic museums and drool-worthy Southern food for at least two days. Just south of Savannah, Georgia's sea islands beckon. Take a culturally rich night on the Gullah-Geechee **Sapelo Island** – you must make prior arrangements and bring your own food – then head south to **St Simons Island**, the largest and most developed of the Golden Isles, full of pretty beaches and wonderful golf courses. Further south is **Jekyll Island** – the historic Jekyll Island Club Hotel was the stomping ground of Gilded Age millionaires. Continue the southern trajectory to **Cumberland Island**, home to the wild and remote Cumberland Island National Seashore. Only 300 people per day are allowed to visit, so you'll have (mostly) your own little piece of paradise here.

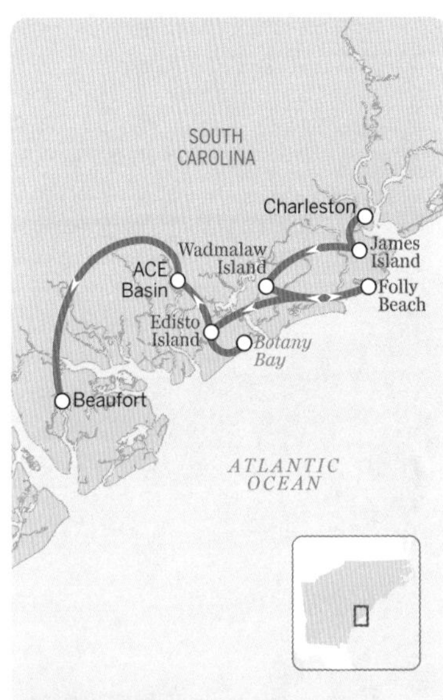

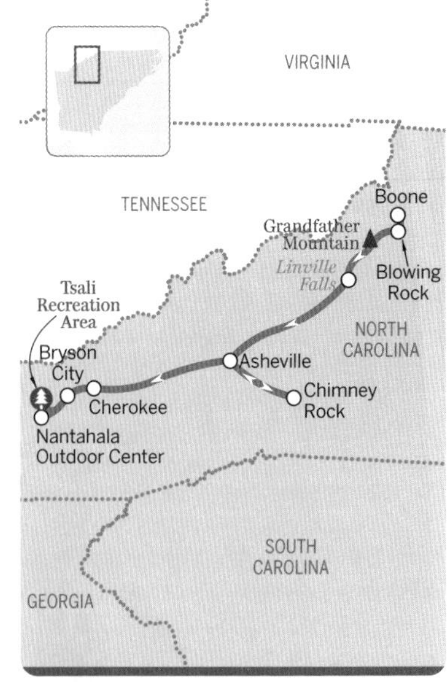

Lowcountry Cruiser

With a good set of wheels and an appreciation for seafood, history and natural beauty you'll be covered on this little trip.

Chances are you'll fly into **Charleston**. Many of the states's best experiences and restaurants are concentrated in and around the city, so spend three days visiting top sights and a couple of the plantations either on the Ashley River or over on **James Island** (hit the Charleston Tea Plantation on **Wadmalaw Island** while you're at it). Then roll over to laid-back **Folly Beach** for a night, where you can get a fabulous rental house or stay in a charming B&B right on the water.

Venture south the next day, with a stop at **Edisto Island** to explore some unadulterated coastline at **Botany Bay**. Double back and make a stop at the seductively swampy **ACE Basin** to look for whooping cranes before pressing on to **Beaufort**, South Carolina's friendliest, most delightful small town. It's sort of like a mini-Charleston, with an adorable downtown and abundant antebellum mansions in The Point neighborhood (see them by carriage). Stay two nights before retracing your steps to Charleston.

1 WEEK

Blue Ridge to the Smokies

Above all – literally – it's the magnificent mountains that make North Carolina special. To savor their full splendor, spend a week driving the Blue Ridge Parkway, hiking and biking and staying in cool college towns such as Asheville and Boone.

Start your road trip with two nights in funky **Boone**, a couple of hours' drive from either Charlotte or the Virginia state line. While in the area, hike up to the Mile High Swinging Bridge at **Grandfather Mountain**, and out to **Linville Falls**, breaking for lunch in **Blowing Rock**. Now cruise on west, and in under half a day you'll reach the mountains' 'capital,' **Asheville**. Allow a (very) good three nights to do Beer City's breweries justice, slurp up some barbecue, and swoon at the opulent Biltmore Estate, plus take a day trip south to **Chimney Rock**. Then follow the parkway west again, pausing to learn about the Trail of Tears in **Cherokee**, and a morning's drive will bring you to your final two-night stop, **Bryson City**. While there, be sure to cycle the lakeshore in the nearby **Tsali Recreation Area**, or raft at the **Nantahala Outdoor Center**, and venture into Great Smoky Mountains National Park before you head home.

Canoeing in Okefenokee Swamp National Wildlife Refuge (p15

Plan Your Trip

Outdoor Activities

With its varied terrain, mild climate and natural splendor, Georgia and the Carolinas is a outdoor lover's paradise. From strenuous hikes to pleasant nature walks, from peaceful islands to white-water rafting – there's an activity for every interest and ability thanks to the varied terrain and miles of coastline. Plus, the mild winters make it possible to get outside almost any time of year.

When to Go

April & May

The South serves up glorious spring wildflowers, mild temps and occasional rain.

June & August

Hottest months of the year – you'll want to be on the water if you're outdoors.

September & October

Fall foliage is in full splendor and temperatures are still mild. Beach days are possible on the coast and bodysurfing is at its best in the Outer Banks.

January & February

Wintry landscapes. Access to some mountain areas may be cut off.

Best Parks

Great Smoky Mountains National Park (p315) The USA's most visited park is fun for all ages.

Providence Canyon (p158) Just 30 minutes outside of Columbus, Georgia's Grand Canyon is a rainbow of otherworldly formations.

Okefenokee National Wildlife Refuge (p158) Canoe, kayak or hike around this primordial environment.

Congaree National Park (p216) Come to behold the meandering waterways of its floodplain ecosystem and its sky-high canopy.

Water Activities & Tours

Thanks to miles of coastline and wild mountain-fed rivers, Georgia and the Carolinas gives water-loving travelers plenty of chances to take a dip.

Fontana Lake (p338) Taking in a unique perspective of the Smokies from a canoe or kayak.

Amicalola Falls State Park (p138) See the Southeast's highest waterfall.

Nantahala Outdoor Center (p299) With well-trained staff and years of experience, there's no better place for family groups to share an exhilarating, and drenching, white-water baptism.

Okefenokee Adventures (p158) Feel like Indiana Jones while cruising these mysterious waterways.

WhiteWater Express (p160) The longest urban white-water rafting experience is in Columbus, with thrilling constructed rapids up to class V.

Hiking

The foothills of the Appalachians are the biggest draws for hikers, but just about every region of Georgia and the Carolinas has a walk or trail that will make you gasp.

Trail Difficulty

We've rated hikes by three levels of difficulty to help you choose the trail that's right for you.

Easy Manageable for nearly all walkers, an easy hike is less than 4 miles, with fairly even terrain and no significant elevation gain or loss.

Moderate Fine for fit hikers and active, older children, moderate hikes have a modest elevation gain – in the range of 500ft to 1000ft – and are usually less than 7 miles in length.

Hard Hikes have elevation gains of more than 1000ft, are mostly steep, may have tricky footing and are often more than 8 miles long. Being physically fit is paramount.

All hikes, from day hikes to backcountry treks, follow well-marked, established trails and, unless otherwise noted, the distance listed in each hike description is for a round-trip journey. The actual time spent hiking will vary with your ability. When in doubt, assume trails will be harder and take longer than you think.

Best Hikes

Appalachian Trail (p319) Hike a piece of the legendary trail, which travels for 71 miles across the Smokies before continuing up to Maine.

Chimney Rock Park (p300) Whether you want to enjoy an easy family hike, or prefer a more demanding backcountry trail, it's hard to beat.

Mt LeConte (p316) No matter which trail you take, it's a great achievement making it to the top.

Cumberland Island Loop (p116) There's ample opportunity to walk on the wild side on Cumberland Island – this 4-mile hike takes you through diverse landscapes.

Upcountry Foothills (p227) Whether you hike the full 76 miles or just a portion, this trail takes you through South Carolina's most beautiful backcountry.

Packing List

If you're doing multi-day or overnight hikes in Georgia and the Carolinas, consider packing some of the items below.

Clothing

➡ Hiking boots with sturdy soles and good ankle support

➡ Wide-brimmed hat in the summer

➡ Fleece or sweater, plus long underwear (merino wool or synthetic)

➡ Lightweight trousers

➡ Waterproof jacket and pants

➡ Warm hat, scarf and gloves in the winter

➡ Gaiters or spare shoes (river sandals) for over-the-ankle creek crossings

➡ Moisture-wicking socks

Equipment

➡ Water bottle and reservoir (such as a Camelbak)

➡ Water filtration system ump or chemical disinfectants)

➡ Trail map and compass

➡ Pocket knife

➡ Safety mirror and whistle to attract attention in emergencies

➡ Walking stick or trekking poles

➡ Sunscreen and lip balm

➡ DEET insect repellent

➡ Backpack with a rain cover

➡ First-aid kit

➡ Crampons (for winter hiking)

➡ High-energy food and snacks

➡ LED headlamp and flashlight with spare batteries

➡ Survival bag or blanket

Overnight Hikes

➡ Sleeping bag and sleeping mat

➡ Lightweight tent, tarp and rain fly

➡ Garbage bags for protecting suspended food bag in the rain

➡ Toilet paper, trowel and sealable plastic bags for packing out trash – note that human waste must be disposed of at least 100 feet from any campsite

➡ Biodegradable soap, toiletries and towel

➡ Cooking, eating and drinking utensils, including a stove, fuel and dehydrated food

➡ Matches and lighter

Optional Gear

➡ Binoculars

➡ Camera and/or cell (mobile) phone plus a portable power supply (such as a solar charger)

➡ GPS receiver and/or altimeter

Beaches

With some 600 miles of coastline, you'll find plenty of chances to chill out with an ocean view in Georgia and the Carolinas.

Ocracoke Beach (p269) Dolphins are frequently spotted on this long, glorious beach.

Kiawah Beachwater Park (p201) An idyllic stretch of sand on this 10-mile barrier island.

Cumberland Island National Seashore (p114) You're likely to have the 17 miles of sandy beach to yourself on this natural paradise.

Cape Hatteras National Seashore (p255) A 70-mile network of interlinked, undeveloped islets, laced through with woods, dunes, marshes and beaches.

North Beach (p91) This peaceful portion of Tybee Island is a great place to relax.

Great Smoky Mountains National Park

The biggest draw for outdoor adventurers in Georgia and the Carolinas is, of course, Great Smoky Mountains National Park. The most visited national park in the USA draws some 11 million visitors annually to its miles of trails, scenic drives and historic areas including Cades Cove. If you're heading to the park, here are a few useful tips.

What to Wear

Take time to plan your clothing well before you hit the road. Don't wait until the last minute to realize that your waterproof jacket isn't warm enough, or that you need a new pair of hiking boots and won't have time to break them in. The main things to keep in mind when planning your wardrobe are to choose garments that are moisture-wicking, breathable, waterproof (and windproof), insulating and, of course, comfortable.

You'll need to strategize carefully, especially if you plan to camp in the backcountry. First-time visitors are often surprised by the weather, which can get quite cold at higher elevations, particularly if the rains arrive. Spring comes late to the mountains, and nighttime temperatures can dip below freezing even in April. At higher elevations snow is possible from November to April, and rain falls year-round – not surprising for a region that receives 55 to 85 inches of rain per year. Come prepared for dramatic shifts in weather regardless of the season.

Best Day Hikes in the Great Smoky Mountains National Park

The Great Smoky Mountains offers some fabulous day hikes. These range from short and flat riverside jaunts to challenging hikes to craggy overlooks with jaw-dropping views. Wherever you go it's best to set out early, as you'll beat the worst of the crowds, and have the best opportunities for wildlife-watching.

Alum Cave Bluffs (p328), Great Smoky Mountains National Park

Alum Cave Bluffs (p328) A fantastic walk crossing log bridges, spying old-growth forest and enjoying fine views.

Laurel Falls Trail (p319) An easy, paved 2.6-mile trek to one of the park's most popular waterfalls.

Anthony Creek Trail (p332) This kid-friendly trail is an easy ramble, and a connector to the Appalachian Trail.

Sugarlands Valley Nature Trail (p320) The only fully wheelchair-accessible trail in the park takes you past the rushing Little Pigeon River.

Kephart Prong Trail (p316) Get a taste of history (and a glimpse of wildflowers) on this 4.2-mile hike.

Rough Fork Trail to Woody Place (p335) This 2-mile hike has several fun creek crossings and is suitable for families with younger kids.

Andrews Bald (p319) Spectacular views await from this high-elevation grassy meadow near Clingmans Dome.

Pulled pork barbecue sandwi

Plan Your Trip

Eat & Drink Like a Local

Along the coast, Lowcountry fare, a historically significant, African-influenced cuisine spawned from the shrimp, crab and crawfish-rich coastal estuaries, dominates dining. Fried chicken, fried green tomatoes and Southern side dishes line steaming lunch buffets or fill the tables at traditional 'meat and three' lunch spots. Charleston has a place on every foodie's bucket list, but farm-to-table offerings excel from Athens to Greenville – and there's a whole lot of BBQ too.

Year in Food

While the eatin' is good year-round in Georgia and the Carolinas, there are particular peaks for fresh produce and the local seafood industry.

March–April

In March, the Food & Wine Festival (p178) in Charleston is a gastronomic throw-down. Local farmers markets start in April, and kick off with everything from squash to zucchini to sweet peas. Late spring is for soft-shell crabs.

May–August

Harvesttime for beloved local produce such as Georgia peaches, field peas and okra, plus many other fresh seasonal favorites.

Mid-June

Shrimp are at their biggest and most bountiful along the coast, staying readily available until the season comes to a close on December 31.

September–November

It's food and wine festival season, with events taking place almost every weekend. Greenville's Euphoria (p221) is a highlight. Oyster season kicks off.

Local Specialties

Carolina Barbecue

The only common denominator on barbecue in Georgia and the Carolinas is this: it's gotta be pig. Yes, your typical barbecue restaurant may also offer chicken and beef, but by their pulled pork ye shall know them.

South Carolina's tangy mustard-based sauce, dubbed 'Carolina Gold,' is found mainly in the central part of the state and was influenced by the region's large number of German immigrants.

Eastern-style barbecue, prevalent near the coast of North Carolina and going down into South Carolina, cooks the whole of the hog, then chops the shredded meat up together, with local variations as to whether the crisped-up skin goes into the mix as well. It's then served with a thin sauce, which, at its most basic, consists solely of vinegar and pepper; some North Carolina chefs throw in a dash of locally made Texas Pete hot sauce too.

Western-style barbecue takes over as you head into the Piedmont, and logically enough is also known as Piedmont style. Here they only cook the dark meat of the pig – usually just the shoulder, but perhaps the butt as well – and they serve it with a sweeter sauce that's made with tomatoes or, commonly, ketchup. This style is prevalent throughout Georgia as well.

Lexington-style barbecue is, depending on who you talk to, either a subtly different take on, or the apotheosis of, Western style. Either way, the small town of Lexington, 20 miles south of Winston-Salem, is considered to be the capital of North Carolina barbecue, and it inspired the 'light' tomato sauces you'll find in nearby parts of South Carolina. October's one-day Lexington Barbecue Festival (www.barbecuefestival.com) attracts more than 100,000 aficionados each year.

Lowcountry Shrimp & Grits

Shrimp and grits is a culinary mainstay all over the Southeastern US, and occasionally even shows up on Southern-inspired menus further afield. It may be claimed as an emblematic dish of the greater South, but its origins stem specifically from the Lowcountry region of South Carolina and Georgia.

While there are tons of takes on seasoning, the quintessential preparation features sautéed, wild-caught local shrimp atop a bed of creamy, stone-ground grits. The beloved, rib-stickin' staple can be enjoyed for any meal, though it was traditionally taken by coastal fishers at breakfast to fuel the pursuit of the day's catch.

Gullah-Geechee history indicates that this meal was consumed by their slave ancestors, who would receive food allowances that included grits.

Maximizing nearby coastal food resources, they would catch seafood in local creeks and prepare them in myriad ways, including with grits.

Developed by the Creek indigenous peoples of the Southeastern Woodlands, grits are a thick porridge of boiled, milled corn – think of it as Italian polenta's American cousin. When it comes to this dish's grits (and in general, really), the more butter and cream, the better. Some chefs add cheeses such as Gouda, goat or Gruyère to scale up the sinfully delicious flavor.

With shrimp and grits, presentation is as important as taste. The dish is typically topped with crumbles of smoky, thick-cut bacon and finished with chopped scallion or parsley, and diced tomato or red-bell pepper for color.

Soul Food & the African American Diaspora

When it comes to perceptions of cuisine from this part of the country, the distinction between what's known as 'Southern' food and 'soul' food can be blurry. While all soul food is Southern food, not all Southern food is soul – the roots of the latter stem from what was developed by African slaves in the Southeastern United States as they made do with whatever was available to them. As their descendants migrated north and west during the postslavery era, they carried the traditional recipes of their forebears with them.

This diaspora brought about what is known today as soul food, a true American immigrant cuisine – in black communities outside the South, it's a celebration of down-home, rural roots, with traditional dishes being served usually only during special occasions. Typical ones include fried chicken and fish, ham hocks, oxtails, chitlins, pigs' feet, hush puppies and greens (collard, mustard or turnip). These parallel with a lot of Southern foods, though the soul variety is often fattier, saltier and spicier.

Traditionally, soul food wasn't as calorically offensive as we find it today. Its antebellum beginnings were based on seasonally available, organic (before the need for such a term was even a thing) produce, and meat was only used to add flavor to the vegetables. If meat was consumed, it was typically baked or boiled – frying was reserved only for celebratory occasions. Processed ingredients such as refined flour, sugar and butter were only incorporated on the rare chance they could be obtained. In fact, with such a reliance on dark leafy greens, legumes, root vegetables and seafood, many of today's health fads and diet trends closely resemble early soul-food fare.

Pecan pie

FROM NORTH CAROLINA, WITH LOVE

Flavorful gifts North Carolina has given to the world include Krispy Kreme doughnuts, which first emerged from the fryer in Winston-Salem in 1937; Mount Olive Pickles, which started out in Mount Olive, NC, in 1926; and Pepsi, invented in New Bern in 1896 and originally promoted with the slogan 'The Taste Born in the Carolinas.'

Pimento cheese sandwich

Fried Green Tomatoes

You may have heard of fried green tomatoes thanks to the 1991 film of the same name, which was shot in Atlanta and environs (though set in Alabama) and nominated for two Academy Awards. If you're traveling through Georgia and the Carolinas, you'll see this dish pop up on menus just about everywhere. From its most basic recipe (unripe or green tomatoes coated with cornmeal and fried), you'll stumble across hundreds of adaptations in every hole-in-the-wall dive and top-end restaurant throughout the city. If the chance to order a fried green tomato BLT comes your way, seize it.

Pimento Cheese

Traditionally served as a spread but awesome on burgers and sandwiches, too, this quintessential Southern dish is made with sharp cheddar cheese, mayonnaise and pimentos, blended into a chunky paste with a variety of add-ins such as cream cheese, Louisiana-style hot sauce, Worcestershire sauce, cayenne pepper, paprika, jalapeños and more. It is not to be ridiculed and not to be missed.

Sweet Treats

There's nothing more Georgian than pecan pie and if you haven't had the state's world-famous pecans in a pie with sugar, butter, eggs, vanilla extract and karo syrup, you haven't lived! And don't forget the peaches. They're most famously associated with Georgia, but South Carolina actually grows more of them. Peach pie or cobbler is a can't-miss ending to a Southern meal. Other Southern staples you'll see on dessert menus include chess pie (flour or cornmeal, butter, sugar and eggs with flavorings such as vanilla, chocolate, lemon and buttermilk) and sweet-potato pie (mashed sweet potatoes with nutmeg and cinnamon along with sugar, eggs, milk and butter).

Leon's Poultry & Oyster Shop (p181)

How to Eat & Drink

When to Eat

Breakfast, lunch and dinner (aka supper) are still the day's three main meals in Georgia and the Carolinas, though on weekends, a noon brunch has edged out both breakfast and lunch to become everybody's favorite meal.

Breakfast and brunch tend to be large meals heavy on carbs – expect heaping portions of biscuits, chicken 'n' waffles, grits and pancakes. The main difference is that breakfast happens earlier than brunch, but menu items tend to look similar.

Lunch is a midday affair, and can be anything from a to-go sandwich to a three-course extravaganza at an upscale restaurant – though, it's probably the least important meal of a Southerner's day.

Dinner (or supper), is often a social affair, either with family and friends in the home or out on the town. In a true Southern household, many dinners will involve 'meat and three,' which is essentially a main meat and three sides. Supper used to be taken around 3pm, but these days people eat it between 6pm and 8pm.

Where to Eat

Cafes Usually smaller establishments that serves coffee and tea along with some baked goods or pre-made sandwiches.

Food trucks Kitchens on wheels, parked anywhere that hungry pedestrians frequent. Orders are taken through a window and you can linger and eat nearby or take it to go.

Seafood shacks These places tend to be holes-in-the-wall made almost entirely of wood, often-times near the sea. They serve mostly fried food of varying quality.

Breweries In most cases, craft breweries are big on offering at least a few snacks to pair with your brew.

Restaurants Sit-down places where somebody takes your order and then brings the food.

Experimental food courts Try out a range of cuisines at places like Workshop (p182) in Charleston, 7th Street Public Market (p239) in Charlotte and Krog Street Market (p64) or Sweet Auburn Curb Market (p61) in Atlanta.

Menu Decoder

Small plates Bigger than an appetizer but smaller than a main dish, these tapas-style dishes are often intended for sharing.

À la carte Choose anything you like from the menu; sides often must be ordered in addition to main dishes.

For the table A very large portion of food, meant to be served family-style.

Tasting menu A series of small plates chosen by the chef; often the whole table must agree to participate in the tasting menu.

Meat and three A choose-your-own-adventure restaurant where one meat and three sides are a fixed price.

Food Experiences

Cheap Treats

Boiled peanuts Green, unripened peanuts boiled in super-salty water over an open fire, most often found on the side of backcountry highways – look for the handmade, roadside signs and pull over to pick up a sack.

Oysters Saddle up to restaurant raw bars downtown and on the islands and devour the delicious bivalves baked, raw, steamed or fried.

Buttermilk biscuits Whether smothered in peppered sausage gravy, smeared with honey or jam, or adorned with a lump crab cake (Narobia's Grits & Gravy (p107) does them best), these billowy bits of buttery bliss always hit the spot.

Meals of a Lifetime

FIG (p182) Charleston's longtime foodie favorite remains one of the country's best.

Wyld (p106) Marsh-side local hangout serving modern, seafood-leaning dishes.

Fox Brothers (p65) Texas-influenced Georgia BBQ whose brisket and pulled pork will floor you.

Gunshow (p66) Kevin Gillespie's unorthodox, dim-sum-style New American hot spot.

PinPoint (p280) An award-winning New Southern restaurant in charming Wilmington.

Mateo (p250) Stunning Southern-style tapas in Durham.

Edmund's Oast (p182) This outstanding gastropub is always packed.

Jianna (p229) Michael Kramer's rustic Italian cuisine is matched by the restaurant's top-notch atmosphere.

Dare to Try

Live blue crab Crack into these crustaceans and get wrist deep in messy innards as you pick for bits of sweet meat. Local fresh seafood markets sell 'em by the dozen and will steam them for you on the spot.

Chitterlings Always pronounced 'chitlins,' the small intestines of a pig (and sometimes cow) are chopped up, boiled down, salted and splashed with vinegar or hot sauce. While they aren't the easiest to find, you can get them at some black-owned soul-food joints on Savannah's west side. Love 'em or hate 'em, ain't no in-between.

Pigs' feet Pickled, stewed, smoked, salted or boiled, gelatinous porky peds were a staple among older generations in the South. They're increasingly difficult to find in restaurants, but you might see them as a daily special at soul-food spots. If you're really curious, pick up a jar of the pickled variety in smaller, locally owned grocery stores.

Best Cheap Eats

Vandy's (p165) Cruise into this restaurant in Georgia, one of the few remaining to cook over an open BBQ pit.

Sunbury Crab Company (p114) Crack open delectable blue crab on the bayou at this rustic restaurant.

Taqueria del Sol (p70) Outstanding tacos, chowder and enchiladas for less than $10.

Sisters of the New South (p103) Superb soul food in a casual, come-as-you-are setting.

Juanita Greenberg's Nacho Royale (p183) Charleston locals go nuts for the nachos at this affordable local hangout.

Waffle House (p71) Not indulging in drunken 2am eats at Atlanta's quintessential greasy spoon is a sin indeed – look for them throughout the region.

Price's Chicken Coop (p239) Is this the best fried chicken in America? Only one way to find out.

Leon's Oyster Shop (p181) This converted body shop is one of the best places to eat off a hangover.

Plan Your Trip

Travel with Children

With so many opportunities to get outdoors and easy accessibility by car, Georgia and the Carolinas is an ideal destination for families. The region's rich history offers educational options as well.

Best Regions for Kids

Great Smoky Mountains

The Smoky Mountains can be a wonderland for small travelers. There are adventures aplenty, with mesmerizing wildflower-filled hikes, horseback rides, rafting trips and star-filled nights around the campfire.

Greenville

Big-city transplant families are flocking to Greenville. Downtown is walkable, with the even, clean sidewalks featuring whimsical quotes. Kids will also get a kick out of Mice on Main (p221), a find-the-bronze-mice scavenger hunt.

Atlanta

Atlanta knows how to keep children entertained, delighted and educated. Many of the city's top attractions are both kid- and adult-friendly (bonus!).

Asheville

Asheville is a family-friendly destination, bursting with opportunities for kids. The surrounding mountain towns hold adventures for active families.

Georgia & the Carolinas for Kids

Bicycling, hiking, urban walks, horseback riding, waterfall swims and even white-water rafting are around every corner. Take a road trip along the Blue Ridge Parkway and stop to stretch your legs (and run off that pent-up energy) on mountain trails or in charming small towns. Or opt for a more urban itinerary: Atlanta's many kid-friendly attractions could fuel a week's vacation, and cities like Charlotte, Greenville, Asheville, Charleston and Savannah offer plenty of museums, sights and activities that will enthrall the younger set. Most restaurants welcome children with special menus, and an increasing number of breweries accommodate families as well.

Children's Highlights

Museums

- Just about everything is hands-on at Charlotte's Discovery Place Science (p233).
- Got a mini astronaut? They'll love the space-themed wonderland that is Coca-Cola Space Science Center (p160).
- One of Atlanta's most unique museums, the Center for Puppetry Arts (p52) has a huge collection of Jim Henson puppets.
- Kids can try to kick a field goal, sing karaoke and more at the College Football Hall of Fame (p48).

➡ Admission includes unlimited plays at the Asheville Pinball Museum (p289), so be prepared to pry those little hands away when their time's up.

➡ Delve into the wonders of the natural world at Fernbank Museum of Natural History (p51).

Outdoors

➡ Older or more adventurous kids can hit the rapids at the Nantahala Outdoor Center (p299).

➡ All ages will enjoy the Great Woodland Adventure Trail at Chimney Rock (p300) and the Sugarlands Valley Nature Trail (p320) in the Smokies.

➡ Ride a Shetland pony at Lawton Stables (p198).

➡ Bicycle the Swamp Rabbit Trail (p221).

➡ Stroll the Atlanta BeltLine (p53) and stop for lunch (or a sweet treat) at Krog Street Market (p64).

➡ Get an education in the outdoors at Great Smoky Mountains Institute at Tremont (p322).

Activities

➡ Participate in a classic American experience at Starlight Drive-In (p82).

➡ Why yes, Tweetsie Railroad (p286) is a Wild West theme park in North Carolina, and yes, kids totally dig it.

➡ Train-loving kids should hop aboard Blue Ridge Scenic Railway (p139).

➡ Roam the massive rooms and even bigger grounds of the Biltmore Estate (p287), the USA's classiest theme park.

➡ Experience the prospecting life at the Foggy Mountain Gem Mine (p287) – you can have any stones you find cut and mounted.

PLANNING TIPS

➡ Most hotels offer cribs or rollaway beds for children. Request when booking.

➡ If traveling by car, rest areas are your best bets for bathroom breaks, although a gas station or fast-food restaurant will do in a pinch.

➡ You can request a mug of hot water to warm a baby bottle in a cafe or restaurant.

➡ If you want to go to a fine-dining establishment with children, it's recommended to book a table for 6pm or earlier.

➡ In Great Smoky Mountains National Park, you'll have to bring your own food and water.

➡ Charleston and Savannah are walking cities; plan accordingly.

Restaurants

➡ Watching the planes take off helps little ones stay in their seats longer at Runway Cafe (p229).

➡ Dinner is interactive at Sunbury Crab Company (p114) – kids will love cracking open crab with a mallet.

➡ Family-friendly brunch in Charlotte can be found at Melanie's Food Fantasy (p288).

➡ Dig into a no-frills pie at Sidewall Pizza Company (p229).

➡ At Monday Night Garage (p78) in Atlanta, there are toys, games and apple juice for kids.

Regions at a Glance

The full spectrum of the South's complex, diverse history, culture and environment is on display in Georgia and the Carolinas.

At its heart is Atlanta, the Hollywood of the South with a strong African American heritage and world-class museums. Artsy Savannah boasts an astonishing range of architecture, while Charleston is a drinking and dining highlight. Spot wild horses and dolphins, explore groovy beach towns or sleep at a swanky resort in the coastal regions.

Intellectual pursuits await in the college-rich Charlotte and the Triangle. Experience Appalachian culture and epic hikes in the North Carolina mountains and Great Smoky Mountains National Park.

More natural wonders and surprisingly tasty wines await in North Georgia, along with the chill college town of Athens. And don't miss the barbecue and offbeat delights to be discovered in South Georgia.

Atlanta

Museums
Nightlife
Sports

World-class Museums

The South's biggest city is home to great museums – many of which are within walking distance of Centennial Park. Don't miss the High Museum of Art, the Martin Luther King Jr National Historic Site or the Center for Civil & Human Rights.

Out on the Town

Entertainment options are endless in Atlanta, which has one of the USA's richest music scenes. From watering holes to clubs to gastropubs, a memorable night out awaits.

Go Team

Atlanta has a spanking-new stadium from which to cheer on two of its most popular teams: the NFL's Atlanta Falcons (football) and the MLS's United FC (soccer).

p46

Savannah & Coastal Georgia

Art & Culture
Architecture
Islands

Art & Culture

The Savannah College of Art & Design draws artsy students from around the world and gives the city an avant-garde edge. On the coast, the Pin Point Heritage Museum gives a glimpse of the unique Geechee culture.

Architecture

Downtown Savannah is one of the largest National Historic Districts in the USA – in the same square mile you can find Colonial homes, 19th-century townhouses, Gothic mansions and art-deco department stores.

Down by the Water

Tybee, Cumberland and Jekyll Islands each offer a distinct coastal experience, from wildlife-watching to marshy hikes to the simple pleasure of a day at the beach.

p89

North Georgia

Outdoors
Small Towns
Wine

Hikes & Hollows

The famed Appalachian Trail ends in these gently rolling mountains. Admire the Southeast's highest cascading water-fall, climb Black Rock Mountain for great views or take a nerve-shattering stroll across a suspension bridge to gaze out over Tallulah Gorge.

Small-town Delights

The villages of North Georgia all have unique personalities. Find Alpine delights in Helen, discover Georgia's mining history in Dahlonega and military history in Toccoa.

Georgia Wine

Vineyards dot the hills of North Georgia. The region's refreshing, mainly semi-sweet wines are usually served up with scenic views.

p125

Augusta & South Georgia

Outdoors
Adventures
Food

Wildlife & White-water

Outdoor adventure awaits in South Georgia. Spot gators and water birds in the wilds of Okefenokee swamp or hike through the rainbow-hued Providence Canyon. Just outside of Columbus, White-Water Express offers the world's longest purpose-built urban rafting experience.

Walking Dead to Presidential Plains

South Georgia offers ample opportunity for off-the-beaten-track experiences – from tours of the *Walking Dead* filming locations to seeing the birth home of a former president.

BBQ Dreams

Georgia's smoke pits are legendary and many of the best can be found in South Georgia.

p151

Charleston & South Carolina

Food
Nightlife
Coastal Charm

Local Food

Charleston's dining scene has earned global accolades, but in-the-know foodies are also flocking to Greenville. Small towns on the coast serve up fresh, simple seafood; inland, you'll find melt-in-your-mouth barbecue doused in the state's signature mustard- or vinegar-based sauce.

Brews & Tunes

Microbreweries and sophisticated cocktail bars abound, especially in Charleston and Greenville.'

Sunny Days

South Carolina packs a lot into its 200 miles of coastline. Find upscale resorts at Hilton Head, historic sites at Fort Sumter or Bulls Island, and a carnival atmosphere on Myrtle Beach.

p166

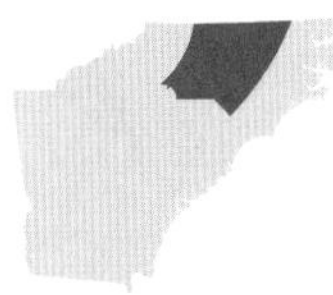

Charlotte & the Triangle

Cities
Sports
Museums

City Life

From the financial capital of Charlotte to the state capital of Raleigh to the academic capitals of Chapel Hill and Durham, there's a range of urban delights to explore.

Sports Scene

Charlotte and the Triangle have the best opportunities to cheer on sports teams. In basketball season, the rivalry between Duke and NC Chapel-Hill is second to none. Charlotte is home to NASCAR and site of one of the circuit's longest races.

Modern Museums

You'll find a museum for every taste. The more traditional highlight the arts and sciences, but there's also a preserved Moravian settlement, and an important Civil Rights site.

p232

Coastal North Carolina

Beaches
Wildlife
Seafood

Coastal Sands

From wild shorelines along the Outer Banks to groovy beach towns such as Wilmington and boardwalk-bedecked Beaufort, the 300 miles of North Carolina's Atlantic Coast offer a variety of ways to soak up the sun.

Animal Adventures

The untouched sections of the North Carolina Coast provide sanctuary to a wide variety of animals. See wild horses on Ocracoke Island and keep the binoculars out for birds in Rodanthe.

Local Seafood

Shrimp, crab and clams plucked fresh from the Atlantic can be found throughout the region, from comfy clam shacks to white-tablecloth elegance.

p254

North Carolina Mountains

Outdoors
Breweries
Landscapes

Bikes & Hikes

Some of the Southeast's best mountain biking and most glorious hikes can be found in this region. Many are accessible as day trips from Asheville, but even the smallest town offers a chance to enjoy the great outdoors .

Beer City, USA

A thriving craft beer scene can be found in many US cities today, but one of the industry's early adopters was Asheville. The city remains one of the country's best and friendliest.

Idyllic Vistas

The foothills of the Appalachians are full of gently curved mountain roads – pull over at one of the many scenic viewpoints along the way for a picture-perfect moment.

p282

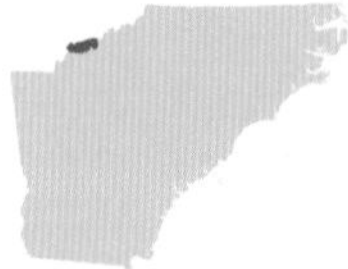

Great Smoky Mountains National Park

Hiking
Scenic Drives
Wildlife

Captivating Climbs

This national park is a hiker's paradise. There are myriad trails for all abilities and experience levels. Be sure to try out the Appalachian Trail (70 miles of it are found here) and experience the view from Clingmans Dome.

Winding Roads

A drive along Newfound Gap Rd reveals the diversity of ecosystems that can be found here. The road climbs some 3000ft and passes through hardwood and evergreen forests.

Birds, Bears & More

Wildlife-spotting opportunities abound. Black bear, dozens of bird species, elk and more!

p313

On the Road

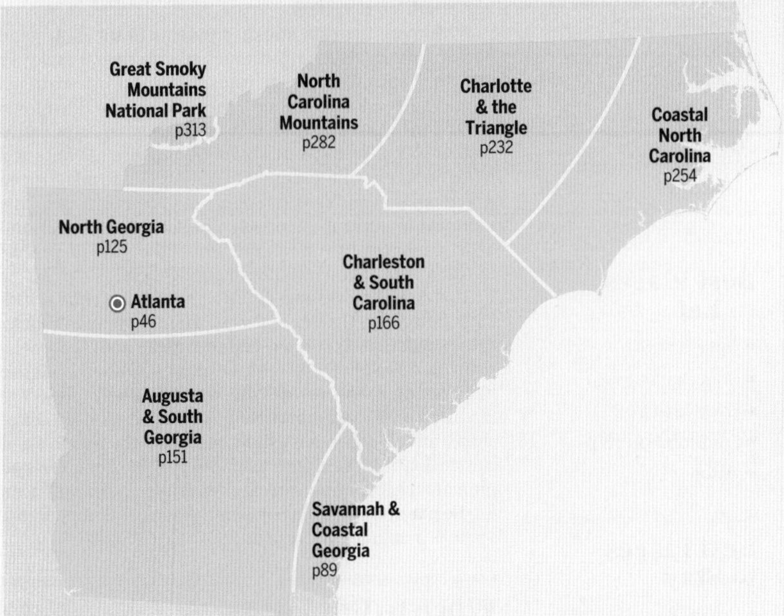

Great Smoky Mountains National Park p313
North Carolina Mountains p282
Charlotte & the Triangle p232
Coastal North Carolina p254
North Georgia p125
Atlanta p46
Charleston & South Carolina p166
Augusta & South Georgia p151
Savannah & Coastal Georgia p89

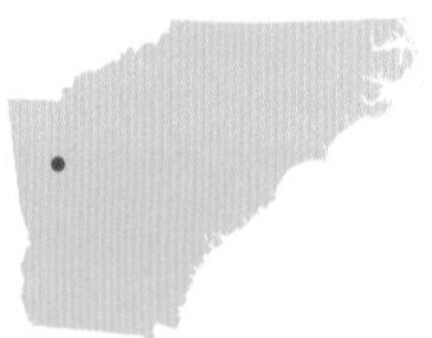

Atlanta

☎ 404, 470, 678, 770 / POP 463,878

Includes ➡

Best Places to Eat

- ➡ Optimist (p70)
- ➡ Staplehouse (p66)
- ➡ Bacchanalia (p72)
- ➡ Fox Brothers (p65)
- ➡ Octopus Bar (p65)

Best Places to Stay

- ➡ Urban Oasis B&B (p58)
- ➡ Stonehurst Place (p60)
- ➡ Sugar Magnolia B&B (p58)
- ➡ Hotel Artmore (p59)

Why Go?

The South's so-called capital isn't nicknamed Hotlanta for nothing, y'all. Charismatic and lush, Atlanta is a feverish, easy-on-the-eyes cavalcade of culture, cuisine and Southern hospitality.

With more than six million residents in the metro and outlying areas, Atlanta continues to experience explosive growth thanks to domestic transplants and international immigrants alike. Beyond the big-ticket Downtown attractions you will find a constellation of superlative restaurants, a palpable Hollywood influence (Atlanta is a hugely popular film-production center) and iconic African American history. That last point can't be overstated: any nationwide African American intellectual, political and artistic movement you can mention either had its genesis in Atlanta, or found a center of gravity here.

Atlanta is a quirky and cultured metroplex, with world-class museums, theater and arts. The economy is robust, the population is young and creative, and the social scene is refreshingly diverse. Distinct neighborhoods are like friendly small towns, rife with pristinely preserved historic homes and thoroughfares of hip bars, cozy coffee shops and independent shopping. And the food? Be it classic Southern eats such as pecan pie, fried chicken and pimento cheese; innovative, chef-driven New American foodie haunts; or ethnic holes-in-the-wall, Atlanta's dining scene is a culinary juggernaut.

When to Go

- ➡ In January, Martin Luther King Day has special significance in the city the man claimed as home.
- ➡ Spring warms up as Atlanta prepares for its annual jazz festival in May.
- ➡ As the weather cools, Atlanta celebrates with the annual Pride Festival in October.

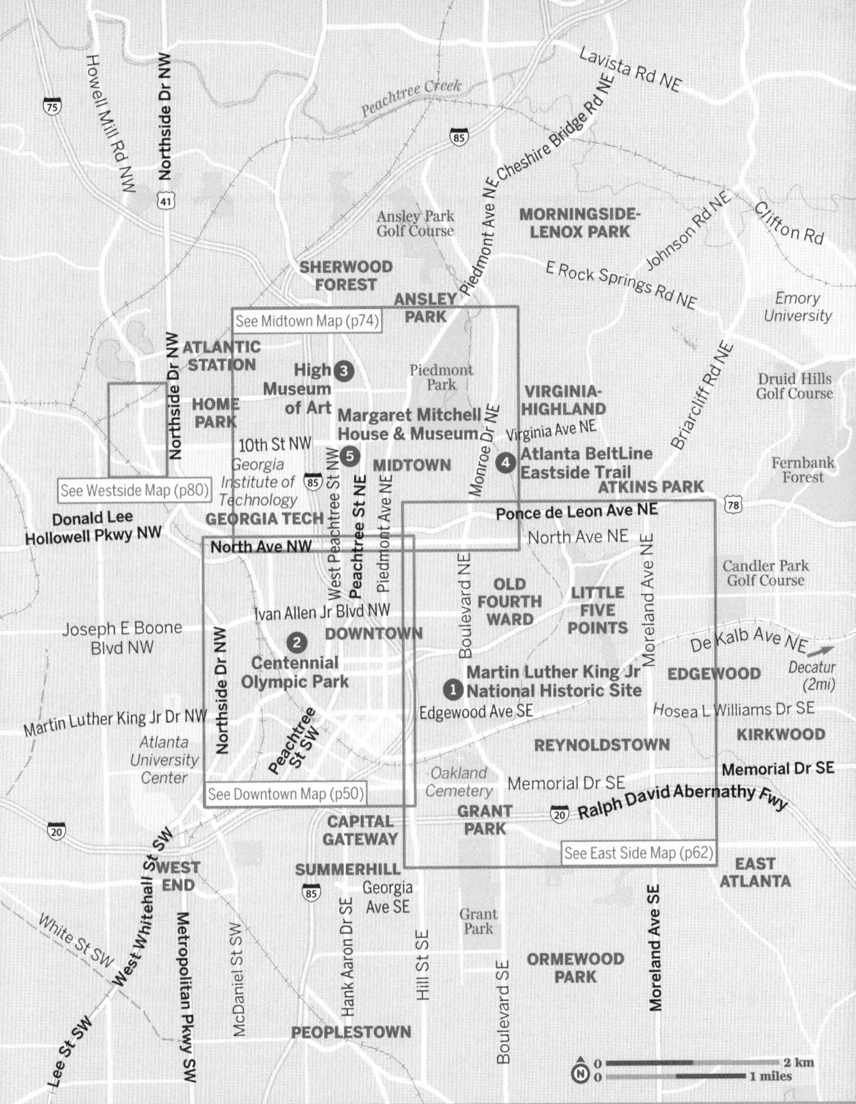

Atlanta Highlights

❶ **Martin Luther King Jr National Historic Site** (p49) Pondering the struggles of the Civil Rights movement.

❷ **Centennial Olympic Park** (p48) Hopping from museum to museum in the center of Atlanta.

❸ **High Museum of Art** (p52) Gawking over galleries in the Southeast's most acclaimed museum.

❹ **Atlanta BeltLine Eastside Trail** (p53) Strolling or biking from major attractions to hip new restaurants.

❺ **Margaret Mitchell House & Museum** (p52) Swooning over the home of the author of *Gone With the Wind*.

History

Originally founded in 1837 as a railway junction called Terminus, Atlanta quickly outgrew its humble beginnings, despite its near-complete destruction during the Civil War. It was a long road from the end of the line to the world-class, multicultural metropolis and iconic center of African American culture that Atlanta is today, but the city emerged bigger and better than before. Young, creative and diverse, Atlanta has risen up.

Sights

Downtown

Atlanta's Downtown packs a whole lot of world-class museums and attractions into a condensed area, something few US cities can boast. Most are around or within easy walking distance of Centennial Olympic Park.

Centennial Olympic Park PARK
(Map p50; www.centennialpark.com; 265 Park Ave NW; 7am-11pm) Atlanta's Centennial Olympic Park is the city's focal point for visitors. The park itself features a dancing Fountain of Rings water fountain, a Quilt of Remembrance in honor of the victims of the 1996 Olympic bombing and a water garden, among other small details. It also contains some of the city's seminal sights, including the Center for Civil & Human Rights, the World of Coca-Cola and the Georgia Aquarium.

> **TRANSPORT TIPS**
>
> ➡ If something is 'on Peachtree,' it's usually the main corridor, Peachtree St NE. But it's best to clarify if it's anything else – Peachtree Battle, Peachtree Center, Peachtree Circle or Peachtree-Dunwoody – before you go.
>
> ➡ Avoid exorbitant downtown parking fees by leaving your car for free at Inman Park MARTA (Metropolitan Atlanta Rapid Transit Authority) station and taking the train; or grabbing free street parking near the Smoke Ring (p60) in Castleberry Hill.

➡ ★ **Center for Civil & Human Rights** MUSEUM
(Map p50; www.civilandhumanrights.org; 100 Ivan Allen Jr Blvd; adult/senior/child $19.99/17.99/15.99; 10am-5pm Mon-Sat, noon-5pm Sun) This striking 2014 addition to Atlanta's Centennial Olympic Park is a sobering $68-million memorial to the American Civil Rights and global human-rights movements. Beautifully designed and thoughtfully executed, the indisputable highlight centers on an absolutely harrowing interactive mock Woolworth's lunch-counter sit-in simulation that will leave you speechless and move some to tears.

➡ **Georgia Aquarium** AQUARIUM
(Map p50; 404-581-4000; www.georgiaaquarium.com; 225 Baker St; adult/child $39.95/33.95; 10am-9pm Mon-Fri, 9am-9pm Sat & Sun) Atlanta's showstopper. It's crowded, but the appeal of this aquarium, the second largest in the US, is hard to deny: whale sharks, playful sea lions at SunTrust Pier 225 and an adorable daily penguin walk. Unfortunately there are also beluga whales and a live dolphin show; keeping cetaceans in captivity is a proven animal-welfare issue. Parking is $10. Book tickets online in advance for discounts.

➡ **World of Coca-Cola** MUSEUM
(Map p50; 404-676-5151; www.woccatlanta.com; 121 Baker St; adult/senior/child $17/15/13; 10am-5pm Mon-Fri, 9am-5pm Sat & Sun) This self-congratulatory museum might prove entertaining to fans of fizzy beverages and rash commercialization. The climactic moment comes when guests sample Coke products from around the world – a taste-bud-twisting good time. But there are also Andy Warhol pieces on view, a 4-D film, company history and promotional materials aplenty.

College Football Hall of Fame MUSEUM
(Map p50; www.cfbhall.com; 250 Marietta St; adult/senior/child $21.99/18.99/17.99; 10am-5pm Sun-Fri, 9am-6pm Sat; P) It is impossible to overstate the importance of college football to American culture. This musem, relocated from Indiana in 2014 and revamped into this three-story, 94,256-sq-ft gridiron sanctuary, is a supremely cool and suitable shrine.

Pledge your allegiance to your team of choice upon entry and your interactive experience is customized as you make your way past famous trophies like the coveted Heisman and hands-on experiences such as Fight Song Karaoke or attempting to kick a 20yd field goal. Needless to say, kids go nuts here.

Skyview Atlanta FERRIS WHEEL
(Map p50; ☎678-949-9023; www.skyviewatlanta.com; 168 Luckie St NW; adult/senior/child $13.89/12.50/9.26; ⏱noon-11pm Sun-Thu, to midnight Fri & Sat; 👪) Soar 200ft above the Atlanta skyline in this 20-story, 42-gondola Ferris wheel.

Georgia State Capitol LANDMARK
(Map p50; ☎404-463-4536; www.libs.uga.edu/capitolmuseum; 206 State Capitol; ⏱8am-5pm Mon-Fri) FREE The gold-domed capitol is Atlanta's political hub. Free self-guided tours give visitors a glance at state-level American politics.

Underground Atlanta LANDMARK
(Map p50; 50 Upper Alabama St; ⏱10am-7pm Mon-Thu, to 8pm Fri & Sat, noon-6pm Sun) This shopping and entertainment district in the Five Points area touted itself as a 'city beneath the streets' when it opened on Atlanta's original post-Civil War Reconstruction Era streets in 1969. A $142-million renovation in 1989 made it the beating heart of downtown Atlanta throughout the '90s, but it has fallen out of favor again – there is almost nothing here besides the Masquerade concert venue, and the lower level is officially closed until further notice.

In 2017 the city sold it off to South Carolinian developers, who are in the midst of redeveloping the site (yet again) to the tune of $300-plus million – and there is citywide hope that Underground will live again in the near future.

Children's Museum of Atlanta MUSEUM
(Map p50; www.childrensmuseumatlanta.org; 275 Centennial Olympic Park Dr NW; $15.95; ⏱10am-4pm Mon-Fri, to 5pm Sat & Sun; 👪) A hands-on museum geared toward kids aged eight and under. It's pretty small, so don't expect much to entertain adults, but it will distract your little ones for a few hours.

WHAT TO WEAR

As with most US cities, Atlanta is as casual, trendy or formal as you want it to be. However, Southern culture and tradition have been known to err on the side of dignified, most notably in top-tier traditional restaurants such as Bacchanalia and top-end steakhouses. Outside formal restaurants and theaters, feel free to express yourself. Smart casual is always safe.

Weather-wise, cool and casual rules in summer but sudden downpours can be common so bring a lightweight waterproof rain jacket. Nights can get chilly from November to March, but with a January average high of 51°F (10°C), winters are normally on the milder side.

East Side

Some of Atlanta's biggest attractions congregate on this side of town. While there is a 1.5-mile long landscaped trail connecting Martin Luther King Jr National Historic Site and the Jimmy Carter Presidential Library & Museum, a vehicle is required for getting to the rest of the area's sights (Fernbank Museum of Natural History is 2 miles east of Jimmy Carter and Clyde Shepherd Nature Preserve is another 4 miles east). Oakland Cemetery sits a walkable 1 mile south of MLK.

★Martin Luther King Jr National Historic Site HISTORIC SITE
(Map p62; ☎404-331-5190; www.nps.gov/malu; 450 Auburn Ave, Sweet Auburn; ⏱9am-5pm; P 👪) FREE The historic site commemorates the life, work and legacy of the Civil Rights leader and one of the great Americans. The site takes up several blocks. Stop by the excellent visitor center to get oriented with a map and brochure of area sites, a 20-minute film, *New Time, New Voice*, and exhibits that elucidate the context – the segregation, systemic oppression and racial violence that inspired and fueled King's work. A 1.5-mile landscaped trail leads from here to the Jimmy Carter Presidential Library & Museum (p52).

Downtown

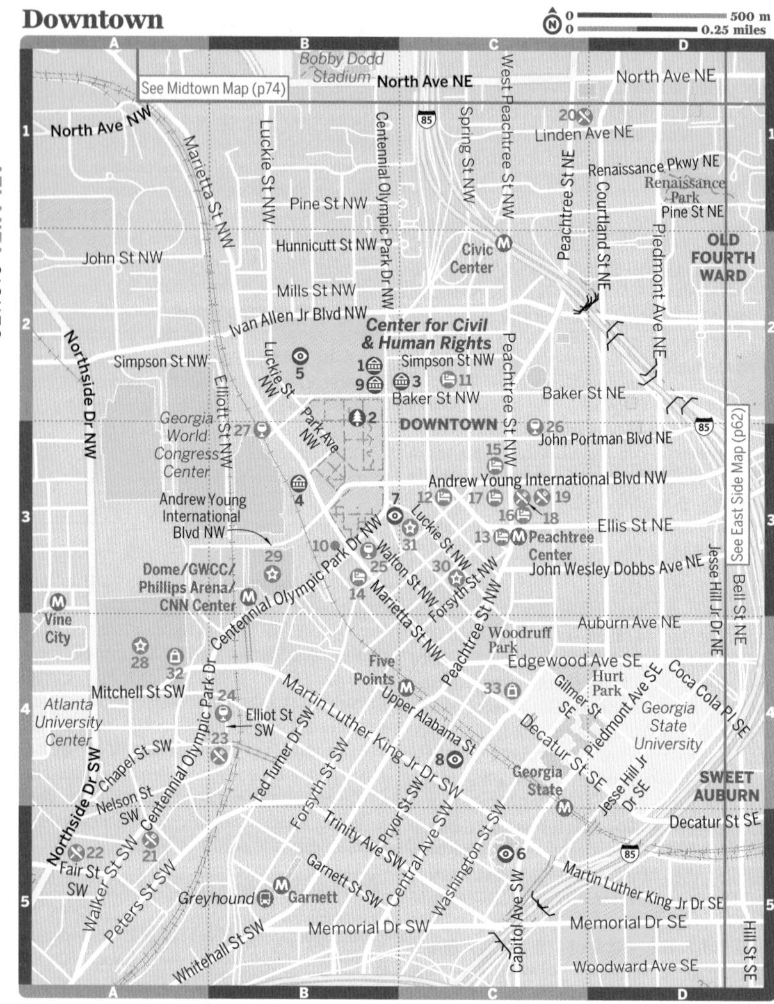

➡ Ebenezer Baptist Church (New) CHURCH

(Map p62; ☎404-688-7300; www.historicebenezer.org; 101 Jackson St NE; ⏰Sun service 9am & 11:30am) The new Ebenezer Baptist Church is the home of the congregation once led by Dr Martin Luther King Jr. As befits one of the most influential church communities in American history, the structure is impressive – light filled, airy and more welcoming than muscular. The church is across the street from the historic Ebenezer Baptist Church, and welcomes visitors to Sunday morning services. Dress nicely.

➡ Martin Luther King Jr Birthplace LANDMARK

(Map p62; 501 Auburn Ave, ⏰10am-4pm) FREE Free, first-come, first-served guided tours of King's childhood home take about 30 minutes to complete and require same-day registration, which can be made at the visitor center at the National Historic Site – arrive early, as slots fill fast. The tours can depart anytime between 10am and 4pm, but you are free to visit the rest of the park at your leisure before your designated tour time.

Downtown

Top Sights
1 Center for Civil & Human Rights B2

Sights
2 Centennial Olympic Park B2
3 Children's Museum of Atlanta C2
4 College Football Hall of Fame B3
5 Georgia Aquarium B2
6 Georgia State Capitol C5
7 Skyview Atlanta B3
8 Underground Atlanta C4
9 World of Coca-Cola B2

Activities, Courses & Tours
10 CNN Center B3

Sleeping
11 Aloft Atlanta Downtown C2
12 American Hotel C3
13 Ellis Hotel C3
14 Glenn Hotel B3
15 Hotel Indigo Downtown C3
16 Ritz-Carlton, Atlanta C3
17 Westin Peachtree Plaza C3

Eating
18 Alma Cocina C3
19 Amalfi Pizza C3
20 Herban Fix C1
21 No Mas! Cantina A5
22 Paschal's A5
23 Smoke Ring B4

Drinking & Nightlife
24 Elliott Street Deli & Pub B4
25 Park Bar Atlanta B3
26 Polaris C3
Red Phone Booth .... (see 19)
SkyLounge .... (see 14)
27 Stats B3

Entertainment
28 Mercedes-Benz Stadium A4
29 Philips Arena B3
30 Rialto Center for the Arts C3
31 Tabernacle C3

Shopping
Coca-Cola Store .... (see 9)
32 Team Store A4
33 Walter's Clothing C4

First Ebenezer Baptist Church — CHURCH

(Map p62; 407 Auburn Ave NE; 9am-5pm) FREE Martin Luther King Jr, his father and grandfather were all pastors here, and King Jr's mother was the choir director. Sadly she was murdered here by a deranged gunman while she sat at the organ in 1974. A multimillion-dollar restoration, brought the church back to the 1960–68 period when King Jr served as copastor with his father. Today looped recordings of King's speeches play in the church building. Sunday services are now held at the new Ebenezer Church (p50) across the street.

King Center for Non-Violent Social Change — MUSEUM

(Map p62; 404-526-8900; www.thekingcenter.org; 449 Auburn Ave NE; 9am-5pm, to 6pm summer) Across from the visitor center of the National Historic Site (p49), this place has information on Martin Luther King Jr's life and work and a few of his personal effects, including his Nobel Peace Prize and Spoken Word Grammy, and exhibitions on Ghandi and Rosa Parks. His gravesite is surrounded by a long reflecting pool and can be viewed anytime.

Fernbank Museum of Natural History — MUSEUM

(Map p84; 404-929-6300; www.fernbankmuseum.org; 767 Clifton Rd; adult/child $20/18; 10am-5pm; P) Fernbank is a supremely kid-friendly museum that explores a bunch of subjects (dinosaurs, geology, IMAX-style theater), all attached to a 65-acre old-growth forest and 10-acre Wildwoods outdoor educational area within – reached by elevated walkway from the museum's terrace. While children will have a blast, Fernbank is so well put together and organized that adults will surely enjoy it as well. The museum is northeast of Downtown, near Decatur.

Historic Fourth Ward Park — PARK

(Map p62; www.h4wpc.org; 680 Dallas St NE; 6am-11pm) Behind Ponce City Market (p65), this below-ground-level 17-acre urban park was one of the BeltLine's first projects. It features a storm-water retention pond which feeds the park's fountains and Splashpad, a playground and outdoor theater, and a skate park partially funded by skateboarding legend Tony Hawk.

It comes with an interesting history as well: the sight was once home to an amusement park, casino and ballpark and people believed Clear Creek, which runs under the park, had therapeutic qualities. But Sears, Roebuck and Co buried it all when it built its massive brick headquarters in 1926 (now Ponce City Market).

Oakland Cemetery CEMETERY
(Map p62; www.oaklandcemetery.com; 248 Oakland Ave SE) In addition to holding the graves of author Margeret Mitchell, golf great Bobby Jones and Atlanta's first African American mayor, Maynard Jackson, Atlanta's historic garden cemetery (dating to 1850) is one of the few graveyards in the world to boast a visitor center and museum shop. It offers themed tours, a music festival called Tunes from the Tombs and other events.

Jimmy Carter Presidential Library & Museum MUSEUM
(Map p62; ☎404-865-7100; www.jimmycarterlibrary.org; 441 Freedom Pkwy, Poncey-Highland; adult/senior/child $8/6/free; ⏲8am-5pm; P) Located on a hilltop overlooking Downtown, this center features exhibits highlighting Jimmy Carter's presidency (1977–81), inclu-ding a replica of the Oval Office and his Nobel Prize. Don't miss the tranquil Japanese garden and butterfly garden out back. The 1.5-mile long, landscaped **Freedom Park Trail** leads from here to the Martin Luther King Jr National Historic Site (p49) through Freedom Park.

Midtown

Midtown's sights aren't as convenient to each other as those in Downtown, but they are still pretty near. With Piedmont Park (and the Atlanta Botanical Garden within) as your centerpiece, the High Museum of Art, Center for Puppetry Arts, the Breman Museum and Margaret Mitchell House & Museum are all within 1.3 miles from the western edge of the park and easily walkable using Peachtree St NE as your main thoroughfare.

Piedmont Park PARK
(Map p74; ☎404-875-7275; www.piedmontpark.org; 400 Park Dr NE; ⏲6am-11pm) FREE A glorious, rambling urban park and the setting of many cultural and music festivals. The park has fantastic bike paths and a Saturday Green Market.

★**High Museum of Art** MUSEUM
(Map p74; www.high.org; 1280 Peachtree St NE; adult/under 5 $14.50/free; ⏲10am-5pm Tue-Thu & Sat, to 9pm Fri, noon-5pm Sun) Atlanta's modern High Museum was the first to exhibit art from Paris' Louvre and is a destination as much for its architecture as its world-class exhibits. The striking whitewashed multilevel building houses a permanent collection of eye-catching late 19th-century furniture, early American modern canvases from the likes of George Morris and Albert Gallatin, and postwar work from Mark Rothko.

Center for Puppetry Arts MUSEUM
(Map p74; ☎tickets 404-873-3391; www.puppet.org; 1401 Spring St NW; museum $12.50, guided tours $16.50; ⏲9am-5pm Tue-Sun; 👪) A wonderland for visitors of all ages and hands down one of Atlanta's most unique attractions, the museum – expanded in 2015 – houses a treasury of puppets, some of which you get to operate yourself. A major addition is the Worlds of Puppetry Museum, housing the most comprehensive collection of Jim Henson puppets and artifacts in the world.

Margaret Mitchell House & Museum MUSEUM
(Map p74; ☎404-249-7015; www.atlantahistorycenter.com; 979 Crescent Ave NE; adult/student/child $13/10/5.50; ⏲10am-5:30pm Mon-Sat, noon-5:30pm Sun) Operated by the Atlanta History Center, this home has been converted into a shrine to the author of *Gone With the Wind*. Mitchell wrote her epic in a small apartment in the basement of this Tudor Revival building, which is listed on the National Register of Historic Places. There are on-site exhibitions on Mitchell's life and writing career, and a two-hour looping documentary, *The Making of a Legend*. A combo ticket (adult/student/child $21.50/18/9) also gets you access to the Atlanta History Center.

Atlanta Botanical Garden GARDENS
(Map p74; ☎404-876-5859; www.atlantabotanicalgarden.org; 1345 Piedmont Ave NE; adult/child $21.95/15.95; ⏲9am-7pm Tue-Sun Apr-Oct, shorter hours winter; P) In the northwest corner of Piedmont Park, this stunning 30-acre botanical garden has a Japanese garden, winding paths and the amazing Fuqua Orchid Center.

Breman Museum MUSEUM
(William Breman Jewish Heritage Museum; Map p74; www.thebreman.org; 1440 Spring St NW; adult/child $12/4; ⏲10am-5pm Sun-Thu, to 4pm Fri; P) Atlanta has the largest Jewish population in the South (outside of South Florida, which is its own region). The Breman Museum explores this history of immigration and

ATLANTA BELTLINE

Transforming the way the city moves, lives, works and plays, the **Atlanta BeltLine** is an enormous sustainable redevelopment project. An existing 22-mile rail corridor encircling the city has been repurposed with light-rail transit and 33 miles of connected multiuse trails. It is the most comprehensive transportation and economic development effort ever undertaken in Atlanta and among the largest, most wide-ranging urban redevelopment programs under way in the US. The trail opened in 2012 and the **Atlanta BeltLine Center** (Map p62; ☎404-446-4404; www.beltline.org; 112 Krog St NE, Suite 14; ⏰4-8pm Mon-Fri, 10am-7pm Sat & Sun) opened in 2018. Located along the Eastside Trail, the center has info and trail maps as well as exhibits and interactive displays highlighting the parks/trails, events/activities, art and history of the BeltLine.

integration and is a major meeting point for the city's Jewish community. The museum also includes a powerful permanent exhibit on the Holocaust.

Greater Atlanta

Stone Mountain Park PARK

(☎800-401-2407; www.stonemountainpark.com; 1000 Robert E Lee Blvd, Stone Mountan; from $34.95; ⏰10am-8pm mid-May–Sep, to 5pm Jan–mid-May) Approximately 20 miles northeast of central Atlanta sits this unique – and controversial – theme park based around the 825ft-high Stone Mountain, the world's largest outcropping of exposed granite. It is best known for the huge carving of Confederate 'heroes' Jefferson Davis, Stonewall Jackson and Robert E Lee (cue the controversial part), which took more than half a century to complete.

Regardless of its potent lack of political correctness (and sordid history with the Ku Klux Klan as well, which was revived here in 1915), the 3200-acre park is wildly popular with families, hikers and outdoor enthusiasts (you can scale the mountain) and tourists alike, especially for the world's largest laser-light show, which takes place in the evenings on Saturdays from April to May, daily from Memorial Weekend through early August, and Saturdays from August through October. It remains one of Atlanta's most unique and fascinating kitsch attractions. Other attractions in the park include camping, golf, fishing, a snow park, a cable car and museums, among others.

Battle of Atlanta Cyclorama PUBLIC ART

(Map p84; www.atlantahistorycenter.com; 130 West Paces Ferry Rd NW, Atlanta History Center, Buckhead; ⏰10am-5:50pm Mon-Sat, noon-5:30pm Sun) Once considered the largest oil painting in the world, this historic, cylindrical panoramic painting of the Civil War's Battle of Atlanta was unavailable for viewing at the time of research, as it was in the process of being restored and moved from its home since 1921 (Grant Park) to the custom-built, 23,000-sq-ft Lloyd and Mary Ann Whitaker Cyclorama Building at the Atlanta History Center. It should be in its new home by the time you read this.

The painting itself, which unrolled measures 42ft (13m) high by 358ft (109m) long, is enhanced by 28 plaster figures that are the focal point of the painting's 3-D diorama, which slowly rotates to tell the story of the epic Civil War battle alongside narration and music. The new Cyclorama will also exhibit the restored *Texas* steam locomotive, an important early Atlanta railroading artifact that played a pivotal role in 1862's Great Locomotive Chase.

Clyde Shepherd Nature Preserve NATURE RESERVE

(Map p84; ☎678-466-0572; www.cshepherdpreserve.org; 2580 Pine Bluff Dr, Decatur; ⏰sunrise-sunset; P 👪) FREE Smack in the middle of the city (well, OK – out in Decatur, but you get the idea), you'll find this 28-acre nature preserve, home of beavers, foxes, box turtles, red-spotted newts, coyotes and veritable clouds of birds. It's a welcome slice of wilderness in the heart of an enormous urban area.

Atlanta History Center MUSEUM

(Map p84; ☎404-814-4000; www.atlantahistorycenter.com; 130 West Paces Ferry Rd NW; adult/child $16.50/11; ⏰11am-4pm Mon-Sat, 1-4pm Sun) This history museum centers on the Swan House, a 1930s mansion designed by iconic Atlanta architect Philip Trammell Shutze. Visitors can wander through the opulent rooms or through 22 acres of pretty on-site gardens. Admission also gets you access to the Margaret Mitchell House.

OFF THE BEATEN TRACK

THE SILVER COMET TRAIL

For cycling enthusiasts, Atlanta's Silver Comet Trail (www.silvercometga.com) is a big day out on two wheels. The nonmotorized, paved trail spans 61.5 miles – you can ride this baby all the way to 'Bama! – following a long-abandoned railroad line built in 1897 through three counties and preserved forests, rural countryside and historic downtowns along the way.

The trail starts 13 miles northwest of Atlanta at Mavell Road Trailhead in Smyrna and ends at the Georgia/Alabama state line near Cedartown at the Esom Hill Trailhead, where it connects with the 34-mile **Chief Ladiga Trail**, eventually connecting Smyrna with Anniston, AL, some 95 miles away. The trail gets its name from the Seaboard Air Line Railroad's luxury *Silver Comet* passenger train, which rode these rails in style from 1947 to 1969.

Highlights along the route include Mableton's **Heritage Park**, a native plant garden, wetlands and historic mill; Dallas' **Pumpkinvine Trestle**, a restored 1901 train trestle; and Rockmart's historic **Brushy Mountain Tunnel** and **Riverwalk Park**. There are also side trails such as the 18-mile mountain-biking trail at Hiram's Caboose trailhead.

Activities

Skate Escape CYCLING

(Map p74; ☎404-892-1292; www.skateescape.com; 1086 Piedmont Ave NE; bicycles & in-line skates per hour from $6; ⏰11am-7pm, to 6pm winter) Rents out bicycles and in-line skates. It also has tandems ($12 per hour) and mountain bikes ($25/40 per 3/24 hours).

Tours

★ **Atlanta Food Walks** FOOD & DRINK

(☎470-223-2203; www.atlantafoodwalks.com; tours from $69; ⏰11am-3pm Thu-Sun) Atlanta is a fantastic city to eat and for the uninitiated, Atlanta Food Walks' Downtown Southern Food Walk and Grant Park Past & Future Food Walk are like a history lesson in your mouth. You'll taste Martin Luther King Jr's favorite meal and more than a mouthful of Southern food, soul food and unique Atlanta culinary oddities. Book online.

★ **Atlanta BeltLine Tours** OUTDOORS

(☎404-446-4404; www.beltline.org; tours free-$25) Runs tours of Atlanta's game-changing BeltLine. There's a three-hour, guided bus tour at 9:30am on Saturdays; a 90-minute Arboretum Walking Tour at 10am during winter (October to May) and 9am the rest of the year; and free three-hour biking tours alternating every Saturday at 9am between Eastside and Westside trails between March and November (bring your own bike). Book online.

Civil Rights Tours Atlanta HISTORY

(☎888-503-5662; www.civilrightstour.com; tour $65) Selma Civil Rights marcher and former MLK aide Tom Houck is your fascinating and fearless leader on what is surely Atlanta's most comprehensive and compelling Civil Rights tour. Besides exploring the obvious Martin Luther King Jr National Historic Site (p49), Houck will introduce you to off-the-beaten-path sights like MLK's last house, Morehouse College and more. Book online.

Urban Atlanta Explorers ADVENTURE

(☎678-636-9310; www.exploreatl.com) This locally owned tour company and adventure-driven social club is one of the most unique ways to see the city – it offers various themed tours, including BeltLine, breweries and Battle of Atlanta; neighborhood-oriented walking and biking tours; as well as nature hikes.

CNN Center TOURS

(Map p50; ☎404-827-2300; http://tours.cnn.com; 1 CNN Center, cnr Marietta St & Centennial Olympic Park Dr; tour adult/senior/child $15/14/12, VIP tour $33; ⏰9am-5pm, VIP tours 9:30am, 11:30am, 1:30pm & 3:30pm Mon-Sat) The 55-minute behind-the-scenes tour through the headquarters of the international, 24-hour news giant is a good time for fans. Although visitors don't get very close to Wolf Blitzer (or his cronies), the 9am and noon time slots offer the best bets for seeing anchors live on air. A VIP tour gets you access to live newsrooms, control rooms and production studios.

Festivals & Events

Inman Park Festival CULTURAL

(770-635-3711; www.inmanparkfestival.org; Inman Park; home tour tickets $20; Apr) One of Atlanta's coolest, most historic and most beautiful neighborhoods takes center stage at this good-time April festival, which counts local art and tours of stunning Victorian homes as highlights in addition to food and drink.

Atlanta Film Festival FILM

(404-352-4225; www.atlantafilmfestival.com; Apr) One of the longest-running film festivals in the country, with over 150 films screened over a seven-day period in various venues such as Plaza Theatre (p81), 7 Stages Theatre, Goat Farm Arts Center (p82) and Callanwolde Fine Arts Center. It's one of only 24 Academy Award qualifiers for narrative short films.

Sweetwater 420 Fest MUSIC

(www.sweetwater420fest.com; Centennial Olympic Park; Apr) Sponsored by one of Atlanta's oldest craft breweries, this weekend music festival with jam-band and environmental-awareness leanings draws hordes to Downtown's Centennial Olympic Park.

Atlanta Dogwood Festival CULTURAL

(404-817-6642; www.dogwood.org; Piedmont Park; Apr) FREE Going strong for over 80 years, the Atlanta Dogwood Festival is one of the city's most well-known annual events and is one of the biggest festivals in the Southeast. While it celebrates the blooming of the city's native dogwood trees, it's certainly more of a weekend about live music, arts and crafts and food these days.

Shaky Knees Music Festival MUSIC

(www.shakykneesfestival.com; Centennial Olympic Park; May) This indie music festival is one of Atlanta's coolest. The 2018 lineup featured LCD Soundsystem, Pixies and Ryan Adams, among others. Two sister festivals, Shaky Boots (currently on hiatus) and Shaky Beats (May), focus on country and EDM (electronic dance music) genres, respectively.

Atlanta Jazz Festival MUSIC

(404-546-6826; www.atlanta.net/events/atlanta-jazz-festival; Piedmont Park; May) FREE One of the largest free jazz festivals in the country has attracted big names such as Miles Davis, Dizzie Gillespie and Nina Simone over its 40-year history. The monthlong event culminates in live concerts in Piedmont Park on Memorial Day weekend.

★ **Peachtree Road Race** SPORTS

(919-242-6802; www.atlantatrackclub.org/peachtree; Jul) This July 4 Atlanta tradition is one of the globe's most famous 10km road races, attracting world-class athletes among its 60,000 annual participants. Started by the Atlanta Track Club in 1970, its coveted official race T-shirt – given only to runners who finish – is designed annually by an *Atlanta Journal-Constitution* contest winner and is an Atlantan status symbol among residents.

Decatur BBQ, Blues & Bluegrass Festival MUSIC, FOOD

(www.decaturbbqfestival.com; cnr 630 East Lake Drive & Harmony Park; Aug) If you are in the South and there is a BBQ, blues and bluegrass festival on, you go. And you gorge on all of it.

★ **Dragon Con** CULTURAL

(404-669-0773; www.dragoncon.org; Aug/Sep) A multigenre convention for freaks and geeks, Dragon Con draws some 80,000 fans of science fiction, fantasy, comic books and other fan-related fantasy genres, who descend on downtown Atlanta often dressed in character over the four-day Labor Day weekend.

★ **Music Midtown** MUSIC

(www.musicmidtown.com; Piedmont Park; from $135; Sep) Atlanta's biggest and best music festival, a two-day Piedmont Park extravaganza that attracts the biggest names in music. The 2017 lineup included Bruno Mars, Mumford & Sons, Wiz Khalifa, Bastille and Weezer.

BEST IN PRINT

Gone with the Wind (Margaret Mitchell; 1936) Though its lens of Southern nostalgia is read more critically today, this epic romance remains an American classic.

A Man in Full (Tom Wolfe; 1998) A 742-page satire of Atlanta high society from a modern American literature great.

A Good Man is Hard to Find (Flannery O'Connor; 1955) O'Connor's seminal work, a grotesque collection of short stories running the gamut from baptism to serial killing.

The Color Purple (Alice Walker; 1982) Georgia-born Walker's 1930s period novel on African American women in rural Georgia won a Pulitzer Prize.

National Black Arts Festival CULTURAL
(☎404-730-7315; www.nbaf.org; ⊙Sep/Nov) Showcases performing arts, literature and visual arts produced by creative artists of African descent. It is considered one of the most important festivals in the world for art and culture of the African diaspora, and big names like Maya Angelou, Wynton Marsalis and Spike Lee have made appearances.

Atlanta Pride Festival LGBTIQ+
(www.atlantapride.org; Piedmont Park; ⊙Oct) Atlanta's annual LGBTIQ+ festival, one of the oldest and largest in the USA.

Wrecking Bar Strong Beer Fest FOOD & DRINK
(☎404-221-2600; www.wreckingbarbrewpub.com; 292 Moreland Ave NE; $55; ⊙Dec;) There are certainly more extravagant beer festivals in Atlanta, but this one is the one that attracts serious hopheads. Expect over 50 high-gravity beers from Georgia-only breweries.

Sleeping

Downtown

If downtown Atlanta has a problem (other than the traffic), it's a lack of interesting options to sleep – there are but a few independent properties here. Very few people sleep downtown beyond the conventioneer crowd, so internationally recognized chain hotels dominate with few exceptions.

Aloft Atlanta Downtown BOUTIQUE HOTEL $
(Map p50; ☎678-515-0300; www.aloftatlantadowntown.com; 300 Ted Turner Dr NW; r $89-159;) Atlanta's supremely located Aloft hotel is steps from Centennial Olympic Park and peppered with personality (rare for the city's hotels). From the odd but interesting outdoor front patio to a colorful lobby brimming with glittery pop art from a formerly homeless artist and a purple-felt pool table, its playful attitude is refreshing and fun. Rooms are more spacious than most.

Due to its size (almost double that of a normal Aloft with 254 rooms), it was a pilot program for the brand's takeout-pot-breakfast concept, and it's one of the few with a happy hour seven days a week ($5 drinks and $5 food items) from 4pm to 6pm. Parking runs $30 to $35.

Westin Peachtree Plaza HOTEL $$
(Map p50; ☎404-659-1400; www.starwoodhotels.com; 210 Peachtree St NW; r from $163;) Occupying Atlanta's most iconic and tallest building, the cylindrical, 73-story Peachtree Plaza, the Westin has been featured in film (1981's *Sharky's Machine* starring Burt Reynolds) and on nearly every postcard of Atlanta there ever was. Being a well-regarded chain, rooms and amenities are unsurprising – the appeal here is the view (it's the fourth-tallest hotel in the Western Hemisphere).

From the the top, the revolving Sun Dial restaurant spins 360 degrees in 30 minutes and surely offers the city's most panoramic accompaniment to a cocktail and a pan-seared scallop or duck breast. Parking is $45. Internet is $14.95 per night for non–Starwood Preferred Guest members.

American Hotel BOUTIQUE HOTEL $$
(Map p50; ☎404-688-8600; www.doubletree3.hilton.com; 160 Ted Turner Dr NW; r $129-229;) The original Americana Motor Lodge that once occupied this space opened in 1962 – funded by Martin Luther King's dentist – and was Atlanta's first integrated hotel (these walls have slept such icons as Aretha Franklin and James Brown). This new mid-century modern throwback to the original hotel features design elements around every turn that evoke the hotel's storied past.

Starburst light fixtures and snazzy blue hallway carpeting lead to 315 rooms with local headboard art and colorful retro Igloo minibars; an Airstream trailer serves as the pool bar. Parking is $38.

Ellis Hotel BOUTIQUE HOTEL $$
(Map p50; ☎877-211-2545; www.ellishotel.com; 176 Peachtree St NW; r $129-249;) With business-chic rooms warmly dressed in blue and gray hues and ostrich-skin headboards, the Ellis is contemporary and subtly boutique. You can sleep inside a magnetic field in the Wellness Room; or pick a room on the pet-friendly floor, women's-only floor or 'Fresh Air' floor (with private access and special cleaning rules for allergy sufferers).

With a better fitness center than most (a real spinning bike, Precor FTS Glide machine) and a location across the street from Peachtree Center MARTA station, it has a lot going for it.

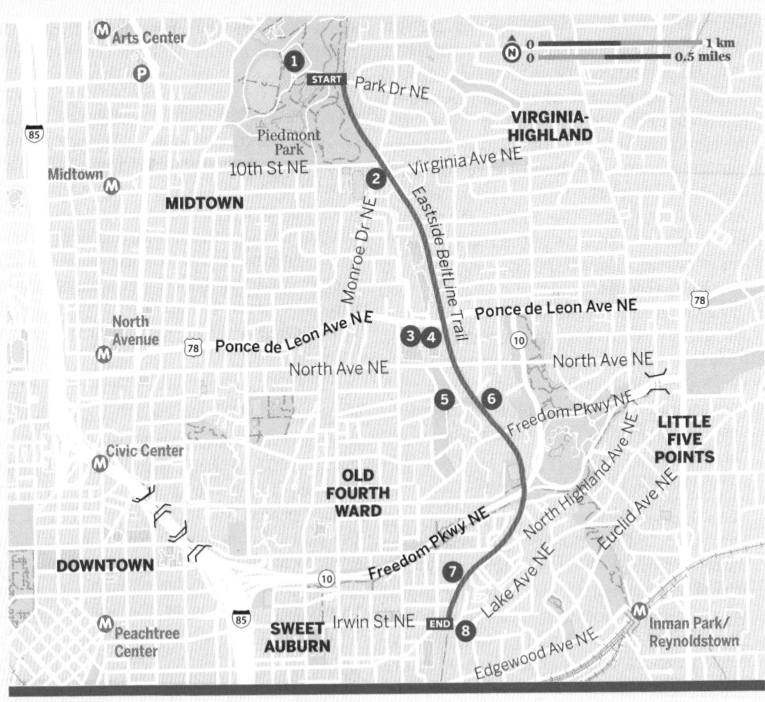

City Walk
Atlanta BeltLine

START PIEDMONT PARK
END KROG STREET MARKET
LENGTH 2 MILES; ONE TO TWO HOURS

The Atlanta BeltLine's awesome 3-mile Eastside Trail connecting Piedmont Park to the hip urban neighborhood of Reynoldstown is a destination-worthy afternoon out. This is the BeltLine's most interesting section from a tourism perspective, taking visitors on a tour through some of the city's hippest districts, hottest restaurants, best bars and breweries, and coolest city markets with pretty scenery and architecture along the way.

Next to **1 Piedmont Park** (p52), juice up on cold-pressed goodness at **2 Arden's Garden** (p78) and hit the BeltLine at the corner of 10th St NE and Monroe Dr. Head south 0.7 miles to **3 Ponce City Market** (p65), the city's newest urban markets, housed inside the former headquarters of Sears, Roebuck and Co. Take some time here to do some boutique shopping or fuel up on caffeine at **4 Spiller Park Coffee** (p76; enter from the trail on the 3rd floor of the market). Cross under North Ave another 0.3 miles and detour west to **5 Historic Fourth Ward Park** (p51), one of the BeltLine's first newly constructed green spaces. Thirsty? Good news – Atlanta's coolest brewery, **6 New Realm Brewing Co** (p75), sits just here on the east side of the trail. Ex–Stone Brewing master-brewer Mitch Steele literally wrote the book on American India pale ales (IPAs), so a pint here is mandatory.

Continuing south another half mile or so, the trail passes under Freedom Pkwy and leans west – you can pop out here and explore the bars and restaurants of Inman Park village or grab the city's favorite popsicle at King of Pops, but don't eat or drink too much, because another 0.3 miles down the trail is **7 Ladybird Grove & Mess Hall** (p76), one of the BeltLine's hippest destinations. You could eat and drink the rest of the day away here, but if you can tear yourself away, continue another 0.2 miles to **8 Krog Street Market** (p64), an abandoned factory turned hip urban market and your final destination. Vendor Hop City has 60 taps of craft beer here.

Glenn Hotel BOUTIQUE HOTEL **$$**
(Map p50; ☎404-521-2250; www.glennhotel.com; 110 Marietta St NW; r $189-269; P ❄ 📶) Modern and elegant, the Glenn is housed in a stately 1923 building that was designed by architect by Waddy B Wood (fantastic name, by the way). Period films loop over the check-in desk, with wafts of lemongrass filling the lobby. Tranquility rocks line the hallways to the rooms, which are a hybrid of contemporary design and historical accents.

Each elevator landing mimics a small art gallery, with carefully curated pieces tucked away in nooks. It's a great choice if you want some individuality mixed with a convenient location almost adjacent to Centennial Olympic Park, with a hip rooftop bar, SkyLounge (p73), to boot. Grab a peach saltwater taffy on the way out!

Hotel Indigo Downtown BOUTIQUE HOTEL **$$**
(Map p50; ☎404-523-7600; www.indigoatlantadowntown.com; 230 Peachtree St NE; r $189-259; P ❄ @ 📶 🐾) Atlanta's second Hotel Indigo has a superb location near Centennial Olympic Park, and a building to match the convenience: a muscular modern structure designed by Atlanta native John Portman. Rooms are crisp and bright, with thoughtful accents like historical photos and splashes of rainbow color.

Ritz-Carlton, Atlanta LUXURY HOTEL **$$$**
(Map p50; ☎404-659-0400; www.ritzcarlton.com/en/hotels/georgia/atlanta; 181 Peachtree St NE; r from $489; P ❄ @ 📶) If you told your author during his college days at the University of Georgia that the fiercely independent coffeehouse Jittery Joe's would someday sit inside a Ritz-Carlton Hotel, he would have had you committed. But here it sits, one of many positives at this 444-room neoclassical luxury downtown hotel.

The sexy lobby – all midnight-blue ban-quettes and chandeliers shrouded in glass drums – leads to richly appointed rooms with marble bathtubs – not exactly common in Atlanta. Parking is $45.

East Side

With numerous historic neighborhoods and atmospheric urban haunts, Atlanta's East Side is where true travelers choose to bed down. Here you'll find historic Queen Anne Victorian homes turned B&Bs, a few independent classics and the city's coolest new boutique hotel – all of which are steps from the city's best food, drinks and nightlife.

Peach House B&B **$**
(Map p62; ☎404-524-8899; www.thepeach.house; 88 Spruce St NE, Inman Park; r $150-250; ❄ 📶) This can't-miss, turquoise-trimmed Georgia Peach of a 1901 Victorian mansion will have you at the porch, a ceiling-fan-cooled, circular-style Southern belle just begging you to accompany it with a glass of wine, cold beer or iced tea. Period furnishings pepper this four-room Inman Park option, with rooms often featuring garden or downtown views.

Highland Inn INN **$**
(Map p62; ☎404-874-5756; www.thehighlandinn.com; 644 N Highland Ave, Virginia-Highland; s/d from $73/103; P ❄ 📶) This European-style, 65-room independent inn, built in 1927, has appealed to touring musicians over the years. Rooms aren't huge, but it has a great location in the Virginia-Highland area and is as affordably comfortable as being Downtown. It's one of the few accommodations in town with single rooms.

★ **Urban Oasis B&B** B&B **$$**
(Map p62; ☎770-714-8618; www.urbanoasisbandb.com; 130a Krog St NE, Inman Park; r $145-215; P ❄ 📶 🏊) Hidden inside a gated and repurposed 1950s cotton-sorting warehouse, this retro-modern loft B&B is urban dwelling at its best. Enter into a huge and funky common area with natural light streaming through massive windows and make your way to one of three rooms, all discerningly appointed with Haywood Wakefield mid-century modern furnishings. It's like sleeping in a Piet Mondrian painting.

A lap pool concealed with louver fencing was recently added. It's on the doorstep of famed Atlanta chef Kevin Rathbun's culinary empire, the Krog Street Market, Edgewood, Inman Park MARTA *and* the BeltLine. Two-night minimum stay.

Sugar Magnolia B&B B&B **$$**
(Map p62; ☎404-222-0226; www.sugarmagnoliabb.com; 804 Edgewood Ave NE, Inman Park; r $155-195; P ❄ @ 📶) This lovely four-room inn occupies an impeccable 1892 Queen Anne Victorian mansion in Inman Park. Five original working fireplaces, a supremely relaxing back porch and firepit are highlights, as is Debbie, hostess with the mostess who whips up Belgian waffles and Dutch baby pancakes for breakfast.

Our favorite room is the blue-curtained Royal Suite with massive terrace and tiled bathroom.

Hotel Clermont BOUTIQUE HOTEL **$$**
(Map p62; ☎470-485-0485; www.hotelclermont.com; 789 Ponce de Leon Ave NE, Poncey-Highland; r $199-319, bunk r $204-314; P❄@📶) With preserved stairwells and unusable original doors, Atlanta's hottest boutique hotel has kept a wink and a nod to this historic 1924 Poncey-Highland building, originally the Bonaventure Arms Apartments. It's decidedly retro and unafraid to be cheeky (the brasserie is named after a former stripper who famously refused to dance with Hitler), and rooms are playful and funky.

Local pop art above the beds, green mid-century-modern-inspired carpeting, gold-plated wallpapering, hand-painted signage and OutKast lyrics inside the in-room safes are just a few of the standout design elements you might stumble across, but it's a tie for the best feature: the awesome rooftop bar versus 15 of the 94 rooms with adult bunk beds that sleep four. Atlanta sleeping disrupter.

Midtown

Midtown is centrally located between Downtown and the nocturnal diversions on both Westside and East Side. There are few sleeping options here, but you'll find a couple of the city's best boutique hotels along with at least one charming top-end B&B.

Hotel Indigo BOUTIQUE HOTEL **$**
(Map p74; ☎404-874-9200; www.ihg.com; 683 Peachtree St NE; r $99-429; P❄@📶🐾) A boutique-style chain hotel, the music-themed Indigo offers a whimsical personality and local in-room touches like custom-stitched patterned bedspreads that echo the iconic Islamic-style domes of the Fox Theatre across the street. The outstanding Midtown location is within walking distance of bars, restaurants and MARTA.

Virginia-Highland B&B B&B **$**
(Map p74; ☎404-892-0434; www.virginiahighlandbb.com; 630 Orme Cir NE, Virginia-Highland; r $139-159, 2-bedroom apt $229; ❄📶) A trestled entry leads to this 1919 arts-and-crafts bungalow, a design-forward time capsule of art deco and mid-century modern furnishings. The three rooms are detailed with atomic rugs, showpiece lampshades, brutalist sculpture and museum-worthy furnishings that look as if they haven't moved in six decades. A screened-in front porch with hammock and backyard meditation labyrinth instill a sense of calm. The somewhat-eclectic owner, Adele, has been hosting travelers for 21 years.

Hotel Artmore BOUTIQUE HOTEL **$$**
(Map p74; ☎404-876-6100; www.artmorehotel.com; 1302 W Peachtree St; r $170-200, ste from $220; P❄@📶) This 1924 Spanish-Mediterranean architectural landmark has been completely revamped into an artistic boutique hotel that's become an urban sanctuary for those who appreciate their trendiness with a dollop of discretion. It wins all sorts of accolades: excellent service, a wonderful courtyard with fire pit and a superb location across the street from Arts Center MARTA station.

Loews Atlanta BUSINESS HOTEL **$$**
(Map p74; ☎404-745-5000; www.loewshotels.com/atlanta-hotel; 1065 Peachtree St; r from $189; P❄@📶) Smart and modern, Atlanta's most boutique business hotel is part of the Loews chain and offers luxury with all the fixins' smack in the heart of the arts in Midtown, walking distance from Woodruff Arts Center and Fox Theatre. The attached Exhale Spa will sooth your weary heart, and the contemporary art adds some high-tech artistic flare.

Georgian Terrace Hotel HISTORIC HOTEL **$$**
(Map p74; ☎404-897-1991; www.thegeorgianterrace.com; 659 Peachtree St NW; r $169-279; P❄@📶🏊) Opened as a hotel in 1911, this 10-story beaux-arts hotel features an airy, light-stealing lobby atrium that beckons travelers to its 326 rooms, which were all in the process of a modern upgrade at the time of research. The most economical rooms are small, but hardwood flooring and newly renovated marble bathrooms ensure a cozy option for solo travelers. Rooftop pool!

In 1939 the hotel's Grand Ballroom hosted the *Gone with the Wind* gala. The film did not premiere across the street at the Fox Theatre but rather at at Loew's Grand Theatre in Downtown. The hotel has a restaurant, coffee shop and fun cocktail bar, Edgar's Proof & Provision (p78).

Twelve Midtown HOTEL **$$**
(Map p74; ☎404-961-1212; www.twelvehotels.com/atlanticstation; 361 17th St NW, Atlantic Station; r $149-449; P❄@📶) Staff isn't all that astute and the hallways need attention, but this 101-room all-suite hotel

at mixed-use Atlantic Station offers sizable rooms for the lower-end price, with full kitchens, a separate living room, spacious bathrooms and hardwood floors. It's great for a long stay or for those who want to be steps from retail and restaurant options. Parking is $28.

★ Stonehurst Place B&B $$$

(Map p74; 404-881-0722; www.stonehurstplace.com; 923 Piedmont Ave NE; r $239-499;) Built in 1896 by the Hinman family, this elegant B&B has all the modern amenities you could ask for and is well located. It's fully updated with ecofriendly water-treatment and heating systems and has original Warhol illustrations on the wall. It's an exceptional choice if you're not on a budget.

W Atlanta – Midtown BOUTIQUE HOTEL $$$

(Map p74; 404-892-6000; www.watlantamidtown.com; 188 14th St NE; r from $299;) One of three Atlanta-area W Hotels, this hip 466-room hotel's big advantage is its prime location on Piedmont Park's doorstep. Rooms feature wine-hued trimmings and all the usual mod cons one would expect from a W, and there's a rooftop pool, Bliss Spa and DJ-spun mixes in the lobby. You know, it's a W.

Greater Atlanta

Solís Two Porsche Drive BOUTIQUE HOTEL $$

(470-466-3300; www.solis2porschedrive.com; Two Porsche Dr, Hapeville; r $179-400, ste $259-900;) Solís' new auto-inspired boutique hotel is next door to Porche's North American headquarters overlooking the 1.6-mile track at the Porsche Experience Center and the runways at Hartsfield-Jackson Inter-national Airport. Common areas are chock-full of vintage Porsche imagery while the 214 rooms feature laser-etched headboards and tailpipe-evoking bedside lamps.

Cool stuff, no doubt, but it's really all about the rooftop Overdrive Lounge, which offers some of the finest transport porn you'll ever see, with views of planes to the right, trains to the left and automobiles in the middle. The 300-sq-ft, 8000-gallon Jacuzzi-like plunge pool isn't bad either and the airport shuttle – with leather seats and USB ports – is one of the classiest you ever did see.

Whitley BOUTIQUE HOTEL $$$

(Map p84; 404-237-2700; www.thewhitleyhotel.com; 3434 Peachtree Rd NE, Buckhead; r from $371;) Converted from one of Atlanta's most storied luxury hotels (Ritz-Carlton, Buckhead) in 2017, the Whitley is named for Atlanta trailblazer John Whitley, who reportedly killed a massive buck in 1840, nailed its head to a tree, and voila! Buckhead was born. Its 507 rooms start at a sizable 360 sq ft with residential-style mahogany flooring and skyline views.

Eating

Downtown

Most Downtown diners aren't really looking for a meal to remember, but for some sustenance between attractions. While no foodie haunt, Downtown is home to old-school classic steakhouses, Southern food staples, a near-endless supply of fast-food and international eats (especially around Peachtree Center station and Georgia State University) and a few diamonds in the culinary rough.

Smoke Ring BARBECUE

(Map p50; www.smokeringatlanta.com; 309 Nelson Street SW, Castleberry Hill; mains $10-15, plates $17-27; 11:30am-10pm Mon-Thu & Sun, to 11pm Fri & Sat;) This sleek Castleberry Hill barbecue restaurant sits in the shadow of Mercedes-Benz Stadium. The pulled pork is divine, especially in the breakfast burrito, but they smoke plenty here beyond the usual suspects, such as ahi tuna, pork belly and lamb belly. The long hardwood bar is ideal for a game-day tipple. It also does a bluegrass brunch on the first Sunday of each month.

Amalfi Pizza PIZZA $

(Map p50; 404-228-7528; www.amalfipizzaatl.com; 17 Andrew Young International Blvd NE; pizzas from $9.50; 11am-10pm Mon-Thu, to 11pm Fri & Sat, noon-10pm Sun;) This new Neapolitan pizzeria makes a for a great Downtown stop for families, with the pies emerging from two dueling, 6000lb wood-burning brick ovens imported from Italy. The way to go here is *carnavale*-style, a star-shaped pizza with a fresh ricotta-stuffed crust – a homage to the original, invented by Pizzeria Attilio in Napoli in the 1930s.

LOCAL KNOWLEDGE

SOUTHERN SPECIALTIES

The most common dish on Atlanta menus is fried green tomatoes – a 1991 smash film of the same name was shot in Atlanta and environs (though set in Alabama) and nominated for two Academy Awards. From its most basic recipe (unripe or green tomatoes coated with cornmeal and fried), there are hundreds of adaptations in every hole-in-the-wall dive and top-end restaurant throughout the city.

A close second is undoubtedly good ol' Southern-fried chicken, probably the single most famous (and most addictive) Southern dish, often marinated in buttermilk for extra oomph. Many of Atlanta's top restaurants have regular fried-chicken events, such as the coveted one at Watershed on Peachtree (p73).

And last but not least, pimento cheese. Traditionally served as a spread but fantastic on sandwiches and burgers too, it's made with sharp cheddar cheese, pimentos and mayonnais, blended into a chunky paste with a variety of add-ins such as jalapeños, cayenne pepper, paprika, cream cheese, Louisiana-style hot sauce, Worcestershire sauce and more. It's not to be missed!

Sweet Auburn Curb Market MARKET **$**
(Map p50; www.thecurbmarket.com; 209 Edgewood Avenue SE; prices vary by vendor; ⏲8am-6pm Mon-Sat, noon-5pm Sun) Atlanta's original historic food hall – it dates to 1924 – is more about fresh produce, meats and seafood than some of the city's other, more gourmet-oriented markets, but there are some favorites here for a meal too, such as Beltline Burritos, Grindhouse Killer Burgers, Venezuelan arepas and soul food aplenty. It's walking distance from Centennial Olympic Park (p48). The whole place smells like sweet caramelized love courtesy of Miss D's New Orleans Pralines!

Herban Fix VEGAN **$$**
(Map p50; www.herbanfix.com; 565 Peachtree St NW; mains $15-19; ⏲1am-3pm & 5-9:30pm Mon-Thu, 11am-3pm & 5-10:30pm Fri & Sat, 11am-3pm Sun; 📶) This contemporary vegan restaurant straddling Midtown and Downtown leans heavily Pan-Asian and will surprise you with its earthy-upscale decor. Dishes are refreshingly creative – grilled eggplant topped with basil and minced garlic, seared pom pom mushroom steak, soy fish with organic kale simmered in laksa curry – and decidedly tasty.

Alma Cocina MEXICAN **$$**
(Map p50; ☎404-968-9662; www.alma-atlanta.com; 191 Peachtree St NW; tacos $15-30, mains $19-21; ⏲11am-3pm & 5-10pm Mon-Thu, 5-11pm Sat, 5-10pm Sun; 📶) 'Soul Kitchen' cooks contemporary tacos and inventive Mexican fare. There might be tequila-poached pear guacamole to start; small plates such as chili-ash-cured Arctic Char with avocado, Fresno chilies, candied ginger and tequila-ginger *aguachile,* or *huitlacoche* empanadas; and mains like achiote-rubbed pork chops and seared scallops in cauliflower-hominy puree. Everything is good. You'll fight for a table during the downtown lunch rush.

Paschal's SOUTHERN US **$$**
(Map p50; ☎404-525-2023; www.paschalsatlanta.com; 180 Northside Dr SW; mains $11-24; ⏲11am-9pm Sun-Thu, to 11pm Fri & Sat) Slinging old-school Southern soul food, Lowcountry cuisine and Cajun/creole staples for six decades, Paschal's touts bone-in fried-chicken sandwiches, slow-cooked ribs and catfish étouffée among its specialties that have been enjoyed by noteworthy entertainers, politicians and folks about town dating all the way back to the Civil Rights movement.

No Mas! Cantina MEXICAN **$$**
(Map p50; ☎404-574-5678; www.nomascantina.com; 180 Walker St SW; mains $13-24; ⏲8am-10pm; 📶 👪) Though the design overkill feels a bit like dining inside a hungover piñata, this festive Downtown Castleberry Hill cantina is popular. Despite its quiet location, it's walking distance from the Mercedes-Benz Stadium, Philips Arena, CNN Center and Centennial Olympic Park.

East Side

A cornucopia of culinary overachievement, Atlanta's East Side is home to the city's hottest table, Staplehouse (p66), which sits atop a near-biblical gastro-mountain of sought-after eats. Wildly popular

East Side

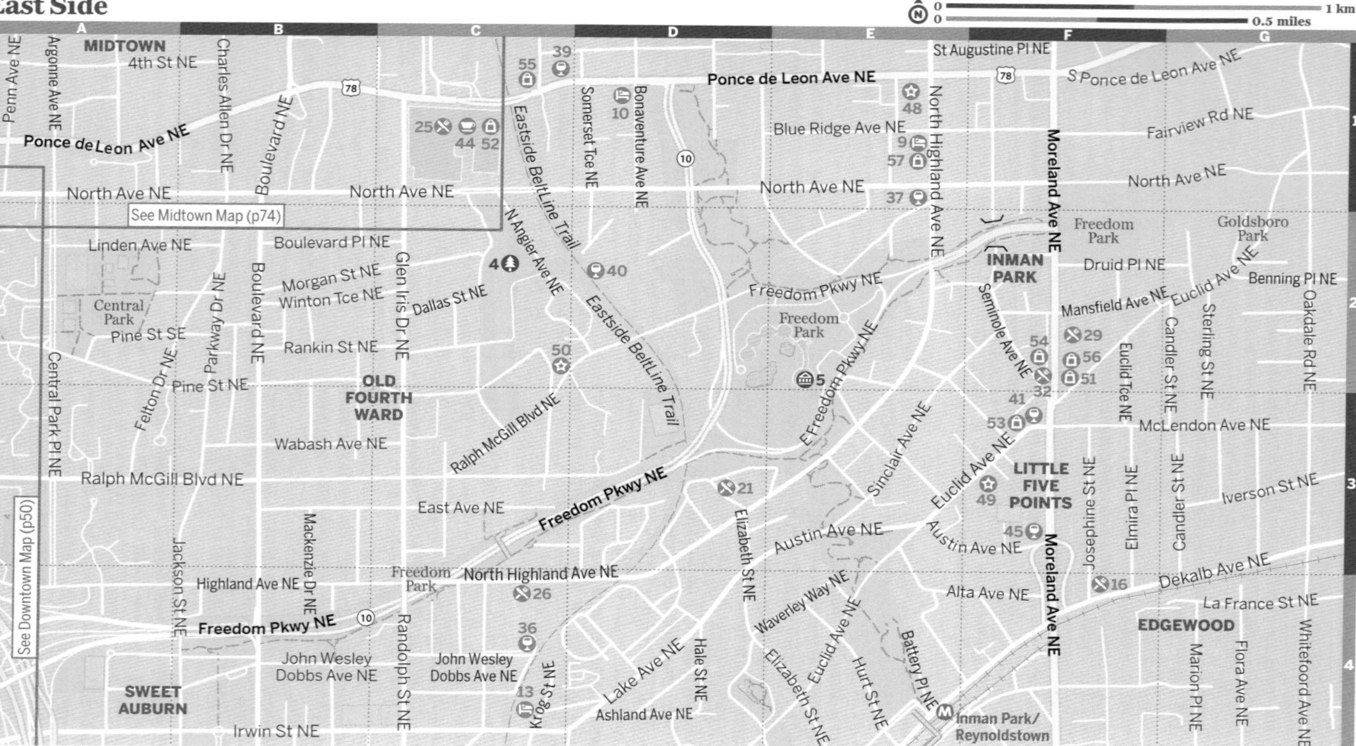
0 1 km
0 0.5 miles
A
B
C
D
E
F
G
1
2
3
4
MIDTOWN
4th St NE
Penn Ave NE
Argonne Ave NE
Charles Allen Dr NE
Boulevard NE
Ponce de Leon Ave NE
78
25
44
52
55
39
Eastside BeltLine Trail
Somerset Tce NE
10
Bonaventure Ave NE
St Augustine Pl NE
S Ponce de Leon Ave NE
48
Blue Ridge Ave NE
9
57
Fairview Rd NE
North Ave NE
See Midtown Map (p74)
37
North Highland Ave NE
Moreland Ave NE
Freedom Park
Goldsboro Park
Linden Ave NE
Boulevard Pl NE
N Angier Ave NE
4
40
INMAN PARK
Druid Pl NE
Benning Pl NE
Morgan St NE
Winton Tce NE
Glen Iris Dr NE
Dallas St NE
Freedom Pkwy NE
Euclid Ave NE
Mansfield Ave NE
Oakdale Rd NE
Central Park
Pine St SE
Parkway Dr NE
Rankin St NE
50
Seminole Ave NE
54
29
56
51
Euclid Tce NE
Candler St NE
Sterling St NE
Pine St NE
OLD FOURTH WARD
Felton Dr NE
Central Park Pl NE
Wabash Ave NE
Ralph McGill Blvd NE
5
E Freedom Pkwy NE
32
41
53
McLendon Ave NE
Sinclair Ave NE
LITTLE FIVE POINTS
49
Josephine St NE
Elmira Pl NE
Iverson St NE
21
East Ave NE
See Downtown Map (p50)
Jackson St NE
Mackenzie Dr NE
Elizabeth St NE
Austin Ave NE
45
Highland Ave NE
26
16
Dekalb Ave NE
Alta Ave NE
La France St NE
EDGEWOOD
Waverley Way NE
36
Lake Ave NE
Hale St NE
Hurt St NE
Battery Pl NE
John Wesley Dobbs Ave NE
Randolph St NE
13
Krog St NE
Ashland Ave NE
SWEET AUBURN
Irwin St NE
Inman Park/Reynoldstown
Marion Pl NE
Flora Ave NE
Whiteford Ave NE

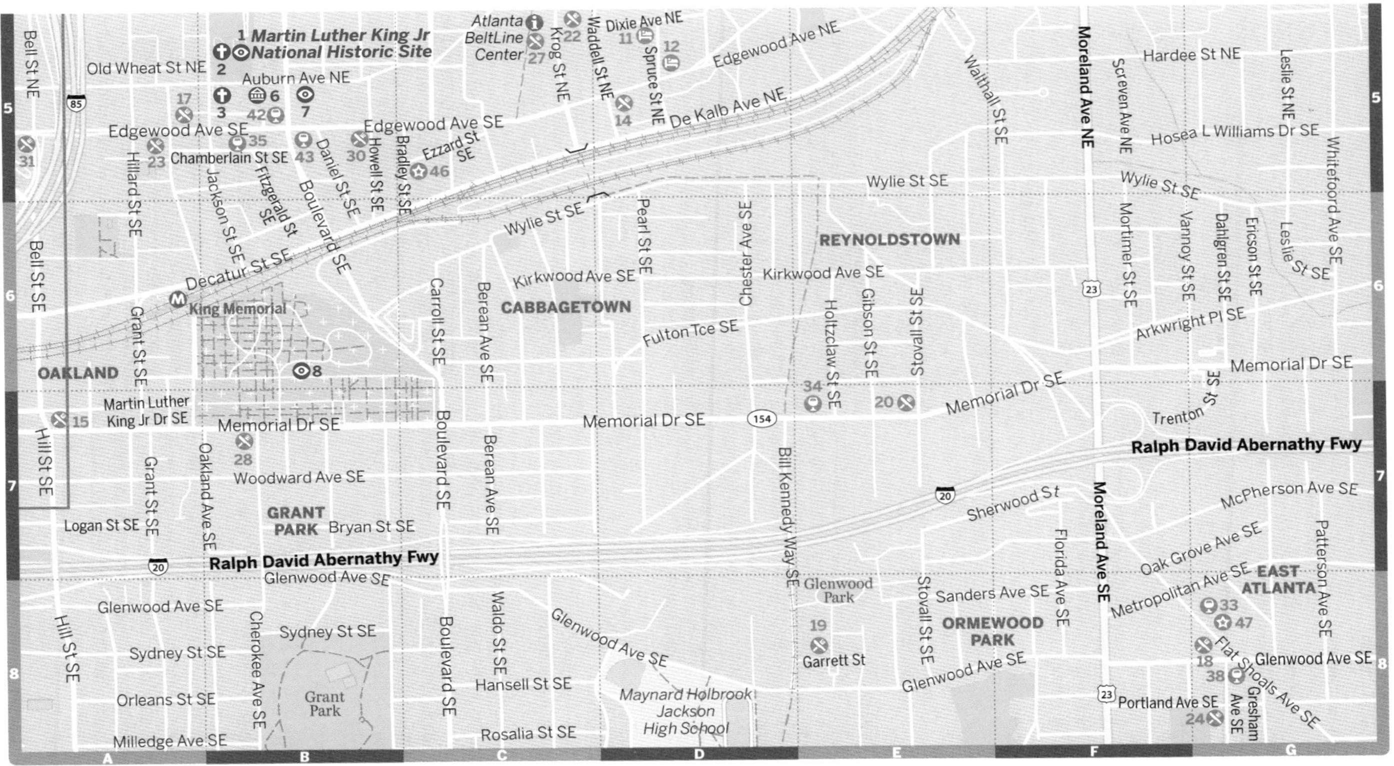
1 Martin Luther King Jr National Historic Site
Atlanta BeltLine Center
Old Wheat St NE
Auburn Ave NE
Edgewood Ave SE
Chamberlain St SE
Jackson St SE
Fitzgerald St SE
Boulevard SE
Daniel St SE
Howell St SE
Bradley St SE
Ezzard St SE
Krog St NE
Waddell St NE
Dixie Ave NE
Spruce St NE
Edgewood Ave NE
De Kalb Ave NE
Walthall St SE
Moreland Ave NE
Screven Ave NE
Hardee St NE
Leslie St NE
Hosea L Williams Dr SE
Whiteford Ave SE
Wylie St SE
Mortimer St SE
Vannoy St SE
Dahlgren St SE
Ericson St SE
Leslie St SE
Arkwright Pl SE
Memorial Dr SE
Trenton St SE
Ralph David Abernathy Fwy
McPherson Ave SE
Bell St NE
Bell St SE
Hillard St SE
Decatur St SE
King Memorial
Grant St SE
OAKLAND
Martin Luther King Jr Dr SE
Hill St SE
Carroll St SE
Berean Ave SE
Kirkwood Ave SE
CABBAGETOWN
Pearl St SE
Chester Ave SE
REYNOLDSTOWN
Fulton Tce SE
Holtzclaw St SE
Gibson St SE
Stovall St SE
Bill Kennedy Way SE
Logan St SE
Oakland Ave SE
Woodward Ave SE
GRANT PARK
Bryan St SE
Glenwood Ave SE
Sherwood St
Florida Ave SE
Moreland Ave SE
Oak Grove Ave SE
Metropolitan Ave SE
EAST ATLANTA
Patterson Ave SE
Sanders Ave SE
ORMEWOOD PARK
Glenwood Park
Garrett St
Waldo St SE
Sydney St SE
Cherokee Ave SE
Orleans St SE
Milledge Ave SE
Grant Park
Hansell St SE
Rosalia St SE
Maynard Holbrook Jackson High School
Flat Shoals Ave SE
Gresham Ave SE
Portland Ave SE
1 2 3 6 7 8 11 12 14 15 17 18 19 20 22 23 24 27 28 30 31 33 34 35 38 42 43 46 47
5 6 7 8
A B C D E F G

ATLANTA

East Side

Top Sights
1 Martin Luther King Jr National Historic Site B5

Sights
2 Ebenezer Baptist Church (New) B5
3 First Ebenezer Baptist Church B5
4 Historic Fourth Ward Park C2
5 Jimmy Carter Presidential Library & Museum E2
6 King Center for Non-Violent Social Change B5
7 Martin Luther King Jr Birthplace B5
8 Oakland Cemetery B6

Sleeping
9 Highland Inn E1
10 Hotel Clermont D1
11 Peach House D5
12 Sugar Magnolia B&B D5
13 Urban Oasis B&B C4

Eating
14 BoccaLupo D5
15 Daddy Dz A7
16 Fox Brothers F4
17 Foxx Original Jamaican Restaurant A5
18 Gaja Korean Bar G8
19 Gunshow E8
20 Home Grown GA E7
21 King of Pops D3
22 Krog Street Market C5
23 Noni's A5
24 Octopus Bar G8
25 Ponce City Market C1
26 Queen of Cream C4
27 Rathbun's C5
28 Ria's Bluebird B7
29 Sevananda F2
30 Staplehouse B5
31 Sweet Auburn Curb Market A5
32 Vortex F2

Drinking & Nightlife
33 Argosy G8
34 Golden Eagle Diner's Club E7
35 Joystick Gamebar B5
36 Ladybird Grove & Mess Hall C4
37 Manuel's Tavern E1
38 Mary's G8
39 MJQ Concourse C1
40 New Realm Brewing Co D2
Paper Crane Lounge .... (see 30)
41 Porter Beer Bar F3
42 Sister Louisa's Church of the Living Room & Ping Pong Emporium B5
43 Sound Table B5
44 Spiller Park Coffee C1
45 Wrecking Bar Brewpub F3

Entertainment
Clermont Lounge .... (see 10)
46 Dad's Garage C5
47 Earl G8
48 Plaza Theatre E1
49 Variety Playhouse F3
50 Venkman's C2

Shopping
51 Abbadabba's F2
52 Citizen Supply C1
53 Criminal Records F3
54 Junkman's Daughter F2
55 Paris on Ponce C1
56 Wish F2
57 Young Blood Boutique E1

gourmet markets, New American foodie haunts, upscale Southern supper clubs and waves of ethnic superstars – Spanish, Italian, Korean fusion, Jamaican, elevated Mexican, old-school Jewish – could fuel your foodie adventures on this side of town for months.

★ Ria's Bluebird AMERICAN $

(Map p62; ☎404-521-3737; www.riasbluebird.com; 421 Memorial Dr SE; breakfast $5-13, sandwiches $11.50; ⊙8am-3pm; P) Ria's makes a big deal about being the kind of business that accepts people of all races, religions and sexual orientations, and supports causes that speak to this commitment. It *also* serves one of the most kick-ass breakfasts in greater Atlanta: enormous skillets and delicious soupy brisket and eggs. For lunch, try a pepper turkey melt. Two thumbs up.

Noni's ITALIAN $

(Map p62; ☎404-343-1808; www.nonisdeli.com; 357 Edgewood Ave SE; mains $6-11; ⊙11:30am-11pm;) At this airy Italian spot with a great outdoor seating area you can have a grappa, then tuck into some homemade tagliatelle Bolognese or grilled shrimp farfalle. Casual, cozy and friendly as hell – we'll be back.

Krog Street Market FOOD HALL $

(Map p62; www.krogstreetmarket.com; 99 Krog St; prices vary by vendor; ⊙7am-9pm Mon-Thu, to 11pm Fri, 8am-11pm Sat, 8am-9pm Sun) This mixed-use complex of hip retail outlets and restaurants is one of the latest anchors of Atlanta's hip and continually gentrifying Inman Park neighborhood. At last count there were 15 food and drink vendors here, offering everything from fried chicken to Chinese dumplings. Favorites include Superica (gourmet Mexican) and Hop City (60 taps of craft beer).

Ponce City Market FOOD HALL $

(Map p62; ☎404-900-7900; www.poncecitymarket.com; 675 Ponce de Leon Ave NE, Midtown; prices vary by vendor; ⊙central food hall 11am-9pm Mon-Sat, noon-8pm Sun) A mixed-use complex housed inside the historic former Sears, Roebuck and Co headquarters in Atlanta, the largest brick structure in the Southeast. Over 20 food vendors occupy this food hall, ranging from candy sellers to Holeman & Finch (Atlanta's best burger), At the Tap (56 taps of craft beer), Spiller Park Coffee, Indian street kabobs and a Moroccan joint.

King of Pops ICE CREAM $

(Map p62; www.kingofpops.com; 337 Elizabeth St NE, Inman Park; popsicles $3; ⊙10am-9pm Mon-Thu, to 10pm Fri & Sat, 11-9pm Sun) Humble beginnings involving a *paleta*-inspired travel dream launched in Central America, a used ice-cream pushcart and routine Twitter frenzies turned King of Pops into Atlanta's most sought-after dessert on a stick. Here at its BeltLine-adjacent HQ, small-batch ice pops in funky flavors like Thai Ice Tea, Coconut Chocolate Sea Salt and Sweet Tea n' Lemonade emerge from its walk-up window.

Queen of Cream ICE CREAM $

(Map p62; www.queenofcream.com; 701 Highland Ave NE, No 1; scoops $3-7; ⊙12:30-9:30pm Mon-Thu, to 10:30pm Fri & Sat, 2-9pm Sun) This sweet creamery sources its dairy daily from Waynesboro and claims to be the only ice-cream parlor in Atlanta whipping up its dense and tasty wares from scratch. There are eight classic flavors (cookies and cream is the most popular but...try cold-brew coffee cocoa nib crunch!) and four rotating in and out (sea-salt caramel); and insane seasonal sundaes (from $7).

Foxx Original Jamaican Restaurant JAMAICAN $

(Map p62; ☎404-523-1331; http://foxxoriginaljamaican.com; 378 Edgewood Ave SE; mains $5.50-17.50; ⊙11:30am-9pm Mon-Thu, to 10:30pm Fri & Sat, 1-7pm Sun) Small and colorful takeout restaurant Foxx doles out some delicious beef patties, oxtail soup, curry goat and fish *escovitch* (vinegar-pepper sauce – gorgeous). On a Hotlanta summer day (or anytime, really), a little bit of that Caribbean goodness, washed down with some coconut water, is pretty damn perfect.

Home Grown GA AMERICAN $

(Map p62; ☎404-222-0455; www.homegrownga.com; 968 Memorial Dr SE; mains $8-22; ⊙7am-3pm Mon-Fri, to 2pm Sat & Sun) Southern favorites stick to your ribs after they're delivered across a bare counter at this friendly spot. Munch on chili-cheese slaw dogs or fried catfish for lunch, or load up on home fries, eggs, pork chops and gravy for breakfast. There's even a vegan sloppy Joe!

Sevananda SUPERMARKET $

(Map p62; ☎404-681-2831; www.sevananda.coop; 467 Moreland Ave NE, Little Five Points; ⊙8am-10pm) Widely considered one of Atlanta's best health-food stores, this is a gold mine for self-caterers.

★ **Octopus Bar** FUSION $$

(Map p62; ☎404-627-9911; www.octopusbaratl.com; 560 Gresham Ave SE, East Atlanta; dishes $6-22; ⊙10:30pm-2:30am Tue-Sat) Leave your hang-ups at the hotel – this is punk-rock dining – and get to know what's good at this unsigned indoor-outdoor patio dive nuanced with graffitied-up walls and ethereal electronica. No reservations, so line up early, and chow down on a Maine lobster roll (drawn butter, tomalley mayo), shoyu ramen (farm egg) or many other innovative executions of fusion excellence.

Do they keep odd hours? Is seating difficult to come by? Does it take forever to get your grub because the chefs are too busy fielding industry complaints from a room full of sous chefs and servers? The answer, of course, is yes. It's hidden within So Ba Vietnamese restaurant and everything – including the cocktails – changes daily.

★ **Fox Brothers** BARBECUE $$

(Map p62; www.foxbrosbbq.com; 1238 DeKalb Ave NE, Inman Park; dishes $10-30; ⊙11am-10pm Sun-Thu, to 11pm Fri & Sat; P) At this longtime Atlanta classic, set in Inman Park, ribs are scorched and smoked perfectly with a hint of charcoal crust on the outside and tender on the inside. It's also known for its exceptional Texas-style brisket and Brunswick-stew-smothered tater tots. Always packed.

★ **BoccaLupo** ITALIAN $$

(Map p62; ☎404-577-2332; http://boccalupoatl.com; 753 Edgewood Ave NE, Inman Park; mains $16-19; ⊙5:30-10pm Tue-Thu, to 11pm Fri & Sat;) There is so much to love about this dark, candlelit Italian-Southern comfort-food haunt led by Mario Batali–trained chef Bruce Logue, but perhaps none more than his Southern-fried-chicken parm with creamy collards and *strano* pasta. It's hands down a top-five Atlanta dish. This Southern soul food with Italian tweak is made with a lotta love and not to be missed. Reserve at least two weeks in advance. If not, the bar accepts walk-ins and is packed as soon as the door opens.

Daddy Dz BARBECUE **$$**

(Map p62; ☎404-222-0206; www.daddydz.com; 264 Memorial Dr SE; sandwiches $7-13, plates $13-23; ⏲11am-10pm Mon-Thu, to 11pm Fri & Sat, noon-9pm Sun; Ⓟ) A juke joint of a barbecue shack, consistently voted one of the top in town, with a central location. From the graffiti murals on the red, white and blue exterior, to the all-powerful smoky essence, to the reclaimed booths on the covered patio, there is soul to spare. Order the succulent ribs with corn bread, and you'll leave smiling.

Vortex BURGERS **$$**

(Map p62; ☎404-688-1828; www.thevortexbarandgrill.com; 438 Moreland Ave NE, Little Five Points; burgers $10.50-19.95; ⏲11am-midnight Sun-Thu, to 2am Fri & Sat) An NC-17 joint cluttered with Americana memorabilia, the godfather of Atlanta burger joints is where alterna-hipsters mingle alongside Texas tourists and Morehouse College steppers. Burgers range from impressive to outlandish but are always some of the most heralded and heart-stopping in Atlanta. The 20ft-tall skull facade is a Little Five Points landmark of pre-Olympic Games outrageousness.

Rathbun's NEW AMERICAN **$$**

(Map p62; ☎404-524-8280; www.kevinrathbun.com; 112 Krog St; mains $15-27; ⏲5:30-10pm Mon-Thu, to 11pm Fri & Sat; 📶) The hip industrial space inside the old Atlanta Stove Works factory plays second fiddle to the diverse menu – eggplant fries with confectioner's sugar, roasted duck with Thai risotto – at this foodie stronghold. Start at the intimate sidecar wine-bar Krog Bar for a tipple before dinner. It's another winner along the BeltLine's Eastside Trail.

Gaja Korean Bar KOREAN **$$**

(Map p62; ☎404-835-2126; www.gajaeav.com; 491 Flat Shoals Ave SE, East Atlanta; dishes $5-15; ⏲5pm-1am Tue-Sat, to 10pm Sun; 📶) This small-plate hipster Korean feels like a find as it's tucked away a bit deeper into the parking lots of Flat Shoals Ave than some of its neighbors. Excellent small plates such as blistered *shishito* peppers in garlic and sweet soy or pan-fried Brussels sprouts with pork belly and *gochujang* honey wash are washed down splendidly with soju.

★**Gunshow** MODERN AMERICAN **$$$**

(Map p62; ☎404-380-1886; www.gunshowatl.com; 924 Garrett St SE, Glenwood Park; dishes $10-18; ⏲6-9pm Tue-Sat; 📶) Celebrity chef Kevin Gillespie's innovative and unorthodox Gunshow is an explosively good night out. Guests choose between over a dozen or so smallish dishes, dreamed up by chefs in the open kitchen, who then hawk their blood, sweat and culinary tears dim-sum-style tableside.

It can be agonizing, turning your nose up at bulgogi baby back ribs because you're holding out for a Japanese bacon and shrimp pancake, but it's a dining experience like no other. Reservations open on Yelp 30 days out.

★**Staplehouse** AMERICAN **$$$**

(Map p62; ☎404-524-5005; www.staplehouse.com; 541 Edgewood Ave SE; dishes $5-36; ⏲5:30-10pm Wed & Thu, to 11pm Fri & Sat, noon-4pm Sun; Ⓟ📶) 🍃 The hottest table in Atlanta and the darling du jour of Southern foodies, Staplehouse dishes up innovative, seasonal New American cuisine. Small to medium plates like chicken-liver tart with burnt honey and blood orange are served with such artful precision you kinda feel bad about eating them (except they're delicious, so not *that* bad). The seasonal menu changes often.

Reservations open online on the second Friday of every month at noon for the next calendar month; walk-ins are only welcome at the eight-person bar – get there by 5pm and wait in front of the Wally World garage. All proceeds from the restaurant go to the Giving Tree, which provides health care for food-and-beverage-industry workers in need.

Midtown

Midtown is not Atlanta's most exciting place to eat (mainly because it's more of a clubbing neighborhood, so most folks eat elsewhere and head in late), but there is plenty of choice here, including a few of the city's best old-school and upscale Southern eats.

Café Intermezzo CAFE $

(Map p74; www.cafeintermezzo.com; 1065 Peachtree St NE, suite 2; desserts $9.75; 9am-1am Mon-Thu, to 2am Fri & Sat, to noon Sun;) This European-style cafe has given Atlantans a dose of high-society class since 1971. The austere atmosphere, punctuated by crystal chandeliers and turn-of-the-century decor, evokes storied Viennese haunts; and both the packed pastry case (three-layer orange torte, tres leches, Italian cream torte!) and 40-page beverage menu overwhelm – but in a good way. It remains a special place for posttheater dessert.

Varsity FAST FOOD $

(Map p74; www.thevarsity.com; 61 North Ave NW; combos $6.75-9.50; 10:30am-10pm Sun-Thu, to midnight Fri & Sat) Presidents have dined here (George W Bush, Bill Clinton, Barack Obama), movies have been filmed here *(We Are Marshall)*, millions have eaten here: this iconic greasy spoon (at it since 1928) is the world's largest drive-in. In response to its famous call to order ('What'll Ya Have?'), you can order dishes such as chili dogs and triple-stack bacon cheeseburgers.

The most famous order? Combo number one (two chili dogs, onion rings and a frosted-orange milkshake/slushie hybrid) although there's a whole lotta other stuff that will clog your arteries but please your palate (especially if your palete is drunk). The franchise has expanded to several additional Atlanta and North Georgia locations over the years but here sits the original.

Ecco EUROPEAN $$

(Map p74; 404-347-9555; www.ecco-atlanta.com; 40 7th St NE; mains $19-33; 5:30-10pm Sun-Thu, to 1pm Fri & Sat;) Sustainable Ecco was named America's best new restaurant in 2006 by *Esquire* and you can certainly have a blowout meal here. But you can also go the tapas route ($7 to $19) and leave with change in your pocket. The fried goat's cheese with honey and black pepper and the chili-braised pork with garlic and homemade pappardelle are both extraordinary.

Einstein's BREAKFAST $$

(Map p74; 404-876-7925; www.einsteinsatlanta.com; 1077 Juniper St NE; brunch $9-21; 11am-11pm Mon-Thu, to 1am Fri, 9am-11pm Sat & Sun;) Eclectic Einstein's is a come-one, come-all, free-spirited microcosm of urban living. Gay couples to the left, hip-hop artists to the right, all noshing on Southern-angled, organic-where-possible brunch dishes such as fried-green-tomato eggs Benedict with goat's cheese and a side of pepper-Jack grits or spicy seafood omelets chased with monstrous Bloody Marys (one of Atlanta's best). The front porch packs 'em in when the weather is nice.

> LOCAL KNOWLEDGE
>
> **BUFORD HIGHWAY EATS**
>
> Get off the beaten path and explore Buford Hwy's ethnic restaurants, markets and shopping centers. You'll feel as if you have stepped into several different countries, yet you're only 20 to 30 minutes from downtown Atlanta.

Empire State South SOUTHERN US $$$

(Map p74; 404-541-1105; www.empirestatesouth.com; 999 Peachtree St NE; mains $31-46; 7-10:30am & 11:30am-10pm Mon-Thu, to 11pm Fri & Sat, 10am-3pm Sun;) This rustic-hip Midtown bistro serves imaginative New Southern fare and it does not disappoint, be it at breakfast ($7.50 to $11) or throughout the remains of the day. It makes its own bagels, the attention to coffee detail approaches Pacific Northwest levels, and it mixes fried chicken, bacon marmalade *and* pimento cheese on a biscuit!

Nan Thai THAI $$$

(Map p74; 404-870-9933; www.nanfinedining.com; 1350 Spring St NW, No 1; mains $18-39; 11:30am-2:30pm & 5:30-10pm Mon-Thu, 11:30am-2:30pm & 5:30-11pm Fri, 5-11pm Sat, 5-10pm Sun;) Straight outta Bangkok, Chef Nan honed her culinary prowess alongside her mother, who ran one of the Thai capital's legendary street-food stalls. Wear a collared shirt – this is highbrow dining – and reserve ahead.

In case you're not convinced, dishes such as *pla sahm rod* (pan-roasted Chilean sea bass with chili sauce, crispy okra, bean curd, green beans and eggplant) and *kai yang* Massaman (grilled lemongrass chicken breast in Massaman curry with avocado, green beans, cashew nuts, pickled shallots and cucumber salad) will do the trick.

Mary Mac's Tea Room SOUTHERN US $$$

(Map p74; 404-876-1800; www.marymacs.com; 224 Ponce de Leon Ave; meals $26.95; 11am-9pm) Fried chicken (often voted Atlanta's best), tomato pie and fried green tomatoes are just a few of the Southern specialties that Mary Mac's has been dishing out family-style since 1945 (cinnamon rolls too, but they're not Southern!). It distinctly feels like dining at grandma's house, but ain't nobody ever complained about that! This old-school eatery has heart and soul.

South City Kitchen SOUTHERN US **$$$**
(Map p74; 404-873-7358; www.southcitykitchen.com; 1144 Crescent Ave NE; mains $18-40; 11am-3:30pm & 5-10pm Mon-Fri, 11am-3:30pm & 5-10:30pm Fri, 10am-3pm & 5-10:30pm Sat, 10am-3pm & 5-10pm Sun;) An upscale, longstanding Southern kitchen featuring tasty updated and elaborated staples like buttermilk-fried chicken served with sautéed collards and red-bliss potatoes, catfish Reubens and shrimp and Geechee Boy grits with tasso ham and smoked tomato-poblano gravy. Start with goat's-cheese-stuffed fried green tomatoes, a Southern specialty *before* the movie.

Westside

Quite frankly, you could spend a week eating in the Westside Provisions District and have consistently mind-blowing food. This is the city's foodie fantasyland.

★ **Busy Bee Café** SOUTHERN US
(Map p84; 404-525-9212; www.thebusybeecafe.com; 810 Martin Luther King Jr Dr NW; mains $12-16; 11am-7pm Mon-Fri, noon-7pm Sun) Politicians, police officers, urbanites and hungry miscreants, along with celebrities (it's had pop-ins by MLK Jr, Obama and OutKast) all converge over the city's best fried chicken paired with soul-food sides such as collard greens, candied yams, fried okra and mac 'n' cheese. This Westside classic has been steeped in hospitality and honest-to-goodness food since 1947.

West Egg Cafe DINER **$**
(Map p80; 404-872-3973; www.westeggcafe.com; 1100 Howell Mill Rd, Westside Provisions District; mains $6-15; 7am-4pm Mon-Fri, 8am-5pm Sat & Sun;) Belly up to the marble breakfast counter or grab a table and dive into black-bean cakes and eggs, turkey-sausage Benedict, pimento-cheese and bacon omelet, or a fried green tomato BLT. It's all reimagined versions of old-school classics, served in a stylish and spare dining room.

City Walk
Peachtree Prowl

START HIGH MUSEUM OF ART
END CENTENNIAL OLYMPIC PARK
LENGTH 2.7 MILES; THREE TO SIX HOURS

The big joke among Atlantans and anyone who visits the city is that the Georgia capital is home to hundreds of streets named Peachtree. Everywhere you turn, Peachtree St, Peachtree Ave, Peachtree Lane, Peachtree this, Peachtree that! While it's not an entirely untrue observation – there are actually 71 streets in metro Atlanta with some variant of Peachtree in their name – there is only one Peachtree that really matters and that is Peachtree St NE, which cuts through the heart of the city from Midtown to Downtown, passing some of the city's most iconic sights along the way.

This walk kicks off at one of Midtown's most notable buildings, the **1 High Museum of Art** (p52) – you can't miss its blinding white facade – and you'll definitely want to pop in for a bit of museum-browsing as it is considered the most important art museum in the Southeast. After you've had your fill of European art and world-class photography, head south on Peachtree St NE where you can pop into **2 Café Intermezzo** (p67) for a gander and an espresso, pause and admire the French-renaissance-revival, Victorian-era **3 Wimbish House** or stop for a game of cornhole at **4 10th St Pocket Park**, also home to an interesting art installation. Venske & Spänle's *Autoeater* was carved from a slab of 16-ton Carrera marble imported from Italy, and can be seen swallowing a Fiat Panda whole – python-style.

After 0.8 miles, you'll arrive at 10th St NE; head a few steps west to the **5 Margaret Mitchell House & Museum** (p52). This protected apartment home on the National Register of Historic Places is where Mitchell lived and composed her famous opus, *Gone with the Wind*. If you spent an hour or so at both museums, you'll be looking at lunchtime, and one of Midtown's best restaurants, **6 Empire State South** (p67), is just across the street at the corner with Peachtree Pl NE. Chef Hugh Acheson's modern takes on upscale Southern dining is the perfect pick-me-up for the afternoon.

Continue south down Peachtree St NE another 0.6 miles, passing several interesting and seemingly out-of-place churches on the left-hand side along the way, including the 1902 gray granite 7 **St Mark United Methodist Church** and the Gothic/art deco 1905 8 **Lutheran Church of the Redeemer**. From the latter, you can just start to make out the ornate Moorish exterior and retro-red marquee of the 9 **Fox Theatre** (p82), originally built in 1928 as a home for Atlanta's Shriners organization. Across the street is the 10 **Georgian Terrace Hotel** (p59), a beaux-arts nod to Paris erected in 1911. It was here in the hotel's Grand Ballroom that the premiere gala for *Gone with the Wind* was held.

As you continue south on Peachtree St NE, you'll cross into downtown Atlanta at North Ave – note the Romanesque 11 **North Ave Presbyterian Church** on your left – and things will get decidedly busier and more hectic. Don't forget to catch a glimpse of the 1897 Romanesque 12 **Basilica of the Sacred Heart of Jesus** just past Ivan Allen Jr Blvd NE (granted minor basilica status by Pope Benedict XVI).

The street splits just before 13 **SunTrust Plaza**, Atlanta's second-tallest building, so stay right to remain on Peachtree St NE. Walk another 0.1 mile and glance left to the Hyatt Regency – you'll see its iconic blue dome, an Atlanta skyline mainstay, as you approach. Inside the dome is 14 **Polaris** (p73), a great spot for a cocktail, but it doesn't open until 5pm. Head west at the next intersection on John Portman Blvd NW, which will run smack into 15 **Centennial Olympic Park** (p48) after about 0.3 miles.

Now you have some serious decisions. Do you quench your thirst inside the 16 **World of Coca-Cola** (p48)? Take a poignant trip back to darker days at the 17 **Center for Civil & Human Rights** (p48)? Ogle sea lions inside the massive 18 **Georgia Aquarium** (p48)? Pledge allegiance to your favorite team at the 19 **College Football Hall of Fame** (p48)? Or get a bird's-eye view of the metro Atlanta area from the 200-ft-high 20 **Skyview Atlanta** (p49)? It's all here surrounding the 21-acre urban park, one of Atlanta's lasting legacies from the 1996 Summer Olympics. If that's too overwhelming, you can wander the park as well – there's a dancing Fountain of Rings water fountain, a Quilt of Remembrance in honor of the victims of the 1996 Olympic bombing and a water garden.

Taqueria del Sol MEXICAN $

(Map p80; www.taqueriadelsol.com; 1200b Howell Mill Rd; tacos $2.30-2.80, enchiladas $3.60; 11am-2pm & 5:30-9pm Tue-Thu, to 10pm Fri & Sat;) Smoked-pork or fried-chicken tacos and to-die-for shrimp corn chowder are highlights of this Mexican-Southern marriage, an incomparable value in a city that can overwhelm with both sides of that culinary coin. It has expanded throughout Georgia and Tennessee since its humble beginnings here in 2000.

Star Provisions Market & Cafe SUPERMARKET $

(Map p84; 404-365-0410; www.starprovisions.com; 1460 Ellsworth Industrial Blvd NW; mains $8-16; 8am-6pm Mon-Sat, to 4pm Sun;) DIY gourmets will feel at home among the cheese shops and butcher cases, bakeries, organic cafe and kitchen-hardware depots attached to the city's finest dining establishment, Bacchanalia (p72). Excellent picnic and craft-coffee accoutrements. It serves breakfast all day, gourmet sandwiches and pizzas.

★ **Cooks & Soldiers** BASQUE $$

(Map p80; 404-996-2623; www.cooksandsoldiers.com; 691 14th St NW; small plates $6-16; 5-10pm Sun-Wed, to 11pm Thu, to 2am Fri & Sat;) A game-changing Westside choice, this Basque-inspired hot spot specializes in *pintxos* (Basque-like tapas) and wood-fired *asadas* (grills) designed to share. Both the food and cocktails are outstanding. Highlights include the house gin and tonics, coal-roasted mushrooms with goat's cheese, crème fraîche and black truffle, and an $84 wood-grilled bone-in rib eye that clocks in at an obviously shareable 2.2lbs (1kg)!

JCT Kitchen & Bar SOUTHERN US $$

(Map p80; 404-355-2252; www.jctkitchen.com; 1198 Howell Mill Rd, Westside Provisions District; mains $17-38; 11am-2:30pm & 5-10pm Mon-Thu, to 11pm Fri & Sat, 4:30-9pm Sun;) Upscaled Southern staples are the backbone at this trendy Westside Provisions District mainstay overlooking one of the city's iconic rail lines. Slow-cooked chicken leg and dumplings, fried chicken with housemade hot sauce, smoky mountain trout and a grown-up grilled cheese are highlights, while the upstairs bar features smaller bites and craft cocktails ($10 to $13). Crowd is trendy.

★ **Marcel** STEAK $$$

(Map p80; 404-665-4555; www.marcelatl.com; 1170 Howell Mill Rd, Westside Provisions District; steaks $49.95-129.95; 5-10pm Mon-Thu, to 11pm Fri & Sat;) Ford Fry's French-style, boxing-themed steakhouse serves unquestionably expensive, unequivocally transcendent cuts of beef from hormone-free, purebred Black Angus cattle from Chicago's Linz Heritage Angus Ranch. Each cut is a labor of love draped over smoldering Georgia hickory wood and finished with salted butter. Perfect order: divinely crusted bone-in filet, brandy *au poivre* sauce, béarnaise fries and burgundy-roasted mushrooms. It's a temple of carnivorous arts unparalleled in Atlanta.

★ **Optimist** SEAFOOD $$$

(Map p80; 404-477-6260; www.theoptimistrestaurant.com; 914 Howell Mill Rd; mains $22-68; 11:30am-2:30pm & 5-10pm Mon-Thu, 5-11pm Fri & Sat, 5-10pm Sun;) In a short space, we could never do this Westside sustainable-seafood mecca justice. In a word, astonishing! Start with crispy calamari with salsa *matcha* and almonds then move on to a duck-fat-poached swordfish or a daring whole grilled octopus with *aji amarillo* and poblano peppers, and finish with a scoop of housemade salted-caramel ice cream.

This is one of the South's most buzzed about hot spots, not a word of it heresy. If you can't get a reservation, plop yourself down at the massive fresh-oyster bar. Alternatively, just practice your putting skills on the three-hole green and smell that miraculous food – arguably a better option than actually eating at lesser establishments.

★ **Miller Union** AMERICAN $$$

(Map p80; 678-733-8550; www.millerunion.com; 999 Brady Ave NW; mains lunch $12-16, dinner $23-36; 11:30am-2:30pm Tue-Sat, plus 5-10pm Mon-Thu, 5-11pm Fri & Sat;) Credit to Miller Union – it takes its farm-to-table locavore ethos seriously. The result is exceedingly delicious Southern-inspired fare: farm egg baked in celery cream with grilled bread; country chicken with Carolina gold rice, coconut, almond and chutney; or chicken, pecan-sage pesto, apple, smoked cheddar and arugula sandwiches. It's nonstop delicious.

Greater Atlanta

★**Desta Ethiopian Kitchen** ETHIOPIAN $
(Map p84; www.destaethiopiankitchen.com; 3086 Briarcliff Rd NE; mains $8-15; 10am-10pm Sun-Thu, to midnight Fri & Sat;) It's worth a trip to the burbs for this authentic Ethiopian – there's a wait list *before* noon – where vibrant dishes like *tibs* (saucy sautéed meat or fish with onion, tomatoes, peppers and berbere chili powder), *misir wot* (spicy red-lentil stew) and *kitfo* (raw minced beef with *mitmita* seasoning and Ethiopian-spiced butter) pop with flavor. Sop it all up with injera bread (a spongy, sourdough-risen flatbread) and toast with beer and wine. It's in Druid Hills, 5 miles north of Decatur.

★**Waffle House** DINER $
(Map p84; www.wafflehouse.com; 2850 E College Ave; breakfast $3-10.70, mains $1-11; 24hr) To say Waffle House is an Atlanta institution is an insult to Waffle House – this quintessential greasy-spoon diner is... everything! And while there are a million locations in Atlanta proper (OK, more like 130-plus), this Avondale Estates location is less than a half mile down the street from the original 1955 location at 2719 E College Ave (now a museum).

There's no Atlantan who hasn't munched down on patty melt (a flattened burger with caramelized onions and cheese on toasted bread) with hash browns covered (with cheese) and topped (with chili); or a sausage, egg and cheese grits bowl; or a pecan waffle at some point in their lives. Some Atlanta-area interstate exits actually feature dueling locations on either side of the highway. There are country songs about Waffle House too. You get the picture – Waffle House is awesome.

Northern China Eatery CHINESE $
(770-458-2282; www.northernchinadoraville.com; 5141 Buford Hwy NE, Doraville; mains $6-18; 10am-10pm) We love a restaurant with an unambiguous name – and cuisine. At the Eatery, you'll find real-deal northern Chinese cuisine from a Tianjin chef: spicy beef lung, *dan dan* noodles, barbecue lamb and more dumplings than you can shake a (chop) stick at. Located on the Buford Hwy, the city's hotbed of ethnic eats, in the far northeastern Atlanta suburbs.

Sam's BBQ1 BARBECUE $
(770-977-3005; www.bbq1.net; 4944 Lower Roswell Rd, Marietta; plates $9-16.50; 11am-7:30pm Mon-Thu, to 8pm Fri & Sat, to 3pm Sun;) Sam's BBQ1 is run by grill-master Sam Huff, who makes pork so tender, sweet and satisfying that he's been immortalized in song (and on the Food Network). He smokes pork, chicken, brisket, ribs, sausages and turkey. But like elsewhere, pork is king, and he has the awards to prove it. Sam's is in Marietta, a suburb far northwest of Atlanta proper.

Ann's Snack Bar FAST FOOD $
(Map p84; 1615 Memorial Dr SE, Kirkwood; burger with fries $9.50; 11am-7pm Tue-Sat) 'Miss Ann' Price, who started Ann's in 1974 and lost a battle with breast cancer 41 years later, was a true Atlanta culinary legend. You didn't cross Ann. You didn't break her rules. Of course, that made her internationally known Ghetto Burger (it has been called the world's greatest by numerous critics on numerous occasions) all the more satisfying. The burger – the messiest, most ridiculous double-stack of beef topped with ketchup, mustard, chili, lettuce, onions, tomatoes, cheese, deep-fried bacon and special seasonings you could ever imagine – lives on at this Kirkwood dive.

Farm Burger BURGERS $
(Map p84; www.farmburger.net; 410b W Ponce de Leon Ave; burgers $7-10; 11:30am-10pm Sun-Thu, to 11pm Fri & Sat;) Southeastern sweetgrass-fed, locally farm-raised beef is the calling at this gourmet farm-to-table burger joint, a trailblazer in an ongoing Atlanta burger war. Build your own from $7 from an unorthodox list that includes oxtail marmalade, roasted bone marrow and pimento cheese (a Southern staple), or go for the daily-changing chalkboard specials. No antibiotics. No hormones.

Chai Pani INDIAN $
(Map p84; 404-378-4030; www.chaipanidecatur.com; 406 W Ponce de Leon Ave, Decatur; mains $9-13; 11am-3pm & 5:30-9:30pm Mon-Thu, to 10pm Fri & Sat, to 9pm Sun;) This casual and fun Indian transplant from Asheville comes with James Beard Award–nominated chef Meherwan Irani, who offers a vibrant menu of homeland street snacks *(chaat)*, creative sandwiches, *uttapam* (rice and lentil crepes) and *thalis* (platter of various dishes). It's toned down for an American palate, but Bombay staples like *bhel puri* and *vada pav* take us to India's west coast!

LOCAL KNOWLEDGE

DINING IN DECATUR

Independent Decatur, 6 miles east of downtown, is a countercultural enclave and a bona-fide foodie destination. As in most traditional Southern towns, the gazebo-crowned Courthouse Sq is the center of the action, with a number of restaurants, cafes and shops surrounding it.

Victory SANDWICHES $

(Map p84; 404-377-9300; www.vicsandwich.com; 340 Church St, Decatur; sandwiches $4-5; 11am-2am;) This spare, converted brick house in Decatur is a wonderful bargain gourmet-sandwich counter where baguettes are stuffed with white anchovies and lemon mayo, or chicken and ghost-pepper Jack, among other intriguing options.

Colonnade AMERICAN $

(Map p84; 404-874-5642; http://colonnadeatlanta.com; 1879 Cheshire Bridge Rd NE; mains $14-27; 5-9pm Mon-Thu, to 10pm Fri, noon-9pm Sat, 11:30am-9pm Sun; P) Colonnade feels like it stepped out of some 1950s mid-century modern handbook on how to create a restaurant. But the clientele runs a demographic gamut – it's a mix of churchy old-timers and silver-fox couples – and the food is hearty Southern fare at its finest. Try the fried chicken and mingle at the bar.

Leon's Full Service FUSION $$

(Map p84; 404-687-0500; www.leonsfullservice.com; 131 E Ponce de Leon Ave; mains $13-28; 5pm-1am Mon, 11:30am-1am Tue-Thu & Sun, to 2am Fri & Sat;) Leon's can come across as a bit pretentious, but the gorgeous concrete bar and open floor plan spilling out of a former service station and on to a groovy heated deck with floating beams remains cooler than thou and fully packed at all times. You may find prosciutto-wrapped trout and braised short ribs on the changing menu.

Everything, from the beer (14 taps), wine and cocktails ($8 to $13, its spirits are all small-batch craft creations) shows love and attention to detail. No reservations.

Iberian Pig SPANISH $$

(Map p84; 404-371-8800; www.theiberianpigatl.com; 121 Sycamore St, Decatur; tapas $4-18; 5-10pm Mon-Thu, to 11pm Fri & Sat, to 9pm Sun) Located smack dab in central Decatur, the Pig serves (surprise, surprise!) a full slate of Spanish cured meat, cheese and tapas, including marinated lamb chops, spiced chicken, butternut-squash *chicharones*, pork-cheek tacos and pan-seared scallops. Wash it all down with a fine red wine or craft cocktail, and live the good life.

General Muir AMERICAN $$

(Map p84; 678-927-9131; www.thegeneralmuir.com; 1540 Avenue Pl; mains lunch $7-12, dinner $12-26; 7am-9pm Mon-Thu, 7am-10pm Fri, 8am-10pm Sat, 8am-9pm Sun;) Decorated with B&W photography and New York–style subway tiling, the General Muir does Jewish deli *par excellence*. Bagels, latkes (potato pancakes), potatoes cooked in *schmaltz* (chicken liver), pastrami on rye and less deli-esque mains (poutine, anyone?), plus an extensive dinner menu featuring mains such as trout, hanger steak and stewed lentils.

Revival SOUTHERN US $$

(Map p84; 470-225-6770; www.revivaldecatur.com; 129 Church St, Decatur; mains $15-36; 5-9pm Wed-Thu, to 10pm Fri & Sat, 10:30am-3pm & 5-9pm Sun;) Serving his grandmother's family-style Sunday-dinner recipes, celebrity Atlanta chef Kevin Gillespie's farm-fresh Southerner in a restored early-1900s Decatur homestead reminds you of slower days. Standouts include the fried chicken (of course), grass-fed beef and pork meatloaf wrapped in bacon, and fried brussels sprouts with cider *gastrique*, banana peppers and feta, but the family-style dinner ($150, feeds four) is the star.

Fat Matt's Rib Shack BARBECUE $$

(Map p84; 404-607-1622; www.fatmattsribshack.com; 1811 Piedmont Ave NE; mains $4.25-15; 11:30am-11:30pm Mon-Thu, to 12:30am Fri & Sat, 12:30pm-11:30pm Sun) Don't leave the Atlanta city limits until you sample Fat Matt's Rib Shack. Although it does serve chopped pork, we suggest a slab of ribs (though a half slab will probably suffice). Take special note of the Brunswick stew, a delicious side dish best described as barbecue soup. And the best part? It has live blues nightly.

★ **Bacchanalia** MODERN AMERICAN $$$

(Map p84; 404-365-0410; www.starprovisions.com/bacchanalia; 1460 Ellsworth Industrial Blvd; prix fixe per person $95; 5:30-10pm Mon-Sat; P) Considered one of the top restaurants in the city, Bacchanalia's menu changes daily, and you may choose from multiple dishes for each of the four courses. Start with Maine lobster with fennel, ginger and lemongrass before moving on to Nantucket Bay scallops, lamb with flowing broccoli and ceci-pea *bagna càuda* or Rohan duck with honey and lavender winter citrus.

Then comes the the decadent cheese course and dessert. Still hungry? You can have courses of caviar (from $90), fresh oysters ($10), extra seafood ($70), a Kobe New York strip ($50) or seared foie gras ($15). Reserve (way) ahead.

Watershed on Peachtree SOUTHERN US **$$$**
(Map p84; ☎404-809-3561; www.watershedrestaurant.com; 1820 Peachtree Rd NW, Buckhead; mains $24.50-32; ⏰11:30am-3pm & 5-10pm Tue-Sat, 11am-3pm Sun; 📶) Co-owned by Indigo Girl Emily Saliers, this pioneering farm-to-table, James Beard Award–winning staple has been reborn in north Atlanta after years in Decatur. Outstanding and simple progressive Southern food is given a classy upgrade by Jean-Georges Vongerichten disciple (and Food Network *Chopped* winner) Zeb Stevenson. Wednesday lunch and dinner is fried-chicken day; reserve ahead for these outstanding birds.

Cakes & Ale MODERN AMERICAN **$$$**
(Map p84; ☎404-377-7994; www.cakesandalerestaurant.com; 155 Sycamore St; mains $9-20.50; ⏰cafe 7am-6pm Mon-Fri, 7:30am-6pm Sat, 8am-4pm Sun, restaurant 6-10pm Tue-Thu, 5:30-10:30pm Fri & Sat; 📶) A Chez Panisse alum and pastry mastermind runs this hip eatery. Proof, the bakery-cafe next door (www.proofbakeshop.com), has life-affirming hot chocolate and a case of delectable pastries, while the restaurant features spare but stunning selections such as gourmet 'sammies' (sandwiches) or a farro bowl at lunch, and crispy quail with za'atar or pork shoulder with rutabaga mash at dinner.

Drinking & Nightlife

Downtown

As with the dining scene, Downtown nightlife won't be as cutting edge as other parts of the city – we're talking mainly sports bars and run-of-the-mill chains such as Hooters and Hard Rock Cafe – but you can scare up a decent cocktail or two.

Elliott Street Deli & Pub BAR
(Map p50; www.elliottstreet.com; 51 Elliott St SW; ⏰11am-2pm & 4pm-midnight Mon & Wed-Thu, to 2am Tue, Fri & Sat, noon-midnight Sun) Gritty and tiny and sitting defiantly in the shadow of Mercedes-Benz Stadium, the Elliott Street Deli & Pub hangs on as one of Atlanta's best dive bars, tucked off the radar in Castleberry Hill. It also does some of the city's best sandwiches.

Red Phone Booth BAR
(Map p50; ☎404-228-7528; www.redphonebooth.com; 17 Andrew Young International Blvd NE; ⏰4pm-2am Mon-Fri, 5pm-2am Sat, to midnight Sun; 📶) You need to dial a secret phone number into the restored London red telephone box to gain access to this speakeasy-themed bar – and they won't give it to you! You'll need to know a member or someone who knows the code (ask your concierge). When inside, you'll find turn-of-the-century craft cocktails made with freshly squeezed juices and hand-chipped double-reverse-osmosis ice, and an extensive cigar menu.

Polaris COCKTAIL BAR
(Map p50; www.hyatt.com/en-US/hotel/georgia/hyatt-regency-atlanta/atlra/dining; 265 Peachtree St NW; ⏰5pm-midnight Mon-Sat; 📶) This iconic blue dome atop the Hyatt Regency – one of Atlanta's ironically historic and space-age-like postcard images – is reached by a 22-story glass-elevator ride. The restored-retro lounge, which rotates (of course it does), has rejuvenated mojo since relaunching in 2014. You'll get craft cocktails, a hell of a view and the feeling you are imbibing inside a flying saucer!

Stats SPORTS BAR
(Map p50; ☎404-885-1472; www.statsatl.com; 300 Marietta St NW; ⏰11am-11pm Mon-Thu, to 1am Fri & Sat, noon-11pm Sun; 📶) With 70 high-definition TVs through the 16,000-sq-ft brewpub, you won't miss a second of the big game. And you don't even have to leave your seat: Stats was the first bar in the US with an at-table beer-tap system (on select tables – reserve ahead) which allows you to pour yourself another cold one without waiting at the bar!

SkyLounge COCKTAIL BAR
(Map p50; ☎404-521-2250; www.glennsskylounge.com; 110 Marietta St, 11th fl, Glenn Hotel; ⏰6-11pm Sun-Thu, to 1am Fri & Sat; 📶) Downtown Atlanta's only true rooftop bar features craft cocktails ($10 to $13), outdoorsy wicker furniture and a 300-degree city view of Mercedes-Benz Stadium, Centennial Olympic Park and the CNN Center that simply wows. Call ahead both to reserve a table and to see if it's not closed due to a private event.

Midtown

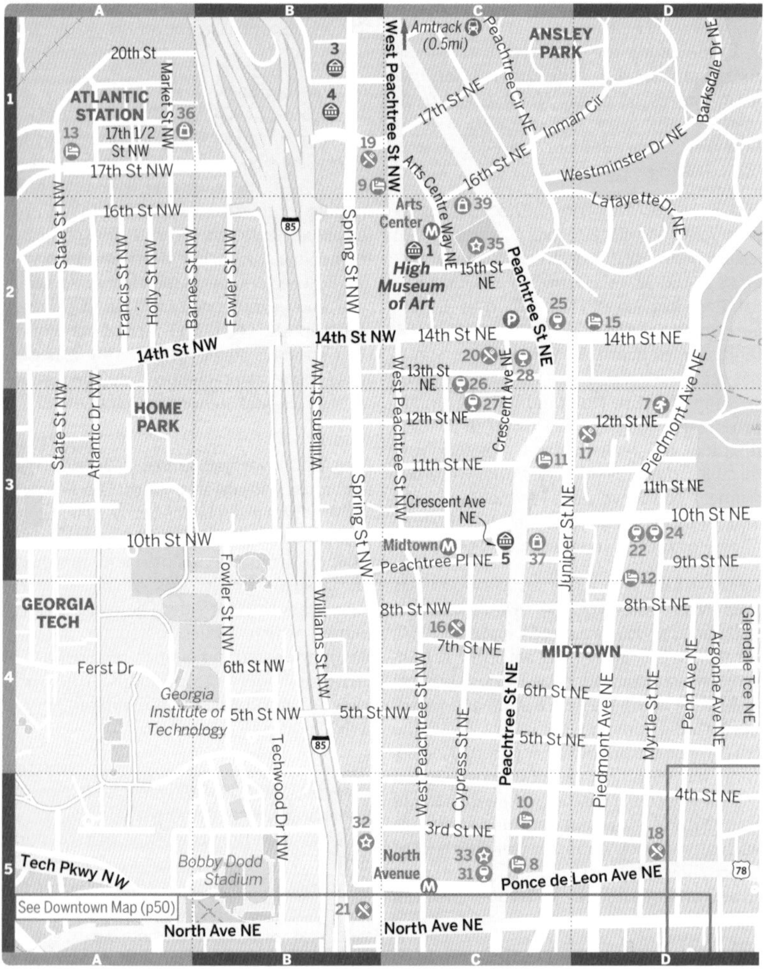

Park Bar Atlanta BAR

(Map p50; www.parkbaratlanta.com; 150 Walton St NW; ⏲11:30am-midnight Mon-Thu, to 2am Fri & Sat, noon-midnight Sun; 🛜) It's not trendy or flashy, but this neighborhood bar located right off Centennial Olympic Park Dr feels like it has been holding out for years while the city grew up around it. The music- and sports-themed pub has 12 taps and is an official US Soccer national-team bar. Plenty of pub grub on offer as well.

East Side

Atlanta's East Side is a boozer bonanza. Whether you want to kick back with a cold pint at a cutting-edge craft brewery, relax with a classic cocktail or do adult shots between epic rounds of Ping-Pong, the East Side's neighborhoods – Inman Park, Old Fourth Ward, East Atlanta Village, Little 5 Points, Virginia-Highland and Decatur, among others – are teeming with excellent options.

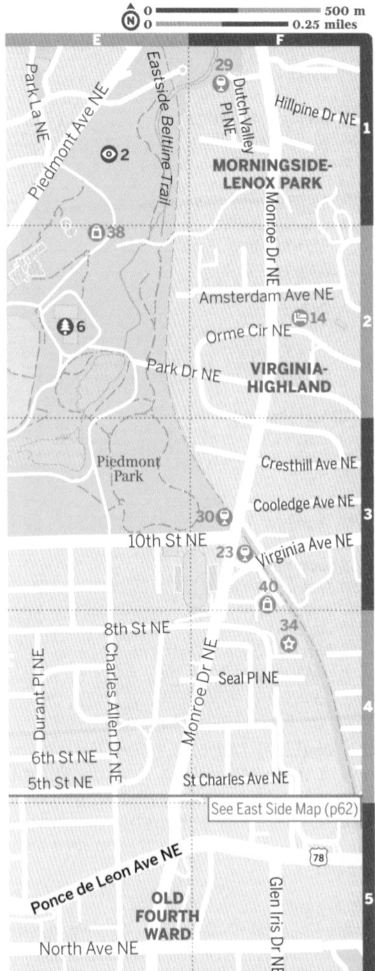

★ New Realm Brewing Co MICROBREWERY

(Map p62; ☎404-968-2778; www.newrealmbrewing.com; 550 Somerset Tce NE, No 101; ⏰5-11pm Mon-Wed, 11am-1am Fri & Sat, 11am-11pm Sun; 📶) Ex-Stone Brewing Co brewmaster Mitch Steele wrote the book on IPAs. His latest venture, a 20,000-sq-ft restaurant and brewery along the BeltLine's Eastside Trail, is a coup for Southern hopheads. Eight taps (four direct from serving tanks behind the bar) harbor triple IPAs and small-batch brews guzzled by a fun crowd ogling the Atlanta skyline from the upstairs terrace.

But the fun doesn't end there: with a serious food menu dishing up kale Caesar salads from the hop garden and heartier mains like lamb sausages with black-eyed pea stew, you could spend all day here. And you will.

★ Porter Beer Bar BAR

(Map p62; ☎404-223-0393; www.theporterbeerbar.com; 1156 Euclid Ave NE, Little Five Points; ⏰11:30am-midnight Mon-Thu, to 2:30am Fri, 11am-2:30am Sat, 11am-midnight Sun; 📶) A bar for the true suds connoisseur, the Porter has an encyclopedic variety of beers from around the world, including 55 taps and a head-spinning nine-page vintage list with beers dating to 1997 (stored in the drool-inducing cellar) The darkly lit space encompasses a huge bar and an atmosphere perfect for the sampling of a brew or five. There's food.

★ Sister Louisa's Church of the Living Room & Ping Pong Emporium BAR

(Map p62; ☎404-522-8275; www.sisterlouisaschurch.com; 466 Edgewood Ave, Edgewood; ⏰5pm-3am Mon-Sat, to midnight Sun; 📶) This cradle of Edgewood's bar revival fosters a church theme, but it's nothing like Westminster Abbey. Sacrilegious art peppers every patch of free wall space, the kind of offensive stuff that starts wars in some parts. Praise the resistance to fancy craft cocktails and join the congregation, chuckling at the artistry or staring at mesmerizing table-tennis matches.

★ Golden Eagle Diner's Club COCKTAIL BAR

(Map p62; www.goldeneagleatl.com; 904 Memorial Dr SE, Reynoldstown; 📶) From the owner of Ladybird Grove & Mess Hall (p76) comes one of Atlanta's hottest new tables, an impossibly retro step back in time set on plaid carpeting inside a gorgeously renovated 1930s-era train depot. The food is throwback continental classics, but we're here for a cocktail ($10 to $12).

Boozy classics are meticulously mixed within a 16-seat horseshoe-shaped bar flanked by pillowy tufted turquoise velvet reminiscent of a *Mad Men*–era workers' tavern. The lighting is moody and the design is instantly Instagrammable – imagine a mid-century-modern American Legion hall, if all its members were Parsons' interior-design grads. Another round, please!

Midtown

Top Sights
1 High Museum of Art ... C2

Sights
2 Atlanta Botanical Garden ... E1
3 Breman Museum ... B1
4 Center for Puppetry Arts ... B1
5 Margaret Mitchell House & Museum ... C3
6 Piedmont Park ... E2

Activities, Courses & Tours
7 Skate Escape ... D3

Sleeping
8 Georgian Terrace Hotel ... C5
9 Hotel Artmore ... B1
10 Hotel Indigo ... C5
11 Loews Atlanta ... C3
12 Stonehurst Place ... D3
13 Twelve Midtown ... A1
14 Virginia-Highland B&B ... F2
15 W Atlanta – Midtown ... D2

Eating
Café Intermezzo ... (see 11)
16 Ecco ... C4
17 Einstein's ... D3
Empire State South ... (see 37)
18 Mary Mac's Tea Room ... D5
19 Nan Thai ... B1
20 South City Kitchen ... C2
21 Varsity ... B5

Drinking & Nightlife
22 10th & Piedmont ... D3
23 Arden's Garden ... F3
24 Blake's ... D3
Edgar's Proof & Provision ... (see 8)
25 Establishment ... C2
26 Foxtrot Liquor Bar ... C2
Lava Lounge ... (see 26)
27 My Sister's Room ... C3
28 Opera ... C2
29 Orpheus Brewing ... F1
30 Park Tavern ... F3
31 Publik Draft House ... C5

Entertainment
Alliance Theatre ... (see 35)
32 Apache Café ... B5
33 Fox Theatre ... C5
34 Midtown Art Cinema ... F4
35 Woodruff Arts Center ... C2

Shopping
36 Atlantic Station ... A1
37 Eco Denizen ... C3
38 Garden Gift Shop ... E2
39 Museum Shop at High Museum of Art ... C2
40 Richards Variety Store ... F3

★ **Wrecking Bar Brewpub** BAR
(Map p62; ☎404-221-2600; www.wreckingbarbrewpub.com; 292 Moreland Ave NE, Little Five Points; ⊙4-11pm Mon-Thu, noon-midnight Fri & Sat, to 10pm Sun, bar closes later;) In the basement of century-old, heroically restored Victorian-style Kriegshaber House (which was a Methodist Protestant church, a dance school and architectural antiques store in its past lives), western-Carolinian-trained brewmaster Neal Engleman makes magical juicy IPAs, cedar-aged cask IPAs, hoppy sours and so much more at this 16-tap Little Five Points favorite wrapped around original stone pillaring.

Farm-to-table pub grub like the house-cured and smoked pastrami sandwich (collard kimchi, Swiss cheese and Korean garlic mayo) and epic charcuterie and cheese plates means food is taken just as seriously as suds, so there is little incentive to leave.

★ **Ladybird Grove & Mess Hall** BAR
(Map p62; ☎404-458-6838; www.ladybirdatlanta.com; 684 John Wesley Dobbs Ave NE; ⊙11am-late Tue-Sun, closed Mon) With an enviable location (and enormous patio) overlooking the BeltLine, Ladybird offers its patrons one of the best drinking views in Atlanta. Complement that cocktail or draft beer with some of the classy pub grub on offer from the kitchen. Last call depends on how busy the bar is.

★ **Argosy** PUB
(Map p62; ☎404-577-0407; www.argosy-east.com; 470 Flat Shoals Ave SE; ⊙5pm-2:30am Mon-Fri, noon-2:30am Sat, to midnight Sun;) This East Atlanta gastropub nails it with an extensive list of rare craft beers (35 taps), elevated bar food – house-cut Kennebec potato fries, miso quinoa burger, wood-fired pizzas – and a vibe that invites you to stay for the rest of the evening. The multiangled bar snakes its way through a rustic-chic space and living-room-style lounge areas. The back bar hosts live jazz once a month – otherwise there's pinball and Skee-Ball back there.

Spiller Park Coffee COFFEE
(Map p62; www.spillerpark.com; 675 Ponce de Leon Ave NE, Ponce City Market; ⊙7am-6pm Mon-Thu, to 8pm Fri, 8am-8pm Sat, 8am-7pm Sun) This connoisseur-level specialty coffeehouse is all the rage in Atlanta, with espresso ($3) that

is indeed special, using top-end roasters such as Intelligentsia (Illinois), Máquina (Pennsylvania) and Heart (Portland). It's an in-the-round coffee bar and prime people-watching perch.

Mary's GAY & LESBIAN
(Map p62; 404-624-4411; www.marysatlanta.com; 1287 Glenwood Ave SE, East Atlanta; 5pm-2:30am Mon-Sat) Mary's is a great playfully campy 'gayborhood' bar. It's laid-back during the week, but cranks into an all-comers-welcome weekend dance party (and karaoke fest around 10:30pm-ish on Saturday).

Joystick Gamebar BAR
(Map p62; www.joystickgamebar.com; 427 Edgewood Ave SE; 5pm-2:30am Mon-Fri, noon-2:30am Sat, noon-midnight Sun) Sure, it's a bar, but it's also an arcade full of old-school video games, pinball machines and the folks who love to play them.

MJQ Concourse CLUB
(Map p62; 404-870-0575; www.facebook.com/mjqconcourse; 736 Ponce de Leon Ave NE; 11pm-3am Wed, Fri & Sat) This club inside a former underground parking garage remains the place for young indie scenester rage – you enter through a small retractable garage door in what looks like an indiscreet toolshed behind a Chipotle – I mean, where else? Think hip-hop, down tempo and rare grooves.

Sound Table CLUB
(Map p62; www.thesoundtable.com; 483 Edgewood Ave SE, Sweet Auburn; 7pm-2:30am Wed-Sat, to midnight Sun;) If you are looking for a mega nightclub with lasers and confetti, head to Opera (p78), but if you want a more intimate night out with cutting-edge DJs, head to this restaurant/club hybrid in Sweet Auburn just steps from everything MLK. Funk, soul, EDM, eletronica, drum and bass – it does it all, including dinner.

Manuel's Tavern BAR
(Map p62; www.manuelstavern.com; 602 N Highland Ave; 11am-midnight Mon, to 1am Tue-Fri, 9am-1am Sat, 9:30am-midnight Sun;) An Atlanta staple since 1956 and still operated by the original family, this classic tavern is always packed with politicians, journalists, actors and creatives. It serves a mean burger on toast (with greasy fries).

Paper Crane Lounge COCKTAIL BAR
(Map p62; www.staplehouse.com; 541 Edgewood Ave SE; cocktails $13-15; 5:30-10pm Wed-Thu, to 11pm Fri & Sat;) In the former private dining room of Atlanta's hottest restaurant (Staplehouse; p66), this cozy first-come, first-served cocktail destination (see Staplehouse host for seating) executes a small menu of near daily-changing libations listed on the menu by flavor profile, not recipe, and mixed from an unorthodox chest-of-drawers bar. The intimate, leathery space is lit by colorful Christmas-tree lights.

Midtown

Midtown mostly caters to club-goers rather than connoisseurs of mixology, oenophiles or hopheads, but there are plenty of fine spots for a cocktail (many inside top-end hotels) or a beer (breweries congregate around Piedmont Park). Midtown is also the epicenter of Atlanta's LGBTIQ+ scene – with the bull's-eye at the intersection of 10th and Piedmont Sts.

Orpheus Brewing BREWERY
(Map p74; www.orpheusbrewing.com; 1440 Dutch Valley Pl NE; 6-10pm Mon-Thu, 5pm-midnight Fri, 1-10pm Sat & Sun;) An elevated patio overlooking an outcrop of Piedmont Park is where the visual experience at Orpheus Brewing ends – a visit here is about the brews, not the views. New double-hop IPAs, wild fermentations, dry-hopped sours and barrel-aged libations are the Orpheus way and the results are a drop-to-one-knee beer blessing! Head brewer Jason Pellet is a hops artist.

Transmigration of Souls is one of the Southeast's best (and best-named) double IPAs and Atalanta, a tart plum saison, was *Atlanta* magazine's Beer of the Year in 2014.

My Sister's Room LESBIAN
(Map p74; 678-705-4585; www.mysistersroom.com; 66 12th St NE; 7pm-midnight Mon, to 2am Wed-Thu, 6pm-3am Fri & Sat, 2pm-midnight Sun) Far and away the city's hottest lesbian bar, in a two-story setting in East Atlanta Village.

Lava Lounge CLUB
(Map p74; 404-873-6189; www.lavaloungeatlanta.com; 45 13th St; 9pm-3am Thu-Sat, 4-11:45pm Sun) In a converted 1920s home, contemporary Lava Lounge offers three levels, each with an independent sound system, and is more design-forward than your average dance club: a main level art deco-esque walnut back bar, vintage Edison bulbs, mosaic pillars and the like. The most famous DJs spin in the lower level Cue Club.

Opera CLUB
(Map p74; www.operaatlanta.com; 1150 Crescent Ave NE; ⌚10pm-3am Wed, Fri & Sat) Opera is Atlanta's hottest megaclub. True to its name, it evokes the lavishness of a European opera house but perhaps with much longer lines to get in. World-class local and international DJs spin everything from Latin fusion to EDM, with confetti and aerial acrobatic dancers. Wednesday nights are hot.

Arden's Garden JUICE BAR
(Map p74; www.ardensgarden.com; 985 Monroe Dr NE; juices $3-10; ⌚7am-8pm Mon-Fri, 8am-9pm Sat, 9am-5pm Sun) Long before cold-pressed juices became trendy (and $12 a pop!), Atlanta had Arden's Garden, which has been firing off affordable and healthy bottles of love since 1995. It's all over the Southeast nowadays, but this location adjacent to Piedmont Park is the original. Activated-charcoal lemonade and the belly-burning ginger- and cayenne-laced firecracker are faves.

Establishment COCKTAIL BAR
(Map p74; www.establishmentatlanta.com; 1197 Peachtree St NW, W Hotel; ⌚11am-3pm & 4:30pm-2am Mon-Thu, 4:30pm-2am Sat, 12:30pm-midnight Sun; 📶) This sophisticated, easy-on-the-eyes cocktail lounge attached to the W Hotel (p60) is teeming with rustic-chic Americana pop art, reclaimed Georgia hardwoods (15 counties' worth of oak, pine and cherrywood), antler lighting, antique iron and pioneer-era memorabilia, all to enlist the feel of a 1800s barnyard bar. Local African American artist Janssen Robinson's striking oil-on-canvas paintings pepper 175-year-old walls.

Edgar's Proof & Provision COCKTAIL BAR
(Map p74; www.proofandprovision.com; 659 Peachtree St NW; ⌚5pm-midnight Tue-Thu, to 2am Fri & Sat; 📶) This basement bar under the Georgian Terrace Hotel (p59) bills itself as a loved-by-locals community drinkery. It is particularly primed for hidden-away imbibing on classy cocktails or curated craft drafts paired with *the* grilled cheese (fontina, cheddar, Swiss, pecorino spread, jalapeño corn bread, bourbon barrel-aged bacon – do it! Do it now!). After a show at Fox Theatre, it's a madhouse.

Park Tavern BAR
(Map p74; ☎404-249-0001; www.parktavern.com; 500 10th St NE; ⌚4:30pm-midnight Mon-Fri, 11:30am-midnight Sat & Sun; 📶) This staple microbrewery-restaurant's outdoor patio can lean preppy, but its location on the edge of Piedmont Park is one of the most beautiful spots in Atlanta to sit back and drink away a weekend afternoon.

Blake's GAY & LESBIAN
(Map p74; ☎404-892-5786; www.blakesontheparkatlanta.com; 227 10th St NE; ⌚3pm-3am Mon-Fri, 1pm-3am Sat, 1pm-1am Sun) Just off Piedmont Park, Blake's bills itself as 'Atlanta's favorite gay bar since 1987.' It's straight-friendly, hosts a drag revue and serves some decent pub grub.

Foxtrot Liquor Bar COCKTAIL BAR
(Map p74; www.foxtrotbar.com; 45 13th St; ⌚5pm-2am Tue-Sat; 📶) This shotgun-style bungalow is awash in plaids and '50s-evoking decor with warm, soothing hardwood floors. Cocktails ($10 to $13) with Kold-Draft square ice cubes (less melting) are the main event, though there is a small beer and wine list. Feels vaguely understated in a neighborhood full of towering skyscrapers.

Publik Draft House BAR
(Map p74; www.publikatl.com; 654 Peachtree St NE; ⌚11am-midnight Mon-Wed, to 2am Thu & Fri, 10am-2am Sat, 10am-midnight Sun) Before and after anything happening at the Fox Theatre, this bourbon-forward bar – alongside the theater structure itself – is elbow to elbow. If it's too crowded on Friday and Saturday, escape upstairs for craft cocktails ($8 to $18) at the more intimate UPbar on the 2nd floor.

10th & Piedmont GAY
(Map p74; www.10thandpiedmont.com; 991 Piedmont Ave NE; ⌚10am-3pm & 5-10pm Mon-Thu, to 11pm Fri, 10am-4pm & 5-11pm Sat, 10am-6pm Sun) This snazzy, airy bar, popular with the local LGBTIQ+ community, serves up Southern favorites and has DJs spinning hip-hop on Sundays.

Westside

With fine dining comes fine drinking and Atlanta's Westside is home to breweries, adult playgrounds, Asian-themed cocktail bars and Third Wave coffee. Once finished, the Lee + White development along the BeltLine's Westside Trail will be Atlanta's brewery barrio.

★ **Monday Night Garage** MICROBREWERY
(Map p84; www.mondaynightbrewing.com; 933 Lee St SW, West End; ⌚4-9pm Mon-Thu, noon-10pm

Fri & Sat, 1-6pm Sun;) One of two locations in Atlanta, Monday Night Brewing's barrel-aging and souring facility in the West End is set to become its go-to destination and the anchor of a future craft-beer hub in the city. Fire pits and a BeltLine-facing patio keep things cozy while inside an Airstream trailer and massive mural evoke a trashy-arty feel. Twenty taps. On Saturday nights, Ok Yaki whips up *okonomiyaki* (savory Japanese street-food pancakes) for hungry hopheads.

★ Painted Duck BAR

(Map p80; 404-352-0048; www.thepaintedduckatl.com; 976 Brady Ave NW; duckpin bowling week/weekend $25/35, shoe rental $4.50; 5pm-midnight Mon-Thu, to 2am Fri, 11am-2am Sat, noon-midnight Sun;) You enter this incredible basement adult playground under a wordless neon green-and-white duck sign and through a graffitied, black-lit hallway that will make you feel like drinking and gaming is an illicit activity. Once inside: jaw drop! Sixteen lanes of chargeable duckpin bowling against a 50ft street-art-mural backdrop of migrating ducks and wildlife.

And the remaining distractions are free: Belgian feather bowling (a sort of curling/bowling hybrid), snookball (a kind of soccer pool), shuffleboard, horseshoes, basketball and more. There is a long and sociable central bar pouring a surprisingly craft lineup of beer and cocktails, and elevated bar food (fried duck-confit nuggets, pulled-pork sandwiches served on Hawaiian rolls) to go with it. There's also a small and seemingly wimpy (by comparison) air-hockey table – ain't nobody got time for that here!

Brash Coffee COFFEE

(Map p80; www.brashcoffee.com; 1168 Howell Mill Rd, Westside Provisions District; coffee $3-5; 7am-6pm Mon-Fri, 8am-6pm Sat & Sun;) This Third Wave specialty caffeine house is a labor of love – the owner built a coffee mill on a farm in El Salvador – inside a bundle of converted shipping containers surrounded by tiered wooden outdoor seating.

Octane CAFE

(Map p80; www.octanecoffee.com; 1009b Marietta St; coffee $2.75-6; 7am-10pm Mon-Wed, to 11pm Thu & Fri, 8am-11pm Sat, 8am-10pm Sun;) This industrial-hip coffeehouse near Georgia Tech's campus, the original of four locations in the city, brews the joe of choice for severe caffeine junkies, following a direct trade philosophy. It remains one of Atlanta's most serious and best coffeehouses, but its 2017 purchase by Revelator Coffee Company has Atlanta on edge (a name change could have occurred by the time you read this).

Little Trouble COCKTAIL BAR

(Map p80; www.little-trouble.com; 1170 Howell Mill Rd, Westside Provisions District; 6pm-late Mon-Sat;) This somewhat-hidden-in-plain-sight drinking den feels a bit like you're drinking cocktails inside a video game – the neon-lit entrance is accessed via several open-air alleyways inside the Westside Provisions District complex, though it remains a bit hard to find – and is a clear *Blade Runner* homage. Inside, Japanese sake, whiskey and craft cocktails are the way to go – slung by wannabe actors – not the Asian-slanted bar bites. But it's really about the design.

Ormsbys BAR

(Map p80; www.ormsbysatlanta.com; 1170 Howell Mill Rd, Westside Provisions District; 11:30am-3pm Mon-Fri, noon-3am Sat, noon-midnight Sun;) With an array of drinking distractions (back-gammon, bocce, darts, pool, shuffleboard and Skee-Ball), this good-time bar attracts a heavy Georgia Tech crowd for fun and games. Atlanta Bocce League does a very serious eight-week bocce season four times a year.

Greater Atlanta

★ Brick Store Pub BAR

(Map p84; 404-687-0990; www.brickstorepub.com; 125 E Court Sq, Decatur; draft beers $5-12; 11am-1am Mon, to 2am Tue-Sat, noon-1am Sun) Beer hounds geek out on Atlanta's best craft-beer selection at this pub in Decatur, with some 30 meticulously chosen drafts (including those in the more intimate Belgian beer bar upstairs). Nearly 300 beers by the bottle are served from a 15,000-bottle vault, drawing a fun, young crowd every night.

★ Scofflaw Brewing Co MICROBREWERY

(Map p84; www.scofflawbeer.com; 1738 MacArthur Blvd NW, Upper Westside; 10am-5pm Mon-Tue, to 9pm Wed-Fri, noon-8pm Sat, 1-5pm Sun;) Named after the hard-to-pronounce word for those who said, 'F-you!' to Prohibition laws and continued drinking anyway, Scofflaw Brewing Co's 30-tap brewery is producing Atlanta's most experimental IPAs and stouts – brewmaster Matt Shirah came up at California's Lost Abbey and Russian

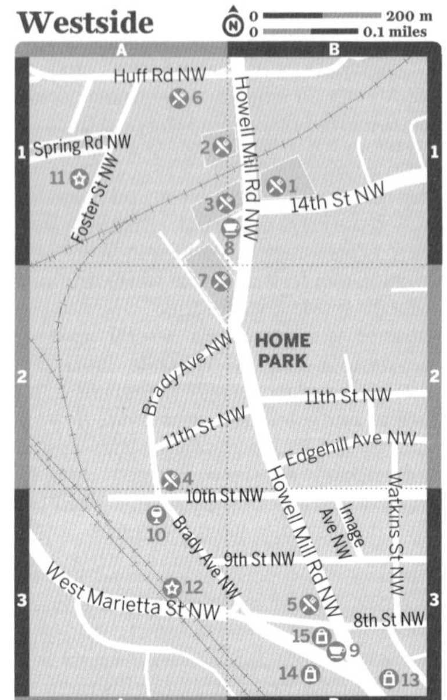

Westside

Eating

1 Cooks & Soldiers B1
2 JCT Kitchen & Bar A1
3 Marcel A1
4 Miller Union A2
5 Optimist B3
6 Taqueria del Sol A1
7 West Egg Cafe A2

Drinking & Nightlife

8 Brash Coffee B1
Little Trouble .... (see 3)
9 Octane B3
Ormsbys .... (see 3)
10 Painted Duck A3

Entertainment

11 Goat Farm Arts Center A1
12 Terminal West A3

Shopping

13 A Ma Maniére B3
Crafted .... (see 7)
14 Hop City B3
Savannah Bee Company .... (see 7)
Seed Factory .... (see 7)
Sid Mashburn .... (see 2)
15 Thomas Wages B3

River Brewing, the latter famous for its world-sought-after triple IPA, Pliny the Younger. Motto? 'No Bullshit. Just Beer.'

The large, open-space brewery is rife with picnic tables and there's a festive outdoor fairy-lit patio that welcomes rotating food trucks on Saturdays.

Kimball House COCKTAIL BAR

(Map p84; 404-378-3502; www.kimball-house.com; 303 E Howard Ave, Decatur; 5pm-midnight Sun-Thu, to 1am Fri & Sat;) Housed in an atmospheric period dining room in a restored train depot slightly off the grid in Decatur, Kimball House harbors a vaguely saloon-like feel under overhead belt-driven fans. It specializes in craft cocktails ($10 to $13), absinthe and a long list of flown-in-fresh oysters.

Monday Night Brewing BREWERY

(Map p84; www.mondaynightbrewing.com; 670 Trabert Ave NW; 4-9pm Mon-Thu, to 10pm Fri, noon-4pm Sat, 1-6pm Sun;) The neighborhood's best brewery sits on the Westside BeltLine and beckons seasoned drinkers with its Saturdays-be-damned slogan, 'Weekends are overrated.' Inside you'll find 12 taps, ritzy chandeliers and worn leather couches, but the real fun here is enjoying the juicy IPAs, sours and Scotch ales on the extensive, fairy-lit patio.

Entertainment

For listings, check out Atlanta Coalition of Performing Arts (www.atlantaperforms.com). The Atlanta Music Guide (www.atlantamusicguide.com) maintains a live-music schedule, plus a directory of local venues and links to online ticketing.

Downtown

Mercedes-Benz Stadium STADIUM

(Map p50; 470-341-5000; www.mercedesbenzstadium.com; 1 AMB Dr NW; tours adult/child $25/20; tours 11am-5pm) Atlanta's state-of-the-art, $1.6-billion multipurpose eight-petal retractable-roof stadium is home to the NFL's Atlanta Falcons (football) and the MLS' Atlanta United FC (soccer). The striking, architecturally wowing stadium resembles a camera's aperture and is the first professional sports stadium to achieve Leadership in Energy and Environmental Design (LEED) Platinum status (a green building certification) in the US.

Daily tours (book online) get you to the locker rooms, the field, Window to the City, Skybridges and 100 Yard Club as well as over 180 works of art curated from the Savannah College of Art & Design.

Rialto Center for the Arts THEATER
(Map p50; ☎404-413-9849; www.rialto.gsu.edu; 80 Forsyth St NW; ⊙box office 10am-4:30pm Mon-Fri) On the campus of Georgia State University, the historic Rialto has produced national and international jazz, world music, orchestra, dance and other performance-arts productions since 1916.

Tabernacle LIVE MUSIC
(Map p50; ☎404-659-9022; www.tabernacleatl.com; 152 Luckie St NW) Guns N' Roses, Bob Dylan, Adele and Kendrick Lamar have all played this storied downtown live-music venue dating to 1910. While it was formerly an infirmary and a Baptist church, today the congregation worships the music amid a vaguely *Moulin Rouge*–like ambience.

Philips Arena BASKETBALL
(Map p50; ☎404-878-3000; www.philipsarena.com; 1 Philips Dr; ⊙box office 10am-4pm Mon-Fri) The home of the Atlanta's Hawks; hosts large-scale arena concerts as well.

☆ East Side

Clermont Lounge DANCE
(Map p62; http://clermontlounge.net; 789 Ponce de Leon Ave NE, Poncey-Highland; ⊙5pm-3am Mon-Sat) The Clermont is a strip club, the oldest in Atlanta. But not *just* a strip club. It's a bedrock of the Atlanta scene that welcomes dancers of all ages, races and body types. In short, it's a strip club built for strippers, although the audience – and *everyone* comes here at some point – has a grand time as well.

The Clermont's dancers are performers in every sense of the word. Yes, they flash skin – but they also joke with the audience, take shots of whiskey or sips of beer when they want, and generally command the venue like a bunch of bosses. They're in control of the evening and invite you to enjoy it with them. Don't pass the offer up.

Variety Playhouse LIVE MUSIC
(Map p62; ☎404-524-7354; www.variety-playhouse.com; 1099 Euclid Ave NE, Little Five Points) A historic, smartly booked and well-run concert venue built in 1940 and fully renovated in 2015. It hosts a variety of touring artists and is one of the main anchors of the Little Five Points scene.

Plaza Theatre CINEMA
(Map p62; ☎631-682-8456; www.plazaatlanta.com; 1049 Ponce de Leon Ave NE; movies from $10) Atlanta's oldest continuously operating movie theater opened in 1939.

Dad's Garage THEATER
(Map p62; ☎404-523-3141; www.dadsgarage.com; 569 Ezzard St, Old Fourth Ward; ⊙Thu-Sat) No, that's not a hipster worship hall. Dad's Garage, Atlanta's most award-winning and longest-standing improv group, took over this former church in the Old Fourth Ward after losing their previous home to mixed-use development. Shows runs Thursday to Saturday; check online for exact schedule.

Venkman's LIVE MUSIC
(Map p62; ☎470-225-6162; www.venkmans.com; 740 Ralph McGill Blvd NE, Old Fourth Ward; ⊙5:30-10pm Tue-Thu, to 10:30pm Fri, 10am-3pm & 5:30-10:30pm Sat, 11am-3pm Sun;) This newer entertainment supper club in the Old Fourth Ward hosts live music and is rather serious about food and drink. Check the schedule online for what's on.

Earl LIVE MUSIC
(Map p62; ☎404-522-3950; www.badearl.com; 488 Flat Shoals Ave SE; shows from $8; ⊙11:30am-3am Mon-Sat, to midnight Sun) It's grimy, it's grotty and it has a great lineup of live music most nights. We love any bar that occupies that perfect juncture between dive and live venue – enter, if you will, the Earl.

☆ Midtown

Apache Café LIVE PERFORMANCE
(Map p74; ☎404-876-5436; www.apachecafe.info; 64 3rd St NW; ⊙7pm-midnight Sun-Mon, 8pm-1am Tue, to 1:30am Wed, 9pm-2am Thu-Sat) An eclectic performance-art venue for hip-hop, spoken-word poetry and soul artists on the rise. It's a must-stop for those looking to dive into Atlanta's diverse African American music scene.

Woodruff Arts Center ARTS CENTER
(Map p74; ☎404-733-4200; www.woodruffcenter.org; 1280 Peachtree St NE; ⊙box office noon-6pm Tue-Sat, to 5pm Sun) This arts complex contains within its campus the High Museum (p52), the Atlanta Symphony Orchestra and the Alliance Theatre.

Alliance Theatre THEATER
(Map p74; ☎404-733-4650; www.alliancetheatre.org; 1280 Peachtree St NW; ⊙box office noon-6pm Tue-Sat, to 5pm Sun) Internationally renowned theater inside the Woodruff Arts Center which produces a diverse bill of 10 or so annual productions, several of which later wind up on Broadway (such as Elton John and Tim Rice's Tony Award–winning *Aida* and the musical version of *The Color Purple*.

Fox Theatre THEATER
(Map p74; ☎855-285-8499; www.foxtheatre.org; 660 Peachtree St NE; ⊙box office 10am-6pm Mon-Fri, to 3pm Sat) A spectacular 1929 movie palace with fanciful Moorish and Egyptian designs. It hosts Broadway shows and concerts in an auditorium holding more than 4500 people. Tours are also available.

Midtown Art Cinema CINEMA
(Map p74; ☎404-879-0160; www.landmarktheatres.com/atlanta/midtown-art-cinema; 931 Monroe Dr NE) One of Atlanta's artier theaters, showing independent as well as big-studio films.

☆ Westside

Terminal West LIVE MUSIC
(Map p80; ☎404-876-5566; www.terminalwestatl.com; 887 W Marietta St, Westside; ⊙box office 11am-5pm Tue-Fri) One of Atlanta's best live-music venues, this concert space is located inside a beautifully revamped 100-year-old iron and steel foundry on the Westside.

Goat Farm Arts Center PERFORMING ARTS
(Map p80; www.facebook.com/pg/thegoatfarmartscenter; 1200 Foster St NW) Embedded in a revamped 19th-century cotton-gin manufacturing factory that previously stood in ruin, Goat Farm Arts Center is the city's most cutting-edge and experimental visual performing-arts studio, set on 12 acres in West Midtown. Think artists-in-residence, contemporary dance, vanguard theater, indie rock concerts and thought-provoking exhibitions. It also home to the avant-garde Imperial Opa Circus.

☆ Greater Atlanta

Blind Willie's BLUES
(Map p84; ☎404-873-2583; www.blindwilliesblues.com; 828 North Highland Avenue NE, Virginia-Highland; ⊙7pm-late Mon-Sat) This divey Virginia-Highland blues bar behind a neon alligator is one of the nation's top spots for the world's best down-and-dirty blues. Taj Mahal, Rufus Thomas and Charles Brown have all graced this stage and regulars Sandra Hall, House Rocker Johnson and the Shadows usually play weekly. It's named after Georgia's own legendary bluesman, 'Blind' Willie McTell.

Starlight Drive-In OUTDOOR CINEMA
(www.starlightdrivein.com; 2000 Moreland Ave SE; adult/child $9/1) Atlanta's only remaining drive-in theater shows double features on every screen. Drive up, tune in via your car radio and enjoy big-tickets movies like the old days. It's 6 miles south of Downtown.

SunTrust Park BASEBALL
(www.mlb.com/braves; 755 Battery Avenue SE; tickets $7-88) Major League Baseball's Atlanta Braves moved into this new, 41,149-capacity stadium 10 miles northwest of downtown Atlanta in Cobb County beginning with the 2016 season, part of a $1.1-billion enter-tainment complex known as the Battery.

Eddie's Attic LIVE MUSIC
(Map p84; ☎404-377-4976; www.eddiesattic.com; 515b N McDonough St, Decatur) This is one of the best venues for live folk and acoustic music, renowned for breaking local artists on to the regional – and sometimes national – scene. Shawn Mullins, Sugarland, Justin Bieber and John Mayer all sowed their musical oats here.

Shopping

Downtown

Uninteresting shops and national chains dominate Downtown's shopping options, but that *could* all change when the revamped Underground Atlanta reopens as a mixed-use development. It was closed for renovation at the time of writing.

Walter's Clothing SHOES
(Map p50; www.waltersclothing.com; 66 Decatur St; ⊙8:30am-6:30pm Mon-Sat) This throwback streetwear shop dates to 1952 and is said to have the biggest collection of street-smart kicks in town. It's often the first shop in Atlanta to receive a hot new shoe. It's certainly not fancy, but it's a Downtown icon and rumored to be a favorite of visiting NBA players. While there are clothes for sale, why it's not called Walter's Shoes, we couldn't tell ya.

Coca-Cola Store GIFTS & SOUVENIRS
(Map p50; www.worldofcoca-cola.com/explore/explore-inside/explore-coca-cola-store; 121 Baker St NW; ⊙10am-5pm Mon-Fri, 9am-5pm Sat & Sun) You don't need a ticket to enter the World of Coca-Cola's adjacent souvenir shop. Fans of Atlanta's world-famous soda can pick up anything and everything here, from Coke-themed spatulas to pajamas to trucker hats.

Team Store CLOTHING

(Map p50; www.mercedesbenzstadium.com/team-store; 1414 Andrew Young International Blvd NW; 10am-6pm Mon-Sat, noon-6pm Sun) One of two official Atlanta Falcons/Atlanta United FC gear shops, but this one is notable as it's inside the city's striking new Mercedes-Benz Stadium (p80) – you can get a peek at the field as well. Enter through gate 2 on Andrew Young International Blvd NW. Pssst…there's free parking near the Smoke Ring (p60) restaurant, which is just a short walk away.

East Side

The neighborhoods of Little Five Points, Decatur, Virginia-Highland and Poncey-Highland offer some of the city's best shopping, especially when it comes to unique boutiques, temples of vintage and independent curators of cool.

★**Criminal Records** MUSIC

(Map p62; 404-215-9511; www.criminalatl.com; 1154 Euclid Ave, Little Five Points; 11am-8pm Mon-Thu, to 9pm Fri & Sat, noon-7pm Sun) This throwback record store is stacked wall to wall with a library's worth of new pop, soul, jazz and metal, on CD or vinyl. It has a fun music-related book section, and a great collection of comic books and graphic novels. Basically, a certain kind of music-lover and genre-loving geek could live here.

Paris on Ponce VINTAGE, ARTS & CRAFTS

(Map p62; www.parisonponce.com; 716 Ponce de Leon Pl NE; 11am-6pm Mon-Sat, noon-6m Sun) Clocking in at over 46,000-sq-ft and 30-plus vendors, this massively cool vintage shop inside an old mattress factory will floor you with its tragically hip ethos. You'll find anything and everything here, and rummaging through the various sections feels like browsing through a gourmet flea market. Local artists are widely featured.

Citizen Supply CLOTHING

(Map p62; www.citizensupply.com; 675 Ponce de Leon Ave NE, Ponce City Market; 10am-9pm Mon-Sat, noon-8pm Sun) This fiercely curated all-under-one-roof flagship shop stocks a dizzying array of top-quality – some say hipster – brands of products you didn't know you wanted until you saw them: foresty pomades from Mail Room Barber Co, Edison electric bikes, Bradley Mountain canvas and leather bags, Wander North Georgia (p147) T-shirts, Atlanta-centric art, Loyal Stricklin leather-bound Aviator mugs and more.

LGBTIQ+ ATLANTA

Atlanta is one of the few places in Georgia with a noticeable and active gay and lesbian population, probably second only to San Francisco in visibility and population. Midtown is the center of gay life; the epicenter is around Piedmont Park and the intersection of 10th St and Piedmont Ave, where you can check out Blake's (p78), Atlanta's classic gay bar, or 10th & Piedmont (p78), good for food and late-night shenanigans. The town of Decatur, east of downtown Atlanta, has a significant lesbian community. For news and information, grab a copy of the weekly *Peach ATL* (www.peachatl.com), monthly *Goliath Atlanta* (www.goliathatlanta.com) or visit www.gayatlanta.com.

Atlanta Pride Festival (p56) is a massive annual celebration of the city's gay and lesbian community. It's held in October in and around Piedmont Park.

Wish FASHION & ACCESSORIES

(Map p62; 404-880-0402; http://wishatl.com; 447 Moreland Ave, Little Five Points; noon-8pm Mon-Thu, to 9pm Fri & Sat, 1-7pm Sun) You wouldn't be the first to spy a famous actor or athlete picking up a new pair of graffitied sneakers, blinged-out bomber jacket or distressed jeans at this streetwise street-wear shop, located in a former public library. The shoe section alone is seriously eye-watering in its immensity.

Young Blood Boutique JEWELRY

(Map p62; 404-254-4127; www.youngbloodboutique.com; 632 North Highland Ave NE, Poncey-Highland; 10am-7pm Mon-Sat, to 6pm Sun) Head to this bright, beautifully set out boutique for handmade, innovative jewelry from Portland to Australia, and feminist-centric accessories brought to you by a full slate of fascinating design brands, including Demimonde and Mikinora.

Junkman's Daughter VINTAGE

(Map p62; 404-577-3188; www.thejunkmansdaughter.com; 464 Moreland Ave NE, Little Five Points; 11am-7pm Mon-Fri, to 8pm Sat, noon-7pm Sun) A defiant and fiercely independent cradle of counterculture since 1982, this 10,000-sq-ft alternative superstore stocks racks of vintage, ornery bumper stickers, kitschy toys and tchotchkes, *Star Wars* lunch boxes, incense, wigs, offensive coffee mugs and a whole lot more. It put Little Five Points on the map.

Greater Atlanta

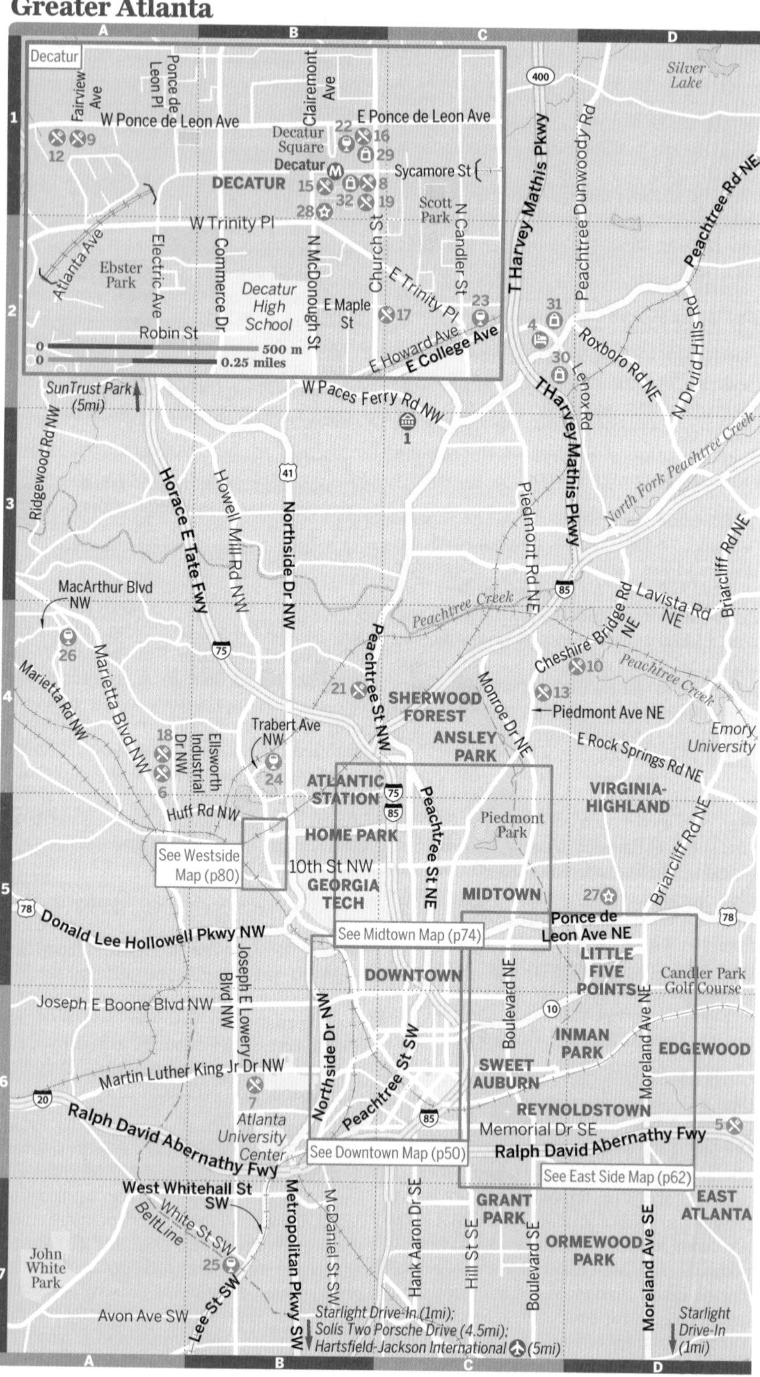

Greater Atlanta

Sights
1 Atlanta History Center C3
Battle of Atlanta Cyclorama........ (see 1)
2 Clyde Shepherd Nature Preserve F4
3 Fernbank Museum of Natural History E5

Sleeping
4 Whitley........................ C2

Eating
5 Ann's Snack Bar D6
6 Bacchanalia A4
7 Busy Bee Café B6
8 Cakes & Ale........................ B1
9 Chai Pani........................ A1
10 Colonnade D4
11 Desta Ethiopian Kitchen........................ E3
12 Farm Burger A1
13 Fat Matt's Rib Shack C4
14 General Muir E4
15 Iberian Pig........................ B1
16 Leon's Full Service........................ B1
17 Revival C2
18 Star Provisions Market & Cafe.......... A4
19 Victory B1
20 Waffle House F5
21 Watershed on Peachtree B4

Drinking & Nightlife
22 Brick Store Pub B1
23 Kimball House C2
24 Monday Night Brewing........................ B4
25 Monday Night Garage B7
26 Scofflaw Brewing Co A4

Entertainment
27 Blind Willie's........................ D5
28 Eddie's Attic........................ B1

Shopping
29 HomeGrown B1
30 Lenox Square C2
31 Phipps Plaza C2
32 Sq/Ft B1

Abbadabba's SHOES

(Map p62; ☎404-588-9577; www.coolshoes.com; 421 Moreland Ave NE, Little Five Points; ⏰10am-7:30pm Mon-Sat, noon-6pm Sun) When you head to a shoe shop in the bohemian-hipster-punk nexus that is Little Five Points, you're not expecting calf-skin loafers – and you're not getting them here. Instead, Day-Glo sneakers, Doc Martens, Converse and Birkenstock.

Midtown

Midtown is no retail paradise – it's mostly the domain of national chains or unworthy local shops of little interest to tourists save the rare exception and a few great gift shops inside museums and attractions.

Richards Variety Store GIFTS & SOUVENIRS, TOYS

(Map p74; www.richardsvarietystore.com; 931 Monroe Dr NE; ⏰10am-8pm Mon-Sat, noon-6pm Sun) There is almost nothing this massive, good-time emporium doesn't have. Hebrew alphabet kits? Ouija boards? Paper pinhole cameras? 3-D White House puzzles? Stuffed penguins? You'll tap into your inner child as you rummage sections devoted to toys, puzzles, housewares, books, art, gadgets – the aisles go on and on. There is *something* in here you didn't know you needed!

Eco Denizen GIFTS & SOUVENIRS

(Map p74; www.ecodenizen.net; 999 Peachtree St NE; ⏰11am-8pm Mon-Sat, noon-6pm Sun) This eco-driven mom- and pop-run gift shop is full of coveted stuff: vegan wallets from Matt & Nat, Tokens & Icons wine openers fashioned from recycled Major League Baseball bats and professional tennis rackets, and local art such as Houston Llew's glass-on-copper pop-art pieces.

Museum Shop at High Museum of Art ART, GIFTS & SOUVENIRS

(Map p74; www.museumshop.high.org; 1280 Peachtree St NW; ⏰10am-5pm Mon-Sat) You don't need a museum ticket to access the great museum shop at High Museum of Art (p52), and parking for the first 30 minutes is free. You'll find high-end, art-centric gifts and souvenirs, and handmade art by local and regional artists.

Atlantic Station MALL

(Map p74; ☎404-410-4010; www.atlanticstation.com; 1371 Market St NW; ⏰11am-9pm Mon-Sat, to 6pm Sun) This massive, multiuse Midtown complex that boasts its own zip code has 35 stores, including an Atlanta Falcons/Atlanta United FC Team Shop, and an 18-screen theater. There is a free shuttle every 10 to 15 minutes from MARTA Arts Center station.

Garden Gift Shop GIFTS & SOUVENIRS

(Map p74; www.atlantabg.org/visit/garden-gift-shop; 1345 Piedmont Ave NE, Atlanta Botanical Garden; ⏰9am-10pm Tue-Thu & Sun, to 11pm Fri & Sat) Unique, botanically themed gift items inside the Atlanta Botanical Garden (p52).

Westside

The Westside Provisions District is chock-full of trendy boutiques, independent haberdasheries and smartly curated design shops.

Hop City ALCOHOL

(Map p80; ☎404-350-9998; www.hopcitybeer.com; 1000 Marietta St NW, No 302, West Midtown; ⏰10am-9pm Mon-Wed, to 10pm Thu-Sat, 12:30-6pm Sun) Features the largest selection of retail craft beer in the Southeast along with 60 taps to drink from on premises. The local inventory is obviously extensive, but there are suds from here to Shanghai.

Sid Mashburn CLOTHING

(Map p80; ☎404-350-7135; www.sidmashburn.com; 1198 Howell Mill Rd, Westside Provisions District; ⏰10am-6:30pm Mon-Sat or by appt) Menswear designer Sid Mashburn has since expanded nationally, but it all started in Atlanta, where 80% of his high-end boutique and haberdashery originates in-house. It's geared toward more conservative fashion – custom-tailored shirts, suits, trousers, sweaters, denim – but there are some funkier products if you browse. Women and children are catered to with Ann Mashburn and Kid Mashburn, respectively.

Thomas Wages CLOTHING

(Map p80; ☎404-892-0302; www.thomaswages.com; 1009a Marietta St NW; ⏰11am-7pm or by appt) Atlanta menswear designer Thomas Wages subscribes to a 'Made in America' ethos and you'll find plenty to love at this hip boutique, where his own light and medium denim button-down shirts, made-to-measure suits and belts are tempting indeed. He also stocks hip accessories such as Topo hats, Dom Vetro sunglasses and Fulton & Roark soaps, among others.

Savannah Bee Company FOOD & DRINKS
(Map p80; www.savannahbee.com; 1100 Howell Mill Rd, Westside Provisions District; ⏲10am-7pm Mon-Sat, noon-6pm Sun; 📶) Help save the bees at this Savannah, GA transplant gone national, where high-quality monofloral and polyforal honeys are the backbone, but the golden-nectar inventory certainly doesn't stop there: books about honey, an impressive mead bar, beeswax candles, tupelo-honey hand creams and soaps – you can even wipe your butt with tupelo-honey wipes if you desire!

Crafted ARTS & CRAFTS
(Map p80; www.craftedwestside.com; 1100 Howell Mill Rd, Westside Provisions District; ⏲11am-6pm Mon-Fri, 10am-6pm Sat, noon-5pm Sun) Featuring Atlanta-centric arts and crafts from local designers, Crafted is a great spot to pick up fun art, clever sloganed tea towels and pillows, hip T-shirts, crafty jewelry and the like.

A Ma Maniére FASHION & ACCESSORIES
(Map p80; ☎404-975-3380; https://a-ma-maniere.com; 969 Marietta St NW, Westside; ⏲noon-8pm Mon-Fri, 11am-8pm Sat, noon-5pm Sun) Head here for some of the freshest street wear in the city: Amiri jackets, NikeLab kicks, Balmain hoodies and Maison Margiela jeans. These are often four-figure items of clothing, although if you understood the last sentence, you probably already knew that.

Seed Factory CHILDREN'S CLOTHING, TOYS
(Map p80; www.seedfactoryatlanta.com; 1100 Howell Mill Rd NW, Westside Provisions District) A finely curated selection of top-quality children's clothing, toys and other baby-centric gifts for kids aged up to eight years old. A must-stop for hip parents toting cargo.

Greater Atlanta

Sq/Ft GIFTS & SOUVENIRS
(Map p84; ☎404-373-6607; www.sqftdecatur.com; 149 Sycamore St, Decatur; ⏲11am-7pm Mon, to 8pm Tue-Thu, to 9pm Fri & Sat, to 6pm Sun) It's hard to pin down the shopping genre of Decatur's Sq/Ft – on one visit, you may find graphic-print shower curtains, Phaidon coffee-table books, hip-hop screen-print shirts, macramé wall hangings, Bones&Blooms tea towels and handmade jewelry. Whatever you find, it's going to be awesome.

HomeGrown ARTS & CRAFTS
(Map p84; www.homegrowndecatur.com; 412 Church St, Decatur; ⏲10am-9pm Mon-Sat, noon-8pm Sun) Locally rooted Homegrown is true to its name: up to 90% of the candles, hipster T-shirts, art prints, turned-wood bowls, natural cosmetics and other fun and funky arts and craft on offer are Georgia born and bred.

Perimeter Mall MALL
(www.perimetermall.com; 4400 Ashford Dunwoody Rd; ⏲10am-9pm Mon-Sat, noon-7pm Sun) In the upscale suburb of Dunwoody, 13.5 miles north of Downtown, Perimeter Mall is Atlanta's best shopping mall outside the Perimeter (OTP) and the second-largest mall in Georgia. It houses over 200 stores and many upscale restaurants as well as a 10-screen cinema complex. It can be easily accessed by MARTA's Dunwoody station.

Lenox Square MALL
(Map p84; www.simon.com/mall/lenox-square; 3393 Peachtree Rd NE, Buckhead; ⏲10am-9pm, to 7pm Sun) Atlanta's biggest shopping mall inside the perimeter (ITP), Lenox Square offers nearly 250 specialty stores, including luxury brands such as Fendi, Burberry, Cartier, Louis Vuitton and Diane von Furstenberg.

Phipps Plaza MALL
(Map p84; www.simon.com/mall/phipps-plaza; 3500 Peachtree Rd NE, Buckhead; ⏲10am-9pm Mon-Sat, noon-5:30pm Sun) One of Atlanta's most upscale shopping malls, with loads of luxury haute couture, a 14-screen AMC movie theater and LEGOLAND Discovery Center.

Information

SAFE TRAVEL

While Atlanta is a big city with big-city crime issues, such activities do not tend to target tourists, and because the city is truly a series of self-contained towns, it's rare for visitors to simply walk into rough neighborhoods. However, keep your wits about you during the evening.

Atlanta's main annoyance is traffic. Millions of vehicles zoom in and out of downtown Atlanta every day, and rush-hour traffic, particularly in the area around Centennial Olympic Park, is a nightmare. Try to avoid driving between 7am and 9am and 4pm and 6pm.

EMERGENCY & IMPORTANT NUMBERS

Police	911
Medical	911
Rape Treatment Center	770-476-7407
Information Assistance	411
American Civil Liberties Union (ACLU) of Georgia	770-303-8111

ETIQUETTE

Greetings Shake hands with men, women and children when meeting for the first time and when saying goodbye.

Queues Americans respect lining up and any attempt to 'cut the line' will surely be frowned upon and likely cause a fuss.

Bargaining Haggling over the price of goods is not common. In shops, if you are buying in bulk or making a large purchase, you can ask if there is any discount available.

Conversing Southerners are a generally polite bunch – you'll hear 'yes, ma'am' and 'no, sir' quite often, though this isn't something visitors need to concern themselves with outside extremely formal interactions.

TOURIST INFORMATION

Atlanta Convention & Visitors Bureau (www.atlanta.net) Maps, information about attractions, restaurants, outdoor recreation and accommodations; operates visitor centers at **Underground Atlanta** (Map p50; 404-577-2148; 65 Upper Alabama St; 10am-6pm Mon-Sat, noon-6pm Sun).

Getting There & Away

Atlanta straddles the intersection of three interstates: I-20, I-75 and I-85. Hartsfield-Jackson International Airport (p370), 9.5 miles south of Downtown, is the world's busiest airport by passenger traffic. The easiest way into the city from the airport is MARTA, the city's rail system, although bus 191 travels between the airport and the Lakewood MARTA station as well. For those traveling by bus or train, Greyhound (Map p50; 404-584-1728; www.greyhound.com; 232 Forsyth St) and Amtrak (p371) both serve the city.

Getting Around

Despite its sprawling layout and debilitating traffic, Atlanta is fairly easy to navigate both with your own set of wheels or on public transportation. The city is well served by the MARTA bus and rail system and a Downtown tram. And once the groundbreaking Atlanta BeltLine completes its loop by 2030, Atlanta's multiuse trail system will be one of the most progressive in North America, if not the world.

BUS

MARTA runs Atlanta's city bus system in Fulton, DeKalb and Clayton counties. You'll need to buy a reloadable silver Breeze Card ($2, valid three years) to ride. Download MARTA On the Go (www.itsmarta.com/marta-on-the-go.aspx) for schedules and real-time bus locations.

CAR & MOTORCYCLE

Atlanta's neighborhoods and business districts are best accessed by car. You can generally find a parking space – even a free one on occasion – but rates can be expensive, especially if you only need a spot for a short time (the removal of meters means there is usually a one-hour minimum).Download the Parkmobile (http://us.parkmobile.com) app to pay for parking with your smartphone.

TAXI

Taxi rates start at $2.50 for the first eighth mile or less, $0.25 for each additional eighth of a mile. Waiting time is $21 per hour. Uber (www.uber.com) and Lyft (www.lyft.com) both operate in Atlanta.

TRAIN

The **MARTA** (www.itsmarta.com; single ride $2.50, 1-/3-/7-day pass $9/16/23.75; 4:45am-1am Mon-Fri, 6am-1am Sat & Sun) trains travel to/from the airport to downtown, and include commuter routes. Each customer must purchase a Breeze Card (www.breezecard.com); you pay $2 for the card, which can then be loaded and reloaded as necessary. MARTA fare is $2.50.

TRAM

The **Atlanta Streetcar** (http://streetcar.atlantaga.gov) is a nice way of getting around downtown Atlanta. Fare is $1 for a one-way ticket (or you can get an all-day pass for $3); the streetcar follows a 2.7-mile loop that covers a dozen stops, from Centennial Olympic Park to the Martin Luther King Jr National Historic Site.

Savannah & Coastal Georgia

Includes ➡

Best Places to Eat

- ➡ Sunbury Crab Company (p114)
- ➡ Halyards (p121)
- ➡ Wyld (p106)
- ➡ Southern Soul BBQ (p120)
- ➡ Indigo Coastal Shanty (p113)

Best Places to Stay

- ➡ Sapelo Island Birdhouses (p124)
- ➡ Sea Camp Beach (p115)
- ➡ Goodbread House (p118)
- ➡ Greyfield Inn (p118)
- ➡ Jekyll Island State Park (p122)

Why Go?

Georgia's coast isn't as vast as those of the neighboring states along the eastern seaboard, but it's wonderfully wild and unique. Fecund sea islands are lapped by salt tides and peppered with marshes, estuaries and mile upon mile of flat beach. The region has a lost-in-time, almost Gothic, beauty; every corner seems to drip with sweat and Spanish moss, and the low whisper of the Atlantic is never far off.

Those are the nice parts, anyway; swathes of the islands have been manicured into country-club golf courses and shopping centers. But it's not hard to escape these developments and head into the seaside wilds.

Each Georgia island has a distinct character all of its own. Sapelo, Jekyll, the Golden Isles and the town of Brunswick all showcase the beauty of the coastline with a different twist, from humid forests and small-town charm to long horizons over the salt marshes.

When to Go

- ➡ The most popular time to visit is summer (June–August), when beaches are hot and water is warm.
- ➡ Celebrate the famous Shrimp & Grits (p122) three-day extravaganza held on Jekyll Island in September.
- ➡ Many attractions close or reduce hours in the colder months (November–March), meaning bargains can be found.
- ➡ The shoulder months of April and October are the best times to visit Savannah.

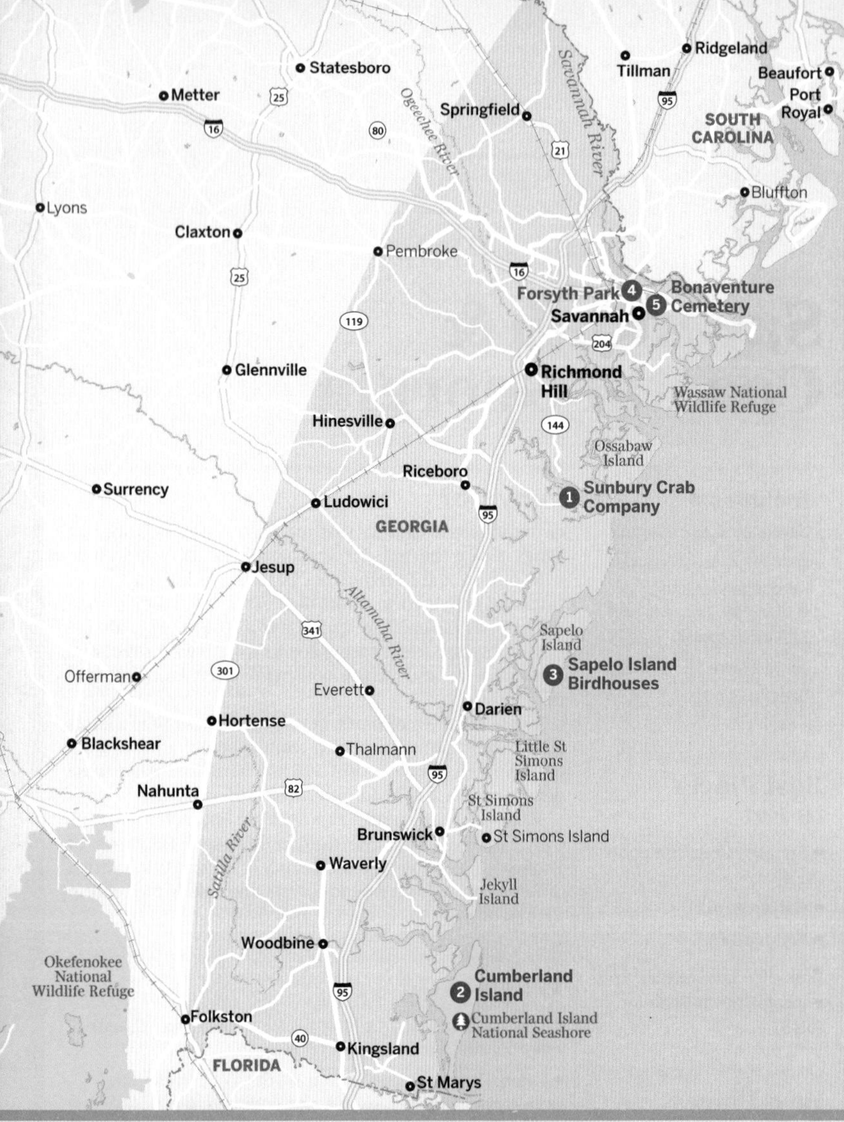

Savannah & Coastal Georgia Highlights

1 Sunbury Crab Company (p114) Devouring a bucket of blue crab at this rare-find fish house.

2 Cumberland Island (p114) Exploring mysterious forests, expansive empty beaches and wilderness campgrounds on this island of adventures.

3 Sapelo Island Birdhouses (p124) Experiencing Sapelo's coastal wilderness at these cottages, tucked away amid the maritime woods and Spanish moss.

4 Forsyth Park (p92) Strolling under live oaks and sweet gum in Savannah's most famous green space.

5 Bonaventure Cemetery (p91) Soaking in the atmosphere of one of the South's eeriest burial grounds.

SAVANNAH

912 / POP 146,763

Rife with elegant townhouses, antebellum mansions, green public squares, pristine tidal freshwater marshes and mammoth oak trees bedecked in moss, Savannah is a beautiful and culturally rich city.

History

Georgia's history as one of the original 13 colonies, and eventually a state, began when James Oglethorpe and a group of inmate settlers sailed from England to Yamacraw Bluff on the banks of the Savannah River. From then on, Savannah's story is one of friendship, diversity, revolution, discrimination, integration and gentrification – and with a couple of hurricanes thrown in. This city, Georgia's first, has seen its share of triumphs and tragedies over an undeniably storied and eventful 285 years.

Sights

East Savannah & the Islands

With such immense natural beauty, this stretch of coastal Savannah is a sight in and of itself. A drive from Thunderbolt, home of Bonaventure Cemetery, to Tybee Island, location of Savannah's beach, is a gorgeously winding, marsh-laden sojourn to the sea.

★ Bonaventure Cemetery CEMETERY

(Map p104; 912-651-6843, Historical Society 912-412-4687; www.bonaventurehistorical.org; 330 Bonaventure Rd; 8am-5pm; P) If you do a Google image search of the term 'Southern Gothic,' the Bonaventure Cemetery pops right up. That should give you an idea of what to expect at this municipal cemetery, plunked on a bluff overlooking the Wilmington River. Forlorn statues and gaunt sculptures in burial shrouds are perched over tombs and mausoleums arranged into a Spanish-moss-drenched necropolis. Bonaventure most famously figured in the novel and film *Midnight in the Garden of Good and Evil* by John Berendt (1994).

The cemetery sprawls over 100 fecund acres located about 4 miles east of downtown Savannah. You can explore the grounds on your own, or take a free guided tour (2pm Saturday, 2pm, 2:30pm and 3pm Sunday). Be on the lookout for family, some 500 Confederate graves, and a Jewish section, which dates to 1909.

Little Tybee Island ISLAND

(Map p104) This uninhabited barrier island, only accessible by boat or kayak, is just south of Tybee Island and is actually double its size. The preserved land is rich with coastal marshland, dunes, wildlife and sub-tropical forests and is a great place to camp. There aren't any facilities on the island, but there's no fee and you can visit any time. Experienced kayakers can rent from any of the outfitters around Tybee, or book a charter service that runs trips to the island.

North Beach BEACH

(Map p108; Railwood Ave, Tybee Island) With fewer services and a vibe that feels more remote, this stretch of beach is a great place to relax. You can watch massive container ships drift in from sea, especially if you take a left once you hit the sand and walk further north up the shore to the point where the Savannah River runs into the Atlantic.

Tybee Island Light Station & Museum LIGHTHOUSE

(Map p108; www.tybeelighthouse.org; 30 Meddin Dr, Tybee Island; adult/child $9/7; 9am-5:30pm Wed-Mon) Take a self-guided tour of Tybee's iconic lighthouse and see panoramic views of the island from its observation deck. Tickets include admission to the nearby cottage and museum. Accepts volunteers to greet visitors, interpret and help with on-site projects. Con-tact Gus Rehnstrom or Art Worden at 912-786-5801 or volunteers@tybeelighthouse.org.

Fort Pulaski National Monument FORT

(Map p104; www.nps.gov/fopu/index.htm; Cockspur Island; adult/child under 16yr $7/free; 9am-5pm) Located on Cockspur Island at the mouth of the Savannah River, Fort Pulaski was constructed after President James Madison ordered coastal fortifications following the War of 1812. For history buffs, it's worth a stop on the way to Tybee.

Tybee Pier & Pavilion PIER

(Map p108; 912-652-6780; 16th St at Strand Ave, Tybee Island; 7am-11pm) Tybee's main beachside hub, with public bathrooms, concessions and a long fishing pier. Tables in the pavilion are available to rent by the hour.

Historic District & Forsyth Park

The sights of Savannah's Historic District are among the best in the country. Monuments, museums and grand homes will keep you wandering in wonder. Sights are scattered around 22 park squares arranged in a grid, and it's easy to walk from one end of the district to the other, with Forsyth Park at the southern edge near the Victorian District, and River St to the far north. Broad St is the eastern boundary and Martin Luther King Jr Blvd is the western, where you'll find the main visitor center and bus hub.

★ Forsyth Park PARK

(Map p98) FREE The Central Park of Savannah is a sprawling rectangular green space, anchored by a beautiful fountain that forms a quintessential photo op.

Mercer-Williams House HISTORIC BUILDING

(Map p98; ☎912-236-6352; www.mercerhouse.com; 429 Bull St; adult/student $12.50/8; ⊙10:30am-4:10pm Mon-Sat, noon-4pm Sun) Although Jim Williams, the Savannah art dealer portrayed by Kevin Spacey in the film version of *Midnight in the Garden of Good and Evil*, died back in 1990, his infamous mansion didn't become a museum until 2004. You're not allowed to visit the upstairs, where Williams' family still lives, but the downstairs is an interior decorator's fantasy.

Telfair Academy MUSEUM

(Map p98; ☎912-790-8800; www.telfair.org/visit/telfair; 121 Barnard St; adult/child $20/15; ⊙noon-5pm Sun & Mon, 10am-5pm Tue-Sat) Considered Savannah's top art museum, the historic Telfair family mansion is filled with 19th-century American art and silver and a smattering of European pieces. The home itself is an artifact in its own right that wows visitors to this day.

Webb Military Museum MUSEUM

(Map p98; ☎912-663-0398; www.webbmilitarymuseum.com; 411 E York St; adult/senior/veteran/child $10/9/8/6; ⊙10am-5pm Mon-Sat, noon-4pm Sun) Get a deeper insight on military history, from the Civil War era through Desert Storm, by viewing this privately owned collection that helps humanize war through artifacts such as uniforms and personal effects.

American Prohibition Museum MUSEUM

(Map p98; ☎912-220-1249; www.americanprohibitionmuseum.com; 209 W St Julian St; adult/child $13/10; ⊙10am-5pm) Learn about the history of Prohibition in the US in this spirited museum, the only one of its kind in the country. Exhibits feature live actors, films, animated portraits and detailed wax figures, and you can round out your visit with a tipple on the top floor at Up, the museum's speakeasy.

First African Baptist Church CHURCH

(Map p98; ☎912-233-6597; www.firstafricanbc.com; 23 Montgomery St; tours $10; ⊙tours 11am, 2pm & 4pm Tue-Sat, 1pm Sun, worship services 10am Sun, 6am Wed) Considered the oldest African American church in the country, this National Historic Landmark played a pivotal role on the Underground Railroad. Offers worship services and tours, where you can see holes in the floorboards that enabled slaves to breathe.

Flannery O'Connor Childhood Home MUSEUM

(Map p98; ☎912-233-6014; www.flanneryoconnorhome.org; 207 E Charlton St; adult/student $6/5; ⊙1-4pm Fri-Wed, closed Thu) This stone row house on Lafayette Sq is where the literary great was born in 1925 and lived until she was 13. Her second short-story collection won the National Book Award in 1972 – eight years after she died.

SCAD Museum of Art MUSEUM

(Map p98; www.scadmoa.org; 601 Turner Blvd; adult/child under 14yr $10/free; ⊙10am-5pm Tue, Wed, Fri & Sat, to 8pm Thu, noon-5pm Sun) Architecturally striking (but what else would you expect from this school of design?), this brick, steel, concrete and glass longhouse delivers your contemporary-art fix. There are groovy, creative sitting areas inside and out, and a number of rotating and visiting exhibitions that showcase some of the most impressive talents within the contemporary-art world.

Cathedral of St John the Baptist CHURCH

(Map p98; ☎912-233-4709; www.savannahcathedral.org; 222 E Harris St; ⊙Mass 7:30am & noon Mon-Fri, noon & 5:30pm Sat, 8am, 10am & 11:30am Sun, in Latin 1pm Sun) Completed in 1896 but destroyed by fire two years later, this impressive cathedral, reopened in 1912, features stunning stained-glass transept windows from Austria depicting Christ's ascension into heaven, as well as ornate Station of the Cross woodcarvings from Bavaria.

'THE WEEPING TIME'

One of the largest slave sales in US history took place in Savannah in March 1859. Known colloquially as 'The Weeping Time' by slaves and their descendants, it's said that the bright and sunny weather turned to rain as the sale began. Torrents continued to fall over what used to be the Ten Broeck Race Course, the site of the auction 2 miles west of Savannah's Historic District, and didn't relent until the last slave was sold the following day. It was believed that the heavens were weeping in response to the dreadful inhumanity being carried out.

Pierce Mease Butler, the man who owned the 436 enslaved men, women, children and infants who were sold, inherited wealth (which included slaves) from his grandfather, Major Pierce Butler. Major Butler was one of the largest slaveholders in the nation at the time and was one of the signatories of the United States Constitution; he authored the Fugitive Slave Clause and played a key role in its inclusion under Article Four of the Constitution.

Pierce M Butler's gambling addiction saw him in a significant amount of debt, necessitating the appointment of a group of trustees who seized control of his assets in 1856. To extricate his debts, they sold off his family properties but couldn't return him to solvency so decided that his 'movable property,' slaves, would be put up for auction to absolve him of his remaining financial obligations. The slaves were brought from the Butler plantations to the racetrack and put in the horse stables, where they waited for the auction to begin.

The auction was advertised for several weeks and filled every hotel in Savannah with potential buyers. They went to the racetrack to preview the slaves, prodding and pinching their muscles to check for strength potential and pulling open their mouths to examine their teeth. Humans were treated like livestock.

On the first day of the auction, the heavy rains slowed the arrival of buyers and the event began two hours late. When it finally began, the first slaves were sold: George, Sue and their two boys, George and Harry, for $600 each. But some families weren't so fortunate to be sold together. By the end of the auction, all 436 people had been sold away, most from their families and the only home they knew.

Despite the abundance of generations-old historic monuments and memorials throughout the South, those that have anything to do with slavery are rare or recent arrivals. The site of 'The Weeping Time' was not marked or commemorated until almost 150 years after it occurred – in 2008 a local man passing out dirt from Nigeria sprinkled some on to the earth and then-mayor Otis Johnson (only the second African American to ever hold that office) poured water over it to consecrate the ground. What you'll see today is an obscurely placed historical marker plaque (p97) in a small triangular park on the corner of Augusta Ave and Dunn St in west Savannah, where many poor African Americans reside.

Jepson Center for the Arts GALLERY
(JCA; Map p98; ☎912-790-8800; www.telfair.org/visit/jepson; 207 W York St; adult/child $20/15; ⏲noon-5pm Sun & Mon, 10am-5pm Tue-Sat; 👪) Designed by the great Moshe Safdie, and looking pretty darn space-age by Savannah's standards, the JCA – rather appropriately, given its architecture – focuses on 20th- and 21st-century art. Be on the lookout for wandering SCAD students and temporary exhibitions covering topics from race to art in virtual-reality video games.

Haitian Monument MONUMENT
(Map p98; Franklin Sq) Built to honor 750 Haitian volunteer infantrymen who fought to try and get Savannah back from the British in 1779 during the American Revolution.

Colonial Park Cemetery CEMETERY
(Map p98; ☎912-651-6843; 200 Abercorn St; ⏲8am-5pm) Established in 1750, Savannah's oldest surviving Revolutionary-era resting place was used for Savannah's white burials for a century, until its closure in 1853.

Waving Girl Statue STATUE
(Map p98; east end of River St at E Broad St, Morrell Park) FREE Florence Martus, aka the Waving Girl, was known for greeting passing ships by waving a handkerchief by day and a lantern by night for more than 40 years. Myth says she was bethrothed to a sailor and the day-in, day-out waving was done in the hopes of being the first to welcome him home.

African American Monument MONUMENT

(Map p98; E Upper Factors Walk, Rousakis Plaza) FREE This solemn monument features a family of four in a close embrace, with broken shackles around their feet that represent emancipation from slavery. The harrowingly evocative inscription was written by renowned poet Maya Angelou.

Ships of the Sea Maritime Museum MUSEUM

(Map p98; 912-232-1511; www.shipsofthesea.org; 41 Martin Luther King Jr Blvd; adult/student $9/7; 10am-5pm Tue-Sun) If you're into boats or naval history, this little museum will hold a lot of interest. Located in an old Savannah mansion, there are several floors of maritime paintings, antiques, artifacts and, most impressive, a large collection of ships painstakingly recreated in miniature (by 'miniature,' we mean several feet long). The educational material is only sort of interesting, but the level of attention given to the model boats is stunning.

Ralph Mark Gilbert Civil Rights Museum MUSEUM

(Map p98; 912-777-6099; www.visit-historic-savannah.com/ralph-mark-gilbert-civil-rights-museum.html; 460 Martin Luther King Jr Blvd; adult/child $8/4; 10am-4pm Tue-Sat) This museum provides a local introduction to the Civil Rights movement as it played out in Savannah – the supposedly genteel city had some fairly savage reactions against the campaign for equal rights. The museum occupies the former Wage Earners Savings & Loan Bank, once the largest bank for local African Americans.

Owens-Thomas House HISTORIC BUILDING

(Map p98; 912-790-8800; www.telfair.org/visit/owens-thomas; 124 Abercorn St; adult/senior/child $20/18/15; noon-5pm Sun & Mon, 10am-5pm Tue-Sat) Completed in 1819 by British architect William Jay, this gorgeous villa exemplifies English Regency–style architecture, known for its symmetry. The guided tour is a little obsessed with details on aristocratic life, but it delivers interesting trivia about the spooky 'haint blue' ceiling paint in the slave quarters, and the number of years by which this mansion preceded the White House in getting running water (nearly 20).

City Walk Savannah's Squares

START: FORSYTH PARK
END: JOHNSON SQ
LENGTH: 1¾ MILES, TWO HOURS

Begin this leisurely stroll at the south entrance of **1 Forsyth Park** (p92) at Bull St and Park Ave. Head north along the main thoroughfare and arrive at the iconic fountain for an obligatory photo op before continuing north past Gaston St, the official boundary where the Victorian District ends and the Historic District begins. Stay north on Bull St toward the intersection of Wayne St, where a tall monument topped with a statue of General Casimir Pulaski greets you in **2 Monterey Square**, one of Savannah's most picturesque. The **3 Mercer-Williams house** (p92), setting of the novel and film *Midnight in the Garden of Good and Evil*, faces its west side – pop in to hear the harrowing history of what went down inside Savannah's most famous haunted house, then continue north for two blocks and hook a right on **4 Jones Street**. From east to west, this street is famous for its cobblestones and high-stooped, Greek Revival homes tucked under a canopy of live oak trees. Take your time admiring the mid-19th-century architecture along this enchanted lane, but don't forget that locals reside in the houses – stick to the sidewalk when taking your snaps.

Hang a left on Abercorn St and continue two blocks north to Charlton St – you'll see the spectacular twin steeples of the **5 Cathedral of St John the Baptist** (p92) as you approach **6 Lafayette Square**. Keep heading north, past Liberty St, to **7 Colonial Park Cemetery** (p93) at the intersection of Perry St – wander past beautiful Gothic tombs and monuments before turning west on McDonough St, where you'll hit **8 Chippewa Square** at the intersection of Bull St. It sits smack in the middle of the Historic District, with a bronze statue of Savannah founder James Oglethorpe overseeing all the action from the center. This square is famous for the park-bench scenes in the 1994 film *Forrest Gump*, which was shot on the north side along Hull St – but the actual bench from the movie was just a prop placed there for the duration of the production, so don't

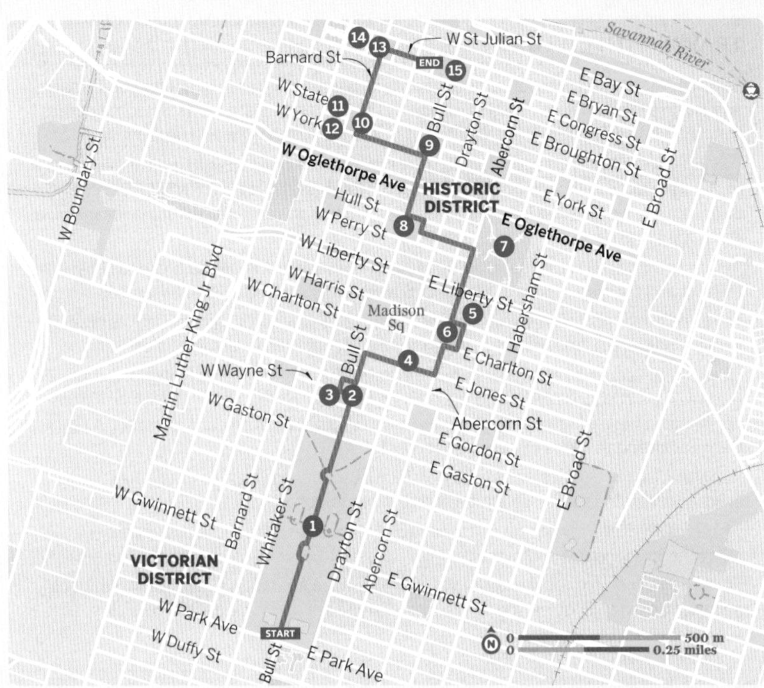

expect to take a seat and compare your life to a box of chocolates.

Keep truckin' north on Bull St, past Oglethorpe Ave, to York St and arrive at 9 **Wright Square**. This was the second square constructed in Savannah and is the burial site of Tomochichi, the Yamacraw tribe leader who befriended Oglethorpe and helped him establish the colony. When Tomochichi died, Oglethorpe ordered that he be buried with military honors and in accordance with the customs of the Yamacraw/Creek peoples. His grave was marked by a pyramid of stones sourced from the surrounding area. In 1883 this demarcation was replaced with an elaborate monument of William Washington Gordon, a Savannah-born lawyer and businessman. Gordon's own wife even recognized this as an insult to Tomochichi and the Yamacraw/Creek nation, and with fellow members of the Colonial Dames of Georgia arranged for a new monument, made of granite sourced from Stone Mountain, to honor him. See this enormous boulder on the southeast corner of the square before heading west on York St for two blocks to 10 **Telfair Square**. You won't find any monuments with a contentious backstory in this square, but you will find creative inspiration all around it – both the 11 **Telfair Academy** (p92) and the 12 **Jepson Center for the Arts** (p93) sit on Barnard St.

Continue north on Barnard St and cross over Broughton St, downtown's main commercial drag, toward Congress St and arrive at 13 **Ellis Square**. Once known as Marketplace Sq (the buzzing 14 **City Market** sits on the west edge), it was a center for commerce from the 1730s through 1950s and in the 1850s housed a slave market that operated prior to General Sherman's arrival to Savannah in 1864. In 1954 a parking garage was built to further serve retail interests in the area and after the expiration of its 50-year lease, it was demolished in accordance with local historic preservation efforts. What exists today is a modern, open public space with a wading fountain and a bronze statue of Johnny Mercer; in that musical spirit, concerts are regularly hosted here. Head back east down St Julian St toward Bull St and end the journey at 15 **Johnson Square**, Savannah's first and largest square. In 1902 the remains of Revolutionary War hero General Nathanael Greene were exhumed from his original grave in Colonial Park Cemetery and reinterred under the obelisk in the center of the square.

TRAVEL WITH CHILDREN

Savannah is a great place for families, with outdoor adventures in beautiful green spaces and kid-friendly activities at sights all across the city. Most restaurants welcome parties with children and there is loads of interesting history to make for an enriching visit.

Savannah Children's Museum (Map p98; http://www.chsgeorgia.org/SCM) This all-outdoor museum, located in Tricentennial Park at the old Central of Georgia Railway Carpentry Shop, is full of exciting and interactive activities, such as an underground archaeology table and a giant lego panel.

Tybee Island (p91) From spotting dolphins and manatees along the shore to playing in the surf and building castles in the sand, Savannah's local beach is a ball for kids.

Forsyth Park (p92) The sprawling green space of Savannah's 'Central Park' is great for games and picnics, and there's a playground where local and visiting kids convene.

River St Savannah's riverfront is great for a stroll, with monuments to explore, such as the Waving Girl Statue (p93), and the exciting Echo Sq in Rousakis Plaza, which kiddos can stand in the middle of and hear their voice reverberate in an echo chamber. A ride on the free Savannah Belles Ferry is also lots of fun.

Jepson Center for the Arts (p93) ArtZeum, the Jepson Center's interactive children's learning gallery, gets little ones excited about art.

Ships of the Sea Maritime Museum (p94) Kids with a fascination for boats will enjoy the large models at this museum.

Fort Pulaski National Monument (p91) This huge fort with educational exhibitions and cool cannons is fun for the whole family. There are trails to walk and bike close by.

Southside & the Moon River District

The Moon River District is home to Low-country sights with rich history and pristine natural beauty.

★Wormsloe Histoic Site HISTORIC SITE
(Map p104; ☎912-353-3023; www.gastateparks.org/wormsloe; 7601 Skidaway Rd; adult/senior/child 6-17yr/child 1-5yr $10/9/4.50/2; ⊙9am-5pm; P) A short drive from downtown, on the beautiful Isle of Hope, this is one of the most photographed sites in town. As soon as you enter, you feel as if you've been roused from an arboreal dream as you gaze at a corridor of mossy, ancient oaks that runs for 1.5 miles, known as the Avenue of the Oaks.

Pin Point Heritage Museum MUSEUM
(Map p104; ☎912-355-0064; www.chsgeorgia.org/phm; 9924 Pin Point Ave; adult/child under 12yr $8/4; ⊙9am-5pm Thu-Sat) Set in what used to be the AS Varn & Son Oyster Seafood Factory, this museum highlights the culture and history of the Gullah-Geechee peoples in the Pin Point community, which was established by first-generation freed slaves and thrived for nearly 100 years. Exhibitions showcase the community's connection to fishing industries, which were a vital part of their livelihood.

Midtown & the Victorian District

Bull St is the main artery running through this area, with Laurel Grove Cemetery being the sight furthest west, just on the edge of the Victorian District. Daffin Park is all the way east down Victory Dr just before you approach East Savannah. Most sights, such as Starland Arts District, right in the center, are easy to navigate by foot; beyond that, a car or bike is the way to roll.

★Laurel Grove Cemetery CEMETERY
(Map p104; 2101 Kollock St; ⊙8am-5pm) Originally part of a plantation, this segregated cemetery has major historical significance to Savannah. From the mid-19th century, whites – including Confederate veterans of the Civil War – were buried in the north section (which has a separate entrance); the south section contains graves of thousands of African Americans, both once-enslaved and free. Laurel Grove South is one of the largest African American cemeteries in the South and many influential figures from the community, including from during the Civil Rights Movement, are interred here. The entrance for Laurel Grove North is located at 802 West Anderson St.

Savannah African Art Museum MUSEUM
(Map p104; ☎912-421-8168; visit.saam@gmail.com; 201 E 37th St; ⊙11am-4pm Thu-Sat) FREE Privately owned museum showcasing 19th- and 20th-century spiritual and ceremonial art objects from 22 African countries, with museum volunteers giving guided tours. It was setting up its new premises at the time of research; check its Facebook page for an update on its reopening before visiting.

Sulfur Studios ART STUDIO
(Map p104; www.sulfurstudios.org; 2301 Bull St; ⊙noon-5pm Thu-Sat) Community art space with a gallery and retail space, plus open artist studios during Starland's First Friday Art March.

Daffin Park PARK
(Map p104; ☎912-351-3851; 1500 E Victory Dr) This large recreational park has good walking paths, a pond, lots of grass for sports and picnics, and a public pool. You can catch baseball games at Grayson Stadium, home to the Savannah Bananas baseball team.

Greater Savannah

Wassaw National Wildlife Refuge WILDLIFE RESERVE
(Map p104; ☎843-784-9911; www.fws.gov/refuge/wassaw; Wassaw Island; ⊙sunrise-sunset) A wild, minimally developed coastal barrier island and 10,053-acre refuge where you can enjoy bird-watching, beachcombing and hiking around the beaches, live-oak and slash-pine woodlands and salt marshes. You can only get there by a 30-minute boat ride (around $50), which can be booked with charter services at marinas around town.

Weeping Time Plaque LANDMARK
(Map p104; cnr Augusta Ave & Dunn St) FREE Historic marker close to the site of the largest slave auction in US history. For more information, see p93.

Activities

McQueen's Island Historic Trail WALKING
(Map p104; US Hwy 80, McQueen's Island) This 6-mile walking and biking trail is built over a stretch of the Savannah & Atlantic Railroad line. It parallels the south channel of the Savannah River and you can spot wildlife such as box turtles, red-tailed hawks, brown pelicans and more. The midpoint entrance is about 15 miles east of Savannah on US Hwy 80 on McQueen's Island, just as soon as you cross the Bull River; park along the road or at Fort Pulaski a little further along.

First Friday Art March WALKING
(Map p104; Starland Arts District, near Bull St at 40th St; ⊙6-9pm 1st Fri of month) FREE On the first Friday of each month, galleries, shops and eateries around the Starland Arts District open their doors for shows, shopping and drinking with local artists and makers.

Old Savannah City Mission VOLUNTEERING
(Map p104; ☎912-232-1979, ask for Connell Stiles; www.oscm.org; 2414 Bull St; ⊙24hr) Help Savannah's needy with a range of tasks. Must apply to volunteer and some positions require special training.

Habitat for Humanity VOLUNTEERING
(Map p98; ☎912-353-8122; www.habitatsavannah.com; 701 Martin Luther King Jr Blvd, ReStore; ⊙9am-5pm Tue-Sat) Work in the ReStore or lend a hand with constructing homes for impoverished residents of Savannah.

Courses & Tours

Chef Darin's Kitchen Table COOKING
(Map p104; ☎912-662-6882; www.chefdarinskitchentable.com; 2514 Abercorn St, Suite 40; 4hr class per person from $75; ⊙11am-6pm Tue-Fri, 10am-6pm Sat) When you tire of eating all that sinful Southern food (OK, that may never happen), try your hand at making it with local top chef Darin Sehnert. Theme-driven classes include Low Country Cuisine, French Bistro and Northern Italian. There's also a store stocked with kitchen accoutrements.

Bonaventure Cemetery Journeys TOURS
(Map p104; ☎912-319-5600; www.bonaafterhours.com; 330 Bonaventure Rd; per person $25-45; ⊙day tours 10am & 2pm, night tour 5pm Sat) Lovers of history and engaging storytelling will enjoy fantastic Bonaventure tours run by local historian Shannon Scott. The three-hour Bonaventure After Hours tour is the only way to see the cemetery at night, where you'll get a different perspective on the history, architecture and traditions of Savannah's most alluring city of the dead. Special private group tours are also available.

Sorrel Weed House HOUSE
(Map p98; ☎912-257-2223; www.sorrelweedhouse.com; 6 W Harris St; ⊙10am-11:30pm) Fans of the paranormal can get their thrills at one of Savannah's spookiest mansions – the ghost tours are genuinely creepy and the grounds hauntingly beautiful.

Savannah

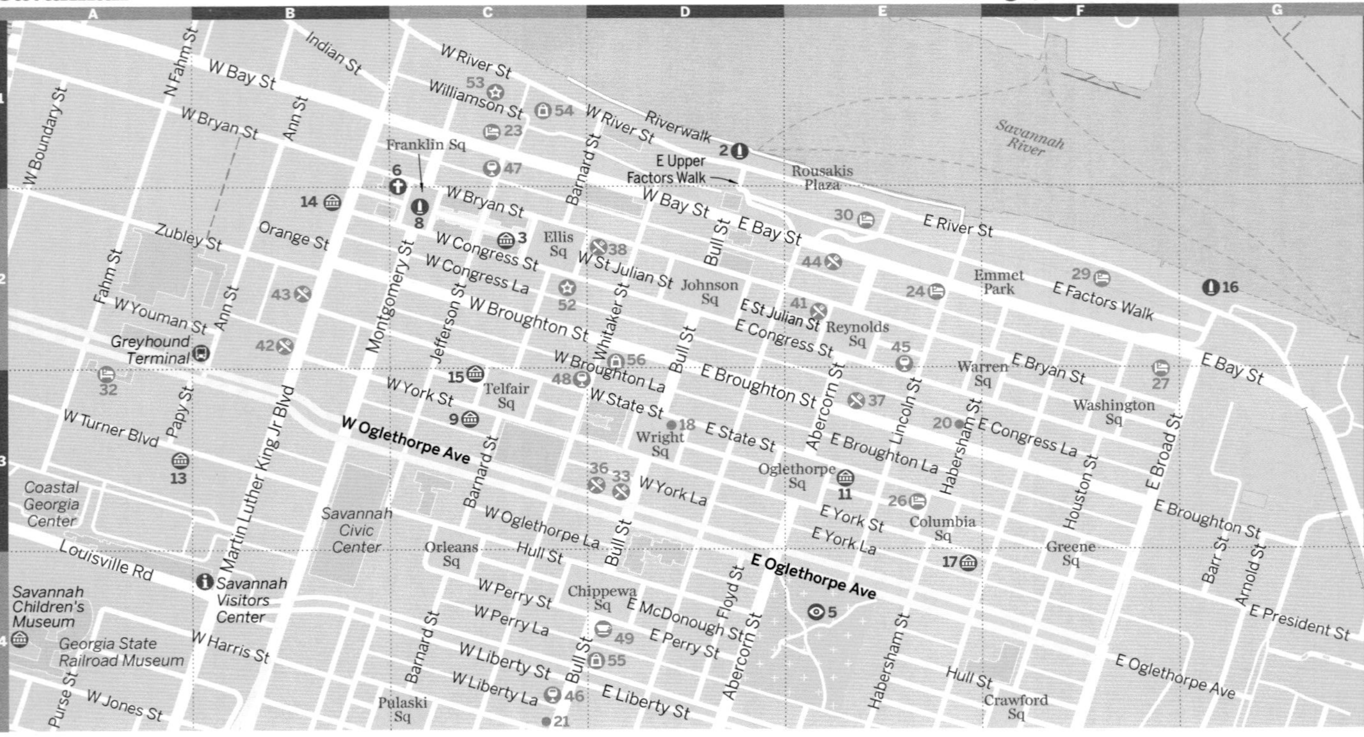
0
400 m
0
0.2 miles
A
B
C
D
E
F
G
1
2
3
4
Savannah River
Riverwalk
Rousakis Plaza
E Upper Factors Walk
E Factors Walk
Emmet Park
Franklin Sq
Ellis Sq
Johnson Sq
Reynolds Sq
Warren Sq
Washington Sq
Telfair Sq
Wright Sq
Oglethorpe Sq
Columbia Sq
Greene Sq
Orleans Sq
Chippewa Sq
Crawford Sq
Pulaski Sq
Savannah Civic Center
Savannah Visitors Center
Coastal Georgia Center
Savannah Children's Museum
Georgia State Railroad Museum
Greyhound Terminal
W River St
W Bay St
E Bay St
E River St
W Bryan St
E Bryan St
W Congress St
W Congress La
E Congress St
E Congress La
W St Julian St
E St Julian St
W Broughton St
E Broughton St
W Broughton La
E Broughton La
W State St
E State St
W York St
W York La
E York St
E York La
W Oglethorpe Ave
E Oglethorpe Ave
W Oglethorpe La
W Perry St
W Perry La
E Perry St
E McDonough St
W Liberty St
W Liberty La
E Liberty St
W Harris St
W Jones St
E President St
Williamson St
Indian St
Ann St
Orange St
Zubley St
W Youman St
W Turner Blvd
Louisville Rd
Martin Luther King Jr Blvd
Montgomery St
Jefferson St
Barnard St
Whitaker St
Bull St
Abercorn St
Lincoln St
Habersham St
Houston St
E Broad St
Barr St
Arnold St
Floyd St
Hull St
Purse St
N Fahm St
Fahm St
Papy St
W Boundary St

HISTORIC DISTRICT
VICTORIAN DISTRICT
MIDTOWN
1 Forsyth Park
Forsyth Park
Mother Mathilda Beasley
Madison Sq
Lafayette Sq
Troup Sq
Chatham Sq
Monterey Sq
Calhoun Sq
Whitefield Sq
Jim Gillis Historic Savannah Pkwy
Selma St
Martin Luther King Jr Blvd
Montgomery St
Berrien St
W Taylor St
W Wayne St
Alice St
Jefferson St
Tattnall St
W Huntingdon St
Lorch St
W Hall St
W Hall La
W Gwinnett St
W Gwinnett La
W Bolton St
W Bolton La
W Waldburg St
W Waldburg La
W Park Ave
W Duffy St
W Duffy La
Barnard St
Howard St
Whitaker St
W Charlton St
W Charlton La
W Jones St
W Jones La
W Wayne St
W Gordon St
W Gordon La
W Gaston St
Bull St
Drayton St
Goodwin St
Abercorn St
Lincoln St
Habersham St
Price St
Blair St
E Broad St
E Macon St
E Liberty La
E Harris St
E Macon St
E Charlton St
E Charlton La
E Jones St
E Jones La
E Taylor St
E Wayne St
E Gordon St
E Gaston St
E Gordon La
E Gaston St
E Gaston La
E Huntingdon St
E Huntingdon La
E Hall St
Nicoll St
E Hall St
E Hall La
E Gwinnett St
E Gwinnett La
E Bolton St
E Bolton La
E Waldburg St
E Waldburg La
E Park Ave
Hitch Dr
Wilder Dr
E Liberty St
E Perry La
Weaton St
Flagler St
Rockerfeller St
Grant St
Burton Crt
Joe La
Paulsen St
Joe St
Hammond St
Wolf St
Wolf La
4
7
10
12
19
22
25
28
31
34
35
39
40
50
51
57
A
B
C
D
E
F
G
5
6
7
8

Savannah

Top Sights
1 Forsyth Park C7

Sights
2 African American Monument D1
3 American Prohibition Museum C2
4 Cathedral of St John the Baptist D5
5 Colonial Park Cemetery E4
6 First African Baptist Church C1
7 Flannery O'Connor Childhood Home D5
8 Haitian Monument C2
9 Jepson Center for the Arts C3
10 Mercer-Williams House C6
11 Owens-Thomas House E3
12 Ralph Mark Gilbert Civil Rights Museum A5
13 SCAD Museum of Art A3
14 Ships of the Sea Maritime Museum B2
15 Telfair Academy C3
16 Waving Girl Statue G2
17 Webb Military Museum E4

Activities, Courses & Tours
18 Footprints of Savannah D3
19 Habitat for Humanity A6
20 Savannah Bike Tours E3
21 Sorrel Weed House C4

Sleeping
22 Azalea Inn D7
23 Bohemian Hotel C1
24 East Bay Inn E2
25 Gastonian D6
26 Kehoe House E3
27 Kimpton Brice F3
28 Mansion on Forsyth Park C7
29 Olde Harbour Inn F2
30 River Street Inn E2
31 Savannah Pensione D7
32 Thunderbird Inn A3

Eating
33 Collins Quarter D3
34 Forsyth Park Farmers Market B8
35 Fox & Fig E5
36 Husk Savannah D3
37 Leopold's Ice Cream E3
38 Little Duck D2
39 Local11Ten B8
40 Mrs Wilkes Dining Room C5
41 Olde Pink House E2
42 Prohibition B2
43 The Grey B2
44 Treylor Park E2

Drinking & Nightlife
45 Abe's on Lincoln E2
46 Artillery C4
47 Club One C1
48 El-Rocko Lounge C3
49 Gallery Espresso D4
50 Original Pinkie Masters D5
Rocks on the Roof .... (see 23)
51 Sentient Bean B8

Entertainment
52 Jinx C2
53 Savannah Smiles Dueling Pianos C1

Shopping
54 Books on Bay C1
55 Satchel D4
56 Savannah Bee Company D2
57 ShopSCAD C5

Footprints of Savannah HISTORY
(Map p98; ☎912-695-3872; www.footprintsofsavannah.com; tours begin in Wright Sq; adult/child $20/7; ⊙daily tours 10am) Learn about the side of Savannah that didn't make it into the history books with Vaughnette Goode-Walker on this 1½-hour walking tour that highlights the city's rich and complex African American history. Call ahead to book; discounted group tours available.

Savannah Bike Tours CYCLING
(Map p98; ☎912-704-4043; www.savannahbiketours.com; 41 Habersham St; tours $25; ⊙varies by season) This outfit offers two-hour bike tours over easy flat terrain on its fleet of cruisers.

Festivals & Events

Savannah Black Heritage Festival PERFORMING ARTS
(☎912-358-4309; www.savannahblackheritagefestival.com; ⊙usually 1st 3 weeks Feb) Every year, during Black History Month (February), this multidisciplinary festival features events that range from cultural educational programs, ethnic cuisine demonstrations and craft fairs to historic tours, visual arts exhibitions and dance and spoken word performances.

Savannah Stopover MUSIC
(www.savannahstopover.com; ⊙usually Mar) If you're into live music, come to this local indie music festival that's held the weekend before Texas' South by

Southwest (SXSW) festival. It's a warm-up for bands en route to Austin. It's held over four days, in more than 10 locations and features more than 75 bands.

Telfair Art Fair MUSIC
(www.telfair.org/artfair; ⌚usually Nov) Free open-air art fair with food trucks, music and children's activities. Preview selections at the Arty Party before the official event.

Sleeping

East Savannah & the Islands

The only sleeping options in this area are on Tybee Island. There are hotels and a handful of B&Bs, plus vacation rentals and private accommodations.

Royal Palm Motel MOTEL $
(Map p108; ☎912-786-4763; www.royalpalmtybee.com; 909 Butler Ave, Tybee Island; s/d $78/95) This budget motel has renovated rooms, air-con and a modest pool, and is just a few minutes' walk to Tybee's beachfront.

★ **Beachview Bed & Breakfast** B&B $$
(Map p108; ☎912-786-5500; www.beachviewbbtybee.com; 1701 Butler Ave, Tybee Island; r from $229; P 📶 🐾) The tastefully themed rooms in this stately home feature bright, breezy decor, clawfoot tubs and comfortable beds, all within walking distance of Tybee's south-end beachfront. Breakfast is farm-to-table and Wendy, the on-site manager and owner's daughter, is as chipper and helpful as they come.

Atlantis Inn INN $$
(Map p108; ☎912-786-8558; www.atlantisinntybee.com; 20 Silver Ave, Tybee Island; s/d $168/189; ❄ 📶) A quirky 1950s-style inn, its rooms have touches such as red-velvet decor, murals and bamboo-lined walls. There's a microwave and minifridge in each room, and it's just a few minutes' walk from the Tybee Pier.

Hotel Tybee HOTEL $$$
(Map p108; ☎912-786-7777; www.hoteltybee.com; 1401 Strand Ave, Tybee Island; r from $279; P ❄ 📶 🏊) Ocean views and a central location are the highlight of this megahotel's 208 modern rooms, which feature private balcony and flat-screen TV, plus two swimming pools and free parking.

Historic District & Forsyth Park

Savannah's finest accommodations are in this part of the city. From modern boutique hotels to historic inns and B&Bs, there's a property that'll fit your needs – and blow your mind with its beauty.

Thunderbird Inn MOTEL $
(Map p98; ☎912-232-2661; www.thethunderbirdinn.com; 611 W Oglethorpe Ave; r $130-160; P ❄ 📶 🐾) 'A tad Palm Springs, a touch Vegas' best describes this vintage-chic 1964 motel that wins its own popularity contest – a 'Hippest hotel in Savannah' proclamation greets guests in the '60s-soundtracked lobby. In a land of stuffy B&Bs, this groovy place is an oasis, made all the better by local Savannah College of Art & Design student art. Doughnuts for breakfast!

River Street Inn HOTEL $$
(Map p98; ☎912-234-6400; www.riverstreetinn.com; 124 E Bay St; r from $199; 📶) This excellent option has historical-chic (but not stuffy) rooms with hardwood floors and four-poster beds, and the best ones have balconies. The interior feels plucked from a history textbook, which makes sense, seeing as the building that the hotel occupies dates to 1817.

East Bay Inn INN $$
(Map p98; ☎912-238-1225; www.eastbayinn.com; 225 E Bay St; r/ste from $180/220; ❄ 📶 🐾) Wedged between corporate rivals, this brick behemoth offers just 28 huge rooms – each with original double-wide wood floors, exposed brick walls, soaring ceilings, slender support columns and flat-screen TV, along with much charm and warmth to spare.

Kimpton Brice BOUTIQUE HOTEL $$$
(Map p98; ☎912-238-1200; www.bricehotel.com; 601 E Bay St; r from $390; ❄ 📶 🏊) Kimpton is known for its design-conscious hotels, so you'd figure it would bring its A game to one of the country's leading design cities. The Kimpton Brice does not disappoint in this, or any other, regard. Modern rooms have playful swatches of color, while the hotel's entrance and lobby feels like it could accommodate a cool club. Amenities include French-press coffee on request, a sweet pool and free rental of an on-site fleet of Public bikes.

Kehoe House B&B $$$

(Map p98; ☎912-232-1020; www.kehoehouse.com; 123 Habersham St; r from $250; ❄📶) This romantic, upscale Renaissance Revival B&B dates from 1892. Twins are said to have died in a chimney here, making it one of America's most haunted hotels (if you're skittish, steer clear of rooms 201 and 203). Ghosts aside, it's a beautifully appointed worthwhile splurge on picturesque Columbia Sq.

Gastonian B&B $$$

(Map p98; ☎912-232-2869; www.gastonian.com; 220 E Gaston St; r from $320; 📶) If you have that 'I want to feel like a 19th-century baron' itch that just *needs* to be scratched, the Gastonian is the hotel you've been waiting for. Opulent, individually designed rooms have a Gilded Age vibe, and feel like they've been lifted from a Disney movie set. Guests are served enormous breakfasts. Rooms have private baths.

Olde Harbour Inn INN $$$

(Map p98; ☎912-234-4100; www.oldeharbourinn.com; 508 E Factors Walk; ste $212-360; 📶🐾) The spiffy suites at this waterfront hotel occupy the golden mean between historic atmosphere and modern sensibilities, from the airy sense of space (a bit of space, actually – from 450 to 650 sq ft) to the subdued color schemes and polished hardwood floors. There's a free wine and cheese reception every evening.

ACCESSIBLE TRAVEL

Cobblestones and bumpy brick paths aside (chalk it up to the city's charm), Savannah is quite wheelchair accessible. Ramps and elevators are available at most multilevel sights and there are reserved parking spaces in the parking garages, plus a few here and there on the streets and squares.

Several of the higher priced hotels are wheelchair accessible, while many B&Bs are not; Kehoe House (p102) is a notable exception. CAT Freedom, Chatham Area Transit's disability services program, has partnered with Savannah Yellow Cab and the City of Savannah to offer ADA-compliant, wheelchair-accessible taxi vans.

Download Lonely Planet's free Accessible Travel guides from http://lptravel.to/AccessibleTravel.

Bohemian Hotel BOUTIQUE HOTEL $$$

(Map p98; ☎912-721-3800; www.bohemianhotelsavannah.com; 102 W Bay St; r weekday/weekend $299/449; P❄@📶) Enjoy sleek, dark, Gothic hallways, a riverside perch and small touches such as driftwood and oystershell chandeliers. Rooms are stunning, though perhaps too low-lit for some. Personalized service makes it feel far more intimate than its 75 rooms indicate. A rooftop lounge and bar area provides excellent views across the river.

Midtown & the Victorian District

This the primary area for sleeping options. You'll find B&Bs, inns and boutique hotels radiating out from Forsyth Park.

Savannah Pensione GUESTHOUSE $

(Map p98; ☎912-236-7744; www.savannahpensione.com; 304 E Hall St; s/d without bath from $57/67; P❄@) It was run as a hostel for some 15 years, but the owner of this basic neighborhood crash pad got tired of backpackers traipsing up and down the historic steps of the 1884 Italianate mansion. Fair enough. Now a bare-bones and vibeless pension, it still offers the cheapest Historic District rooms, though its potential is unrealized. Dorms beds can be had for $26, but only for groups of three or more who know each other.

Mansion on Forsyth Park BOUTIQUE HOTEL $$$

(Map p98; ☎912-238-5158; www.mansiononforsythpark.com; 700 Drayton St; r weekday/weekend $220/380; P❄@📶🏊) A choice location and chic design highlight the luxe accommodations on offer at the 18,000-sq-ft Mansion – the sexy bathrooms alone are practically worth the money. The best part of the hotel-spa is the amazing local and international art that crowds its walls and hallways – over 400 pieces in all.

Azalea Inn INN $$$

(Map p98; ☎912-236-6080; www.azaleainn.com; 217 E Huntingdon St; r/villas from $299/379; P❄📶🏊) We love this canary-yellow historic inn, a humble stunner on a quiet street near Forsyth Park. The 10 rooms aren't huge, but are well done with varnished dark-wood floors, crown moldings, four-poster beds and a small dipping pool out back. Three new villas offer more modern luxury for long-term stays.

LOCAL KNOWLEDGE

ETIQUETTE

Savannahians ooze Southern charm and politeness. Don't be alarmed by people wanting to chat to you and learn your life story – and tell you theirs – anywhere you go.

Greetings Handshakes are common when meeting men and women for the first time. Say 'hello' and 'goodbye' to staff when visiting shops, restaurants and sights.

Queues Known as 'lines,' these are dutifully respected. Odds are you'll make a few friends while standing in them.

Taboo Topics It may be best to keep thoughts on US politics to yourself – while Savannah is largely a blue city, you never know who you might offend. And, being the South, Christian culture is overt; tread conscientiously with topics relating to religion.

Gratuity Savannah runs on hospitality. Tipping is compulsory.

Eating

East Savannah & the Islands

All the seafood in Savannah is great, but this is where you'll find it in abundance. There are also good spots serving standard American fare, with a few decent ethnic options here and there.

Breakfast Club BREAKFAST $

(Map p108; ☎912-786-5984; www.thebreakfastclubtybee.com; 1500 Butler Ave, Tybee Island; mains $8-14; ⏰7am-1pm) The line gets long (for a reason) but tables turn quickly at this breakfast favorite. Staples such as omelets are prepared with fresh ingredients, and sausages and burger patties are ground in-house; the Blackhawk breakfast burrito is stellar.

Sisters of the New South SOUTHERN US $

(Map p104; ☎912-335-2761; www.thesistersofthenewsouth.com; 2605 Skidaway Rd; mains $6-14; ⏰6am-9pm Mon-Thu, to 10pm Fri & Sat, 8am-9pm Sun) This laid-back cafe beloved of locals serves up Southern soul-food favorites for breakfast, lunch and dinner. The red-velvet cake is among the best we've tried.

Crab Shack SEAFOOD $$

(Map p104; ☎912-786-9857; www.thecrabshack.com; 40 Estill Hammock Rd, Tybee Island; mains $8-25; ⏰11:30am-9pm Sun-Thu, to 10pm Fri & Sat) This hidden favorite slings bountiful peel-and-eat seafood platters in a multishack complex along an alligator lagoon. Tables have a hole in the center with a giant Rubbermaid trashcan underneath, so you know it's legit (don't worry, the cats comin' for your scraps are kempt and dearly beloved members of the family). Get a spot on the patio, if you can.

Tybee Island Social Club AMERICAN $$

(Map p108; ☎912-472-4044; www.tybeeislandsocialclub.com; 1311 Butler Ave, Tybee Island; mains $9-18; ⏰noon-10pm Mon-Thu, to midnight Fri & Sat, 11am-10pm Sun) Inventive starters, burgers, tacos and seafood dishes are best washed down with a signature cocktail at this laid-back haunt. The decor is modern with a touch of rustic, and a bluegrass band plays during brunch. It's a good spot to camp out and enjoy a bottle of wine (if you can nab a parking spot in the tiny front lot).

Historic District & Forsyth Park

The Historic District is home to some of Savannah's most celebrated dining establishments. From classic Southern dishes to fine international fare, your appetite will be appeased no matter your fancy.

Forsyth Park Farmers Market MARKET

(Map p98; www.forsythfarmersmarket.com; Forsyth Park; ⏰9am-1pm Sat) This popular farmers market showcases fresh, local goodies in one of the city's prettiest public spaces. It's at the south end of the park at the intersection of Bull St and Park Ave.

Fox & Fig VEGAN $

(Map p98; ☎912-297-6759; www.foxandfigcafe.com; 321 Habersham St; mains $7-16; ⏰8am-9pm Tue-Sun, to 3pm Mon) A range of internationally inspired dishes get plant-based treatments at this charming cafe. Try the seared Southern seitan (wheat gluten) with French toast if you want a fix of something more indulgent.

Greater Savannah

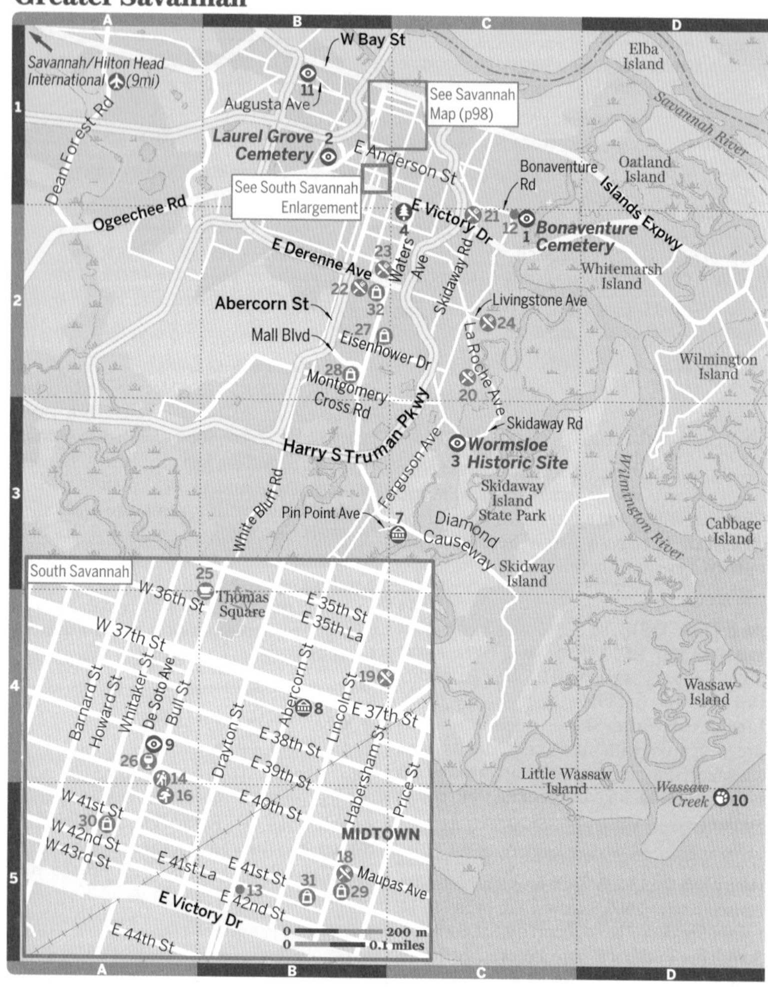

Treylor Park SOUTHERN US $

(Map p98; ☎912-495-5557; www.treylorparksavannah.com; 115 E Bay St; mains $6-14; ⊙noon-midnight Mon-Wed, from 10am Sat & Sun) All the hip young things pack into this 'Treylor Park,' which revels in a retro-chic, Airstream aesthetic. The food? Southern classics simply done well: fried chicken on a biscuit with sausage gravy and spicy collard greens, or a grilled apple-pie sandwich. Take your pick and wash it down with an excellent cocktail in the warmly lit courtyard.

Leopold's Ice Cream ICE CREAM $

(Map p98; ☎912-234-4442; www.leopoldsicecream.com; 212 E Broughton St; scoops $4-5.50; ⊙11am-10pm Sun-Thu, to 11pm Fri & Sat;) This classic American ice-cream parlor has been scooping up its creamy Greek recipes since 1919. Tutti Frutti was invented here, but we dig coconut, ginger, and honey and almond cream. Hurry up and wait.

Little Duck DINER $

(Map p98; ☎912-235-6773; www.littleduckdiner.com; 150 W Saint Julian St; mains $8-15; ⊙10am-3pm & 5-10pm Mon-Fri, 9am-10pm Sat &

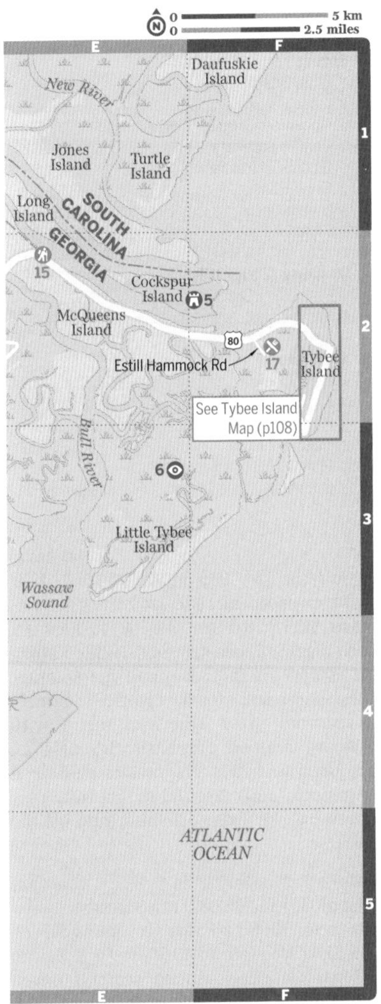

Sun) Classic diner fare gets reimagined in this bright, airy, art deco-inspired space. We love its dedicated grilled-cheese menu, where you can scale up the traditional variety with Gruyère and Havarti cheeses, or go all out with indulgent ingredients such as duck or smoked salmon – plus a bowl of tomato soup, as you do. Tacos, bowls and breakfast are all top notch.

Collins Quarter CAFE **$$**
(Map p98; ☎912-777-4147; www.thecollinsquarter.com; 151 Bull St; dinner mains $17-32; ⏰6:30am-5pm Mon, to noon Tue, to 10pm Wed-Sun; 📶) If you have ever talked coffee with an Australian, you know they are particularly fussy about their java. This wildly popular newcomer is Australian-owned and turns Australian-roasted Brooklyn coffee into beloved flat whites and long blacks. Beyond Savannah's best coffee, it serves excellent fusion fare, including a drool-inducing brisket burger. There's booze too!

Mrs Wilkes Dining Room SOUTHERN US **$$**
(Map p98; www.mrswilkes.com; 107 W Jones St; lunch adult/child $22/11; ⏰11am-2pm Mon-Fri Feb-Dec; 👪) The line outside can begin as early as 8am at this first-come, first-served Southern comfort-food institution. Once the lunch bell rings and you are seated family-style, the kitchen unloads on you: fried chicken, beef stew, meatloaf, cheese potatoes, collard greens, black-eyed peas, mac 'n' cheese, rutabaga, candied yams, squash casserole, creamed corn *and* biscuits. It's like Thanksgiving and the Last Supper rolled into one massive feast, chased with sweet tea.

★ **Husk Savannah** SOUTHERN US **$$$**
(Map p98; ☎912-349-2600; www.husksavannah.com; 12 W Oglethorpe Ave; mains $25-36; ⏰5-10pm Sun-Thu, to 11pm Fri & Sat) After acclaimed success with Charleston, Nashville and Greenville locations, celebrity-chef Sean Brock brings Husk's hyperlocal, agriculturally driven Southern food sorcery to Savannah. This outpost is the only one boasting a raw seafood bar and is the biggest of all, set in a historic, three-story space that hosts 200 people. Like all locations, the daily menu depends on what's locally available.

Prohibition AMERICAN **$$$**
(Map p98; ☎912-200-9255; www.prohibitionsavannah.com; 125 Martin Luther King Jr Blvd; dinner mains $15-36; ⏰11am-2:30pm, 5pm-1am) Sleek, dimly lit throwback restaurant and bar in a speakeasy style serves upmarket small plates, hearty comfort-food-style mains and bespoke cocktails for lunch, brunch and dinner. There's a stage for live bands, and a Sunday supper club is in the works.

The Grey MODERN AMERICAN **$$$**
(Map p98; ☎912-662-5999; www.thegreyrestaurant.com; 109 Martin Luther King Jr Blvd; mains $14-38; ⏰5:30-10pm Sun & Tue-Thu, to 11pm

Greater Savannah

Top Sights
1 Bonaventure Cemetery C2
2 Laurel Grove Cemetery B1
3 Wormsloe Historic Site C3

Sights
4 Daffin Park C2
5 Fort Pulaski National Monument F2
6 Little Tybee Island E3
7 Pin Point Heritage Museum C3
8 Savannah African Art Museum B4
9 Sulfur Studios A4
10 Wassaw National Wildlife Refuge D5
11 Weeping Time Plaque B1

Activities, Courses & Tours
12 Bonaventure Cemetery Journeys C2
13 Chef Darin's Kitchen Table B5
14 First Friday Art March A4
15 McQueen's Island Historic Trail E2
16 Old Savannah City Mission A5

Eating
17 Crab Shack F2
18 Green Truck B5
19 Narobia's Grits & Gravy B4
20 Pearl's Saltwater Grille C2
21 Sisters of the New South C2
22 Sugo Rossa B2
23 Sweet Spice B2
24 Wyld C2

Drinking & Nightlife
25 Foxy Loxy Cafe B3
26 Wormhole A4

Shopping
27 Byrd Cookie Company B2
28 Clutter B2
29 Habersham Antiques Market B5
30 House of Strut A5
31 Picker Joe's Antique Mall B5
32 Savannah Wine Cellar B2

Fri & Sat;) A wonderfully retro makeover of the 1960s Greyhound Bus Terminal gives us one of Savannah's culinary darlings, where chef Mashama Bailey's 'Port City Southern' cuisine is a delightful, immigrant-infused take on local grub. Bearded hipsters work the best seats in the house, around the U-shaped centerpiece bar, where scrumptious lamb shoulder and a gargantuan pork shank are standouts. Reservations essential.

Olde Pink House SOUTHERN US **$$$**
(Map p98; 912-232-4286; 23 Abercorn St; mains $15-43; 11am-2:30pm & 5-10:30pm, closed lunch Sun & Mon) Classic Southern food done upscale in one of Savannah's most consistently great restaurants. Our favorite appetizer is the Southern sushi: shrimp and grits rolled in a coconut-crusted nori roll. Dine in the slender digs upstairs, or go underground to the fabulous tavern where the piano player rumbles and the room is cozy, funky and perfect. The building is a 1771 landmark.

Southside & the Moon River District

There are tons of standard, all-American franchise restaurants around this part of town and some decent locally run options, plus solid spots featuring various ethnic cuisines.

★ **Wyld** SEAFOOD **$$**
(Wyld Dock Bar; Map p104; 912-692-1219; www.thewylddockbar.com; 2740 Livingston Ave; mains $13-17; 5-9pm Tue-Thu, to 10pm Fri, noon-10pm Sat, noon-4pm Sun) Hidden along an estuary of the Savannah marshlands, this laid-back, local favorite features a seasonal, New American menu with a heavy seafood emphasis. It's also an ace spot to catch live music, chill in a hammock, rally around a fire pit, play bocce ball, or drop a fishing line off the dock.

Pearl's Saltwater Grille SEAFOOD **$$**
(Map p104; 912-352-8221; www.pearlssaltwatergrille.com; 7000 La Roche Ave; mains $12-29; 5-10pm Mon-Thu, to 10:30pm Fri & Sat, to 9:30pm Sun) This hidden seafood haven has been a local favorite for more than 20 years. Try the crab-stuffed flounder, parmesan-crusted grouper or fried jumbo shrimp – or a tasty steak or pasta dish for landlubbers – with spectacular views of the marsh.

Sugo Rossa ITALIAN **$$**
(Map p104; 912-417-2330; 5500 Abercorn St, Twelve Oaks Shopping Center; mains $16-25; 4:30-9:30pm Mon-Sat, from 4pm Sun) Classic Italian dishes such as authentic wood-fired pizzas are served in a relaxed, elegant space.

Midtown & the Victorian District

The Historic District can no longer stake claim to all Savannah's great restaurants. Over the last few years, fantastic options have sprouted up from the stretch of town between Forsyth Park and Victory Dr, giving the downtown scene a run for its money.

Green Truck PUB FOOD **$**
(Map p104; ☎912-234-5885; www.greentruckpub.com; 2430 Habersham St; mains $9-14; ⊙11am-11pm Mon-Sat) Casual pub serving locally sourced and housemade fare (right down to the ketchup). Its burgers are the best in town – we love the Trailer Park, adorned with pimento cheese and bacon.

Narobia's Grits & Gravy BREAKFAST **$**
(Map p104; ☎912-231-0563; 2019 Habersham St; ⊙7am-1pm Mon-Fri, to 2pm Sat) Lovers of soul food, seafood and breakfast food will get their fill with the simple, hearty plates at this humble hole in the wall. The French toast and crab biscuit aren't to be missed.

Sweet Spice JAMAICAN **$**
(Map p104; ☎912-335-8146; www.sweetspicesavannah.net; 5515 Waters Ave; mains $6-14; ⊙11am-8pm Mon-Thu, to 9pm Fri & Sat) This easygoing Jamaican spot, about 4.5 miles southeast of downtown, is a welcome break from all the American and Southern fare you get around here. A large platter of curry goat or jerk chicken costs just a smidge more than a fast-food meal and it's utterly delicious. It will also keep you filled up for a long time.

★**Local11Ten** MODERN AMERICAN **$$$**
(Map p98; ☎912-790-9000; www.local11ten.com; 1110 Bull St; mains $26-40; ⊙6-10pm;) Upscale, sustainable, local and fresh: these elements help create an elegant, well-run restaurant that's one of Savannah's best.

Start with a blue-crab soufflé, then move on to the seared sea scallops in chive-lemon beurre blanc or the honey and brown-sugar-rubbed pork chop and a salted-caramel pot de crème to finish. Wait. Scratch that. The menu already changed. After dinner, head up to the rooftop bar for a digestif among the oak trees.

Drinking & Nightlife

Historic District & Forsyth Park

There's no shortage of bars in the Historic District, known as 'downtown' to locals. River St is popular with out-of-towners, while Congress St sees a mixture of townies and tourists. There are several spots – both dives and upscale joints – south of Broughton St for those who dare to wander. There are a handful of proper nightclubs, none much to write home about.

★**El-Rocko Lounge** COCKTAIL BAR
(Map p98; ☎912-495-5808; www.elrockolounge.com; 117 Whitaker St; ⊙5pm-3am Mon-Sat) One step in the door and you feel the '70s-inspired swank, but then realize the vibe – in true Savannah fashion – is absolutely chill. Friendly barkeeps mix fancy cocktails while DJs keep the energy high and dance moves steady with diverse jams on vinyl. The crowd is superhip and delightfully unpretentious, and the owner is as rad as they come.

Artillery COCKTAIL BAR
(Map p98; www.artillerybar.com; 307 Bull St; ⊙4pm-midnight Mon-Sat) Talented mixologists craft novel, quality cocktails in this opulent space where elements of 19th-century eclecticism and romanticism meld with modern design touches. To drink here, abide by the house rules: no hats, sandals, tank tops, noisy phones, or shots. The signature Artillery Punch – a concoction of rye whiskey, gin, brandy and rum – packs a powerful punch. Sip slowly.

Original Pinkie Masters BAR
(Map p98; ☎912-999-7106; www.theoriginalsavannah.com; 318 Drayton St; ⊙3pm-3am Mon-Thu, noon-3am Fri & Sat) Cheap, cash-only drinks and great people-watching make this hometown dive the best in town. It's far away enough from the River St ruckus, but easy enough to walk (err, stumble) to when you're ready to close out the night with the locals.

Abe's on Lincoln BAR
(Map p98; ☎912-349-0525; www.abesonlincoln.com; 17 Lincoln St; ⊙4pm-3am Mon-Sat) Pop back a beer or 10 with SCAD students and locals at this dark, dank, all-wood bar. Attracts an eclectic crowd that stares through boozy

Tybee Island

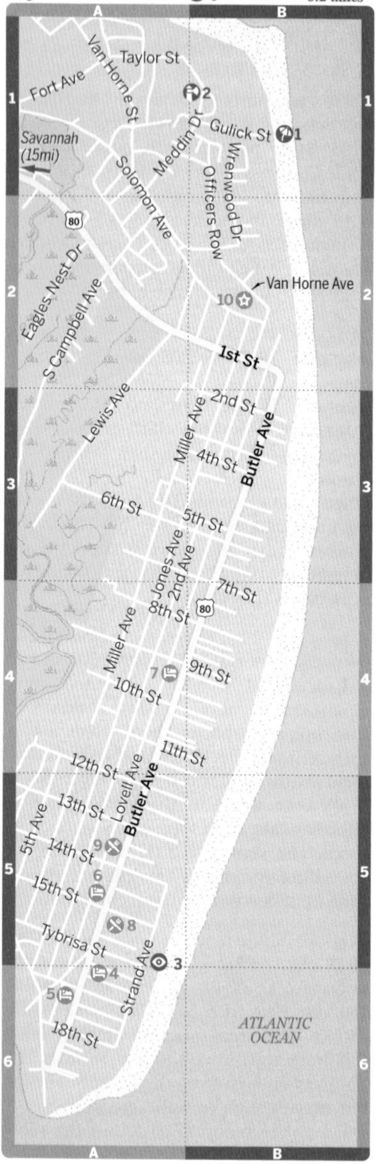

0 — 400 m
0 — 0.2 miles

goggles at whatever weird behavior the bartenders are inevitably tolerating that night. Good times.

Tybee Island

Sights

1 North Beach B1
2 Tybee Island Light Station & Museum B1
3 Tybee Pier & Pavilion A5

Sleeping

4 Atlantis Inn A6
5 Beachview Bed & Breakfast A6
6 Hotel Tybee A5
7 Royal Palm Motel A4

Eating

8 Breakfast Club A5
9 Tybee Island Social Club A5

Entertainment

10 Tybee Post Theater B2

Gallery Espresso COFFEE

(Map p98; ☎912-233-5348; www.galleryespresso.com; 234 Bull St; ⏰7:30am-10pm Mon-Fri, 8am-10pm Sat & Sun) SCAD students, tourists, the downtown business crowd and Savannah's artistic elite all camp out in the cozy wingback chairs of this bohemian corner cafe, where – as the name suggests – the walls are adorned with rotating artists' exhibitions. In addition to coffee and espresso drinks, there's a wide selection of teas and libations, plus sandwiches, salads and light bites.

Rocks on the Roof BAR

(Map p98; ☎912-721-3821; www.bohemianhotelsavannah.com/dining/lounge; 102 W Bay St, Bohemian Hotel; ⏰11am-midnight Sun-Thu, to 1am Fri & Sat; 📶) The expansive rooftop bar at the Bohemian Hotel (p102) is breezy, fun and best when the weather is fine and the fire pit is glowing.

Club One LGBTIQ+

(Map p98; ☎912-232-0200; www.clubone-online.com; 1 Jefferson St; ⏰5pm-3am) Drag shows (late resident star Lady Chablis appeared in *Midnight in the Garden of Good and Evil*), ripping dance nights and plenty of flirting kick off pretty regularly at this gay bar, which is otherwise a laid-back place where a mix of locals and SCAD students play pool and shoot the breeze.

Midtown & the Victorian District

The nightlife in this area has a distinctively local flavor. Coffee houses double as venues, and the bars of the fantastic restaurants are great places to chill out.

Foxy Loxy Cafe CAFE
(Map p104; ☎912-401-0543; www.foxyloxycafe.com; 1919 Bull St; ⏰7am-11pm Mon-Sat, 8am-6pm Sun) Buzzing cafe and art-print gallery full of students and creatives set in an old Victorian house. The courtyard out back is the loveliest in this area. It has tasty tacos for when you get peckish, and freshly baked kolaches (fruit pastries) that are positively addictive. There's Sunday brunch, weekday happy hour, and monthly vinyl nights and poetry slams.

Sentient Bean CAFE
(Map p98; ☎912-232-4447; www.sentientbean.com; 13 E Park Ave; ⏰7am-9pm; 📶) Everything you want, or expect, from an indie coffeehouse: terrific brew, gourmet breakfasts, spacious boho interior, and hipster clientele and baristas, all awash in sustainability. It's one of Savannah's favorite and just across from Forsyth Park. Live music often pops off.

Wormhole BAR
(Map p104; ☎912-349-6770; www.wormholebar.com; 2307 Bull St; ⏰noon-3pm Mon-Sat) Locally loved watering hole hosting live bands, comedy, DJs, trivia, open mike, karaoke and more. There's pool, darts and video games to keep you plenty entertained while you catch a buzz, and it serves a full menu of food until late.

☆ Entertainment

Tybee Post Theater THEATER
(Map p108; ☎912-472-4790; www.tybeeposttheater.org; 10 Van Horne Ave, Tybee Island; ⏰hours vary by event, check schedule) Historic theater constructed in 1930 as a movie house for army soldiers, it went dark in the '60s and dodged the wrecking ball at the turn of the century. Now the landmark serves as a concert hall, cultural and educational performance venue, theater and film-screening stage.

Savannah Smiles Dueling Pianos LIVE MUSIC
(Map p98; ☎912-527-6453; www.savannahsmilesduelingpianos.com; 314 Williamson St; ⏰7pm-3am Wed-Sat) This dueling piano bar, where patrons decide what's played on the stage, brings the party crowd from far and wide. The lively space can host up to 450 people and it's a ruckus on a busy night, when everyone's that special kind of turnt: crammed cheek by jowl and singing up a storm.

Jinx LIVE MUSIC
(Map p98; ☎912-236-2281; www.facebook.com/thejinx912; 127 W Congress St; ⏰4pm-3am) A good slice of odd-duck Savannah nightlife, the Jinx is popular with students, townies, musicians, and basically anyone else who has a thing for dive-y watering holes with live music – from rock to punk to alt-country to hip-hop – and funky stuff decorating the walls.

Shopping

Historic District & Forsyth Park

There's great shopping throughout the Historic District. Many well-known brands have storefronts along West Broughton St. Boutiques dot the squares and the riverfront, and City Market has some decent souvenir shops.

Books on Bay BOOKS
(Map p98; ☎912-236-7115; www.booksonbay.com; 224 W Bay St; ⏰10am-6pm) Junkies of that old-book smell will get a great fix at this quaint shop specializing in titles that date from the 17th century through the 1920s. Find first-edition runs of classics, plus poetry collections, foreign manuscripts, religious and political texts.

Satchel FASHION & ACCESSORIES
(Map p98; ☎912-233-1008; www.shopsatchel.com; 4 E Liberty St; ⏰10am-6pm Mon-Sat, 11am-3pm Sun) Handbag obsessives should duck into Satchel, owned and operated by the designer herself. She also manufactures her own goods and is a patron of all things design in Savannah.

ShopSCAD ARTS & CRAFTS
(Map p98; ☎912-525-5180; www.shopscad.com; 340 Bull St; ⏰9am-5:30pm Mon-Fri, 10am-6pm Sat, noon-5pm Sun) All the wares at this funky, kitschy boutique are designed by students, faculty and alumni of Savannah's prestigious college of art and design. There are a lot of awesome finds to be uncovered.

Savannah Bee Company FOOD
(Map p98; ☎912-233-7873; www.savannahbee.com; 104 W Broughton St; ⏰10am-7pm Mon-Sat, 11am-6pm Sun) This internationally renowned honey dreamland is one of Savannah's must-stops. Expect artisanal honey of infinite variety, and limitless free tastings.

Southside & the Moon River District

Malls and chain retailers abound in the area, but there are a handful of unique shops with goods you can't get elsewhere.

Byrd Cookie Company FOOD & DRINKS
(Map p104; 912-355-1716; www.byrdcookiecompany.com; 6700 Waters Ave; 9:30am-5:30pm Mon-Fri, 10am-5pm Sat, noon-5pm Sun) A souvenir bowl of shrimp and grits won't keep on the way home, but a tin of Savannah's favorite cookies will. We love the classic chocolate-chip, key-lime and Georgia-peach flavors.

Savannah Wine Cellar WINE
(Map p104; 912-355-9463; www.savannahwinecellar.com; 5500 Abercorn St, Twelve Oaks Shopping Center) Boutique bottle shop with more than 400 wines; offers try-before-you-buy tastings and classes.

Clutter VINTAGE
(Map p104; 912-354-7556; www.cluttersav.com; 714 Mall Blvd; 10am-5:30pm Mon-Sat) You may not be able to buy a townhouse here, but you can outfit your home like a Savannah mansion. Start by purchasing the perfect Savannah bedroom at this furniture consignment store.

PARKING IN THE HISTORIC DISTRICT

There are several parking garages (some 24hr) across Savannah's Historic District; if you park in a garage on the fringes, use the Chatham Area Transit (www.catchacat.org) free 'dot' shuttle to hitch a ride to various points of interest around the Historic District and Forsyth Park.

You can purchase parking passes ($15/24 one/two days) from the Savannah Visitors Center, the Mobility & Parking Services Department, and various hotels and inns. The pass allows for meter parking of one hour or more, free parking in the city's lots and garages (upon availability), and forgives exceeding allowed time in time-limit zones. Note that passes aren't valid during special events. Call the City of Savannah Mobility & Parking Services at 912-651-6470 for more information.

Midtown & the Victorian District

This part of town is a retro junkie's delight. With sweet vintage shops and a host of antiques markets, a shopping trip here is one of a kind.

★**House of Strut** VINTAGE
(Map p104; 912-712-3902; www.houseofstrut.com; 17 W 41st St, lower unit, ring bell to enter; 11am-7pm Mon-Fri, 10am-6pm Sat, noon-4pm Sun) Our favorite vintage shop in town occupies the sprawling 1st floor of an old Victorian home, where each room is thoughtfully curated with hand-picked fashion finds that are also available for rent. The space doubles as a venue for local art and music events.

Picker Joe's Antique Mall ANTIQUES
(Map p104; 912-239-4657; www.pickerjoes.com; 217a E 41st St; 10am-6pm Mon-Sat, noon-5pm Sun) Pickin' and siftin' for antique and vintage treasures is a delight in this bright, clean, organized mall that was once a mattress factory. Military and aviation memorabilia is especially abundant due to owner Jim Plumlee's aviation background, and there's a room dedicated to architectural ornaments and fixtures.

Habersham Antiques Market ANTIQUES
(Map p104; 912-238-5908; 2502 Habersham St; 9:30am-5:30pm Mon-Fri, 10am-5pm Sat) There are plenty of great souvenirs to be found in Savannah, but we think you should snag an opulent chandelier or a Russian egg or some cool '70s cups or...look, whatever you want, really. Someone gave it up in the past, and it's now sold at this market.

Information

EMERGENCY & IMPORTANT NUMBERS

Emergency services (fire, police, ambulance)	911
Nonemergency police line	912-652-6500
Local directory	411
Municipal offices & information	311
Operator	0

SAFE TRAVEL

Dangerous and violent crime is a reality in Savannah, with one of the highest rates – across communities of all sizes – in the US. Cases of rape, murder, armed robbery and aggravated assault, and property crime continue to rise.

- Practice vigilance and avoid walking alone at night in areas where there aren't a lot of people; that being said, robberies have been known to happen in broad daylight and even in parts of downtown with heavy tourist traffic.
- Don't leave valuables in vehicles, as car break-ins and theft happen frequently.

TOURIST INFORMATION

Savannah Visitors Center (Map p98; ☎912-944-0455; www.savannahvisit.com; 301 Martin Luther King Jr Blvd; ⏲9am-5:30pm) Excellent resources and services are available in this center, based in a restored 1860s train station. Many privately operated city tours start here. There is also a small, interactive tourist-info kiosk in the visitor center at Forsyth Park.

Getting There & Away

For a city of its size, Savannah is quite well connected and easy to access by bus or train, and even easier by plane or car. Flights, cars and tours can be booked online at lonelyplanet.com/bookings.

AIR

The Savannah/Hilton Head International Airport (p370) is about 5 miles west of downtown, off I-95; service is mainly domestic flights to eastern seaboard, Southern and Midwestern cities.

BUS

Greyhound (p370) has connections to Atlanta (about five hours), Charleston, SC (about two hours) and Jacksonville, FL (2½ hours).

TRAIN

The Amtrak (p371) station is just a few miles west of the Historic District; trains run to Charleston, Jacksonville, and from there to points beyond.

Getting Around

Within the downtown area, Savannah is very foot friendly. Areas south of Midtown are best accessed by car or bus. Motorcycles are also seen citywide. Note that there is no local train or subway system in Savannah.

TO/FROM THE AIRPORT

Chatham Area Transit (CAT, www.catchacat.org) offers cheap and convenient transport to and from the airport with its 100X Airport Express route ($8 return). Many hotels, particularly the chains in the vicinity of the airport, offer free shuttle services; inquire directly with your hotel for details.

BOAT

The free Savannah Belles Ferry (www.catchacat.org), designed in an old riverboat-ferry style, connects downtown with Hutchinson Island across the Savannah River. It has the following stops:

- River St at City Hall
- Waving Girl Landing at the Savannah Marriott Riverfront Hotel
- Hutchinson Island at the Savannah International Trade & Convention Center, near the Westin Savannah Harbor Resort & Spa

BUS

Chatham Area Transit operates local buses that run on bio-diesel, including a free shuttle (the dot) that makes its way around the Historic District and stops within a couple of blocks of nearly every major site.

COASTAL GEORGIA

Brunswick

☎912 / POP 16,400

With its large shrimp-boat fleet and downtown historic district shaded by lush live oaks, Brunswick has charms you might miss when sailing by on I-95 or the Golden Isle Pkwy (Hwy 17). The town dates from 1733, and it feels very different from its neighbors. There were several plantations nearby, and a large African American population worked on the farms as slaves. Brunswick is not as tourism-oriented as other parts of the coast, and visitors may find multicultural Brunswick, with its West Indian flavors and rich local art scene, a refreshing change of pace.

Sights

Marshes of Glynn Overlook Park PARK
(Map p112; Glynn Ave & Gloucester St; ⏲dawn-dusk; P) This small park is a great spot to take in the sprawling, subtle beauty of the sea-island salt marshes. A fishing pier, picnic tables and small educational exhibit are on-site.

Mary Ross Waterfront Park PARK
(Map p112; F St, near Bay St) During WWII, Brunswick shipyards constructed 99 Liberty transport ships for the navy. Today, a 23ft scale model at Mary Ross Waterfront Park stands as a memorial to those ships and their builders. Enjoy the sunset across the marshes from the benches here.

Coastal Islands

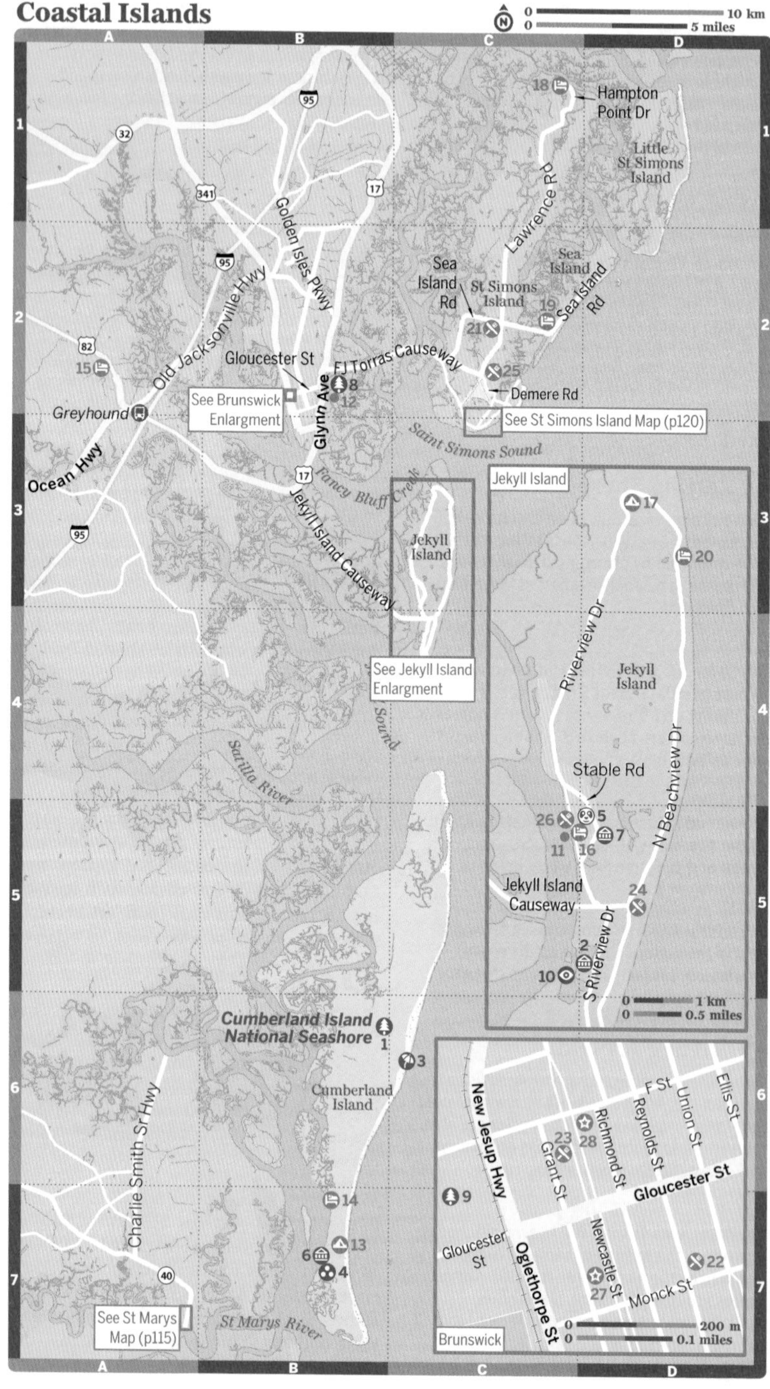

Coastal Islands

Top Sights

Sights

Activities, Courses & Tours

Sleeping

Eating

Entertainment

Lady Jane Shrimp Boat TOURS

(Map p112; 912-265-5711; www.shrimpcruise.com; 1200 Glynn Ave, next to Marshside Grill; adult/child under 6yr $40/35;) On this odd but alluring combination of nature tour and working-shrimp-boat experience, you'll trawl for morsels along the St Simons Sound. At the end of the day, you'll have lungs full of salt-marsh air and you might even have some shrimp to take home. The *Lady Jane* also does dolphin-spotting and crabbing tours.

Festivals & Events

First Friday FAIR

(www.brunswickgeorgia.net; Newcastle St; 5-8pm) If you happen to be in Brunswick for First Friday, held the first Friday of the month, peruse the local art and antique galleries and enjoy wine and bites with the locals.

Sleeping

Chain hotels cluster both downtown and along the highway; budget travelers have one solid option, a hostel.

Hostel in the Forest HOSTEL $

(Map p112; 912-264-9738; www.foresthostel.com; 3901 Hwy 82; d $30, plus lifetime membership for 1st-time visitors $10; P) The only budget base in the area is this set of bare-bones octagonal cedar huts and tree houses (sans air or heat) on an ecofriendly, sustainable campus. You must pay a lifetime member fee to stay, and dinner is included. As you might guess, the hostel is in the woods, about 10 miles outside Brunswick. Phone reservations only.

Eating

The town claims to be the originator of Brunswick stew, a southern staple of tomatoes, corn, okra and all kinds of goodness. There's also a notable Caribbean influence here, with West Indian curry and jerk chicken to be found. Restaurants can be found throughout the Historic District near Gloucester St.

Indigo Coastal Shanty FUSION $

(Map p112; 912-265-2007; http://indigocoastalshanty.com; 1402 Reynolds St; mains lunch $8-13, dinner $12-17; 11am-3pm Tue-Fri, 5-9pm Fri & Sat;) You can't miss this funky setting, with its faded turquoise windows and doors, and higgledy-piggledy rainbow-colored fence. The exterior is matched by an eclectic and delicious menu of international influences: Bahamian chicken curry served over jasmine rice, jerk tostadas and classic Southern pimento-cheese burgers.

Island Jerk CARIBBEAN $

(Map p112; 912-267-4742; www.facebook.com/islandjerkbrunswickga; 1519 Newcastle St; mains $5.50-14; 10am-7:30pm Mon-Wed, 10am-8pm Thu & Fri, 11am-7pm Sat) Jerk chicken, West Indian curry, oxtail in gravy and spicy *escovitch* (vinegar-pepper sauce) with shrimp or snapper (plus habanero-pepper

DON'T MISS

BLUE CRAB & BAY VIEWS

Sunbury Crab Company (912-884-8640; www.sunburycrabco.com; 541 Brigantine Dunmore Rd, Sunbury; mains $9-25; 5-10pm Wed-Fri, noon-10pm Sat, noon-8:30pm Sun;), inside a ramshackle building of reclaimed wood and offering views over Sunbury Harbor, is a truly special find. The menu is whatever is fresh that day: peel-and-eat shrimp, fried oysters or a bucket of local blue crab – to be devoured with the help of a wooden mallet. Sunbury is located about 50 miles north of Brunswick and 40 miles south of Savannah.

sauce) are just some of the things you can experience at Island Jerk. The setting is low-key, just six simple white tables, green walls and a big Jamaican flag. Finish your meal with some rum cake.

☆ Entertainment

Art Downtown SoGlo Gallery ARTS CENTER
(Brunswick Actors' Theatre; Map p112; gallery 912-262-0628, theater 912-280-0023; www.sogloallery.com; 1413 Newcastle St; show tickets $25; theater performances take place at 8pm Sat & 3pm Sun) This production company is an ambassador of local and regional artists, actors, writers and directors. SoGlo hosts regional creative types and holds seminars and workshops in its large art gallery. Theatrical performances take place in a 111-seat theater. Book tickets in advance on the SoGlo Gallery website.

The Historic Ritz Theatre THEATER
(Map p112; 912-262-6934; www.goldenislesarts.org; 1530 Newcastle St; tickets from $17; box office 9am to 5pm Tue-Fri) Back in 1899, this was an opera house; today it's a gorgeously restored three-story venue that hosts theater performances, movie screenings, art shows and the like. It's managed by the Golden Isles Arts & Humanities society, which is involved with arts programs across the coastal region.

Getting There & Away

Brunswick is located off Hwy 17. **Greyhound** (Map p112; 800-231-2222; 2990 Hwy 17 S) buses stop at the Flying J gas station, 10 miles west of town. Destinations include Savannah (from $12, two hours, twice daily) and Jacksonville ($12, 70 minutes, twice daily). You can catch onward buses from either city.

Cumberland Island & St Marys

A hundred years ago the southernmost barrier island in Georgia was once an exclusive playground for the wealthy elite. It's still privately owned, but now this section of coastal wilderness is managed by Cumberland Island National Seashore, which has preserved it for the ages.

Visitors can access it via daily ferries from St Marys for day trips or longer stays, and explore the ancient 17-mile-long stretch of moss-covered oak forests, salt marshes and untouched beach. Wild horses roam around, sea turtles hatch here, and ruins still stand begging to be discovered.

With plenty of trails to explore, it's a lovely, lonely escape, and a quiet departure from civilization and any trace of the modern world, aside for the diminishing bars of mobile-phone reception you may notice (on that note, you're on Cumberland Island – put away the phone).

Sights

★ **Cumberland Island National Seashore** NATURE RESERVE
(Map p112; 912-882-4336; www.nps.gov/cuis; Cumberland Island; $7) Georgia's largest and southernmost barrier island is an unspoiled paradise. A campers' fantasy, place for family day trips and secluded retreat for couples – it's no wonder the wealthy Carnegie family used Cumberland as a retreat (Dungeness Ruins) in the 1800s.

The 36,415 acres consist of marsh, mudflats and tidal creeks. Plus, 17 miles of wide, sandy beach (p115) that you'll likely have to yourself. The interior has maritime forest, and mysterious jagged tree-lined pathways that would be at home in a *Game of Thrones* episode.

Dungeness Ruins RUINS
(Map p112; Cumberland Island; free with entry to Cumberland Island) This derelict, but spectacular, mansion was built by Thomas Carnegie and his wife, Lucy, in 1884. It became the base of a vibrant social scene, a semitropical setting where senators, statesmen and celebrities were hosted at parties. Find it on the southwest side of the island, roughly a 20-minute bike ride from the ferry landing.

St Marys

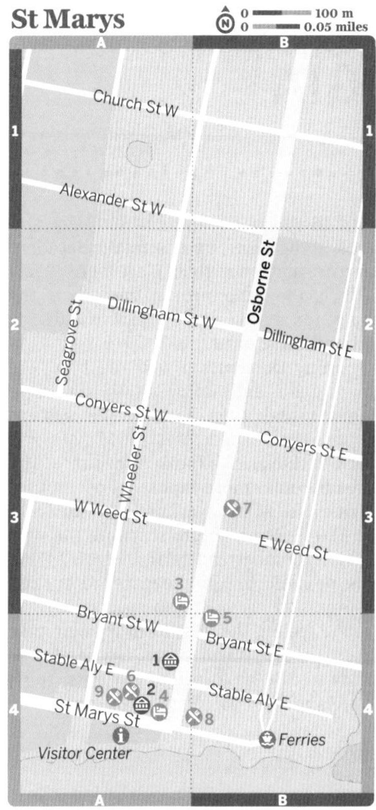

St Marys

Sights

1 Cumberland Island National Seashore Museum A4
2 St Marys Submarine Museum A4

Sleeping

3 Goodbread House A3
4 Riverview Hotel A4
5 Spencer House Inn B4

Eating

6 Bessies A4
7 Cedar Oak Cafe B3
8 Pauly's Cafe B4
9 Riverside Cafe A4

Cumberland Island Beach BEACH
(Map p112; Cumberland Island; free access with island entry fee) Cumberland Island's pristine, expansive and almost-empty beach runs for 17 miles. There's ample opportunity to see wildlife here. Look out for osprey, loggerhead turtles, ghost crabs and enormous horseshoe crabs. Swimming is allowed at your own risk. There are no lifeguards and currents can be strong.

Cumberland Island National Seashore Museum MUSEUM
(Map p115; 129 Osborne St, St Marys; 1-4pm, hours subject to staff availability) FREE If you have time to spare after checking in for the ferry, this little museum offers some background info on the area's military history, plus early settlers – indigenous tribes, African Americans, plus the Stafford and Carnegie families.

St Marys Submarine Museum MUSEUM
(Map p115; www.facebook.com/stmaryssubmuseum; 102 St Marys St W, St Marys; adult/child 6-12yr/child under 6yr $5/3/free; 10am-5pm Tue-Sat, noon-5pm Sun) Learn about St Marys 'Silent Service' through a collection of 20,000 artifacts, including vintage submarine equip-ment, war relics and deep-sea diving suits.

Ice House Museum MUSEUM
(Map p112; Cumberland Island; free with entry to the island) Used by the Carnegies to store ice, which was cut from frozen ponds and lakes in the winter months. The structure is now a small museum with information about the island and Carnegie era.

Sleeping

On Cumberland Island itself, your accommodations options are elegant luxury or camping, which in these mysterious forests has as elegance all of its own (as well as mosquitoes). If you're just visiting on a day trip, there are a few hotels in St Marys that are worth checking out.

Cumberland Island Camping CAMPGROUND $
(Map p112; 912-882-4336, ext 1; www.recreation.gov; Cumberland Island; campsites $9-22) There are multiple campgrounds set among the island's magnificent live oaks: Sea Camp Beach, Stafford Beach Campground and Wilderness Campgrounds. The more expensive options have picnic tables, grill sites, drinkable water and restrooms, while the cheapest choices are in the wild campgrounds with no designated tent sites. The max stay is seven consecutive nights.

HIKING IN COASTAL GEORGIA

CUMBERLAND ISLAND HIKE

START ICE HOUSE MUSEUM
END ICE HOUSE MUSEUM
DURATION ONE TO 1½ HOURS
DISTANCE 4 MILES
DIFFICULTY EASY

Start at the **Ice House Museum** (p115). It's at this small historic building the Carnegie family stored their frozen water. Step inside for exhibits on how the family lived.

After looking around, walk back onto the main pathway, and continue right (south) for five to 10 minutes to the spectacular **Dungeness Ruins** (p114). The building's skeleton dates back to the late 19th century and, though dilapidated, is still impressive. It's a peaceful spot surrounded by well-maintained lawns. Take a pew on one of the benches in the grounds, near an original fountain, and soak in the scene, imagining the decadent parties that once took place here. Some sketch the structure if they have the time. You may see wild horses wandering around these parts.

From Dungeness, walk back to the main path and follow it to the right (south) and then toward the eastern shore. The shaded forest-lined path will turn to thick sand, flanked by dunes. The area becomes more exposed. Look out for birds and wildlife around the adjacent St Marys River, before reaching the wild 17-mile Cumberland Island Beach (p115). It's possible to spot loggerhead turtles, osprey and various crab species here. If you're feeling the heat from the sun, take a dip in the warm ocean (swimming is allowed, but be aware of currents; these waters are not patrolled by lifeguards).

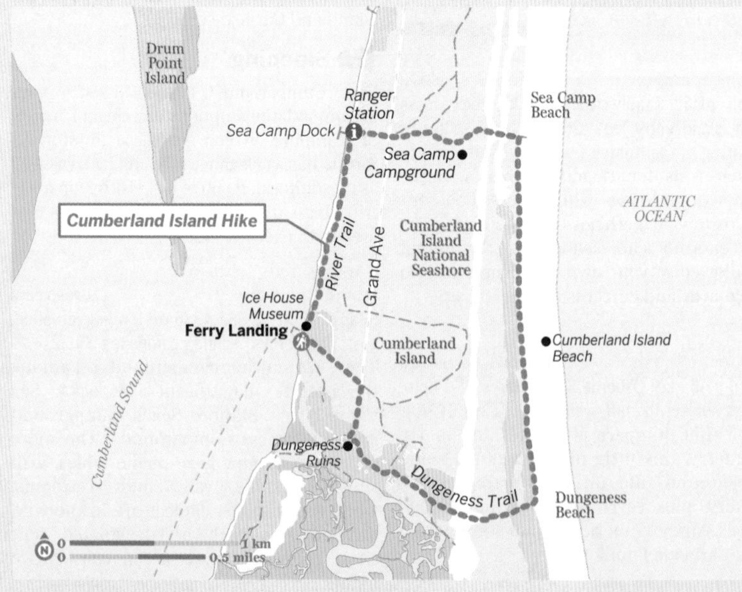

An easy stroll through one of Georgia's most pristine natural environments.

BOB POOLT/SHUTTERSTOCK ©

Hiking on Cumberland Island

Walk north for 20 to 30 minutes until you see a main pathway on the left, which will pass the primitive campgrounds of **Sea Camp Beach** (p115). It's an atmospheric trot through the undergrowth and untamed woodlands, with green ferns on the forest bed and twisted live oak trees covered with Spanish moss. Keep walking along the path for 10 to 20 minutes and it will bring you to the west shoreline and Ranger Station and Sea Camp dock, where there are information boards.

Follow the main dirt and sandy pathway going left (south) from the Ranger Station through the ancient forest. It runs parallel to the Fancy Bluff Creek shoreline. You'll see signs pointing you in the direction of places of interest. After 20 minutes' walk, you'll reach the Ice House Museum and the dock.

Goodbread House B&B $
(Map p115; ☎912-882-7490; www.goodbreadhouse.com/; 209 Osborne St, St Marys; r $119-139) You can't miss this eclectically styled bed and breakfast: it has a life-sized pirate and mini cannon out front. Brilliantly chintzy, cozy and eccentric, the beautiful double story blue-and-white clapboard property (with verandas on each level) has stood here since 1870. Owner Mardja will certainly make you feel at home among all the antiques.

Riverview Hotel HISTORIC HOTEL $
(Map p115; ☎912-882-3242; www.riverviewhotelstmarys.com; 105 Osborne St, St Marys; r $84-115; P 📶) The Riverview sits opposite the ferry for Cumberland Island in St Marys. Its attractive veneer conceals some pretty-standard rooms, but you get a soft bed, cable TV, a continental breakfast and a good rate for your money. The hotel's Captain Seagles Restaurant serves seafood, shrimp and grits, and gator tail.

Spencer House Inn INN $$
(Map p115; ☎912-882-1872; www.spencerhouseinn.com; 200 Osborne St, St Marys; r $150-245; P 📶) At this historic inn (c 1872) there are 14 spacious rooms on three floors, with slightly less personality and clutter than other local options. It's also more up to date with flat-screen TVs and top-end bath products. Staff book ferry reservations, pack lunches for day-trippers and serve a full gourmet breakfast each morning.

Greyfield Inn INN $$$
(Map p112; ☎904-261-6408; www.greyfieldinn.com; Cumberland Island; r incl meals $525-635) Want to live as the Carnegies did? You can either make a few million dollars and buy your own island, or simply stay in this romantic mansion built in 1900. The gorgeous rooms seem to have leapt out of an interior-design article on how to best mix an old oaky aesthetic with contemporary design. Two-night minimum stay. The rates are high, but they do include use of bicycles, kayaks and other equipment, three meals each day, and guided tours of the island.

Eating & Drinking

Unless you're staying at the Greyfield Inn, you will need to bring your own food to Cumberland Island. There are grocery stores near St Marys. Alternatively, fill up at the seafood-oriented restaurants or order a packed lunch from one of the many cafes in St Marys before your ferry.

Pauly's Cafe ITALIAN $
(Map p115; ☎912-882-3944; www.facebook.com/paulyscafe; 102 Osborne St, St Marys; menu items $6.35-16; ⏰11am-9pm Sun-Thu, to 10pm Fri & Sat; 🖉) On the main intersection in St Marys, this friendly, chintzy cafe serves big sandwiches to go, with a side of either potato salad or pasta. Plus, it does a good selection of Italian pasta dishes – carbonara, tortellini and chicken parmigiana, spinach lasagne and more. The tiny interior with bookshelves filled with trinkets is a little dingy for dining in, however.

Bessies AMERICAN $
(Map p115; ☎912-439-3232; 106 St Marys St W, St Marys; hotdogs $3, sandwiches from $5, mains $9-14; ⏰11am-8pm Tue-Sat, 11am-4pm Sun) Right next to the Riverside Cafe and opposite the Visitor Center, this simple cafe serves up unpretentious American classics: burgers, steak sandwiches, chili cheese fries and hotdogs, plus wraps and sandwiches. The crab-cake sandwich is our favorite – it's homemade from scratch, served on a potato bun, with Cajun sauce and *concasse* salsa.

Cedar Oak Cafe CAFE $
(Map p115; ☎912-882-9555; www.facebook.com/cedaroakcafe; 304 Osborne St, St Marys; bagels from $2.49, breakfast from $4.95, sandwiches from $6.25; ⏰7:30am-4pm; 📶) Small cubbyhole cafe serving reasonably priced breakfasts, plus sandwiches and bagels for your Cumberland Island trip. You can't go wrong with the grilled tuna with salad, onion, tomato and Swiss on rye bread.

Riverside Cafe GREEK $$
(Map p115; www.riversidecafesaintmarys.com; 106 St Marys St, St Marys; mains $8-20; ⏰11am-9pm) A Greek cafe that does a take on the gyro: pork, lamb or beef are seasoned and pounded into gyro-like strips (it doesn't have a rotisserie), piled with lettuce, feta and tzatziki, and folded into a fresh pita. There's Greek salad, fried fish, crab cakes and fried jumbo shrimp too. They'll pack a lunch to go for the ferry.

Information

Visitor Center (Map p115; ☎877-860-8767; www.cumberlandislandferry.com; 113 St Marys St, St Marys; ⏰9am-4pm) Book tickets for the Cumberland Island ferry via the website. Visitors are required to check in here at the St Marys dock at least an hour before the ferry departure. Find it opposite the Riverside Cafe (p118). Park your car one block west before getting the ferry. Also conducts tours of the island and facilitates camping on the island.

Getting There & Away

The only public access to the island is by ferry to/from the mainland town of St Marys, located off Exit 1 on I-95.

Convenient and pleasant **ferries** (Map p115; ☎877-860-6787; www.nps.gov/cuis; E Saint Marys St & Ready St, St Marys; round-trip adult/senior/child $28/26/16) leave from the St Marys dock at 9am and 11:45am and return at 10:15am and 4:45pm; the crossing takes 45 minutes. Visitors are required to check in at the visitor center at the dock at least 60 minutes prior to departure.

There is an extra 2:45pm departure March 1 to September 30, and no service at all on Tuesday and Wednesday from December 1 to February 28. Reservations are staunchly recommended well before you arrive.

St Simons Island

St Simons Island is the largest and most developed of the Golden Isles. There are pretty beaches galore, majestic live oaks, and different neighborhoods to explore – spanning retail parks to cute villages. However, the sheer natural beauty of St Simons isn't as easy to access compared to other nearby islands, given the presence of heavy residential and resort development. For example, the island of Little St Simons is an all-natural jewel, but it's only accessible to guests staying at the exclusive Lodge on Little St Simons. That said, golf fans will be in their element – it has some fine courses.

Sights

Lighthouse Museum MUSEUM
(Map p120; ☎912-638-4666; www.saintsimonslighthouse.org; 610 Beachview Dr; adult/child 5-11yr $12/5; ⏲10am-5pm Mon-Sat, 1:30-5pm Sun) Built in 1807 and standing 85ft tall, the first lighthouse here was destroyed by Confederates when Union troops landed in 1862. The second lighthouse, which you'll be able to tour, was built in 1872. The 104ft tower has a spiral 129-step cast-iron staircase and an adjacent keeper's residence. Otherwise it's, y'know, a lighthouse.

Massengale Park BEACH
(Map p120; 1350 Ocean Blvd; ⏲sunrise-sunset; P 👪) East Beach, the island's best tract of sand, is accessible from Massengale Park, which itself has a playground and some live oak trees. There's a nice pier too, making for a pretty place to watch the sunset.

Activities

Neptune Park AMUSEMENT PARK
(Map p120; ☎912-279-3720; www.glynncounty.org; 550 Beachview Dr & Mallery St; adult/child under 3yr $8/free; ⏲11am-5:30pm Wed-Fri, to 6pm Sat, 1pm-5:30pm Sun May-early Sep; 👪) This park is a good spot for parents: there's a playground, mini-golf course ($8 per round, in addition to entry fee), and, during the summer, a small water park with waterslides and floaties. Hours may vary; call ahead or check the county website for details.

King and Prince Golf Course GOLF
(Map p120; ☎912-634-0255; www.kingandprince.com/georgia-golf-resort.aspx; 100 Tabbystone; resort guest/nonguest incl cart $75/115; ⏲8am-5pm) A par 72 course set amongst salt marshes and coastal ecosystems, the King and Prince is one of Georgia's best-regarded golf courses. The course is owned and operated by the King and Prince Golf Beach & Golf Resort (located at 201 Arnold Rd, back in the center of town).

Tours

Ocean Motion KAYAKING
(Map p120; ☎912-638-5225; www.stsimonskayaking.com; 1300 Ocean Blvd; kayaking tours $49, bicycles half-/full day $15/19) Kayak through the island's marshes on two-hour tours with this knowledgeable outfitter. Also organizes bicycle rental.

Sleeping

Beach View House GUESTHOUSE $$
(Map p120; ☎603-524-4000; www.beachviewhouse.com; 537 Beachview Dr; houses from $193-493; ❄📶🐾) This unique two-story abode with porch and wooden veranda looks utterly out of place in its surroundings, and for good reason. Originally built in 1892 on Cumberland Island, in 1923 it was transported via the Atlantic to its present location, then reconstructed. Rooms have vintage furniture and cozy Southern style. A relaxing balcony area offers rocking chairs and ocean views.

St Simons Inn By The Lighthouse INN $$
(Map p120; ☎912-638-1101; www.saintsimonsinn.com; 609 Beachview Dr; r $159-269; P❄📶🏊) This cute and comfortable good-value inn is accented with white wooden shutters and a general sense of seaside breeziness. It's well located next to the downtown drag and a short pedal from East Beach. Continental breakfast included.

St Simons Island

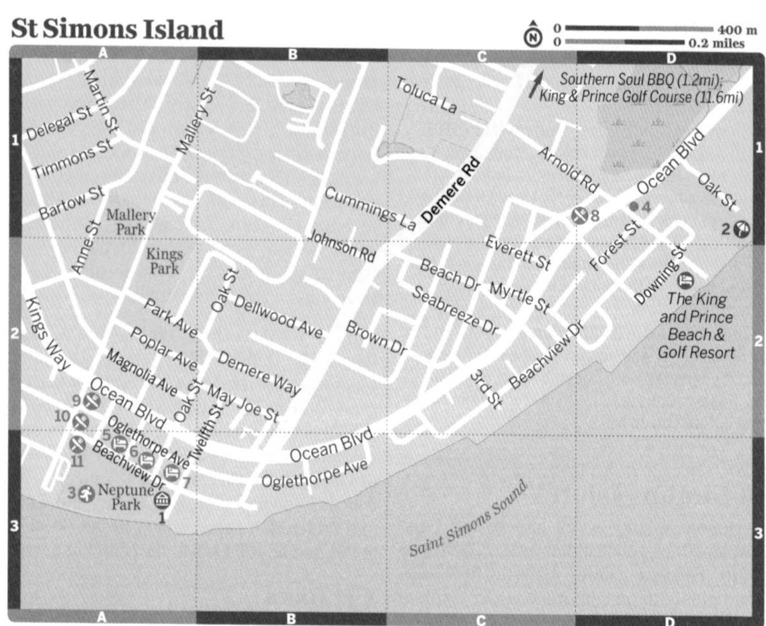

St Simons Island

Sights
1 Lighthouse Museum........A3
2 Massengale Park........D1

Activities, Courses & Tours
3 Neptune Park........A3
4 Ocean Motion........D1

Sleeping
5 Beach View House........A3
6 Ocean Inn and Suites........A3
7 St Simons Inn By The Lighthouse........A3

Eating
8 Crab Trap........D1
9 Palm Coast........A2
10 St Simons Sweets........A2
11 The Half Shell........A3

Ocean Inn and Suites INN $$
(Map p120; ☎912-634-2122; www.oceaninnsuites.com; 599 Beachview Dr; r $169-219; P 📶 🏊) Rooms are a little dated, but clean and comfortable. There are hardwood floors throughout, plus a lovely roof terrace with views of the lighthouse. Next to St Simons Inn By The Lighthouse.

Lodge on Little St Simons Island LODGE $$$
(Map p112; ☎888-733-5774; www.littlestsimonsisland.com; ferry dock 1000 Hampton River Club Marina Dr, hotel Little St Simons Island; d all inclusive from $425-700; ❄📶) This isolated historic lodge sits on pristine and private Little St Simons. Stays include accommodations, boat transfers to and from the island, three prepared meals daily, beverages (including soft drinks, beer and wine), all activities (including naturalist-led excursions) and use of recreation equipment. Rooms have a rustic, cabin vibe, with modern amenities. It's only accessible by boat. Prebooking is essential.

The Cloister RESORT $$$
(Map p112; ☎855-572-4975; www.seaisland.com; Sea Island Dr, Sea Island; d $399-749, ste $799-3249) The whole island is private and occupied by The Cloister and requires a reservation to get in. It has horse stables, a 56,000-sq-ft spa complex and enough golf to satisfy a PGA tour. No luxurious stone is left unturned at this Mediterranean-inspired resort, where the rooms, atmosphere and rates could have you imagining you're a dignitary or royal.

Eating

Southern Soul BBQ BARBECUE $
(Map p112; 912-638-7685; www.southernsoulbbq.com; 2020 Demere Rd; mains $7.50-17; 11am-9pm Mon-Sat, to 6pm Sun; P) Housed inside a former gas station at the side of a roundabout, Southern Soul BBQ serves succulent slow oak-smoked pulled pork, burnt-tipped brisket, full slab of sticky ribs, and daily specials like jerk chicken burritos. There's a number of wonderful housemade sauces – sweet and firey BBQ, tangy mustard and big vinegar pepper – which 'cue fans can slather over their meat.

St Simons Sweets BAKERY $
(Map p120; 912-638-0150; www.stsimonssweets.com; 229 Mallery St; cupcakes from $3.50; 10am-6pm Mon-Sat) Every good village needs a confectionery, and St Simons Sweets doesn't disappoint. Step inside for rows of pretzel twists covered in chocolate; milk, dark and white chocolate turtles; homemade pralines; attractively decorated cupcakes; piles of fudge pieces; plus countless other candies. Look around for giant goodies: specials include a 6ft long 'Party Python' – an enormous gummy snake (for $175).

Palm Coast CAFE $
(Map p120; 912-634-7515; www.palmcoastssi.com; 318 Mallery St; mains $9-14.50; cafe 8am-3pm, bar to midnight, later on weekends) For simple and affordable eats in the village, choose from healthy breakfast plates, wraps, sandwiches and main salads at this tasty coffeehouse set in a cottage on the main drag. Its cozy bar draws a crowd and it has a rather expansive dining patio out back and rockers on the concrete front porch. Ask about upcoming live music and events.

The Half Shell SEAFOOD $$
(Map p120; 912-268-4241; www.thehalfshellssi.com; 504 Beachview Dr; mains $9-27; 11:30am-10pm) The seafood at this down-to-earth oyster bar is pretty impressive, especially given the reasonable prices on otherwise-swish St Simons. Shrimp baskets, fish sand-wiches and, of course, oysters (from $10 for half dozen) are all given solid preparation. Operating hours may vary October to April.

Crab Trap SEAFOOD $$
(Map p120; 912-638-3552; www.thecrabtrapssi.com; 1209 Ocean Blvd; dishes $13-26; 5-10pm Mon-Sat;) A stripped-down seafood house, with pebbled concrete floors, a dank beamed wooden interior, nautical memorabilia, plus vintage diving and fishing gear on display. Shrimp, oysters, scallops, crab and a single fresh catch of the day are grilled, steamed or fried. The crab soup (read: not bisque!) is locally beloved.

★ **Halyards** SEAFOOD $$$
(Map p112; 912-638-9100; www.halyardsrestaurant.com; 55 Cinema Lane; mains $18-42; 5-9pm Mon-Thu, to 10pm Fri & Sat;) Chef Dave Snyder's classy, sustainable, seasonal seafood consistently hogs best-of-everything awards on St Simons, and for good reason. The menu changes with the seasons, but may include dishes like sautéed black grouper, with broccoli, leek and mascarpone *farrotto*, and roasted tomato butter.

Getting There & Away

St Simons is about 9 miles from Brunswick. To get here, take Sea Island Rd from Hwy 17.

Jekyll Island

An exclusive refuge for millionaires in the late 19th and early 20th centuries, Jekyll is a 4000-year-old barrier island with 10 miles of beaches. Today it's an unusual clash of wilderness, preserved historic buildings, modern hotels and a massive campground. It's an easily navigable place – you can get around by car, horse or bicycle.

Sights

4-H Tidelands Nature Center MUSEUM
(Map p112; 912-635-5032; http://tidelands4h.org; 100 S Riverview Dr; $5; 9am-4pm Mon-Fri, 10am-2pm Sat & Sun; P) Run by a staff of peppy University of Georgia science students, the Tidelands is a kid-friendly nature center with some neat display cases on local ecology and resident wildlife, including a baby alligator, loggerhead turtle and snakes. Your children can lift, look inside and open various interactive exhibits and even feel or hold certain animals in the touch tanks.

Georgia Sea Turtle Center WILDLIFE RESERVE
(Map p112; 912-635-4444; www.georgiaseaturtlecenter.org; 214 Stable Rd; adult/child/child under 3yr $8/6/free, tours from $22; 9am-5pm; P) An endearing attraction is the Georgia Sea Turtle Center, a conservation center and turtle hospital where patients are on view for the public. Behind the Scenes tours (3pm)

and Turtle Walks (Wednesday, Friday and Saturday) are also available, among other programs.

Summer Waves Water Park AMUSEMENT PARK
(Map p112; 912-635-2074; www.jekyllisland.com; 210 S Riverview Dr; adult/child $20/16; 10am-6pm Mon-Fri, to 8pm Sat, 11am-7pm Sun Jun & Jul, shorter hours May, Aug & Sep; P) Waterslides, lazy rivers, wave pools and other aquatic attractions await you and the kids at Summer Waves. Plus, a gift shop and fast-food outlets.

Jekyll Island Museum MUSEUM
(Map p112; 912-635-4036; www.jekyllisland.com/history/museum; 100 Stable Rd; 9am-5pm; P) FREE Interesting exhibits at this museum include local history and ecology. Visitors can take a tram tour of the area and historic buildings (adult/child $16/10).

At the time of research, the museum was closed for refurbishment. The gift shop remains open across the street at 101 Old Plantation Rd, and conducts tram tours.

Tours

★ Kayak Tours & Canoe Rentals BOATING
(Map p112; 912-635-5032; http://tidelands4h.org/tours.html; 100 S Riverview Dr; 2hr single/tandem kayak tours $59/114, canoes per hour $20, aqua bikes per hour $20) The 4-H Tidelands Nature Center conducts highly recommended three-hour tours of the salt marshes; on any given day, you may paddle past wood storks, great blue herons, pelicans and dolphins. This is by far the best local means of accessing the understated beauty of the barrier-island salt marshes. Canoe rentals and aqua bikes are also available.

Captain Phillip Boat Tours BOATING
(Map p112; 912-635-3152; www.captainphillip.com; tours from adult/child $25/15; tour times vary, phone to check schedules) Narrated 90-minute sunset and sightseeing boat tours depart from Jekyll Wharf. There's also the chance to see the local bottlenose dolphins playing in these waters.

Festivals & Events

Shrimp & Grits Festival FOOD & DRINK
(www.jekyllisland.com; National Historic Landmark District; parking $4; mid-Sep) FREE Celebrating the famous Southern dish, this three-day festival take place every year on the third weekend of September. It not only includes bucketloads of shrimp and grits, but also craft beer, wildlife demonstrations, live music and local art.

Sleeping

Resort-y beach hotels constitute the majority of the interesting accommodations – these spots may not be as Gatsby-esque as the area's history implies, but they're a step up from the mainland's chain hotels. Head to the north of the island for cheaper camping options.

Jekyll Island State Park CAMPGROUND $
(Map p112; 912-635-3021; www.jekyllisland.com/lodging/jekyll-island-campground; 1197 Riverview Dr; tent sites with/without electricity $41/26) Situated in the quiet north of the island and surrounded by forest, the state park offers 158 campsites with on-site shower and bathroom facilities, plus a laundry and small supplies store. The campground is within easy walking distance of Clam Creek and Driftwood Beach. Up to six people are allowed on each site; two-night minimum on weekends.

Villas By The Sea VILLA $$
(Map p112; 912-635-2521; www.villasbythesearesort.com; 1175 N Beachview Dr; r/condos from $149/294; P) A nice choice on the north coast, close to the best beaches. Rooms are spacious and the one-, two- and three-bedroom condos, set in a complex of lodge buildings sprinkled over a garden, aren't fancy but they're plenty comfy.

Jekyll Island Club Hotel HISTORIC HOTEL $$$
(Map p112; 855-535-9547; www.jekyllclub.com; 371 Riverview Dr; d/ste from $192/305, resort fee $15; P@) From a distance, with its turrets and balconies, this hotel could be a castle. This posh and storied property is the backbone of the island, featuring a rambling array of rooms spread out over five historic structures. Each building feels plucked from a novel about Jazz Age decadence, although the current vibe is a little more Hilton Head Island country club.

Eating

Jekyll Market MARKET $
(Map p112; 912-635-2253; www.jekyllmarket.com; 11 Main St; meals $10; 8am-8pm Sun-Thu, to 9pm Fri & Sat) This gourmet grocery store is a great place to stock up on fresh, well-made, often-organic produce, ingredients, snacks and even plate meals, from BBQ dishes to shrimp bowls.

The Wharf SOUTHERN US $$

(Map p112; ☎912-635-3612; http://jekyllwharf.com; 371 Riverview Dr; mains $12-28; ⊙11:30am-9:30pm Tue-Sun; P) The prettiest dining setting on the island is this wooden boathouse-style restaurant situated on a pier. There's indoor seating and an airy nautical-themed vibe, plus outdoor seating overlooking the water. Unpretentious seafood and Southern mains include Southern chicken, cathead biscuits, grilled ahi tuna, broiled sea scallops and chipotle lobster mac 'n' cheese. Live music takes place weekly.

Driftwood Bistro SOUTHERN US $$

(Map p112; ☎912-635-3588; www.driftwoodbistro.com; 1175 N Beachview Dr; mains $9-16.50; ⊙5-9pm Mon-Sat; P) Driftwood Bistro serves decent Lowcountry-style seafood in an old-school, family-friendly setting. Local Georgia shrimp is usually on the menu, and you shouldn't miss these plump, sweet delicacies.

Getting There & Away

Jekyll Island can be accessed via Hwy 17 and GA-520 (use Exit 29 on I-95). To get here, you'll have to cross a toll bridge and pay for a parking pass ($6/28 per day/week).

Sapelo Island

The beauty of Georgia's sea islands achieves a sort of wilderness apotheosis on Sapelo Island, a patchwork of salt marsh, estuarine rivulets and coastal forest that is only accessible by plane or boat. Four thousand years ago, the island was home to indigenous people, and in the 16th century, a Franciscan mansion was built here. Some 97% of the island is owned by the state and managed by Georgia Department of Natural Resources.

Around 50 locals live in Hog Hammock; most are descendants of enslaved Africans who worked the island's plantations in centuries past. These descendants are known as Geechee or Gullah-Geechee, a nod to the cultural ties they share with the Gullah in neighboring South Carolina.

Visitors to Sapelo must arrive on pre-arranged tours or be guests of Sapelo Island residents (the latter includes staying in an island hotel or guesthouse).

Tours

All sights must be visited as part of a pre-arranged Sapelo Island tour. Points of interest include a Native American **shell ring** – a bleached-out white structure built of shells, bones and pottery, 13ft high at its tallest, 300ft in diameter, 3000 to 4200 years old, and utterly mysterious in its purpose; it's accessible via Sapelo Island Tours. A little way south are the ruins of the evocatively named **Chocolate Plantation**. The other main sight is the **RJ Reynolds Mansion** (http://gastateparks.org/reynoldsmansion), the palatial home of the tobacco magnate of the same name.

Sapelo Island National Estuarine Research Reserve ECOTOUR

(Sinerr; ☎912-437-3224; http://sapelonerr.org; 1766 Landing Rd SE, Darien; adult/child incl ferry fee $15/10; ⊙tours 8:30am-12:30pm Wed, 9am-1pm Sat) Some 6100 acres of Sapelo are managed and researched by this organization, which also runs tours of the island.

The reserve also manages a **Visitor Center** (http://sapelonerr.org/visitor-center; 1766 Landing Rd SE, Darien; ⊙7:30am-5:30pm Tue-Fri, 8am-5:30pm Sat) on the mainland, where the ferry departs from.

Geechee Tours CULTURAL

(☎912-485-2197; www.sapeloislandga.org; tours $25, bike rental per day $35) This outfit can arrange tours that explore the history and folkways of Georgia's Geechee sea islanders. Staff can also connect you to local lodging options, and organize Lowcountry boils and oyster roasts. Affiliated with Sapelo Island Cultural & Revitalization Society.

> **OFF THE BEATEN TRACK**
>
> **GEORGIA'S FIRST FORT**
>
> **Fort King George** (☎912-437-4770; http://gastateparks.org/fortkinggeorge; 302 McIntosh Rd SE, Darien; adult/senior/child 6-18yr/child under 5yr $7.50/7/4.50/free; ⊙9am-5pm Tue-Sun; P) is a fully reconstructed version of Georgia's first fort (and British outpost dating back to 1721), overlooks a vast estuary and is surrounded by mossy oaks. Visitors can wander around the reconstructed buildings, including a blockhouse – the basement of which was where soldiers would store their munitions, rum, salt and meat. Meanwhile, cannons are poised to fire on the 2nd floor. Points of interest include 18th-century bunkhouses, dining rooms and the graveyard for those who defended the Southern English Frontier.

Sapelo Island Tours ECOTOUR
(☎912-506-6463; www.toursapelo.com; tours from $25; times vary) Sapelo native JR Grovner runs these excellent tours, which take in both the elegant natural history of Sapelo and Geechee culture and history.

South East Adventure Outfitters CULTURAL
(☎912-638-6732; http://southeastadventure.com; min 4 people, prices vary per group size) An operator offering custom overnight tours for groups. Pre-arrangement necessary.

Sleeping

The Wallow GUESTHOUSE $
(☎912-485-2206; www.gacoast.com/geecheetours.html; Church Rd; r $55-70, ste $100, 6-room houses $500; ❄) This guesthouse consists of five comfy, individually appointed guest rooms, all maintained by Cornelia Walker Bailey, a Sapelo native, historian, cook and all around force of nature. Affiliated with Geechee Tours. Self-catering options only.

★ **Sapelo Island Birdhouses** COTTAGE $$$
(☎912-223-6515; www.sapeloislandbirdhouses.com; Bailey Rd; cottages $150-375; ❄📶) These beautiful cottages, tucked away amid the maritime woods and Spanish moss, feel like an outgrowth of Sapelo's coastal wilderness. The properties include flat-screen TVs, beach gear, outdoor showers, brightly decorated interiors and screened porches. Golf carts to access the island's different attractions are available. Two-night minimum stay.

Information

You need to bring your own food to Sapelo. If you're staying on the island, contact your accommodation provider; they may be able to provide meals.

There is very little mobile-phone coverage on the island, so get ready to disconnect.

Sapelo Island Cultural & Revitalization Society (SICARS; ☎912-485-2197; www.sapeloislandga.org) A nonprofit dedicated to the preservation of Geechee culture and involved in many of the island's tourism initiatives and infrastructure.

Getting There & Away

Sapelo Island can only be accessed via a 20- to 30-minute **ferry** (☎912-485-2251; https://ugami.uga.edu/ferry; 1766 Landing Rd; round-trip $5; ⏰3 times daily, twice on Sun) ride, which departs from Meridian, 8 miles northeast of Darien, off GA Hwy 99. From the mainland, the ferry runs return trips from Sapelo Island with the same frequency. The ferry does not run on state holidays. Check online for exact times. Day-trippers can only go out to the island on the first ferry of the day, the other ferries are reserved for those with overnight bookings. Book your ferry in advance of travel.

Getting Around

You can rent bicycles through **Geechee Tours** (p123) for $35 per day.

North Georgia

Includes ➡

Best Places to Eat

- Home.made from Scratch (p131)
- National (p132)
- Fortify Kitchen & Bar (p147)
- Sawmill Place (p143)
- Spirits Tavern (p136)

Best Places to Stay

- Len Foote Hike Inn (p138)
- White Birch Inn (p146)
- Amicalola Falls Lodge (p138)
- Mountain Crossings at Walasi-Yi (p142)

Why Go?

Elevation seekers should head to North Georgia, which sits at the southern end of the great Appalachian Range. Those mountains, and their surrounding foothills and upcountry, provide superb mountain scenery, as well as some decent wines and frothing rivers. Fall colors emerge late here, peaking in October. A few days are warranted to see sites such as the 1200ft-deep Tallulah Gorge, and the mountain scenery and hiking trails at Vogel State Park and Unicoi State Park.

When to Go

- Georgia's Appalachian Trail through-hikers get moving anytime from late March to mid-April; the region blooms with pretty dogwoods.
- College-football season kicks off in September – Athens is a notable good time.
- Sweltering heat and summer prices retreat; go in November, before the holidays.

North Georgia Highlights

1 Amicalola Falls State Park (p138) Feeling the spray of these mighty falls, the Southeast's tallest.

2 Tallulah Gorge State Park (p147) Hiking deep into the permit-only gorge floor of this gorgeous, waterfall-peppered canyon.

3 Athens (p130) Eating, drinking and pledging devotion to the Georgia Bulldogs in this immensely cool, musically inclined college town.

4 Dahlonega (p135) Vineyard-hopping through Georgia's surprisingly beautiful, up-and-coming wine country.

5 **Blue Ridge** (p139) Riding the rails on the Blue Ridge Scenic Railway from this pretty mountain town.

6 **Clayton** (p146) Taking in vistas of four states from Black Rock Mountain, Georgia's highest state park.

7 **Helen** (p143) 'Shooting the Hooch' on a leisurely tubing trip in this kitschy German village in 'Alppalachia'.

8 **Toccoa** (p148) Taking on the famous '3 miles up, 3 miles down' climb to the top of Currahee Mountain in this historic military town.

HIKING IN TALLULAH GORGE

SLIDING ROCK TRAIL

START/END JANE HURT YARN INTERPRETIVE CENTER
DURATION 3 HOURS
DISTANCE 3.4 MILES
DIFFICULTY DIFFICULT

This challenging, rocky, boulder-filled trail will take you deep into remote parts of Tallulah Gorge State Park (p147) most visitors don't see. Leave the families and amateur walkers to the rim trails, take a gallon (4L) of water and get yourself a gorge-floor permit – only 100 are available per day – and dive deep into one of the most spectacular canyons in the Eastern US. Check the weather before setting out: no permits are issued if it is raining or the trail is wet, or on dam-release days. Pets and children under eight years old are not allowed.

Begin at the Jane Hurt Yarn Interpretive Center then head left to Overlook 1 to take in views of Bridal Veil Falls. Retrace your steps back past the Interpretive Center and turn left (south) on the Tallulah Gorge Rim Trail to take the 310 metal stairs that descend steeply into the canyon and its 80ft-high suspension bridge over the Tallulah River. From here, you can see three of the park's six waterfalls.

After crossing the bridge, the trail hangs a left and drops down another grueling set of 221 metal stairs to the thundering base of Hurricane Falls. From here, you ascend back up the stairs and head left along the Hurricane Falls Trail (comprising of another 347 stairs) in order to reach the South Rim Trail.

Take the the South Rim Trail eastbound. Around 0.5 miles later, veer left to enter the Sliding Rock Trail. Shortly after passing the South Wallenda tower, the trail begins a sharp, 45-degree decline strewn with boulders (be extremely careful if they are wet). At this point, the trail isn't really

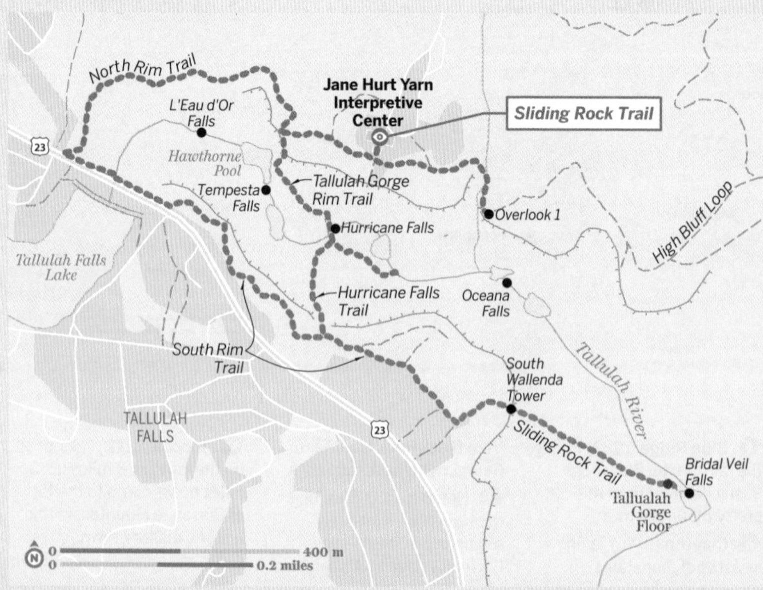

A challenging hike deep into one of the most stunning natural features in the eastern USA.

SEAN PAVONE/SHUTTERSTOCK ©

Tallulah Gorge

marked anymore – you'll need to navigate via trail-spotting for the 500ft, 0.4-mile drop.

Two miles into the trail, you'll reach the Tallulah Gorge floor. Here you can pop into a swimming hole formed at the bottom of Bridal Veil Falls – the only spot you're permitted to swim in the park. To return, head back up Sliding Rock Trail to reach the south rim and follow the South Rim Trail to the North Rim Trail to return to the Interpretive Center.

Athens

706, 762 / POP 119,980

A beery, artsy and laid-back college town, Athens has an extremely popular football team (the University of Georgia Bulldogs, College Football Playoff National Championship runners-up in 2018), a world-famous music scene, a bona fide restaurant culture and surprisingly diverse nightlife. The university – UGA – drives the culture of Athens and ensures an ever-replenishing supply of young bar-hoppers and concert-goers, some of whom stick around long after graduation and become 'townies.' The pleasant, walkable downtown offers a plethora of funky choices for eating, drinking and shopping.

Sights

★Georgia Museum of Art MUSEUM
(706-542-4662; www.georgiamuseum.org; 90 Carlton St; 10am-5pm Tue, Wed, Fri & Sat, to 9pm Thu, 1-5pm Sun) FREE A smart, modern gallery where brainy, arty types set up in the wired lobby for personal study, while art hounds gawk at modern sculpture in the courtyard garden as well as the tremendous collection from American realists of the 1930s.

State Botanical Garden of Georgia GARDENS
(www.botgarden.uga.edu; 2450 S Milledge Ave; 8am-6pm) FREE Truly gorgeous, with winding outdoor paths and a sociohistorical edge, Athens' gardens are a gift for a city of this size. Signs provide smart context for its amazing collection of plants, which includes rare and threatened species. There are nearly 5 miles of top-notch woodland walking trails too. The visitor center, cafe and gift shop are closed on Mondays but the grounds are open.

> DON'T MISS
>
> **OUTDOOR ATHENS**
>
> Opened in 2017, the **Firefly Trail** (www.fireflytrail.com) is the first leg of a 39-mile multiuse trail that will connect Athens to Union Point, GA. Accessible by foot and bike, it's the beginning of a great little recreational pathway for the city.
>
> The most recent sections of the trail to open are around Winterville.

University of Georgia UNIVERSITY
(UGA visitor center 706-542-0842; www.uga.edu; 405 College Station Rd) Take in a football game at the hallowed grounds of Sanford Stadium, walk around the 160-year-old cast-iron arch (depending on who you are – only UGA grads are supposed to walk *through* the landmark!), or just take in the hip and fun atmosphere around campus and downtown. Whatever you do, it is the 37,000-student University of Georgia, founded in 1781, that keeps Athens' heart beating. The address and phone connects you to the UGA visitor center.

Festivals & Events

Twilight Criterium CYCLING
(www.athenstwilight.com; Apr) FREE An annual top stop on the national cycling-tour circuit nearing its 40th year, this nighttime, 80km professional cycling race draws 150 international top riders to downtown Athens.

Sleeping

Most hotels in Athens seem to cater to parents visiting young Timmy or Tammy, or alums in town for a Bulldogs game. There are a lot of chain hotels in town and on the outskirts, and most are clean and serviceable. Some cheap motel options can also be found around town, but our research leads us to conclude that you get what you pay for.

★Graduate Athens INN $$
(706-549-7020; www.graduateathens.com; 295 E Dougherty St; r $129-249, ste $280-500; P@) This wonderfully designed boutique hotel, the first of a college-campus chain, is drowning in sexy retro hipness, from potted plants inside old-school Dewey decimal card-catalog filing cabinets in the lobby to the sweet Crosley turntables and classic video games in the suites.

Hotel Indigo BOUTIQUE HOTEL $$
(706-546-0430; www.indigoathens.com; 500 College Ave; r/ste from $179/279; P@) Rooms are spacious, loftlike pods of cool at this eco-chic boutique hotel. Part of the Indigo chain, it's a Leadership in Energy and Environmental Design (LEED) gold-certified sustainable standout. Green elements include regenerative elevators and priority parking for hybrid vehicles – 30% of the building was constructed from recycled content.

OFF THE BEATEN TRACK

MUSIC NOTES

For a glimpse of a classic Athens musical legend, do a drive-by of 748 Cobb St, a Second Empire Victorian home painted 12 different colors. Known as Buck Manor, REM guitarist Peter Buck lived here until his divorce from his wife, Barrie. REM filmed the 'Nightswimming' video here as well as a prerelease promotional video for *Out of Time*. Nirvana spent the night here when they played the 40 Watt Club in 1991. Other REM pilgrimage-worthy sights include the *Murmur* album railroad trestle (Dudley Park); Weaver D's Delicious Fine Foods (1016 E Broad St), whose slogan – 'Automatic for the People!' – spawned the title of the band's 1992 album; and the steeple of the long-demolished St Mary's Episcopal Church, where REM played their first show, at 394 Oconee St.

Eating

Ideal Bagel Co BREAKFAST $
(706-353-0005; 815 W Broad St; bagels $1.25-5; 7am-3pm Mon-Fri, 8am-8pm Sat & Sun; P) They may never allow us past the Hudson River again after writing this, but the bagels here give anything in New York a run for its money. We stand by that, and dare you, dear reader, to try one of Ideal's onion bagels with schmear and tell us any different.

White Tiger BARBECUE $
(www.whitetigergourmet.com; 217 Hiawassee Ave; mains $6.75-11; 11am-3pm Mon-Sat, 6-8pm Thu, 10am-2pm Sun;) The 100-year-old structure doesn't invite confidence, but this off-the-beaten-path local favorite does killer wood-smoked pulled-pork sandwiches – add pimento cheese (and send us a thank-you note!) – plus burgers and even barbecue-smoked tofu and a whole lot more for vegetarians. Chef Ken Manring honed his skills in much higher-brow kitchens before settling in Athens.

Grit VEGETARIAN $
(199 Prince Ave; mains $7.75-8.95; 8am-9:30pm Mon-Wed, to 10pm Thu & Fri, 10am-10pm Sat, 10am-9:30pm Sun;) A Normaltown vegetarian/vegan staple long before it was trendy, this somewhat divey institution is dressed up with the building's original tinplated ceilings (owned by Michael Stipe, incidentally). The wide-ranging dishes on offer (tofu Reubens, veggie banh mi, noodle bowls, Middle Eastern plates) don't perform culinary miracles, but the vibe makes it a classic city must.

Pouch PIES $
(706-395-6696; www.pouchpies.com; 151 E Broad St; pies $5.50; 11am-10pm Mon-Wed, to 11pm Thu-Sat;) In the South, 'pie' usually means something sweet, buttery and served after dinner. For the South African owners of Pouch, 'pie' means savory pastries from around the world: Aussie pies with beef and gravy, Portuguese pies with piripiri white-wine sauce, chorizo and spicy chicken, and even a local offering with pulled pork and peach BBQ sauce! Makes for a great budget meal.

Big City Bread Cafe DELI $
(706-353-0029; www.bigcitybreadcafe.com; 393 N Finley St; mains $7.75-12; 7am-9:30pm Mon-Sat, to 3pm Sun;) As you may have gathered, the bread at this restaurant-bakery is awesome, but so are the creations derived from said bread: lamb burgers, grilled cheese and mozzarella, tomato and basil sandwiches etc. Throw in fantastic coffee and a great slate of meal-sized salads and you have a winner.

Ted's Most Best ITALIAN $
(www.tedsmostbest.com; 254 W Washington St; mains $8-9; 11am-10pm Mon-Wed, to 11pm Thu-Sat, noon-10pm Sun) This atmospheric eatery occupies a former Michelin tire shop and is a great spot for cheap eats. Pizzas and paninis are what drives it, but the outdoor patio and sandbox/bocce court (when the little ones haven't commandeered it) is the real star of the show.

★**Home.made from Scratch** SOUTHERN US $$
(706-206-9216; www.homemadeathens.com; 1072 Baxter St; mains $16-24; 11am-2pm & 5:30-9:30pm Tue-Sat;) Home.made is upping the game when it comes to nouveau-Southern cuisine. The menu constantly changes based on ingredient availability, but whatever these folks source is always turned into something creative, delicious, rooted in local flavors and often playfully over the top. At lunch,

Athens

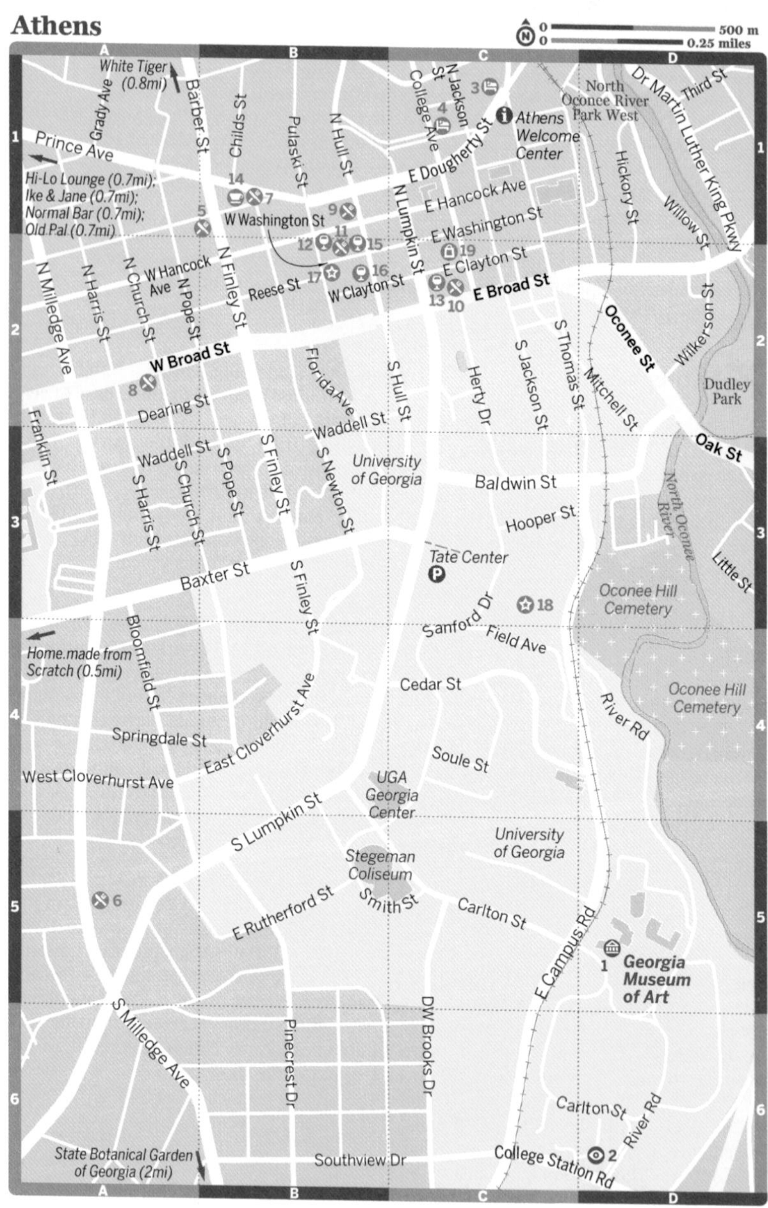

don't miss the fried chicken and pimento-cheese sandwich with a side upgrade to tomato pie.

At dinner, think shrimp and andouille sausage with tomatoes, celery, onions and sweet peppers over grits or boneless chicken thighs with smoked hoppin' John (black-eyed peas, rice, chopped onion and sliced bacon).

National MODERN AMERICAN $$
(706-549-3450; www.thenationalrestaurant.com; 232 W Hancock Ave; mains $20-29; 11:30am-10pm Mon-Thu, to late Fri & Sat,

Athens

Top Sights
1 Georgia Museum of Art........D5

Sights
2 University of Georgia........D6

Sleeping
3 Graduate Athens........C1
4 Hotel Indigo........C1

Eating
5 Big City Bread Cafe........B1
6 Five & Ten........A5
7 Grit........B1
8 Ideal Bagel Co........A2
9 National........B1
10 Pouch........C2
11 Ted's Most Best........B2

Drinking & Nightlife
12 Creature Comforts Brewing Co........B2
13 Cutter's........C2
14 Hendershots........B1
15 Manhattan Bar........B2
16 Trapeze Pub........B2
World Famous........(see 15)

Entertainment
17 40 Watt Club........B2
18 Sanford Stadium........C3

Shopping
19 Wuxtry Records........C2

5-10pm Sun;) An effortlessly cool bistro on the downtown outskirts, favored for its daily changing, eclectic menu that jumps from roasted monkfish to roasted chicken on jeweled Carolina Gold rice with dried apricot, pistachio, currants, *schug* hot sauce, yogurt, cucumber, marinated onion and cilantro (got it?). Outstanding vegetarian choices too. Spanish and Middle Eastern accents abound. The bar is one where you may want to sit and sip a while.

Five & Ten AMERICAN **$$$**
(706-546-7300; www.fiveandten.com; 1073 S Milledge Ave; mains $22-48; 5:30-10pm Sun-Thu, to 11pm Fri & Sat, 10:30am-2:30pm Sun;) Sustainably driven, James Beard Award–winning Five & Ten ranks among the South's best restaurants. Its menu is earthy and slightly gamey: Georgia quail with pickled *yacón* and white-miso aioli, and Frogmore stew (stewed corn, sausage and potato). Vegetarians should try baked Crescenza cheese with confit parsnips and blue collard greens or pasta ribbons with grilled tomato sauce, jalapeños and Parmesan.

Drinking & Nightlife

Nearly 100 bars, restaurants and breweries dot the compact downtown area, so it's not hard to find a good time. To escape students, head to Normaltown, a mile or so west of downtown along Price Ave, where 'townies' and locals tend to hang out.

★**Creature Comforts Brewing Co** MICROBREWERY
(www.creaturecomfortsbeer.com; 271 W Hancock Ave; pints $5.50-7.50; 5-9pm Tue-Thu, to 10pm Fri, 1-6pm Sat & Sun;) Athens' best craft beer emerges from 33 taps at this cutting-edge, dog-friendly former tire shop which excels at staples – Indian Pale Ales (IPAs), amber ales – but isn't afraid to play around with suds (tart blonde ale aged in wine barrels, mixed fermentation ale aged in bourbon barrels with blackberries). Local ingredients often form the backbone of the memorable brews.

There's live music most nights and free tours (hourly 6pm to 9pm). Start with one of Georgia's best IPAs (Tropicália) and then move on to a bevy of innovative pints. Note that there's a no-sample policy.

Trapeze Pub CRAFT BEER
(www.trappezepub.com; 269 N Hull St; 11am-2am Mon-Sat, to midnight Sun;) Downtown's best craft-beer bar installed itself well before the suds revolution. You'll find dozens of taps spanning regional, national and international brews, and another 100 or so at any given time in bottles. Soak it up with their Belgian-style fries ($3.50), the best in town.

Old Pal BAR
(www.theoldpal.com; 1320 Prince Ave; 4pm-2am Mon-Sat;) This is Normaltown's thinking-person's bar, devoted to seasonal craft cocktails ($9) and a thoughtfully curated bourbon list. It's a beautiful, dark space that has many local preservation awards.

Hi-Lo Lounge BAR

(www.hiloathens.com; 1354 Prince Ave; ⏲4pm-2am Mon-Thu, noon-2am Fri & Sat, 11am-midnight Sun) This chilled-out Normaltown bar and grill has an atmosphere that's somewhere between a dive, a grill and a cool party your friends never told you about. There's an extensive whiskey menu, solid cocktails ($5 to $7), and a good list of craft beers on 14 taps.

Manhattan Bar BAR

(337 N Hull St; ⏲4pm-2am Mon-Sat) This busy little bar is a good spot to soak up some Athens counterculture, find a strong drink and, during winter, sip on some spiked hot chocolate (divine).

World Famous COCKTAIL BAR

(www.facebook.com/theworldfamousathens; 351 N Hull; ⏲11am-2am Mon-Sat, 11:30am-midnight Sun; 📶) This bustling spot serves commendable craft cocktails in mason jars amid retro French farmhouse decor. Also hosts intimate comedy and live-music events.

Hendershots COFFEE

(www.hendershotscoffee.com; 237 Prince Ave; ⏲6:30am-11pm Mon-Thu, to midnight Fri, 7:30am-midnight Sat, 7am-10pm Sun; 📶) This fantastic coffeehouse pulls triple duty as a great bar and live-music venue. Pick your poison.

Normal Bar BAR

(www.facebook.com/normal.bar.7; 1365 Prince Ave; ⏲4pm-2am Mon-Sat; 📶) This lovable dark storefront bar is not very student-like but still very much Athens. The beer goes from cheap Pabst Blue Ribbon (PBR) to sophisticated local craft IPA. There's a terrific wine list and the crowd is cute, young – but not *too* young; think grad students or even young professors – and laid-back. A cooler version of the quintessential neighborhood bar.

Cutter's SPORTS BAR

(120 E Clayton St; ⏲3pm-2am Mon-Fri, noon-2am Sat) If you can't get a ticket to a football game, make your way to this popular sports bar with gargantuan flat-screen TVs. Before the game it's buzzing, and if victory is grasped, the interior becomes a sloshed dance hall of depravity (but in a good way).

☆ Entertainment

Athens gave us the B-52's and REM, but the live-music scene didn't stop in the '90s – this town both creates and attracts lots of bands. During the fall, football mania takes over the town. Pick up a free copy of *Flagpole* (www.flagpole.com) to find out what's on.

40 Watt Club LIVE MUSIC

(☎706-549-7871; www.40watt.com; 285 W Washington St; $5-25) Athens' most storied joint has lounges, a tiki bar and $2.50 PBRs. The venue has welcomed indie rock to its stage since REM, the B-52's and Widespread Panic owned this town and today this is still where the big hitters play when they come to town. It has recently embraced comedy as well.

Sanford Stadium STADIUM

(☎706-542-9036; www.georgiadogs.com; 100 Sanford Dr) Football games happen on Saturdays in fall at Sanford Stadium, in the middle of the lovely, leafy campus that rambles over rolling hills east of a pleasant downtown.

Shopping

Wuxtry Records MUSIC

(www.wuxtryrecords.com; 197 E Clayton St; ⏲10am-8pm Mon-Thu, to 9pm Fri & Sat, noon-6pm Sun) REM guitarist Peter Buck once worked these hallowed halls of vinyl and CDs, and it is here where he and singer/customer Michael Stipe first forged the relationship that would become one of the most important alternative music acts in history. The ceiling is peeling, the carpets rotting, the music superb – just the way it should be.

ℹ Information

Athens Welcome Center (☎706-353-1820; www.athenswelcomecenter.com; 280 E Dougherty St; ⏲10am-5pm Mon-Sat, noon-5pm Sun) This visitor center, in a historic antebellum house at the corner of Thomas St, provides maps and information on local tours.

ℹ Getting There & Away

This college town is about 70 miles east of Atlanta. There's no main highway that leads here, so traffic can be an issue on secondary state and county roads. The local **Greyhound station** (☎706-549-2255; www.greyhound.com; 4020 Atlanta Hwy, Bogart) is actually about 6 miles west of downtown Athens. Buses leave for Atlanta (from $15, 7½ hours, twice daily) and Savannah (from $36, 14 hours, twice daily).

Groome Transportation (☎706-612-1155; https://groometransportation.com; 3190 Atlanta Hwy, Suite 22) operates 23 shuttles per day year-round between Athens and Hartsfield-Jackson Atlanta International Airport ($39, 2¼ hours). Shuttles leave from the **UGA Georgia Center** (1197 S Lumpkin St) and its Athens office between 2:25am and 9:25pm.

DON'T MISS

WINE TASTING IN THE DAHLONEGA PLATEAU

Old-world wine enthusiasts may scoff, but North Georgia wine has come a long way in the last decade. When most folks think of wine tasting in Georgia, images of tipsy frat boys and their dates swigging sweet muscadine wines on a Saturday afternoon might spring to mind. We're not saying that never happens, but times have changed. Dahlonega, known as the Heart of Georgia Wine Country, helped secure a Dahlonega Plateau appellation (technically called an American Viticultural Area) from the Alcohol and Tobacco Tax and Trade Bureau for the region's wines in 2018. The town's nine wineries – **Frogtown**, **Three Sisters**, **Wolf Mountain**, Monteluce, Kaya, Cavender Creek, Blue Mountain, the Cottage and Accent Cellars – have won plenty of awards when competing against more famous American wine regions (Frogtown bills itself as the most awarded non-Californian winery in the US). Not only that, but the wineries are gorgeous: blink twice and you might swear you're in Napa Valley or Europe.

To get to the wineries on an organized tour from Dahlonega, **Appalachian Transportation** (706-864-0021; www.appalachiantransportation.com; 27 S Park St; per person from $65; 11am-5pm) is your best bet. There are a few companies doing the same from Atlanta but prices are exorbitant – you are better off organizing an Uber for the day.

Getting Around

Downtown Athens is a compact and walkable grid system, but those with a car will find parking a challenge. There is metered parking (per hour $1, 8am to 10pm), pay lots (two of which, on College Ave and Washington St, are free for the first 30 minutes) but free spots are hard to find (there are a few on College Ave next to Hotel Indigo). You can also park at the Tate Center parking deck for free for 30 minutes with a $10 purchase at the bookstore – that means you can snag a Georgia Bulldog hoodie, pop across the street and take a gander at Sanford Stadium and get out of there without a booted car!

Dahlonega

706, 762 / POP 6050

In 1828 Dahlonega was the site of the first gold rush in the USA (locals are known as 'Nuggets'). These days the boom is in tourism, as it's an easy day excursion from Atlanta and a fantastic mountain destination. Not only is Dahlonega a hotbed of outdoor activities, but downtown in Courthouse Sq is an attractive mélange of wine-tasting rooms, gourmet emporiums, great food, countrified shops and foothill charm. Wine tasting in the surrounding vineyards is on the rise too. There's a vaguely artistic vibe permeating throughout town (especially when it comes to music), often fueled by students at the University of North Georgia, located off the square. Tack on Amicalola Falls State Park just 18 miles west and you have a pretty irresistible bundle of mountain fun.

Sights

★ Wolf Mountain Vineyards WINERY

(706-867-9862; www.wolfmountainvineyards.com; 180 Wolf Mountain Trail; tastings $20, mains $13-15, brunch $35; tastings 11am-5pm Thu-Sat, 12:30-5pm Sun, cafe noon-3pm Thu-Sat, Sun brunch 12:30pm & 2:30pm) Wolf lures a hip and trendy 30-something crowd to its gorgeous, 30-acre winery that frames epic sunsets over Springer Mountain from its tasting-room terrace. Top wines like its *méthode champenoise* 100% chardonnay Blanc de Blanc and crisp and fresh Plentitude (an unoaked chardonnay/Viognier blend) are the way to go. Reservations required for cafe and brunch.

Three Sisters WINERY

(706-865-9463; www.threesistersvineyards.com; 439 Vineyard Way; tastings from $15; 11am-5pm Thu-Sat, 1-5pm Sun; P) A wonderfully unpretentious vineyard where Cheetos, overalls and bluegrass tunes – or fine cheese and great views – pair just fine with the wine.

Frogtown Cellars WINERY

(706-865-0687; www.frogtownwine.com; 700 Ridge Point Dr; tastings $14-24; noon-5pm Mon-Fri, 11-6pm Sat, 12:30-5pm Sun) This beautiful winery has a killer deck where you can sip libations and nibble cheese. It bills itself as the most awarded American winery *not* in California, which we can't confirm, but the wine does go down a treat with a mountain sunset.

Dahlonega

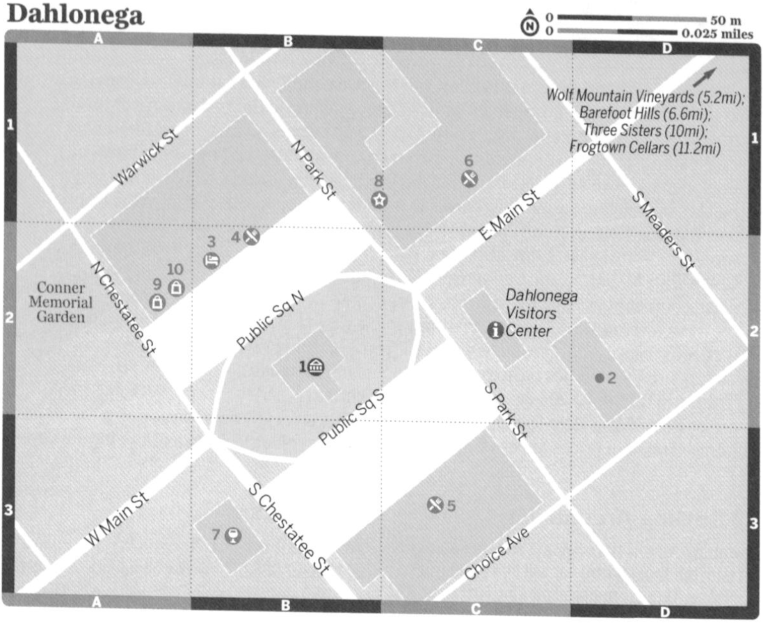

Wolf Mountain Vineyards (5.2mi); Barefoot Hills (6.6mi); Three Sisters (10mi); Frogtown Cellars (11.2mi)

Warwick St · N Park St · E Main St · S Meaders St · N Chestatee St · Public Sq N · Public Sq S · S Park St · W Main St · S Chestatee St · Choice Ave · Conner Memorial Garden · Dahlonega Visitors Center

Dahlonega Courthouse Gold Museum MUSEUM
(www.gastateparks.org/dahlonegagoldmuseum; Public Sq; adult/child $7/4.50; 9am-4:45pm Mon-Sat, 10am-4:45pm Sun) If you have a thing for coins, currency or financial history, pop into this museum. Dahlonega has gold-mining roots and the town prospered with each strike. In 1838 the federal government opened a mint in the town square, where more than $6 million in gold was coined before the operation was closed at the dawn of the Civil War.

Sleeping

Barefoot Hills HOTEL $
(470-788-8043; www.barefoothills.com; 7693 Hwy 19 N; dm $42, r from $115, cabins $150-180; P ❄ 📶) On Hwy 19 N, 7 miles or so north of town, this revamped option could be known as the Boutique Hotel Formerly Known as Hiker Hostel. New owners upgraded this former backpackers in 2017, transitioning the converted log cabin to a near boutique-level hotel – but maintaining a hiker focus with a four-bed bunk room, supply store and shuttles to trailheads.

Three stylish shipping-container cabins are built from reclaimed materials found throughout Georgia. They offer mountain, sunset or sunrise views and long-stay amenities (kitchenette, some with washer and dryer). The vibe and traveler camaraderie are gone and the bunk prices have sky-rocketed, but it's still a wonderful option. There's a shuttle service from Atlanta.

Hall House Hotel INN $$
(706-867-5009; www.hallhousehotel.com; 90 Public Sq; r $165-195; P ❄ 📶) A charming historic nest on the square dating to 1881. There are five bright and charming rooms, each uniquely decorated, some with four-poster beds.

Eating

You'll find most of the town's eating options concentrated downtown, near the Public Sq, with a diverse and generally quite good smattering of options, from Mediterranean fare to seafood to Cajun/creole.

★ **Spirits Tavern** BURGERS $
(706-482-0580; www.spirits-tavern.com; 19 E Main St; burgers $12-15; 11am-11pm Sun-Thu, to 1am Fri, to midnight Sat; 📶) This full bar dishes up surprisingly creative burgers made from Angus beef or free-range, hormone-free turkey and veggies, including gooey mac 'n' cheese, Greek and Cajun versions. With eight taps and a seasonally changing list of serious cocktails, it's also the best 'bar' in town.

Dahlonega

Picnic Cafe & Dessertery CAFE $
(https://thepicniccafe.wixsite.com/picniccafe; 30 Public Sq; sandwiches $8.49; 7:30am-7pm Sun-Thu, to 8pm Fri & Sat;) Owned by Dahlonega mayor Sam Norten and the absolute best spot around to mingle with town characters and university students engrossed in local gossip. Picnic does simple and quick biscuit sandwiches for breakfast, and sandwiches such as honey-ham salad, pimento cheese and sweet Georgia peach chicken salad for lunch.

Capers on the Square MEDITERRANEAN $
(www.facebook.com/capersonthesquare; 84 Public Sq N; mains $9-20; 11am-9pm Mon, Tue & Thu-Sat, noon-7pm Sun;) This tasty little newcomer on the square leans casual Greek (lamb kabobs, moussaka, shrimp orzo) but each month, it takes on a different Mediterranean country for its specials, almost none of which are otherwise represented in North Georgia other than Italian.

Bourbon Street Grille CAJUN $$
(706-864-0086; www.thebourbonstreetgrille.com; 90 Public Sq N; mains $10-22; 11am-8pm Mon, Wed, & Thu, to 10pm Fri & Sat, 9am-8pm Sun;) This intimate, Cajun-inspired eatery on the creaky, uneven 2nd floor of the historic Hill House dishes out jambalaya and gumbo and gets many of its wares shipped in from Louisiana purveyors (fresh Apalachicola oysters, redfish, andouille sausage, alligator).

Drinking & Nightlife

Dahlonega bills itself as the Official Wine Tasting Room Capital of Georgia and there are nine wineries in the immediate environs. Additionally, you'll find distilleries (musician Zac Brown, a Dahlonega native, owns one) and a meadery. Othe4rwise, there are no bars per se in Dahlonega – only restaurants with alcohol.

Gold City Growlers CRAFT BEER
(www.goldcitygrowlers.com; 10 S Chestatee St; 11am-7pm Tue-Wed, to 8pm Thu, to 9pm Fri & Sat, 1-6pm Sun) Dahlonega's best craft-beer destination has 20 taps of mostly Georgia suds but there's a catch: city ordinances only allow growler fill-ups to go, or tastings, which run $6 for four 2oz pours.

But all is not lost. Growlers in 32oz or 64oz sizes can be rented for $1 and a 32oz fill-up (two beers, basically) starts at $6 – so more or less the price of a single pint in many places. So tucking away in your hotel room with a growler and a partner or some friends isn't such a bad deal.

Naturally Georgia WINE BAR
(770-231-5783; www.naturallygeorgia.com; 90 Public Sq N; noon-6pm Mon & Thu, 11am-8pm Fri & Sat, 12:30-6pm Sun) If you're in need of some wine, head to this tasting room, which pours wines from around the state, from dry whites to robust, Portuguese-style reds.

Entertainment

Crimson Moon Café LIVE MUSIC
(www.thecrimsonmoon.com; 24 N Park St; 10am-3pm Mon, to 9pm Thu, to 10:30pm Fri & Sat, to 9:30pm Sun;) An organic coffeehouse offering great Southern comfort food (and brunch every day, mains $6.50 to $18) that doubles as an intimate live-music venue. Thursday night is open-mike night and old-time jam sessions take place every second Sunday.

Shopping

Giggle Monkey Toys TOYS
(www.gigglemonkeytoys.com; 104 Public Sq N; 11am-6pm Mon-Fri, 10am-6pm Sat, noon-6pm Sun) If you are toting little ones, do *not* go

WEST RIDGE TRAIL

The best option for a quick view of the falls is the **West Ridge Trail**. Drive a half mile north on Top of the Falls Rd from the visitor center and park in the first parking lot on the right-hand side. From there, the 0.3-mile recycled-rubber (wheelchair-accessible) trail leads to a spectacular viewpoint bridge that traverses the falls. Those more able or with more time can opt for the 2-mile loop to the top of the falls via the first mile of the **Appalachian Approach Trail**, returning via 604 stairs along the **East Ridge Trail**. The aforementioned Appalachian Approach Trail is an 8.5-mile jaunt to **Springer Mountain**.

in this store. Giggle Monkey's co-owner, Tammy Clower, is a Certified Play Expert and this dizzying wonderland is teeming with extremely well-curated, outside-the-norm toys, games, puzzles and books.

Paul Thomas Chocolates CHOCOLATE
(www.paulthomaschocolates.com; 102 Public Sq N; per pound from $22.95; 10am-6pm Sun-Thu, to 7pm Fri & Sat) This Florida transplant chocolatier does over 80 types of handmade artisan chocolates. Think delicious sea-salt turtles, wasabi and jalapeño dark-chocolate bark and endless rows of truffles.

Information

Dahlonega Visitors Center (706-864-3711; www.dahlonega.org; 13 S Park St; 9am-5:30pm Mon-Fri, 10am-5pm Sat & Sun) Has plenty of information on area sights and activities, including hiking, canoeing, kayaking, rafting and mountain biking.

Getting There & Away

Dahlonega is about 70 miles north of Atlanta; the quickest way here is via Hwy 19. There is no public bus service, but folks traveling from Atlanta often take a Metropolitan Atlanta Rapid Transit Authority (MARTA) train to North Springs station in Atlanta and catch an Uber from there ($50 to $75). The nearest Amtrak station is in Gainesville, 21 miles south.

Amicalola Falls State Park

This 829-acre privatized state park, 18 miles west of Dahlonega on Hwy 52, is one of Georgia's most spectacular. It features the mighty 729ft Amicalola Falls. While most folks visit on a day trip from Atlanta or Dahlonega, the park is worth at least an overnight – it offers offers spectacular scenery, a lodge and excellent hiking and mountain-biking trails.

Sights

Amicalola Falls WATERFALL
(706-265-4703; www.gastateparks.org/amicalolafalls; 280 Amicalola Falls State Park Rd, Dawsonville; per vehicle $5; 7am-10pm; P) The tallest cascading waterfall in the Southeast is a spectacular sight. It tumbles 729ft through protected North Georgia mountain scenery within Amicalola Falls State Park. You can also watch it fall right under foot from the viewpoint bridge on the West Ridge Trail.

Sleeping

Len Foote Hike Inn LODGE $$
(800-581-8032; www.hike-inn.com; 280 Amicalola Falls State Park Rd, Dawsonville; s/d $127/180) You will be far, far from the rat race at this hike-in-only lodge, 5 miles from the nearest road and technically outside Amicalola Falls State Park. You'll need to carry in everything, haul out your own trash and reserve in advance.

Rooms are comfortable and cozy – a welcome break from the trails – and two hot meals are served each day. All guests hiking in must check in at the Amicalola Falls State Park Visitor's Center by 2pm.

Amicalola Falls Lodge LODGE $$
(800-573-9656; www.amicalolafallslodge.com; 418 Amicalola Falls State Park Rd, Dawsonville; campsites $30-40, r from $139, 1-/2-/3-bedroom cabins $159/189/219; P) This lodge is a full-service hotel with beautiful mountain views from every room (though not of the falls); the rustic cottages sleep four to 10. You can eat buffet-style at the on-site Maple Restaurant, and take advantage of local ziplines, archery courses and other adventure activities.

Eating

Dining options within the park are limited to snacks at the visitor center and Maple Restaurant at Amicalola Falls Lodge.

Maple Restaurant AMERICAN $
(www.amicalolafallslodge.com; 418 Amicalola Falls State Park Rd, Amicalola Falls Lodge, Dawsonville; buffet $11-17, mains $16-28; ⏲7-11am, 11:30am-3pm & 5:30-9pm;) The Maple Restaurant at Amicalola Falls Lodge caters both to guests and hungry park visitors and through-hikers. There's a buffet option for all three meals, or à la carte menu of steaks and chops, mountain trout, spaghetti and pizzas (from $12).

Information

Amicalola Falls State Park Visitor's Center
(☎706-265-4703; www.amicalolafallslodge.com; 280 Amicalola Falls State Park Rd, Dawsonville; ⏲8:30am-5pm) Through-hikers must register at the park visitor's center. Park info, clothing and gear, and snacks are also on offer.

Getting There & Away

The park is 18 miles west of Dahlonega on Hwy 52. There is no public transportation, so it's best to have your own wheels.

Blue Ridge

☎706, 762 / POP 1400

Cutesy and wildly popular Blue Ridge was founded in 1866 as a railroad junction (its historic depot, rebuilt in 1906, still sits across from its postcard-perfect Main St). This little town draws hordes of fans in summer for its charming linear downtown rife with restaurants, bars, antique shops and locally owned businesses.

While it's hard to believe it was once promoted as the 'Switzerland of the South,' it *is* easy on the eyes and offers more quality distractions than other North Georgia towns. It's known as Georgia's trout capital, and year-round river and stream fly-fishing in the surrounding countryside is a big draw.

The town is often considered Atlanta's backyard – a hotbed for wealthy Atlantans to lay down roots with a second home in the mountains.

Sights

Mercier Orchards FARM
(☎800-361-7731; www.mercier-orchards.com; 8660 Blue Ridge Dr; ⏲7am-6pm;) The largest apple orchard in the Southeast is a 300-acre fourth-generation family farm that's a kick for the kiddies – especially the tractor tours. 'U-pick' events run on weekends from late April/early May to September, starting with strawberries then blueberries, blackberries, peaches and apples (don't worry, there's hard cider for mom and dad). There's also a cafe.

Activities

Fly-fishing draws serious anglers to Blue Ridge. If you're looking for an outlet to get you out on the water, try Blue Ridge Fly Fishing.

Popular day hikes around Blue Ridge include **Falls Branch Falls**, a 0.5-mile round-trip hike that's part of the Benton MacKaye trail system (www.bmta.org), to a double waterfall, and **Long Creek Falls**, a 2.4-mile round-trip hike on the Appalachian Trail. The 3290-acre, aquamarine **Lake Blue Ridge**,1.5 miles from downtown Blue Ridge, offers kayak and paddleboard rentals at Morganton Point Recreation Area from April through October.

Blue Ridge Fly Fishing FISHING
(☎706-258-4080; www.blueridgeflyfishing.com; 490 E Main St; half-/full-day from $275/375; ⏲8:30am-6pm) Fly-fishing expert Jeff Turner runs half- and full-day fly-fishing outings in Blue Ridge, Ellijay, McCaysville, Suches, Copper Hill and Chattanooga, and float trips on the Toccoa River. Stop by his fly shop smack downtown.

Tours

Blue Ridge Scenic Railway RAIL
(☎877-413-8724; www.brscenic.com; 241 Depot St; adult $44-79, child $29; ⏲mid-Mar–Dec) Starting from the historic 1905 downtown depot at 11am on most days (check the schedule online), this scenic-railway ride takes you along 1886-laid tracks to the quaint sister border towns of McCaysville, Georgia and Copperhill, TN, winding along the bank of the Toccoa River, returning at 3pm.

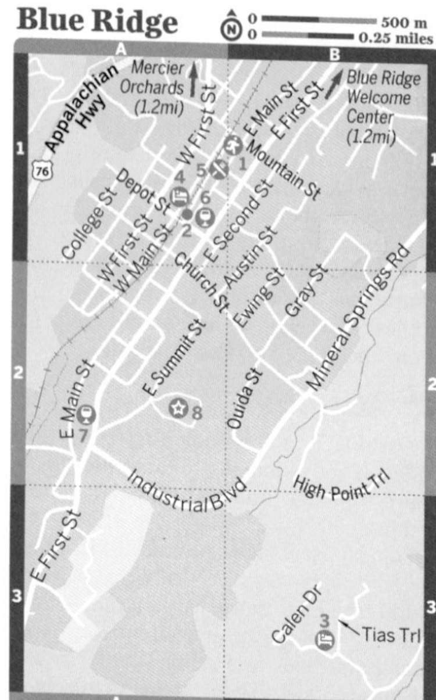

Blue Ridge

Activities, Courses & Tours

1 Blue Ridge Fly Fishing B1
2 Blue Ridge Scenic Railway A1

Sleeping

3 Aska Lodge B3
4 Blue Ridge Inn A1

Eating

5 Harvest on Main A1
Southern Charm .... (see 4)

Drinking & Nightlife

6 Chester Brunnenmeyer's Bar & Grill A1
7 Grumpy Old Men A2

Entertainment

8 Swan Drive In A2

Sleeping

Blue Ridge is home to 1500 mountain homes in addition to B&Bs, motels and chain hotels. While some small and rustic traditional cabins are available, most are luxury mountain homes. To peruse them all in one place, check out www.blueridgemountains.com/wheretostay.html.

Aska Lodge B&B **$$**
(☎706-632-0178; www.askalodge.net; 178 Calen Dr; r $160-180; P❄📶) This idyllic, two-story pinewood lodge is run by a friendly, well-traveled climber couple. The four rooms all feature highly regarded trade-offs – do you choose the wraparound porch with swing or the in-room Jacuzzi? The wooden sliding bathroom doors and other woodwork throughout the house are produced on-site and there's an outstanding front-yard firepit.

Blue Ridge Inn B&B **$$**
(☎706-661-7575; www.blueridgeinnbandb.com; 477 W First St; r $175-240; P📶) Bang downtown is this epic three-story Victorian home dating to the 1890s and awash in 12ft ceilings, original hand-carved woodwork and heart-pine flooring. The town's classy choice, it has impeccable rooms with features such as claw-foot tubs or four-poster beds, antique vanities and hardwood bathroom floors. Think quaint, historic and oh so comfortable.

Eating

If Blue Ridge has anything, it's places to eat. Main St is lined with restaurants – everything from down-home country kitchens to sophisticated New American choices and plenty of highfalutin pub grub in between.

Harvest on Main NEW AMERICAN **$$**
(☎706-946-6164; www.harvestonmain.com; 576 E Main St; mains $18-29; ⏲11am-3pm & 4-8pm Sun, Mon, Wed & Thu, 11am-4pm Tue, 11am-3pm & 4-9pm Fri & Sat; 📶) With more creative flair than most, this rustic-chic eatery in the heart of the action does hearty mains – seared fish with sesame spinach over chickpea stew, smoked bone-in pork chop with apple BBQ sauce, duck two ways – alongside a hefty wine, craft-beer and bourbon list. Tree-limb chairs, a big fireplace and Southern service keep things cozy.

Southern Charm SOUTHERN US **$$**
(☎706-632-9090; www.eatsoutherncharm.com; 224 W Main St; mains $10-17; ⏲11am-8pm Mon-Wed, to 3pm Thu & Sun, to 9pm Fri & Sat; 📶) In a big, bright-yellow house across the railroad tracks from E Main St, this friendly Southern eatery excels at the classics: fried green tomato with a shrimp po'boy, fried chicken, blackened rainbow trout (and don't forget grandma's biscuit chicken pot pie).

Drinking & Entertainment

You'll find at least three breweries and two farm wineries in addition to a whole lot of drinking action along Main St in all the bars and restaurants. Even Mercier Orchards (p139) has hard cider on tap.

★ **Grumpy Old Men** CRAFT BEER
(www.grumpyoldmenbrewing.com; 1315 E Main St; pints $5; 1-5pm Thu & Fri, to 6pm Sun;) With cornhole courts, outdoor picnic seating and a DIY ethos, this excellent hop headquarters is a quintessential Southern-brewing good time. There are 18 taps, which often include small-batch or one-off experimental brews (the Grasshoppa Imperial IPA and Hell's Holler Porter are both great).

The indoor ski and toilet-seat benches make for fun Instagram moments.

Chester Brunnenmeyer's Bar & Grill BAR
(www.chestersblueridge.com; 733 E Main St; 4-11:30pm Mon-Fri, 11:30am-11:30pm Sat, 12:30-11:30pm Sun;) This is one of the town's most popular bars, mainly for its long and social 30-stool bar facing 18 taps of mainly local and regional craft beer.

It also does a mean Bloody Mary that drinks like a meal (pepper vodka, Bloody Mary mix, seasoned-salt rim, cheddar cheese, pickled green beans, drunken tomato, stuffed olives, pickled okra, celery, beef stick).

Swan Drive In THEATER
(706-632-6690; www.swan-drive-in.com; 651 Summit St; films $8) Dating to 1955, this old-school drive-in theater is one of three still operating in Georgia.

Information

Blue Ridge Welcome Center (800-899-6867; www.blueridgemountains.com; 152 Orvin Lance Dr; 8:30am-5pm Mon-Fri, 9am-5pm Sat, 1-5pm Sun) Pick up information on Blue Ridge, Fannin County, the North Georgia Mountains and the Southern Blue Ridge.

Getting There & Away

Just a 90-minute drive north of Atlanta on I-75/I-575, Blue Ridge is probably the most easily accessed of North Georgia's mountain towns.

Blairsville

706, 762 / POP 660

Easygoing Blairsville sits deep in the heart of the Chattahoochee National Forest and North Georgia's Blue Ridge Mountains. The town is home to a slightly unorthodox rounded town 'square' which wraps itself around Blairsville's historic courthouse, dating to 1899. Like similar North Georgia mountain towns, the great outdoors plays big in Blairsville, the closest city to Brasstown Bald, Georgia's highest mountain and its biggest draw. Blairsville is also close to Vogel State Park, Blood Mountain and a plethora of waterfalls, lakes, hiking and biking trails. While nearby Dahlonega was considered the first-known gold site in the USA, Blairsville's nuggets were said to be the purest of them all.

Sights

Vogel State Park STATE PARK
(706-745-2628; www.gastateparks.org/vogel; 405 Vogel State Park Rd; per vehicle $5; 7am-10pm; P) Located at the base of the evocatively named Blood Mountain, this is one of Georgia's oldest parks, and constitutes a quilt of wooded mountains surrounding a 22-acre lake. There's a multitude of trails to pick from, catering to beginners and advanced hikers. Many of the on-site facilities were built by the Civilian Conservation Corp; a seasonal museum tells the story of these work teams, who both built the park and rescued the local economy during the Great Depression.

Helton Creek Falls WATERFALL
(www.fs.usda.gov; Hwy 129 S) FREE On a good day, this double waterfall barrels out of the woods over a rocky outcrop, tumbling 100ft into a moss creek valley below. But on a rainy day, it rages spectacularly, so much that it actually feels both thrilling and suspiciously dangerous. Either way, if you're visiting during a nasty spell, don some rain gear and head straight for it. Don't get too close! It's a 0.3-mile trail from the parking area. To reach here from Blairsville, ignore the GPS: take Hwy 19/129 S 11 miles and turn left on Helton Creek Rd on the left-hand side just past the entrance to Vogel State Park. Go 2.2 miles to a small pullout parking area. The trailhead is on your right.

Brasstown Bald MOUNTAIN
(https://cfaia.org/brasstown-bald-recreation-area-visitor-centers-in-georgia; 2941 GA-180 Spur, Hiawassee; adult/child incl shuttle $5/3; ⏲10am-5pm May-Nov, as weather allows Dec-Apr) Some-what of a pilgrimage for born and bred Georgians, Brasstown Bald is Georgia's highest point, rising 4784ft above sea level. On a clear day, you can see four states: Georgia, North Carolina, Tennessee and South Carolina. There is a trail to the top (and a shuttle service during working hours). Outside the season/hours, you can still access the top parking lot and foot trail to the observatory, but the museum and facilities will be closed.

Museum of Mountain Life MUSEUM
(www.unioncountyhistory.org; 25 Veterans Memorial Dr; ⏲11am-4pm Thu-Sat) FREE This small museum is divided among several structures: a less interesting 1906 Grapelle Butt Mock House, a restored 1900s family home with original heirlooms, and the far more intriguing 1806 John Payne Cabin, a half-dovetail notch cabin that depicts the home of a Confederate soldier just before the Civil War. There's nothing distinctly riveting here, but it's free and worth a pop in. It's part of the Union County Historical Society.

Grandaddy Mimm's DISTILLERY
(www.mimmsmoonshine.com; 161 Pappy's Plaza; tours & tasting $5; ⏲11am-6pm Mon-Sat) This good-time distillery churns out a moonshine for all desires: 40-, 93-, 100- and 140-proof liquid served from a bar that was one of the original four used to film *Coyote Ugly*. Check the schedule for weekend concerts (inside in winter, outside in summer) – that's when the place really gets going.

HIKER'S HAVEN

Top of Georgia Hostel & Hiking Center (☎706-982-3252; www.topofgeorgiahostel.com; 7675 Rose Haven, Hiawassee; dm/cabins $30/70; 📶), an economical hiker hostel, is one of North Georgia's few. Stays are one night only unless 'slackpacking' is arranged in advance. It's just a half mile west of the Appalachian Trail at Dicks Creek Gap, so is an ideal stopover or spot for laundry ($5) or just a shower ($10). Shuttles from Unicoi Gap and Dicks Creek Gap are available as well. Hiawassee is about 15 miles northeast of Blairsville and about 20 miles north of Helen.

Sleeping

In Blairsville proper, there aren't any places to sleep beyond a few chain hotels and motels. In the surrounding countryside, you'll find more charming options, including cabins, camping and other outdoorsy-geared options.

Mountain Crossings at Walasi-Yi HOSTEL $
(☎706-745-6095; www.mountaincrossings.com; 9710 Gainesville Hwy; per person per night $20; ⏲store 9am-5pm) This hostel is the one and only human-made intrusion on the Appalachian Trail. Parched and sore hikers will be happy it isn't a mirage, as they follow the AT directly through the store, which has served as an outfitter to hikers since it was completed by the New Deal's Civilian Conservation Corps in 1937.

There is a 14-bed bunkhouse for those who'd like to do the first part of the trail and then hike (or hitchhike) back to Springer Mountain. If you're a through-hiker and already blown through gear or forgot something vital, they'll have it here.

Paradise Hills, Winery Resort & Spa CABINS $
(☎877-745-7483; www.paradisehillsga.com; 366 Paradise Rd; 1-/2-3-bedroom cabins from $119/169/179; P 📶) These roomy, well-to-do forest-green cabins feature full kitchenettes (albeit with dated appliances), whirlpool bathtubs, fireplaces and expansive front porches with wooded views. Wi-fi is lodge-only, where you'll also find the on-site winery's tasting room and friendly staff. No breakfast. It's about 4 miles from downtown Blairsville.

Seasons Inn MOTEL $
(☎706-745-1631; www.seasons-inn.com; 94 Town Sq; r $60-85; P ❄ 📶 🐾) This mom-and-pop operation is unremarkable beyond a typical roadside motor inn at first sight, but attentive owners have spruced it up beyond typical offerings, with Amish rocking chairs, fresh new carpet, hiker and pet-friendly ($10 extra) services and a devout commitment to cleanliness. With a position on the square, it's the best budget bang for the buck.

Eating

Nearly everything of note in Blairsville is on the rounded town square, where you'll find Southern dining, Italian, great burgers and the oldest diner in Union County. Chains abound elsewhere around town, broken up by the occasional Mexican joint.

★ **Sawmill Place** BREAKFAST $

(☎706-745-1250; www.thesawmillplace.com; 1150 Pat Haralson Dr; breakfast $2-9.30; ⏲6:30am-2pm Mon-Fri, to 11:30am Sat) This farm-to-table cabin eatery does high-quality, creative breakfast scrambles, sandwiches, biscuits and pancakes that will sooth a breakfast-lover's soul – with sweet, country-style service to boot. The Notterly Scramble (spicy collard greens, onions, bacon and cheddar cheese scrambled into three large farm-fresh eggs) and sweet-potato pancakes are top choices. Rock it off on that big front porch!

Hole in the Wall DINER $

(www.holeinthewallga.com; 12b Town Sq; breakfast $3-11; ⏲7am-2:30pm Mon & Tue, to 8:30pm Wed-Sat, 7:30am-2:30pm Sun; 📶) This historic greasy spoon has been at it since the Great Depression. Eggs, hash browns, pancakes and French toast stuffed with cheesecake pudding (what?) provide the morning pick-me-up for nearly everyone in town. Pay attention to the walls – they're full of historic anecdotes and hilarious Southern euphemisms. Cash only.

Michaelee's Italian Life Cafe ITALIAN $$$

(☎706-400-5603; www.italianlifecaffe.com; 6c Town Sq; mains $13-44; ⏲11am-8pm Mon-Thu, to 9pm Fri & Sat; 📶) This BYOB (nice wine shop next door) town-square mainstay is everything that's wrong *and* right with Italian-American restaurants. Michelangelo would be turning over in his grave, but this fusion mix of totally unorthodox Italian recipes (blackened shrimp and scallop carbonara with Sicilian cream sauce? Linguini Bolognese? White-chocolate shrimp with chocolate balsamic?) might shock Italians, but it's damn tasty.

Drinking & Nightlife

Blairsville goes to bed early. On the lovely town square, there's a swanky wine shop. There's little else – Union Country is dry on Sundays.

Cabin Coffee COFFEE

(www.cabincoffeecompany.com; 44a Town Sq; coffee $1.80-5.20; ⏲7am-4:40pm Mon-Fri, 8am-4pm Sat; 📶) This Iowa-based coffee chain is a caffeine godsend in Blairsville, serving up a long list of single-origin coffees from Latin America, Africa and Indonesia, along with blended drinks and healthier-than-average (for these parts) biscuits, bagels and sandwiches ($2.75 to $7). Western-themed, saddled seating and northern white cedar armchairs and couches are mighty cozy.

> **OFF THE BEATEN TRACK**
>
> **STOP FOR SOUL FOOD**
>
> Pork, ribs and chicken are served in a log cabin with a chimney pumping out smoky essence of pit BBQ. In addition to BBQ, the **Pink Pig** (www.budspinkpig.com; 824 Cherry Log St, Cherry Log; mains $7.50-15.50; ⏲11am-9pm Thu-Sun) does soul food such as chicken and dumplings, chicken livers, cured ham and fried green tomatoes. Jimmy Carter is known to be a fan. Cherry Log is about 8 miles southeast of Blairsville.

ℹ Information

Blairsville Welcome Center (☎706-745-5789; www.visitblairsvillega.com; 129 Union County Recreation Rd; ⏲9am-5pm Mon-Fri, 10am-1pm Sat Memorial Day-Oct)

Brasstown Bald Visitor's Center (☎706-896-2556; https://cfaia.org/brasstown-bald-recreation-area-visitor-centers-in-georgia; 2941 GA-180 Spur, Hiawassee; ⏲10am-5pm)

Vogel State Park Visitor's Center (☎706-745-2628; www.gastateparks.org/vogel; 405 Vogel State Park Rd; ⏲8am-5pm Dec-May, to 6pm Sun-Thu, to 8pm Fri & Sat Jun-Nov) Park info, trail maps, firewood, camping provisions and bike rentals (per day $20) are available from the park's visitor center.

ℹ Getting There & Away

Blairsville is nearly a straight shot 97 miles north of Atlanta near the Tennessee and North Carolina borders along State Rd 19. There is no Greyhound station or public transportation, so having your own wheels is essential.

Helen

☎706, 762 / POP 510

Awash in lederhosen and *fahrvergnügen* (driving pleasure) and lots of other questionable German cliches, gingerbread-trimmed Helen is a little bit of Bavaria in Appalachia (call it 'Alppalachia', if you will). It is certainly a startling, out-of-place sight. In the grand tradition of other touristy German villages like Colonia Tovar (Venezuela) and Gramado (Brazil), here scores of North Georgians and Atlanta day-trippers (some 1.5 million per year) run amok among German-style architecture fueled by steins of Dunkelweizens, Doppelbocks and Pils like it's Oktoberfest year-round. This kitschy, Epcot-style Alpine playground was dreamed up in the 1960s by a few local businesspeople wanting to revitalize the town. In 1969 local businesses and carpenters got to work – with help from a local artist with German roots – transforming this former mill town into the self-proclaimed best little German town in America.

Sights

Helen's main sight is downtown itself, a small and tiny Bavarian-style village full of confectionery shops; pottery, jewelry, woodworking and leather boutiques; old-time photo studios; and restaurants and pubs. Just outside town, a bevy of interesting and beautiful historic and natural sights abound.

★ Anna Ruby Falls WATERFALL
(☎706-878-1448; https://cfaia.org; 3455 Anna Ruby Falls Rd; adult/child $3/free; ⏲9am-5pm Nov-Mar, to 6pm Apr-May, to 7pm Jun-Oct, gate closes 1hr before; 👪) Not to be confused with Tennessee's far more famous Ruby Falls, Georgia's Anna Ruby Falls is tucked away in Unicoi State Park (part of the Chattahoochee-Oconee National Forest) 5.7 miles north of downtown Helen. Here twin waterfalls spawned by dueling creeks – Curtis Creek and York Creek – drop 153ft and 50ft, respectively. The falls are reached by a gorgeous 0.4-mile paved hiking trail (read: kid and stroller friendly, though uphill) from the visitor center.

The falls and the state park have separate entry fees – if you are only visiting the falls, you can drive through the park for free. The recreation area includes picnic facilities.

Unicoi State Park STATE PARK
(☎706-878-2201; www.gastateparks.org/unicoi; 1788 Hwy 356; per vehicle $5; ⏲7am-10pm; P 👪) At this adventure-oriented park, visitors can rent kayaks ($10 per hour), take paddleboard lessons ($25), hike some 12 miles of trails, mountain bike, or take a zipline safari through the local forest canopy ($59).

Habersham Vineyards & Winery WINERY
(☎706-878-9463; www.habershamwinery.com; 7025 S Main St; tastings $7.50; ⏲10am-6pm Mon-Sat, 12:30-6pm Sun) One of Georgia's pioneering wineries dating all the way back to 1983. Winemaker Andrew Beaty is University of California, Davis– and California-trained and his juice often wins awards. Seek out its Creekstone label, which produces a Viognier, chardonnay, cabernet sauvignon and merlot, among others. Of course, there's a gewürztraminer in the house!

Hardman Farm FARM
(http://gastateparks.org/hardmanfarm; 143 Hwy 17, Sautee Nacoochee; adult/child $12/7; ⏲10am-4pm Thu-Sun Mar-Dec) This 1870 Italianate farmhouse set on 173 acres, 2 miles southeast of downtown Helen, is Georgia's newest state historic site. The nearby gazebo-topped Nacoochee Mound and cow pasture hearkens to Cherokee roots. Tours take in the 19th-century parlor with original lighting (check the fascinating telephone and climate-control system), the bedroom of Anna Ruby Nichols (for whom nearby Anna Ruby Falls was named) and the withered dairy barn (there are 19 outbuildings in all).

Activities

Besides eating, drinking and shopping, the number-one activity in Helen – in summer, anyway – is undoubtedly river tubing on the Chattahoochee River, which winds through the village.

Cool River Tubing Co TUBING
(☎706-878-2665; www.coolrivertubing.com; 590 Edelweiss Strasse; tubing per trip/day $8/12; ⏲9am-6pm) One of two outfitters in Helen that can set you up with 'shootin' the Hooch' – river tubing on the Chattahoochee River. It makes for a damn fine afternoon floating down the river with fellow travelers on a 1½- or 2½-hour trip (alcohol is prohibited but that doesn't mean people aren't buzzed). Cool Tubing also has a booth on Main St.

Festivals & Events

Oktoberfest CULTURAL
(☎706-878-1619; www.helenchamber.com; 1074 Edelweiss Strasse, Helen Festhalle; week/weekend $8/10; ⏲Sep-Oct) Helen goes all out for its annual celebration of German music, food, drinks and dancing (waltzes, polkas, chicken dances), but the dog-friendly *biergarten* is where you want be – nearly 30 breweries pour their wares. The festival starts on weekends in September, switching to a daily party from September 27 to October 28.

Sleeping

As one of North Georgia's most touristy locales, Helen suits all types of lodgings and budgets. Chain motels, B&Bs, cabins, riverside lodges and cottages and German-themed inns are in abundance. Prices increase significantly during Oktoberfest and during fall foliage.

Unicoi State Park & Lodge LODGE **$**
(☎800-573-9659; www.unicoilodge.com; 1788 Hwy 356 Rd; camping/r/cabins from $15/124/159) Two miles north of the Alpine village, this state-run adventure lodge has something for everyone: 100 cozy rooms, 30 one-, two- and three-bedroom cabins with full kitchen and wood-burning fireplace (our favorite), 82 campsites and 51 RV sites with water, electricity and dump stations. There's a restaurant and tavern on-site and outdoor adventures (paddleboarding, mountain biking etc) from your doorstep. There's a $10 lodging fee which includes park access.

Nacoochee Adventures TREEHOUSE, CAMPGROUND **$**
(☎706-878-9477; www.nacoocheeadventures.com; 7019 S Main St; camping $49) Whether you opt for a treehouse forged from recycled materials, a pioneer-style covered wagon or a gypsy vardo, this primitive campground (no water or electricity) is one of Helen's most unique sleeps. Most options are located a half-mile hike into the woods from the office (golf-cart/utility vehicles are available for rent). There is a $95 refundable deposit. You'll need supplies – this is structure and mattress only.

Alpine Hilltop Haus B&B **$**
(☎706-878-2388; www.alpinehilltop.com; 362 Chattahoochee Strasse; r from $120; P ❄ ☎) Barbara and Frankie are the charming hosts of this B&B tucked away in the woods just behind town, but still close enough to walk. Rooms, in an Alpine-inspired annex, vary from a bit froufrou to more modern and luxurious. There's a fantastic wooden back patio with town views – perfect for morning coffee or a glass of wine.

Eating

Helen has carved itself an Alpine niche and the gastronomy on offer here is no exception: hearty German restaurants dominate the culinary landscape. If that's not your thing – or you're all wursted out – there is a handful of gastropubs, BBQ spots and a smattering of ethnic eats (Thai, Mexican etc).

Bodensee GERMAN
(☎706-878-1026; www.bodenseerestaurant.com; 64 Munich Strasse; mains $16-20; ⏱11am-9pm Sun-Thu, to 10pm Fri & Sat; ☎) Widely considered the best of Helen's German restaurants, Bodensee even boasts a Romanian-trained chef with considerable Bavarian experience. Pork specialties feature aplenty: *hauspfannle* (pork tenderloin with bacon and mushroom-cream sauce, *rouberspiess* (pork loin with paprika, onion and spicy 'Gypsy' sauce) and, of course, schnitzel. But there are beef (*sauerbraten* with potato dumplings and red cabbage, Hungarian goulash) and veggie choices as well. Get your German on!

Mully's Nacoochee Grill AMERICAN **$$**
(☎706-878-1020; www.mullysnacoocheegrill.com; 7277 S Main St; mains $14-34; ⏱4:30-8:30pm Tue, to 9pm Wed & Thu, 11:30am-2:30pm & 4:30-9pm Fri & Sat, 11:30am-2:30pm & 4:30-8pm Sun; ☎) Occupying a relocated rural farmhouse, Helen's foodie find serves a classic menu of globally influenced dishes stereotypically considered fine dining before the New American culinary movement (wedge salads, chicken masala, grilled rib eyes) but ups the ante with slightly more chef-driven, Southern-angled dishes like peppercorn-crusted pork tenderloin with brandy-cream sauce, and shrimp sautéed with red onions, poblano and red peppers and served with grits.

It's 1.4 miles southeast of the Alpine village. If you are around for Wednesday, Friday, Saturday or Sunday brunch, former Bon Jovi touring guitarist Kent Johnston provides the soundtrack.

Drinking & Nightlife

As you might guess, big steins of German beer and popular German beer brands like Paulaner, Erdinger, Weihenstephan, Schneider Weisse and Spaten Oktoberfest are big business in Helen. The most atmospheric *biergarten* is probably the one at pretty White Horse Sq.

Information

Anna Ruby Falls Welcome Center (☎706-878-1448; https://cfaia.org; 3455 Anna Ruby Falls Rd; ⏱9am-4:30pm Nov-Mar, to 5:30pm Apr-May, to 6:30pm Jun-Oct) In addition to gifts and falls information, check here about May and June nighttime walks to see the rare *Orfelia fultoni* (known locally as foxfire), a bioluminescent species of fly whose larvae glows spectacularly at night.

Helen Welcome Center (☎800-858-8027; www.helenga.org; 726 Bruckenstrasse; ⏲9am-5pm Mon-Sat, 10am-4pm Sun) The Alpine Helen/White County Convention & Visitors Bureau runs the town welcome center. Pick up brochures on restaurants, activities and accommodations as well as tourist info for the area.

Getting There & Around

Helen is tucked away in the North Georgia mountains 86 miles northeast of Atlanta and most easily reached by car via Hwy 19 S.

City parking lots charge $2 (private lots run $5)

Clayton

☎706, 762 / POP 2270

One of North Georgia's most charming depots, Clayton is on the rise. Founded as Claytonsville by European-American settlers in 1821, today the small town has become somewhat of a Blue Ridge Mountain refuge for outdoor-enthusiast escapees from Atlanta, Athens and beyond. Its adorable downtown and main street are lined with independent businesses and fun restaurants. Clayton's location, surrounded by Rabun County's 20 or so publicly accessible waterfalls and several state parks, makes it a magnet for outdoor distractions. Tallulah Gorge State Park, just 11 miles south, and Georgia's highest state park, Black Rock Mountain State Park (5 miles north), are the big draws in the immediate area.

Sights

Black Rock Mountain State Park STATE PARK

(☎706-746-2141; www.gastateparks.org/blackrockmountain; per vehicle $5; ⏲7am-10pm Mar 16-Dec 16) Reaching altitudes of 3640ft, Georgia's highest state park is 5 miles north of Clayton. At that height, its obvious draws are the vistas. Like Brasstown Bald (Georgia's highest point), you can see four states from the park's various lookouts on a clear day. There are 11 miles of trails spread over four routes as well as a campground and primitive backcountry camping sites. A picnic from its summit visitor center is the way to go.

Foxfire Museum & Heritage Center CULTURAL CENTER

(www.foxfire.org; 98 Foxfire Lane; adult $8, child 7-10/under 6 $3/free; ⏲8:30am-4:30pm Mon-Sat) Fancy living off the grid? Since 1966, this important, hands-on experiential museum telling the story of Appalachian Culture has been solely focused on lost-art-type, back-to-basics Appalachian living skills that have been passed down for generations. There are 10 authentic pioneer log cabins along with artifacts, tools and handcrafted housewares, toys and folk art. It's located on Black Rock Mountain in Mountain City 3.4 miles north of Clayton.

Sleeping

Clayton proper is home to two B&Bs, with another four in Rabun County. The usual chain hotels are here and camping resorts and campgrounds are within 10 to 15 minutes of downtown. Generally speaking, Clayton has some of the top B&Bs in North Georgia.

York House Inn B&B $

(☎706-746-2068; www.yorkhouseinn.com; 416 York House Rd, Rabun Gap; r $105-190; 📶) Opened in 1896, this is Georgia's oldest B&B and sits on the the National Register of Historic Places. Inviting, rocking-chair-peppered porches lead to 14 spacious rooms with amenities such as Ralph Lauren bedding and original heart-pine floors. Breakfast is serious business: how does baked shaved-ham cups with spinach Parmesan filling, topped with fresh eggs and heavy cream sound? It's 4.8 miles north of Clayton in Rabun Gap.

White Birch Inn B&B $$

(☎706-782-4444; www.thewhitebirchinn.net; 28 E Savannah St; r week/weekend night from $215/222; P❄📶) Owned and designed by an architect/interior-designer power couple, this cozy inn is a real stunner, especially where woodwork is concerned. A tree-bark wall forms the backdrop of the fireplace-warmed lounge under tree-limb-wrapped rust-orange lighting. Each of the six rooms is different, but highlights include a copper sink-in bathtub, a tree-branch bed frame and a gorgeous custom wooden vanity.

Eating

Clayton is one of the best small towns in North Georgia for a meal. Along the main drag, there are a couple of fantastic choices, ranging from higher-end New Southern farm-to-table offerings to scrumptious burgers and highbrow pub grub. Further afield you'll find a wide array of choices, including BBQ, Mexican and Italian.

Universal Joint BURGERS $

(www.ujclayton.com; 109 N Main St; burgers $9.50-11.50; ⏲11:30am-10pm Sun-Thu, to midnight Fri & Sat; 📶) Laidback 'Ujoint' is a local favorite – best outdoor patio in town, 17 taps of local and regional craft beers and perfectly charred burgers adorned in righteously Southern ways. Try the Steinbeck (half pound of Angus beef, housemade pimento cheese, bacon, lettuce, onions, tomato, pickled jalapeño and a pickle). Add a bevy of sassy bartenders and you have yourself an afternoon.

Fortify Kitchen & Bar NEW AMERICAN $$$

(☎706-782-0050; www.fortifyclayton.com; 69 N Main St; mains $22-35; ⏲Tue-Sat; 📶) Clayton's best night out is this stylish farm-to-table supper club from chef Jamie Allred, North Georgia's top kitchen dog. Some of the Southeast's best purveyors form the foundation for incredible fried green tomatoes with blackened Gulf shrimp or cornmeal-crusted Carolina mountain trout with dill pesto. Serious cocktails ($10) and desserts (pecan tart with blood-orange caramel) bookend an evening here. If you're looking for something more casual, it does gourmet pizza ($12 to $22) next door at Fortify Pi. Dinner reservations essential.

Drinking & Nightlife

Clayton's charming downtown has a trifecta of great spots for a drink, all within a few feet of each other. On the higher end, the intimate bar at Fortify Kitchen & Bar is perfect for serious farm-to-cocktail-type mixology. You'll find 17 taps at Universal Joint.

White Birch Provisions CAFE

(www.whitebirchprovisions.com; 60 E Savannah St; coffee $1.50-5; ⏲7:30am-5pm Mon, Tue, Thu & Fri, to 2pm Wed, 8am-2pm Sat; 📶) This adorable cafe and gourmet shop serves Clayton's best espresso, and it's a cute and quaint hang space as well. In addition to coffee, you'll find local provisions from around the Southeast, a bakery and a wine cave, all surrounded by local art.

Shopping

★ **Wander North Georgia** CLOTHING

(www.wandernorthgeorgia.com; 33 N Main St; ⏲11am-5pm Mon-Thu, to 6pm Fri & Sat, noon-5pm Sun) What started as an outdoorsy mountain blog and Instagram page has turned into one of Georgia's coolest start-ups. The fantastic T-shirts are the main attraction (it's co-owned by a graphic designer), plus the trucker hats, but there are all kinds of meticulously curated woodsmen-type gear here (candles, books like *Cabin Porn* and *Van Life*, beard balm).

Information

Rabun County Welcome Center (☎706-782-4812; www.explorerabun.com; 232 Hwy 441 N; ⏲8am-5pm Sun-Thu, to noon Fri) Maps, lodging info, brochures on Rabun County.

Getting There & Away

Clayton sits in Georgia's northeast corner, 108 miles northeast of Atlanta and not that far from the Tennessee, North Carolina and South Carolina borders. It's accessed via Hwy 23 N from I-85 and best reached by car.

Tallulah Gorge State Park

This 2739-acre state park is home to a spectacular gorge nearly 1000ft deep and 2 miles long. It protects six endangered plant species, including the persistent trillium (there are at least 22 species in Georgia) and harbors six waterfalls collectively known as the Tallulah Falls. In the mid-19th century, Tallulah Gorge became a resort area for coastal residents on the run from yellow fever. The introduction of the railroad in 1882 increased access and ushered in the 'Grand Era' of hotels on the rim of the gorge. The damming of the river in the early 1900s to create electricity for Atlanta reduced the flow by 90% or more and killed off a devastating chunk of tourism. Today, it's one of North Georgia's most popular destinations for outdoor adventure, including hiking, biking and climbing. Scenes from 1972's *Deliverance* were filmed here.

Sights

Tallulah Gorge GORGE

(☎706-754-7981; www.gastateparks.org/tallulahgorge; 338 Jane Hurt Yarn Dr, Tallulah Falls; per vehicle $5; ⏲8am-sunset; P) 🍃 The 1000ft-deep Tallulah Gorge carves a dark scar across the wooded hills of North Georgia. Walk over the *Indiana Jones*–worthy suspension bridge, and be on the lookout (literally) for rim trails to overlooks (see p128). Or get a first-come, first-served permit to hike to the gorge floor – only 100 are given out each day (arrive early, they're usually gone in the morning) and not offered on water-release dates (check schedule online).

Activities

There are some 20 miles of hiking trails in this gorgeous park, including short, easy walks on the rim of the gorge, passing five waterfalls along the way. In addition to the north- and south-rim trails, the 2-mile **Hurricane Falls Trail** is a moderate, family-friendly hike that will get you deep into the canyon (via 310 steps) to the suspension bridge (from which three waterfalls can be seen), as well as to the base of Hurricane Falls (via a second set of 221 stairs). To go deeper, you'll require a free gorge-floor permit, limited to 100 per day.

Sleeping

Terrora Campground CAMPING

(706-754-7979; www.gastateparks.org/tallulahgorge; 300 Jane Hurt Yarn Dr; campsites from $32) Tallulah Gorge's one full-service campground contains 50 sites with electricity and water along with two comfort stations. It sits about about a mile from the Jane Hurt Yarn Interpretive Center.

Information

Jane Hurt Yarn Interpretive Center (706-754-7981; www.gastateparks.org/tallulahgorge; 338 Jane Hurt Yarn Dr; 8am-5pm) One of the better state-park welcome centers you'll come across, this one hosts exhibits on the park, and the people and cultures of the region, and has a small gift and snack shop. Stop here for gorge-floor permits. A 15-minute film, *Tallulah Gorge*, is screened every 30 minutes from 8am to 4pm.

Getting There & Away

Tallulah Gorge State Park sits off Hwy 441, about 97 miles northeast of Atlanta and 65 miles north of Athens. The closest you can get without your own wheels is the **Amtrak** (800-872-7245; www.amtrak.com/stations/tca.html; 47 N Alexander St) station in Toccoa, 18 miles south.

Toccoa

706, 762 / POP 8500

Founded shortly after the Civil War, tiny Toccoa – believed to mean 'beautiful' in a Native American dialect – is a small-time North Georgia town with big-time history and hospitality. It's perhaps most famous as the site of WWII's Camp Toccoa at Currahee, the inaugural US Army paratrooper training camp and the inspiration for Tom Hanks' and Steven Spielberg's Emmy- and Golden Globe-winning war-drama miniseries, *Band of Brothers*. The paratroopers' intense training regime involved a daily '3 miles up, 3 miles down' to the top of Currahee Mountain just outside town, which affords a panoramic North Georgia view for those who climb it. Toccoa's historic downtown boasts an epic restored art deco theater and emblematic low-rise late 19th-century architecture along its main drag, Doyle St. Toccoa Falls, one of the tallest free-falling waterfalls east of the Mississippi River, wows travelers on the campus of Toccoa Falls College. Toccoa is a pleasant surprise.

Sights

★ **Toccoa Falls** WATERFALL

(www.cityoftoccoa.com/toccoa-falls.cfm; 77 Azalea Ct, Toccoa Falls College; adult/child $2/free; sunrise-5pm Jan–mid-Feb, to sunset mid-Feb–mid-Dec) This dramatic 186ft-high waterfall, reached along a 500ft path from the visitor center on the campus of Tocca Falls College, is one of the tallest free-falling waterfalls east of the Mississippi River (it's taller than Niagara – a paltry 167ft). It's a definite wow moment as the falls come into view. But this beauty does not come without tragedy: a dam above the falls failed in 1977 – the resulting flood killed 39 people, Georgia's worst natural disaster in more than 40 years.

Though there is a nominal fee to access the falls, they are free outside visitor-center opening hours (the gate should be open).

Currahee Military Museum MUSEUM

(www.toccoahistory.com; 160 N Alexander St; adult/child $10/free; 10am-4pm Mon-Sat, 1-4pm Sun) Toccoa's pride and joy is this 14,000-sq-ft museum dedicated to the inaugural US Army paratrooper training camp, located here during WWII, and the four Parachute Infantry Regiments who trained here, and went on to be the first American boots on the ground during the Invasion of Normandy. Visitors come from far and wide thanks to *Band of Brothers*, inspired by Camp Toccoa.

The museum not only houses the original 70ft-long Aldbourne stables (disassembled in the UK and reassembled in Toccoa in 2005) and all manner of Camp Toccoa military paraphernalia, but includes a small city museum which reveals a loaded list of surprising Toccoa-related history: soul singer James Brown was sent to juvenile detention near Toccoa, where he joined his first R&B group, the Famous Flames; 1956 Olympic weightlifting gold-medalist Paul Anderson – who still owns a Guinness World Record for the greatest weight ever raised by a human being (6270lb) – hails from here. There is also a small exhibit hall dedicated to local veterans and other wars.

Currahee Vineyard & Winery WINERY

(☎706-768-5383; www.curraheevineyards.com; 3301 W Currahee St; tastings $4-10; ⊙noon-6pm Thu, Fri & Sun, 11am-6pm Sat) This small, family-owned and -operated winery does brisk business in the region for its sweet fruit and muscadine wines. While they aren't likely to be fawned over by Robert Parker anytime soon, the Georgia Sunrise peach wine and the Georgia Ole Blue (with blueberries, pomegranate and muscadine) are surprisingly tasty and refreshing, and the 18% alcohol Currahee Apple is a real heart-warmer.

There's often live music on weekends with wine slushies. A BBQ pit-master is brought in on holiday weekends and for other special events throughout the year. Tastings are free with a bottle purchase.

Traveler's Rest State Historic Site HISTORIC SITE

(www.gastateparks.org/travelersrest; 4339 Riverdale Rd; adult/child $5/1; ⊙9am-5pm Sat & Sun) The only surviving traveler's rest along the Unicoi Turnpike (a once-busy thoroughfare over the Appalachian Mountains), this stagecoach inn and plantation was built in 1805. it is extremely well preserved, and you can just imagine exhausted travelers doing everything from tying up their road-weary horses for the night to having gunfights over the last swig of moonshine by the fireplace à la Quentin Tarantino's *Hateful Eight*. The inn includes numerous original artifacts and furnishings, many crafted by renowned Massachusetts cabinet-maker Caleb Shaw.

Activities

Veterans, military enthusiasts and many others consider the hike up **Currahee Mountain** – made famous by the rallying cry of the WWII Parachute Infantry Regiments ('3 miles up, 3 miles down') – to be a pilgrimage. If you're short on time, you can drive to the top as well. Either way, expansive North Georgia views are on offer at the top.

Paddling along the **Tugaloo Corridor** on the Tugaloo River is also popular.

Festivals & Events

Currahee Military Weekend CULTURAL

(www.visittoccoa.com; ⊙Oct) In addition to a celebration of honorary veterans, Toccoa's biggest party is this military-themed weekend, when the town goes all out with BBQs, swing dances, a veterans parade, memorabilia show and, most hard-core of all, the Currahee Challenge Run, a 5km and 10km run from the base of Currahee Mountain on the Colonel Robert Sink Trail to the top.

Sleeping

Toccoa doesn't offer a lot of beds. There is the wonderful and historic Simmons-Bond Inn, right off the main square, and two uneventful chain hotels.

Simmons-Bond Inn B&B $

(☎706-282-5183; www.simmons-bond.com; 74 W Tugalo St; r week night $99-129, weekend night $129-149; P 📶) This historic two-story, 1903 mansion is rife with interesting and quirky details, such a built-in china cabinet that once served as a pie safe, a hidden bathroom in the Colleen room (which is also home to famed journalist Nellie Bly's original oak traveling-writing desk), and late 18th-century heirlooms, ornate woodwork and leaded glass throughout.

The blue-toned Tiffany room (with color-coordinated claw-foot bathtub) is our favorite of the five rooms, but it's hard to go wrong surrounded by this much history.

Eating

Casual dining is the apex of restaurant choices in Toccoa. The best options are along historic Doyle St, the main downtown drag. Throughout Toccoa, think bar-and-grill-type pub grub and Southern comfort food – burgers, shrimp and grits, catfish plates – and BBQ, mostly.

X-Factor Grill AMERICAN $

(www.xfactorgrill.com; 27 E Doyle St; mains $6-14; ⊙11am-5pm Mon-Wed, to 9pm Thu-Sat, to 2:30pm Sun;) On historic Doyle St, X-Factor Grill is Toccoa's mainstay bar and grill. It's nothing fancy but it does a decent job with American staples – pecan trout, fish tacos, burgers, catfish, Rueben sandwiches, fettuccine Alfredo – and craft beer (four taps plus a good few dozen in bottles). You even get a fluffy biscuit served before your meal.

Ping's Grill AMERICAN **$**
(www.facebook.com/pingsgrill; 201 Black Mountain Rd; mains $6.50-10; 11:30am-8pm Tue-Sat, to 4pm Sun;) In a pretty setting on Lake Toccoa, this casual, clubhouse-style restaurant dishes up good burgers, sandwiches and chicken wings over creaky hardwood floors and a roaring fireplace. In summer sit outside on the lakeside patio. It's a convenient option combined with Toccoa Falls (p148) – just 2.5 miles away.

Drinking & Nightlife

The only real bar in town is at X-Factor Grill (p149), which also happens to be the best restaurant in town. So, it's a short pub crawl. The county's only winery, Currahee Vineyard & Winery (p149), is a fun place for a tasting with occasional live music.

Shopping

All Things Currahee ARTS & CRAFTS
(www.facebook.com/allthingscurrahee; 46 Doyle St; 10am-6pm Mon-Fri, to 4pm Sat) Pop into this charming main-street shop for locally forged arts, crafts and gifts – nearly everything comes from within 100 miles of Toccoa. A few of our favorite things include ceramics, soaps and cosmetics, hand-turned pens and artisanal knives.

Information

Toccoa-Stephens County Welcome Center
(706-886-2132; www.visittoccoa.com; 160 N Alexander St; 8:30am-5pm Mon-Fri, 10am-4pm Sat) Run by the Toccoa-Stephens County chamber of commerce. Pop in for info and excellent Southern hospitality.

Getting There & Away

Toccoa is 94 miles southeast of Atlanta and 50 miles north of Athens and reached via the recently expanded Hwy 17 – also known as the Currahee Pkwy.

The town is one of three Georgia stops on the Crescent City Amtrak (p148) line from New York to New Orleans.

Augusta & South Georgia

Includes ➡

Best Places to Eat

➡ Fresh Air (p165)

➡ Vandy's (p165)

➡ Nic & Norman's (p164)

➡ Frog Hollow Tavern (p158)

➡ Bee's Knees (p157)

Best Places to Stay

➡ Florence Marina State Park (p162)

➡ Rothschild Pound House Inn (p162)

➡ Veranda Historic Bed & Breakfast Inn (p164)

➡ Days Inn & Suites Peachtree City (p163)

Why Go?

Driving through South Georgia's expansive wide-open pastures, cotton fields and fruit farms is a chance to see the 'Peach State' in all its glory. Surprisingly, South Georgia actually produces more blueberries and peanuts than it does peaches, and there's plenty of opportunity to experience local produce grown in these fertile parts. Come for the region's simple, warm country-style hospitality, excellent barbecue and a number of underrated natural sights.

Kayak along the untamed waters of Okefenokee's alligator-ravaged swamp, and trek around Providence Canyon's remarkable orange, red and purple formations. Meanwhile, visitors from around the world flock to Plains, the birthplace of former US President Jimmy Carter, and the sleepy historic town of Senoia, dubbed the 'Hollywood of the South' (it doubles as Woodbury and Alexandria in the wildly popular zombie series *The Walking Dead*).

On the border with South Carolina, the city of Augusta offers a charming Riverwalk and a glimpse into the early days of soul singer James Brown.

When to Go

➡ The most pleasant average temperatures in the area are from March–May.

➡ To sample plump, juicy peaches and flavorsome blueberries, visit from May–August.

➡ Pecans, squash and parsnips are best from September–March, and hotel rates are at their lowest.

Augusta & South Georgia Highlights

1 Okefenokee National Wildlife Refuge (p158) Spotting alligators on a boat trip through mysterious swampy waters.

2 Fresh Air (p165) Heading to Jackson for some of the best smoked pork on the planet, paired with tangy barbecue sauce.

3 WhiteWater Express (p160) Getting your thrills in Columbus rafting on the longest human-made urban white-water rafting experience in the world.

4 Providence Canyon (p158) Hiking through otherworldly formations inside Georgia's spectacular 'Little Grand Canyon.'

5 Georgia Tour Company (p163) Exploring the 'Hollywood of the South' in Senoia visiting movie locations and filming spots from *The Walking Dead*.

6 Coca-Cola Space Science Center (p160) Learning about life beyond earth's orbit at this fascinating museum in Columbus filled with NASA kit and interactive exhibitions.

7 Sibley Mill (p154) Admiring the neo-Gothic style of this 1882 textile mill in Augusta.

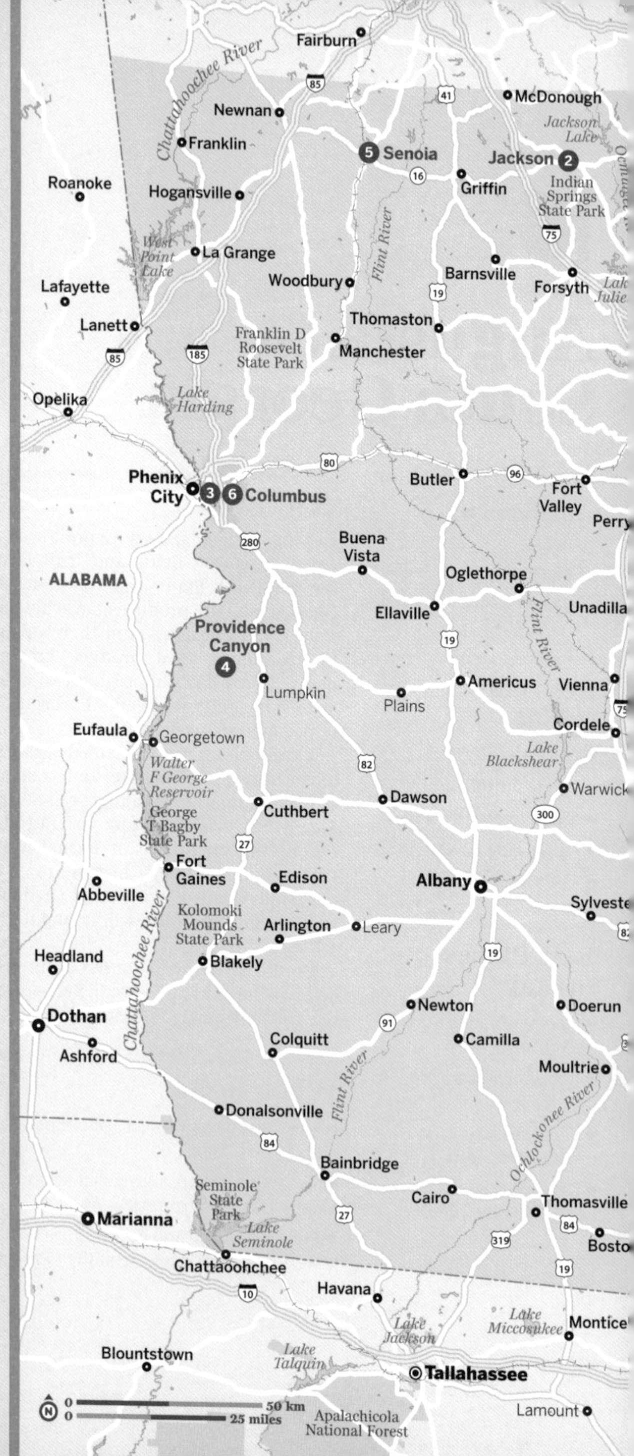

Greensboro
J Strom Thurmond Lake
Aiken
Little River
Thomson
Augusta
7
Williston
Lake Oconee
Warrenton
Monticello
Eatonton
Sparta
Barnwell
Oconee National Forest
Lake Sinclair
Ogeechee River
Wrens
SOUTH CAROLINA
Savannah River
Waynesboro
Milledgeville
Gray
Sandersville
Louisville
Allendale
Wadley
Macon
Millen
Oconee River
Sylvania
Wrightsville
Jeffersonville
Twin City
Warner Robins
Swainsboro
George L Smith State Park
Ogeechee River
Dublin
Statesboro
Metter
Cochran
Soperton
Springfield
GEORGIA
Hawkinsville
Vidalia
Lyons
Eastman
Alamo
Claxton
Pembroke
McRae
Abbeville
Rhine
Richmond Hill
Lumber City
Rochelle
Glennville
Hazlehurst
Hinesville
Ocmulgee River
Altamaha River
Baxley
Riceboro
Surrency
Ludowici
Fitzgerald
Ashburn
Broxton
Jesup
Ocilla
Alma
Douglas
Tifton
Offerman
Alapaha
Everett
Darien
Hortense
Omega
Lenox
Pearson
Blackshear
Thalmann
Satilla River
Reed Bingham State Park
Waycross
Nashville
Nahunta
Brunswick
Adel
Waverly
Lakeland
Homerville
Banks Lake
Woodbine
Valdosta
Folkston
Kingsland
Quitman
1
Okefenokee National Wildlife Refuge
Lake Park
Fargo
Suwanee River
Yulee
Fernandina Beach
Withlacoochee River
Callahan
Jasper
Moniac
St. George
Madison
FLORIDA
Osceola National Forest
Jacksonville
Live Oak
20
1
25
441
129
88
49
301
16
1
21
441
25
16
341
301
16
441
341
1
95
84
23
341
84
441
23
82
82
75
84
95
441
23
10

Augusta

☎706, 762 / POP 197,182

On top of the world for one week out of the year and fairly quiet the other 51, Augusta has traditionally been content with its annual flash in the spotlight during the Masters golf tournament. Augusta moves and shakes with the best of 'em during that April week, but the rest of the year, it's lowland downtown, an amalgamation of 19th-century Sullivan-esque and art deco architecture. But the city is in the midst of a renaissance, mainly due to a tech boom that is positioning Augusta as a major regional cybersecurity and data center. Spearheaded by multiple private and government cyber institutions and facilities in the works, downtown is experiencing growth not seen in two decades.

Sights

Butted up against the Riverwalk, downtown Augusta harbors most sights of note, including the city's two best museums and historic buildings. But pay attention while strolling downtown as Augusta has a developed art scene. Visitors will notice murals and photos spread among the streets, restaurants and local businesses, honoring the life of the artist or community. **Art the Box** has done up eyesore electricity- and signal-control boxes throughout downtown. Download the interactive **Public Art Map** (http://gismap.augustaga.gov/auggagis/storymaps/index.html) for locations of 40 works of public art.

OFF THE BEATEN TRACK

LITERARY LEGACY

Novelist Flannery O'Connor (1925–64) was raised on **Andalusia** (☎478-454-4029; www.andalusiafarm.org; 2628 N Columbia St, Milledgeville; adult/child $7/free; ⏰10am-4pm Tue-Sat, 2-4pm Sun; Ⓟ), a 544-acre estate. After attending the Writers Workshop at the University of Iowa, she returned to this pretty home, set amid a quilt of beautiful, wooded hills, to write. Hourly tours give info on O'Connor's short yet prolific career. Milledgeville is about 90 miles southeast of metro Atlanta.

★Sibley Mill HISTORIC BUILDING

(1717 Goodrich St) The fact that this historic building is closed to the public won't stop you from curiously approaching if you see it in the distance. The massive textile mill, completed in 1882, features a striking, ornate and eclectic architectural style evoking neo-Gothic and seemingly out of place in Augusta.

In front is the original obelisk chimney of the Confederate Powder Works, which predated the mill and was the only permanent edifice constructed by the Confederate States of America. It was the largest supplier of gunpowder for Confederate troops during the Civil War and was in operation until 1865. Get your Instagram ready: standout photogenic highlights include towering turrets, the chimney itself and the cast-iron coat of arms of the Sibley family emblazoned with the Latin saying *esse quam videri* (to be, rather than just seem). The mill is slated to be turned into a new cybersecurity and technology center.

Augusta Museum of History MUSEUM

(www.augustamuseum.org; 560 Reynolds St; adult/child $4/2; ⏰10am-5pm Thu-Sat, 1-5pm Sun) Augusta's well-done history museum has exhibitions on local celebrities and city history, but is of most interest for its extensive James Brown exhibit, the world's most comprehensive exhibition dedicated to the Godfather of Soul (featuring personal effects like his diabetes kit, stage outfit and costumes, and numerous audiovisual stations); and its golf exhibit, with fun galleries chronicling the evolution of tees, clubs and balls (the 1618 Featherie looks like a hacky sack!), and a Masters Green Jacket.

Augusta Riverwalk PARK

(www.augustaga.gov/292/riverwalk; 8th & Reynolds Sts; ⏰24hr) This multilevel brick trail parallels the pretty Savannah River through downtown Augusta from 11th St to the Gordon Hwy Bridge and is peppered with attractions like the Morris Museum of Art and Augusta Museum of History along the way. It's a picturesque spot to sit and ogle the river and impressive riverside mansions on the South Carolina side. On Saturdays in spring, summer and fall, the **Augusta Market** (www.theaugustamarket.com) runs here from 8am to 2am.

OFF THE BEATEN TRACK

HISTORY & THE ARTS IN MACON

Culture seekers in South Georgia should consider a detour to **Macon**, about 1½ hours southeast of Atlanta on I-75. Highlights include the **Tubman Museum** (478-743-8544; www.tubmanmuseum.com; 310 Cherry St, Macon; adult/child $10/6; 9am-5pm Tue-Sat) downtown, with a collection of more than 7000 artworks and artifacts from African American history on display. Across the street at the beautifully restored 1921 **Douglass Theater**, a small walk of fame highlights African American musical greats with ties to Georgia, including Otis Redding.

Fans of Southern rock can check out the **Big House Museum**, home to the Allman Brothers Band and their families from 1970–73. Some of the mansion's 18 rooms are furnished with personal belongings and others with memorabilia. 'Ramblin' Man' and 'Midnight Rider' were both written while the band was living here.

For an idea of what life was like for Georgia's earliest inhabitants, **Ocmulgee National Monument** offers a glimpse through its archeological museum and a reconstructed ceremonial earth lodge. A short walk takes you to the Great Burial Mound.

James Brown Statue STATUE

(www.augustamuseum.org/the-james-brown-statue; Broad St, btwn James Brown Blvd & 8th St; 24hr) This life-size bronze statue of the Godfather of Soul features Augusta's favorite son with signature cape and microphone. It was originally set to be unveiled in 2004, but Brown was jailed after reportedly pushing his wife to the floor and threatening her with a chair, so the city shelved the idea until a year later. The James Brown CAM will take your photo with the soul and funk pioneer and send it to your cell phone within minutes.

Morris Museum of Art MUSEUM

(www.themorris.org; 1 10th St, 2nd fl; adult/child $5/free, Sun free; 10am-5pm Tue-Sat, 1-5pm Sun) This refreshingly not overwhelming museum is dedicated to art and artists of the South, chronologically displayed from 19th-century portraits to contemporary art in the South, touching on the Civil War, impressionism, abstraction and still lifes along the way, among others.

Activities

Augusta Aviation SCENIC FLIGHT

(706-733-8970; www.augustaaviation.com; 1775 Highland Ave, Daniel Field Airport; $110; 10am-4pm) The only way to get a peak over the walls of Augusta National if you are not a member, ticket holder or very good golfer is on a 30-minute aerial tour from Augusta Aviation – and even then you'll need to specifically request a flyover.

Patriot Riverboat Tours BOATING

(803-730-9739; www.patriottourboat.net; 1 5th St; adult/child $12/6; 3-4pm Wed-Sun Mar-Oct, Sat only by reservation Nov-Feb) Offers one-hour narrated riverboat tours and two-hour sunset tours along the pretty Savannah River, departing from the Riverwalk Marina.

Festivals & Events

Masters Tournament SPORTS

(706-667-6700; www.masters.com; 2604 Washington Rd, Augusta National Golf Club; tickets $115; Apr) One of four major professional-golf championships and the most prestigious by a landslide, the Masters Tournament at Augusta National Golf Club ranks up there with the Super Bowl, Kentucky Derby, Daytona 500 and the National Collegiate Athletic Association (NCAA) Final Four as one of the most iconic American sporting events, with its famed Green Jacket one of the most coveted sporting awards on earth.

If you want to go, you'll need to apply for the ticket lottery at https://tickets.masters.com in May the previous year. If you can't get tournament tickets, you might be able to finagle $75 tickets for the practice rounds. Either way, it's the only way you'll be getting into the world's most famous golf course unless you are a member of the exclusive, invitation-only Augusta National Golf Club.

Arts in the Heart of Augusta ART

(www.artsintheheartofaugusta.com; Broad St, at the Auga Common; $7-12; Sep) Augusta's most important nongolf event is this three-day bash featuring a three-city-block arts and crafts market, a Global Village with grub cooked by local ethnic associations representing 20 countries and live music on five stages. The festival attracts nearly 100,000 attendees annually.

Augusta

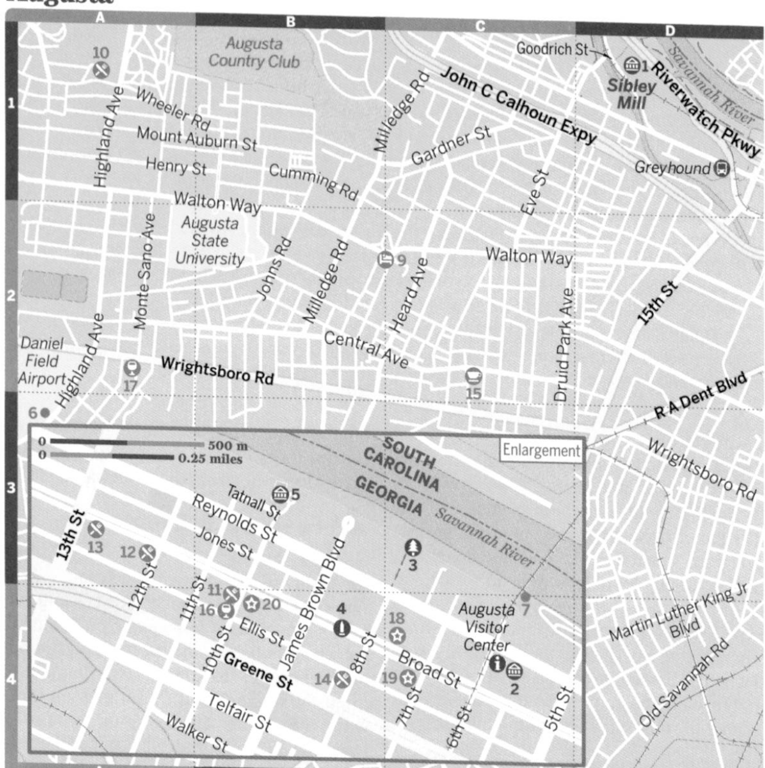

Sleeping

Olde Town Inn B&B $

(706-828-5600; www.oldetowninnaugusta.com; 349 Telfair St; r $109; P ❄ 📶) The slogan goes, 'this ain't your mama's B&B – this is a Bed & Bar!' This old-town charmer offers five rooms, well appointed with hardwood floors and four-poster beds, named after notorious women in Augusta history. But the real coup of this 1896 Italianate Revival that sits in Georgia's oldest neighborhood is the cozy basement bar, the **Fox's Lair**. With live music nightly, it's one of the city's liveliest bars. Friendly innkeepers to boot!

Partridge Inn HISTORIC HOTEL $$

(706-737-8888; www.partridgeinncurio.com; 2110 Walton Way; r $159-179, ste $189-209; P ❄ @ 📶 🏊) Dating to the 1890s, whitewashed Partridge Inn is Augusta's most storied hotel. This grand, piecemeal-built Southern charmer is dressed somewhat in arts-and-crafts style and is an unusual hodgepodge of asymmetric verandas, balconies and porches that clocks in at city-block size. A modern makeover has given the rooms a contemporary flourish, with abstract local art and subway-tiled shower floors. The **restaurant** is excellent (mains $20 to $37), with some unusual dishes (blackened ostrich). The rooftop bar is a social focal point for well-to-do Augustans.

Eating

Many of Augusta's better restaurants are along Broad St, the downtown main drag and social epicenter of the city, and its offshoots. A lot of hot spots are closed Sunday and Monday.

Farmhaus Burger BURGERS $

(www.farmhausburger.com; 1204 Broad St; burgers $6.75-10.75; 11am-10pm Mon-Thu, to 11pm Fri & Sat; 📶) Whether you build your own or spring for one of its creations, your gut will thank you for choosing this gourmet, locally steeped burger joint. Think custom-

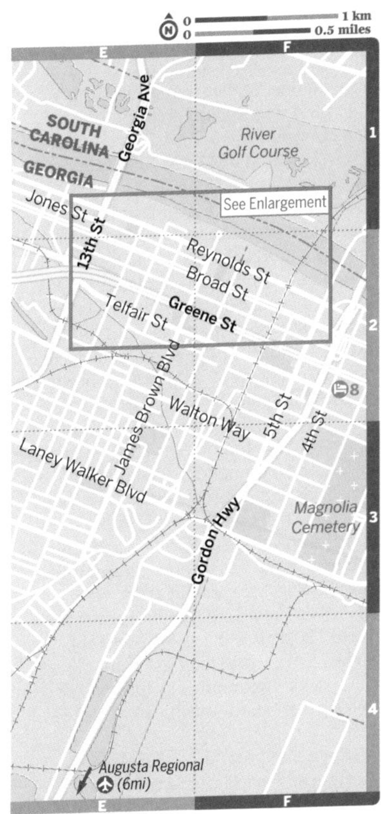

Augusta

Top Sights

1 Sibley Mill D1

Sights

2 Augusta Museum of History C4
3 Augusta Riverwalk C3
4 James Brown Statue B4
5 Morris Museum of Art B3

Activities, Courses & Tours

6 Augusta Aviation A3
7 Patriot Riverboat Tours C4

Sleeping

8 Olde Town Inn F2
9 Partridge Inn C2

Eating

10 Abel Brown A1
11 Bee's Knees B4
Craft & Vine .... (see 12)
12 Farmhaus Burger A3
13 Frog Hollow Tavern A3
14 Humanitree House Juice Joint B4

Drinking & Nightlife

15 Buona Caffé C2
16 Hive B4
17 Indian Queen A2

Entertainment

18 Imperial Theatre C4
19 Miller Theater C4
20 Soul Bar B4

ground Southeastern Angus double stacks (or organic Sea Island red-pea patties) with sunny-side-up local farm egg, heirloom-smoked bacon and smoked Gouda, and house-cut Russet fries with sea salt and cracked pepper.

Craft & Vine GASTROPUB $

(706-496-8442; www.craftandvine.com; 1204 Broad St; small plates $9-13, pizzas $14; 5pm-midnight Wed-Thu, to 1am Fri & Sat;) Craft & Vine's impressive list of artisanal cheeses and charcuterie, unusual small plates like blackened beef tongue and creative wood-fired pizzas (vegetarians could do worse than roasted cauliflower, Asiago mornay sauce, garlic, red onion and pepper flakes) pairs very well with craft beer and cocktails in the trendy, old-wood-meets-metal interior.

Humanitree House Juice Joint VEGAN $

(www.humanitreehouse.com; 305 8th St; mains $7.50-9; 8am-7pm Tue-Fri, 9:30am-5pm Sat;) This bohemian and artsy juice joint is deadly serious about its cold-pressed, No High Pressure Processing (HPP) nectars and vegan wraps and sandwiches. It doubles as an art gallery, live-music venue and performance space as well, and a general social gathering point for like-minded alternative folks.

Bee's Knees FUSION, TAPAS $$

(706-828-3600; www.beeskneestapas.com; 211 10th St; tapas $6-12, mains $15-18; 5-10pm Mon-Thu, to 11pm Fri & Sat, 11am-3pm & 5-10pm Sun, bar open late;) Innovative, often-vegetarian-focused fusion tapas keep this locally owned hot spot hopping day and night. Highlights include spicy tempeh 'wings' (buffalo organic soy cakes), sweet-potato hummus and tofu pad thai, but the eclectic menu rarely misses no matter what you choose.

An ever-changing craft-beer list, seasonal cocktails and sweet daily drink specials draw a fun, slightly alternative herbivore and carnivore crowd.

DON'T MISS

GO WILD IN SOUTH GEORGIA

Two glorious natural areas – Okefenokee Swamp National Wildlife Refuge and Providence Canyon – provide some of South Georgia's most memorable outdoor experiences. Don't forget your hat, sunscreen and bug spray!

Nearly a half-million acres in size, **Okefenokee Swamp** (912-496-7836; http://okeswamp.com/; 2700 Suwannee Canal Rd, Folkston; private vehicle $5, on foot or bicycle $1; 30min before sunrise to 7:30pm Mar-Oct, to 5pm Nov-Feb; P) is a magnificent environment to explore, with something for travelers of all abilities. Choose from hiking trails and wildlife drives to boardwalks and canoe or motorboat trips through some 120 miles of prehistoric canals. Look for movement between the carpet of green lily pads and you might clap eyes on Georgia's living dinosaurs: alligators. Otters, water moccasins, anhingas, osprey and black bears also share this wilderness.

There are three main entrances to Okefenokee Swamp. The Kingfisher Landing entrance is just south of Waycross, the Suwannee Canal Recreation Area is in Folkston and the Stephen C. Foster State Park entrance is to the west. The Kingfisher entrance includes a 1.5-mile railroad system, with train tours on a replica steam engine. The Suwannee entrance has a self-guided 7.5-mile wildlife drive through the park leading to the Chesser Homestead, where early settlers named 'Swampers' lived in the mid-19th century. From the Stephen C. Foster entrance, visitors can reach the 5-mile wide Billys Island, which is only accessible by boat or canoe through 'gator-infested waters. Human occupancy here dates to AD 1200; today the only trace of former inhabitants is a modest cemetery. Boat tours and kayak and bike rental can be prearranged with **Okefenokee Adventures** (866-843-7926; www.okefenokeeadventures.com; 4159 Suwannee Canal Rd, Folkston; canoes & kayaks half-/full day from $25/35, 90min boat tours adult/child from $19.50/12; 30min before sunrise to 7:30pm Mar-Oct, to 5pm Nov-Feb), located inside the park at the Suwannee (Folkston) entrance. Wilderness camping is possible inside the park if a permit is applied for at least two months in advance (visit www.recreation.gov to apply). For boat tours, hiking and board-walking, wear closed-toed shoes.

Only 30 minutes from Columbus sits **Providence Canyon** (229-838-4244; http://gastateparks.org/providencecanyon; 8930 Canyon Rd, Lumpkin; parking $5; 7am-6pm; P), Georgia's 'Little Grand Canyon.' This 1003-acre state park is something to behold. Otherworldly formations include gullies as deep as 150ft, with beautiful layers of orange, red, purple and pink sediment. Visitors can explore via a variety of hikes, including an easy rim trail with spectacular views over the canyon, plus a 1-mile canyon-floor trail, and longer 3-mile and 7-mile canyon-floor trails.

Evidence suggests this area was once the bottom of the sea. The canyon we see today formed due to mass erosion over the years, as a result of bad farming practices. Now, it's a natural wonder. Keep your eyes peeled for the local residents: armadillos, deer, raccoons and butterflies. Hikers can stay overnight at basic campgrounds inside the canyon; book in advance at the **visitor center** (8416 Canyon Rd, Lumpkin; 8am-6pm Wed-Sun Oct-Mar, to 9pm Wed-Sun Apr-Sep, subject to change). The closest is the Pioneer Camping site ($40 per night), and the furthest is the Primitive Camping site ($10 per night): neither have water facilities. There's a small exhibition at the visitor center, where you can also buy drinks and get free information and hiking maps. Parking areas around the rim of the canyon have picnic facilities and restrooms.

★ **Frog Hollow Tavern** SOUTHERN US $$$
(706-364-6906; www.froghollowtavern.com; 1282 Broad St; mains $22-34; 5-10pm Wed-Thu, to 10:30pm Fri & Sat;) Chef Sean Wight's attention to local bounty completely transformed Augusta's dining scene at this classy tavern. The regionally focused dishes include golden tilefish with roasted baby turnips and greens, or wild-caught shrimp and grits with housemade andouille sausage. Organic and biodynamic juice are favored on the lengthy wine list and there are barrel-aged whiskey cocktails.

Abel Brown SOUTHERN US $$$

(☎706-738-6491; www.abelbrownaugusta.com; 491 Highland Ave; mains $23-38; ⏰5-10pm Mon-Thu, to 11pm Fri & Sat, 12:30am-9pm Sun; 📶) Despite its location in an uneventful strip mall 3.5 miles west of downtown, this staple is one of Augusta's signature Southern kitchens. It serves fresh oysters from throughout the eastern seaboard and Canada; scrumptious, souped-up Southern dishes with occasional international flourishes; and commendable local beer and international wines.

Drinking & Nightlife

Nearly all the action takes place along Broad St and its vicinity, although Indian Queen and Fox's Lair (p156) are worth detours to the Summerville and Olde Town districts, respectively.

★ **Hive** CRAFT BEER

(www.hiveaugusta.com; 215 10th St; ⏰11:30am-2:30pm & 5pm-2:30am Mon-Thu, 11:30am-2:30am Fri & Sat; 📶) With 78 taps topped by funky, totem-pole-evoking ceramic handles fired by Tire City Potters across the street, Augusta's hophead stomping ground keeps things stylish, local and craft-dedicated. Current selections are scrolled painfully slowly on the gastropub's electronic board – you're better off with one of its tablets or consulting its real-time list online at www.hiveaugusta.com/tap-list. In addition to nationwide craft suds, there's wine, kombucha and sodas on tap.

Buona Caffé COFFEE

(www.buonacaffe.com; 1858 Central Ave; coffee $1.70-3.30; ⏰7am-7pm Mon-Fri, 8am-5pm Sat; 📶) Getting something besides caffeinated drip dredge in Augusta remains challenging, but this hipster haunt in a repurposed house 2.5 miles east of downtown gets the job done. Italian grammar error aside (it should be Buon Caffé), it is the city's only local roaster and specializes in espresso, pour over and cold brews. It also serves a limited menu of panini, quiche and breakfast sandwiches.

Indian Queen BAR

(www.theindianqueen.com; 2502 Wrightsboro Rd; ⏰3pm-2am Mon-Sat) A youngish crowd flocks to this rough-hewn log cabin slapped with Native American imagery in the toney Summerville neighborhood, where a small but excellently executed menu of classic cocktails (from $8) is the way to go rather than its somewhat-uninspiring beer selection. It does a mean and generous Old Fashioned – upgrade to Bulleit Bourbon. If there's not a cocktail that suits, ask for the secret menu.

Entertainment

For entertainment listings, pick up a copy of the free independent weekly, *Metro Spirit* (www.metrospirit.com).

Miller Theater LIVE MUSIC

(☎706-842-4080; www.millertheateraugusta.com; 708 Broad St; ⏰box office noon-6pm Mon-Fri) This historic, 1300-seat, art deco–style theater was the second-largest theater in Georgia behind Atlanta's Fox Theatre when it originally opened in 1940. It was completely restored after a 23-year hiatus, reopening in 2018 to host fairly big-name concerts and the Symphony Orchestra Augusta.

Imperial Theatre THEATER

(☎706-722-8341; www.imperialtheatre.com; 745 Broad St; ⏰box office 10am-4pm Tue-Fri) With a gilded awning, and a staged graced by actors/comedians Charlie Chaplin and Milton Berle as well as ballet-dancer Anna Pavlova, the 100-year-old Imperial Theatre hearkens to glamorous times of vaudeville and photoplays. It was James Brown's home theater as well. Today it's been restored and hosts plays, shows and a free summer film series.

Soul Bar LIVE MUSIC

(www.soulbar.com; 984 Broad St; ⏰4pm-3am Mon-Fri, to 2am Sat) Dark and seedy, Soul Bar is a James Brown–dedicated Broad St staple lit by little more than a beckoning red light at the entrance and rows of colorful Christmas lights lining its walls. The long bar has seen it all, including Brown himself, who is said to have shot a mean game of pool here on occasion. Brown cover acts are often featured and the place gets jam-packed.

Information

Augusta Visitor Center (☎706-724-4067; www.visitaugusta.com; 1010 Broad St; ⏰10am-5pm Mon-Sat, 1-5pm Sun) Helpful for city insights, brochures and accommodations listings.

Getting There & Away

Augusta straddles the Georgia–South Carolina border 152 miles east of Atlanta on I-20. **Augusta Regional Airport** (706-798-3236; www.flyags.com; 1501 Aviation Way), 8 miles south of downtown, is served by regional flights by Delta Airlines from Atlanta and American Airlines from Charlotte.

Greyhound (706-722-6411; www.greyhound.com; 1546 Broad St) operates five or so buses per day to Atlanta (from $27, three hours) and five to Columbia, SC (from $15, 1½ hours).

Columbus

706 / POP 197,500

Set along the Chattahoochee River, the boundary between Georgia and Alabama, Columbus is the third-largest city in Georgia. Nicknamed 'Fountain City' due to its unusually large number of water features, it has an easily walkable historic center. Coca-Cola inventor John Pemberton settled here in the 1850s and is buried here at the Linwood Cemetery. The city's other claim to fame is its human-made rafting course – the longest urban white-water rafting experience in the world.

Around 7000 students attend Columbus State University, and the local residents and academics champion the local arts. Venues of note include the old (and supposedly haunted) Springer Opera House and Riverside Theatre Complex.

Sights

Coca-Cola SpaceScience Center — MUSEUM

(706-649-1470; www.ccssc.org; 701 Front Ave; adult/child $6/4; 10am-4pm Mon-Fri, 10:30am-6pm Sat;) Operated by Columbus State University, this space-themed wonderland is full of interactive exhibits that your kids will love, plus some of the most expensive NASA kit on public display – worth around $20 million. See the main engine nozzle of a space shuttle, operations management consoles, plus a general onboard computer, among other serious bits of tech. The center is also home to the Omnisphere Planetarium Theater – an advanced immersive video experience with a sphere dome for viewing high-res 360-degree images. Also on-site is the WestRock Observatory and the Space Shuttle Odyssey launch simulator, plus actual space suits worn by astronauts.

The River Market Antiques & Lunch Box Museum — MUSEUM

(706-653-6240; http://therivermarketantiques.com; 3218 Hamilton Rd; $5, under 12yr free; 10am-6pm Mon-Sat) This bizarre emporium is home to more than 2000 colorful lunch boxes. The most valuable are estimated to fetch in the region of $2500 if they were to ever go to auction. Peruse dozens of nostalgic designs from Star Trek and Pac-Man to Hulk, Popeye and vintage Disney characters. Allen Woodall started collecting them in the 1990s after he inherited a number from a friend who died.

National Civil War Naval Museum — MUSEUM

(706-327-9798; www.portcolumbus.org; 1002 Victory Dr; adult/senior/under 6yr $7.50/6.50/free; 10am-4:30pm Mon-Sat, 12:30-4:30pm Sun; P) This museum, dedicated to the naval history of the nation's bloodiest conflict, includes the CSS *Jackson,* an 1862 ironclad Confederate navy ship that was hauled up after 95 years underwater, plus a replica of the turret of the ironclad USS *Monitor*. You'll also find a collection of mid-19th-century American and Confederate flags, unearthed from an attic in Massachusetts.

Carson McCullers Center for Writers & Musicians — MUSEUM

(706-565-1200; www.mccullerscenter.org; 1519 Stark Ave; $5; by appointment) The future literary lioness Carson McCullers moved here with her family in 1925, when she was just eight years old, and lived here for 19 years. It's also the base of operations for the Carson McCullers Center, which runs a McCullers-based archive and offers fellowships to aspiring writers and artists. Email or call well in advance to arrange a tour.

Activities

WhiteWater Express — RAFTING

(706-321-4720; www.whitewaterexpress.com; 1000 Bay Ave; from $38.50; 9am-6pm;) Adrenaline junkies rejoice! WhiteWater Express has you covered with loads of adventure activities plus its main event – the longest urban white-water rafting experience in the world. The human-made course has thrilling class II to V rapids for different abilities. Rafters must be seven or older and weigh more than 60 pounds.

Columbus

Columbus

Sights

1 Carson McCullers Center for Writers & Musicians D2
2 Coca-Cola Space Science Center A2
3 National Civil War Naval Museum C4
4 The River Market Antiques & Lunch Box Museum C1

Activities, Courses & Tours

5 Chattahoochee RiverWalk A1
6 WhiteWater Express A1

Sleeping

7 Rothschild Pound House Inn B2

Eating

8 Iron Bank Coffee Co. A1
9 The Cannon Brew Pub A1

Entertainment

10 Riverside Theatre Complex A1
11 Springer Opera House B1

Choose from a Classic, Challenge or Carnage run on the same 2.5-mile stretch of Chattahoochee River. On the more challenging afternoon sessions the water can be five to 15 times faster, due to the gallons of water being released from a nearby dam. WhiteWater Express also offers bike rental ($10 per day), stand up paddleboard (SUP) rental ($19 per two hours), tubing ($12 including shuttle) and fly-fishing clinics ($150 half-day).

Chattahoochee RiverWalk WALKING

(Woodruff River Front Park, 1000 Bay Ave) Follow the 15-mile pathway on a self-guided walk along the Chattahoochee River, separating the states of Alabama and Georgia. Take in the gorgeous views: colorful boats on the river's rapids, pretty park areas, fountains and cascading dams. Attractions en route include the Civil War Naval Yard, the Coca-Cola Space Science Center and Phoenix City Amphitheater. Cyclists are welcome on the route. There are plenty of picnic benches and bathrooms along the walk too.

Sleeping

Florence Marina State Park CAMPGROUND $

(229-838-4244; http://gastateparks.org/florencemarina; 218 Florence Rd, Omaha; campsites/cottages from $28/75; park 7am-10pm; P) Ten minutes from Providence Canyon (p158; 35 minutes from Columbus), this campground is open year-round and is on the northern end of the 45,000-acre Lake Walter F. George. It's the best-value place to stay in the area, with lots of facilities: 43 campsites and 15 basic, cosy cottages. Activities include pontoon-boat rental ($35 for four hours), fishing and mini-golf ($4). Wildlife tours ($5) run at the weekend, with the chance to spot alligators and native birds.

Rothschild Pound House Inn B&B $$

(706-322-4075; www.thepoundhouseinn.com; 201 7th St; r/ste/cottages from $165/175/300; P) Dating back to the 1870s, this atmospheric mansion has Victorian features throughout and is just a few blocks from the Chattahoochee River and downtown Columbus. It has rooms dressed in period furniture and original features, and guests can make use of the parlors and big porch area. The free breakfast includes options like waffles and bacon or eggs Benedict.

WORTH A TRIP

PRESIDENTIAL PLAINS

Only one US president, Jimmy Carter (1977–81), hails from Georgia. It's worth a trip to the tiny town of Plains (population around 700) to see **Jimmy Carter's boyhood home** (229-824-4104; www.nps.gov/jica/index.htm; 402 Old Plains Hwy, Plains; 10am-5pm, except public holidays) FREE, now part of the Carter National Historic Site, and to shop for presidential (and peanut-related) souvenirs on the quaint Main St. If you come on the right weekend, you could also meet President Carter himself: at research time, the 93-year-old was still teaching Sunday School twice a month at Maranatha Baptist Church. Check the website (www.mbcplains.org) for dates. Plains is about 60 miles southeast of Columbus on Hwy 280.

Eating

Iron Bank Coffee Co. COFFEE $

(706-992-6609; https://ironbankcoffee.com; 6 W 11th St; menu items from $1.50; 7am-9pm Mon-Thu, to 11pm Fri & Sat, 8am-6pm Sun;) Hip cafe in an old bank with high ceilings, chandeliers, big wooden tables and a jumble of different style chairs. The best place to sit is inside the old bank vault, complete with the original bank-vault door. It serves Stumptown coffee (from $1.75), sandwiches, pastries, salads, plus craft beer (from $4.25) and wine.

Cannon Brew Pub GASTROPUB $

(706-653-2337; www.facebook.com/cannonbrewpub; 1041 Broadway; pizzas from $9.95, Turning Blue Burger Challenge $30; 11am-10pm Mon-Thu, to 11pm Fri & Sat, noon-10pm Sun) This old-world-style pub has enormously high ceilings, a large beer hall and a copper bar. It brews its own hops in an on-site microbrewery. Try the homemade amber ale, pale ale and American red. Beer samplers available. Fresh pizzas are baked in a brick oven, but people with an enormous appetite should try the legendary Turning Blue Burger Challenge.

Entertainment

Springer Opera House THEATER

(706-324-5714; https://springeroperahouse.org; 103 E 10th St; tours $5, tickets from $20;) This historic 1871 theater is an atmospheric place to catch a show. Its interiors remain opulent, with crescent double balconies and ornate details. Previous performers in the main hall include Edwin Booth, Oscar Wilde and Ethel Barrymore, while more recent shows include *The Great Gatsby* and *West Side Story*. Tours of the building take place on Monday and Wednesday at 3:30pm.

Riverside Theatre Complex THEATRE

(706-507-8444; https://theatre.columbusstate.edu; 6 W 10th St; adult from $17, under 12yr $12; box office noon-6pm Mon-Fri & 1hr before shows start) A modern theatre showing a variety of theatrical productions, from William Shakespeare to modern comedies such as *The Last Night of Ballyhoo* by Georgia native and Pulitzer Prize–winning playwright Alfred Uhry.

Getting There & Away

I-185 runs through Columbus, connecting with I-85 to Atlanta. Greyhound buses (visit www.greyhound.com to book) connect Atlanta to Columbus seven times a day (from $18, one hour 40 minutes).

Senoia

770 / POP 4100

The quaint town of Senoia dates back to 1860. It's a popular destination for those who want to unwind from city life. Historic Main St is a lovely place to amble around of an afternoon, perusing the smart boutiques and antique stores, catching up with friends in the pleasant coffee shops or wandering around local exhibitions.

In recent years, however, it's become an epicenter for zombie geeks. Much of the hit TV show *The Walking Dead* was filmed in and around Senoia – and all die-hard fans will know that it doubles as both the fictional town of Woodbury and the 'safe-zone' of Alexandria in the series.

Visitors will find an unlikely marriage of businesses catering to a cult fan following of a gory bloodsucking show and a sophisticated older crowd attracted by the quintessential Southern setting.

Sights

Woodbury Shoppe MUSEUM

(770-727-9394; www.woodburyshoppe.com; 48 Main St; 11am-5pm Mon-Thu, 10am-6pm Fri & Sat, noon-6pm Sun) FREE This official *Walking Dead* mini-museum and souvenir shop is your one-stop shop for all things related to the extremely popular AMC TV show. It's located right in the heart of Senoia, the live set of the fictional town of Woodbury from season three. The museum includes props from the show, such as a model zombie, the mirror Beth breaks in season two and a prison cell from season three, among other items.

In the gift shop, fans can pick up everything from life-sized cardboard cutouts of their *Walking Dead* heroes, to their very own version of Negan's barbed-wire baseball bat, 'Lucille,' made famous by the goriest scene of the show.

OFF THE BEATEN TRACK

TECHNICOLOR DREAMLAND

After experiencing visions in which he was chosen by 'people of the future' to depict their culture of peace and love, self-taught artist Eddie Owens Martin turned his mother's 19th-century farmhouse, **Pasaquan** (706-507-8306; https://pasaquan.columbusstate.edu; 238 Eddie Martin Rd, Buena Vista; suggested donation adult/senior/student $10/5/3; 10am-5pm Fri-Sun), into a psychedelic wonderland over the course of three decades. The site – which includes six buildings – is an explosive, rainbow-hued fusion of African, pre-Columbian Mexican and Native American motifs. Definitely worth a detour for fans of unusual photo ops and connoisseurs of outsider art.

The site was restored in 2014 and is now managed by Columbus State University. Buena Vista is about 50 miles southeast of Columbus.

Activities

Georgia Tour Company WALKING

(770-599-0091; www.georgiatourcompany.com; 53 Main St; tours from $25; 10am-5pm) Locals call Senoia the 'Hollywood of the South,' and this company will show you why on its filming tours. Choose from *The Walking Dead* fan tour (with guides dressed in cosplay as members of the cast) or the Big Screen walking tour, featuring locations from movies *Fried Green Tomatoes, Drop Dead Diva, The Fighting Temptations* and other films.

Tours run for 1½ to 2½ hours. The Georgia Tour Company shop sells plenty of zombie-themed calendars, fridge magnets and key rings to take home as a souvenir, plus weirdly refreshing pickle ice for 50¢.

Sleeping

Days Inn & Suites Peachtree City MOTEL $

(770-632-9700; www.wyndhamhotels.com; 976 Crosstown Dr, Peachtree City; r $80-91; P) Yes it's a chain, but it's clean, comfortable, inexpensive and only a 10-minute drive north from all *The Walking Dead* action in Senoia. Rooms are well presented with dark wood furnishings, crisp white linen and good heaters (for those visiting in winter).

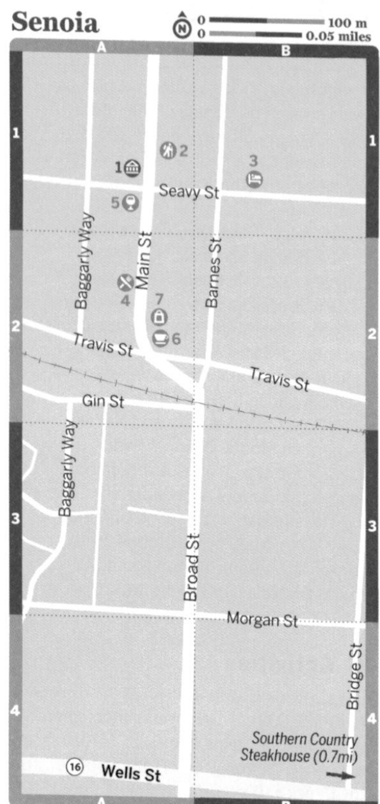

Senoia

Sights

Activities, Courses & Tours

Sleeping

Eating

Drinking & Nightlife

Shopping

★ **Veranda Historic Bed & Breakfast Inn** B&B $$

(☎770-599-3905; http://verandabandbinn.com; 252 Seavy St; queen/king r from $125/135) To really feel like a resident of the fictional town of Woodbury (minus the zombies), book a stay at this impressive two-story white wooden mansion. Built in 1906, in Greek Revival style, it has original features throughout: ornate tin ceilings, vintage furnishings and fireplaces in the nine guest bedrooms. Ask the owners about its famous guests over the years.

Eating

Main Street Fudge & Ice Cream Shop ICE CREAM $

(☎770-599-3168; 42 Main St; scoops of ice cream from $2.55; ⏱noon-6pm Tue-Thu, to 7pm Fri, 11am-7pm Sat, 1-6pm Sun; 👪) Your one-stop shop for a sweet treat in Senoia. Choose from 12 flavors of ice cream, 21 kinds of fudge, brownie bombs, cheesecake and banana pudding. Plus fried pies, cinnamon rolls, cookie sandwiches, pineapple upside-down cake and even Turkish-style baklava. Homemade hot cocoa and hot apple cider is served in the winter months.

Nic & Norman's AMERICAN $$

(☎770-727-9432; http://nicandnormans.com; 20 Main St; mains $12-24; ⏱11am-10pm Mon-Thu, to 11pm Fri & Sat, to 9pm Sun) 🌿 Owned by Greg Nicotero (*The Walking Dead* special-effects creator) and Norman Reedus (the actor who plays Daryl in the series), this restaurant is one of the most atmospheric hangouts in town. The setting is upmarket yet unpretentious, with exposed brick walls, a vintage bar area, chandeliers and leather booths. The kitchen has an emphasis on sustainable food.

It uses mostly locally sourced, non-GMO ingredients. While the menu's not revolutionary, it offers simple tried-and-tested dishes: salads, grilled flatbreads and gourmet burgers. Plus, there's a rotation of six other mains – items like grilled salmon, steak and penne pasta.

WORTH A TRIP

BEST BBQ

Barbecue is king in South Georgia. The traditional smoke pits here are some of the finest in the world, and these two joints deserve a detour.

Fresh Air (770-775-3182; www.freshairbarbecue.com; 1164 Hwy 42, Jackson; BBQ pork sandwiches from $2.95, mains $6.50-7.50; 8am-7:30pm Mon-Thu, to 8:30pm Fri & Sat, to 8pm Sun;) A glorious warm and friendly pioneer-style wooden roadside shack with outdoor seating and sawdust out front. Only three things are served here: chopped pork, Brunswick stew and coleslaw. No ribs. No shoulder. The result is transcendent, vinegary BBQ – and it's even better with a dash of hot sauce.

Vandy's (912-764-2444; www.vandysbbq.com; 22 W Vine St, Statesboro; mains $8-14; 6am-2pm Mon-Thu, to 3pm Fri & Sat;) The real deal – it uses one of only six open BBQ pits left in the state. The chopped-pork sandwich is served with a vinegar-and-mustard-based sauce on two slices of Sunbeam white bread (baked next door). The hog is smoked overnight in the massive block-and-brick pit out back to beat the Georgia heat. Ribs are available on Tuesdays.

Southern Country Steakhouse STEAK $$

(770-599-9616; www.facebook.com/SOCO Senoia; 34 Chestlehurst Rd; mains $9-20; 4pm-2am Thu-Sat) This dive bar/restaurant just outside Senoia's main town has a classic American roadhouse look, with an old rusty farm truck outside, and is decorated with wooden garden tables, wagon wheels and farm memorabilia. Regular karaoke and occasional line dancing take place here (call ahead, schedules vary). However, the menu is unexceptional, with standard rib eye and hamburgers, plus service can be slow.

Drinking & Nightlife

Senoia Coffee & Cafe CAFE

(770-599-8000; www.senoiacoffeecafe.com; 1 Main St; coffee from $1.45; 7am-5pm Mon-Sat, 9am-4pm Sun;) This beloved cafe is situated mere steps from *The Walking Dead* film set. Fortunately, it's better known for its excellent coffee and airy interior than harrowing decisions about which survivor to rescue or leave behind. You might see members of the cast and crew in here during filming season.

Fun menu items (from $5) that *Walking Dead* fans will love include the Maggie's Farmhouse breakfast, with two eggs and a choice of meat; the Hershel's Hash, potatoes, corned beef and all the trimmings; plus the Alexandria Sunrise – with two eggs, sausage and biscuit 'safely tucked behind a "wall" of our famous sausage gravy.'

Maguire's IRISH PUB

(https://maguiresirishpub.com; 42 Main St, enter via Seavy St; 11am-until late) Your best chance for a pint in this sleepy town is Maguire's basement bar, which usually has craft ale and local brews on tap. There's trivia on Wednesdays and sometimes live music at the weekends. There is food available (mains $10–$18, kitchen open until 9pm Sunday to Thursday, to 10pm Friday and Saturday).

Shopping

FoxxHollow Antiques ANTIQUES

(770-599-0606; www.facebook.com/foxx hollowantiques; 7 Main St; 11am-5pm Wed-Sat) You can't miss this place – there's a big metal giraffe out front. Get locally made and sourced gifts and trinkets for your home at this cozy store, plus larger pieces of furniture.

Getting There & Away

Some companies run filming location tours to Senoia from Atlanta, but travelers can access the area via car. Take I-85 to Rte 16.

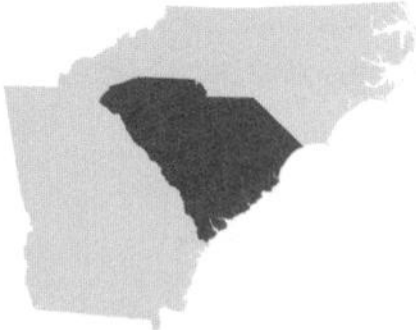

Charleston & South Carolina

POP 4.9 MILLION

Includes ➡

Best Places to Eat

- ➡ 167 Raw (p182)
- ➡ FIG (p182)
- ➡ Edmund's Oast (p182)
- ➡ TW Graham & Co (p194)
- ➡ Ribaut Social Club (p207)

Best Places to Stay

- ➡ Zero George Street (p179)
- ➡ Wentworth Mansion (p180)
- ➡ Water's Edge Inn (p201)
- ➡ Anchorage 1770 (p206)
- ➡ Swamp Rabbit Inn (p228)

Why Go?

Moss-draped oaks. Stately mansions. Wide beaches. Rolling mountains. And an ornery streak as old as the state itself. Ah yes, South Carolina, where the accents are thicker and the traditions more dear. From its Revolutionary War patriots to its 1860s secessionist government to its outspoken legislators, the Palmetto State has never shied away from a fight.

Most travelers stick to the coast, with its splendid antebellum cities and palm-tree-studded beaches. But the interior has a wealth of sleepy old towns, wild and undeveloped state parks and spooky black-water swamps. Along the sea islands you hear the sweet songs of the Gullah, a culture and language created by former slaves who held on to many West African traditions through the ravages of time.

From well-bred, gardenia-scented Charleston to up-and-coming Greenville to bright, tacky Myrtle Beach, South Carolina is always a fascinating destination.

When to Go

- ➡ Catch sun without the crowds between spring break and summer vacation in May.
- ➡ A 17-day barrage of world-class performing arts fills Charleston's historic venues at Spoleto from late May to mid-June.
- ➡ School back in session and cooler days make peeping at fall foliage a peaceful proposition in October.

Information

South Carolina Department of Parks, Recreation & Tourism (☎803-734-0124; www.discoversouthcarolina.com) Can mail you the state's official vacation guide on request. The state's nine highway welcome centers offer free wi-fi (ask inside for the passwords).

Getting There & Away

South Carolina's three main gateways are **Charleston International Airport** (Map p196; ☎843-767-7009; www.chs-airport.com; 5500 International Blvd), **Greenville–Spartanburg International Airport** (☎864-877-7426; www.gspairport.com; 2000 GSP Dr, Greer) and **Myrtle Beach International Airport** (☎843-448-1580; www.flymyrtlebeach.com; 1100 Jetport Rd). Regional hubs include **Columbia Metropolitan Airport** (☎803-822-5000; www.columbiaairport.com; 3250 Airport Blvd) and **Savannah/Hilton Head International Airport** (☎912-964-0514; www.savannahairport.com; 400 Airways Ave), which is actually located in Georgia but is the major airport for the Hilton Head region.

Amtrak and Greyhound serve a few of the major metropolitan areas.

Getting Around

The best way to see South Carolina is by car. Rental companies can be found in major cities and at the Greenville–Spartanburg and Charleston airports.

Public transportation in South Carolina cities is limited, but ridesharing apps are widely used.

CHARLESTON

☎843 / POP 134,400

The zenith of old-world charm, Charleston whisks you into the nation's tumultuous past and nourishes your mind, heart and stomach in roughly equal measure.

This lovely city will embrace you with the warmth and hospitality of an old and dear friend – who lived in the 18th century. We jest, but the cannons, cemeteries and carriage rides absolutely conjure an earlier era. Here, signers of the Declaration of Independence puffed cigars and whispered of revolution in the withdrawing rooms of historic homes, and the first shots of the Civil War rang out over Fort Sumter in Charleston Harbor. The city itself was built on slave labor, and several related sights are among the nation's most important educators on the long-standing oppression of African Americans.

Its chefs are regular contenders for James Beard awards. Its restaurants and dishes frequently get the nod from magazines like *Bon Appétit*. And with culinary roots in Europe, the Caribbean and West Africa, is it any wonder that every year millions of people pack a toothbrush just to eat in Charleston? But reading or hearing about delicious things never quite satisfies the way, say, slurping a raw oyster can. Or tearing into a fried green tomato. Or swirling the cream and sherry in a bowl of she-crab soup...

The streets of Charleston's downtown are often characterized as a living museum, and that's entirely accurate. Historic homes, churches and landmarks pepper the city, with many of them concentrated in the city's Historic District. Other important sites can be found clustered on the city's eastern side, near and within the Aquarium Wharf.

Outside the city, the plantations are all worth visiting, each for different reasons. To the west, the Charleston Tea Plantation (p201) and Angel Oak Tree (p200) are fascinating sights well worth the drive.

History

In strolling the tidy, peaceful streets of Charleston today, it's sometimes difficult to imagine the terrors that came before: the earthquakes, the fires, the hurricanes, slavery, the Revolutionary War and the Civil War, just to name a few. The city has managed to survive it all, and to rebuild stronger each time. Today Charleston is a living museum, and its battle scars teach important lessons. Perhaps that is exactly the reason so many people feel compelled to visit.

Sights & Activities

South of Broad & the French Quarter

Whether you're bouncing around in a horse-drawn carriage, poking around a palatial historic home or peering through a wrought-iron gate at a flourishing garden, you'll understand that the storybook Southern charm of the peninsula's southeastern tip cannot be exaggerated.

South of Broad is simply awash in quiet elegance, and has long been considered the zenith of Charlestonian prosperity. In the French Quarter, romance emanates from cobblestone streets, and the city's oldest buildings perch among delicious restaurants and vibrant galleries.

Charleston & South Carolina Highlights

❶ **Charleston** (p167) Admiring the historic beauty of one of the US's most hospitable cities.

❷ **Lowcountry cuisine** (p195) Filling up on seafood-centric, African-influenced eats.

❸ **Beaufort** (p203) Losing yourself on the charming streets of this small Southern coastal town.

❹ **Greenville** (p219) Strolling through the dynamic, river-centered downtown or setting off on an outdoor adventure.

❺ **Hilton Head** (p197) Relaxing on the 12 miles of beaches that make up South Carolina's largest barrier island.

❻ **Congaree National Park** (p216) Paddling around this otherworldly inky-black swamp.

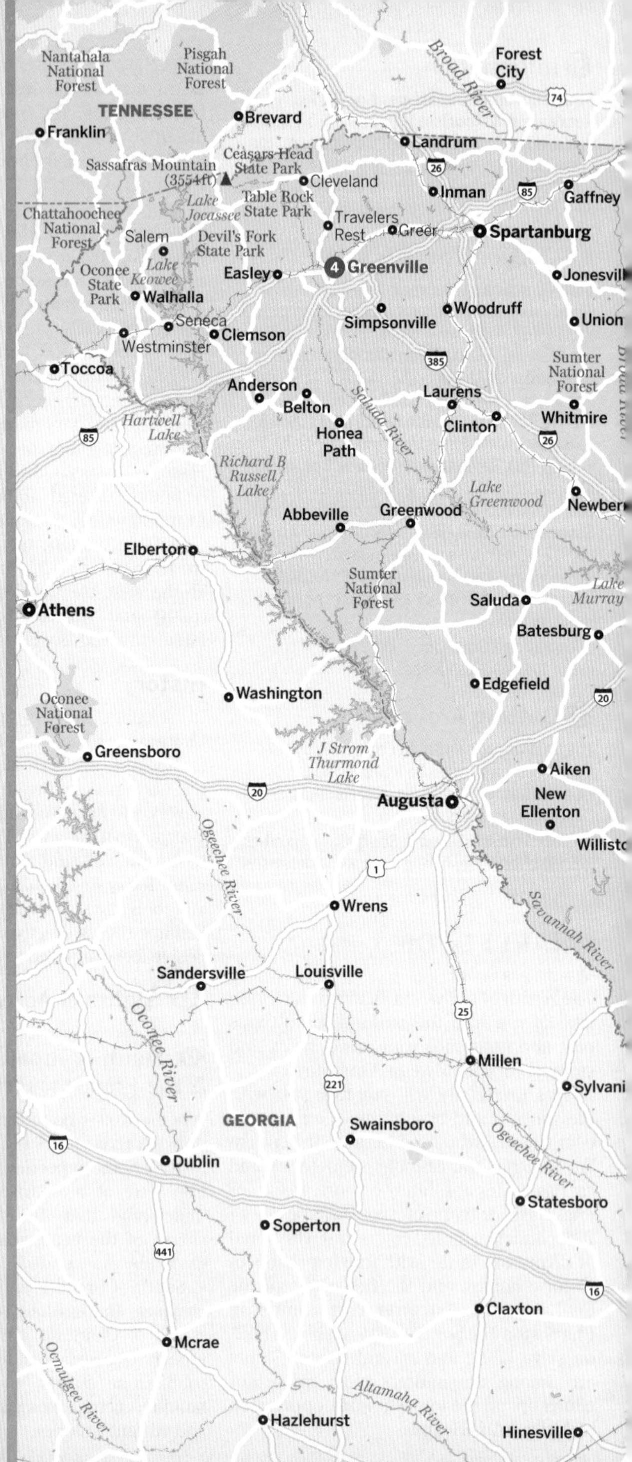

Kings Mountain
Charlotte
Albemarle
Carthage
NORTH CAROLINA
Fayetteville
Kings Mountain National Military Park
York
Monroe
Raeford
Rockingham
Rock Hill
Catawba River
Laurinburg
Lando
Chester
Lancaster
Lynches River
Cheraw
Great Pee Dee River
Beenettsville
Little Pee Dee River
Great Falls
Kershaw
Wateree Lake
Dillon
Winnsboro
Hartsville
Darlington
SOUTH CAROLINA
Camden
Bishopville
Mullins
Nichols
Tabor City
Florence
Marion
Loris
Wateree River
Columbia
Sumter
Lake City
Conway
Gadsden
Manchester State Forest
Myrtle Beach
Congaree National Park
Hemingway
Myrtle Beach State Park
North Fork Edisto River
St Matthews
Manning
Kingstree
Black River
Murrells Inlet
Huntington Beach State Park
Orangeburg
Lake Marion
St Stephens
Georgetown
Santee River
Pawleys Island
Denmark
Holly Hill
Lake Moultrie
Barnwell
St George
Moncks Corner
Francis Marion National Forest
Edisto River
McClellanville
Lowcountry
Summerville
Allendale
Bulls Bay
Cape Romain National Wildlife Refuge
Walterboro
Mt Pleasant
Hampton
Isle of Palms
Charleston
Sullivans Island
Estill
Jacksonboro
Yemassee
Folly Island
Edisto Beach State Park
Tillman
Ridgeland
Beaufort
Springfield
Port Royal
Hunting Island State Park
ATLANTIC OCEAN
Bluffton
Hilton Head Island
Daufuskie Island
Savannah
Richmond Hill
100 km
50 miles

★ Heyward-Washington House HISTORIC BUILDING

(Map p174; ☎843-722-0354; www.charlestonmuseum.org; 87 Church St; adult/child 13-17yr/child 3-12yr $12/10/5; ⏲10am-5pm Mon-Sat, noon-5pm Sun) As the name hints, this 1772 Georgian-style town house is kind of a big deal because George Washington rented it for a week, and visitors can stand in what was likely his bedroom. The owner, Thomas Heyward, Jr, was one of South Carolina's four signers of the Declaration of Independence, and it's fun to think about all the talk of revolution that must have taken place in the withdrawing room.

★ Old Slave Mart Museum MUSEUM

(Map p174; ☎843-958-6467; www.oldslavemart.org; 6 Chalmers St; adult/child 5-17yr $8/5; ⏲9am-5pm Mon-Sat) Formerly called Ryan's Mart, this building once housed an open-air market that auctioned African American men, women and children in the mid-1800s, the largest of 40 or so similar auction houses. South Carolina's shameful past is unraveled in text-heavy exhibits illuminating the slave experience; the few artifacts, such as leg shackles, are especially chilling.

Joggling Board PUBLIC ART

(Map p174; 51 Meeting St, Nathaniel Russell House; ⏲10am-5pm) FREE In the yard of the Nathaniel Russell House sits a fine specimen of a super-Charlestonian porch furnishing – the joggling board. It consists of a 16ft plank set on rockers, and was apparently used in the early 1800s to cure rheumatoid arthritis and aid in courtship. You'll have to try it out to understand.

Calhoun Mansion MUSEUM

(Map p174; ☎843-722-8205; www.calhounmansion.net; 16 Meeting St; $17; ⏲11am-5pm) If you've ever wondered what the wealthiest, fanciest, most well-traveled hoarder's house might look like, visit the Calhoun Mansion. With 35 rooms and 24,000 sq ft, this Gilded Age, Italianate manor is Charleston's largest single family residence, and nearly every inch of it brims with the eccentric homeowner's collected furnishings, art and antiques from around the world.

Nathaniel Russell House HISTORIC BUILDING

(Map p174; ☎843-724-8481; www.historiccharleston.org; 51 Meeting St; adult/child 6-16yr $12/5; ⏲10am-5pm, last tour 4:30pm) A spectacular, self-supporting spiral staircase is the highlight at this 1808 Federal-style house, built by a Rhode Islander, known in Charleston as 'King of the Yankees.' A meticulous ongoing restoration honors the home to the finest details, such as the 1000 sheets of 22-karat gold leaf in the withdrawing room. Twenty layers of wall paint were peeled back to uncover the original colors, and handmade, fitted, contoured rugs were imported from the UK, as originally done by the Russells. The small but lush English garden is also notable, as is the square-oval-rectangle footprint of the home.

Edmondston-Alston House HISTORIC BUILDING

(Map p174; ☎843-722-7171; www.edmondstonalston.com; 21 E Battery; adult/child 6-16yr $12/6; ⏲1-4:30pm Sun & Mon, 10:30am-4:30pm Tue-Sat) Charles Edmondston built this Federal-style home in 1825 for a mere $25,000, and fell on hard times in 1837, forcing him to sell it to Charles Alston for $15,500. The Alston family upgraded the home in Greek Revival style, and it remains in their possession, with one member continuing to reside on the 3rd floor. A couple of other rooms and a carriage house out back operate as a high-end B&B.

St Michael's Church CHURCH

(Map p174; ☎843-723-0603; http://stmichaelschurch.net; 71 Broad St) St Michael's is the oldest church in town, dating back to 1752, and its beloved bells have been announcing the time and various events, including earthquakes, hurricanes, fires and attacks on the city, for more than 250 years.

John Rutledge and Charles Cotesworth Pinckney (both signers of the US Constitution) are buried here, and the steeple was painted black during the Revolutionary War to prevent it from being used as a target.

Rainbow Row AREA

(Map p174; 83 E Bay St) With its 13 candy-colored houses, this stretch of Georgian row houses on lower E Bay St is one of the most photographed areas in Charleston. The structures date back to 1730, when they served as merchant stores on the wharf, a sketchy part of town at the time. Starting in the 1920s the buildings were restored and painted over in pastels. People dug it, and soon much of the rest of Charleston was getting a similar makeover.

CHARLESTON IN...

One Day

Spend a couple of hours meandering around Charleston's awe-inspiring Historic District, following our self-guided South of Broad walking tour (p184) or jumping on one with **Charleston Footprints** (p176). Take lunch at **Gaulart & Maliclet** (p181) or **Poogan's Porch** (p183).

For a crucial history lesson on antebellum Charleston, visit the **Old Slave Mart Museum**, in the same building where enslaved Africans were once auctioned to the highest bidder. Next, tour the **Nathaniel Russell House** (with a heightened appreciation of the slave labor on which it was built), or time-travel to the 1700s at the **Heyward-Washington House**.

For dinner, consider making a reservation well in advance at **FIG** (p182). Otherwise, drop into **167 Raw** (p182), which doesn't take reservations.

After dinner, stroll the city a bit more, popping in and out of any cocktail bar that catches your eye. And for a great view of the city at night, be sure you make a stop at a rooftop place like **Pavilion Bar** (p186) or **Rooftop at the Vendue** (p187).

Two Days

Have a wander through history in the (p172; founded in 1773, it's America's oldest), and if you're still keen on touring 19th-century homes, spring for the combo ticket that includes the **Joseph Manigault House** (p172). For lunch, stroll along King St browsing menus, and choose your spot. For Nashville-style hot quail legs, head straight for **Virginia's on King** (p184).

Visit with some otters, rehabbing sea turtles and an albino alligator in the **South Carolina Aquarium** (p172) then jump on the afternoon **Fort Sumter Boat Tour** (p177) to see where the Civil War began.

Reserve a table at **Zero Café + Bar** (p182) well in advance for dinner, and splurge on the tasting menu (with wine pairings).

After dinner, hit up a craft cocktail bar or two – **Proof** (p188) is great, and at **Prohibition** (p188), you can also swing dance – before settling in at **Theatre 99** (p189) for some sidesplitting improv.

Old Exchange & Provost Dungeon HISTORIC BUILDING
(Map p174; ☎843-727-2165; www.oldexchange.org; 122 E Bay St; adult/child 7-12yr $10/5; ⏲9am-5pm; 👪) Kids love the creepy dungeon, used as a prison for American patriots held by the British during the Revolutionary War. The cramped space sits beneath a stately Georgian Palladian customs house completed in 1771. Costumed guides lead the dungeon tours. Exhibits about the city are displayed on the upper floors. Combination tickets with the Old Slave Mart Museum cost adult/child $15/8.

Battery & White Point Garden GARDENS
(Map p174; cnr East Battery & Murray Blvd) The Battery is the southern tip of the Charleston Peninsula, buffered by a seawall. Stroll past cannons and statues of military heroes in the gardens, then walk the promenade and look for Fort Sumter.

Waterfront Park PARK
(Map p174; ☎843-724-7321; 1 Vendue Range; ⏲24hr) A lovely, eight-acre park on the Cooper River, notable for its landscape architecture and eye-catching, pineapple-shaped fountain. During summer it's a great place to stroll and cool off in.

St Philip's Church CHURCH
(Map p174; www.stphilipschurchsc.org; 146 Church St) An Episcopal church erected in 1835, considered all-important by the first city residents. Lots of famous people were buried in the church cemetery and also the one across the street, known as the 'strangers churchyard.' The body of former Vice President John C Calhoun has been buried, moved away and reburied here.

A loose path, the Gateway Walk (p176), winds through several church grounds and graveyards between St John's Lutheran Church and St Philip's Church.

HOUSE HUNTERS

Unless you're an antiques fanatic, don't take more than a couple of tours inside historical homes. A lot of the same information gets repeated, and it's far more romantic to be wandering the city.

East Side, NoMo & Hampton Park

Most of the must-see sights in these neighborhoods ('No Mo' stands for North Morrison) are clustered on the East Side and tend to be historical in nature – the Aiken-Rhett House (p172), the Charleston Museum (p172) and the Joseph Manigault House are all top notch. The South Carolina Aquarium is great for kids, and at the wharf next door boats leave for Fort Sumter. The Hampton Park area offers less-visited sights including the Citadel and Hampton Park.

★ Fort Sumter National Monument HISTORIC SITE
(Map p196; ☎843-883-3123; www.nps.gov/fosu) The first shots of the Civil War rang out at Fort Sumter, on a pentagon-shaped island in the harbor. A Confederate stronghold, this fort was shelled to bits by Union forces from 1863 to 1865. A few original guns and fortifications give a feel for the momentous history here.

★ Aiken-Rhett House HISTORIC BUILDING
(Map p174; ☎843-723-1159; www.historiccharleston.org; 48 Elizabeth St; adult/child 6-16yr $12/5; ⏲10am-5pm, last tour 4:15pm) The only surviving urban town-house complex, this 1820 abode gives a fascinating glimpse into antebellum life on a 45-minute self-guided audio tour. The role of slaves is emphasized and visitors wander into their dorm-style quarters behind the house before moving on to the lifestyle of the rich and famous.

The Historic Charleston Foundation manages the property 'preserved as found,' conserving but not restoring it. There have been few alterations and you get it as is, peeling Parisian wallpaper and all.

Redux Contemporary Art Center ARTS CENTER
(Map p174; ☎843-722-0697; www.reduxstudios.org; 1056 King St; ⏲10am-6pm Tue-Fri, noon-5pm Sat) A contemporary-art hub and event space, with three galleries, a few dozen studios and some classrooms.

South Carolina Aquarium AQUARIUM
(Map p174; ☎843-577-3474; http://scaquarium.org; 100 Aquarium Wharf; adult/child $30/23; ⏲9am-5pm; 👪) A showcase of South Carolina's wildlife, with creatures hailing from the mountain forest, piedmont, salt marsh, coastal and undersea habitats. Although the facility is rather small in comparison with some of the country's more prominent aquariums, there are plenty of fish and other creatures. Noteworthy residents include otters, rattlesnakes, sharks and an albino alligator.

Hampton Park PARK
(Map p174; ☎843-724-7327; 30 Mary Murray Dr) A big, awesome park that locals love for its arboreal and floral displays, fitness trail and large swaths of open space, often utilized for things like Frisbee matches. It has public restrooms and parking, and is rarely crowded.

Charleston Museum MUSEUM
(Map p174; ☎843-722-2996; www.charlestonmuseum.org; 360 Meeting St; adult/child 3-17yr/child 3-12yr $12/10/5; ⏲9am-5pm Mon-Sat, noon-5pm Sun) Founded in 1773, this is the country's oldest museum. It's helpful and informative if you're looking for historical background before strolling through the Historic District. Exhibits spotlight various periods of Charleston's long and storied history.

Joseph Manigault House HISTORIC BUILDING
(Map p174; ☎843-722-2996; www.charlestonmuseum.org; 350 Meeting St; adult/child 13-17yr/child 3-12yr $12/10/5; ⏲10am-5pm Mon-Sat, noon-5pm Sun, last tour 4:30pm) This three-story Federal-style house from 1803 was once the showpiece of a French Huguenot rice planter. There's a tiny neoclassical gate temple in the garden and the house is full of 19th-century furnishings from the collection of the Charleston Museum, which runs the site.

Citadel Campus & Museum SCHOOL
(Map p174; ☎843-953-6845; www.citadel.edu/root; 171 Moultrie St; ⏲7:30am-10pm Mon-Thu, to 5pm Fri, 9am-3pm Sat, noon-10:30pm Sun) FREE South Carolina's military-college campus is set in historic buildings and is replete with uniformed cadets and various memorials. There's a small museum on the 3rd floor of the library that displays mostly military apparel and a recreation of historic barracks.

SK8 Charleston SKATING

(☎843-406-6971; www.ccprc.com/1725/SK8-Charleston; 1549 Oceanic St; per skater/spectator $3/1; ⏲2-10pm Mon-Fri, 10am-10pm Sat & Sun) SK8 Charleston is a 32,500-sq-ft skate park just north of NoMo, overlooking the Ashley River. There's a 200ft snake run, a pro bowl, an intermediate bowl and a 315ft street course. There's also live music, concessions, giveaways and skateboarding demonstrations.

Harleston Village & Upper King

These neighborhoods don't have have any of the big-name attractions. But places of worship and offbeat museums and galleries abound.

Marion Square SQUARE

(Map p174; ☎843-724-7327; www.nps.gov/nr/travel/charleston/mar.htm; 329 Meeting St; ⏲24hr) Charleston's most frequented park is 10 acres of green space in the middle of downtown, bordering on King, Calhoun, Meeting and Tobacco Sts. It's the home of the wildly popular Farmers Market (p191) and also houses several monuments, including a soaring statue of former Vice President John C Calhoun.

Karpeles Manuscript Library Museum MUSEUM

(Map p174; ☎843-853-4651; www.rain.org/~karpeles; 68 Spring St; ⏲11am-4pm Tue-Sun) FREE An outpost of the world's largest private collection of important original manuscripts and documents, housed in a former Methodist church built in 1856. Exhibits rotate three times a year, making this a popular stop with locals. They include Einstein's Theory of Relativity, Freud's manuscript on dreams and Darwin's conclusion to his Theory of Evolution.

College of Charleston COLLEGE

(Map p174; ☎843-805-5507; www.cofc.edu; 66 George St) Spread over a few city blocks at the center of Charleston's downtown, this university was founded in 1770 and is the oldest in the state. The campus is notable for its lush landscaping, which includes live oaks draped in Spanish moss, as well as its historic mansions and homes, some of which contain residence halls and Greek institutions.

George Gallery ART STUDIO

(Map p174; ☎843-579-7328; http://georgegalleryart.com; 50 Bogard St; ⏲10am-5pm Tue-Fri, 11am-5pm Sat) A neighborhood favorite, this contemporary-art gallery displays mostly abstract and nonobjective work of artists from the East Coast with some connection to Charleston. There are no actual rules, though – just whatever the owner feels like.

Gibbes Museum of Art GALLERY

(Map p174; ☎843-722-2706; www.gibbesmuseum.org; 135 Meeting St; adult/child $15/6; ⏲10am-5pm Tue & Thu-Sat, to 8pm Wed, 1-5pm Sun) Houses a decent collection of American and Southern works. The contemporary collection includes works by local artists, with Lowcountry life as a highlight. A 2016 renovation added a new museum store and cafe as well as 30% more gallery space.

Kahal Kadosh Beth Elohim SYNAGOGUE

(Map p174; ☎843-723-1090; www.kkbe.org; 90 Hasell St; ⏲10am-4pm Sun-Fri) The oldest continuously used synagogue in the country, complete with a museum and gift shop. A tour costs $10 for adults and is free for children; check the website for tour times.

Urban Nirvana SPA

(Map p174; ☎843-724-6555; www.urbannirvana.com; 141 Wentworth St; ⏲9am-7pm Mon-Sat, 11am-6pm Sun) On the grounds of the Wentworth Mansion (p180) in gorgeously converted former stables, this elegant, relaxing spa is defined by brick and exposed wood beams. Complete with heated blankets and aromatic oils, the treatments are nothing short of transportive. The woman who does the facials is a real pro (facials from $60).

Alley BOWLING

(Map p174; ☎843-818-4080; www.thealleycharleston.com; 131 Columbus St; per lane per hour Sun-Thu $35, Fri & Sat $45; ⏲4pm-2am Mon-Wed, 11am-2am Thu-Sun) Superfun bar to play Skee-Ball, table hockey, bowling and Pop-A-Shot. It also has arcade games and decent pub food. Wednesday is trivia night and Tuesday has $2 bowling lanes after 9pm.

Charleston

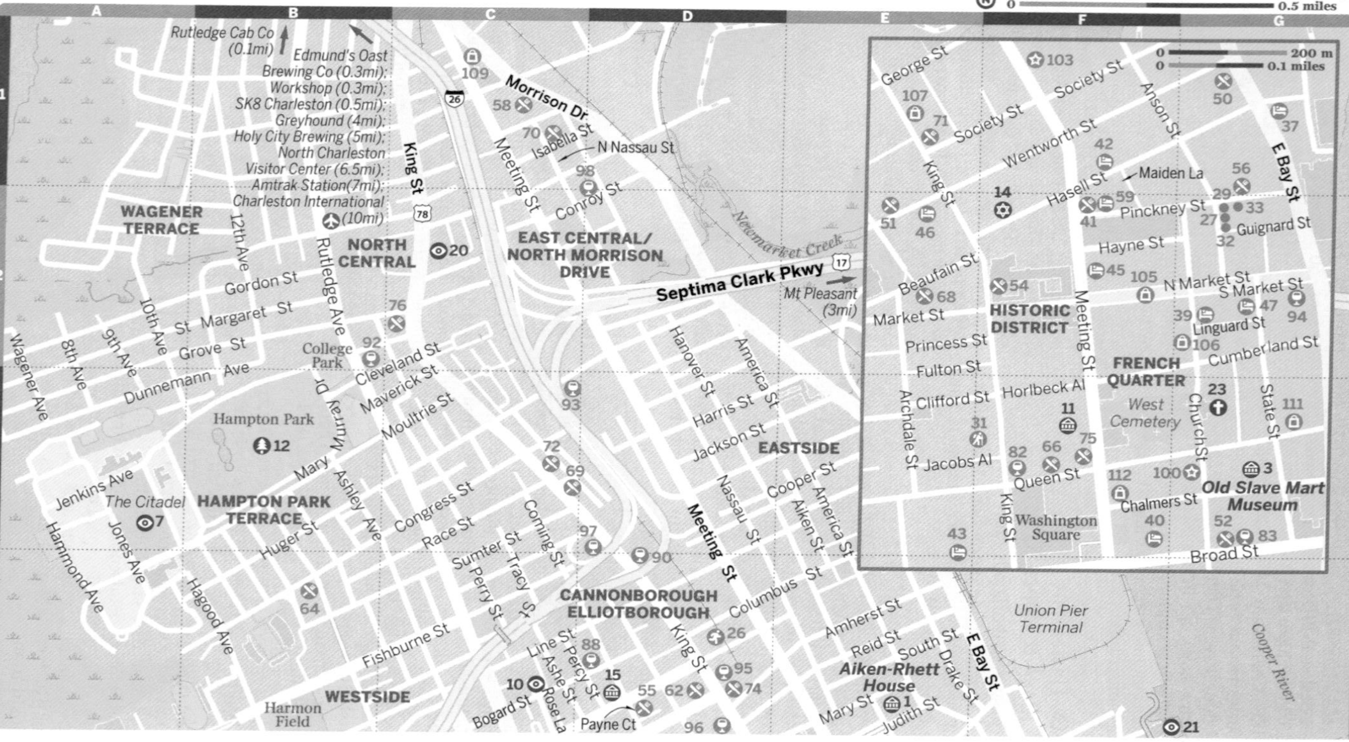
0 1 km
0 0.5 miles
0 200 m
0 0.1 miles
A
B
C
D
E
F
G
1
2
3
4
Rutledge Cab Co (0.1mi)
Edmund's Oast Brewing Co (0.3mi); Workshop (0.3mi); SK8 Charleston (0.5mi); Greyhound (4mi); Holy City Brewing (5mi); North Charleston Visitor Center (6.5mi); Amtrak Station (7mi); Charleston International (10mi)
WAGENER TERRACE
NORTH CENTRAL
EAST CENTRAL/ NORTH MORRISON DRIVE
HAMPTON PARK TERRACE
EASTSIDE
CANNONBOROUGH ELLIOTBOROUGH
WESTSIDE
HISTORIC DISTRICT
FRENCH QUARTER
Old Slave Mart Museum
Aiken-Rhett House
Hampton Park
College Park
The Citadel
Harmon Field
Union Pier Terminal
Cooper River
Newmarket Creek
West Cemetery
Washington Square
Mt Pleasant (3mi)
Septima Clark Pkwy
Morrison Dr
King St
Meeting St
Rutledge Ave
E Bay St
Isabella St
N Nassau St
Conroy St
12th Ave
10th Ave
9th Ave
8th Ave
Wagener Ave
Gordon St
Margaret St
Grove St
Dunnemann Ave
Cleveland St
Maverick St
Moultrie St
Murray Dr
Mary St
Ashley Ave
Congress St
Race St
Sumter St
Coming St
Tracy St
Perry St
Huger St
Jenkins Ave
Jones Ave
Hammond Ave
Hagood Ave
Fishburne St
Line St
Percy St
Ashe St
Rose La
Bogard St
Payne Ct
Hanover St
America St
Harris St
Jackson St
Nassau St
Cooper St
Aiken St
Columbus St
Amherst St
Reid St
South St
Drake St
Mary St
Judith St
George St
Society St
Wentworth St
Anson St
Hasell St
Maiden La
Pinckney St
Guignard St
Hayne St
N Market St
S Market St
Beaufain St
Market St
Linguard St
Cumberland St
Princess St
Fulton St
Horlbeck Al
Clifford St
Archdale St
Jacobs Al
Queen St
Church St
State St
Chalmers St
Broad St
1
3
7
10
11
12
14
15
20
21
23
26
27
29
31
32
33
37
39
40
41
42
43
45
46
47
50
51
52
54
55
56
58
59
62
64
66
68
69
70
71
72
74
75
76
82
83
88
90
92
93
94
95
96
97
98
100
103
105
106
107
109
111
112

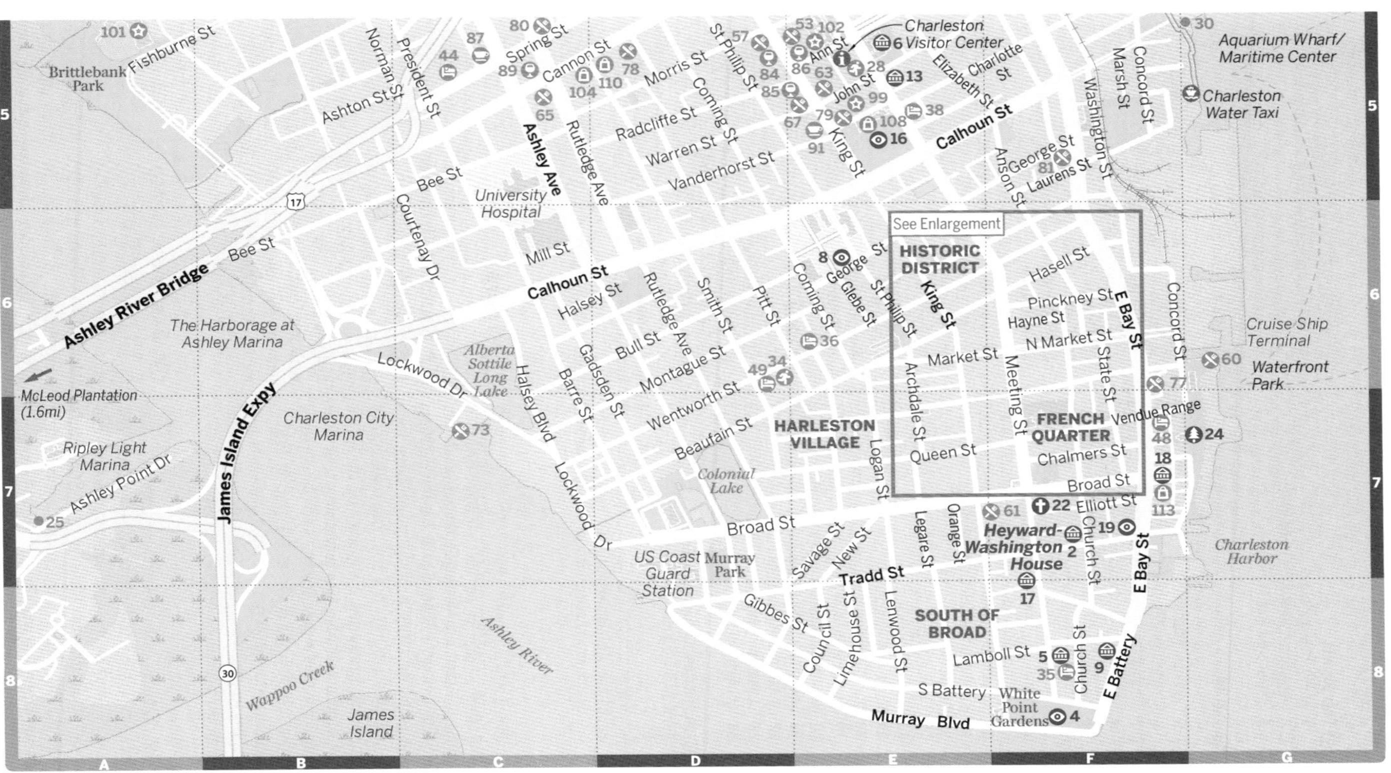
Brittlebank
Park
Fishburne St
Ashton St
Norman St
President St
Spring St
Cannon St
Morris St
St Philip St
Coming St
Radcliffe St
Warren St
Vanderhorst St
Ann St
John St
King St
Charleston
Visitor Center
Elizabeth St
Charlotte
St
Calhoun St
Washington St
Marsh St
Concord St
Aquarium Wharf/
Maritime Center
Charleston
Water Taxi
Ashley Ave
Rutledge Ave
Bee St
University
Hospital
Anson St
George St
Laurens St
Courtenay Dr
Mill St
Bee St
Ashley River Bridge
Calhoun St
Halsey St
The Harborage at
Ashley Marina
See Enlargement
HISTORIC
DISTRICT
George St
Glebe St
St Philip St
King St
Hasell St
Pinckney St
Hayne St
N Market St
Market St
E Bay St
Concord St
Cruise Ship
Terminal
Waterfront
Park
Rutledge Ave
Smith St
Pitt St
Coming St
Bull St
Montague St
Gadsden St
Barre St
Wentworth St
Lockwood Dr
Alberta
Sottile
Long
Lake
Halsey Blvd
McLeod Plantation
(1.6mi)
James Island Expy
Charleston City
Marina
Archdale St
Meeting St
State St
Vendue Range
FRENCH
QUARTER
HARLESTON
VILLAGE
Beaufain St
Logan St
Queen St
Chalmers St
Broad St
Ripley Light
Marina
Ashley Point Dr
Colonial
Lake
Lockwood Dr
Elliott St
Broad St
Heyward-
Washington
House
Church St
E Bay St
Charleston
Harbor
US Coast
Guard
Station
Murray
Park
Savage St
New St
Legare St
Orange St
Tradd St
Gibbes St
Council St
Limehouse St
Lenwood St
SOUTH OF
BROAD
Ashley River
Lamboll St
Church St
E Battery
Wappoo Creek
S Battery
White
Point
Gardens
Murray Blvd
James
Island

Charleston

Top Sights

1 Aiken-Rhett House ... E4
2 Heyward-Washington House ... F7
3 Old Slave Mart Museum ... G3

Sights

4 Battery & White Point Garden ... F8
5 Calhoun Mansion ... F8
6 Charleston Museum ... E5
7 Citadel Campus & Museum ... A3
8 College of Charleston ... E6
9 Edmondston-Alston House ... F8
10 George Gallery ... C4
11 Gibbes Museum of Art ... F3
12 Hampton Park ... B3
Joggling Board ... (see 17)
13 Joseph Manigault House ... E5
14 Kahal Kadosh Beth Elohim ... F2
15 Karpeles Manuscript Library Museum ... D4
16 Marion Square ... E5
17 Nathaniel Russell House ... F8
18 Old Exchange & Provost Dungeon ... F7
19 Rainbow Row ... F7
20 Redux Contemporary Art Center ... C2
21 South Carolina Aquarium ... G4
22 St Michael's Church ... F7
23 St Philip's Church ... G3
24 Waterfront Park ... G7

Activities, Courses & Tours

25 Adventure Harbor Tours ... A7
26 Alley ... D4
27 Bulldog Tours ... G2
28 Charleston Brews Cruise ... E5
Charleston Footprints ... (see 112)
29 Culinary Tours of Charleston ... G2
30 Fort Sumter Boat Tour ... G5
31 Gateway Walk ... F3
32 Old South Carriage Co ... G2
33 Palmetto Carriage Works ... G2
34 Urban Nirvana ... D6

Sleeping

35 15 Church Street ... F8
36 1837 Bed & Breakfast ... E6
37 Ansonborough Inn ... G1
38 Dewberry ... E5
39 French Quarter Inn ... G2
40 Historic Charleston B&B ... F3
41 Indigo Inn ... F2
42 Jasmine House Inn ... F1
43 John Rutledge House Inn ... E3
44 Not So Hostel ... C5
45 Planters Inn ... F2
46 Restoration ... E2
47 Spectator ... G2
48 Vendue ... F7
49 Wentworth Mansion ... D6
Zero George Street ... (see 81)

Eating

50 167 Raw ... G1
51 Basic Kitchen ... E2
52 Brown Dog Deli ... G3
53 Callie's Hot Little Biscuit ... E5
54 Charleston Grill ... F2
55 Chez Nous ... D4
Circa 1886 ... (see 49)
56 Cru Cafe ... G1
57 Darling Oyster Bar ... D5
58 Edmund's Oast ... C1

Charleston Brews Cruise CRUISE
(Map p174; ☎843-860-7847; https://charlestonbrewscruise.com; 375 Meeting St; drinker/nondrinker $65/25; ⊙tours 1:30pm Sun & Tue-Thu, 12:30pm Fri & Sat) The city's most popular beer tour runs buses around to a rotating selection of four local breweries every day of the week but Monday. It also has a walking tour that visits three pubs downtown ($40 per person), and a happy-hour crawl at 5:15pm on Friday and Saturday ($50 per person) involving just two breweries: Holy City Brewing (p187) and Palmetto Brewing Company (p187).

Gateway Walk WALKING
(Map p174) A loose, natural-feeling path, the Gateway Walk winds through several church grounds and overgrown graveyards between St John's Lutheran Church and St Philip's Church. The walk is particularly lovely during spring, when the wildflowers are in bloom.

Tours

South of Broad & the French Quarter

Charleston Footprints WALKING
(Map p174; ☎843-478-4718; www.charlestonfootprints.com; 2hr tour $20) An excellent walking tour of historical Charleston sights led by a knowledgeable and theatrical local. Tours begin at the Shops of Historic Charleston Foundation (p190).

East Side, NoMo & Hampton Park

Palmetto Carriage Works TOURS
(Map p174; ☎843-853-6125; https://palmettocarriage.com; 8 Guignard St; tours adult/child $26/16; ⊙9am-5pm, departing every 15 min)

59	FIG	F2
60	Fleet Landing	G6
61	Gaulart & Maliclet	F7
62	Grocery	D4
63	Halls Chophouse	E5
64	Harold's Cabin	B4
65	Hominy Grill	C5
66	Husk	F3
67	Juanita Greenberg's Nacho Royale	E5
68	Le Farfalle	E2
69	Leon's Oyster Shop	C3
70	Lewis Barbecue	C1
71	Leyla Fine Lebanese Cuisine	E1
72	Little Jack's Tavern	C3
73	Marina Variety Store	C7
74	Ordinary	D4
75	Poogan's Porch	F3
76	Rodney Scott's BBQ	C2
77	Slightly North of Broad	F6
78	Sugar Bakeshop	D5
79	Virginia's on King	E5
80	Xiao Bao Biscuit	C5
81	Zero Café + Bar	F5

Drinking & Nightlife

	Bar at Husk	(see 66)
82	Bin 152	F3
83	Blind Tiger	G3
84	Charleston Distilling Co	D5
85	Closed for Business	E5
86	Dudley's on Ann	E5
87	Eclectic	C5
88	Elliotborough Mini Bar	D4
89	Fuel	C5
90	High Wire Distilling	D4
91	Kudu	E5
92	Moe's Crosstown Tavern	B2
93	Palmetto Brewing Company	C3
94	Pavilion Bar	G2
95	Pour Taproom	D4
96	Prohibition	D4
	Proof	(see 67)
97	Recovery Room	D3
98	Revelry Brewery	D1
	Rooftop at the Vendue	(see 48)

Entertainment

99	Charleston Music Hall	E5
100	Dock Street Theatre	G3
101	Joseph P Riley, Jr Park	A5
102	Music Farm	E5
103	Theatre 99	F1

Shopping

104	Beads on Cannon	C5
	Blue Bicycle Books	(see 99)
105	Charleston City Market	F2
106	Charleston Crafts Cooperative	G2
107	Croghan's Jewel Box	E1
	Edmund's Oast Exchange	(see 58)
108	Farmers Market	E5
109	Goat. Sheep. Cow. North.	C1
110	Indigo & Cotton	D5
111	Robert Lange Studios	G3
112	Shops of Historic Charleston Foundation	F3
	Tavern at Rainbow Row	(see 113)
113	W Hampton Brand Gallery	F7

Charleston's oldest and most respected carriage-tour company. Packages including harbor cruises and plantations are also available.

Culinary Tours of Charleston FOOD & DRINK

(Map p174; ☎843-727-1100; www.culinarytoursofcharleston.com; 18 Anson St; 2½hr tour from $60) Sample grits, pralines and barbecue on food-centric walking tours of restaurants and markets. Also available: dessert tours and a celebrity-chef experience.

Old South Carriage Co TOURS

(Map p174; ☎843-723-9712; www.oldsouthcarriage.com; 14 Anson St; adult/child $25/15; ⏲after 5:30pm) This carriage-tour company has introduced a new horse-and-buggy excursion that take places in the evening. It focuses on the settlers who built Charles Town and the events that shaped the Colonial era. For incredibly brave souls there's also a nighttime haunted carriage tour.

Bulldog Tours WALKING

(Map p174; ☎843-722-8687; https://bulldogtours.com; 18 Anson St; ghost tour adult/child $25/15) Highly regarded tour com-pany offering history, food and (most imp-ortantly) ghost walks, which include stops at the Old City Jail and Provost Dungeon, along with the city's oldest graveyard.

Fort Sumter Boat Tour BOATING

(Map p174; ☎boat tour 843-722-2628, park 843-883-3123; www.fortsumtertours.com; 340 Concord St; adult/child 4-11yr $22/14) The only way to get to Fort Sumter is by this boat tour. Departure times vary throughout the year; check the website to plan your trip.

CHARLESTON FOR CHILDREN

Charleston is an imaginative city and as such a great place to bring kiddos of all ages, with plenty of attractions, museums and green spaces to stimulate their rapidly expanding minds and bodies. The visitor center has given a lot of thought to which activities are best for families, and put together a five-day itinerary at www.charlestoncvb.com/itineraries/family-playcation.

South Carolina Aquarium (p172) Kids of all ages will adore sea-creature touch tanks and the turtle rehab center.

Middleton Place (p190) For kids that will like kayaking by the Ashley River and frolicking in America's oldest manicured gardens.

Old South Carriage Co (p177) Young children will enjoy bouncing on your lap, and older ones may have their curiosity about history piqued.

Festivals & Events

ArtWalk ART
(☎304-340-4253; www.artwalkcwv.com; ⊙usually 5-8pm 3rd Thu of the month) Downtown Charleston holds a slew of art events, openings, activities and special programming, with more than 40 galleries and shops participating.

2nd Sunday on King STREET CARNIVAL
(☎843-303-1113; www.facebook.com/2ndSundayonKingSt; King St; ⊙1-5pm, 2nd Sun of the month) On the second Sunday of every month, King St closes to cars and the whole city descends for shopping, eating and merriment.

Bill Murray Look-a-Like Polar Plunge COMEDY
(Folly Beach; ⊙Jan 1) A subzero swim that pays homage to Charleston's most distinguished resident, Bill Murray, with participants attempting to resemble him in various roles. Everyone is encouraged to 'freeze your bills off' and prizes are given to the best costumes.

Southeastern Wildlife Exposition ART
(SEWE; ☎843-723-1748; http://sewe.com; ⊙Feb) The country's largest wildlife event, with three days of nature-focused art, exhibits, demonstrations and social events around the city, with an eye toward conservation.

Food & Wine Festival FOOD & DRINK
(☎843-727-9998; https://charlestonwineandfood.com; ⊙Mar) An elaborate series of dinners, wine tastings, food workshops, culinary excursions and eating seminars around Charleston during the first week in March.

Festival of Houses & Gardens FAIR
(☎843-722-3405; www.historiccharleston.org/blog/events/category/festival-houses-gardens; ⊙Mar/Apr) Run by Historic Charleston, this showcase of the city's distinctive architecture, history, gardens and culture features house and garden tours of up to 10 properties a day.

Cooper River Bridge Run SPORTS
(☎843-856-1949; www.bridgerun.com; ⊙Apr) A world-class and well-attended race from Mt Pleasant to downtown Charleston.

Spoleto USA PERFORMING ARTS
(☎843-579-3100; www.spoletousa.org; ⊙May/Jun) This 17-day performing-arts festival is South Carolina's biggest event, with operas, dramas and concerts staged across the city.

MOJA Arts Festival PERFORMING ARTS
(☎843-724-7305; www.mojafestival.com; ⊙Sep/Oct) Spirited poetry readings and gospel concerts mark this two-week celebration of African American and Caribbean culture.

Sleeping

South of Broad & the French Quarter

Options are limited in South of Broad, a residential hood where residents aren't interested in having tourists next door. There are a couple of B&Bs, however, and it's a lovely place to base yourself. The French Quarter offers a handful of suitable hotels, though you'll need some deep pockets to swing it.

Historic Charleston B&B ACCOMMODATION SERVICES $$
(Map p174; ☎843-722-6606; www.historiccharlestonbedandbreakfast.com; 55 Broad St, Suite 100; ⊙9am-5pm Mon-Fri) One of the best

ways to get to know Charleston is to stay at a small home where the owners serve up authentic Southern breakfasts and dole out great local information. They fill up fast though, so try using this agency to get a booking.

★**15 Church Street** B&B $$$
(Phillips-Yates-Snowden House; Map p174; ☎843-722-7602; www.facebook.com/FifteenChurch; 15 Church St; r $235-325; ❄📶) Tucked into a historic home in the heart of South of Broad, this charming B&B largely flies under the radar. But those who stumble upon it are treated to a very Charleston experience complete with history lessons, dainty accommodations, and a wine-and-cheese hour run by a host couple who might as well write a guidebook on Southern hospitality.

Vendue INN $$$
(Map p174; ☎843-577-7970; www.thevendue.com; 19 Vendue Range; r $149-389; P❄📶) This 84-room boutique inn exudes an inviting, smart, modern style. Reimagined as an art hotel after a renovation, it displays artwork property-wide (all for sale), is home to an in-house artist studio, and the inn itself unfurls like a masterpiece of architecture and design. It also has a fine-dining restaurant, the Drawing Room.

French Quarter Inn HOTEL $$$
(Map p174; ☎843-722-1900; https://fqicharleston.com; 166 Church St; r $300-700; ❄📶) Under the same ownership as the nearby Spectator, this genteel, welcoming hotel is not historic (it was built in 2002), but it is well placed for exploring downtown. Its dramatic spiral staircase is a joy to climb and the verdant rooftop terrace is lovely to visit around sundown, during the wine hour. Comfy rooms and superfriendly service round out offerings.

Spectator BOUTIQUE HOTEL $$$
(Map p174; ☎843-724-4326; www.thespectatorhotel.com; 67 State St; r $400-500; P❄📶) One of the city's swankiest newest hotels offers above-and-beyond service and amenities (including things like personal butlers and warming towel racks), plus a bit of Jazz Age flair. Furnishings and common areas are decidedly plush, and the central location is great for sightseers. Parking is $30 a night.

East Side, NoMo & Hampton Park

There aren't too many options in Hampton Park or NoMo, but the East Side has some of the city's most desirable and reasonably priced inns. Backpackers will be out of luck, though.

★**Ansonborough Inn** HOTEL $$
(Map p174; ☎800-522-2073; www.ansonboroughinn.com; 21 Hasell St; r from $169-329; P❄@📶) Droll neo-Victorian touches such as the closet-sized British pub and the formal portraits of dogs add a sense of fun to this intimate Historic District hotel, which also manages to feel like an antique sailing ship. Huge guest rooms mix old and new, with worn leather couches, high ceilings and flat-screen TVs.

Indigo Inn BOUTIQUE HOTEL $$
(Map p174; ☎843-577-5900; www.indigoinn.com; 1 Maiden Lane; r $209-359; P❄📶🐾) This snazzy 40-room inn enjoys a prime location in the middle of the Historic District and an oasis-like private courtyard, where guests can enjoy free wine and cheese by the fountain. Decor gives a nod to the 18th century and is a tad frilly, but the beds are comfy and renovated bathrooms have been modernized. Pets are $40 per night.

★**Zero George Street** BOUTIQUE HOTEL $$$
(Map p174; ☎843-817-7900; www.zerogeorge.com; 0 George St; r from $699; ❄📶) Live – if only for a night – like a well-heeled Charlestonian at this lovingly restored, C 1804 property in quiet, residential Ansonborough. The adorable stucco homes and brick carriage houses contain 16 unique rooms arranged in neutral tones and contemporary furnishings, but the true draws are the dreamy piazzas, lush courtyard gardens and the tiny, candlelit Zero Café + Bar (p182).

WHAT TO PACK

➡ Pack a bathing suit – there are five beaches within an hour of Charleston's downtown.

➡ Don't forget comfortable shoes. Walking is the best way to experience the city, and sometimes parking can be a bummer downtown.

➡ If you've got your own shucker, bring it, and try to get involved in an oyster roast; they are ubiquitous and good fun.

Planters Inn HISTORIC HOTEL $$$
(Map p174; ☎843-722-2345; www.plantersinn.com; 112 N Market St; r from $359; P ☎) Elegant and centrally located, this upscale historic hotel has added some fabulous new rooms, including the most sumptuous quarters in the city. The 1460-sq-ft pied-à-terre, dubbed the St Philip Suite, comes with a David Boatwright mural, the best view in the city, regally arched doorways and much more. It's pretty ridiculous, ya'll.

Dewberry LUXURY HOTEL $$$
(Map p174; ☎843-558-8000; www.thedewberrycharleston.com; 334 Meeting St; r from $300; P) Once an abandoned federal office building, this former eyesore was tinkered with by architects for eight years before reopening as a glistening ode to mid-century modern design. It's a postbellum breath of fresh air, ingeniously curated with the finest of local furnishings, textiles and hand-painted wallpaper. Rooms are opulent but homey, with floor-to-ceiling windows, plush mattresses and all-marble bathrooms.

Jasmine House Inn B&B $$$
(Map p174; ☎843-577-0041; www.jasminehouseinnbnb.com; 64 Hasell St; r from $339; P) A sister property of the lovely Indigo Inn (p179), this Greek Revival, apricot-colored mansion across the street offers a bit more intimacy and privacy with its 11 well-appointed rooms. Furnishings and antiques channel the mid-1800s, and the piazzas and back courtyard are excellent spots to take breakfast and relax. No children allowed.

Harleston Village & Upper King

Cannonborough Elliotborough contains the city's only hostel, and Harleston Village offers its most lavish Gilded Age mansion. There are a few stays in between, and basing yourself around these parts is a lovely way to enjoy a quieter side of Charleston.

CULTURAL FIRSTS

Charleston is home to the nation's first public college (the College of Charleston), first museum (the Charleston Museum) and first theater (the Dock Street Theatre).

Not So Hostel HOSTEL $
(Map p174; ☎843-722-8383; www.notsohostel.com; 156 Spring St; dm $28, r $65-106; P) Housed mainly in a wonderful 1840 dwelling complete with atmospheric blue porches and an odd, twin-matching architecture setup, Charleston's one hostel is creaky and inviting. A couple of eight-bed co-ed dorms, various four-bed male and female dorms, and nice but cramped private rooms (some with private baths) are spread over three buildings with guest kitchens throughout. Green initiatives abound.

1837 Bed & Breakfast B&B $$
(Map p174; ☎843-723-7166; www.1837bb.com; 126 Wentworth St; r $139-275; P) Close to the College of Charleston, this B&B may bring to mind the home of your eccentric, antique-loving aunt. The 1837 has nine charmingly overdecorated rooms, including three in the old brick carriage house. And, no, you're not drunk – those warped porches are lopsided as hell and full of history.

★ **Wentworth Mansion** HISTORIC HOTEL $$$
(Map p174; ☎843-853-1886; www.wentworthmansion.com; 149 Wentworth St; r from $400; P) Routinely named a top stay in the country, this Gilded Age mansion would be the ideal setting for an elaborate Clue dinner party – and who wouldn't die for a glimpse of these Tiffany stained-glass windows, Italian crystal chandeliers and hand-carved mahogany moldings? An enclosed cupola on the roof offers breathtaking cityscapes, and the service here redefines Southern hospitality.

Restoration BOUTIQUE HOTEL $$$
(Map p174; ☎843-518-5100; www.therestorationhotel.com; 75 Wentworth St; ste from $399;) Spanish-moss-draped, 200-year-old B&Bs are cool and all, but if you skew more hip and contemporary than antebellum and antique, this all-suite hipster enclave steeped in Americana arts-and-crafts kitsch is for you. Reclaimed wood-bound hallways lead to 54 rooms over a few buildings, which grow from 500 sq ft and are awash in modern indigo, some with kitchenettes and washers and dryers.

John Rutledge House Inn B&B $$$
(Map p174; ☎843-723-7999; www.johnrutledgehouseinn.com; 116 Broad St; r $289-399) Governor John Rutledge was one of four South Carolinian signers of the US Constitution. Why not stay in his grand, lovingly restored mansion? The central downtown location is

ideal, the service is impeccable and the inn is exquisite, with soaring ceilings, breezy piazzas and a lovely courtyard. Each room is uniquely charming, with parquet floors and marble fireplaces.

Eating

South of Broad & the French Quarter

South of Broad is fairly devoid of restaurants, but the French Quarter offers quite a few, particularly along E Bay St. Some are decent, a few are delicious and most are fairly pricey.

★ Gaulart & Maliclet FRENCH $
(Map p174; ☎843-577-9797; www.fastandfrenchcharleston.com; 98 Broad St; breakfast $5-11, lunch & dinner mains $11-14; ⏲8am-4pm Mon, to 10pm Tue-Thu, to 10:30pm Fri & Sat) Ooh la la. Locals crowd around the shared tables at this tiny spot, known as 'Fast & French,' to nibble on Gallic cheeses and sausages, fondues or nightly specials ($21 to $24) that include bread, soup, a main dish and wine.

Brown Dog Deli SANDWICHES $
(Map p174; ☎843-853-8081; www.browndogdeli.com; 40 Broad St; sandwiches $8-14; ⏲11am-6pm Mon-Thu, to 8pm Fri & Sat, to 4pm Sun) Really tasty gourmet sandwiches, packed with fresh and creative ingredients. A favorite is the Boar's Head mesquite turkey with a brie spread, bacon, sprouts, red onions and cranberry-pepper jelly. The salads and wraps are also worthwhile, and there's a second location over on the corner of Calhoun and Smith Sts.

Fleet Landing SEAFOOD $$
(Map p174; ☎843-722-8100; www.fleetlanding.net; 186 Concord St; lunch mains $9-24, dinner $13-26; ⏲11am-3:30pm daily, 5-10pm Sun-Thu, 5-11pm Fri & Sat; 📶) Come here for the perfect Charleston lunch: a river view, a cup of she-crab soup with a splash of sherry, and a big bowl of shrimp and grits. Housed in a former naval degaussing building on a pier, it's a convenient and scenic spot to enjoy fresh fish, a fried seafood platter or a burger after a morning of downtown exploring.

Slightly North of Broad SOUTHERN US $$$
(SNOB; Map p174; ☎843-723-3424; http://snobcharleston.com; 192 E Bay St; mains $28-36; ⏲11:30am-2:30pm & 5pm-late Mon-Sat, 10:30am-2pm & 5pm-late Sun) A tried-and-true French Quarter mainstay, with a rotating menu of Lowcountry comfort dishes reinvented with flair. Best bets include the peach salad (served with prosciutto, goat's cheese and pecans) and the duck breast, which comes over seasonal veggies.

LOCAL KNOWLEDGE

FOWL PLAY

Lamboll St in South of Broad is home to a rogue and famous band of guinea fowl, and locals delight in their presence.

East Side, NoMo & Hampton Park

There are some real gems sprinkled throughout these hoods, everything from tasting menus to soul food to one of America's top three burgers (according to *Bon Appétit*). In fact, you'd be hard pressed to find a bad meal.

★ Leon's Poultry & Oyster Shop SOUTHERN US $
(Map p174; ☎843-531-6500; http://leonsoystershop.com; 698 King St; oysters from $1, fried chicken meal $15, scalloped potatoes $5; ⏲11am-10pm) In a converted old body shop reimagined as an industrial-chic eatery, Leon's is a Charleston favorite for three distinct and delicious items: oysters, fried chicken and scalloped potatoes. There is no better place to eat off a hangover, and the rosé on tap is a classy way to keep the party going.

Lewis Barbecue BARBECUE $
(Map p174; ☎843-805-9500; https://lewisbarbecue.com; 464 N Nassau St; mains $8-21; ⏲11am-10pm Tue-Sun) Lewis Barbecue is a bit north of downtown, but Charlestonians regularly venture out and line up for this oh-so-delicious meat. Favorites include the Texas-style, cut-to-order brisket, pulled turkey and 'hot guts' (ie homemade sausages), and the industrial-chic space includes an expansive bar and backyard patio.

Rodney Scott's BBQ BARBECUE $
(Map p174; ☎843-990-9535; www.rodneyscottsbbq.com; 1011 King St; mains $9-14; ⏲11am-9pm) *Top Chef* alum and legendary whole-hog pitmaster Rodney Scott's BBQ joint is regularly swarmed with fans clamoring for succulent pulled pork, fried catfish, chicken and rib plates and rib-eye sandwiches. It teeters and totters along a fine line between gentrified (slick T-shirts, IPAs on draft) and old school (peg-board menu).

Little Jack's Tavern BURGERS $

(Map p174; ☎843-531-6868; http://littlejackstavern.com; 710 King St; tavern burger $8; ⏲11am-10pm Sun-Thu, to 11pm Fri & Sat) A classy neighborhood cocktail bar and restaurant, with one helluva hamburger (in 2017 *Bon Appétit* named it one of the top three burgers in America). The butter-soaked bun is toasted just right, and the oversized patty is smothered in a fantastic tangy sauce and savory fried onions.

Workshop FOOD HALL $

(☎843-996-4500; https://workshopcharleston.com; 1503 King St; mains from $5; ⏲11am-9pm Mon-Thu, to 10pm Fri & Sat, 10am-9pm Sun) Workshop has kitchen space for six within the Pacific Box & Crate development, and these mini-restaurants rotate regularly, offering restaurateurs and chefs a chance to try out new dishes. Eclectic and exploratory offerings have included offerings like avocado fries, brisket enchiladas and spicy pork vindaloo over green chili grits.

★ **167 Raw** SEAFOOD $$

(Map p174; ☎843-579-4997; http://167raw.com/charleston; 289 E Bay St; oysters each $2.75, mains $14-27; ⏲11am-10pm Mon-Sat) There are no reservations at this tiny hole-in-the-wall that unassumingly serves up the city's best seafood. People wait in lines down the block for the delicious lobster roll, and the tuna burger and sea-scallop po'boy are also off-the-charts toothsome. Oysters arrive fresh daily from Nantucket (where the restaurant runs its very own oyster farm), and the service is truly on point.

★ **Edmund's Oast** PUB FOOD $$

(Map p174; ☎843-727-1145; www.edmundsoast.com; 1081 Morrison Dr; mains $14-29; ⏲4:30-10pm Mon-Thu, to 11pm Fri & Sat, 10am-10pm Sun; 📶) Occupying a gutted former hardware store in gentrifying NoMo, Charleston's highest-brow brewpub got a fancy new executive chef, Bob Cook, in 2017. The new grub: Southern faves like salt chicken skins, hanger steaks and hot-and-sour tilefish. The drink pairings: 64 taps (eight devoted to cocktails, meads and sherries, and a dozen proprietary craft beers, among other craft offerings). Pints are $6 to $9.

Harold's Cabin AMERICAN $$

(Map p174; ☎843-793-4440; www.haroldscabin.com; 247 Congress St; mains $8-20; ⏲11am-10pm Tue-Fri, 9am-10pm Sat & Sun; 🖉) It goes without saying that if Bill Murray is a co-owner, the place is probably dope. That's the case for this former corner store, which remains a rustic (if newly chic) neighborhood haunt offering locally sourced grocery items – and now it's also a restaurant and bar. The veggie-driven meals are largely made up of ingredients from a rooftop garden.

Rutledge Cab Co AMERICAN $$

(☎843-720-1440; http://rutledgecabco.com; 1300 Rutledge Av; mains $10-26; ⏲11:30am-11pm Mon-Fri, 10am-midnight Sat & Sun) An unpretentious eatery set in a former service station in North Charleston, with delicious burgers that are cheap on Monday, mimosas that are cheap on Saturday, ultimate Bloody Marys that are cheap on Sunday, and a ringing endorsement from Bill Murray (who co-owns the place).

Cru Cafe AMERICAN $$

(Map p174; ☎843-534-2434; http://crucafe.com; 18 Pinckney St; mains $10-25; ⏲11am-3pm & 5-10pm Tue-Thu, to 11pm Fri & Sat) Innovative comfort food, served in a two-story, historic home with a charming porch. This place is beloved for its healthy salads and unusual takes on local specialties, for example the deeply fried green tomatoes with pork-belly croutons, sheep's-milk feta and smoky caramel drizzle. The General Tso's Caesar wrap is also a winner.

★ **FIG** SOUTHERN US $$$

(Map p174; ☎843-805-5900; www.eatatfig.com; 232 Meeting St; mains $30-36; ⏲5-10:30pm Mon-Thu, to 11pm Fri & Sat; 📶) 🍃 FIG has been a longtime foodie favorite, and it's easy to see why: welcoming staff, efficient but unrushed service and top-notch, sustainably sourced nouvelle Southern fare from James Beard Award–winner Mike Lata. The six nightly changing dishes embrace what's fresh and local from the sea and local farms and mills. FIG stands for Food is Good. And the gourmets agree. Book well in advance.

Zero Café + Bar AMERICAN $$$

(Map p174; ☎843-817-7900; www.zerogeorge.com; 0 George St; 6-course tasting menu with wine $135, vegetarian $125; ⏲5-10pm Tue-Sun; 🖉) The kitchen at the Zero George Street (p179) hotel might be diminutive, but the dining experience provided by Food Network celebrity chef Vinson Petrillo is enormously memorable. The chef assumes his diners are intrepid and sends out dainty plates of pressure-cooked octopus, ricotta *gnudi* (gnocchi-like dumplings) and scallop tartare. Vegetarians are well served too.

Harleston Village & Upper King

So little time, so much deliciousness. Narrowing down where to eat on Upper King is the great Charleston challenge. The varied and eclectic eateries of Cannonborough Elliottborough don't make things easier.

★ Xiao Bao Biscuit ASIAN $
(Map p174; www.xiaobaobiscuit.com; 224 Rutledge Ave; mains lunch $12, mains $12-16; 11:30am-2pm & 5:30-10pm Mon-Sat) Housed in a former gas station, with exposed brick walls and concrete floor, this casual but stylish eatery hits the hipster high marks. But the food? Now we're talking. The short but palate-kicking menu spotlights simple pan-Asian fare enhanced by local ingredients and spicy flavors. For something different and memorable, try the *okonomiyaki* – a Japanese cabbage pancake – with egg and bacon.

Juanita Greenberg's Nacho Royale MEXICAN $
(Map p174; 843-723-6224; https://juanitagreenbergs.com; 439 King St; nachos $9-11; 11am-2am) Nachos are front and center at this tasty, affordable Mexican joint on King St, and locals go wild for it with good reason. The nacho royales arrive Mexican-pizza-style, with corn or flour chips and your choice of veggies, beans, steak, tofu, shrimp, pulled chicken and basically anything else you can dream of. Boring people can also get burritos or tacos.

Marina Variety Store SOUTHERN US $
(Map p174; 843-723-6325; www.varietystorerestaurant.com; 17 Lockwood Dr; mains from $6; 6:30am-4pm & 5-9pm Mon-Sat, 6:30am-3pm Sun) A long-standing, down-home, greasy-spoon kinda place, with harbor views and Southern hospitality as warm as the buttermilk biscuits. Thumbs up to the grits, fried green tomatoes and crab-cake Benedict. Put the gravy on everything.

Sugar Bakeshop BAKERY $
(Map p174; www.sugarbake.com; 59 1/2 Cannon St; cupcakes $3.25; 10am-6pm Mon-Fri, 11am-5pm Sat) The staff are as sweet as the cupcakes at Sugar, a teensy space north of downtown Charleston. Try to visit on a Thursday, when the Lady Baltimore cupcakes are on – a retro Southern specialty with dried fruit and white frosting.

Callie's Hot Little Biscuit SOUTHERN US $
(Map p174; 843-737-5159; http://calliesbiscuits.com; 476 1/2 King St; biscuit sandwiches $7; 7am-2pm Mon-Fri, from 8am Sat & Sun, 10pm-2am Fri & Sat) Locals rave about this tiny little kitchen on King St, and it's a real Charleston staple. If you're a fanatic for pimento cheese, country ham and buttermilk, you'll probably understand.

★ Basic Kitchen HEALTH FOOD $$
(Map p174; 843-789-4568; https://basickitchen.com; 82 Wentworth St; mains breakfast & lunch $8-14, dinner $13-23; 8-10:30am, 11am-3pm & 5:30-9pm Mon-Fri, 9am-3pm & 5:30-9pm Sat, 9am-3pm Sun;) With dishes like avo toast, fresh sesame kale and rainbow bowls (which come with sweet-potato noodles, veggies, herbs and Thai peanut sauce), this healthy and delicious little cafe feels like something you'd stumble across in Bali. The surfboard decor and yummy fresh fruit juices do nothing to dispel that impression; and clearly, vegetarians are well served here.

Darling Oyster Bar SEAFOOD $$
(Map p174; 843-641-0821; http://thedarling.com; 513 King St; mains $10-27; 4pm-late) Not all oysters are created equal in Charleston, but the Darling serves up the raw goodness. Its light, flavorful selections originate in places like Prince Edward Island and arrive at the table with a mild ginger mignonette. The Creole shrimp channels N'awlins and kills it, the lightly cured ceviche is highly refreshing, and the cocktails are crafty and delicious.

Poogan's Porch SOUTHERN US $$
(Map p174; 843-577-2337; www.poogansporch.com; 72 Queen St; mains brunch $10-14, dinner $21-34; 10:30am-2:30pm & 5-9:30pm Mon-Fri, 9am-2:30pm & 5-9:30pm Sat & Sun) It's very Charlestonian to take brunch on the terrace of this cozy but elegant two-story Victorian, where the homemade buttermilk biscuits are out of control and the chicken and waffles are second to none. Boozy brunchers have their pick of mimosas, cocktails, craft beer and 1500 bottles of wine in the cellar.

Ordinary SEAFOOD $$
(Map p174; 843-414-7060; www.eattheordinary.com; 544 King St; dishes $10-33; 5-10:30pm Tue-Sun) Inside a cavernous 1927 bank building, this buzzy seafood hall and oyster bar feels like the best party in town. The menu is short, but the savory dishes

are prepared with finesse – from the oyster sliders to the lobster rolls to the nightly fish dishes.

Chez Nous FRENCH $$

(Map p174; ☎843-579-3060; www.cheznouschs.com; 6 Payne Ct; mains $20-29; ⊙11:30am-3pm & 5:30-10:30pm Tue-Sun) A diminutive neighborhood restaurant with a tiny, nearly illegible menu of dishes and wine hailing from southern France, northern Italy and northern Spain. Just two appetizers and two mains are served each day in the charming dining rooms (one on the first level, one upstairs) or on a pleasant patio. It's highly unlikely you'll go wrong.

Virginia's on King SOUTHERN US $$

(Map p174; ☎843-735-5800; www.virginiasonking.com; 412 King St; fried quail legs $12, mains $14-24; ⊙7am-9pm Mon-Thu, to 10pm Fri, 8am-10pm Sat, 10am-3pm Sun) Delicious Southern cooking served in an elegant dining room with exposed brick, dark wood and tasteful paintings. But if you do spicy, the absolute best thing about this place (and maybe the best snack in the entire city) is the fried quail legs, Nashville-hot-chicken-style.

Hominy Grill SOUTHERN US $$

(Map p174; ☎843-937-0930; www.hominygrill.com; 207 Rutledge Ave; breakfast $4.50-14, lunch & dinner mains $9-22; ⊙7:30am-3pm Mon-Fri, 9am-3pm Sat & Sun; ✍) Slightly off the beaten path, this neighborhood cafe serves modern, vegetarian-friendly Lowcountry cuisine in an old barbershop. The shaded patio is tops for brunch, and the 'nasty biscuit' is a crowd-pleaser.

Leyla Fine Lebanese Cuisine LEBANESE $$$

(Map p174; ☎843-501-7500; http://leyla-charleston.com; 298 King St; mains $24-38; ⊙11:30am-9pm Tue-Thu & Sun, to 10pm Fri & Sat; ✍) A welcome respite from all the Lowcountry and fried food, this elegant Lebanese restaurant is a favorite with locals. You can't really go wrong, so you might as well do it all with a sampler of hummus, tabouleh, baba ghanoush, falafel, fried kibbe and lots of other goodness. There are plenty of good vegetarian options.

Le Farfalle TUSCAN $$$

(Map p174; ☎843-212-0920; http://lefarfallecharleston.com; 15 Beaufain St; pastas $17-26, mains $28-42; ⊙11:30am-2:30pm & 5:30-11pm Mon-Sat, 10:30am-2:30pm & 5:30-11pm Sun) Seafood charcuterie doesn't get better than

City Walk
South of Broad

START OLD EXCHANGE & PROVOST DUNGEON
END FOUR CORNERS OF LAW/ ST MICHAEL'S CHURCH (INTERSECTION OF MEETING & BROAD STS)
LENGTH 1.5 MILES; ONE HOUR

Begin at the ❶ **Old Exchange & Provost Dungeon** (p171), where costumed guides lead tours of the dungeon where Stede Bonnet, the Gentleman Pirate, and Revolutionary War prisoners were once imprisoned. Contemplate the glorious freedom of walking around, and then head south to the picturesquely pastel ❷ **Rainbow Row** (p170), where you can snap your shot of these redone 1730s merchant stores that inspired the birth of the Charleston Preservation Society, along with a restoration of the entire city in the 1920s. Make a right on ❸ **Tradd St** and take note of the gorgeous pre-Revolutionary homes, built very close together in a decidedly English style, some with deep lots and elaborate gardens.

On Church St, take a right and the ❹ **Heyward-Washington House** (p170), where the first president himself shacked up in 1791, will be on your left. The Georgian-style town house is now a museum and well worth a tour, particularly for the old-timey furnishings collection, which includes the priceless Holmes bookcase and a chair that belonged to Francis Marion, the Swamp Fox. The next couple of homes on your left are collectively referred to as ❺ **Cabbage Row**, because African Americans who lived in these tenements displayed vegetables for sale on the windowsills. In his novel *Porgy*, Dubose Heyward based 'Catfish Row' on this location, which Gershwin then based the opera *Porgy and Bess* on. A crippled man named Goatcart Sammy lived in the neighborhood, and was a real-life version of the character Porgy.

Double back south to brick-paved ❻ **Stolls Alley** (it'll be on your left) and take in the impressive wrought-iron gates, comely walls, and stately homes all dripping with moss and flanked by wildflowers. Return to Church St, go south, and make a left on Atlantic St. Have a look down the windy Zig-Zag Alley before heading right along East Battery, and the federal-style

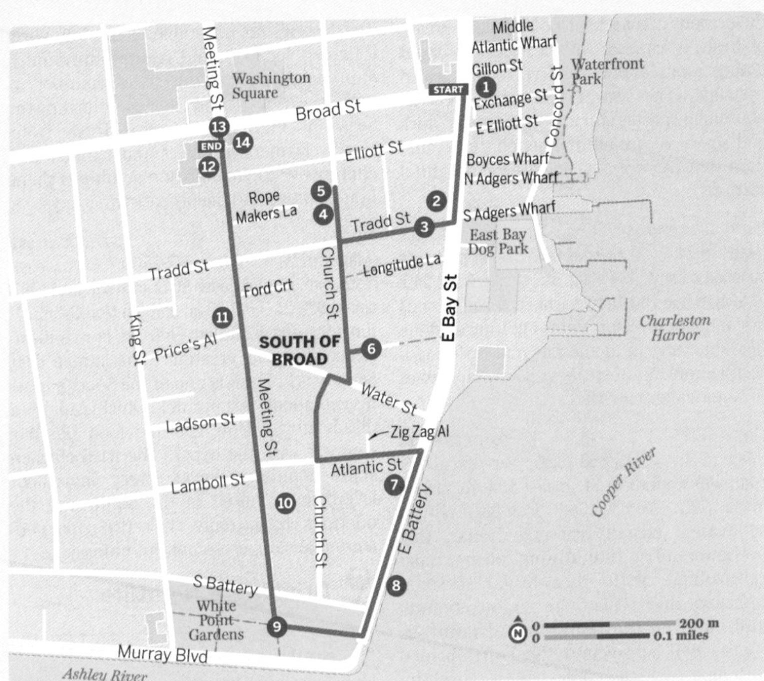

7 **Edmondston-Alston House** (p170), now a museum, will appear on your right. Inside, a docent-led tour brings guests through the public rooms, where they can view intricate woodwork, family artifacts and an original print of the Ordinance of Secession. Upstairs, the 2nd-floor piazza is ideal for viewing the harbor. Back outside and walking south along **8** **Charleston Harbor**, the confluence of the Ashley and Cooper Rivers will be at your left, and on a clear day you'll be able to see all the way to Fort Sumter, the target of the first shots of the Civil War.

Continue south to approach the **9** **Battery & White Point Garden** (p171), named for the fortifications that used to line the seafront and for the mounds of oyster shells once piled over the point. Notice the cannons and monuments in the park; they represent Charleston's wars and heroes. Cut through the park and make your way north along Meeting St, and the **10** **Calhoun Mansion** (p170), a Gilded Age manor and Charleston's largest single family residence, will be unmistakable on your right. This place overflows with over-the-top souvenirs from the eccentric owner's far-flung travels, and those who tour it often find their jaws on the floor.

Continuing north, the **11** **Nathaniel Russell House** (p170) will appear on the left, and a tour here is worthwhile for its square-oval-rectangle footprint and free-flying spiral staircase. Don't miss the joggling board in the yard, and take note that the exterior bricks, like many others in Charleston, were all made by slaves on local plantations. Heading north again, you'll notice an elaborate display of **12** **sweetgrass baskets** to your left. For centuries, the Gullah people have been making these from sweetgrass, pine needles and palmetto leaves.

The final stop is just ahead at the intersection of Broad St and Meeting St, and it is famously referred to as the **13** **Four Corners of Law**. On each corner of this intersection stands a building representing a different sort of law: City Hall on the northeast corner is city law, the Charleston County Courthouse on the northwest corner is state law, the US Court House and Post Office to the southwest are federal law, and **14** **St Michael's Church** (p170) on the southeast corner is God's law. St Michael's is the oldest church in town, and its bells have been announcing earthquakes, hurricanes, fires and attacks on the city for more than 250 years.

the octopus carpaccio at Le Farfalle, a breath of fresh Tuscan air with a spacious, bright dining room and cheeky yet sophisticated waitstaff. The warm rosemary focaccia, housemade pastas and mains (ie roasted duck and sea bass) are all dreams on plates, and the extensive wine list makes for delightful pairings.

Halls Chophouse STEAK **$$$**

(Map p174; 843-727-0090; https://hallschophouse.com; 434 King St; steaks from $40; 5-11pm Sun-Thu, to midnight Fri & Sat) Hands down the best restaurant for getting all done up, squeezing in at the bar and ordering a sizable, rare cut of steak with several glasses of Napa Valley cabernet.

Circa 1886 SOUTHERN US **$$$**

(Map p174; 843-853-7828; www.circa1886.com; 149 Wentworth St; mains $34-40, tasting menu $90; 5:30-10pm Mon-Sat) In a renovated, elegant carriage house, this is Lowcountry fine dining at its most rewarding, with healthful, seasonal offerings that reflect the region's bounty and build on its traditions. Adventurous diners will appreciate the coffee-brined antelope, which comes with sorghum sweet-potato mousseline and *shishito* peppers. Everybody will lose it for the benne-crusted (sesame-crusted) duck breast with white peach grits.

Charleston Grill GRILL **$$$**

(Map p174; 843-577-4522; www.charlestongrill.com; 244 King St; mains $32-68; 5-10pm;) Fine dining, with dishes inspired by Southern and French cooking, along with live jazz. This is one of the city's most elegant restaurants. The foie gras and smoked-duck appetizer is divine and the tasting menu rarely disappoints, but the whole table must sign on.

Grocery AMERICAN **$$$**

(Map p174; 843-302-8825; www.thegrocerycharleston.com; 4 Cannon St; mains $28-30; 5-10pm Tue-Sat, 10am-2:30pm & 5-10pm Sun;) Set in an industrial-chic space adorned with mason jars of pickled everything, this is Charleston's farm-to-table champion, with a fiercely locavore and vegetarian-friendly approach, and cooking styles channeling both the South and the Mediterranean. Seasonal ingredients arrive fresh from nearby farmers, foragers and fishers, and chef/owner Kevin Johnson combines them in innovative and deeply satisfying ways.

Husk SOUTHERN US **$$$**

(Map p174; 843-577-2500; www.huskrestaurant.com; 76 Queen St; brunch & lunch $10-17, dinner $29-34; 11:30am-2:30pm Mon-Sat, 5:30-10pm Sun-Thu, 5:30-11pm Fri & Sat, brunch 10am-2:30pm Sun) The creation of acclaimed chef Sean Brock, Husk is one of the South's most buzzed-about restaurants, which can be a disadvantage. How can the food possibly compete with the hype? (The fried chicken skins definitely don't.) Every ingredient is grown or raised in the South and the offerings change daily. The setting, in a two-story mansion, is elegant but unfussy.

> **DUELING DINNERS**
>
> Locals fall into two categories: Rodney Scott's BBQ (p181) people or Lewis Barbecue (p181) people. You must decide for yourself.

Drinking & Nightlife

South of Broad & the French Quarter

The French Quarter's rooftop establishments offer views of South of Broad, which doesn't have any of its own bars to speak of. You can, however, do tastings of local moonshine at Tavern at Rainbow Row (p190) on the weekends.

Pavilion Bar ROOFTOP BAR

(Map p174; 843-723-0500; www.marketpavilion.com; 225 E Bay St; cocktails from $9; 11:30am-midnight) Complete with an infinity pool, illuminated umbrellas and stunning city views, this swanky rooftop bar tends to attract a well-heeled set. But people sometimes end up barefoot when the hotel throws plexiglass over the pool and converts it into a dance floor.

Blind Tiger PUB

(Map p174; www.blindtigerchs.com; 36-38 Broad St; 11am-2am) Opened in 1893, this cozy and atmospheric former dive, reborn in 2016 after an extensive restoration, seduces with stamped-tin ceilings, good pub grub and barrels of history. The expansive back courtyard is a popular place for a blind mule cocktail, which comes with vodka, ginger beer, lime juice and a candied ginger garnish.

Rooftop at the Vendue BAR

(Map p174; www.thevendue.com; 23 Vendue Range; 11:30am-10pm Sun-Thu, to midnight Fri & Sat) This rooftop bar has sweet views of downtown and the crowds to prove it. Enjoy craft cocktails, and live music on Sundays from 2pm to 5pm.

East Side, NoMo & Hampton Park

NoMo and Hampton Park offer a fine selection of local breweries and watering holes, and many of the popular restaurants also make for good boozing.

Palmetto Brewing Company MICROBREWERY

(Map p174; 843-937-0903; www.palmettobrewery.com; 289 Huger St; 4-8pm Tue-Thu, noon-10pm Fri & Sat) Charleston's first microbrewery (since Prohibition, anyway) produces four main craft beers with fresh barley malts and hops: an amber ale, a pilsner and a couple of India Pale Ales (IPAs). It also has rotating special ales and even a 'Brose' radler (shandy). Tours are available on weekdays at 5pm, and the tap room and outdoor beer garden are lively on weekends, particularly Fridays.

Recovery Room BAR

(Map p174; 843-727-0999; www.recoveryroomtavern.com; 685 King St; 3pm-2am Mon-Sat, noon-2am Sun) Not what it sounds like. Instead, it's a late-night dive that often swells with college students and boozy regulars in search of cheap whiskey. Various theme nights include trivia games, live music and bocce ball.

Moe's Crosstown Tavern SPORTS BAR

(Map p174; 843-641-0469; https://moescrosstowntavern.com; 714 Rutledge Ave; 11am-2am Mon-Sat, 10:30am-2am Sun) Considered Hampton Park's best dive bar, this place fills with loyal patrons on game days. The burgers and Sunday brunch are tasty; the craft beer and camaraderie are even tastier.

Revelry Brewery MICROBREWERY

(Map p174; www.revelrybrewingco.com; 10 Conroy St; 4-10pm Mon-Thu, noon-midnight Fri & Sat, noon-10pm Sun) Probably the hippest of the Northern Peninsula breweries. It's hard to beat knocking back a few artfully crafted cold ones on Revelry's fairy-lit and fire-pit-heated rooftop, which affords expansive views all the way to the cable-stayed Ravenel Bridge. The downstairs bar, seemingly owned by the brewery's black Lab, is a mere 5ft from the tanks.

OFF THE BEATEN TRACK

CHEERS FOR BEER

It's worth venturing a few miles further north to check out one of Charleston's best craft breweries, **Holy City Brewing** (843-225-5623; www.holycitybrewing.com; 4155 Dorchester Rd, North Charleston; 11am-8pm Sun-Thu, to 9pm Fri & Sat;). Church on Sunday or craft beer and yoga? Holy City ain't scared! Sunday-morning yoga at 10am ($15) is par for the course at this North Charleston microbrewery that loves to shake things up with its product as well: smoked porters with BBQ rub, barrel-aged pilsners, hoppy brown ales etc. There are 25 taps (pints $5).

Edmund's Oast Brewing Co BREWERY

(843-718-3224; http://edmundsoast.com/brewing-co; 1505 King St Ext; 11am-10pm) Edmund's Oast (p182) in NoMo has this new baby brewing cousin just down the street, set in a 20,000-sq-ft facility with 26 boozy beverages on tap and two hangover-prevention chambers (a wood-fired brick oven and a Polish smokehouse). Brews are ambitious and at times, downright medieval: Domesday is brewed with yarrow, mugwort, lavender and marshmallow flower.

Harleston Village & Upper King

Craft cocktail joints, distilleries, craft-beer haunts and even a wine bar flank Upper King, while little neighborhood spots are sprinkled throughout Cannonborough Elliottborough. Harleston Village isn't so drinky – the college kids must need to study.

★ **Eclectic** COFFEE

(Map p174; 843-202-0666; www.eclecticcafeandvinyl.com; 132 Spring St; 7am-7pm Mon & Wed, to 9pm Thu & Fri, 8am-9pm Sat, 9am-5pm Sun;) Our favorite Charleston coffeehouse, this indigo-trimmed Cannonborough Elliott-borough establishment is gorgeous: the walls are lined with vinyl records for sale, and it has a perfect juxtaposition of hardwood flooring, exposed brick and silver-gilded ceilings, plus a gorgeous hand-hewed wooden workstation area reclaimed from an old South Dakota horse corral. Coffee, wine, beer and cafe grub mean you can stay here all day.

ALL ABOUT BILL

When in these parts, visit all the things Bill Murray owns and you might just spot the man himself. Check out the RiverDogs baseball team, Harold's Cabin (p182) and Rutledge Cab Co (p182).

Prohibition COCKTAIL BAR

(Map p174; 843-793-2964; https://prohibitioncharleston.com; 547 King St; 5pm-1am Mon-Thu, to 2am Fri, 11am-2am Sat, 11am-1am Sun) This delightful Jazz Age gastropub serves up excellent craft cocktails (from $10) that tend to pair well with the lip-smackin' Southern grub. Think a 'bacon maple old-fashioned' cocktail with some deviled eggs, or a mint julep with shrimp and grits. There's also a sweet dance floor, and free swing-dancing lessons are offered Wednesday and Sunday at 6:30pm. It's a total hoot.

High Wire Distilling DISTILLERY

(Map p174; 843-755-4664; http://highwiredistilling.squarespace.com; 652 King St; 9am-6pm Tue-Fri, 11am-6pm Sat) A bright downtown tasting room where you take shots of small-batch gin, whiskey, vodka and amaro, right in a row. Tasty cocktails are also available, and the 'bee's knees' (with botanical gin, lemon, honey and lavender) is a doozy.

Proof COCKTAIL BAR

(Map p174; 843-793-1422; www.charlestonproof.com; 437 King St; 4pm-2am Mon-Fri, 6pm-2am Sat & Sun) It may be snug in here, but the cocktails ($9 to $13) sure are first-class and their mixologist is some kind of visionary. Case in point: the 'knuckleball' has Old Grand-Dad, a spicy cola reduction, orange bitters and pickled boiled peanuts.

Closed for Business PUB

(Map p174; 843-853-8466; www.closed4business.com; 453 King St; 11am-midnight Sun-Wed, to 2am Thu-Sat) A 42-tap selection of local and national craft brews (from $4.25) and hipster-rustic decor give this inviting 'draft emporium' a neighborhood vibe and just the right amount of edge.

Dudley's on Ann GAY & LESBIAN

(Map p174; 843-577-6779; www.dudleysonann.com; 42 Ann St; 4pm-2am) A great little bar, full of glitz and glam, with drag karaoke nights on Wednesday. Definitely a haven for gender-bending pop stars.

Pour Taproom CRAFT BEER

(Map p174; 843-779-0810; www.charleston.pourtaproom.com; 560 King St; 4-11pm Mon-Thu, noon-1am Fri & Sat, noon-11pm Sun) A new brewpub with a cool concept: on-tap, self-serve craft beer, wine and cocktails, where you pour it yourself and pay by the ounce. It's downtown, on the 9th floor of the Historic District Hyatt. There are also appetizers and sandwiches.

Charleston Distilling Co DISTILLERY

(Map p174; 843-718-1446; www.charlestondistilling.com; 501 King St; 11am-7pm, closed Wed & Sun) A farm-to-bottle, independently owned, small-batch distillery on King St. Grab a flight of spirits or a cocktail and take a tour ($5) of the distillery, a sleek space with inlaid brick and wood paneling. Do it fast, though. Word on the street is that the business may move to John's Island to expand its operations.

Bin 152 WINE BAR

(Map p174; 843-577-7359; www.bin152.com; 152 King St; 4pm-2am) From the same couple behind Chez Nous comes this elegant downtown wine bar (glasses from $15). It's low-lit, chic and festooned in impressive, rotating art and antiques (all for sale). But the best reason to go is to pair the adventurous wine selections with imported cheese (from $10), freshly baked bread and other charcuterie bits.

Fuel BAR

(Map p174; 843-737-5959; www.fuelcharleston.com; 211 Rutledge Ave; 11am-11pm) An island-themed neighborhood bar and restaurant (mains $12 to $14), tucked into what used to be a 1950s filling station and illuminated with gas-pump light fixtures. The jerk chicken's good, and so are the tacos, but the best reason to come is to sip rum drinks (especially mojitos) on the patio.

Elliotborough Mini Bar BAR

(Map p174; 843-577-0028; 18 Percy St; 5-10pm Mon-Thu, to 11pm Fri & Sat, 3-8pm Sun) A supercozy neighborhood bar with quirky art and festive lights. Live music happens regularly; only beer and wine are served.

Kudu COFFEE, CRAFT BEER

(Map p174; www.kuducoffeeandcraftbeer.com; 4 Vanderhorst St; 6:45am-9pm Mon-Fri, 7am-9pm Sat, 8am-8pm Sun) Rock up at 6:45am and order an excellent espresso or craft booze – we're not judging – at this hipster cafe and beer bar just off Marion Sq.

Bar at Husk BAR

(Map p174; ☎843-577-2500; www.huskrestaurant.com/about/bar; 76 Queen St; ⊙4pm-late) Adjacent to the restaurant Husk (p186), this intimate brick-and-worn-wood spot recalls a speakeasy, with classic cocktails ($10 to $15), sphere ice and passionate attention to detail.

☆ Entertainment

☆ South of Broad & the French Quarter

Dock Street Theatre THEATER

(Map p174; ☎843-720-3968; www.charlestonstage.com; 135 Church St) Dock Street Theatre is an exquisite place to see theater. It has plenty of history – a previous iteration opened in 1736 on the same spot, becoming the first theater in America. The current performing-arts center is also historic; it was built in 1809 and first occupied by the Planter's Hotel.

Today it's the last (former) hotel from the antebellum period. Its Regency-style facade looks like it's straight out of New Orleans, and the wrought-iron balcony and brownstone columns channel the 1800s. There's a lovely grand staircase too.

It's now home to South Carolina's largest professional theater production company (Charleston Stage Company), and also contains the city's Cultural Affairs office and the City Gallery, which exhibits local art.

☆ East Side, NoMo & Hampton Park

Joseph P Riley, Jr Park BASEBALL

(The Joe; Map p174; ☎843-723-7241; www.riverdogs.com; 360 Fisburne St; ⊙Apr-Sep) Home of the RiverDogs minor-league baseball team and the Citadel team. The stadium is a namesake of a longtime former Charleston mayor who regularly attends games, but it is more often referred to as 'the Joe.' On ladies night anyone wearing a skirt gets in free. Bill Murray is a part-owner of the RiverDogs.

Theatre 99 COMEDY

(Map p174; ☎843-853-6687; www.theatre99.com; 280 Meeting St; from $5; ⊙shows 8pm Wed-Sat, sometimes 10pm) Performances and classes in improv comedy. Very funny stuff, to the point where locals drop in multiple times a week.

☆ Harleston Village & Upper King

Charleston Music Hall LIVE PERFORMANCE

(Map p174; ☎843-853-2252; www.charlestonmusichall.com; 37 John St; ⊙box office 10am-3pm Mon-Fri) An intimate performance venue with great acoustics and not a bad seat in the house. Ideal for live music or theater.

Music Farm CONCERT VENUE

(Map p174; ☎843-577-6989; http://musicfarm.com; 32 Ann St; ⊙varies) A popular downtown concert venue, with local and national acts from every imaginable genre. The place isn't very big; in the summertime it often fills up and gets pretty sweaty.

Shopping

South of Broad & the French Quarter

South of Broad has a few good souvenir shops tucked away, though it's not particularly commercial. The French Quarter's got the famous Charleston City Market, as well as plenty of good galleries, which are especially fun to explore during the city's ArtWalk.

★ **Robert Lange Studios** ART

(Map p174; ☎843-805-8052; http://robertlangestudios.com; 2 Queen St; ⊙11am-5pm) Some of the city's best contemporary art regularly appears in this long-standing downtown gallery. Artist Nathan Durfee's experimental work is a highlight, and during ArtWalk (p178) this place is a madhouse.

Charleston City Market MARKET

(Map p174; ☎843-937-0920; www.thecharlestoncitymarket.com; 188 Meeting St; ⊙day market 9:30am-6pm year-round, night market 6:30-10:30pm Fri & Sat Apr-Dec) With more than 300 vendors hawking everything from sweetgrass baskets to piping-hot biscuits, this vibrant, open-air market is one of the nation's oldest, getting its start in 1804. Some travelers may feel it's a bit schlocky, but over the four blocks there are interesting finds and locally made products (all marked with a 'Certified Authentic Handmade in Charleston' seal).

W Hampton Brand Gallery ARTS & CRAFTS

(Map p174; ☎843-327-6282; 114 E Bay St; ⊙9am-2pm Thu-Mon) An excellent place to unearth unique souvenirs and gifts, such as likenesses of the homes of Rainbow Row, painted on reclaimed slate roof tiles.

WORTH A TRIP

ASHLEY RIVER PLANTATIONS

Three significant plantations line the Ashley River about a 20-minute drive northwest from downtown Charleston. All offer talks and tours concerning the role of slavery.

Drayton Hall (Map p196; ☎843-769-2600; www.draytonhall.org; 3380 Ashley River Rd; adult/child $22/10, grounds only $12; ⏲9am-3:30pm Mon-Sat, 11am-3:30pm Sun, last tour 3pm) This 1738 Palladian brick mansion is the country's oldest preserved plantation house open to the public. Yep, it's older than the nation. Drayton Hall was the only structure of its kind on the Ashley River to survive the Revolutionary and Civil Wars and the great earthquake of 1886. Tours enlighten visitors about the lives of the era's super-rich, along with the African Americans they enslaved. Guided tours explore the unfurnished house, which has been preserved but not restored.

Middleton Place (Map p196; ☎843-556-6020; www.middletonplace.org; 4300 Ashley River Rd; gardens adult/child 6-13yr $28/10, house-museum tour extra $15, carriage tour $18; ⏲9am-5pm) Designed in 1741, this plantation's vast gardens are the oldest in the US. Countless slaves spent years terracing the land and digging the precise geometric canals for the owner, wealthy South Carolina politician Henry Middleton. The bewitching grounds are a mix of classic formal French gardens and romantic woodland, bounded by flooded rice paddies and rare-breed farm animals. Union soldiers burned the main house in 1865; a 1755 guest wing, now housing the **house museum**, still stands.

Magnolia Plantation (Map p196; ☎843-571-1266; www.magnoliaplantation.com; 3550 Ashley River Rd; adult/child 6-10yr $20/10, tours $8; ⏲8am-5:30pm Mar-Oct, to 4:30pm Nov-Feb) Somewhat incongruously, this 500-acre plantation, which has been owned by the Drayton family since 1676, is a veritable theme park. Enjoy a tram tour, a petting zoo and a guided house tour. At the reconstructed slave cabins, the Slavery to Freedom Tour traces the African American experience. The most popular attraction, an Audubon Swamp Garden Tour, involves a spooky stroll along the boardwalk through the trees and bog.

Sleeping

Inn at Middleton Place (Map p196; ☎800-543-4774; www.theinnatmiddletonplace.com; 4290 Ashley River Rd; r from $229; P❄📶🏊) This dreamy property adjacent to Middleton Place is family friendly for its serene, riverside locale, relaxing pool and convenient kayak rentals. There's a main lodge with games and a big-screen TV as well. Rooms are comfy, with contemporary furnishings, floor-to-ceiling windows and wood-burning fireplaces.

Town & Country Inn & Suites (Map p196; ☎843-571-1000; www.thetownandcountryinn.com; 2008 Savannah Hwy; r $129-299, ste $249-299; P❄@📶🏊) About 5 miles west of downtown Charleston, Town & Country offers modern and stylish rooms at a reasonable price. The inn is a good launchpad if you want to get a jump on traffic for a morning visit to the Ashley River plantations.

Tavern at Rainbow Row ALCOHOL
(Map p174; ☎843-722-4800; www.charlestonspirits.com; 120 E Bay St; ⏲10am-7pm Mon-Sat) America's oldest liquor store has been getting people drunk since 1686. There are free tastings of local whiskey and moonshine on weekends.

Shops of Historic Charleston Foundation GIFTS & SOUVENIRS
(Map p174; ☎843-724-8484; www.historiccharleston.org; 108 Meeting St; ⏲9am-6pm Mon-Sat, noon-5pm Sun) This place showcases jewelry, home furnishings and furniture inspired by the city's historic homes, much of which is based on Blue Canton porcelain.

🔒 East Side, NoMo & Hampton Park

Edmund's Oast Exchange ALCOHOL
(Map p174; ☎843-990-9449; 1081 Morrison Dr; ⏲11am-8pm Tue-Sat, noon-5pm Sun) Formerly known as Charleston Beer Exchange, this beer and wine retail store opened near its parent brewery (p182) in 2017. The two-story space has more than 1000 different varieties of booze available in cans, bottles, kegs and growlers.

Goat. Sheep. Cow. North. CHEESE
(Map p174; ☎843-203-3118; https://goatsheepcow.com; 804 Meeting St; ⏰11am-9:30pm Mon-Sat) A gourmet cheese shop that triples as a cafe and wine bar. Get your pasteurized Spanish goat's milk and thermized Italian sheep's milk here.

Harleston Village & Upper King

King Street is the city's most celebrated shopping corridor, with plenty of chains but also boutique retailers you won't encounter elsewhere. Cannonborough Elliottborough is peppered with quaint shops and galleries and Harleston Village offers decent corner stores and shops.

Beads on Cannon JEWELRY
(Map p174; ☎843-723-5648; www.beadsoncannon.com; 87 Cannon St; ⏰11am-5pm) A massive bead store, with two floors full of stones, Czech glass, wire, leather, chains, Swarovski crystal, tools and rhinestones. The store also offers jewelry-making classes.

Indigo & Cotton CLOTHING
(Map p174; ☎843-718-2980; https://indigoandcotton.com; 79 Cannon St; ⏰11am-6pm Mon-Fri, to 5pm Sat) Stocks high-end and innovative brands of clothing, footwear and accessories: for instance, Raleigh Denim, a company that stitches its jeans on vintage sewing machines.

Croghan's Jewel Box JEWELRY
(Map p174; ☎843-723-3594; www.croghansjewelbox.com; 308 King St; ⏰10am-5:30pm Mon-Fri, to 5pm Sat) Long-standing, family-owned jewelry store offering pricey but gorgeous antique pieces, estate finds, engagement rings and other one-of-a-kind gifts on Upper King.

Farmers Market MARKET
(Map p174; www.charlestonfarmersmarket.com; Marion Sq; ⏰8am-2pm Sat Apr-Nov) Stop by Charleston's terrific farmers market on Saturdays for local produce, homemade food and drinks, art, music, boiled peanuts and more.

Charleston Crafts Cooperative ARTS & CRAFTS
(Map p174; ☎843-723-2938; www.charlestoncrafts.org; 161 Church St; ⏰10am-6pm) A pricey, well-edited selection of contemporary South Carolina–made crafts, such as sweetgrass baskets, hand-dyed silks and wood carvings.

Blue Bicycle Books BOOKS
(Map p174; ☎843-722-2666; www.bluebicyclebooks.com; 420 King St; ⏰10am-7:30pm Mon-Sat, 1-6pm Sun) Excellent new-and-used bookstore with a great selection on Southern history and culture.

Information

EMERGENCY & IMPORTANT NUMBERS

Police, fire, ambulance	☎911
Hurricane hotline	☎843-402-5800
Emergency preparedness hotline	☎843-202-7100

ETIQUETTE

Charlestonians are incredibly genteel people, and they expect visitors to be on their best behavior as well.

Greetings Don't be surprised or take offense if locals are inquisitive about your last name or probe your political leanings. They live in a small place where everybody knows each other, and these are common ways to become acquainted.

Open container law One thing locals get angry about (particularly in the South of Broad neighborhood) is people carrying on after dark. Be aware that it's illegal to drink alcohol in the street and rude to make too much noise.

Sensitivity about race Charleston was a center of the slave trade and places connected with that history should be treated with respect. For instance, when touring the Old Slave Mart Museum, it is not funny or OK to ask where you can get yourself a slave. (People have actually done this.)

INTERNET ACCESS

The City of Charleston offers free public wi-fi access in most city parks. Otherwise, it's easily accessible at most hotels and coffee shops, and the occasional restaurant.

LGBTIQ+ TRAVELERS

The city of Charleston is very accepting of people from all different backgrounds and has a large and vibrant LGBTIQ+ community. Beau Magazine (https://beau-magazine.com) is a Charleston-based online resource that offers suggestions for LGBTIQ+ friendly businesses and events and shares stories.

MEDICAL SERVICES

Bon Secours St Francis Hospital (☎843-402-1000; www.rsfh.com/st-francis-hospital; 2095 Henry Tecklenburg Dr; ⏰24hr) Another good hospital with an emergency room.

University Hospital (Medical University of South Carolina; ☎843-792-1414; www.

muschealth.org; 171 Ashley Ave; ⏲24hr) Has an emergency room.

SAFE TRAVEL

Charleston is a safe city with a relatively low crime rate.

➡ Take the same precautions as you would in most cities – be aware of your surroundings at night or when alone, especially in North Charleston.

➡ The biggest annoyance here is that sidewalks and cobblestone- and brick-paved alleys are often uneven. When people trip over these, they are said to be doing 'the Charleston shuffle.'

TOURIST INFORMATION

Charleston Visitor Center (Map p174; ☎843-724-7174; www.charlestoncvb.com; 375 Meeting St; ⏲8:30am-5:30pm Apr-Oct, to 5pm Nov-Mar) Find help with accommodations and tours or watch a half-hour video on Charleston history in this spacious renovated warehouse.

North Charleston Visitor Center (☎843-853-8000; www.charlestoncvb.com; 4975b Centre Point Dr; ⏲10am-5pm Mon-Sat, 1-5pm Sun) A visitor center with brochures, maps and staff who can help you plan your trip.

ℹ Getting There & Away

The vast majority of travelers arrive in Charleston in their own vehicles, but other visitors get here via planes, trains and buses. Flights, cars and tours can be booked online at lonelyplanet.com/bookings.

Charleston International Airport Getting downtown from the airport is easy and fast with shuttles, taxis, buses, ridesharing and a rental-car center at your service. The airport is about 10 miles northwest of the center of the city.

Greyhound Station From this bus station in North Charleston, it's simple to take a rideshare downtown, and there's a Charleston Area Regional Transportation Authority (CARTA) stop (route 11) in front of the station if you'd rather save money.

Amtrak Station Taking a rideshare from this station in North Charleston is simple, and so is hopping on the adjacent CARTA stop (route 10) to get to the downtown area.

ℹ Getting Around

Bicycle A great way to get around, with plenty of city bike-share stations, rental shops and racks.

Boat A ferry service makes four stops around Charleston Harbor.

Bus City buses cost $2 a ride, and there's also a free streetcar that makes loops from the visitor center.

Car & Motorcycle There are car-rental companies at the airport. Note that parking can be difficult downtown.

Taxi Ridesharing apps are usually cheaper and easier than calling or finding taxis.

LOWCOUNTRY

The southern half of the South Carolina coast is a tangle of islands cut off from the mainland by inlets and tidal marshes. Here, descendants of West African slaves known as the Gullah maintain small communities in the face of resort and golf-course develop-ment. The landscape ranges from tidy stretches of shimmery, oyster-gray sand to wild, moss-shrouded maritime forests.

The southernmost stretch of South Carolina's coast is popular with a mostly upscale set of golfers and B&B aficionados, but the area has quirky charms aplenty for everyone.

Sights

★Bulls Island ISLAND

(Map p196; ☎843-881-4582; www.bullsislandferry.com; Awendaw; ferry ride $40) Part of Cape Romain National Wildlife Refuge, this pristine barrier island offers a haunting 'boneyard beach' (pines and myrtles poke out of the sand, having been stripped of their leaves by the salty air), great shelling, gator sightings and hiking trails. One trail leads to a pile of oyster shells stacked long ago by Native Americans. The ferry captains' main role is transport, but they're often knowledgeable guides as well.

★Daufuskie Island ISLAND

(Map p196; www.hiltonheadisland.org/daufuskie-island) For those looking for an escape just a touch less discovered than Hilton Head Island, this idyllic island offers a sublime day trip and a window into the Lowcountry's slower-paced past. The attractions of the island – a historical trail, a few restaurants, a couple of golf clubs, some art galleries, a winery and a rum distillery – are best visited via golf cart, the primary mode of transport on the island. Its shores are only accessible by boat.

Center for Birds of Prey ANIMAL SANCTUARY

(Map p196; ☎843-971-7474; www.thecenterforbirdsofprey.org; 4719 Hwy 17 N, Awendaw; tour & flight demonstration adult/child 6-12yr $18/12; ⏲10am-5pm Thu-Sat) Make friends with owls, hawks, falcons, kites, vultures and eagles at this 152-acre conservation area, and watch

OFF THE BEATEN TRACK

BULLS ISLAND & MCCLELLANVILLE

Travelers with an affinity for the natural world may eventually bristle at visiting yet another historic house or museum, and that's when it's time to head to **Bulls Island**. Its pristine shores can be reached via ferry (a 15-minute ride), and captains often share their wealth of knowledge on the island's attractions, which include hiking trails, great shelling, numerous alligators and a 'boneyard' beach with spooky, bare trees poking up through the sand. It's wise to bring sunscreen, comfy shoes, a beach towel and some food. The boat stays at the island for a little over three hours, then heads back to the mainland.

If you've still got energy at this point, it's totally worth it to continue driving north to McClellanville, a quaint little fishing town with oak-lined streets and lovely Victorians. The superlative seafood joint **TW Graham & Co** (p194) has expertly fried seafood and decadent key lime pie. Those who really like to make the most of their travels should consider a drive over a dirt road through the woods to the **St James Santee Parish Church**, a little brick house of worship built in 1768 for the French Huguenots. Another worthwhile attraction in the area is the **Center for Birds of Prey**, where owls, hawks, falcons, kites, vultures and eagles are rehabilitated. Those that cannot be released stay within the 152-acre conservation area, and some birds do flying demonstrations.

them soar overhead during flying demonstrations. The center treats injured birds, and those that cannot be released become residents.

ACE Basin National Wildlife Refuge WILDLIFE RESERVE

(Map p196; ☎843-889-3084; www.fws.gov/refuge/ace_basin; 8675 Willtown Rd; park sunrise-sunset, office 8am-4pm) FREE Formerly occupied by large rice plantations, this area fell out of use after the Civil War and was bought up by sportsmen who turned it into a hunting retreat. They managed the land wisely, and when it became a wildlife refuge in 1990 the wetland ecosystem was still thriving. Over the refuge's 12,000 acres, visitors can spot alligators, endangered storks and whooping cranes.

There's an 1828 plantation house at the entrance that contains the refuge's main office.

Colleton Museum & Farmers Market MUSEUM, MARKET

(☎843-549-2303; www.colletonmuseum.com; 506 E Washington St, Walterboro; $5; noon-6pm Tue, 10am-5pm Wed-Fri, 10am-2pm Sat) A quirky little museum with interesting exhibits on South Carolina nature, history, art and agriculture. Highlights include megalodon teeth, a 'Dave pot' (stoneware made by an exceptionally talented enslaved man), and an exhibit on the Tuskegee Airmen, many of whom did their training in the town. It's located in the town of Walterboro, about 50 miles west of Charleston.

The unusual museum also includes a cafe, a commercial kitchen for chefs looking to start new businesses and a seasonal farmers market (open 2pm to 6pm Tuesday and 10am to 2pm Saturday from May through October; Saturday only in November and December).

St James Santee Parish Church CHURCH

(Brick Church at Wambaw; Old Georgetown Rd, McClellanville) In a secluded spot within Francis Marion National Forest (about 40 miles northeast of Charleston) sits this lovely brick church. It was built in 1768 for the French Huguenots and is very well preserved. Getting there on the sandy road through the woods is half the fun. Beware of the dog in the yard.

Heyward House Museum & Welcome Center HISTORIC BUILDING

(Map p196; ☎843-757-6293; www.heywardhouse.org; 70 Boundary St, Bluffton; adult/student house tours $10/5, neighborhood tours $18/12; 10am-5pm Mon-Fri, to 4pm Sat) The Bluffton Historical Preservation Society has meticulously preserved this circa-1841 Carolina-farmhouse-style home, converting it into a welcome center and museum in the heart of the Bluffton's historic district. Visitors can pick up maps, information and menus for local restaurants here, and 45-minute house tours and 1½-hour neighborhood walking tours are available during opening hours.

Festivals & Events

Summerville Sweet Tea Festival FOOD & DRINK
(843-821-7260; www.summervilledream.org/sweet-tea-festival.html; Hutchinson Sq; Sep) A celebration of all things sweet tea, accompanied by music, art, food and merriment.

Sleeping & Eating

Kiss your grits – you're in fine eatin' country. Lowcountry cuisine dominates the South Carolina and Georgia coastlines, drawing from land (okra, field peas, rice and corn) and sea (shellfish), and heavily influenced by West/Central African traditions brought via the slave trade. Try the classics: shrimp and grits, she-crab soup, chicken perloo (a regional chicken and rice dish), shrimp, crawfish and/or crab boils (or Frogmore stew).

Hampton House B&B $
(843-542-9498; http://hamptonhousebandb.com; 500 Hampton St, Walterboro; r incl breakfast $125-145; ) Set in a 1912 colonial home, this elegant but quirky B&B features three charming guest rooms with queen canopy beds and tasteful antique furnishings and art. The full country breakfast is tasty, and the backyard offers cheerful gardens and a relaxing pool.

★ **TW Graham & Co** SEAFOOD $
(843-887-4342; http://twgrahamcoseafood.webs.com; 810 Pinckney St, McClellanville; mains $7-12; 11am-2:30pm Tue-Sun & 5:30-9:30pm Thu-Sat) In sleepy McClellanville, this here's where you get the best fried veggies and seafood in the whole damn state. It's a straightforward kinda place: service sweeter than the tea, and fried okra, fried green tomatoes, fried shrimp, fried calamari, fried crawfish tails, and a few other things fried. Oh, and some fried crab balls.

Bluffton BBQ BARBECUE $
(843-757-7427; www.bluffton-bbq.com; 11 State of Mind St, Bluffton; BBQ $6-10; 11am-7pm Wed-Fri, noon-7pm Sat) This slow-cookin' BBQ joint makes no bones about the occasionally lengthy wait time; for this tangy pulled pork, baby back ribs and rotisserie roasted chicken, ya'll have some patience, ya hear? It's nothin' fancy here, but dang it's good.

Cottage SOUTHERN US $$
(843-757-0508; http://thecottagebluffton.com; 38 Calhoun St, Bluffton; mains $13-16; 8am-3pm Mon-Sat, 5-8pm Fri & Sat, 8am-2pm Sun;) A charming if slightly cramped Southern kitchen, with pet-friendly patio seating and a killer Sunday brunch. Think flavorful gumbo, spicy jambalaya and creative things like blue crab, corn and bacon pot pie. The place is famous for its omelet specials and occasionally throws in other wildcards, like frog legs, too.

Shopping

South Carolina Artisans Center ARTS & CRAFTS
(843-549-0011; www.scartisanscenter.com; 318 Wichman St, Walterboro; 9am-5pm Mon-Sat) The South Carolina Artisans Center is a rambling house with folk art, fine art and traditional crafts filling several rooms.

Information

Welcome Center (843-538-4353; www.walterborosc.org; 1273 Sniders Hwy, Walterboro; 9am-5pm Mon-Sat) Walterboro calls itself the the 'Front Porch of the Lowcountry,' and a red rocking chair greets guests here at its welcome center.

Getting There & Away

Charleston International Airport (p167) and Savannah/Hilton Head International Airport (p167) in Savannah, 40 miles east of Hilton Head Island, are the main gateways to South Carolina's Lowcountry from the north and south, respectively. Amtrak (p371) trains and **Greyhound** (843-744-4247; www.greyhound.com; 3610 Dorchester Rd) buses also run from Charleston.

Mt Pleasant

843 / POP 84,200

Across the Cooper River from Charleston is the residential and vacation community of Mt Pleasant, originally a summer retreat for early Charlestonians, along with the slim barrier resort islands of Isle of Palms and Sullivan's Island. Though increasingly glutted with traffic and strip malls, the area still has some charm, especially in the historic downtown, called the Old Village, and along Shem Creek.

Sights & Activities

Boone Hall Plantation HISTORIC BUILDING
(Map p196; ☎843-884-4371; www.boonehallplantation.com; 1235 Long Point Rd; adult/child 6-12yr $24/12; ⊙8:30am-6:30pm Mon-Sat, noon-5pm Sun early Mar-Aug, shorter hours Sep-Jan) Just 11 miles from downtown Charleston on Hwy 17N, Boone Hall Plantation is famous for its magical Avenue of Oaks, planted by Thomas Boone in 1743. Boone Hall is still a working plantation, though strawberries, tomatoes and peaches long ago replaced cotton as the primary crop. The main house, built in 1936, is the fourth house on the site. The most compelling buildings are the Slave St cabins, built between 1790 and 1810 and now lined with exhibits.

Patriot's Point Naval & Maritime Museum MUSEUM
(☎843-884-2727; www.patriotspoint.org; 40 Patriots Point Rd; adult/child 6-11yr $22/14; ⊙9am-6:30pm) This museum is home to the USS *Yorktown,* a giant aircraft carrier used extensively in WWII. You can tour the ship's flight deck, bridge and ready rooms and get a glimpse of what life was like for its sailors. Also on-site are a submarine, naval destroyer, the Medal of Honor Museum and a re-created 'fire base' from Vietnam, which all add a unique touch to merely touring a decommissioned ship. You can also catch the Fort Sumter Boat Tour (p177). Parking is $5.

Nature Adventures Outfitters KAYAKING
(☎843-568-3222; www.kayakcharlestonsc.com; Shrimp Boat Lane; tours adult/child from $45/35; ⊙8am-8pm May-Sep, hours vary rest of year) These outfitters lead saltwater kayak and canoe trips through Shem Creek Shrimping Village, Rantowles Creek and Morris Island. There are blackwater tours to Wambaw Creek Wilderness Area, Quemby Creek and Wadboo, as well as lengthier overnight trips down the Edisto River and to Capers Island and the privately owned Adventure Island.

Festivals & Events

Lowcountry Oyster Festival FOOD & DRINK
(www.charlestonrestaurantassociation.com/lowcountry-oyster-festival; 1235 Longpoint Rd, Boone Hall Plantation, Mt Pleasant; ⊙Jan) Oyster lovers feast on 80,000lb of the salty bivalves at this festival in January (oyster buckets are $12 to $14). There's also oyster shucking and eating contests, live music, local food and a whole lotta beer.

Sleeping

Mt Pleasant obviously cannot match the oodles of historic B&Bs found in Charleston, but it has a few, along with a wealth of more standard-issue chain hotels (Hampton Inn, Days Inn etc) that are easier on the wallet than Charleston's options.

Old Village Post House Inn B&B **$$**
(☎843-388-8935; http://oldvillageposthouseinn.com; 101 Pitt St; r from $168; P❄︎☜) In affordable Mt Pleasant, this pale yellow-and-blue clapboard house is a homey, relaxing option tucked into a historic fishing community. It's under the same ownership as Charleston's Halls Chophouse (p186), and its restaurant is (unsurprisingly) highly recommended.

Shem Creek Inn INN **$$**
(☎843-701-1488; www.shemcreekinn.com; 1401 Shrimp Boat Lane; r from $219; P❄︎☜≋) Renovated in 2017, this glistening white dockside retreat on Shem Creek is close to all the waterfront restaurants, with awesome views of the harbor and marshlands. Activities on the creek include paddleboarding, kayaking and fishing, and guests return to an expanded lobby and 51 accommodations – all relaxed spaces, with nods to nautical themes and wildlife. Expect oyster roasts and lots of boozin'.

Eating

Some good seafood restaurants overlook the water at Shem Creek, where it's fun to dine creekside at sunset and watch the incoming fishing-boat crews unload their catches.

Mt Pleasant Farmers Market MARKET **$**
(☎843-884-2528; 645 Coleman Blvd, Mt Pleasant; meals from $5; ⊙3:30-7pm Apr-Sep) Held in a spacious pavilion at Moultrie Middle School, this local food market gives a platform to 40 vendors and farmers (but no artisans, jewelers or anyone else non-food-related). The stalls are lined with fruits, vegetables, seafood, baked goods and freshly prepared meals, and you'll recognize many of the products and faces from Charleston's Farmers Market (p191).

Wreck of the Richard & Charlene SEAFOOD **$$$**
(☎843-884-0052; www.wreckrc.com; 106 Haddrell St; mains $18-29; ⊙5-8:30pm Tue-Thu, to 9pm Fri-Sun) There are no signs, no split checks,

Lowcountry

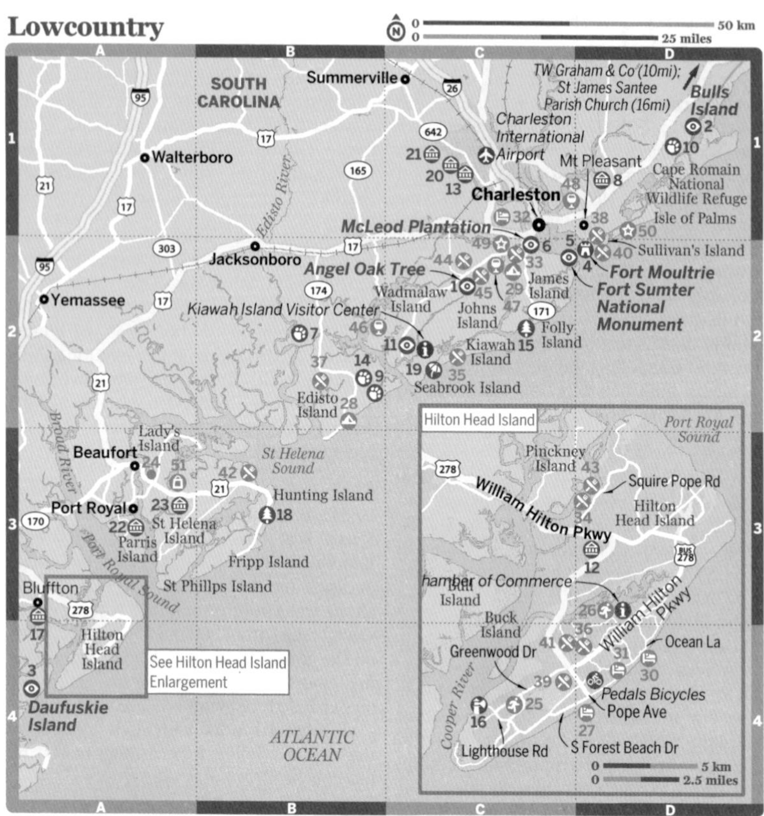

no air-conditioning, no cell-phone use and no nonsense at Shem Creek's best seafood shack. Just heaping paper plates of shrimp, scallops, fish, oysters, deviled crab and stone crab. Get 'em fried, boiled or grilled, and throw in some decadent fried hominy or hush puppies for good measure. Hit the patio in good weather.

Drinking & Nightlife

In summertime the bars lining Shem Creek are packed with boozing locals, especially Red's Ice House. Also, there are a few microbreweries that call Mt Pleasant home, the best of which is Two Blokes Brewing.

★**Two Blokes Brewing** MICROBREWERY
(Map p196; ☎843-654-4564; www.twoblokesbrewing.com; 547 Long Point Rd; ⏰4-9pm Mon-Thu, 3-10pm Fri, noon-10pm Sat, noon-6pm Sun, longer hours in summer; 📶) Two blokes – an American-Australian duo – founded this great Mt Pleasant brewery, one of three (and counting) in town. The Aussie brewmaker steeps 6.5lb of chipotle peppers for the excellent and well-balanced Chipotle Amber Ale, but any of the 12 on-tap offerings willl also suit just fine.

Red's Ice House BAR
(☎843-388-0003; www.redsicehouse.com; 98 Church St; ⏰11am-1am) When the weather's cooperating, the patio at this easygoing seafood joint is the place to party on Shem Creek. The crow's nest is a great spot to watch the boats go by blasting their country music.

Information

Mt Pleasant Visitor Center (☎800-774-0006; www.charlestoncvb.com; 99 Harry M Hallman Jr Blvd; ⏰9am-5pm) Located just across the Ravenel Bridge from Charleston, here you can

Lowcountry

Top Sights
1 Angel Oak Tree ... C2
2 Bulls Island ... D1
3 Daufuskie Island ... A4
4 Fort Moultrie ... D2
5 Fort Sumter National Monument ... C2
6 McLeod Plantation ... C2

Sights
7 ACE Basin National Wildlife Refuge ... B2
8 Boone Hall Plantation ... D1
9 Botany Bay Plantation Wildlife Management Area ... B2
10 Center for Birds of Prey ... D1
11 Charleston Tea Plantation ... C2
12 Coastal Discovery Museum ... D3
13 Drayton Hall ... C1
14 Edisto Island Serpentarium ... B2
15 Folly Beach County Park ... C2
16 Harbour Town Lighthouse ... C4
17 Heyward House Museum & Welcome Center ... A3
18 Hunting Island State Park ... B3
19 Kiawah Beachwater Park ... C2
20 Magnolia Plantation ... C1
21 Middleton Place ... C1
22 Parris Island Museum ... A3
23 Penn Center ... A3

Activities, Courses & Tours
Gullah-N-Geechie Mahn Tours ... (see 23)
24 Higher Ground ... A3
25 Lawton Stables ... C4
26 Outside Hilton Head ... D3

Sleeping
27 Beach House ... D4
28 Edisto Beach State Park ... B2
Hunting Island State Park Campground ... (see 18)
Inn at Middleton Place ... (see 21)
29 James Island County Park ... C2
30 Omni Oceanfront Resort ... D4
Sanctuary at Kiawah Island Golf Resort ... (see 35)
31 Sonesta Resort ... D4
32 Town & Country Inn & Suites ... C1

Eating
33 Cory's Grilled Cheese ... C2
34 Hudson's ... D3
35 Jasmine Porch ... C2
36 Java Burrito ... D4
37 King's Farm Market ... B2
38 Obstinate Daughter ... D1
39 One Hot Mama's ... C4
40 Poe's Tavern ... D2
41 Red Fish ... C4
42 Shrimp Shack ... B3
43 Skull Creek Dockside Restaurant ... D3
44 Tattooed Moose ... C2
45 Wild Olive ... C2

Drinking & Nightlife
46 Deep Water Vineyard ... B2
Firefly Distillery ... (see 46)
Lodge ... (see 39)
47 Low Tide Brewing ... C2
48 Two Blokes Brewing ... C1

Entertainment
Jazz Corner ... (see 36)
49 Pour House ... C2
50 Windjammer ... D1

Shopping
51 Carolina Cider Company & Superior Coffee ... A3

get tourism info and help with accommodations and tours throughout the area.

Getting There & Away

Mt Pleasant is located just across the Cooper River from Charleston and reached via the cable-stayed Ravenel Bridge on Hwy 17, 9 miles east of the peninsula. City bus 41 from the corner of Meeting and Mary Sts in downtown Charleston services Mt Pleasant.

Hilton Head Island

843 / POP 40,500

Across Port Royal Sound, tony Hilton Head Island is South Carolina's largest barrier island and one of America's top golf spots. There are dozens of courses, many enclosed in posh private residential communities (historically known as 'plantations,' now often called 'resorts').

The island was the first eco-planned destination in the USA. Founder Charles Fraser believed a resort should blend with nature, so subdued colors, strict zoning laws (no building over five stories high, signage must be low and lit from below) and a distinct lack of streetlights characterize the environment here. But while summer traffic and miles of stoplights can stifle an appreciation of the beauty of the island, you can find some lush nature preserves, wide, white beaches hard-packed enough for bike riding, and a whole lot of dolphins.

Sights

Coastal Discovery Museum MUSEUM

(Map p196; 843-689-6767; www.coastaldiscovery.org; 70 Honey Horn Dr; 9am-4:30pm Mon-Sat, 11am-3pm Sun) FREE A Smithsonian Affiliate, this museum is well worth a trip for its exhibits highlighting the island's rich Gullah history, natural wonders and other coastal treasures. A trail system on the 62-acre property winds past ancient oak trees, lush gardens and historic buildings. The museum suggests a donation of $5.

Harbour Town Lighthouse LIGHTHOUSE, MUSEUM

(Map p196; www.harbourtownlighthouse.com; 149 Lighthouse Rd; adult/child $4.25/free; 10am-sunset) Hilton Head's lighthouse, with the only female lighthouse keeper in North America, was built in 1970 and is prettily perched at the Harbour Town marina on the island's southern end, tucked away on Sea Pines Plantation. The 114 steps to the top are a museum, filled with Civil War artifacts, island history and regional lighthouse history, which certainly makes climbing them more interesting than otherwise. In addition to the admission, you'll pay a $6 day-pass fee for Sea Pines.

Activities

★ **Outside Hilton Head** WATER SPORTS

(Map p196; 800-686-6996; www.outsidehiltonhead.com; 1 Shelter Cove Lane; 8am-6pm summer, shorter hours rest of year) Boasting 40 years of experience and five locations on the island, this is the go-to outfitter for getting out on the water, be it boating, kayaking, charter fishing, stand up paddling (SUP) or dolphin tours. A great trip to Daufuskie Island (p192) includes a historian guide and a golf-cart tour, with stops at artisan workshops, a rum distillery and a museum.

Lawton Stables HORSEBACK RIDING

(Map p196; 843-671-2586; www.lawtonstables.com; 190 Greenwood Dr; trail rides per person $65, pony rides $10; 8am-5pm) The best way to explore the forests and lakes of the 600-acre Sea Pines Nature Preserve is on horseback. The horses here are surefooted and well cared for, and the verdant surrounds are a fantastic showcase of the Lowcountry's natural beauty. Rides on Shetland ponies are available to kids aged seven and under, and there's a farm that kids will love.

Sleeping

Beach House RESORT $$

(Map p196; 843-785-5126; www.beachhousehhi.com; 1 S Forest Beach Dr; r $160-300, ste $200-400; P@) This independently owned Holiday Inn is the most affordable (and closest to the beach) of Hilton Head's sandside resorts. Earth-toned and whimsical (note the massive room numbers), it attracts a young and fun crowd, especially at the beach volleyball courts and the Tiki Hut bar (there's live music day and night in season).

Omni Oceanfront Resort RESORT $$$

(Map p196; 843-842-8000; www.omnihotels.com/hotels/hilton-head; 23 Ocean Lane; r from $359; P) A great choice for those seeking a sporty but low-key spot, this beachfront hideaway was revamped in 2016 and features some of the largest rooms on the island, each of which comes with a mini-kitchen and balcony. Other sweet amenities include 56 holes of golf, 24 tennis courts, two beachside hot tubs and three pools (one is adults-only).

Sonesta Resort RESORT $$$

(Map p196; 843-842-2400; www.sonesta.com/hiltonheadisland; 130 Shipyard Dr; r from $329; P@) With its soothing rust-orange and beige color palette, outdoor fire-pit lounges and calming ponds throughout, Shipyard Plantation's Sonesta Resort and its laid-back vibe complement the Lowcountry better than most on Hilton Head. Rooms – 340 clean-lined, contemporary hideaways – are spacious and stylish; the heated shade pool neutralizes the odd cold day and the beach is postcard-perfect.

Eating

★ **Java Burrito** MEXICAN $

(Map p196; 843-842-5282; www.javaburritoco.com; 1000 William Hilton Pkwy; mains $7-14; 7:30am-9pm Mon-Sat) Like a sustainably tricked-out Chipotle, this family-owned, farm-to-table burrito Eden is impossible not to love, which is why in-the-know islanders are addicted to it. Choose your method (burrito, bowl, taco etc), choose your protein (chicken, steak, veggies, eggs, local fish etc), choose your fixings (rice, beans, queso etc), then die happy.

★ **Hudson's** SEAFOOD $$

(Map p196; ☎843-681-2772; www.hudsonsonthedocks.com; 1 Hudson Rd; lunch $9-24, dinner $14-34; ⏰11am-3pm & 5-9pm; 📶) Hilton Head's go-to seafood shack is a doozy, with a wonderful dockside deck on the water that brims with revelry (old-time islanders stick to the cozy indoor bar), all of which is centered on the bounties of the sea. Anything with shrimp, (seasonal) soft-shell crab or fresh oysters (they cultivate and harvest their own seasonally) will woo you.

Skull Creek Dockside Restaurant SEAFOOD $$

(Map p196; ☎843-785-3625; www.docksidehhi.com; 2 Hudson Rd; mains $15-29; ⏰11am-10pm Mon-Thu, to 11pm Fri & Sat, 10am-10pm Sun) Set in a renovated old river house, the latest addition to Hilton Head's dining scene raises the (already high) bar for seafood with its mouthwatering amalgam of American, Italian and Southern dishes. Think heaping plates of meat-heavy crab cakes, scallops seared in citrus butter and colossal stuffed shrimp, paired with sides like pimento-cheese grits and creamy collard greens.

One Hot Mama's BARBECUE $$

(Map p196; ☎843-682-6262; www.onehotmamas.com; 7a Greenwood Dr; wings each $1, sandwiches & burgers $9-13; ⏰11am-2am, food served to 10pm, plus brunch 10:30am-2pm Sun) Known for serving up the best BBQ on Hilton Head Island, along with incredible chicken wings doused in sauces like strawberry jalapeño and holy hula hula, this 'Barmuda Triangle' establishment also fills with revelers on weekend nights. *Food Network Star* finalist Orchid Paulmeier is at the helm, and the Sunday brunch is legendary.

Red Fish SEAFOOD $$$

(Map p196; ☎843-686-3388; www.redfishofhiltonhead.com; 8 Archer Rd; mains $24-39; ⏰11:30am-2pm & 5-9pm Mon-Sat; 📶) Equal parts bottle shop, art gallery and intimate seafooder, Red Fish hosts power-lunch cronies by day and islander foodies by night, both of whom come for hook-to-table seafood (a co-owner's husband does the fishing himself), paired with excellent Californian and Oregonian wines. Start with the baked pimento-cheese appetizer, then go for whatever's freshest, which is often prepped with Asian and Latin touches.

Drinking & Entertainment

Most of the independent nightlife on the island is concentrated on the south end in an area known as the 'Barmuda Triangle.' Jazz Corner is also a great spot for live music and a martini.

Lodge CRAFT BEER

(Map p196; ☎843-842-8966; www.hiltonheadlodge.com; 7d Greenwood Dr; ⏰3pm-1:45am Thu-Sat, to 11pm Sun-Wed, food served 4-10pm; 📶) Themed as a hunting lodge but with the added bonus of seafaring games such as shuffleboard and giant Jenga, the island's best craft-beer bar is a hopped-up bridge between the mountains and the sea. There are 36 rotating regional-brew taps (growlers welcome) overseen by *Food Network Star* finalist Orchid Paulmeier.

Jazz Corner LIVE MUSIC

(Map p196; ☎843-842-8620; www.thejazzcorner.com; 1000 William Hilton Pkwy; ⏰6-11pm) Jazz Corner is an intimate, elegant venue tucked into a nondescript shopping plaza, but it's regularly listed among the best jazz clubs in the country. Top talent swings by regularly, and the Southern cuisine and oversized martinis also earn high marks from guests.

Information

Hilton Head Island–Bluffton Chamber of Commerce (Map p196; ☎843-523-3373; www.hiltonheadisland.org; 1 Chamber of Commerce Dr; ⏰8:30am-5:30pm Mon-Fri) Has a small desk with information and brochures.

Getting There & Away

Savannah/Hilton Head International Airport (p167) is located in Savannah, 40 miles west of Hilton Head Island across the state line in Georgia. A rideshare costs between $50 and $60. Most people arrive with their own wheels.

Getting Around

Pedals Bicycles (☎888-699-1039; www.pedalsbicycles.com; 71 Pope Ave; per day/week from $12/21; ⏰9am-5pm) Offers a variety of bikes for rent (tandems, Burleys, beach cruisers, mountain bikes – even adult tricycles!) and can deliver in advance to your choice of lodging. It's also a full-service bicycle shop.

Charleston County Sea Islands

A dozen islands within an hour's drive of Charleston make up the Charleston County Sea Islands. Around 10 miles by road southeast of Charleston on the Mt Pleasant side, Sullivan's Island and Isle of Palms beckon day-trippers for sand-lounging and reveling on blue-sky days. Around 4 miles in the other direction brings you to James Island, one of the most urban of Charleston's barrier sea islands. A further 9 miles south of Charleston, Folly Beach is good for a day of sun and sand. The other end of the island is popular with surfers.

Upscale rental homes, golf courses and the swanky Sanctuary resort mark Kiawah Island, 26 miles southwest of Charleston, where you'll find those lucky enough to stay here cruising on their bikes along one of the most gorgeous beaches in the South. Nearby Edisto Island (*ed*-is-tow) is a homespun family vacation spot without a single traffic light.

Sights

Plantations, distilleries, vineyards and beaches – lots of beaches! At its southern tip, Edisto Beach State Park has a gorgeous, uncrowded beach and oak-shaded hiking trails and campgrounds, along with an environmental learning center featuring interactive displays and tanks containing alligators, snakes and turtles.

James Island County Park is a superb little recreation spot for biking and kayaking. Kiawah Beachwater Park offers Kiawah's only public-access beach.

Edisto Island

Botany Bay Plantation Wildlife Management Area WILDLIFE RESERVE
(Map p196; 843-442-8140; sunrise-sunset Wed-Sun;) FREE An avenue of regal live oaks flanks the entrance to this 4687-acre wildlife preserve, where a mix of pine forests, agricultural fields, coastal islands and 2 miles of undeveloped beach await for in-the-know visitors and nature enthusiasts. There's a 6.5-mile wildlife drive through the forest, which features plenty of birds and fox squirrels. And the beach, which can only be accessed on foot, offers a peek at some coastline that looks similar to how it did when the original settlers arrived.

Edisto Island Serpentarium ZOO
(Map p196; 843-869-1171; www.edistoserpentarium.com; 1374 Hwy 174, adult/child $15/11; 10am-6pm Mon-Sat Jun-early Sep, hours vary Thu-Sat spring & fall) Around 50 years of reptile obsession by owners Ted and Heyward Clamp culminate in this serpentarium, which differs from most in that you can see snakes living in their natural habitats, separated from visitors by low-walled enclosures rather than glass. Alligators, lizards, turtles and crocodiles also call the outdoor serpentarium home. Think of it as a reptilian Disneyland.

Folly Beach & James Island

Folly Beach County Park PARK
(Map p196; 843-762-9960; www.ccprc.com; 1100 W Ashley Ave, Folly Island; parking $5-15; 9am-8pm May-Aug, shorter hours rest of year) At the far west end of Folly Beach, this scenic county park features a serene swimming beach and a pelican rookery. Public changing areas and beach-chair rentals are available. Lifeguards are on duty seasonally.

★ **McLeod Plantation** PLANTATION
(Map p196; 843-795-4386; www.ccprc.com/1447/McLeod-Plantation-Historic-Site; 325 Country Club Dr, James Island; adult/child $15/6; 9am-4pm Tue-Sun) This James Island plantation offers an honest and frankly devastating account of the lives of the enslaved and later (theoretically) emancipated African Americans who lived and worked here between 1851 and 1990. Yes, you read that right. The last African American resident, who worked as a nurse for the grandson of the man who enslaved her great-great-grandparents, moved out of the former slave quarters only a few decades ago.

Johns Island

★ **Angel Oak Tree** HISTORIC SITE
(Map p196; 843-559-3496; www.angeloaktree.com; 3688 Angel Oak Rd, Johns Island; 9am-5pm Mon-Sat, 1-5pm Sun, gift shop till 4:30pm) FREE Some folks reckon this Southern live oak tree is 1500 years old (others says it's 400 to 500 years old). Whatever the case, it's one of the oldest living organisms east of the Mississippi, standing 66.5ft tall and measuring 28ft around. Its thick branches shoot off in all directions, in many cases twisting to the ground and back up again. Although there's no climbing allowed, you can take tree selfies.

Kiawah Island

Kiawah Beachwater Park BEACH

(Map p196; www.ccprc.com; 8 Beachwalker Dr, Kiawah Island; parking $5; ⏲9am-8pm May-Sep, shorter hours rest of year) This idyllic stretch of sun-toasted sand at the southern end of Kiawah Island has been called one of the top 10 beaches in the USA and is the only publicly accessible beach on Kiawah. Take a bike – the compact sand is perfect for a ride along the 10-mile barrier island.

Sullivan's Island

★ **Fort Moultrie** FORT

(Map p196; ☎843-883-3123; www.nps.gov/fosu; 1214 Middle St, Sullivan's Island; adult/child $3/free; ⏲9am-5pm) This layered fort encapsulates the history of US coastal defense spanning nearly 200 years and four wars. Aspects of the fort have been restored to help visitors understand the evolution of architecture, weaponry and engineering during a range of time periods, with special attention given to the Revolutionary War, the Civil War, WWI and WWII periods.

Wadmalaw Island

Charleston Tea Plantation PLANTATION

(Map p196; ☎843-559-0383; www.charlestonteaplantation.com; 6617 Maybank Hwy, Wadmalaw Island; trolley tour adult/child under 13yr $12/6; ⏲10am-4pm Mon-Sat, noon-4pm Sun) There's only one large-scale, working tea plantation in the US, folks, and this is it. A trolley tour takes visitors around the property, offering plenty of information on the history and process of growing tea plants, while a free tour of the production facility gives insight into the magic behind green, oolong and black tea.

The gift shop has lots of goodies and souvenirs, including free, bottomless hot and cold tea.

Tours

Adventure Harbor Tours BOATING

(Map p174; ☎843-442-9455; www.adventureharbortours.com; 56 Ashley Point Dr, Charleston; adult/child 3-12yr $55/30) Runs harbor cruises, sunset cruises and fun trips to uninhabited Morris Island – great for shelling.

Sleeping

There are a handful of resorts, inns and beach hotels on the various islands, but the majority of travelers stay in upscale vacation homes reserved via online booking services. Kiawah Island has the least options, and Folly Beach has the most.

Edisto Beach State Park CAMPGROUND $

(Map p196; ☎843-869-2156; www.southcarolinaparks.com; 8377 State Cabin Rd, Edisto Island; adult $5, child 6-15yr $3, tent & RV sites $24-72, cabins $100-220; 📶) Edisto Beach State Park has a gorgeous, uncrowded beach and oak-shaded hiking trails and campgrounds.

James Island County Park CAMPGROUND $

(Map p196; ☎843-795-4386; www.ccprc.com; 871 Riverland Dr, James Island; tent sites from $32, 8-person cottages $193; 📶) A great budget option, this 643-acre park southwest of downtown Charleston has meadows, a marsh and a dog park. You can rent bikes ($4 per hour) and kayaks ($5.50 per hour), go for a run or frolic with your pup. The park offers shuttle services to downtown and Folly Beach ($10). Reservations are highly recommended. There are 125 campsites and 10 marsh-adjacent rental cottages.

★ **Water's Edge Inn** B&B $$$

(☎843-588-9800; www.innatfollybeach.com; 79 W 2nd St, Folly Beach; r $249-329, villas $399-699; P❄📶) This playful B&B is defined by its Tommy Bahama flair, with lots of wicker and rattan furnishings, surfboard decor and Jimmy Buffett on repeat in the parking lot. Rooms are unique and cozy, with fireplaces, Jacuzzis and some with views out over Folly River. A communal hot tub overlooks the river, and a nightly social hour includes wine and special island punch.

Regatta Inn BOUTIQUE HOTEL $$$

(☎843-588-0101; http://regattainnfollybeach.com; 64 W 9th St Ext, Folly Beach; r from $277; P❄📶) A romantic, nautical-themed boutique property overlooking the Folly River. The 10 rooms on three floors all have comfy king beds with headboards made from sails, and cozy fireplaces. Some also have Jacuzzis and incredible views over the water, occasionally with dolphins and fiery sunsets. Each evening there's a wine and snacks social hour. No guests under 18.

Sanctuary at Kiawah Island Golf Resort RESORT $$$

(Map p196; ☎800-654-2924; www.kiawahresort.com; 1 Sanctuary Beach Dr, Kiawah Island; r/ste from $560/1100, villas from $260, houses per week from $5500;) Ready to swank it up? Consider an idyll at the Sanctuary, sitting prettily by the sea 21 miles south of downtown Charleston. Hotel rooms glow with freshly classic decor – think soft greens, four-poster beds, Italian linens, custom-made mattresses and marble showers. Villas and houses are also available. Amenities include two tennis complexes, 90 holes of golf, a spa and kids' Kamp Kiawah.

Eating

Great seafood is everywhere you look, from local oyster-shucking beach shacks like Bowens Island Restaurant (p202) to top-end steak and lobster experiences with stupendous views. While Kiawah Island is gate-controlled for guests and homeowners only, nonguests can get a day pass for the island's restaurants (and thereby access to the beach at their leisure).

★ **Bowens Island Restaurant** SEAFOOD $

(www.bowensisland.biz; 1870 Bowens Island Rd, Folly Island; mains $8-18; 5-9:30pm Tue-Sat) Down a long dirt road through Lowcountry marshland near Folly Beach, this unpainted wooden shack is one of the South's most venerable seafood dives – grab an oyster knife and start shucking! A half/full tray runs $12/17. Cool beer and friendly locals give the place its soul.

Poe's Tavern PUB FOOD $

(Map p196; ☎843-883-0083; www.poestavern.com; 2210 Middle St, Sullivan's Island; mains $9-13; 11am-midnight) On a sunny day the front porch of Poe's on Sullivan's Island is the place to be. The tavern's namesake, master of the macabre Edgar Allan Poe, was once stationed at nearby Fort Moultrie. The burgers are good, and the Amontillado comes with guacamole, jalapeño jack, pico de gallo and chipotle sour cream. Quoth the raven: 'Gimme more.'

King's Farm Market MARKET $

(Map p196; ☎843-869-3600; www.kingsfarmmarket.com; 2559 Hwy 174, Edisto Island; 9am-5pm Mon-Sat, to 4pm Sun Feb-Dec) It's not just about the fresh produce, the macadamia-nut cookies, the key lime pie, the blackberry cobbler, the jalapeño-pimento cheese, or the sandwiches and casseroles. It's also about the easygoing friendliness. C'mon in.

Jack of Cups PUB FOOD $

(☎843-633-0042; www.jackofcups.com; 34 Center St, Folly Beach; mains $9-12; kitchen noon-10pm Wed-Mon, bar open later) This local watering hole looks like your average neighborhood pub, with a sunny back patio to boot. But the from-scratch menu, which changes daily, really sets it apart. The curries are excellent, and the mulligatawny soup – a red-lentil concoction with Indian spices and apple puree on top – is rightfully famous.

Tattooed Moose SANDWICHES $

(Map p196; ☎843-952-7591; http://tattooedmoose.com; 3328 Maybank Hwy, Johns Island; sandwiches $8-11; 11:30am-2am) Your best bet for a lunch stop on Johns Island, with refreshingly exotic sandwiches including a Lowcountry Cuban, a Moroccan gyro and the wildly popular Lucky #1 (with pork belly and kimchi). There's a second location in downtown Charleston, in the NoMo neighborhood.

★ **Obstinate Daughter** AMERICAN $$

(Map p196; ☎843-416-5020; www.theobstinatedaughter.com; 2063 Middle St, Sullivan's Island; pizzas from $15, mains $10-27; 11am-10pm Mon-Fri, 10am-10pm Sat & Sun;) Sullivan's Island wasn't on the region's culinary map till this place showed up and made serious waves. The chef/owner, who also received high praise for Wild Olive, has demonstrated considerable range here, refocusing on light and playful plates of fresh veggies, pasta, seafood and unusual ingredients. Raw oysters are flown in from top locales, and vegetarians will leave exuberant.

Wild Olive ITALIAN $$

(Map p196; ☎843-737-4177; www.wildoliverestaurant.com; 2867 Maybank Hwy, Johns Island; pastas $13-22, mains $20-37; 5:30-10pm Sun-Thu, to 11:30pm Fri & Sat, bar from 4pm; P) This cozy Italian kitchen on Johns Island is whipping up some of the best homemade pastas and ambitious mains outside of Tuscany. The *carne crudo* is light and artful, and the lamb-sausage lasagna is a gooey delight that warmed us from the inside. Other favorites include charred octopus and ricotta gnocchi, and the homemade *limoncello* was a lovely touch.

Jasmine Porch SOUTHERN US $$$

(Map p196; ☎843-768-6330; https://kiawahresort.com/dining/jasmine-porch; Kiawah Island; small plates $10-16, mains $26-36; 6:30-11am, 11:30am-2pm & 5:30pm-late Mon-Sat, 6:30-10:15am, 11:45am-2pm & 5:30pm-late Sun)

Kiawah Island is a private island, mostly for fancy golfers and other well-off folks. But tell 'em at the gate you're headed to Jasmine Porch and, boom, you're in. The charming Southern kitchen is ensconced in the Sanctuary resort and its spacious dining room is defined by a sky-high ceiling, oak-plank flooring and elegant brick.

Drinking & Entertainment

Folly Beach is the best (and edgiest) for nightlife, with a few bars in the island's center by the Tides Hotel. Sullivan's Island skews yuppie and has great people-watching. Isle of Palms has a good scene as well, particularly in the summer. There are a few good craft breweries on Johns Island, including Low Tide Brewing.

★ Firefly Distillery DISTILLERY
(Map p196; 843-557-1405; http://fireflyspirits.com; 6775 Bears Bluff Rd, Wadmalaw Island; 11am-5pm Tue-Sat) The world's first hand-crafted sweet-tea-flavored vodka came from this gem of a distillery, tucked into the forest on Wadmalaw Island. Sampling this classic, which is made with tea grown on the nearby Charleston Tea Plantation (p201), distilled four times and blended with sugarcane from Louisiana, is what brings most people to the door. Tastings are $6.

Chico Feo PUB
(843-906-2710; www.chicofeos.com; 122 E Ashley Ave, Folly Beach; noon-2am Mon-Thu, 11am-2am Fri-Sun) A laid-back local favorite serving beer and wine, and also a range of tasty international dishes, from acai bowls to tacos to burritos to *bun cha* (a Vietnamese stew).

Low Tide Brewing BREWERY
(Map p196; 843-501-7570; http://lowtidebrewing.com; 2836 Maybank Hwy, Johns Island; 3-10pm Mon-Thu, noon-midnight Fri & Sat, noon-10pm Sun) A friendly neighborhood brewery with 12 taps spouting solid craft beers, including stouts, sours, ales and lagers. We like the Romance in the Dark, a dark sour with a hint of cherry flavor. A flight of four costs $7.

Deep Water Vineyard WINERY
(Map p196; 843-559-6867; www.deepwatervineyard.com; 6775 Bears Bluff Rd, Wadmalaw Island; 10am-5pm Tue-Sat) OK, so muscadine wine isn't usually at the top of an oenophile's list. It is, however, a fine product of South Carolina, and at this here winery (the only one in the Charleston area, mind you), a few of them aren't that terrible. The owners bring in some grapes from California to make interesting blends with their own. Tastings are $7.

Pour House CONCERT VENUE
(Map p196; 843-571-4343; http://charlestonpourhouse.com; 1977 Maybank Hwy, James Island; concerts from $12; 4pm-2am Mon-Fri, to midnight Sat, 11am-2am Sun) An intimate local music venue, with a very chill back patio. College kids and twenty-somethings dig it.

Windjammer LIVE MUSIC
(Map p196; 843-886-8596; www.the-windjammer.com/wp; 1008 Ocean Blvd, Isle of Palms; tickets from $5; 11am-1:30am) A long-standing beach bar with good live music Thursday through Saturday nights. Occasional karaoke too.

Information

Kiawah Island Visitor Center (Map p196; 800-774-0006; www.charlestoncvb.com; 4475 Betsy Kerrison Pkwy, Kiawah Island; 9am-3pm) Has maps, tourist info and helps with accommodations and tours in the Charleston area.

Getting There & Away

Charleston's barrier sea islands are all accessed via a series of byways and bridges from the city, though not always with a connection from one to another. You'll need to take the long way round if you want to go from Sullivan's Island to Kiawah or Edisto Islands, for example. Coming from the south, Edisto (via SC 174), Kiawah and Johns (via SC 17) can be accessed without going through Charleston. From the north coast, SC 17 also reaches Sullivan's and Isle of Palms without going through the city.

Beaufort

843 / POP 13,400

On Port Royal Island, darling colonial Beaufort (byoo-furt) is the second-oldest city in South Carolina, and perhaps the nation's greatest educator on the turbulent post–Civil War period. In 2017 President Obama established four Reconstruction Era National Monuments within the county, and in pockets of the city and neighboring islands Gullah culture still thrives.

The streets of this fair city are lined with gorgeous antebellum homes, restored 18th-century mansions and twisting magnolias that drip with Spanish moss. Unsurprisingly, Beaufort is often used as a backdrop for Hollywood films, and is best explored either on foot or from the perch of a horse and buggy.

Beaufort

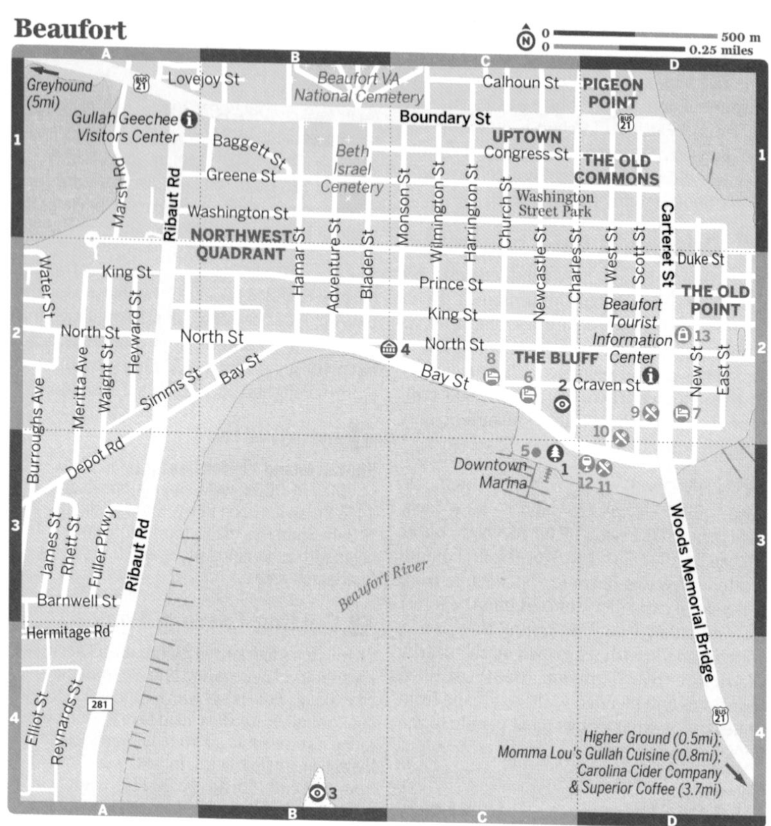

The riverfront downtown has gobs of linger-worthy cafes and galleries, and the Southern hospitality here is at its finest. Expect to be invited by perfect strangers to hop on a boat and drink beer at everybody's favorite sandbar in the middle of Port Royal Sound.

History

In November 1861, Union forces prevailed in the Battle of Port Royal, laying siege to Confederate forts on Hilton Head Island and St Helena Island. When slave owners in Beaufort caught wind of this, they all skipped town in what a newspaper columnist famously dubbed Beaufort's 'Great Skedaddle.'

As tour guides tell it, white people left so fast that Union soldiers found half-eaten suppers on the tables. There was fear of a revolt, because back then Beaufort's population was 85% enslaved people. These newly freed African Americans were left behind to tend to the homes, all of which remain standing today. For this reason, Beaufort is an exceptional place to visit not only to view magnificent antebellum homes, but also to learn about the Reconstruction Era and the culture of the Gullah people, who are descendants of the ex-slaves.

After the war, Beaufort's infrastructure was largely converted into hospitals where soldiers and former slaves got medical care. Over on St Helena Island, Penn School was established to educate ex-slaves and provide social services and employment assistance. Darrah Hall, the oldest standing structure on the school grounds, is one of four sites that in 2017 was named a Reconstruction Era National Monument by President Obama. Others include the Brick Church, where classes were held; the Old Beaufort Fire House, a social and economic hub of the time; and Camp Saxton in Port Royal, where 5000 African Americans (many of whom were ex-slaves) were recruited to join the Union army.

Beaufort

Notable figures with connections to Beaufort include Harriet Tubman, conductor of the Underground Railroad, who worked here to liberate slaves and recruit them into the army. On carriage tours, visitors also pass the former home of Robert Smalls, an ex-slave who commandeered a Confederate ship, turned it over to the Union and became the period's most inspiring African American politician.

Sights & Activities

The most authentic way to learn about the city's history is on one of the historic carriage tours (p206). Film buffs can pick up a Hollywood movie site guide at the Beaufort Tourist Information Center, and Pat Conroy's Beaufort Tour is highly recommended for fans of the author. Daredevils will enjoy Vintage Biplane Tours.

Sandbar NATURAL FEATURE

(Map p204; Beaufort River) At low tide on a warm day, Beaufort's sandbar is the place to drink and be drunk. It's only about a mile south of the Henry C Chambers Waterfront Park and people show up in all manner of watercraft, including boats, kayaks and paddleboards. They bring coolers with enough booze to last long after the tide goes out, and on some days there are even concerts performed on a floating stage.

Henry C Chambers Waterfront Park PARK

(Map p204; 843-525-7011; Bay St) Overlooking the bay, this iconic downtown anchor is flanked by dining options, shops and art galleries. Many of Beaufort's festivals and events are held here, and it's a beautiful place to watch the sun dip behind the marina.

Santa Elena History Center MUSEUM

(Map p204; 843-379-1550; https://santa-elena.org; 1501 Bay St; $10; 10am-4pm Tue-Sat;) Tucked into an old federal courthouse, this history museum tells the largely unfamiliar story of the earliest Europeans to settle in North America, and we're not talking about Jamestown. Back in 1562 the French landed on present-day Parris Island and dubbed it Charlesfort. They abandoned the site, but in 1566 the Spanish moved in and renamed it Santa Elena. This museum describes the early rivalry between these nations, and how the colonialists lived.

Pat Conroy Literary Center ARTS CENTER

(Map p204; 843-379-7025; http://patconroyliterarycenter.org; 308 Charles St; noon-4pm Thu-Sun) Until his death in 2016, South Carolina's literary great Pat Conroy called Beaufort home. The city inspired some of his most famous works, including *The Great Santini* and *The Prince of Tides*, and this newly established literary center offers exhibits on his life and work, including his writing desk and chair.

★ **Higher Ground** WATER SPORTS

(Map p196; 843-379-4327; https://highergroundoutfitters.com; 95 Factory Creek Ct, Lady's Island; tours per person from $50, rental kayak or SUP half-full day $40/60; 10am-6pm Mon-Sat, 1-4pm Sun) In Beaufort you're eventually gonna need a way to get on the water. And there's nobody better to paddle with than Tim Lovett, an avid outdoorsman and all-around nice guy who has been leading standup paddling (SUP) and kayak tours here since 2003. His noble dog Hobie often joins, and your dog is welcome, too!

Vintage Biplane Tours SCENIC FLIGHTS

(904-910-6369; www.beaufortbiplanetours.com; 30min flight $200; 11am-6pm) Seeing the Lowcountry from above is a treat, particularly from a seat in the bright-yellow De Havilland Tiger Moth aircraft, first flown in 1931. Pilot Michael Rainey is a retired marine aviator and Topgun graduate.

WATER SPORTS

You haven't experienced Beaufort if you haven't seen it from the water. Do a kayak or stand up paddling tour with Higher Ground (p205), or rent some equipment and head for the sandbar (p205).

Tours

★ Pat Conroy's Beaufort Tour WALKING
(843-838-2746; www.beauforttoursllc.com; adult/child 4-12yr $30/15; 2pm Thu-Sun) A highly recommended tour run in conjunction with the Pat Conroy Literary Center (p205), showcasing sights that were important in the writing life of the author. Stops include his high school (where he later taught), homes in the Point neighborhood where he lived and wrote, and Pat's grave on St Helena.

Historic Carriage Tours TOURS
(Map p204; 843-524-2900, 843-476-7789; 1002 Bay St; tour $23; hours vary) Two virtually identical carriage companies share a small office in Henry C Chambers Waterfront Park (p205) and alternate sending out tours every 20 minutes in high season (less frequently in winter months). Guides are engaging and knowledgeable, and focus on the historic Point neighborhood, which is chock-full of restored antebellum mansions, enormous oaks draped with Spanish moss and fascinating stories.

Festivals & Events

Gullah Festival CULTURAL
(www.theoriginalgullahfestival.org; late May) Celebrate Lowcountry African American culture on Memorial Day weekend in Beaufort.

Pat Conroy Literary Festival LITERATURE
(http://patconroyliteraryfestival.org; 308 Charles St; day pass from $73.50; Oct) A celebration of author Pat Conroy's legacy, held yearly in his adopted hometown, at the Pat Conroy Literary Center (p205). This multiday gathering includes readings, writer panels, book signings, live performances, film screenings, exhibitions and workshops.

Sleeping

Besides the standard chain hotels and motels, Beaufort is home to a dozen or so lovely and historic B&Bs and restored mansions, which are definitely the way to go.

City Loft Hotel BOUTIQUE HOTEL $$
(Map p204; 843-379-5638; www.cityloft hotel.com; 301 Carteret St; r/ste $169/209; P ❄ ✈ ✈) The chic City Loft Hotel adds a refreshing dash of modern style to a town heavy on historic homes and stately oak trees. Enjoy flat-screen TVs in the bedroom and bathroom, artisan-tile showers and memory-foam beds. Other perks include a gym, complimentary bicycle use and an on-site coffee shop ($5 voucher included in rates).

★ Anchorage 1770 INN $$$
(Map p204; 877-951-1770; https://anchorage1770.com; 1103 Bay St; r $235-375; ❄ ✈) The city's most sought-after stay is a lovingly restored 18th-century Federalist mansion on the waterfront that once belonged to the well-respected and hard-partying Admiral Beardslee. He built nooks into the tabby walls to hide booze from his wife, and there are other fun surprises (for example, delicious Butterfinger cookies at turndown) from the inn's gracious hosts.

Cuthbert House Inn B&B $$$
(Map p204; 843-521-1315; www.cuthberthouseinn.com; 1203 Bay St; r $190-325; P ❄ ✈) The most romantic of Beaufort's B&Bs, this sumptuously grand white-columned mansion is straight out of *Gone with the Wind*. Antique furnishings are found throughout, but monochromatic walls add a fresh, modern feel. Some rooms have a river view (three have fireplaces). On his march through the South in 1865, General William T Sherman slept at the house.

Eating

Beaufort may have a smaller culinary scene than Charleston, but it isn't short on Lowcountry scrumptiousness or fresh seafood. A handful of good restaurants offer outdoor dining with views of the river, and the elegant Ribaut Social Club leads the pack. Note that many restaurants are closed on Sunday and Monday.

Plums SOUTHERN US $
(Map p204; 843-525-1946; http://plumsrestaurant.com; 904 Bay St; mains $10-15; 11am-9pm) A solid waterfront bistro serving creative Lowcountry cuisine whipped up with local, seasonal ingredients. Great sandwiches, salads and seafood, and the shrimp-and-crab dip served with warm pretzel-y bread is a mouth's dream.

Lowcountry Produce SOUTHERN US $

(Map p204; ☎843-322-1900; www.lowcountryproduce.com; 302 Carteret St; breakfast $9-15, sandwiches $10-18; ⊙8am-3pm;) A fantastic cafe and market for picnic rations such as pies, housemade relishes, local cheeses and all kinds of Lowcountry-spun awesomeness (including a bizarre but wildly popular cream-cheese lasagna). Or eat in and indulge in an Oooey Gooey, a grilled pimento-cheese sandwich with bacon and garlic-pepper jelly (one hot mess!), or a tasty crab-cake sandwich with brussels-sprouts slaw.

★ **Ribaut Social Club** AMERICAN $$

(Map p204; ☎877-951-1770; https://anchorage1770.com/dining.aspx; 1103 Bay St; mains $20-32; ⊙5-7:30pm Wed-Sat, 11am-2pm Sun) A refined yet homey Lowcountry restaurant, set in the refurbished mansion – Anchorage 1770 – that once belonged to Admiral Beardslee (and named after his boisterous gentleman's club). The executive chef brings a personal touch to regional, seasonal dishes, and excels with seared sea scallops with Carolina gold rice and a tender duck breast in a pomegranate bourbon glaze.

Old Bull Tavern GASTROPUB $$

(Map p204; ☎843-379-2855; http://oldbulltavern.com; 205 West St; mains $13-18; ⊙5-9:30pm Tue-Thu, to 10pm Fri & Sat) The Old Bull Tavern offers some of the tastiest food and cocktails in Beaufort, with a wood-fired pizza oven and low-lit, worldly aesthetic to boot. The menu changes daily but always features playful American and European comfort dishes, prepared with fresh seasonal ingredients, often with a clever twist. Start with the wasabi deviled eggs and prosciutto, and continue with the braised lamb shank.

Drinking & Nightlife

Beaufort is called a 'two-liver town,' meaning you'll actually need two livers to do this place right. The Sandbar (p205) is the drinking spot of choice on warm days, and Hemingway's is a hub regardless of the weather. Locals you have just met may invite you along: just go.

Hemingway's BAR

(Map p204; ☎843-521-4480; www.hemingways.org; 920 Bay St; ⊙10am-2am;) Beaufort's best little dive fills nightly with local characters (even after the place flooded during Hurricane Irma, it converted to a swim-up bar and several people arrived on paddleboard). Jello shots ($1) are served early and often, and there's a decent patio brunch on Sunday (served from 11am to 3pm).

Shopping

Chocolate Tree FOOD

(Map p204; ☎843-524-7980; www.thechocolatetree.us; 507 Carteret St; ⊙10am-6pm Mon-Sat, 1-5pm Sun) Apparently Tom Hanks became a big fan of this chocolate shop during the filming of *Forrest Gump*, and he still orders a box every year despite knowing exactly what he's gonna get. The confections are prepared in-house daily, with favorite assortments (gift assortments from $16) including tigerpaws, rocky roads and dark sea-salt caramels.

Information

Beaufort Tourist Information Center (Map p204; ☎843-525-8500; www.beaufortsc.org; 713 Craven St; ⊙9am-5pm Mon-Sat) Inside the Beaufort History Museum, offering maps, brochures and advice.

Gullah Geechee Visitors Center (Map p204; ☎843-379-9407; 1908 Boundary St; ⊙9am-5:30pm Mon-Sat) Connects visitors with the history and culture of the area's Gullah inhabitants. Maps and brochures are available, and the staff can recommend tours and restaurants.

Getting There & Away

Beaufort is 71 miles southwest of Charleston International Airport (p167) and 46 miles northeast of Savannah/Hilton Head International Airport (p167).

Greyhound (☎800-231-2222; www.greyhound.com; 3448 Trask Pkwy) also serves the town.

Parris Island, St Helena Island & Hunting Island

Within day-tripping distance from Beaufort, a cluster of marshy, rural islands offers an enticing amalgam of history, culture and nature, with a splash of Marine Corps action and some supertasty shrimp burgers to boot.

Across the bridge to the east, St Helena Island is the heart of Gullah country, where the descendants of slaves have meticulously preserved their language and culture, and where two Reconstruction Era National Monuments were established by President Obama in 2017. Further east, on Hunting Island, you'll discover one of the state's most breathtaking coastal parks, and perhaps

OFF THE BEATEN TRACK

WALTERBORO

The 'Front Porch of the Lowcountry' isn't on most vacationers' agendas, but if you're road-trippin' from Beaufort to Columbia, it's well worth a stop. Top attractions include the South Carolina Artisans Center (p194), a giant house full of folk art, fine art and traditional crafts, and the quirky Colleton Museum & Farmers Market (p193), which is actually a few other things too, including a commercial kitchen space and a cafe. If you're stuck here for the night, the Hampton House (p194) is a strange but wonderful place to stay. Visit the Welcome Center (p193) in Walterboro for more info.

a shark tooth. To the south, Parris Island features a Marine Corps training ground and museum, and an archaeological site where the country's first European settlers landed.

As if all that isn't enough, the sweeping views from the bridges connecting these lowland isles are beyond postcard-pretty.

Sights

Parris Island Museum MUSEUM

(Map p196; ☎843-228-2951; www.parrisislandmuseum.com; 111 Panama St; ⏲10am-4:30pm) FREE This fascinating museum covering Marine Corps history contains antique uniforms and weaponry, but is most engaging for its exhibits chronicling the grueling, intense and scary (that CS gas-chamber exercise!) 13-week Marine basic training, which takes place here and at a second facility in San Diego, California. It's far worse than in *An Officer and a Gentleman!*

Hunting Island State Park STATE PARK

(Map p196; ☎843-838-2011; www.southcarolinaparks.com/huntingisland; 2555 Sea Island Pkwy; adult/child 6-15yr $5/3; ⏲park 6am-6pm, to 9pm Mar-Sep, visitor center 9am-5pm Mon-Fri, 11am-5pm Sat & Sun, nature center 9am-5pm Tue-Sat, daily Jun-Aug) Lush and inviting Hunting Island State Park impresses visitors with acres of maritime forest, tidal lagoons and a bone-white beach littered with seashells and the occasional shark tooth. The Vietnam War scenes from *Forrest Gump* were filmed in the marsh, a nature-lover's dream. Campgrounds fill quickly in summer. Climb the lighthouse ($2) for sweeping coastal views. Much of the park was affected by Hurricanes Matthew and Irma, but has largely recovered.

Penn Center MUSEUM

(Map p196; ☎843-838-2432; www.penncenter.com; 16 Penn Center Circle W, St Helena Island; $7; ⏲9am-4pm Tue-Sat) Once the home of one of the nation's first schools for freed slaves, the Penn Center has a small museum that covers Gullah culture and traces the history of Penn School. Two sites on the property became part of the National Reconstruction Era Site in 2017: Darrah Hall, the school building, and Brick Baptist Church, which was originally constructed by slaves who were not allowed to worship inside. Freed slaves took control of it in 1861.

Tours

Gullah-N-Geechie Mahn Tours CULTURAL

(Map p196; ☎843-838-7516; www.gullahngeechietours.net; 16 Penn Center Circle W, St Helena Island; per person from $32, minimum 2 people; ⏲tours 9am, 11:30am & 1:45pm Mon-Sat) This long-standing tour company offers a glimpse into the area's Gullah culture via storytelling, arts and crafts demonstrations and a driving tour of St Helena Island.

Sleeping & Eating

There are a few spots to rest your head, including some chain hotels and a lovely state-park campground, but the quaint inns over in Beaufort are a better option.

Fried ocean goodness abounds in roadside seafood places, and Gullah restaurants are easy to come by on St Helena and Lady's Islands. If you're headed to Hunting Island State Park, pick up snacks and coffee at Carolina Cider Company & Superior Coffee.

Hunting Island State Park Campground CAMPGROUND $

(Map p196; ☎office 843-838-2011, reservations 866-345-7275; www.southcarolinaparks.com; 2555 Sea Island Pkwy; RV sites $24-45, cabins from $249; ⏲6am-9pm early Mar-early Nov, 6am-6pm rest of year) At one of South Carolina's most visited parks, you can park your RV under pine trees or palm trees. Several sites have views of the beach. All sites are available by walk-up, but reservations are advisable in summer.

Shrimp Shack SEAFOOD $

(Map p196; ☎843-838-2962; 1929 Sea Island Pkwy; mains from $3, shrimp burgers $8; ⏲11am-2pm Mon-Sat) If you've ever wished your hamburger was made of shrimp, your prayers are answered at this here roadside shack on stilts. The fresh shrimp is delivered daily to a wharf across the street, and this place grinds 'em up, makes patties, fries them and finishes it off with a bun and some mayo, tartar or cocktail sauce. So perfect.

Shopping

★ **Carolina Cider Company & Superior Coffee** FOOD & DRINKS

(Map p196; www.carolinaciderco.com; 507 Sea Island Pkwy, St Helena Island; ⏲8am-6pm Mon-Sat, from 8:30am Sun, open longer hours in summer) This must-stop shop between Beaufort and Hunting Island State Park is known for its wealth of housemade ciders (peach, blackberry, blueberry etc), but beyond that it's just a happening local spot for all kinds of Lowcountry goodness (salsas, relishes, jams, jellies, grits, baked goods and so on), which are perfect to take back home. There's great coffee as well from Superior Coffee.

Getting There & Away

You'll need your own wheels to make the rounds on these islands, which are strung along the Sea Island Parkway and Ribaut Rd.

MYRTLE BEACH

☎843 / POP 32,200

The towering SkyWheel spins fantastically beside the sea in downtown Myrtle Beach, anchoring a 60-mile swath of sun-bleached excess known as the Grand Strand. This stretch of coastline is now infamously overdeveloped and littered with innumerable mini-golf courses, pancake houses, beach resorts and T-shirt shops – an alarming departure from its beginnings as a laid-back summer retreat for working-class Southerners.

Love it or hate it, Myrtle Beach offers one all-American vacation. Enormous outlet malls, water parks and daiquiri bars compete for attention, bikini-clad teenagers play video games and eat hot dogs in arcades, and Midwestern families roast on the white sand. North Myrtle Beach, actually a separate town, is slightly lower-key, with a thriving culture based on the 'shag' – a jitterbug-like dance invented here in the 1940s.

Sights

The beach itself – wide, hot and crowded with umbrellas – is pleasant enough, and you can also escape to the relatively undeveloped southern tip, where a mile-long stretch has been preserved within Myrtle Beach State Park.

Beachfront Ocean Blvd has the bulk of the hamburger stands and seedy gift shops. Hwy 17 is choked with over-the-top mini-golf courses. Several amusement-park-shopping-mall hybrids teem with people at all hours.

★ **Brookgreen Gardens** GARDENS

(☎843-235-6000; www.brookgreen.org; 1931 Brookgreen Garden Dr, Murrells Inlet; adult/child 4-12yr $16/8; ⏲9:30am-5pm) These magical gardens, 16 miles south of Myrtle Beach on Hwy 17S, are home to the largest collection of American sculpture in the country, amid more than 9000 acres of rice-plantation-turned-subtropical-garden paradise. Seasonal blooms are listed on the website.

Myrtle Beach State Park BEACH, STATE PARK

(☎843-238-5325; https://southcarolinaparks.com/myrtle-beach; 4401 S Kings Hwy; adult/child 6-15yr $5/3; ⏲6am-10pm Mar-Nov, to 8pm Dec-Feb) Escape the madness to this relatively undeveloped mile of coastline 3 miles south of central Myrtle Beach. There's also a nice boardwalk, a nature center, a 750ft fishing pier and some short hiking trails through the maritime forest.

The cabins and campground are quite popular; reserve months in advance.

HURRICANE FLORENCE

On September 14, 2018, Hurricane Florence made landfall outside of Wilmington, North Carolina. The 500-mile-wide storm dropped about 35 inches of rain as it crept westward over the next three days. Damage was not confined solely to the coast. In the days following the storm flooding took a toll on inland communities, including significant damage to state and local highways.

SkyWheel AMUSEMENT PARK
(☎843-839-9200; www.myrtlebeachskywheel.com; 1110 N Ocean Blvd; adult/child 3-11yr $14/9; ⊙11am-midnight, varying shorter hours in low season) The 187ft-high SkyWheel overlooks the 1.2-mile coastal boardwalk. One ticket includes four revolutions in an enclosed glass gondola; it lasts about 10 to 15 minutes. At night the wheel is bewitching, with more than a million dazzling colored lights.

Family Kingdom AMUSEMENT PARK
(☎843-626-3447; www.family-kingdom.com; 300 S Ocean Blvd; combo pass $38; ⊙varies seasonally, closed winter;) Family Kingdom is an old-fashioned amusement-and-water-park combo overlooking the ocean.

Festivals & Events

World Famous Blue Crab Festival FOOD & DRINK
(☎843-249-6604; www.bluecrabfestival.org; 4469 Mineola Av, Little River; ⊙May) The World Famous Blue Crab Festival draws a crowd of around 50,000 for beach music, arts and crafts, local food and business expos. It happens every May on the Little River Waterfront.

Sleeping

Myrtle Beach specializes in tacky, high-rise beachfront resorts. On the south end, heading toward Murrells Inlet, Pawleys Island and Georgetown, you'll see more vacation rentals, inns and B&Bs. Camping options are dotted throughout, including at Myrtle Beach State Park and Huntington Beach State Park on the south side. Prices vary widely by season.

Best Western Plus Grand Stand Inn & Suites HOTEL $
(☎843-448-1461; www.myrtlebeachbestwestern.com; 1804 S Ocean Blvd; r from $66, ste $69-237;) We're not accustomed to championing chain hotels, but the rates here are reasonable, the beach is steps away, there's a fitness and business center and the front desk is professional and friendly. The hotel sprawls across two buildings, one of them oceanfront and one just across Ocean Blvd.

Myrtle Beach State Park CAMPGROUND $
(☎843-238-5325; https://southcarolinaparks.com/myrtle-beach; 4401 S Kings Hwy; tent & RV sites from $30, cabins $65-205, rustic tent Easter-Labor Day from $25;) Sleep beneath the pines or rent a cabin, all just steps from the shore. During summer, cabins must be rented on a weekly basis, and there's a two-night minimum the rest of the year. Reserve months in advance.

Hampton Inn & Suites Oceanfront HOTEL $$$
(☎843-946-6400; http://hamptoninn3.hilton.com; 1801 S Ocean Blvd; r from $279;) A fantastic option along Ocean Blvd for its elaborate system of pools (nine!) and floor-to-ceiling windows overlooking the ocean.

Hampton Inn Broadway at the Beach HOTEL $$$
(☎843-916-0600; www.myrtlebroadway.hamptoninn.com; 1140 Celebrity Circle; r/ste from $249/389;) The bright, renovated rooms overlooking the lake and Broadway at the Beach are a great choice at this hotel. If you're traveling with preteens, you may feel more comfortable letting them roam the adjacent shops and attractions rather than the boardwalk, particularly at night.

Eating

The hundreds of restaurants are mostly high volume and low quality – think buffets longer than bowling alleys and 24-hour doughnut shops. For fresh seafood, locals go to nearby Murrells Inlet, the source of much of South Carolina's seafood. Restaurants here, like Wicked Tuna, are known for basement fish kitchens, where fishers pull right up to the docks to hand their catch to cooks.

Magnolias at 26th BUFFET $$
(☎843-839-3993; www.magnoliasat26th.com; 2605 N Ocean Blvd; breakfast buffet from $8, lunch buffet from $10, dinner buffet $14; ⊙6:30am-9pm) OK, if you insist on doing a buffet, do this one. Locals confide that it's their go-to, the service is superfriendly and there's all the Southern-fried yum you can handle.

Prosser's BBQ SOUTHERN US $$
(☎843-357-6146; www.prossersbbq.com; 3750 Hwy 17 Business, Murrells Inlet; buffet breakfast $7, lunch $10-11, dinner $13-15; ⊙6:30-10:30am & 11am-2pm daily, plus 4-8pm Thu-Sat) It's weird to come to Murrells Inlet's 'restaurant row' and not spring for seafood, but who are we to judge? The gut-busting lunch buffet here is down-home delicious. It includes fried fish and chicken, sweet-potato souffle, mac 'n' cheese, green beans and vinegary pulled pork.

★ **Wicked Tuna** SEAFOOD $$$
(☎843-651-9987; www.thewickedtuna.com; 4123 Hwy 17 Business, Murrells Inlet; mains $14-42;

11am-midnight, shorter hours in winter;) Murrells Inlet is full of kitschy seafooders and, at first glance, the Wicked Tuna looks no different. Guess again! You are in for a real treat at this trip-worthy spot overlooking the beautiful inlet – it employs six fishing boats that go out for three- to six-day stints and bring back upward of 600lb of fresh fish each.

Aspen Grille SOUTHERN US **$$$**
(843-449-9191; www.aspen-grille.com; 5101 N Kings Hwy; mains $18-50; 4:30pm-late Tue-Sun;) At Aspen Grille you can impress your palate, escape the madness and shake off the fried-seafood baskets that bind you. Sophisticated yet inviting, it seems worlds away from the roar of the Kings Hwy. Chef Curry Martin serves fresh and locally sourced fare with style and Southern sensibilities. Think shrimp and cheddar grits with pan gravy and andouille sausage.

Drinking & Entertainment

On and in close vicinity to the boardwalk in central Myrtle Beach is a decent area to start – you'll find decades-old classics such as the Bowery, known for live music. During summer, free concerts, street performers and fireworks shake things up on the boardwalk.

New South Brewery MICROBREWERY
(843-916-2337; www.newsouthbrewing.com; 1109 Campbell St; 4:30-7pm Tue-Fri, 1-5pm Sat) Tucked behind a lumberyard in a warehouse district 1 mile inland from Ocean Blvd, this hyperlocal brewery has been at it since before craft was a thing (since 1998). It's a simple taproom overlooking the brewery with 12 taps – go for the bestseller, the Dirty Myrtle DIPA.

American Tap House CRAFT BEER
(843-712-2301; www.americantaphouse.com; 1320 Celebrity Circle; 11am-2am;) If you prefer your craft-beer experience to come supersized, you'll find 53 taps of national options (pints $5.50 to $9) at this chef-driven gastropub at Broadway at the Beach.

★ **Fat Harold's Beach Club** DANCE
(843-249-5779; www.fatharolds.com; 212 Main St; 4pm-late Sun-Thu, 11am-late Fri & Sat, from 1pm in winter) Folks groove to doo-wop, old-time R&B and beach music at this North Myrtle institution, which calls itself 'Home of the Shag.' The dance, that is. Free shag lessons are offered at 7pm every Tuesday. On Monday they're $10 per person.

Bowery LIVE MUSIC
(843-626-3445; http://thebowery.com; 110 9th Ave N; 11am-4am Mar-Oct, shorter hours rest of the year) From March through October, live country and rock shows ($3 entry) happen nightly at this long-standing honky-tonk institution. The place is decidedly Southern, and serves burgers and wings to help mitigate your future hangover.

Shopping

Broadway at the Beach MALL
(843-444-3200; www.broadwayatthebeach.com; 1325 Celebrity Circle; 10am-11pm Jun-Sep, shorter hours rest of the year) With shops, restaurants, nightclubs, rides, an aquarium and a giant-screen digital-movie theater, this mini-Disney-like outdoor fun mall is Myrtle Beach's nerve center. Note that walking late at night in this area is not considered safe.

Information

Myrtle Beach Visitor Information (843-626-7444; www.visitmyrtlebeach.com; 1200 N Oak St; 8:30am-5pm) Has maps and brochures.

Getting There & Away

Myrtle Beach International Airport (p167) is located within the city limits, as is the **Greyhound station** (843-448-2472; www.greyhound.com; 511 7th Ave N); the airport receives direct flights from more than 30 domestic destinations.

The traffic coming and going on Hwy 17 Business/Kings Hwy can be infuriating. To avoid 'the Strand' altogether, stay on the Hwy 17 bypass, or take Hwy 31/Carolina Bays Pkwy, which parallels Hwy 17 between Hwy 501 and Hwy 9.

COLUMBIA

803 / POP 134,300

South Carolina's state capital, affectionately dubbed 'Cola,' is a quiet place, with wide, shady streets and the kind of old-fashioned downtown where pillbox hats are still on display in the windows of family-run department stores. The University of South Carolina (USC) adds a youthful vibe, and campus-side bars fill with college students whooping it up over football wins, and, more recently, basketball too (both the men's and women's teams made Final Four appearances in 2017, and the women clinched the title).

Columbia

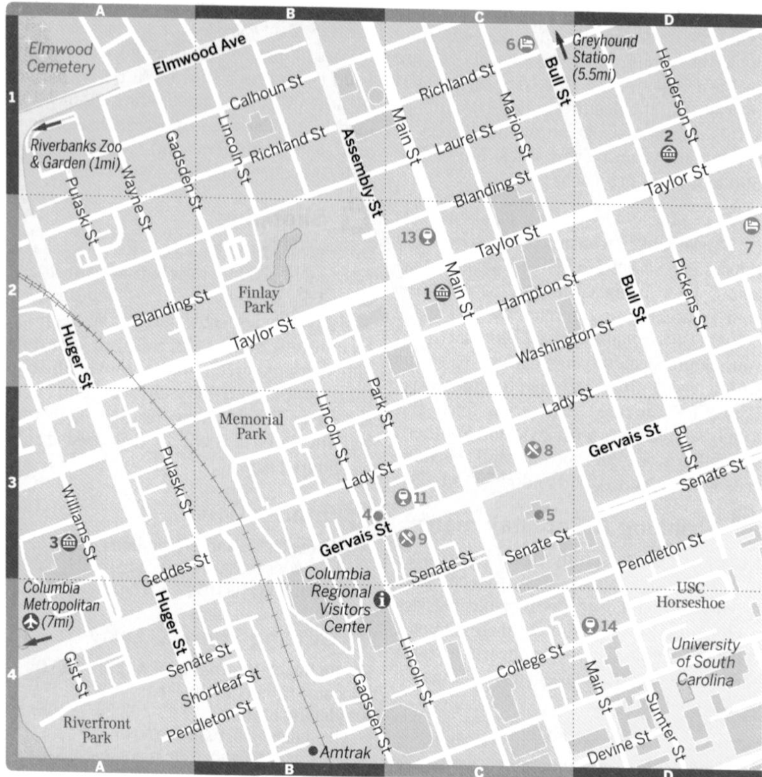

Columbia is a pleasant stop, with some decent restaurants, a renowned zoo and some interesting historical sites. But most visitors, like General Sherman's troops, charge on through to the coast.

Sights

History buffs will appreciate a tour of the capital's historic homes, and particularly should not miss the Robert Mills House. The abodes have been lovingly restored by Historic Columbia, a nonprofit that preserves the city's heritage and offers house tours.

Further edification on the state's history and culture can be achieved at the South Carolina State Museum.

City Roots FARM

(803-254-2302; www.cityroots.org; 1005 Airport Blvd; 9am-5pm Mon-Fri) An 3.5-acre organic, sustainable farm just southeast of Columbia. Produce, herbs, flowers and mushrooms are all grown here, and there is also got a farm store on-site.

Riverbanks Zoo & Garden ZOO

(803-779-8717; www.riverbanks.org; 500 Wildlife Pkwy; adult/child $15.95/13.50; 9am-5pm, plus to 6pm Fri & Sat Mar 18-Oct 1) Considered one of America's top zoos, Riverbanks regularly wins awards for design, animal care and breeding of endangered species. Popular exhibits include the reptile aquarium, which houses species like Galápagos tortoises and Komodo dragons, and an Africa-themed feature with elephants, gorillas and meerkats.

There's also a stunning botanical garden reached by crossing a footbridge over the Saluda River. It contains more than 4000 species of native and exotic plants. The zoo is just west of downtown Columbia.

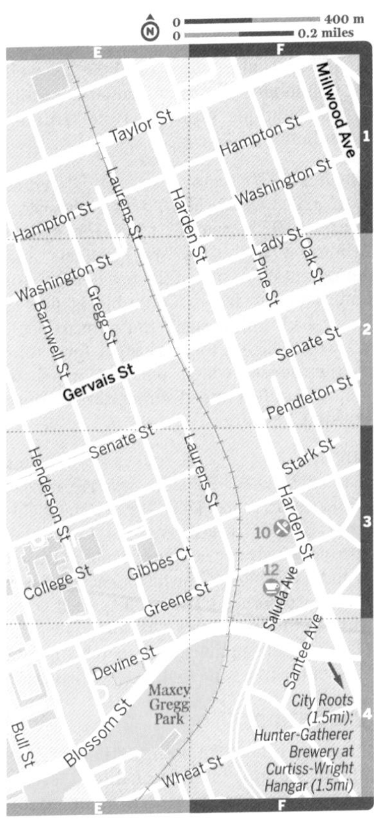

Columbia

Sights

1 Columbia Museum of Art C2
2 Robert Mills House & Gardens D1
3 South Carolina State Museum A3

Activities, Courses & Tours

House Tours .... (see 2)
4 River Runner Outdoor Center B3
5 South Carolina State House C3

Sleeping

6 1425 Inn C1
7 Chesnut Cottage D2

Eating

8 Bourbon C3
9 Motor Supply Co C3
10 Southern Belly BBQ F3

Drinking & Nightlife

11 Art Bar C3
12 Drip F3
13 Grand C2
14 Hunter-Gatherer Brewery D4

Robert Mills House & Gardens HISTORIC BUILDING

(Map p212; ☎803-252-7742; www.historiccolumbia.org/robert-mills-house-and-gardens; 1616 Blanding St; tour $8; ⏱tours 10am & 1pm Tue-Sat, 1pm & 4pm Sun) Robert Mills is best known for designing the Washington Monument, and he's also the architect of this Classical Revival town house. The restored, stately edifice, filled with period furniture and dripping with ornate chandeliers, hammers home just how skilled Mills was. It is now a museum surrounded by lovely gardens, and is one of Columbia's five National Historic Landmarks.

Columbia Museum of Art MUSEUM

(Map p212; ☎803-799-2810; www.columbiamuseum.org; 1515 Main St; adult/student $6/2.50; ⏱11am-5pm Tue-Fri, 10am-5pm Sat, noon-5pm Sun) One of South Carolina's most impressive collections of European and American art, the CMA was undergoing a $5-million permanent gallery expansion at the time of research. The expanded collection, which includes works by Monet, Dale Chihuly and Canteleto, will include several new galleries.

South Carolina State Museum MUSEUM

(Map p212; ☎803-898-4921; http://scmuseum.org; 301 Gervais St; adult/child from $8.95/6.95; ⏱10am-5pm Mon, Wed & Fri, to 10pm Tue, to 6pm Sat, noon-5pm Sun) A Smithsonian-affiliated museum exhibiting collections on the history, culture and geography of South Carolina. Kids will gawk at 'Finn,' the megalodon replica, and there's also a planetarium and a 4-D movie theater.

 Tours

River Runner Outdoor Center OUTDOORS

(Map p212; ☎803-771-0353; www.shopriverrunner.com; 905 Gervais St) Offers kayak and canoe rental for self-guided trips in Congaree National Park for $40 for the first day, and $20 for each additional day, along with custom guided trips. There's also an outdoor retail shop, with kayaks for sale.

House Tours HISTORY

(Map p212; ☎803-252-7742; www.historiccolumbia.org/take-a-tour/house-tours; 1616 Blanding St; tours $8-28; ⏱10am-4pm Tue-Sat, 1-5pm Sun) For a historical deep dive into the Old South, tour some painstakingly restored 19th-century homes. The Robert Mills House (p213) is the most impressive one,

OFF THE BEATEN TRACK

AN URBAN FARM & A BREWING HANGAR

Columbia is cooler than you think, and the best proof is slightly out of town, near the Jim Hamilton–LB Owens Airport. This is where in-the-know locals head for their gardening and boozing needs, which go surprisingly well together. First stop is City Roots (p212), the state's self-proclaimed 'first urban farm,' where you can wander around, buy farm items and talk to people about all things agriculture. With that out of the way, it's time to head across the street to **Hunter-Gatherer Brewery at Curtiss-Wright Hangar**, a brewery and taproom inside a massive and beautifully restored 13,000-sq-ft airplane hangar. The booze is delightful and the high-heat oven cooks up some delicious thin-crust pizza.

and has been converted into a museum. But you can also visit the Hampton-Preston Mansion, the Mann-Simons Site and the Woodrow Wilson Family Home. Tours begin at the Robert Mills House gift shop.

South Carolina State House TOURS
(Map p212; ☎803-734-2430; https://southcarolinaparks.com/education-and-history/state-house; 1100 Gervais St; ⊙hours vary) Home to the Governor's office and the House and Senate Chambers, downtown Columbia's State House offers free guided and self-guided tours. There's a 15-minute film on the history and Greek Revival architecture, and stops at monuments, paintings and other displays with historical significance. Check the website for hours; they vary depending on whether the legislature is in session.

Festivals & Events

Indie Grits Festival CULTURAL
(www.indiegrits.com; ⊙Apr) Columbia's best time is a South by Southwest-style three-day party celebrating art, tech, film, food and music around the city.

Sleeping

Traditional hotels and boutique properties are concentrated within the Vista and Main St districts. There's a handful of quiet inns and B&Bs along downtown's edge, including 1425 Inn and Chesnut Cottage in the historic-homes district. There are plenty of chain hotels off I-26, as well as Columbia's first independent, locally owned boutique property, Hotel Trundle (www.hoteltrundle.com).

★**Chesnut Cottage** B&B $$
(Map p212; ☎803-256-1718; www.chesnutcottage.com; 1718 Hampton St; r $150-179; P❄📶) Brimming with Civil War artifacts and period antiques, one of the few antebellum homes to survive in Columbia is now a lovely B&B and a small museum to boot. It's worth asking the innkeeper for a tour of the house, which once belonged to famous confederate documentarian Mary Boykin Chestnut.

1425 Inn B&B $$$
(Map p212; ☎803-252-7225; www.1425inn.com; 1425 Richland St; r from $249; P❄📶) This eight-room B&B is tucked away in Columbia's historic-homes district, and, while not itself historic, was built to the historical standards of the neighborhood. The extralarge bedrooms with hardwood floors are our favorites. There's a scrumptious front porch to sip a glass of the free wine that's always on hand.

Eating

Columbia is home to both Southern staples and a vibrant international-food scene. Chefs flock here for year-round farm-fresh ingredients, increasing Columbia's repu-tation as a foodie destination. Head down Gervais St to the Vista, a hip, renovated warehouse district popular with young professionals, or to Five Points, where Harden, Greene and Devine Sts meet Saluda Ave, for coffee and cheap international food.

Southern Belly BBQ BARBECUE $
(Map p212; ☎803-764-3512; www.southernbellybbq.com; 819 Harden St; sandwiches $8.75-14.75; ⊙11am-10pm; 📶) Pulled pork reimagined! Normally when you hit a Carolina BBQ spot, the pulled pork comes one way: pulled! But this innovative joint offers eight different sloppy-as-hell versions (such as the D'Jango, with pepper-jack cheese, applewood bacon, grilled onions, roasted red peppers and jalapeños) and seven excellent sauces to make it even messier. Bring a bib!

★**Bourbon** SOUTHERN US $$
(Map p212; ☎803-403-1404; www.bourboncolumbia.com; 1214 Main St; small plates $8-15,

mains $21-42; ⌚4pm-midnight Mon-Thu, to 1am Fri, 11am-3pm & 5pm-midnight Sat, 11am-3pm & 5-10pm Sun) To rub elbows with state lawmakers, attorneys and other people wearing suits, pull up a chair at Bourbon's whiskey bar. The selection of more than 350 mostly bourbon, rye and Tennessee whiskeys tends to pair well with the expertly prepared Cajun and Creole cuisine, with standout items like crispy boudin balls, grilled cab bavette steak and étouffée.

Motor Supply Co MODERN AMERICAN $$$
(Map p212; ☎803-256-6687; www.motorsupplycobistro.com; 920 Gervais St; mains $21-34; ⌚11:30am-2:30pm & 5:30-9:30pm Tue-Thu, to 10:30pm Fri & Sat, 10:30am-2:30pm Sun; 📶) Not only did Motor Supply Co flip a former auto-part shop into a restaurant long before most hipsters were born, it was doing farm-to-table fare before the term existed – since 1989, in fact. Heroic local farms such as Manchester (quail) and Geechie Boy (grits, farro and other grain) often star in the daily-changing menu.

Drinking & Nightlife

Neighboring North Main and Vista districts offer the best nightlife concentration and folks tend to bounce between them. Five Points, just off the USC campus, has the most college bars. Columbia has several breweries near USC's Williams-Brice Stadium, but the most popular, Hunter-Gatherer Brewery, is downtown behind Main St.

★Hunter-Gatherer Brewery at Curtiss-Wright Hangar BREWERY
(☎803-764-1237; http://huntergathererbrewery.com; 1402 Jim Hamilton Blvd; ⌚5-11pm Wed-Fri, 11am-11pm Sat, 11am-6pm Sun) The raddest new thing in Columbia is this old airplane hangar that's been converted into a 13,000-sq-ft brewery, taproom and observation deck overlooking the airport (craft beers from $5). There's food too, most notably some delicious thin-crust pizzas made in a fancy high-heat oven.

Grand BAR
(Map p212; ☎803-726-2233; www.thegrandonmain.com; 1621 Main St; ⌚9am-midnight Sun-Thu, to 2am Fri & Sat) Inspired by the variety of entertainment provided in a 1900s vaudeville house that once stood in its place, this venue triples as a gastropub, game center and boutique bowling alley (bowling lane $25 to $40; shoe rental $4). The upstairs bartender is a hoot, and downstairs guests serve themselves craft beer and wine from the tap and get charged by the ounce.

Art Bar BAR
(Map p212; ☎803-929-0198; www.artbarsc.com; 1211 Park St; ⌚5pm-2am Mon-Fri, 8pm-2am Sat & Sun) If it's getting late in Columbia and you're thinking of calling it a night, go to Art Bar instead. This is a quintessential second-wind kinda place with its ubiquitous twinkly lights, junkyard sculptures and patrons less ordinary. Karaoke and live music are frequent, and the dance floor is enormous.

Drip COFFEE
(Map p212; ☎803-661-9545; www.dripcolumbia.com; 729 Saluda Ave; ⌚7am-10pm Mon-Sat, 8am-6pm Sun) Belly up to the framed chalkboard menu of seven or so daily caffeine-delivery options from Peru, Colombia, Papua New Guinea, Rwanda and the like at this cozy and artsy Five Points coffeehouse. It uses the pour-over method for its java – meticulous and slow, but immensely satisfying.

Hunter-Gatherer Brewery MICROBREWERY
(Map p212; ☎803-748-0540; www.huntergathererbrewery.com; 900 Main St; ⌚4-10pm Mon-Thu, to 11pm Fri & Sat; 📶) True to its name, this microbrewery is all taxidermy and lodgy hardwoods. It produces five beers (pints $5 to $6) at any given time, plus one cask-conditioned selection, and offers up salads and hearty pub grub (think lamb gyros and pan-seared duck) to go along with it.

Information

Columbia Regional Visitors Center (Map p212; ☎803-545-0002; www.experiencecolumbiasc.com; 1101 Lincoln St; ⌚8:30am-5pm Mon-Fri; 📶) Pick up historical walking-tour maps, brochures and other information inside the Columbia Convention Center.

Getting There & Away

Columbia Metropolitan Airport (p167), which receives nonstop flights from nine domestic destinations, is located 7 miles southwest of downtown.

An **Amtrak station** (Map p212; ☎800-872-7245; www.amtrak.com; 850 Pulaski St) sits smack downtown while the **Greyhound bus station** (☎803-569-6522; www.greyhound.com; 710 Buckner Rd) is 5.5 miles north.

CONGAREE NATIONAL PARK

Inky-black water, dyed with tannic acid leached from decaying plant matter. Bone-white cypress stumps like the femurs of long-dead giants. Spanish moss as dry and gray as witches' hair. Encompassing nearly 27,000 acres, **Congaree National Park** (☎803-776-4396; www.nps.gov/cong; 100 National Park Rd, Hopkins) FREE is the largest expanse of old-growth, bottomland hardwood forest in the Southeastern US. Visitors come to behold the meandering waterways of its floodplain ecosystem and its sky-high canopy replete with champion trees – the largest of a species, based on height, trunk width and crown spread.

Congaree offers up the most champions of any park in North America, and they grow this big and tall thanks to waters from the adjacent Congaree and Wateree Rivers, which occasionally rush over the floodplain, nourishing the whole place with sediment.

The park was established in 1976 to save it from loggers, and remains an excellent place to canoe and hike, as you occasionally glance skyward at upland pines, bald cypresses and water tupelos. Be sure to check the 'mosquito meter' at the visitor center so you know what you're getting into.

Look carefully at the Blue Sky mural in the visitor center – the scene seems to change as you move. From mid-May through mid-June, the *Photinus carolinus*, a rare species of firefly, blink in unison, turning the forest floor into a twinkling light show. The phenomenon only occurs in a handful of spots around the world.

Activities

Popular activities in Congaree National Park include hiking, canoeing, wildlife-spotting, camping and recreational fishing (which requires a state license).

Hiking

All ages and levels of athleticism are served, with long backcountry treks, short hikes in the woods and a popular boardwalk saunter. There are 10 walking trails in total, ranging from half a mile to nearly 12 miles. At the heart of the park, the 6.6-mile Oakridge Trail is among the best hikes in the state, with its lofty oaks and scenic creeks.

Boardwalk HIKING

Congaree National Park's elevated, 2.4-mile boardwalk begins at the visitor center and brings guests through the bluff and onto the floodplain. Bald cypress and tupelo trees abound, and when the floodwaters rise, visitors get a close look at the dynamic and lively results. It takes about an hour to complete the loop, and wheelchairs, strollers and dogs are all welcomed.

Oakridge Trail HIKING

This excellent 6.6-mile hike begins about a mile from the visitor center, winding through a towering, old-growth oak forest and across innumerable creeks, which carry floodwaters in and out of Congaree National Park as the Congaree River rises and falls. There are good opportunities for spotting deer, wild boar and owls, and the loop normally takes between three and four hours to complete.

Canoeing

Cedar Creek's ink-black waters wind through 27 miles of wilderness within Congaree National Park, and canoeing a stretch of it is an ideal way to explore the park, particularly on the seasonal, ranger-led Wilderness Canoe Tour. Another option is to rent a canoe or do a guided tour with Columbia-based River Runner Outdoor Center (p213).

Wilderness Canoe Tour CANOEING

Free, ranger-led canoe tours of Cedar Creek typically set out a few times a week between April and June, and September and November, but are heavily dependent on weather and flood conditions. These four-hour excursions are an excellent way to learn about Congaree National Park's history and wildlife, and the 12 spaces often book up fast.

Dates for each month's tours can be found on the park's online event calendar (www.nps.gov/cong/planyourvisit/calendar.htm). Reservations must be made online at www.recreation.gov. The tour starts from South Cedar Creek Canoe Landing. From the park entrance, turn right on Old Bluff Rd, then right on South Cedar Creek Rd and follow it to the landing.

Sleeping

Within the parking, tent camping is the only overnight option in Congaree National Park. Longleaf Campground is easily accessible by car along the entrance road, and the further-flung Bluff Campground requires a mile hike. Backcountry camping is also available and free; guests must register with the Harry Hampton Visitor Center.

For those who prefer a bed and walls, nearby Columbia has plenty of good hotel options, including some lovely historic inns.

Longleaf Campground CAMPGROUND $

(☎877-444-6777; www.recreation.gov; Congaree National Park; campsites for up to 8/24 people $10/20) A three-minute drive from the visitor center, along the entrance road to Congaree National Park, this leafy but sometimes-crowded campground offers 14 sites and provides a couple of toilets, picnic tables and fire rings, but no running water (which is available at the visitor center 24 hours a day). Reservations must be made in advance online or by phone.

Bluff Campground CAMPGROUND $

(☎877-444-6777; www.recreation.gov; Congaree National Park; tent sites for up to 8 people $5) It's about a mile hike along the Bluff Trail to reach this relaxing, secluded campground. Its six sites each offer a fire ring and picnic table, but there are no restrooms or running water. Reservations must be made in advance online or by phone.

Eating

You'll need to bring the food you plan on eating in the park, but snacks like trail mix are available for purchase in the Harry Hampton Visitor Center.

JD's Place SOUTHERN US $

(☎803-353-0061; 7727 Bluff Rd, Gadsen; mains $9.25-11.25; ⌚8am-7:30pm) This hidden gem of a Southern kitchen serves up tasty fried chicken, oxtail and other meat-heavy dishes. It's the perfect stop after a hike or a paddle through Congaree National Park.

Information

Harry Hampton Visitor Center (☎803-776-4396; www.nps.gov/cong; 100 National Park Rd, Hopkins; ⌚9am-5pm) A helpful stop for Congaree National Park information and brochures, this elegant visitor center also contains an auditorium where an 18-minute film on the park is shown, a museum chock-full of interactive exhibits on the park's history and wildlife, and a bookstore selling field guides, snacks, souvenirs and other items.

The helpful 'mosquito meter' outside will let you know on a scale of one to six how buggy the park will be.

OFF THE BEATEN TRACK

MUSEUM OF THE CHEROKEE IN SOUTH CAROLINA

At least 29 tribes of Native Americans have lived in what is now South Carolina, and for hundreds of years they hunted and gathered, fished, planted crops and traded with each other. In the Upcountry, the Cherokee Nation was strong for centuries, and its history is contained in the **Museum of the Cherokee in South Carolina** (☎864-710-9210; www.cherokeemuseumsc.org; 70 Short St, Walhalla; ⌚11am-4pm Thu-Sat) FREE, in the northwestern corner of the state. It's the only museum in South Carolina dedicated solely to the history of the indigenous peoples. The organized and tidy exhibits tell the story of 'lower town,' so named because it was lower in elevation than neighboring Cherokee settlements in the Appalachian Mountains. The museum has been working to excavate one of the 'lower towns' and has plans to expand.

Getting There & Away

The park is a 30-minute drive from downtown Columbia.

UPCOUNTRY

The Cherokee Nation once roamed South Carolina's mountain foothills, which they called the 'Great Blue Hills of God.' The region today is known as the Upcountry. Geographically, it's the spot where the Blue Ridge Mountains drop dramatically to meet the Piedmont. The region is anchored by the city of Greenville (p219).

Sights

★ **Table Rock State Park** STATE PARK

(☎864-878-9813; www.southcarolinaparks.com; 158 Ellison Lane, Pickens; adult/child 6-15yr $5/3; ⌚7am-7pm Sun-Thu, to 9pm Fri & Sat, extended hours mid-May–early Nov) The Upcountry's marquee natural attraction is Table Rock Mountain, a 3124ft-high mountain with a striking granite face. The 7.2-mile round-trip hike to its summit is a popular local challenge. For overnight stays, there is the Table Rock State Park Campground & Cabins (p219).

OFF THE BEATEN TRACK

DIVING LAKE JOCASSEE

South Carolina isn't a top state for scuba diving. But a few creative underwater enthusiasts over at Lake Jocassee Dive Shop have put it on the map. A sunken Chinese junk, a deepwater graveyard and haunted dive sites over Halloween make Lake Jocassee more interesting than the average lake dive. (Bonus fact: the creation of this artificial lake was captured in a scene from the film *Deliverance*).

Devils Fork State Park STATE PARK
(☎864-944-2639; https://southcarolinaparks.com/devils-fork; 161 Holcombe Circle, Salem; adult/child $5/3; ⏱7am-9pm late spring–mid-fall, to 6pm late fall–mid-spring) The highlight of this alluring, 622-acre park is the crystal-clear, spring-fed Lake Jocassee, which was artificially created in the early '70s, when the movie *Deliverance* was being filmed (in certain scenes, you can see the construction in the background). Trout fishing is big here, as is scuba diving to view underwater treasures and oddities, such as a sunken Chinese junk and a submerged cemetery.

Kings Mountain National Military Park PARK
(☎864-936-7921; www.nps.gov/kimo; Hwy 216; ⏱9am-5pm daily, plus to 6pm Sat & Sun Jun-Aug) FREE A 1.5-mile paved trail explores the forested battlefield where Major Patrick Ferguson and his army fought 900 frontiersmen, a key event in the Revolutionary War. The visitor center features the screening of a short film detailing the fight, and a small museum showcases the key players. In 2017 a monument honoring African Americans who fought in the battle was installed on the trail. For more information, see p222.

Caesars Head State Park STATE PARK
(☎864-836-6115; www.southcarolinaparks.com; 8155 Geer Hwy, Cleveland; trail access $2; ⏱9am-9pm mid-Mar–early Nov, to 6pm rest of year, visitor-center hours vary) Plenty of great hikes, bike paths and accessible, sweeping views of regional mountains and foothills (p226).

Hagood Mill Historic Site & Folklore Center HISTORIC SITE
(☎864-898-2936; www.co.pickens.sc.us; 138 Hagood Mill Rd, Pickens; ⏱10am-4pm Wed-Sat, petroglyph exhibit closed Thu) FREE A stream-side historic mill with a petroglyph display and occasional bluegrass music.

Cowpens National Battlefield MEMORIAL
(☎864-461-2828; www.nps.gov/cowp; 4001 Chesnee Hwy, Gaffney; ⏱9am-5pm, auto loop closes 4:30pm) FREE Don't limit yourself to the auto loop, which skirts the central fighting area. Markers placed across the battlefield signify the positions of the different companies and showcase American commander Daniel Morgan's strategy during a battle with the larger and better-equipped British forces during the Battle of Cowpens. Morgan's rousing success inspired Colonial forces, setting them on a path to a victory at Yorktown. Even if you're not fascinated by military history, the strange tranquility of the place makes it worthy of a stroll.

World of Energy MUSEUM
(☎800-777-1004; www.duke-energy.com/worldofenergy; 7812 Rochester Hwy, Seneca; ⏱9am-5pm Mon-Fri) FREE To see how the region's electricity has been produced in a variety of different ways, take a fascinating self-guided tour of Duke Energy's World of Energy at the Oconee Nuclear Station. The plant has generated more than 500 million megawatt-hours of electricity since it went online in 1973.

Activities

★**Lake Jocassee Dive Shop** DIVING
(☎864-944-9255; http://jocasseediveshop.com; 710 Dive Buddy Lane, Salem; 2 lake dives without/with equipment rental $40/90, 4 Charleston dives from $120; ⏱9am-5pm Mon, Thu & Fri, 8am-6pm Sat & Sun) An excellent dive shop offering some of the best underwater adventures in the Southeastern US, including haunted dive sites during Halloween week. Dives to varying depths take place year-round on Lake Keowee's 'Hot Hole' site, a cove fed by heated water, and are seasonally available for other sites in Lake Keowee, Lake Jocassee and the Cooper River in Charleston.

BMW Performance Center SPORTS
(☎864-968-3000; www.bmwperformancecenter.com; 1155 Hwy 101 S, Greer; 1-/2-day school from $849/1699; ⏱8:30am-8pm Mon-Fri) Your need for speed is quenched at America's only BMW performance-driving academy. Delve into fast and furious behind-the-wheel

experiences over the course of one- or two-day classes with various vehicles, including the high-performance M series, or drive a Mini in stunt-driving school – *The Italian Job* will have nothing on you.

Sleeping

Swamp Rabbit Inn INN $
(864-517-4617; www.swamprabbitinn.com; 426 S Main St, Travelers Rest; r with/without private bath $115/105, houses $125, cottages $200;) Like its sister property (p228) in Greenville, this charming and well-appointed inn is just off the popular Swamp Rabbit Trail and contains a variety of accommodations. The main house features three comfy rooms and a full kitchen, while there's also a private house, a cottage and a studio. A relaxing pool and backyard gazebo are communal.

Table Rock State Park Campground & Cabins CAMPGROUND $
(864-878-9813; www.southcarolinaparks.com; 158 Ellison Lane, Pickens; campsites $16-21, cabins $155-181;) The 14 cabins here, built by the Civilian Conservation Corps, range from one to three bedrooms and have air-conditioning, kitchenettes and coffeemakers. Campers have a choice of 93 campsites with water and hookups, spread across two separate wooded camping areas. There are also five walk-in sites (from $18). All sites can be reserved.

Sunrise Farm B&B B&B $$
(864-944-0121; www.sunrisefarmbb.com; 325 Sunrise Dr, Salem; r $106-197, cottages $134-183;) Join Cisco the Bolivian llama and a sheep, a potbellied pig, three pygmy goats, two miniature horses and four cats on 10 acres of pastoral lands. Stay in a 1890s Victorian farmhouse while you're at it, or a more private cottage with a cozy fireplace and private deck, perfect for relaxing and watching the birds flit by. Breakfast is included in room (but not cottage) prices.

Hotel Domestique BOUTIQUE HOTEL $$$
(864-516-1715; http://hoteldomestique.com; 10 Road of Vines, Travelers Rest; r $295-495;) In French, *domestique* means 'servant'. In road cycling, it means competing for the benefit of the team leader. So it's fitting that Lance Armstrong's *domestique*, George Hincapie (also caught up the doping scandal, FYI), used this name for his mountain-view hotel in Travelers Rest. More European than South Carolinian, the place is inspired by Hincapie's travels and, ahem, devoted service.

Eating & Drinking

Pumpkintown Mountain Opry CAFE $
(864-836-8141; www.pumpkintownopry.com; 3414 Hwy 11, Pickens; ice-cream scoops $3, lattes from $3.50; 11am-5pm Thu-Mon) This country store looks like a green-and-yellow gingerbread house. After a hike up Table Rock, it's the perfect stop for a hot pumpkin latte in the winter, or a scoop of pumpkin latte ice cream in the summer. At 7pm on Saturday nights the upstairs becomes a dinner theater, with rotating comedic acts of varying amusement.

Swamp Rabbit Brewery & Tap Room MICROBREWERY
(864-610-2424; www.theswamprabbitbrewery.com; 26 S Main St, Travelers Rest; 4-9pm Tue & Wed, to 10pm Thu, noon-10pm Fri & Sat, noon-7pm Sun) This microbrewery's malty Märzen is just the thing after cycling 10 miles from Greenville to Travelers Rest up the Swamp Rabbit Trail. The German-trained brewer has collected several awards and been around for more than two decades, conjuring up Belgian ales and English-style double IPAs.

Getting There & Away

Greenville–Spartanburg International Airport (p167) is the area's main gateway. Amtrak (p231) and Greyhound (p231) also serve Greenville.

Greenville

864 / POP 67,500

In the foothills of the Blue Mountains, Greenville is home to one of the most photogenic downtowns in the South. The Reedy River twists through the city center, and its dramatic falls tumble beneath the sleek Liberty Bridge at Falls Park. Downtown Main St rolls past a lively array of colorful facades beckoning visitors into indie shops, good restaurants and craft-beer pubs.

The city's newfound splendor has been splashed across prominent magazine and newspaper travel sections with such regularity that its curious marketing campaign, 'Yeah, *that* Greenville,' has seemingly become irrelevant. Meanwhile, the swift population growth – which earned the city the controversial nickname G-Vegas – has condos flying up all over town.

The development has stretched into the village of West Greenville, which is seeing a revival thanks to an influx of art galleries, restaurants and boutiques.

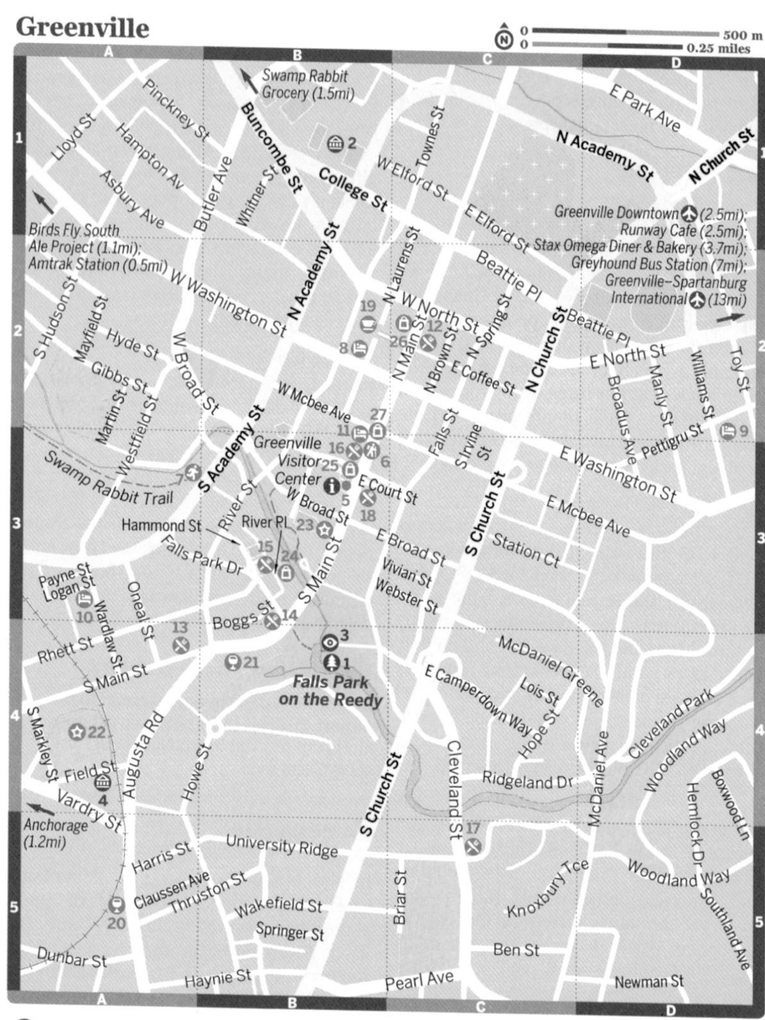

Sights

★Falls Park on the Reedy PARK

(Map p220; ☎864-467-4355; www.fallspark.com; 601 S Main St; ⏲7am-9pm) In the epicenter of downtown Greenville, this stunning 32-acre oasis is a joy to wander. Be sure to cross the park's Liberty Bridge, a modern wonder offering picture-perfect views of the Reedy River and its dramatic waterfalls.

Liberty Bridge BRIDGE

(Map p220; www.fallspark.com/175/The-Liberty-Bridge; Falls Park on the Reedy) Do not leave Greenville without a stroll across this dazzling, modern bridge, suspended and curving over the Reedy River Falls. The silvery 345ft-long marvel is supported by cables on just one side, offering an unobstructed view of the falls on the other. At night it's aglow in colored lights.

Shoeless Joe Jackson Museum MUSEUM

(Map p220; ☎864-346-4867; www.shoelessjoejackson.org; 356 Field St; ⏲10am-2pm Sat, by appointment during the week) FREE If you move it closer to the baseball stadium, they will definitely come. That was the theory behind dismantling, relocating and reconstructing Shoeless Joe Jackson's former Greenville home, which now contains a small museum

Greenville

Top Sights

1 Falls Park on the Reedy B4

Sights

2 Greenville County Museum of Art B1
3 Liberty Bridge B4
4 Shoeless Joe Jackson Museum A4

Activities, Courses & Tours

5 Greenville History Tours B3
6 Mice on Main B3
7 Swamp Rabbit Trail A3

Sleeping

8 Aloft Greenville Downtown B2
9 Pettigru Place D2
10 Swamp Rabbit Inn A3
11 Westin Poinsett B2

Eating

12 Coffee Underground C2
13 Husk A4
14 Jianna B3
15 Lazy Goat B3
16 Nose Dive B3
17 Sidewall Pizza Company C5
18 Soby's B3

Drinking & Nightlife

19 Methodical Coffee B2
20 Upstate Craft Beer Co A5
21 Vault & Vator B4

Entertainment

22 Fluor Field at the West End A4
23 Peace Center B3

Shopping

24 Art Crossing at RiverPlace B3
25 M Judson Booksellers & Storytellers B3
26 Mast General Store C2
27 Saturday Market B2

next to Fluor Field. On display are records, artifacts, photographs, film and other paraphernalia associated with the star outfielder and his monumental career.

Greenville County Museum of Art MUSEUM
(Map p220; ☎864-271-7570; http://gcma.org; 420 College St; ⊙10am-5pm Wed-Sat, 1-5pm Sun) FREE This little American art museum holds its own, with the world's largest public collection of watercolors by Andrew Wyeth and a great many original paintings and prints from homegrown icon Jasper Johns. Parking is 50¢ per half hour.

Activities

Pedal along the river on the 22-mile Swamp Rabbit Trail on one of Greenville's B-Cycle bike-share bicycles (https://greenville.bcycle.com).

★ **Swamp Rabbit Trail** CYCLING, HIKING
(Map p220; ☎864-288-6470) Bike, run or saunter along the bed of a former railroad, converted into 22 miles of greenway stretching from Greenville to Travelers Rest along the Reedy River. Local businesses dot the trail and sell delicious food and craft beer, and a couple of good inns at either end offer bike rentals and comfy beds.

Mice on Main WALKING
(Map p220; ☎864-271-7843; www.miceonmain.com; Main St; 👪) A kid-focused scavenger hunt for mouse art, based on the book *Goodnight Moon*. Essentially, there are nine bronze mice placed around the city's main drag by artist Jimmy Ryan, and with a set of clues and some determination, you and your kids will likely discover them all.

Tours

Greenville History Tours WALKING
(Map p220; ☎864-567-3940; www.greenvillehistorytours.com; 206 S Main St; history/food tour $20/39) Local John Nolan literally wrote the book on Greenville history. Since he started doing neighborhood walking and driving tours in 2006, he's gotten glowing reviews and expanded to offer a range of culinary journeys, including a breakfast tour, a BBQ tour and a West End walking tour ($12).

Festivals & Events

Artisphere ART
(www.artisphere.org; ⊙May) A three-day celebration and showcase of local artistic talent in 17 different mediums. More than 250 artists attend from around the world and there are demonstrations, performances and concerts held around Greenville. There's also a special children's area called Kidsphere.

Euphoria FOOD & DRINK
(☎864-233-5663; www.euphoriagreenville.com; 135 S Main St; ⊙Sep) Four days of tastings, cooking demonstrations, wine seminars, multicourse dinners, celebrity-chef sightings, live music and general revelry. Edwin McCain (yes, the singer/songwriter) is one of the founders of the event, and it's been going on for more than a decade.

ROAD TRIP: GREENVILLE & CHEROKEE FOOTHILLS

Cherokees once roamed these foothills, which they called the 'Great Blue Hills of God.' Known as the Blue Ridge escarpment, it's the spot where the Blue Ridge Mountains drop dramatically to meet the Piedmont. This trip begins with the site of a battle, rolls through woodland valleys and ends with dramatic cascades in the center of Greenville, the heart of the region.

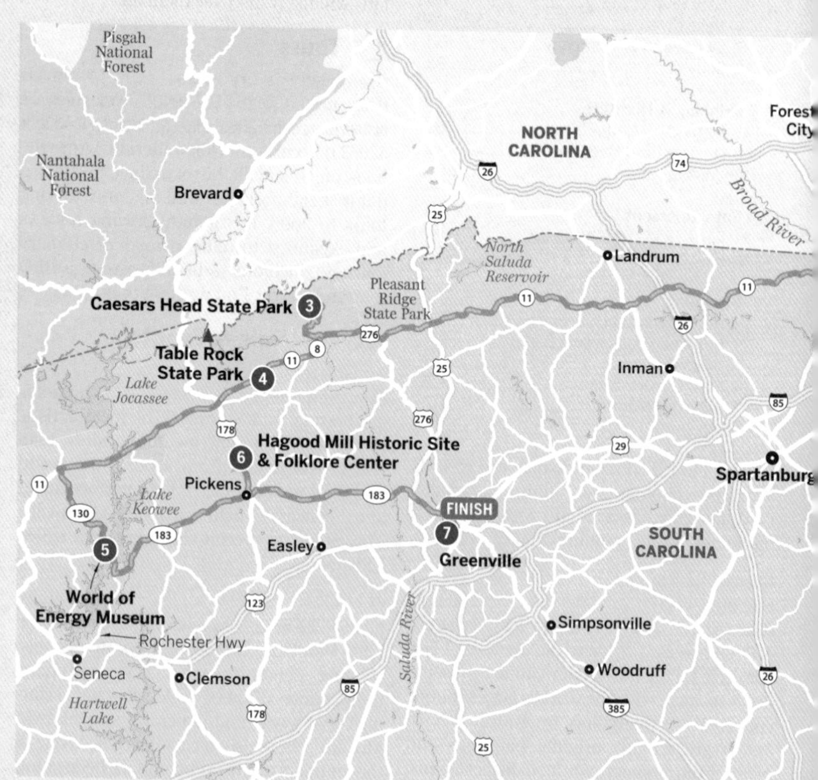

2 Days 172 miles / 277km

Great for... Photos of Table Rock Mountain.

Best Time to Go Apr-Nov for leafy canopies and waterfall hikes; September to November for the Hawk Watch.

1 Kings Mountain National Military Park

As Major Patrick Ferguson learned on the summit of Kings Mountain, threatening American patriots is never a good idea. In the fall of 1780, General Lord Cornwallis ordered Ferguson to subdue the frontier militias of the western Carolinas. In a message to the patriots, who were known as the Overmountain Men, Ferguson proclaimed, 'If you do not desist your opposition to the British Arms, I shall march this army over the mountains, hang your leaders and lay waste your country with fire and sword.'

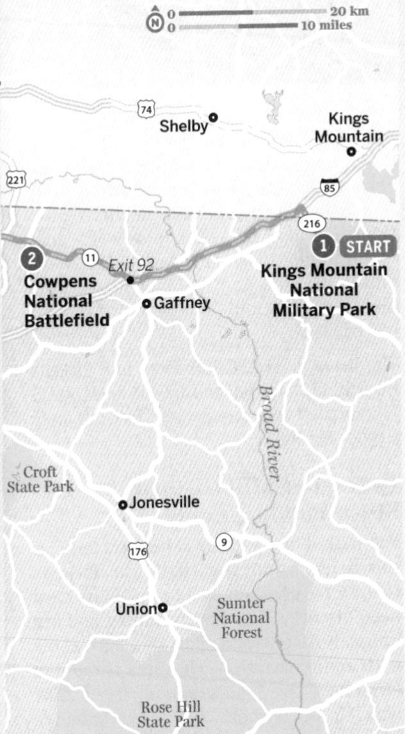

In response, 900 annoyed frontiersmen crossed the mountains, joined forces and surrounded Ferguson and his 1000-man army. Comfortable with close-range combat, the patriots used thick trees as cover as they climbed the mountainous slopes. After a short period of intense fighting, Ferguson was dead, his troops decimated.

At **Kings Mountain National Military Park** (p218) a 1.5-mile paved interpretative trail explores the forested battlefield, and in 2017 a monument honoring African Americans who fought in the battle was installed on the trail. At the visitor center, a 26-minute film describes the fight, which was a turning point in the Revolutionary War. A small museum spotlights the battle's major players.

The Drive > Take SC 216 to I-85 south. Follow it to exit 92 and SC 11 south, which is the Cherokee Foothills Scenic Hwy (if you get to the giant Peach – aka the peach butt – you've gone too far). The profile of a Cherokee is emblazoned on markers along the byway. Drive 10 miles.

2 Cowpens National Battlefield

On January 17, 1781, American commander Daniel Morgan executed a brilliant tactical maneuver – the double envelopment – against a larger, better-equipped British force during the Battle of Cowpens. His resounding success inspired Colonial forces and propelled them on their path to final victory at Yorktown. At **Cowpens National Battlefield** (p218), the auto loop skirts the central fighting area. Signs scattered across the actual battlefield mark the positions of the different companies and explain Morgan's tactics.

The Drive > From the park, continue west 50 miles on SC 11. The byway passes farms, fields, produce stands and Baptist churches before rolling into the woods. Follow US 276 as it twists upward through the park.

3 Caesars Head State Park

Sometimes you want to earn your stunning view – with a 10-mile hike or an all-day bike ride. Other times you just want to step out of your car, walk 30 steps and say 'Wow!' The overlook at **Caesars Head State Park** (p218) falls cheerfully into the latter category. This lofty viewpoint atop the Blue Ridge Escarpment offers a sweeping panorama of regional mountains and foothills. From here, Table Rock Mountain juts into view almost dead ahead. During the fall Hawk Watch (September 1 to December 1), migrating hawks catch thermals here – and impress visitors – as they travel south for winter. If you do want to exercise, try the 4.4-mile round-trip hike to a view of 420ft Raven Cliff Falls.

The Drive > Take Hwy 8 to SC 11 south then drive 4.6 miles.

4 Table Rock State Park

Table Rock Mountain is the region's marquee natural attraction. A 3124ft-high mountain with a striking granite face, it's ready-made for photographs. According to Cherokee legend the mountain served as a table for a giant chieftain, who ate there after a hunt. While dining, he used Stool Mountain as his seat.

The 7.2-mile round-trip hike to its summit at **Table Rock State Park** (p217) is a popular local challenge. For a good view of the mountain take a seat at the park visitor center, which is also an information center for the scenic highway.

Visitors can spend the night in one of 14 cabins constructed by the Civilian Conservation Corps. On the second Saturday of the month catch a bluegrass jam here as part of the Music on the Mountain Series. Need more options? There's camping, swimming and fishing in Pinnacle Lake.

The Drive > Return to SC 11 south and drive 19 miles to SC 130. Turn left and continue south 10 miles, passing through Salem. SC 130 becomes Rochester Hwy.

5 World of Energy Museum

After all those trees and waterfalls, it just seems right to stop and stretch your legs at...a nuclear power plant. But hey, why not? The self-guided tour inside Duke Energy's **World of Energy** (p218) at the Oconee Nuclear Station provides a pretty darn interesting look at electricity and how it has been produced in the region, from the use of water power to coal to uranium. The nuclear plant went online in 1973, and has since generated more than 500 million megawatt-hours of electricity.

The Drive > Take SC 130 south to E Pickens Hwy/SC 183. Turn left and drive 14 miles. At US 178, turn left and drive 3 miles. Turn left on to Hagood Mill Rd.

6 Hagood Mill Historic Site & Folklore Center

You'll find more than a historic mill at this stream-side **site** (p218) in Pickens County. Several hundred petroglyphs have been discovered in the Upcountry, and are uniquely displayed as part of a light show with audio narration. The site's namesake attraction, the 1845 gristmill, has a 20ft wooden waterwheel (the state's largest). The mill was in continuous commercial

KEVIN RUCK/SHUTTERSTOCK ©

Liberty Bridge (p220)

operation until 1966. Today it's back in production on the third Saturday of every month, when there's also live bluegrass music.

The Drive > Return to SC 183 and follow it east 20 miles into downtown Greenville.

7 Greenville

Greenville has one of America's most inviting downtowns. The Reedy River winds through the city center, and its epic falls tumble beneath Main St at **Falls Park** (p220). For a photo of the falls, stroll on to the graceful **Liberty Bridge** (p220), a 345ft-long suspension bridge.

Main St itself rolls past an energetic array of boutiques, eateries and craft-beer pubs. Whimsical quotes from notables such as Oscar Wilde, Erma Bombeck and Will Rogers – called 'Thoughts on a Walk' – dot the sidewalk. In the evening the trees are illuminated by twinkling white lights. Stop by the **Greenville Visitor Center** (p231) for a public-art map and clues for **Mice on Main** (p221).

For exercise, try the **Swamp Rabbit Trail** (p221), a 22-mile path for hikers and cyclists on an old railway line that links downtown to Furman University. Pop into the regionally famed **Mast General Store** (p231) for outdoor gear and old-time candy. The secretive upland corner of Greenville County, which was famed for its bootlegging and hardscrabble Scots-Irish residents, is nicknamed the Dark Corner.

CYCLING & HIKING IN SOUTH CAROLINA

CYCLING THE SWAMP RABBIT TRAIL

START SPANCO DR (NEAR CONESTEE PARK)
END TATE RD (TRAVELERS REST)
DURATION 1½ HOURS
DISTANCE 22 MILES
DIFFICULTY EASY

You can walk it, jog it or even skate it, but the most popular way to experience the fabulous former railway corridor now known as the Swamp Rabbit Trail is on two wheels. The multi-use greenway seems ever-expanding, but at the time of research it began at Spanco Dr near Conestee Park and meandered north along the Reedy River and past Furman University's campus before arriving in Travelers Rest.

Along the 22-mile route, cyclists cross scenic bridges and pedal through verdant stretches of countryside, with picnic areas, water fountains, bike racks and public bathrooms all along the way. Local businesses have sprung up to cater to the half-million people who use the trail each year; some of our favorites include **Swamp Rabbit Grocery**; (p228; a health-food store and cafe), the **Birds Fly South Ale Project** (p230; brewery and yoga) and the **Swamp Rabbit Brewery & Tap Room** (p219; don't miss the malty Märzen!).

For those cyclists traveling from out of town, the **Swamp Rabbit Inn** (p228) offers excellent lodgings in Greenville and a newer outpost in **Travelers Rest** (p219), both of which rent bicycles and are a short hop from the trail.

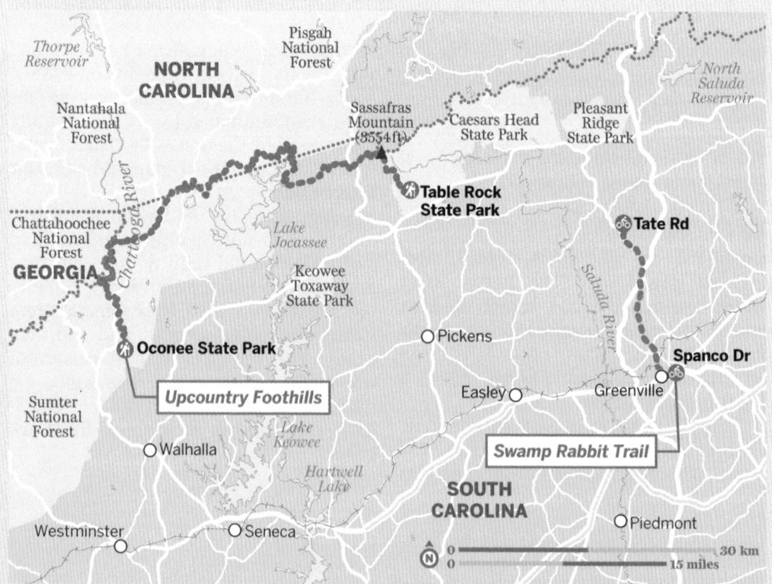

The Upcountry offers South Carolina's best opportunity for outdoor exploration. Enjoy the natural beauty while hiking the mountain trails of the area's stunning state parks, or pedaling along the 22-mile Swamp Rabbit Trail.

HIKING THE UPCOUNTRY FOOTHILLS

START OCONEE STATE PARK
END TABLE ROCK STATE PARK
DURATION FIVE TO 10 DAYS
DISTANCE 76.2 MILES
DIFFICULTY HARD

South Carolina's most beloved hiking trail winds over what the Cherokee Indians called the Blue Wall, a dazzling escarpment that *Backpacker* magazine has said is one of the best 50-plus-mile trails in the country, and area outdoor enthusiasts say has no equal – it is simply the best backcountry wilderness in the state.

Many weekend warriors do short stretches of the trail, but it's well worth attempting the whole thing, which takes five to 10 days, depending on your pace. (Less experienced hikers should begin in Oconee State Park and end at **Table Rock State Park** (p217), while hard-core hikers can do the trek in either direction.) Rewards include old-growth glens, rushing rivers, plummeting waterfalls and scenic gorges rich in biodiversity. The trail runs along the Chattanooga River for 8.5 miles and climbs South Carolina's highest peak (Sassafras Mountain; 3553ft), offering ample opportunities to view rarely seen salamanders, birds and wildflowers, including the cherished Oconee Bell, a wildflower endemic to this region alone.

Although much of the trail has been stomped for centuries by Native Americans, hunters and fishermen, it was in the 1960s that area hiking aficionados thought of linking and improving the series of unmarked paths. After two decades of collaboration with Duke Energy, the US Forest Service, South Carolina's State Parks Department, the Sierra Club, and citizen volunteers and activists, the Foothills Trail was completed and opened to the public in the early 1980s.

The trail's backbone extends nearly 77 miles, but there are also more than 30 miles of outshoots that lead hikers to waterfalls, overlooks and various points of interest. Camping areas pepper the way and usually offer access to cisterns and firewood. Hikers should still pack lots of water, particularly in summer months, and should bring multiple layers of clothing in winter. During hunting season, which runs intermittently from September to January, stick to the trail and wear bright colors. Always shake out boots; there are scorpions.

Major trailheads are located at Table Rock State Park, US 178, SC 130, SC 107 and Oconee State Park, and can be accessed via I-85, I-26 and SC Hwy 11. Volunteer shuttle drivers and commercial drivers can offer transport and don't charge set fees, but should be reimbursed fairly for the number of miles they travel. For more info, see https://foothillstrail.org/shuttle-service.

GREENVILLE FOR CHILDREN

With all the big-city transplant families flocking to more affordable Greenville, you can bet it's one kid-friendly destination. The city is generally safe and walkable, with the even, clean sidewalks featuring whimsical quotes called 'Thoughts on a Walk.' Kids will also get a kick out of Mice on Main (p221), a find-the-bronze-mice scavenger hunt inspired by the book *Goodnight Moon*.

In the winter an outdoor **ice-skating rink** on Main St (www.iceonmain.com) is popular with older children, while in summer the Saturday Market (p231) is a huge hit with kids (and parents) of all ages. The **South Carolina Children's Theatre** (https://scchildrenstheatre.org) and the **Greenville Zoo** (www.greenvillezoo.com) appeal to kiddies year-round, and even the local breweries tend to be family-oriented.

A great place for lunch is **Runway Cafe**, where your aviation-obsessed youngster can watch planes come in while munching on a corn dog.

Greenville Craft Beer Festival BEER
(www.greenvillecraftbeerfestival.com; Fluor Field; ⏲Nov) A lively craft-beer festival that draws an intoxicating array of microbrewery samples from all over the South. There's also music, food and 'beer college' classes.

Sleeping

For the most part, chain hotels are the standard in Greenville, albeit hip (Aloft Greenville Downtown) and historic (Westin Poinsett), but there are a few artsy guesthouses and historic B&Bs around downtown and the Pettigru Historic District.

★ **Swamp Rabbit Inn** B&B $$
(Map p220; ☎864-345-7990; www.swamprabbitinn.com; 1 Logan St; r $115-200; P❄📶) This fun six-room inn occupies a '50s-era former boarding house downtown. It feels like a hostel but features colorfully decked-out private rooms that are as cozy and quirky as any in the South. Wonderful common spaces include a modern guest kitchen and wooden patio with barbecue.

Pettigru Place B&B $$
(Map p220; ☎864-242-4529; www.pettigruplace.com; 302 Pettrigru St; r $175-249; P❄📶) A six-room downtown B&B with quaint themed rooms. We dig the downstairs Brass Giraffe room, with epic walk-in shower, and the upstairs Green Rabbit and Hummingbird rooms, with great patios overlooking charming gardens, and a good mix of modern (shared Keurig coffeemaker, flat-screen TV) and retro conveniences (a shared 1929 GE refrigerator stocked with sodas etc).

Aloft Greenville Downtown BOUTIQUE HOTEL $$$
(Map p220; ☎864-297-6100; www.aloftgreenvilledowntown.com; 5 N Laurens St; r from $249; ❄📶🐾) Hip and centrally located, downtown Greenville's Aloft is defined by well-placed, brightly colored pillows and over-the-top dog-friendliness (its signature 'Arf Program' provides canine friends with royal beds, bowls, treats and toys). The rooms are small but comfy, and stumbling distance from the hotel bar W XYZ, a gathering spot for cocktails, acoustic guitar music and live DJs.

Westin Poinsett HOTEL $$$
(Map p220; ☎864-421-9700; www.westinpoinsettgreenville.com; 120 S Main St; r $189-309; P❄@📶🐾) This grand hotel, which originally opened in 1925, is in the heart of downtown Greenville, just steps from the Reedy River Falls. Past guests include Amelia Earhart, Cornelius Vanderbilt and Bobby Kennedy. There's fresh carpeting and wall vinyl throughout the hotel, while rooms tilt toward the basic (bathrooms are set for a remodel).

Eating

Downtown Greenville is the central hub of dining, with more than 120 locally owned restaurants and dozens of relatively recent openings. West Greenville is also coming into its own with a couple of hot new Southern joints.

Swamp Rabbit Grocery HEALTH FOOD $
(☎864-255-3385; http://swamprabbitcafe.com; 205 Cedar Lane Rd; sandwiches $7.50-9; ⏲7:30am-7pm Mon-Fri, to 6pm Sat, 8am-6pm Sun) You don't have to bicycle along the

Swamp Rabbit Trail to make a stop at the eponymous, adjacent grocery, but it's definitely the most fun way to visit. This local-focused health-food store, cafe and bakery serves up incredible homemade bread and sandwiches. Go for the 'jolly goat,' with herb-roasted turkey, cranberry and local goat's cheese.

Runway Cafe AMERICAN **$**
(☎864-242-4777; www.runwaycafegmu.com; 21 Airport Rd; kid's meals $3.99, mains from $7; ⌚11am-2:20pm Sun-Tue, 11am-2:30pm & 5-8:30pm Wed & Thu, 11am-8:30pm Fri & Sat) On the south ramp of the Greenville Downtown Airport, this is the place for your child to devour a corn dog or a grilled cheese sandwich with a front-row seat for those exhilarating plane landings. There's also an aviation-themed playground next door, with a mini-golf course in the works.

Stax Omega Diner & Bakery DINER **$**
(☎864-297-6639; www.staxs.net; 72 Orchard Park Dr; breakfast $4-14, lunch & dinner $9-15; ⌚6:30am-9pm; 📶) Nobody quite does breakfast excess like the USA and this bustling family-owned diner 4 miles east of downtown Greenville is everything fantastic about that very fact. It's massive – capacity 500! – and they do it all really well: omelets, pancakes, French toast, eggs Benedict, scrambles – the list goes on and on…and on…

Coffee Underground CAFE **$**
(Map p220; ☎864-298-0494; www.coffeeunderground.info; 1 E Coffee St; pastries & desserts $2-5, sandwiches $8.55; ⌚7am-10pm Mon-Thu, to 11:30pm Fri, 8am-11:30pm Sat, 8am-10pm Sun; 📶) Try the Marabella chicken wrap and the Black Tiger milkshake at this welcoming indie coffee shop. The chocolate-chunk cookies are darn good too. It's located at the bottom of the stairs at the corner of Main and Coffee Sts.

★ **Anchorage** AMERICAN **$$**
(☎864-219-3082; www.theanchoragerestaurant.com; 586 Perry Av; plates $12-17; ⌚5-9:30pm Tue-Thu, to 10pm Fri & Sat, 10am-3pm Sun) In the up-and-coming village of West Greenville, local food and booze reigns supreme, and that's particularly true at the Anchorage (impossible to miss thanks to its enormous, bright mural depicting produce). Standout dishes include the playful triggerfish crudo and the heaping charcuterie board complete with bourbon liver mousse.

★ **Nose Dive** GASTROPUB **$$**
(Map p220; ☎864-373-7300; www.thenosedive.com; 116 S Main St; mains $9-24; ⌚11am-10pm Mon-Thu, to 11pm Fri, 10am-11pm Sat, 10am-9pm Sun; 📶) This downtown gastropub does decadent and daring urban comfort food, and has daily changing specials such as burgers with pork belly, caramelized onions, bacon jam and Gouda cheese (decadent!), or pig-ear tacos (daring!). There are 18 craft-beer taps as well as Crafted, its hip upstairs cocktail bar (cocktails $8 to $13).

Sidewall Pizza Company PIZZA **$$**
(Map p220; ☎864-558-0235; www.sidewallpizza.com; 99 Cleveland St; pizzas from $13; ⌚11am-9pm Mon-Sat) Pizza. Salad. Ice cream. That's all the food on offer at this laid-back hangout in a former service station, but what the menu lacks in variety it makes up for in quality: all three are made fresh daily and just about perfect. Gluten-free crusts are available.

Jianna ITALIAN **$$**
(Map p220; ☎864-720-2200; https://jiannagreenville.com; 600 S Main St; mains $18-27; ⌚5-10pm Tue-Thu, to 11pm Fri, 11am-11pm Sat, 11am-9pm Sun) Chef Michael Kramer serves up rustic Italian cuisine and oysters galore in this cheerful 2nd-floor restaurant. The large balcony looks out onto bustling Main St, and the bar is buzzing on weekends. Don't miss the warm ricotta and truffle honey starter or the housemade pastas (especially if agnolotti is on the menu).

Soby's SOUTHERN US **$$**
(Map p220; ☎864-232-7007; www.sobys.com; 207 S Main St; mains $18-31; ⌚5-9pm Mon-Wed, to 10pm Thu-Sat, 10am-1:30pm & 5-9pm Sun; 📶) Book yourself one of the intimate, brick-walled banquettes at this downtown Greenville bastion of New Southern cuisine that also caters to wine lovers (the 5000-bottle list has been awarded a *Wine Spectator* Award of Excellence 20 years running). The oft-changing menu is steeped in the wares of local farmers, foragers and ranchers.

Lazy Goat MEDITERRANEAN **$$**
(Map p220; ☎864-679-5299; www.thelazygoat.com; 170 River Pl; lunch $8-14, dinner small plates $7-12, dinner mains $10-28; ⌚11am-9pm Sun-Thu, to 10pm Fri & Sat) Nibble on fried goat's cheese and sip wine beside the river at this stylish spot, known for its Mediterranean small plates and winning paellas.

ACCESSIBLE TRAVEL

Greenville is generally accommodating to travelers with disabilities, particularly after hosting the Para-Cycling Road Championships in 2014, which drew 300 athletes from around the world.

In particular, the Swamp Rabbit Trail (p221) is a big attraction for adaptive cyclists due to its flatness and the existence of a roundabout designed specifically for hand cyclists who wish to change direction. Another city initiative, **Camp Spearhead** (https://greenvillerec.com/therapeutic-special-needs), is an all-ages weekend and summer camp offering a wide range of outdoor activities to people with disabilities.

All that said, there can be challenges for travelers relying on public transportation, as many of the city's bus stops are not wheelchair accessible. And while most of the area businesses abide by ADA (Americans with Disabilities Act) regulations, some have yet to comply.

Husk SOUTHERN US **$$$**
(Map p220; ☎864-627-0404; http://huskgreenville.com; 722 S Main St; mains $25-38; ⏲5-10pm Sun-Thu, to 11pm Fri & Sat) The latest addition to executive chef Sean Brock's Southern food empire is often declared Greenville's best restaurant, and the original inlaid brick and expansive murals in its elegant, painstakingly refurbished dining room certainly beckon.

The fried chicken skins are just OK, though (maybe there's a reason people don't usually eat just skin?), and the cornmeal-dusted catfish needed a kick.

Drinking & Nightlife

Greenville has a dozen-plus craft breweries and a number of specialty taprooms, with more in the works. Like Asheville to the north, it's become a thing. Although, unlike Asheville, breweries in Greenville are spread all over town. The Brewery Experience (www.thebreweryexperience.com) is a good bet if you want a tour company as your designated driver!

★ **Birds Fly South Ale Project** BREWERY
(☎864-412-8825; https://bfsbeer.com; 1320 Hampton Av; ⏲4-9pm Thu, noon-9pm Fri & Sat, noon-6pm Sun) For Greenville's best Saisons and sours, hop off the Swamp Rabbit Trail in Greenville's West End Water District and look for people carrying yoga mats into the expansive, refurbished cotton warehouse. Yes, yoga pairs well with beers, especially the delicious ones like coconut grinder (a dark Belgian brewed with coconut milk).

★ **Vault & Vator** COCKTAIL BAR
(Map p220; ☎864-603-1881; www.vaultandvator.com; 655 S Main St; ⏲5pm-midnight Tue-Thu, to 1:30am Fri & Sat) Hidden away in the subterranean basement of an old Dr Pepper factory, this speakeasy regularly brims with Greenville's hipster sophisticates, mainly because its pink- and purple-haired mixologists churn out innovative and delicious libations like the 'melancholy ninja' (Fernet-Branca, bourbon, Ninja Warrior cold brew and habanero honey). The bar offers occasional Saturday-afternoon cocktail classes for $35.

Methodical Coffee COFFEE
(Map p220; ☎864-735-8407; www.methodicalcoffee.com; 101 N Main St; ⏲7am-6pm Mon-Thu, 7am-10pm Fri, to 10pm Sat, 8am-5pm Sun; 📶) This is Greenville's most serious house of caffeine, as evidenced by the epic hand-built Slayer espresso machine, which costs around the price of a four-door Toyota! The perfect espresso is served in snifter-like glasses.

Upstate Craft Beer Co MICROBREWERY
(Map p220; ☎864-609-4590; www.upstatecraftbeer.com; 400 Augusta Rd; ⏲3-9pm Mon-Wed, 11am-10pm Thu-Sat, noon-7pm Sun; 📶) Located in the historic 1930s former Claussen Bakery building, with a modern facade that looks like it was built last Tuesday, this part homebrewing shop, microbrewery and taproom has the industrial-chic market cornered. There are 20 taps, split between proprietary beers and invitees, as well as an extensive international bottle list – rare for a microbrewery.

☆ Entertainment

Top-tier entertainment acts regularly blow through Greenville, often performing at either the Peace Center or the Bon Secours Wellness Arena, while local musicians and DJs regularly strum and spin away in local bars and breweries. Baseball season (April to September) is a hoot – you can catch a minor-league game at Fluor Field at the West End for as little as $8.

Peace Center ARTS CENTER
(Map p220; ☎864-467-3000; www.peacecenter.org; 300 S Main St) An expansive downtown cultural hub and performing-arts center, complete with a concert hall, theater and amphitheater (all with great acoustics). Drop in for classical concerts, dance, jazz, country, bluegrass, folk, pop, comedy and a packed schedule of Broadway theater productions.

Fluor Field at the West End BASEBALL
(Map p220; ☎864-240-4528; 945 S Main St; baseball tickets from $8) Home of the Greenville Drive minor-league baseball team, this 5700-seat stadium is modeled after Fenway Park.

Shopping

Greenville is a shopping mecca, with commercial districts for different budgets and tastes throughout the city. Augusta Rd is all high-end specialty boutiques; Haywood Rd is for furniture and home improvement (and Haywood Mall has department stores); Magnolia Park and the Shops at Greenridge are a mix of specialty stores and chains; and the West End area offers offbeat mom-and-pop stores and galleries.

Saturday Market FOOD & DRINKS
(Map p220; ☎864-467-4494; www.saturdaymarketlive.com; cnr Main St & McBee Av; ⏲8am-noon Sat May-Nov; 👪) In the warmer months traffic shuts down and the tents go up on Main St each Saturday as part of a lively farmers market. Organic produce, artisanal cheese, homemade soup, yummy tacos, local art and a whole lot more are on offer, and the whole city seems to show up. There's often live music as well; it's perfect for kids and families.

Art Crossing at RiverPlace ART
(Map p220; ☎864-423-8863; www.artcrossing.org; 300 River St; ⏲11am-6pm Tue-Sat) On the lower level of RiverPlace, in studios converted from parking garages, around a dozen artists can be viewed at work and even befriended. Visitors may also purchase or commission pieces.

M Judson Booksellers & Storytellers BOOKS
(Map p220; ☎864-603-2412; www.mjudsonbooks.com; 130 S Main St; ⏲9am-9pm Mon-Thu, to 10pm Fri & Sat, 11am-5pm Sun) This sunny, woman-owned bookstore inside the former courthouse has a wide selection of books and book-related gifts, plus a charming cafe.

Mast General Store SPORTS & OUTDOORS
(Map p220; ☎866-367-6278; www.mastgeneralstore.com; 111 N Main St; ⏲10am-6pm Mon-Thu, to 9pm Fri & Sat, noon-6pm Sun) Sells outdoor gear and old-time candy.

Information

SAFE TRAVEL

Greenville's rates of violence and property crimes are higher than the national average.

Keep your wits about you and drive or take a rideshare at night rather than walking, particularly in further-flung neighborhoods like the West End.

TOURIST INFORMATION

Greenville Visitor Center (Map p220; ☎864-233-0461; www.visitgreenvillesc.com; 206 S Main St; ⏲8am-5pm Mon-Fri, 9am-5pm Sat, noon-4pm Sun) Stop by for a public-art map, travel brochures and clues for Mice on Main (p221).

Getting There & Away

Greenville–Spartanburg International Airport (p167) is 13 miles east of the city, nearly halfway between Greenville and Spartanburg.

The **Greyhound bus station** (☎864-235-4741; www.greyhound.com; 9 Hendrix Dr) is also out that way, 7 miles southeast of downtown.

The **Amtrak train station** (☎800-872-7245; www.amtrak.com; 1120 W Washington St) is more conveniently located, just west of downtown.

Getting Around

Red-and-blue, open-air vintage **trolley cars** (☎864-467-5001; www.greenvillesc.gov/597/Trolley; ⏲6-11pm Thu & Fri, 10am-11pm Sat, 1-8pm Sun) run up and down and around Main St for limited hours from Thursday through Sunday. They're free.

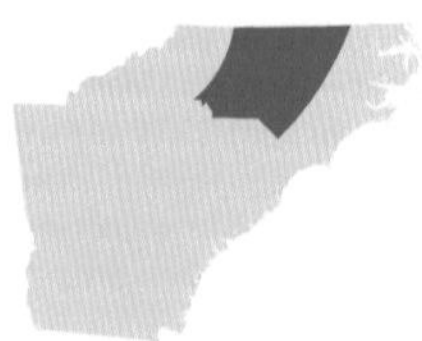

Charlotte & the Triangle

Includes ➡

Best Places to Eat

- ➡ Soul Gastrolounge Tapas (p240)
- ➡ Lantern (p252)
- ➡ Dame's Chicken & Waffles (p250)
- ➡ Mateo (p250)
- ➡ La Farm Bakery (p244)

Best Places to Stay

- ➡ Ivey's Hotel (p237)
- ➡ Duke Mansion (p237)
- ➡ Carolina Inn (p252)
- ➡ Durham (p249)

Why Go?

Charlotte, Winston-Salem and the so-called 'Triangle' cities of Raleigh, Durham and Chapel Hill anchor North Carolina's cosmopolitan heartland, which is the hub of its finance and academic world.

Charlotte, named after the wife of George III – hence its nickname, the Queen City – boomed when gold was discovered nearby, and later prospered from cotton and textiles. Having pioneered interstate banking in the 1980s, it's now the third-largest banking center in the US.

When to Go

- ➡ March is either the best or worst time to visit this basketball-obsessed region – if you come, be prepared to discuss your bracket.
- ➡ Summer's the best time for fun at the US National Whitewater Center, and that's when you really start appreciating the region's abundant beer gardens too.
- ➡ Crowds disperse and weather cools in September, but there's still plenty of sunshine.

CHARLOTTE

☎704 / POP 859,400

North Carolina's largest city, Charlotte sprawls 15 miles in every direction from its compact, high-rise core. Futuristic skyscrapers pepper downtown Charlotte, which is officially known as 'Uptown,' supposedly because it sits upon a barely visible ridge, but really because the council decided that sounds cooler. Uptown holds several fine museums plus the high-octane NASCAR Hall of Fame, while more museums and historic sites are scattered further afield. Hotels and restaurants are also concentrated Uptown, though funkier neighborhoods within easy reach include Plaza Midwood, just east, with its boutiques and restaurants, and hip NoDa, along North Davidson St, where former textile mills hold breweries and cafes.

Sights

Mint Museum Randolph MUSEUM

(☎704-337-2000; www.mintmuseum.org; 2730 Randolph Rd; adult/child 5-17yr $15/6, 5-9pm Wed free; ⏲11am-9pm Wed, 11am-6pm Thu-Sat, 1-5pm Sun; P) The US Mint opened its first-ever outpost in Uptown Charlotte in 1837, using gold mined from the mountains nearby. Transported 3 miles southeast a century later, the building now holds treasures ranging from ceramic masterpieces from Britain and North Carolina to stunning modern American decorative glasswork. Best of all are the wonderful pre-Columbian artifacts created by the Aztecs and Maya. Admission tickets also cover the Mint Museum Uptown, and are valid for two days.

Levine Museum of the New South MUSEUM

(Map p238; www.museumofthenewsouth.org; 200 E 7th St; adult/child 6-18yr $9/5; ⏲10am-5pm Mon-Sat, from noon Sun; P) Tracing the story of the 'New South' that emerged from the ashes of the Civil War, this committed museum explores the years of Reconstruction, Jim Crow and the Civil Rights movement. Haunting Dorothea Lange photos illuminate the Depression era on North Carolina's plantations, while changing exhibits highlight current issues such as the 2016 shooting of Keith Lamont Scott by police. Visitors are encouraged to respond to questions such as 'Does everyone have equal rights in the South today?' Tip: they validate two hours of parking at the 7th Street Station garage next door.

Historic Latta Plantation PLANTATION

(☎704-875-1391; www.lattaplantation.org; 5225 Sample Rd, Huntersville; $8; ⏲tours 11am, noon, 1pm, 2pm, 3pm & 4pm Tue-Sat, 2pm, 3pm & 4pm Sun; P) This 19th-century cotton plantation occupies a small corner of a scenic nature preserve, a dozen miles north of Uptown Charlotte. Exhibits in the visitor center tell the story of the Latta family and their 32 slaves, while guided tours lead through their small clapboard home. You're then free to wander around neighboring structures such as the imposing carriage barn.

Discovery Place Science SCIENCE CENTER

(Map p238; ☎704-372-6261; http://science.discoveryplace.org; 301 N Tryon St; adult/child 2-13yr $17/13; ⏲9am-4pm Mon-Fri, 9am-5pm Sat, noon-5pm Sun; P 👪) Illustrating simple scientific principles with eye-catching displays, Discovery Place is targeted largely at kids. It centers on a steamy rainforest that's inhabited by live macaws, and crossed by a swaying (not at all scary) rope bridge. Pretty much everything, including some docile snakes, is hands-on, though the 'Fantastic Frogs' and pulsating moon jellies remain safely behind glass.

Carolina Raptor Center BIRD SANCTUARY

(☎704-875-6521; www.carolinaraptorcenter.org; 6000 Sample Rd, Huntersville; $12; ⏲10am-5pm Mar-Oct, 10am-5pm Wed-Sat, from noon Sun Nov-Feb; P) A pleasant woodland stroll within the Latta Plantation Nature Preserve leads past aviaries holding predatory birds that have suffered injuries – you may come across volunteers taking a vulture for a walk. En route you'll learn about the 'disgusting habits' of black vultures, that bald eagles aren't really bald – they're white – and that owls are 'not the brightest of birds.'

Mint Museum Uptown MUSEUM

(Map p238; ☎704-337-2000; www.mintmuseum.org; 500 S Tryon St; adult/child 5-17yr $15/6, 5-9pm Wed free; ⏲11am-9pm Wed, 11am-6pm Thu-Sat, 1-5pm Sun) A stunning modernist edifice tucked between mighty skyscrapers, the Uptown portion of Charlotte's Mint Museum consists of two distinct halves. One makes a chronological journey through American art from the 18th century onwards, with a room devoted to local painter Romare Bearden. The other covers crafts and design, and holds some extraordinary contemporary works in glass, wood and clay. Admission tickets remain valid for two days, and also cover the Mint Museum Randolph.

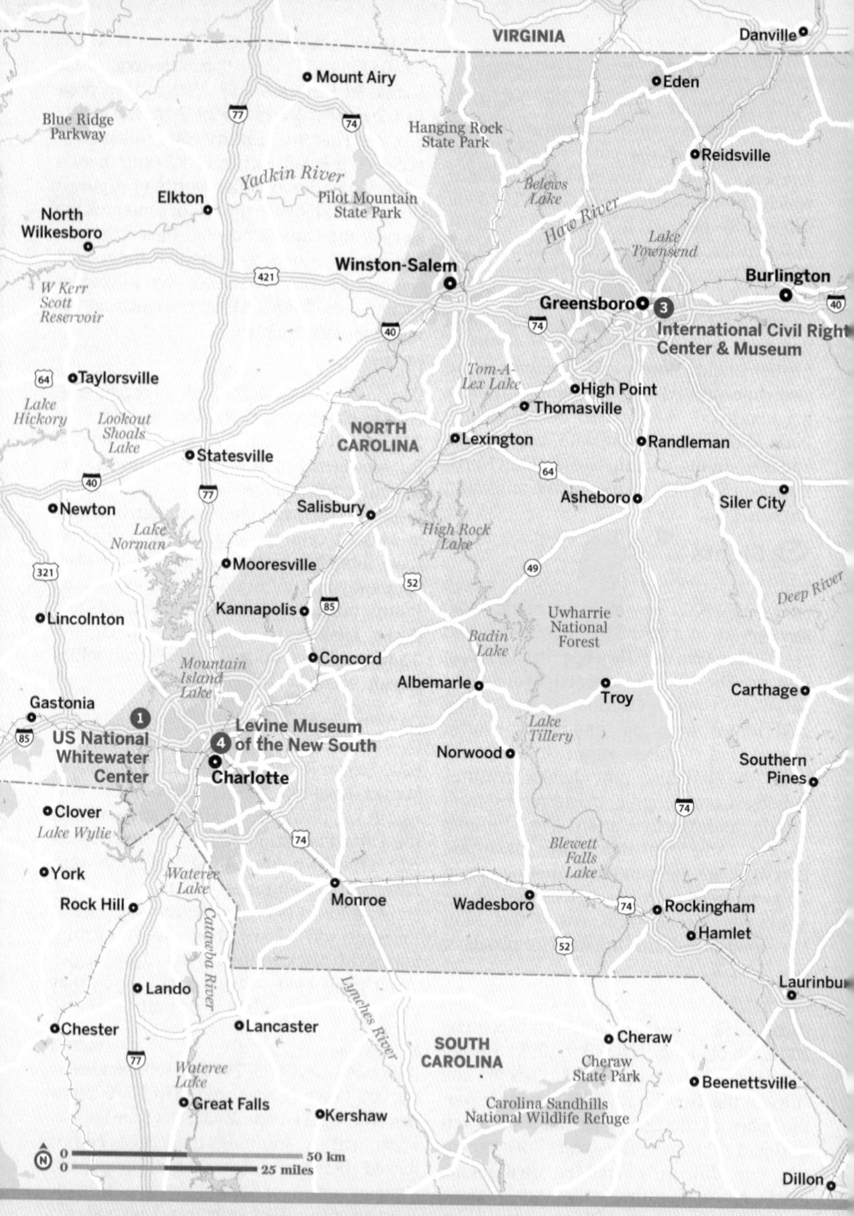

Charlotte & the Triangle Highlights

1 US National Whitewater Center (p237) Paddling the rapids alongside Olympic canoeists and kayakers.

2 Historic Stagville Plantation (p247) Confronting the reality of slavery on a fact-facing tour.

3 International Civil Rights Center & Museum (p251) Discovering where the sit-in campaign began.

4 Levine Museum of the New South (p233) Grappling with the issues that shaped the South.

5 North Carolina Museum of Art (p244) Admiring a world-spanning collection of art at this superb museum.

CHARLOTTE IN TWO DAYS

Start your first morning Uptown, getting your bearings – and a coffee – at the **7th Street Public Market** (p239). Learn about contemporary Charlotte at the ever-stimulating **Levine Museum of the New South** (p233) next door, before strolling a few blocks to enjoy the paintings and crafts in the **Mint Museum Uptown** (p233). Watch the world go by over lunch in its cafe, **Halcyon Flavors from the Earth** (p240), then check out some modern art at the neighboring **Bechtler Museum** (p236). Up the pace by racing the simulators at the **NASCAR Hall of Fame** (p236), before unwinding with a local craft beer or two at the **NoDa Brewing Co** (p240). Round things off by returning Uptown for a romantic dinner at the **Asbury** (p240).

Day two kicks off with a leisurely French-style breakfast at **Amélie's French Bakery & Cafe** (p240), before admiring the art treasures at the **Mint Museum Randolph** (p233). Be sure to grab some succulent take-out fried chicken at **Price's Chicken Coop** (p239) as you head out for an afternoon of wet and very wild adventures at the **US National Whitewater Center** (p237). Back in town, treat yourself to gourmet global snacks at **Soul Gastrolounge Tapas** (p240), then try out a few more breweries or catch a gig at the **AvidXchange Music Factory** (p242).

Bechtler Museum of Modern Art MUSEUM
(Map p238; ☎704-353-9200; www.bechtler.org; 420 S Tryon St; adult/child 11-18yr $8/4; ⏲10am-5pm Mon & Wed-Sat, from noon Sun) An Uptown landmark, thanks to sculptor Niki de Saint Phalle's huge mirror-tiled *Firebird* out front, this showcase for 20th-century art was donated to the city by the Bechtlers, a family of Swiss industrialists. Highlights of its permanent collection, displayed on the 3rd floor, include ceramics and lithographs by Picasso, and tiny gilded bronzes by Alberto Giacometti, a family friend. Look out for top-class temporary exhibitions on the 2nd and 4th floors.

NASCAR Hall of Fame MUSEUM
(Map p238; ☎704-654-4400; www.nascarhall.com; 400 E Martin Luther King Jr Blvd; adult/child 3-7yr/8-12yr $25/12/18; ⏲10am-5pm) The race-car simulator ($5) at this rip-roaring Uptown museum hurtles you onto the track and into an eight-car race that feels surprisingly real. Learn the history of an American-born sport whose roots lie in moonshine running, check out six generations of race cars on 'Glory Road,' and test your pit-crew skills.

Harvey B Gantt Center MUSEUM
(Map p238; ☎704-547-3700; www.ganttcenter.org; 551 S Tryon St; adult/child 6-17yr $9/7; ⏲10am-5pm Tue-Sat, from 1pm Sun) This thriving Uptown art museum was named in honor of former city mayor and civil rights champion Harvey Gannt. Its three small galleries host changing exhibitions of cutting-edge contemporary African American art, from North Carolina and beyond.

Charlotte Museum of History MUSEUM
(☎704-568-1774; http://charlottemuseum.org; 3500 Shamrock Drive; adult/child 6-17yr $10/7; ⏲11am-5pm Tue-Sat; P) There's a lot to read at Charlotte's history museum, in a restored mansion 6 miles east of the center. Wordy displays explain the city's origins, and its role in the American Revolution, in great detail. There's little to look at, though, other than a model of Charlotte as a simple rural crossroads in 1775. Hourly tours lead visitors out to the 1774 Hezekiah Home at the rear – the oldest stone building in the county.

Romare Bearden Park PARK
(Map p238; 300 S Church St) This small park celebrates the African American artist and writer Romare Bearden, born in Charlotte in 1911. A pretty spot to admire the Uptown skyline or watch the sunset, it hosts free live music in summer (noon to 1:30pm Tuesday and Friday, 6pm to 9pm Wednesday).

Billy Graham Library RELIGIOUS SITE
(☎704-401-3200; www.billygrahamlibrary.org; 4330 Westmont Dr; ⏲9:30am-5pm Mon-Sat, last tour 3:30pm) FREE This multimedia 'library' celebrates superstar evangelist and 'pastor to the presidents' Billy Graham, who was born in Charlotte in 1918 and died just short of his 100th birthday in 2018. The engaging and informative 90-minute tour opens with a gospel-preaching animatronic cow, then spotlights key moments in Graham's ministry, including the 1949 tent revival in Los Angeles, where he inspired the hero of *Unbroken*, Louis Zamperini.

Titled the 'Journey of Faith,' and imbued of course with Christian proselytizing, the tour explores Graham's journey and the roots of modern Evangelicalism. Graham's boyhood home, which originally stood 4 miles away, has been relocated here, following a pit stop for a few years in South Carolina.

Activities

★US National Whitewater Center ADVENTURE SPORTS
(☎704-391-3900; www.usnwc.org; 5000 Whitewater Center Pkwy; all-sport day pass adult/child under 10yr $59/49, individual activities $25, 3hr canopy tour $89; ⏲dawn-dusk) A beyond-awesome hybrid of nature center and water park, this 1300-acre facility is home to the largest artificial white-water river in the world. You can paddle its rapids – which serve as training grounds for Olympic canoeists and kayakers – as part of a guided rafting trip, or enjoy a range of other adventure activities.

As well as several rope courses, an outdoor rock-climbing wall, paddle surfing and ziplines, it holds miles of wooded hiking and mountain-biking trails. Or you could just sip a craft brew while you watch the kayaks in action from the Pump House Biergarten. The center is 14 miles west of Charlotte. Parking costs $6.

Festivals & Events

Charlotte Pride Festival & Parade LGBTIQ+
(www.charlottepride.org) North Carolina's largest gay celebration spreads across a (very) full weekend in mid-August, culminating in a massive street parade on the Sunday that attracts crowds of 150,000-plus. The organizers also stage an annual LGBTIQ+ film festival, Reel Out Charlotte, in May.

Taste of Charlotte FOOD & DRINK
(www.tasteofcharlotte.com; S Tryon St) For a long weekend in early June, Uptown swivels its focus from finance to food, as more than 100 local restaurants and producers set up stalls along six blocks of Tryon St. All that plus live music, kids' entertainment and craft vendors.

Sleeping

Because a high proportion of Uptown hotel guests tend to be business travelers, lower room rates are often available at weekends. Clusters of budget chain hotels can be found off I-85, both west of Uptown near the airport and northeast of Uptown near the UNC campus.

Grand Bohemian Charlotte LUXURY HOTEL
(Map p238; www.kesslercollection.com; W Trade St, cnr Church St) This luxury Uptown hotel, soars 16 stories above Uptown, with 254 rooms between its ground-level restaurant and rooftop bar.

Duke Mansion INN $$
(☎704-714-4400; www.dukemansion.com; 400 Hermitage Rd; r $121-341; P ❄ 📶) The century-old former home of the Duke family, including legendary heiress Doris Duke, is now a delightful B&B inn. Set in wooded gardens in the attractive Myers Park neighborhood, a couple of miles south of Uptown, it holds 20 light-filled rooms. Many still have their original tiled bathrooms, and some upstairs open onto their own screened sections of porch. Rates include a buffet breakfast; there's no on-site restaurant, but there are dining options within walking distance.

Omni Charlotte Hotel HOTEL $$
(Map p238; ☎704-377-0400; www.omnicharlotte.com; 132 E Trade St; r from $159; 📶 🏊) With almost 400 comfortable, contemporary rooms, this recently revamped 16-story hotel offers some of the lowest Uptown rates you'll find, particularly on weekends. Besides a spacious pool deck, there's complimentary gym access.

★Ivey's Hotel BOUTIQUE HOTEL $$$
(Map p238; ☎704-228-1111; www.theiveyshotel.com; 127 N Tryon St; r $299-499; P @ 📶 🐾) The Ivey's 42 Parisian-inspired rooms – all on the 2nd floor of a 1924 department-store building – are steeped in history (the 400-year-old oak-wood floors were sourced from a French winery) but have modern flair (55in Sony TVs, Bose soundbars). The balcony executive corner suites, awash in natural-light-sucking windows and exposed brick, are divine. Crown-molded doors and hallways, unique watch-face art, Frette linens, custom-designed furniture – the meticulously curated decor leaves no detail to chance.

Dunhill Hotel BOUTIQUE HOTEL $$$
(Map p238; ☎704-332-4141; www.dunhillhotel.com; 237 N Tryon St; r from $270; P ❄ @ 📶) The staff shine at this heart-of-Uptown hotel, which has been welcoming guests since 1929

Charlotte

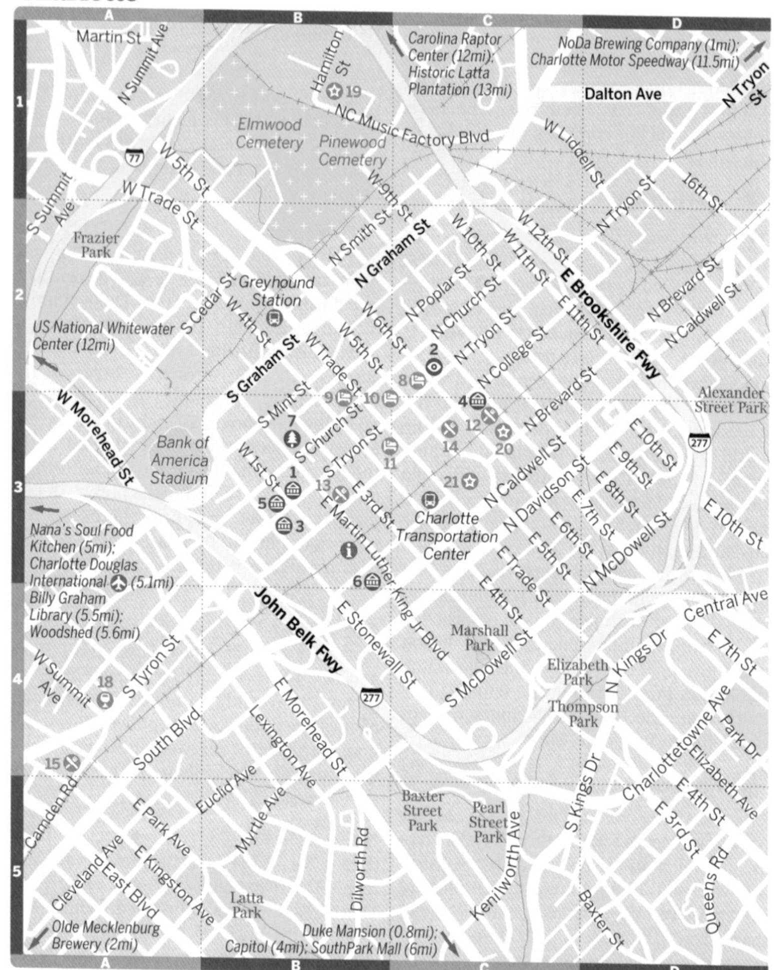

– this was the first hotel in Charlotte to have en-suite bathrooms. The classic decor offers a nod to the 1920s, but large flat-screen TVs, Keurig coffee makers and phone docking stations keep the rooms firmly in the 21st century. Parking is $23 per night.

Eating

Charlotte being a Southeastern culinary capital, it's home to numerous James Beard–nominated restaurateurs and inventive chefs, many of them graduates of the local Johnson & Wales University campus. Uptown's largely upscale options draw the preppy young banker set, while NoDa and Plaza Midwood offer laid-back bistros. Thanks to steady immigration, Charlotte also has ethnic restaurants from Greek to Vietnamese.

Mert's Heart & Soul SOUTHERN US $

(Map p238; ☎704-342-4222; www.mertscharlotte.com; 214 N College St; mains $11-16; ⏲11am-9pm Mon-Fri, 9am-11:30pm Sat, 9am-9:30pm Sun) Down at street level, beneath Uptown's soaring skyscrapers, this cozy, homely diner buzzes with bankers and bohos alike. Its Lowcountry classics include shrimp and grits, barbecue beef ribs and

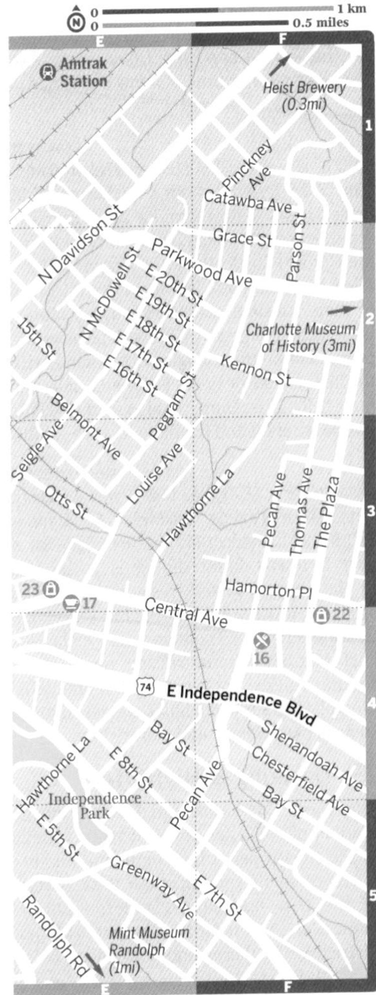

fried catfish, but we love the spicy salmon cakes best.

7th Street Public Market FOOD HALL $
(Map p238; ☎704-230-4346; www.7thstreetpublicmarket.com; 224 E 7th St; mains $10-15; ⏲7am-8pm Mon-Thu, 7am-9pm Fri, 8:30am-9pm Sat, 8:30am-5pm Sun) This indoor food hall's aromatic, irresistible kitchens and cafes entice Uptown palates with everything from gourmet coffee and craft beer to imported cheese and specialties from Orvieto, Italy. Pick and mix a roasted-broccoli burger here, a raw cold-pressed juice there, and settle down at the central tables to enjoy.

Charlotte

Sights
1 Bechtler Museum of Modern Art....... B3
2 Discovery Place Science.................... C2
3 Harvey B Gantt Center....................... B3
4 Levine Museum of the New South..... C3
5 Mint Museum Uptown........................ B3
6 NASCAR Hall of Fame........................ B3
7 Romare Bearden Park......................... B3

Sleeping
8 Dunhill Hotel....................................... C2
9 Grand Bohemian Charlotte................ B3
10 Ivey's Hotel.. B3
11 Omni Charlotte Hotel........................ B3

Eating
12 7th Street Public Market.................... C3
13 Amélie's French Bakery & Cafe......... B3
Asbury...(see 8)
Halcyon Flavors from the Earth..(see 5)
14 Mert's Heart & Soul............................ C3
15 Price's Chicken Coop......................... A4
16 Soul Gastrolounge Tapas.................. F4

Drinking & Nightlife
17 Central Coffee Co.............................. E3
18 Wooden Robot.................................... A4

Entertainment
19 AvidXchange Music Factory.............. B1
20 Children's Theater of Charlotte......... C3
21 Spectrum Center................................ C3

Shopping
22 Book Buyers.. F4
23 Lunchbox Records.............................. E3

Price's Chicken Coop SOUTHERN US $
(Map p238; ☎704-333-9866; www.priceschickencoop.com; 1614 Camden Rd; mains $3.25-12.25; ⏲10am-6pm Tue-Sat) A timeless throwback in ever-gentrifying South End, this scruffy, cash-only takeout is a true Charlotte institution, regularly making 'Best Fried Chicken in America' lists. Order your 'dark quarter' or 'white half' from the white-jacketed cooks, then carry your bounty outside and start looking for a place to eat – leafy Latta Park is 10 minutes' walk east on Park Ave.

Nana's Soul Food Kitchen SOUTHERN US $
(☎704-357-3700; www.nanassoulfoodkitchen.com; 2908 Oak Lake Blvd; mains $9-17; ⏲11am-9pm; P✎) With tempting sides such as mac and cheese, lima beans or black-eyed peas to match its succulent fried chicken and juicy beef ribs, Nana's offers treats to

LOCAL KNOWLEDGE

NEIGHBORHOOD KNOW-HOW

Uptown, as Charlotte's skyscraper-filled downtown area is universally known, is home to banks, hotels, museums and restaurants, and cut through by busy Tryon St. The renovated textile mills of the NoDa neighborhood (named after its principal thoroughfare, North Davidson St) have a hipper vibe, as do the funky mix of boutiques and restaurants in the Plaza Midwood area, just east of Uptown.

suit any appetite – veggie plates are a real bargain. Its bright cafeteria dining room is busiest during the weekday after-work rush, and Sunday lunchtimes once church is over.

The one drawback is that its quiet strip-mall location – just off Billy Graham Pkwy, not far from the airport – can be a little hard to find.

Amélie's French Bakery & Cafe CAFE **$**
(Map p238; ☎704-899-0088; www.ameliesfrenchbakery.com; 380 S College St; pastries $1-6, sandwiches $6.50; ⏲7am-10pm Mon-Thu, to midnight Fri & Sat, to 8pm Sun; 📶) This new, shiny and very big outlet of a much-loved local bakery chain is the perfect spot to rest your feet or meet friends Uptown. The sandwiches and toasted tartines are great value, but it's the decadently voluptuous pastries that draw the crowds, from the simple almond cake known as a *financier* to the house version of a brioche. Their vintage-styled original branch, at 2424 N Davidson St in the NoDa neighborhood, stays open 24 hours.

★ **Soul Gastrolounge Tapas** SUSHI, SANDWICHES **$$**
(Map p238; ☎704-348-1848; www.soulgastrolounge.com; 1500 Central Ave; small plates $7-20, sushi $4-14, sandwiches $9-15; ⏲5pm-2am) This sultry but welcoming Plaza Midwood speakeasy serves a globally inspired selection of small plates. Choices are wide-ranging, from skewers and sushi rolls to Cuban and Vietnamese sandwiches, but the kitchen takes care to infuse each little gem with unique, satisfying flavors. The dancing tuna rolls, with jalapeños and two spicy mayos, are highly recommended if you like heat.

With no reservations, the wait can be maddening – 187 minutes for us! But they use the NoWait app (http://nowait.com), so you can pass that time in a few breweries.

Halcyon Flavors from the Earth AMERICAN **$$**
(Map p238; ☎704-910-0865; www.halcyonflavors.com; 500 S Tryon St; salads & sandwiches $11-18, mains $32-44; ⏲11am-10pm Tue-Sat, to 3pm Sun) A perfect people-watching perch overlooking the Uptown bustle, the Mint Museum's light-filled restaurant is ideal for a zestful lunch or more substantial (and expensive) dinner. Ingredients sourced from local farmers are prominent on the changing daily menu, with the likes of kale or brussels-sprout salads and pork-belly BLTs. Dinner mains might include saddle of rabbit and halibut with crab soufflé.

Asbury SOUTHERN US **$$$**
(Map p238; ☎704-342-1193; www.theasbury.com; 235 N Tryon St; sandwiches $8-14, mains $20-38; ⏲11am-10pm Mon-Fri, from 5pm Sat & Sun) Uptown's finest dining is to be had in the Dunhill Hotel's restaurant, opening straight onto Tryon St. Rooted in Carolinian classics, but given a contemporary makeover, chef Matthew Krenz' cuisine ranges from sorghum-glazed duck with walnut and garlic gremolata to simpler staples, served anytime, such as mac, cheese and country ham.

Drinking & Nightlife

The Queen City has acquired a phenomenal number of breweries in recent years, with 25 in the city proper at last count, and another 20 or so in the metropolitan area. Several of the best line North Davidson St, the namesake artery of NoDa, Charlotte's hippest district, while there's another concentration in South End.

★ **NoDa Brewing Company** MICROBREWERY
(☎704-900-6851; www.nodabrewing.com; 2921 N Tryon St; ⏲4-9pm Mon-Thu, 4-10pm Fri, noon-10pm Sat, noon-7pm Sun; 📶) Charlotte's best craft-beer playground is hidden behind NoDa's new and easy-to-overlook North End brewery. We Uber'ed up on a Friday night and it looked abandoned. At the back, however, we found a packed playhouse of brews (pints $4 to $7) and boccie ball, plus cornhole, Frisbee golf, a fire pit, a massive patio and Charlotte's top food truck, Tin Kitchen.

Their Hop, Drop 'n Roll bested more than 200 international American IPAs to take gold at the 2014 World Beer Cup, but NoDa's got more; give their DIPA with Vermont Maple Syrup or chocolate, raspberry and habanero stout a try, too. When it eventually reopens, their original brewery, at 2229 North Davidson St, will concentrate on barrel-aged and sour beers.

Olde Mecklenburg Brewery MICROBREWERY
(☎704-525-5644; www.oldemeckbrew.com; 4150 Yancey Rd; ⊙11am-10pm Sun & Mon, to 11pm Fri & Sat; 📶) Everything's distinctly German-flavored here, from the huge wood-paneled beer hall and the sunny beer garden, via the sausages ($7) and schnitzel ($13), to the beer itself (pints from $4.50). Be sure to try their Hornet's Nest *hefeweizen* (wheat beer), which picked up a medal at 2017's Great American Beer Festival.

Woodshed GAY
(☎704-394-1712; www.woodshedlounge.com; 4000 Queen City Dr; ⊙5pm-2am) Charlotte's best-known gay men's bar, an old-school Levis 'n' leathers place with a welcoming neighborhood vibe, is near the airport, 6 miles west of Uptown.

Central Coffee Co COFFEE
(Map p238; ☎704-335-7288; www.centralcoffeeco.com; 719 Louise Ave; ⊙6am-8pm Mon-Sat, 7am-7pm Sun) From its ultra-friendly staff to its fresh-baked pastries, this local coffee bar is guaranteed to make you feel at home. Small and cosy, with exposed brickwork and ramshackle air-conditioning, it's next to a confusing five-way intersection on the main road through Plaza Midwood. Be sure to try their signature 'Central Shorty,' a 6oz latte with vanilla.

Wooden Robot MICROBREWERY
(Map p238; www.woodenrobotbrewery.com; 1440 S Tryon St; ⊙4-10pm Tue-Thu, 3pm-midnight Fri, noon-midnight Sat, noon-9pm Sun; 📶) One of Charlotte's most sociable taprooms – when the South End scene descends, it can feel like a sophisticated singles bar, full of hot millennials – this was voted the city's best by Untappd users. It's all brick and beautiful hardwoods and serious suds, often brewed with local coffee, chocolate, malt and syrups (small/medium/large beer from $2/4/6).

Heist Brewery MICROBREWERY
(☎704-375-8260; www.heistbrewery.com; 2909 N Davidson St; ⊙11am-midnight Mon-Wed, 11am-2am Thu-Sat, 10am-midnight Sun; 📶) Set in a former mill, Heist is one of several good-time NoDa breweries. With 36 taps spread over three bars (pints from $4.50), it offers some exceptionally juicy IPAs, craft cocktails ($9 to $13) and an extensive menu of inventive, farm-to-table pub food (dinner mains $10 to $16). The beer focus is on small-batch Belgians, saisons, imperial IPAs and stouts.

☆ Entertainment

Charlotte enjoys a year-round program of cultural activities, courtesy of arts institutions including the **Charlotte Symphony** (www.charlottesymphony.org), the **Charlotte Ballet** (www.charlotteballet.org) and **Opera Carolina** (www.operacarolina.org).

Big-name touring musicians tend to appear at the Spectrum Center (p241), while there's always something on at Uptown's AvidXchange Music Factory (p242). For current listings, check out the free alt-weekly *Creative Loafing* (www.clclt.com).

Spectrum Center STADIUM
(Map p238; ☎704-688-9000; www.spectrumcentercharlotte.com; 333 E Trade St) The Charlotte venue of choice for the biggest music tours, this 20,000-seat arena is also the home of the NBA's Charlotte Hornets.

Charlotte Motor Speedway SPECTATOR SPORT
(☎704-455-3200; www.charlottemotorspeedway.com; 5555 S Concord Pkwy; major events from $49; ⊙Apr-Nov) At the very heart of National Association for Stock Car Auto Racing (NASCAR) country, 14 miles northeast of Uptown, Charlotte's prestigious motorsports arena accommodates almost 90,000 spectators. The season lasts from April to November, with daily speedway tours and

LGBTIQ+ CHARLOTTE

While Charlotte is a gay-friendly city, its LGBTIQ+ community is spread out across the metropolitan area. There's no high-profile gay nightlife district, so the best neighborhoods to find gay and lesbian bars and clubs are Plaza Midwood and NoDa. That said, the best-known men's bar, the Woodshed, is 6 miles west of Uptown.

Charlotte Pride Festival & Parade (p237) is the largest such event in the state.

Qnotes (www.goqnotes.com), a free biweekly newspaper, is a great resource for listings and news coverage.

WORTH A TRIP

WANDER WINSTON-SALEM

In its tobacco-processing heyday, a century ago, Winston-Salem was the largest city in North Carolina. Since then, the city that gave the world Camel cigarettes (and Krispy Kreme doughnuts!) has slipped back to fifth place, leaving its pocket-sized downtown looking a little faded but charming nonetheless. For visitors, though, the big attraction lies immediately south, in the verdant streets of Salem ('peace') itself, founded in 1766 by German Protestants from the Moravian sect. Their settlement remains remarkably intact, despite the encroachment of the nearby industrial city of Winston, which by 1913 had crept so close that there was only just room to squeeze a hyphen between the two, and create Winston-Salem.

At about 80 miles from either Charlotte or the Triangle (and about halfway between them, if you're road-tripping), Winston-Salem is worth a day trip.

The beautifully preserved core of the Moravian settlement of **Salem** (☎336-721-7350; www.oldsalem.org; 900 Old Salem Rd; all-in-one ticket adult/child under 19yr Tue-Sat $27/13, Sun $22/11, 2-stop ticket Tue-Sat $18/9; ⏲9:30am-4:30pm Tue-Sat, from 1pm Sun; P) extends across several blocks south of downtown. You're not obliged to pay for admission if you simply want to admire the architecture, eat in the **Tavern** (☎336-722-1227; www.thetaverninoldsalem.ws; 736 S Main St, Old Salem; lunch mains $10, dinner mains $18-25; ⏲11am-3:30pm & 5-9pm Tue-Sat, 11am-3pm Sun), or shop in the wonderful Winkler Bakery or various craft shops. You'll have a much richer experience, though, if you pay for access to the on-site museums, houses and workshops, where costumed guides explain and demonstrate Moravian traditions, such as gardening, doctoring and gunsmithing.

If you plan to visit any of the paying attractions, start by buying tickets at the large modern visitor center, across the main road from Old Salem proper, at the southern end of a large parking lot. And if your time is short, prioritize the **Museum of Early Southern Decorative Arts** (☎336-721-7369; www.mesda.org; 924 S Main St, Old Salem; all-in-one ticket adult/child under 19yr Tue-Sat $27/13, Sun $22/11, two-stop ticket Tue-Sat $18/9; ⏲9:30am-4:30pm Tue-Sat, from 1pm Sun; P) and the rewarding displays on Salem's African American population in and around St Philips Church.

lesser events supplementing showcase NASCAR races such as May's Coca-Cola 600.

AvidXchange Music Factory LIVE MUSIC
(Map p238; ☎704-916-8970; www.avidxchangemusicfactory.com; 1000 NC Music Factory Blvd; ⏲individual venues vary) This huge complex on the northern edge of Uptown incorporates multiple entertainment venues, ranging from the open-air, 5000-seat Charlotte Metro Credit Union Amphitheatre, via midsize music theaters including the Fillmore and the Underground, to the Comedy Zone, ROC's Jazz Bar and several bars and nightclubs.

Children's Theater of Charlotte THEATER
(Map p238; ☎704-973-2828; www.ctcharlotte.org; 300 E 7th St) Based in the dazzling high-tech Imaginon – a reinvented Uptown library complex that's more relevant to local schoolkids than it is to visitors – the Children's Theater puts on an acclaimed year-round program of shows for kids of varying ages.

Shopping

Uptown Charlotte not being an especially fertile shopping destination, anyone looking for unusual or interesting stores in the city needs to be prepared to do quite a bit of driving. The greatest concentration of big-name retailers is in the South Park neighborhood, 6 miles southwest of Uptown and home to the enormous **SouthPark Mall** (www.simon.com/mall/southpark) at 4400 Sharon Rd.

Capitol CLOTHING
(☎704-366-0388; www.capitolcharlotte.com; 4010 Sharon Rd; ⏲10am-6pm Mon-Sat) Charlotte's best-known luxury clothing store has earned a national reputation for its impeccable array of women's fashion and jewelry, much of it the work of international designers otherwise barely available in the US.

Lunchbox Records MUSIC
(Map p238; ☎704-331-0788; www.lunchboxrecords.com; 825 Central Ave; ⏲noon-8pm

Mon-Thu, noon-9pm Fri & Sat, 1-6pm Sun) Apart perhaps from its giant robot sign and blue-brick facade, this Plaza Midwood store is just like the local record stores you used to love. Rack upon rack of vinyl, plus CDs and DVDs – they buy, too – as well as information and tickets for live shows, and occasional in-store gigs. They even run their own record label.

Book Buyers BOOKS

(Map p238; ☎704-344-8611; www.facebook.com/bookbuyersclt; 1306 The Plaza; ⏰10am-8pm Mon-Sat, noon-6pm Sun) There's only one downside to this large Plaza Midwood second-hand bookshop – Page, the loud and aggressive cat who prowls the aisles. Find a place to hide, and browse for regional classics, general fiction and the unexpected, all cut-price and some even free.

Information

Charlotte's main **visitor center** (Map p238; ☎800-231-4636; www.charlottesgotalot.com; 501 S College St, Charlotte Convention Center; ⏰9am-5pm Mon-Sat) is in Uptown. There's also an information desk at the airport.

ACCESSIBLE TRAVEL

The most recent edition of *Access North Carolina* can be downloaded from www.ncdhhs.gov, the website of North Carolina's Department of Health and Human Services. This invaluable 500-page guide to facilities throughout the state, for visitors with hearing, mobility, sight and other issues, details access to Charlotte's main Uptown attractions. The NASCAR Hall of Fame (p236), for example, has a fully accessible race-car simulator.

All Charlotte's fixed-route buses and trains are accessible to travelers with disabilities (www.ridetransit.org).

EMERGENCY & IMPORTANT NUMBERS

Police, fire, ambulance	☎911
Police non-emergency number	☎704-336-7600

TRAVEL WITH CHILDREN

In the words of its tourist slogan, Charlotte's got a lot to entertain and interest kids. If yours aren't old enough to go rafting at the US National Whitewater Center (p237) or ride the simulators at the NASCAR Hall of Fame (p236), head instead to Uptown's Discovery Place Science (p233) – as well as hands-on science experiments bursting with buttons, there's a whole rainforest to explore – or take in a show at the Children's Theater of Charlotte. Outdoorsy kids may also enjoy seeing the rescued birds out at the Carolina Raptor Center (p233).

Getting There & Away

Charlotte Douglas International Airport (p370), 7 miles west of Uptown, is an American Airlines hub that welcomes nonstop flights from continental Europe and the UK. Both the **Greyhound** (Map p238; ☎704-372-0456; www.greyhound.com; 601 W Trade St) and **Amtrak** (www.amtrak.com; 1914 N Tryon St) stations are handy to Uptown.

Getting Around

Charlotte's public transport system, known as CATS (Charlotte Area Transit System), encompasses city buses; a streetcar line known as the CityLYNX Gold Line; and the LYNX Blue Line light-rail line, which extends to the UNC campus, 9 miles northeast of Uptown. One-way fares range $2.20 to $4.40. The **Charlotte Transportation Center** (Map p238; ☎704-336-7433; www.ridetransit.org; 310 E Trade St), the system's Uptown interchange, can be accessed from Brevard St between 4th and Trade St.

Charlotte also operates a shared-bike network called **Charlotte B-cycle** (https://charlotte.bcycle.com).

THE TRIANGLE

The cities of Raleigh, Durham and Chapel Hill form a rough triangle in the central Piedmont region. Three top research universities – Duke, University of North Carolina and North Carolina State – are located here, as is the 7000-acre computer and biotech-office campus known as Research Triangle Park. Swarming with egghead computer programmers, bearded peace activists and hip young families, each town has its own unique personality, despite being only a few miles apart. In March, everyone – we mean *everyone* – goes crazy for college basketball.

Raleigh

☎919, 984 / POP 458,880

Founded in 1792 as a new capital for North Carolina, and named for Sir Walter Raleigh – whose image crops up in all sorts of unlikely places around the city – Raleigh remains a somewhat staid government town with major sprawl issues. Downtown is undeniably handsome, though, and is home to some top-notch (and free!) museums and galleries, while the food and music scenes are on a definite upswing.

Sights

★North Carolina Museum of Art MUSEUM
(☎919-839-6262; www.ncartmuseum.org; 2110 Blue Ridge Rd; ⊙10am-5pm Tue-Thu, Sat & Sun, to 9pm Fri, park dawn-dusk; P) FREE Expanded in 2010 with the completion of the stunning, glass-and-steel West Building, this superb museum stands 6 miles west of downtown. Ranging far and wide, from ancient Egypt to modern Africa, its permanent collection includes works credited to Giotto and Botticelli – albeit with 'assistance' – and even a 17th-century 'Golf Player' etched by Rembrandt. The museum also holds around 20 jet-black Rodin bronzes, and a gallery celebrating alumni of the pioneering Black Mountain College near Asheville, including Robert Rauschenberg. Look out for Michael Richards' sculpture of a Tuskegee airman pierced by airplanes, which hauntingly prefigured Richards' own death in the 9/11 attacks.

North Carolina Museum of History MUSEUM
(Map p245; ☎919-807-7900; www.ncmuseumofhistory.org; 5 E Edenton St; ⊙9am-5pm Mon-Sat, from noon Sun) FREE For a comprehensive, even-handed and engaging look at the story of North Carolina, immerse yourself in the state history museum. Starting with a 3000-year-old dugout canoe, it continues through to the Civil Rights era by way of the European arrival and the Revolutionary and Civil wars. Look out for the cannon retrieved from the 1718 wreck of Blackbeard's ship, *Queen Anne's Revenge,* and the Woolworth's lunch counter that witnessed a sit-in in 1960.

North Carolina Museum of Natural Sciences MUSEUM
(Map p245; ☎919-707-9800; www.naturalsciences.org; 11 W Jones St; ⊙9am-5pm Mon- Sat, from noon Sun) FREE Whale skeletons hang from the ceiling. Butterflies flutter past your shoulder. Emerald tree boas make you shiver. And be warned: if you arrive after 10am on a school day, swarms of elementary-school children rampage all over the place. Skywalks lead to a glossy extension, the Nature Research Center, where you can watch scientists at work on their projects (and displays make it clear they're in no doubt as to the reality of climate change). Don't miss the exhibit on the Acrocanthosaurus dinosaur, a 3-ton carnivore nicknamed the Terror of the South. Its toothy skull is the stuff of nightmares.

State Capitol HISTORIC BUILDING
(Map p245; ☎919-733-4994; www.nchistoricsites.org/capitol; Union Sq; ⊙9am-5pm Mon-Fri) FREE A fine example of Greek Revival architecture, North Carolina's handsome state capitol was completed in 1840. Despite the risk of running into legislators and lobbyists skulking in strange corners, visitors can wander at will on weekdays, peeping into assorted historic chambers. Saturday visits are on (free) guided tours only.

Sleeping

Downtown Raleigh being short on lodgings of any kind – there are no central boutique hotels, for example – most visitors opt for one of the moderately priced chain properties that stand just off the interstates circling the city. These are especially abundant near exit 10 off I-440, 5 miles north of town, and off I-40 near the airport, 15 miles northwest.

Eating

Besides holding several James Beard Award nominees, Raleigh is home to a range of ethnic restaurants, thanks perhaps to the number of global tech companies based in the Research Triangle. Whether you fancy traditional North Carolina whole-hog BBQ, elevated Southern cuisine or Laotian delicacies, the city's culinary landscape is an evolving surprise.

★La Farm Bakery BAKERY $
(☎919-657-0657; www.lafarmbakery.com; 4248 NW Cary Pkwy, Cary; dishes $6-10; ⊙7am-8pm; 📶) This much-loved French bakery is hard to find, halfway to Chapel Hill and inconspicuous even once you spot the right strip mall. Its breads and pastries are truly out of this world, though – whether you grab a classic baguette or apple chollah, or linger over a miso pork and kimchi brioche or a fig and prosciutto tartine.

Beasley's Chicken & Honey SOUTHERN US $
(Map p245; ☎919-322-0127; www.ac-restaurants.com/beasleys; 237 S Wilmington St; mains $7-13; ⊙11:30am-10pm Sun-Wed, to midnight Thu-Sat) You'll need to loosen your belt after a meal at this crispy venture from James Beard Award–winning chef Ashley Christensen. Inside her airy downtown canteen, fried chicken is the star – on a biscuit, with waffles, in a potpie. The sides

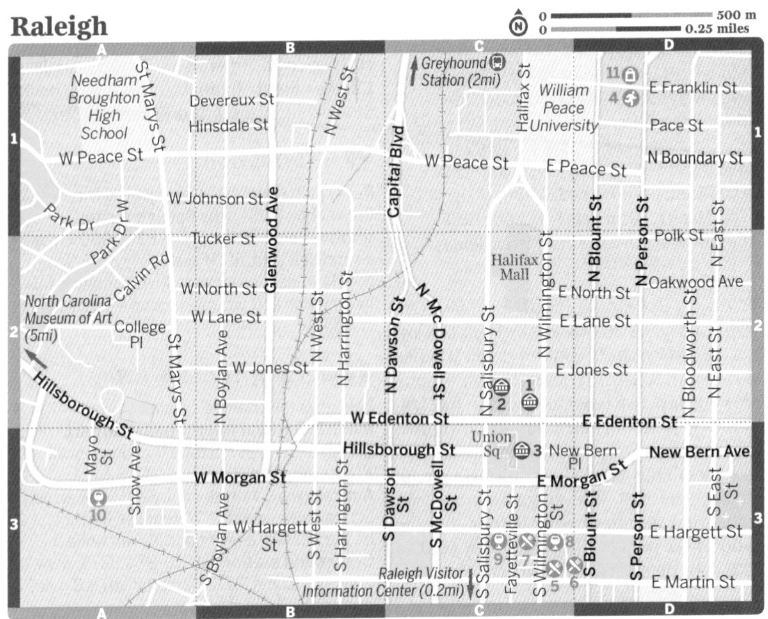

Raleigh

Sights

1 North Carolina Museum of History C2
2 North Carolina Museum of Natural Sciences C2
3 State Capitol C3

Activities, Courses & Tours

4 Oak City Cycling Project D1

Eating

5 Beasley's Chicken & Honey C3
6 Bida Manda D3
7 Raleigh Times C3

Drinking & Nightlife

8 Green Light C3
9 Raleigh Raw C3
10 Trophy Brewing & Pizza A3

Shopping

11 Lumina Clothing Co D1

are decadent too – the creamed collard greens make a perfect introduction for nervous neophytes.

Raleigh Times PUB FOOD $

(Map p245; ☎919-833-0999; www.raleightimesbar.com; 14 E Hargett St; mains $9-15; ⏲11am-2am; 📶) Chase plates of BBQ nachos or (cat)fish 'n' chips with pints of North Carolina craft brews at this popular and very central downtown pub.

Bida Manda LAOTIAN $$

(Map p245; ☎919-829-9999; www.bidamanda.com; 222 S Blount St; lunch mains $11-22, dinner mains $18-30; ⏲11:30am-2pm & 5-10pm Mon-Thu, 11:30am-2pm & 5pm-midnight Fri, 5pm-midnight Sat; 📶) The food at this artfully decorated establishment – one of very few Laotian restaurants in the US – looks as gorgeous as the space itself. Enhanced with Thai, Vietnamese and Chinese flavors, it tastes wonderful too. From pumpkin curry to lemongrass sausage or crispy pork-belly soup, everything's bold and very satisfying. The little shot of Laos-style coffee is a nice touch, too.

Drinking & Nightlife

Wake County is home to almost 30 craft breweries and all manner of great bars, dotted especially around Raleigh's compact downtown, as well as the city's up-and-coming Warehouse District, Glenwood South and North Hills areas.

LET'S GO RIDE A BIKE

More than 150 miles of intersecting greenways and trails lace through the Raleigh area. Rent a bike at **Oak City Cycling Project** (Map p245; ☎919-436-0527; www.oakcitycycling.com; 212 E Franklin St; per hr/week $25/100; ⏰11am-7pm Mon-Fri, 10am-5pm Sat), and check out the RGreenway App for trail details.

★ **Trophy Brewing & Pizza** CRAFT BEER
(Map p245; ☎919-803-4849; www.trophybrewing.com; 827 W Morgan St; ⏰4pm-midnight Mon-Thu, noon-2am Fri & Sat, noon-midnight Sun) Trophy Brewing have two other locations in Raleigh, a brewery taproom and a classier downtown pub, but their original space, with six taps and a small but delectable craft-pizza menu, remains the best. The gorgeous wood bar, made from reclaimed wine barrels, and the patio are a perfect place for pizza ($10 to $22) with their excellent Teacher's Pet IPA.

Green Light COCKTAIL BAR
(Map p245; www.architectbar.com/the-green-light; 108 E Hargett St; ⏰5pm-2am; 📶) The Green Light is a bar within a bar, an intimate cocktail lounge hidden within the larger and less interesting Architect bar in downtown Raleigh. An intriguing, speakeasy-like experience, it's behind the bookcase – if the green light is on, head on in! Considering the focus on classic and craft cocktails, the bartenders are a little pushy with the tequila shots (gourmet ones, but still).

Raleigh Raw JUICE BAR
(Map p245; ☎919-400-0944; www.raleighraw.com; 7 W Hargett St; ⏰7:30am-7pm Mon-Fri, 8am-7pm Sat, 8am-6pm Sun) This funky little 100% raw and organic cold-pressed juice bar takes its blended brews seriously, mixing up fruit and vegetables, and setting out to improve liver function, blood circulation and the like. It's the taste that'll get you coming back, though. They also serve coffee, *matcha* and kombucha, plus small farm-to-table bites.

Shopping

Lumina Clothing Co CLOTHING
(Map p245; www.luminaclothing.com; 215 E Franklin St; ⏰noon-5pm Mon & Sun, 11am-7pm Tue-Sat) Raleigh born and bred, this hip, mostly men's clothing boutique made a name for itself by dishing out its own shirt designs in half sizes. Along with their own stuff, including denim and pants, the fiercely curated collection includes cutting-edge Americana brands such as Ebbets Field flannels, Topo backpacks, Shuron sunglasses and Filson clothing.

Information

Really just a small counter adjoining the Convention Center, the **Raleigh Visitor Information Center** (☎919-834-5900; www.visitraleigh.com; 500 Fayetteville St; ⏰9am-5pm Mon-Sat) is stocked with maps and local information that you can pick up even when it's closed.

Getting There & Away

Raleigh is the Triangle's main gateway. **Raleigh-Durham International Airport** (p370) is 15 miles northwest of downtown, a route served by local bus 100 ($2.25). **Amtrak** (www.amtrak.com; 320 W Cabarrus St) trains arrive in the Warehouse District on the western edge of downtown, while the **Greyhound station** (☎919-834-8275; www.greyhound.com; 2210 Capital Blvd) is 3 miles northeast of downtown.

Durham

☎919, 984 / POP 263,016

Home a century ago to the world's largest tobacco company – American Tobacco – Durham remains at heart a working-class Southern city. Its fortunes collapsed in the 1960s, however, along with the cigarette industry, and Durham's recent revival owes much to the presence of the prestigious Duke University.

The city's downtown has been comprehensively rebuilt, and transformed into a hot spot for gourmands and artists, gays and lesbians. The changing winds were epitomized in 2017, when protesters toppled the Confederate monument that had stood outside the former county courthouse since 1924.

Sights

★ **Historic Stagville Plantation** PLANTATION
(☎919-620-0120; www.stagville.org; 5828 Old Oxford Hwy; ⏰9am-5pm Tue-Sat, tours 11am, 1pm & 3pm; P) FREE Exceptional in prioritizing the 1000 or so 'enslaved persons' who worked here above the families that claimed their ownership, Stagville Plantation ranks among North Carolina's most important historic sites. What survives today, 10 miles

north of downtown, is just a fragment of the huge plantation where the state's largest enslaved population lived in scattered groups. The fascinating guided tours drive in convoy to an emotive cluster of slave homes, along with a massive barn, a mile from the main house.

★Duke Lemur Center ZOO

(Map p248; ☎919-401-7240; http://lemur.duke.edu; 3705 Erwin Rd; adult/child under 8yr $12/9; ⏲9am-4pm, by appointment; 👪) Durham's coolest attraction has to be this research and conservation center, home to the largest collection of lemurs outside their native Madagascar. No one could fail to melt at the sight of these big-eyed fuzzy creatures. Visits are by guided tour only, and must be reserved well in advance. Call at least three weeks ahead for weekdays, or one to two months for weekends.

Nasher Museum of Art GALLERY

(Map p248; ☎919-684-5135; http://nasher.duke.edu; 2001 Campus Dr; adult/child under 16yr $7/free, Thu free; ⏲10am-5pm Tue, Wed, Fri & Sat, 10am-9pm Thu, noon-5pm Sun; P) Set amid the Duke University campus woods, this impressive futuristic cube displays art from around the world and across the ages. Only a small portion of the university's collection is on show at any one time, but you're sure to see magnificent Maya ceramics and statues from the ancient Mediterranean, as well as contemporary works. Prestigious temporary exhibitions charge additional fees.

Museum of Life & Science MUSEUM

(☎919-220-5429; www.lifeandscience.org; 433 W Murray Ave; adult/child 3-12yr $18/13; ⏲10am-5pm, closed Mon Sep-May; P 👪) There's something to appeal to every child at Durham's Museum of Life & Science, 3 miles north of downtown. Its main building, stuffed with everything from live snakes to a lunar lander, serves as an appetizer for treats such as the sailing lake, dinosaur-dotted woodland trail, and bear and butterfly enclosures, which spread across its gardens. An open train tours the whole ensemble, through the woods ($5).

Duke Homestead HISTORIC SITE

(☎919-627-6990; http://dukehomestead.org; 2828 Duke Homestead Rd; ⏲9am-5pm Tue-Sat; P) FREE After the Civil War, Confederate veteran Washington Duke returned to his farm and built an astonishing fortune, astonishingly fast. Tobacco manufacturing operations moved downtown in 1874, so the Duke Homestead, 4 miles north, remains intact. Hourly tours lead through barns and outbuildings, but you're free to wander the farm, after enjoying a museum of tobacco history that barely mentions health issues.

American Tobacco Campus HISTORIC SITE

(Map p248; http://americantobaccocampus.com; 300 Blackwell St) The massive former American Tobacco factory has been transformed into a million-square-foot cavalcade of restaurants, bars and entertainment venues. Still dominated by the towering 'Lucky Strike' chimney, but now centering on gardens traversed by artificial cascades, it's a lively combination of thriving mall and urban park. On the south side of downtown, it's just steps across the tracks from Main St. Look out for the observational beehive that marks the headquarters of international cosmetics company Burt's Bees.

Duke University UNIVERSITY

(Map p248; www.duke.edu; Chapel Dr) Although it can trace its history back to 1838, Duke University became a university, and took its current name, in 1926, thanks to a major endowment from the Duke cigarette family. Spreading across the Georgian-style East Campus and the neo-Gothic West Campus, 1 and 2 miles respectively west of downtown, it has just over 15,000 students.

Sarah P Duke Gardens GARDENS

(Map p248; www.gardens.duke.edu; 420 Anderson St; ⏲8am-dusk) FREE These heavenly gardens on the Duke University campus include 55 acres of koi ponds, terraced rose gardens and magnolia groves. On warm afternoons, they fill with students and visitors playing Frisbee.

Duke Chapel CHAPEL

(Map p248; ☎919-681-9488; http://chapel.duke.edu; 401 Chapel Dr; ⏲8am-8pm, to 10pm in semester) The major landmark on Duke University's west campus, and the epitome of its neo-Gothic style, is the 210ft tower of Duke Chapel. Erected in the 1930s, the chapel is worth visiting even if you don't coincide with the weekly service, held at 11am on Sunday. Until 2017, a statue of Confederate general Robert E Lee stood among those guarding the chapel entrance. After being vandalized, it was removed to reflect the school's 'abiding values.'

Durham

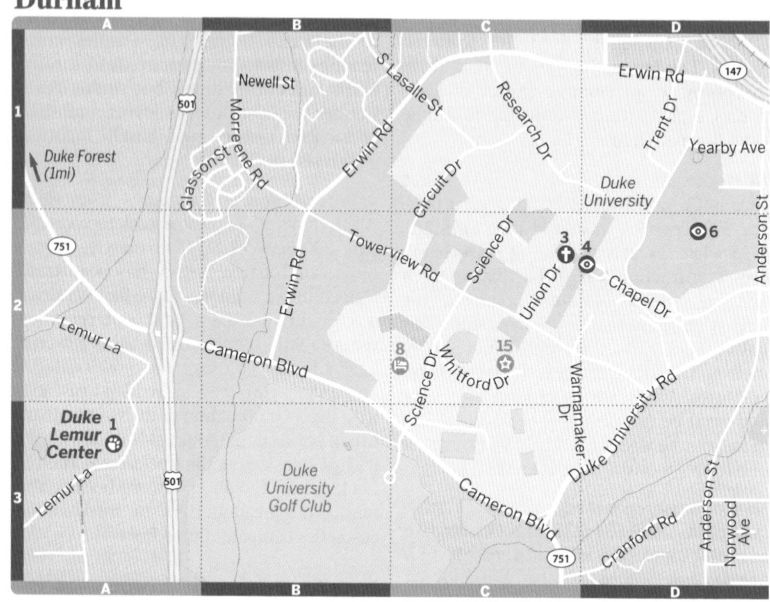

Durham

Top Sights
1 Duke Lemur Center A3

Sights
2 American Tobacco Campus G3
3 Duke Chapel C2
4 Duke University D2
5 Nasher Museum of Art E2
6 Sarah P Duke Gardens D2

Sleeping
7 Durham H2
8 JB Duke Hotel C2

Eating
9 Dame's Chicken & Waffles H2
10 Dashi H2
11 Mateo G2
12 Toast G2

Drinking & Nightlife
13 Cocoa Cinnamon H1
14 Fullsteam Brewery H1

Entertainment
15 Cameron Indoor Stadium C2
16 Durham Bulls Athletic Park G3
17 Motorco Music Hall H1

Shopping
18 Brightleaf Square G2

Activities

Duke Forest HIKING
(http://dukeforest.duke.edu; NC 751) From the 1920s onwards, Duke University bought up farms and forestland south and west of Durham to create what's now Duke Forest. Its six separate tracts now hold numerous hiking and cycling trails, including the popular and newly restored Shepherd Nature Trail, a mile-long loop that starts from Gate C on NC 751, 1.3 miles northwest of I-15.

Sleeping

Durham's accommodation options consist largely of chain hotels, with budget motels concentrated especially off I-85 north of the center. Recently though, boutique hotels have been popping up both downtown and on Duke University's campus, and there are more on the way.

★**Durham** BOUTIQUE HOTEL $$
(Map p248; 919-768-8830; www.thedurham.com; 315 E Chapel Hill St; r from $176; P ❄ @ 🛜) When the suave, 53-room Durham turned

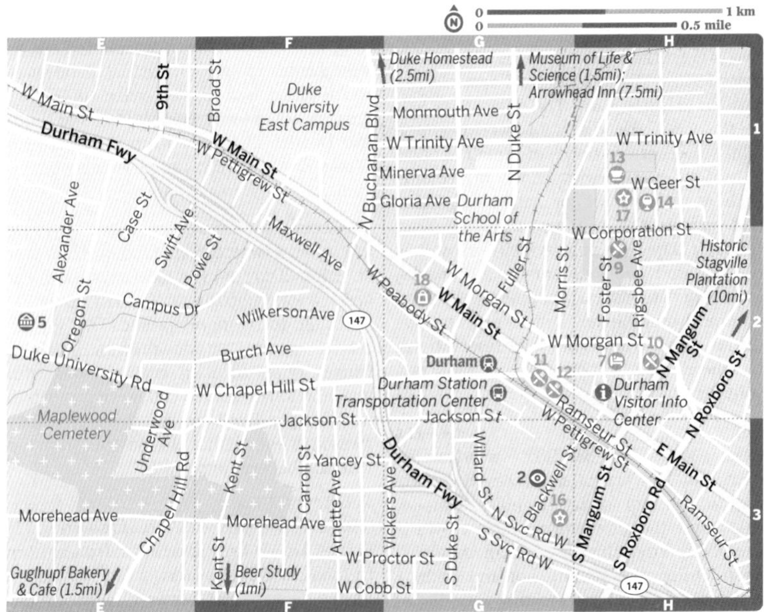

a former bank building – a marvel of mid-century modernist might – into a supremely retro, fiercely local haven in 2015, it marked the moment when Durham's revitalized downtown finally got an independent hipster sleep. Raleigh Denim bedspreads, music programming by Durham-based Merge Records – it's go local or go home. Award-winning chef Andrea Reusing runs the food and beverage program, best enjoyed on the fantastic open-air rooftop terrace.

Arrowhead Inn B&B **$$**
(☎919-477-8430; www.arrowheadinn.com; 106 Mason Rd; r $159, cottages/cabins $269/299; ❄📶) Set in an imposing white clapboard home dating back to 1775, this plush B&B is 9 miles north of downtown. Every antique-furnished room in the main house has its own fireplace, and several have private spa baths; there's a separate cottage and cabin in the grounds. Rates include a sumptuous breakfast; dinner is also available from $45 (Thursday to Saturday, by reservation only).

JB Duke Hotel BOUTIQUE HOTEL **$$**
(Map p248; ☎919-660-6400; www.jbdukehotel.com; 230 Science Dr; r/ste from $212/387; P❄@📶🐾) This slick hotel on Duke's campus rides a fine line between modern and woodsy. Its soothing carpeted lobby comes complete with rough-cut walnut tables and a dark quartzite and metallic-tiled bar, while the spacious rooms offer work desks, coffee machines and campus views. There's also a huge fitness center, plus an outdoor back patio, with fire pits facing the woods.

Eating

Downtown Durham is peppered with nationally renowned restaurants and quirky diners. Appetizing options line West Chapel Hill St downtown, while the former tobacco warehouses of the American Tobacco Campus (p247), nearby, have been attractively renovated as an entertainment and dining complex.

★ **Dame's Chicken & Waffles** CHICKEN **$**
(Map p248; ☎919-682-9235; www.dameschickenwaffles.com; 530 Foster St; mains $10-15; ⏲10am-4pm Mon & Sun, to 9pm Tue-Thu, to 10pm Fri, 9am-10pm Sat) While they can't claim to have invented chicken and waffles – it's been a 'thing' for a couple of centuries – Dame's has raised the ultimate comfort food to a fine art. Their relocation to these larger premises should mean customers won't have to wait before enjoying crispy Southern fried chicken atop, yes, fluffy, syrup-drenched, breakfast-style waffles.

Dashi JAPANESE $

(Map p248; 919-251-9335; www.dashiramen.com; 415 E Chapel Hill St; noodles $12-15, small plates $8-15; 11:30am-2:30pm & 5pm-midnight Mon-Thu, to 1am Fri & Sat) The downstairs half of this cool, friendly, split-level Japanese joint serves sizable bowls of ramen noodles in various broths, with added ingredients such as pulled pork or catfish. Upstairs, and open in the evenings only, there's an *izakaya* (Japanese pub), which – as well as noodles and delicious small-plate snacks, including octopus hush puppies (deep-fried cornmeal dumplings) – offers an extensive drinks menu. They don't take reservations, but there's usually room to drink while you wait for a table.

Toast SANDWICHES $

(Map p248; 919-683-2183; www.toast-fivepoints.com; 345 W Main St; sandwiches $8; 11am-3pm Mon, to 8pm Tue-Sat) Families, couples, solos and the downtown lunch crowd – everybody loves this tiny Italian sandwich shop. Order your panini (hot and grilled), *tramezzini* (cold) or crostini (bundle of joy) at the counter, then grab a table by the window – if you can – for people-watching.

★ **Mateo** TAPAS $$

(Map p248; 919-530-8700; www.mateotapas.com; 109 W Chapel Hill St; small plates $8-15; 11:30am-2:30pm & 5-10:30pm Tue-Thu, 11:30am-2:30pm & 5pm-midnight Fri, 5pm-midnight Sat, 5-9:30pm Sun) A poster child for Durham's remarkable comeback, this James Beard–nominated 'bar de tapas' is downtown's culinary anchor. Many dishes come with a Southern bent, and revelations include the *pan com tomate* with Manchego cheese; the brussels sprouts with pine nuts, raisins and saffron yogurt; and the fried egg and cheese (in which the 'whites' are fried farmer's cheese!).

Guglhupf Bakery & Cafe BAKERY $$

(919-401-2600; www.guglhupf.com; 2706 Durham-Chapel Hill Blvd; breakfast mains $6-9, lunch mains $5-11, dinner mains $11-29; 8am-9:30pm Tue-Sat, 9am-5pm Sun;) We like this superior German-style bakery and cafe for lunch, when skirt-steak sandwiches with blue cheese, homemade bratwurst on sub rolls and vegan mushroom salads bring an upbeat crowd to the sunny patio. Add a German pilsner and a chocolate-mousse tart – with salted caramel – and call it a day.

Drinking & Nightlife

In downtown Durham, if you started out as a mechanic's garage or industrial metal shop, you're probably a hipster coffee shop, craft brewery or bar today. Further west, the Ninth Ave District, along the main drag between Duke's East and West campuses, also buzzes at night.

★ **Cocoa Cinnamon** COFFEE

(Map p248; www.cocoacinnamon.com; 420 W Geer St; 8am-10pm;) If a local says you *must* order a hot chocolate at Cocoa Cinnamon, ask them to be more specific. This former service station, on downtown's northern fringes, offers so many cocoas (along with teas and single-source coffee) that newbies may be paralyzed by the sheer chocolaty awesomeness. All that plus pastries from top Durham bakery Guglhupf!

Fullsteam Brewery BREWERY

(Map p248; 919-682-2337; www.fullsteam.ag; 726 Rigsbee Ave; 4pm-midnight Mon-Thu, 2pm-2am Fri, noon-2am Sat, noon-midnight Sun;) Calling itself a 'plow-to-pint' brewery, Fullsteam has gained national attention for pushing the boundaries of beer with wild, Southernized concoctions. Going out of its way to support local farmers, neighborhood foragers and agricultural entrepreneurs, it uses Carolinian ingredients wherever possible. The excellent taproom features ping-pong, arcade games, cafeteria-style seating and killer T-shirts, and there's live music Sunday evenings.

Beer Study CRAFT BEER

(918-219-7538; http://starpointbrewing.com; 2501 University Dr; 10am-10pm Mon-Thu, 10am-midnight Fri & Sat, noon-10pm Sun;) Part bottle shop, part craft-beer bar, Starpoint Brewing's second Triangle location is a lively oasis, in the otherwise uneventful Rockwood Center strip mall on Durham's south side. Pints cost $5 to $9. They also have a Chapel Hill location (p253).

Entertainment

The intersection of Rigsbee Ave and Geer St, half a mile north of downtown, is a hotbed of bars and music venues. For Triangle entertainment listings, pick up the free weekly *Indy Week* (www.indyweek.com).

Cameron Indoor Stadium BASKETBALL

(Map p248; box office 919-681-2583; www.goduke.com; 115 Whitford Dr) Fans of the Duke University Blue Devils worship inside

Cameron Indoor Stadium, which opened in 1940 and is perhaps the nicest basketball arena on the planet. When there's no scheduled event, you can step inside during normal business hours, and with luck sit in on practice. Off the court, check out old photos and the Duke Hall of Fame.

Motorco Music Hall LIVE MUSIC
(Map p248; ☎919-901-0875; www.motorcomusic.com; 723 Rigsbee Ave; ⊙5pm-midnight Mon, 11:30am-midnight Tue, Wed & Sun, 11:30am-2am Fri & Sat; 📶) This rather beautiful former auto-garage hosts gigs almost every night by local and touring bands, in every conceivable genre. The on-site restaurant, Parts & Labor, sells burgers and world street food.

Durham Bulls Athletic Park STADIUM
(Map p248; ☎box office 919-956-2855; www.dbulls.com; 409 Blackwell St; tickets $7-10) While away a quintessentially American afternoon of beer and watching the Durham Bulls minor-league baseball team, as seen in the 1988 Kevin Costner movie *Bull Durham*. They play between April and early September.

Shopping

Brightleaf Square MALL
(Map p248; www.historicbrightleaf.com; 905 W Main St) Occupying what were originally the Watts and Yuille tobacco warehouses, Brightleaf Square is home to boutiques selling everything from vinyl to gourmet olive oils, plus a few restaurants and breweries.

Information

Set in a former bank building downtown, the **Durham Visitor Info Center** (Map p248; ☎919-687-0288; www.durham-nc.com; 212 W Main St; ⊙9am-5pm Mon, to 6pm Tue-Fri, 11am-7pm Sat, noon-4pm Sun, closed Sun Nov-Mar) offers information, maps and interactive displays.

Getting There & Away

Raleigh-Durham International Airport (p370) is 13 miles southeast of downtown Durham – a ride that costs around $20 in an off-peak Uber. **Greyhound** (☎919-687-4800; www.greyhound.com; 515 W Pettigrew St) sits across the street from **Amtrak** (www.amtrak.com; 601 W Main St), in the **Durham Station Transportation Center** (Map p248; ☎919-485-7433; www.godurhamtransit.org; 515 W Pettigrew St; ⊙8am-midnight Mon-Sat, 7am-9pm Sun), which is also the main downtown interchange for Durham's local bus network.

DON'T MISS

SEE WHERE THE SIT-INS STARTED

The FW Woolworth store where four black students from North Carolina A&T State University sparked the 'sit-in' campaign by ordering coffee on February 1, 1960, is now the **International Civil Rights Center & Museum** (☎336-274-9199; www.sitinmovement.org; 134 S Elm St, Greensboro; adult/child under 13yr $12/8; ⊙10am-6pm Mon-Sat) honoring the 'birthplace of the Civil Rights movement.' Its highlight is the original lunch counter, downstairs, while other exhibits include a no-holds-barred Hall of Shame displaying harrowing photos of atrocities from the era.

Call in advance if you're visiting on a weekday morning; when it's filled with local school groups, independent visitors may not be allowed in. Greensboro is about 50 miles west of Raleigh and 30 miles east of Winston-Salem.

Chapel Hill & Carrboro

☎919 / POP 59,246

While smaller and homier than Raleigh and Durham, its Triangle cohorts, Chapel Hill is a pretty college town that bubbles with life and energy. That's largely due to the 30,000 students – and Tar Heels basketball team – of its University of North Carolina, founded in 1789 as the nation's first state university. While commercialization has increasingly cost Chapel Hill's short downtown strip some of its former charm, its near-neighbor Carrboro remains as appealing as ever. Between the two, they boast some great restaurants and bars, and continue to nurture a dynamic indie rock scene.

Sights

Carolina Basketball Museum MUSEUM
(☎919-962-6000; www.goheels.com; 450 Skipper Bowles Dr, Ernie Williamson Athletics Center; ⊙10am-4pm Mon-Fri, 9am-1pm Sat, hours vary on game days; 🅿) FREE Regardless of allegiances, any basketball fan will appreciate this small but well-done temple to Tar Heel hoops. The numbers say it all – six national championships, 20 final-four appearances, 31 Atlantic Coast Conference (ACC) regular-season championships and 47 NBA first-round draft

picks. Memorabilia, trophies and video footage abound, including Michael Jordan's original signed national letter of intent and other recruiting documents.

University of North Carolina UNIVERSITY
(www.unc.edu) The imposing antebellum buildings of America's oldest public university center on a quad lined with flowering pear trees. Pick up a map either at the university's **visitor center** (919-962-1630; www.unc.edu/visitors; 250 E Franklin St; 9am-5pm Mon-Fri) or the Chapel Hill Visitor Center.

Sleeping

There are frustratingly few hotels close to the action in Chapel Hill, but there are several chain properties within a couple of miles.

★ **Carolina Inn** HOTEL $$$
(919-933-2001; www.carolinainn.com; 211 Pittsboro St; r from $246; P ❄) Even if you're not a Tar Heel, this lovely on-campus inn will win you over with its hospitality and historic touches. The charm starts in the snappy lobby and continues through hallways lined with photos of alumni and championship teams. Classic decor – inspired by Southern antiques – feels fresh in the 185 bright rooms. June through mid-October, stop by on Friday afternoon for live music and food trucks.

Eating

Famously hailed as 'America's foodiest small town,' Chapel Hill is great for dining, with options ranging from budget ethnic places to James Beard Award winners. Cheaper options abound on E Franklin St, close to campus, while W Franklin St becomes more upscale the further west you go – a trend that continues as it segues into E Main St and enters Carrboro.

Vimala's Curryblossom Café INDIAN $
(919-929-3833; www.curryblossom.com; 431 W Franklin St; mains $10-18; 11am-9pm Mon-Thu, to 10pm Fri & Sat;) With its laid-back off-street location and welcoming namesake owner, this courtyard curry house is a hugely popular hideaway for local students. With beef, chicken and lamb on the menu, it's hardly a no-go zone for meat eaters, but the sourdough pancakes in particular make it a haven for vegetarians.

Neal's Deli DELI $
(919-967-2185; www.nealsdeli.com; 100 E Main St, Carrboro; breakfast dishes $3.50-6, lunch dishes $6-9.50; 8am-4pm Tue-Sun;) Start your day by digging into a delicious buttermilk breakfast biscuit at this tiny deli in downtown Carrboro. The egg, cheese and bacon is some kind of good. For lunch, Neal's serves sandwiches and subs, including chicken salad, pastrami and a three-cheese pimento with a splash of bourbon.

★ **Lantern** ASIAN $$$
(919-969-8846; www.lanternrestaurant.com; 423 W Franklin St; mains $25-32; 5:30-10pm Mon-Sat) A strong contender for best dining spot in the entire Triangle, this modern, dinner-only, Asian-fusion spot is very much a farm-to-table affair, with all ingredients sourced from North Carolina. Thank chef Andrea Reusing, a James Beard Award winner, for triumphs such as crispy whole black bass with hot chili, fresh turmeric, dill, fried shallots and roasted peanuts. For dessert? High Rock Farm chestnut crème caramel with poached pears and sorghum snaps.

Drinking & Nightlife

Chapel Hill is renowned for its excellent music scene; look for listings in the free weekly *Indy Week* (www.indyweek.com). As with dining, the most interesting nightlife is concentrated along or just off Franklin St in Chapel Hill and its extension, Main St in Carrboro.

★ **Glasshalfull** WINE BAR
(919-967-9784; http://glasshalfull.net; 106 S Greensboro St, Carrboro; 11:30am-2:30pm & 5-9:30pm Mon-Fri, 5-10pm Sat) OK, so the name doesn't quite roll off the tongue, but everything else about this Carrboro wine bar – sorry, 'wine-centric restaurant' – oozes sleek sophistication. The food is exquisite, with pan-seared scallops or duck confit for dinner, but it's the majestic array of international wines in the adjoining shop, also sold at the bar, that really draws in the crowds.

Crunkleton COCKTAIL BAR
(919-969-1125; www.thecrunkleton.com; 320 W Franklin St; 4pm-2am;) Connoisseurs of classic cocktails should plant themselves down at this long and very serious Chapel

Hill bar, the best in town for mulling over mixology. A perfectly balanced blend of tang and bite, the Modern Cocktail – blended whiskey, sloe gin, fresh-squeezed lemon, absinthe and bitters – deserves a Nobel Peace Prize. Cocktails go for $10 to $14.

Beer Study CRAFT BEER
(919-240-5423; www.facebook.com/BeerStudyNC; 106 N Graham St; noon-midnight Sun-Thu, noon-1am Fri, 11am-1am Sat;) Half bar, half bottle shop, and a refreshingly grungy alternative to Chapel Hill's smattering of breweries, this place offers 18 taps of local and regional craft beer and more than 500 bottles. City ordinances impose plastic cups on dog-friendly establishments, but that's a small price to pay for pup. Pints cost $3 to $7, and you can buy burgers next door.

Open Eye Cafe COFFEE
(919-968-9410; www.openeyecafe.com; 101 S Greensboro St, Carrboro; 7am-11pm Mon-Thu, to midnight Fri & Sat, 8am-10pm Sun;) The best coffeehouse in both Chapel Hill and Carrboro has been a fixture for 20 years, and its single cavernous space buzzes with students from early morning onwards. It sells beer and wine as well as coffee, but the only food is a small array of baked goods.

Top of the Hill PUB
(919-929-8676; www.thetopofthehill.com; 100 E Franklin St; 11am-2am) The 3rd-story patio of this downtown restaurant and microbrewery, nicknamed TOPO and serving organic spirits from its own distillery, is where the Chapel Hill preppy set flock to see and be seen after football games. Consider yourself warned – it can get very fratty.

Entertainment

Dean Smith Center STADIUM
(919-962-2296; www.goheels.com; 300 Skipper Bowles Dr; box office 8am-5pm Mon-Fri) There are no tours of the Tar Heels' home, but basketball fans can visit the 2nd and 3rd floors during business hours. It's named for legendary coach Dean Smith, who retired with 879 career wins and two national titles. Current coach Roy Williams has now won three titles, picking up the third in 2017, which puts him ahead.

Cat's Cradle LIVE MUSIC
(919-967-9053; www.catscradle.com; 300 E Main St, Carrboro) Everyone from Nirvana to Arcade Fire has played the Cradle, which has been hosting the cream of the indie-music world for four decades. Most shows are all-ages.

Shopping

Weaver Street Market MARKET
(919-929-0010; www.weaverstreetmarket.com; 101 E Weaver St, Carrboro; 7am-10pm;) The grocery co-op at Weaver Street Market serves Carrboro as an informal town square, with live music and free wi-fi, and the gift and crafts stores of the restored Carr Mill alongside.

Information

The friendly staff at the **Orange County Visitor Center** (919-245-4320; www.visitchapelhill.org; 501 W Franklin St; 8:30am-5pm Mon-Fri, 10am-3pm Sat) offer copious amounts of information and advice on Chapel Hill and the surrounding area.

Getting There & Away

Raleigh-Durham International Airport (p370) is 18 miles east of Chapel Hill, a journey that costs around $25 in an off-peak Uber.

ONLY CONNECT

Carrboro is especially wired, with wi-fihot spots in assorted businesses and locations all over town joining to create one big free network. Connect to 'tocwireless.net.'

Coastal North Carolina

Includes ➡

Best Places to Eat

- ➡ PinPoint (p280)
- ➡ Dank Burrito (p276)
- ➡ Kill Devil Grill (p264)
- ➡ Eduardo's Taco Stand (p271)
- ➡ Little Dipper (p280)

Best Places to Stay

- ➡ Inn on Turner (p275)
- ➡ Sanderling Resort & Spa (p263)
- ➡ Sea Monkey Hostel & Kite School (p271)
- ➡ Pam's Pelican B&B (p271)
- ➡ CW Worth House (p279)

Why Go?

The coastline of North Carolina stretches more than 300 miles. Remarkably, it remains underdeveloped and the beach is often visible from coastal roads. Yes, the wall of cottages stretching south from Corolla to Kitty Hawk can seem endless, but for the most part the state's shores remain free of flashy, highly commercialized resort areas. Instead you'll find rugged, windswept barrier islands, Colonial villages once frequented by pirates, and laid-back beach towns full of locally owned ice-cream shops and mom-and-pop motels. Even the most touristy beaches have a small-town vibe.

For solitude, head to the isolated Outer Banks (OBX), where fishermen and women still make their living hauling in shrimp and the older locals speak in an archaic British-tinged brogue. Further south, groovy Wilmington is known as a center of film and TV production, and its surrounding beaches are popular with local spring breakers and tourists.

When to Go

- ➡ Few hotels and restaurants remain open between November and March, but there's a blustery beauty about the region.
- ➡ In April and May, the weather is turning fine but accommodation deals can still be found.
- ➡ The sun is out, towns are busy and major events take place from July to September.

OUTER BANKS

The Outer Banks are fragile ribbons of sand tracing the coastline for more than 100 miles, separated from the mainland by sounds and waterways. From north to south, barrier islands Bodie (pronounced 'body'), Roanoke, Hatteras and Ocracoke, essentially large sandbars, are linked by bridges and ferries. The far-northern communities Corolla (kur-all-ah), Duck and Southern Shores are former duck-hunting grounds for the wealthy, and are quiet and upscale. Nearly contiguous Bodie Island towns Kitty Hawk, Kill Devil Hills and Nags Head are developed and more populated. Roanoke Island, west of Bodie, offers Colonial history and the quaint waterfront town Manteo (p266). Further south, Hatteras Island is a protected national seashore with tiny villages and a wild, windswept beauty. At Outer Banks' southern end, shuck oysters and weave hammocks on Ocracoke Island (p268), accessible only by ferry.

Sights

Corolla, the northernmost town on Hwy 158, is famed for its wild horses. Descendants of Colonial Spanish mustangs, the horses roam the northern dunes, and numerous commercial outfitters go in search of them. The ribbon of Cape Hatteras National Seashore, broken up by villages, is home to several noteworthy lighthouses. A meandering drive down Hwy 12, which makes up part of the Outer Banks National Scenic Byway (and its 21 villages), is one of the great American road trips.

If you're driving on some beaches in the Outer Banks, or within Cape Hatteras National Seashore, you'll need an off-road-vehicle (ORV) permit ($50 valid for 10 days). See www.outerbanks.org/plan-your-trip/beaches/driving-on-beach for more info.

Cape Hatteras National Seashore ISLAND

(Map p260; ☎252-475-9000; www.nps.gov/caha) Extending 70 miles from south of Nags Head to the south end of Ocracoke Island, this necklace of islands remains blissfully free from overdevelopment. Natural attractions include local and migratory water birds, marshes, woodlands, dunes and miles of empty beaches; historic lighthouses such as those on Cape Hatteras (p258), Bodie Island (p258) and Ocracoke (p270) are also part of the park.

> **HURRICANE FLORENCE**
>
> On September 14, 2018, Hurricane Florence made landfall outside of Wilmington, North Carolina. The 500-mile-wide storm dropped about 35 inches of rain over the next three days. Damage was not confined solely to the coast. As rivers rose, flooding took a toll on inland communities, including significant damage to state and local highways .

Wright Brothers National Memorial PARK, MUSEUM

(Map p260; ☎252-473-2111; www.nps.gov/wrbr; Prospect Ave off 1000 N Croatan Hwy, Kitty Hawk; adult/child under 16yr $7/free; ⏰9am-5pm) Self-taught engineers Wilbur and Orville Wright launched the world's first successful airplane flight on December 17, 1903 (it lasted 12 seconds). A boulder marks the take-off spot. Climb a nearby hill, where the brothers conducted glider experiments, for fantastic views of sea and sound. The on-site Wright Brothers Visitor Center has a reproduction of the 1903 flyer and exhibits, but was under renovation at the time of research. It should be open again by the time you read this.

Whalehead Club HISTORIC BUILDING

(Map p260; ☎252-453-9040; www.visitcurrituck.com; 1160 Village Lane, Corolla; adult/child 6-12yr $7/5; ⏰tours 10am-4pm Mon-Sat) The sunflower-yellow, art nouveau-style Whale-head Club, built in the 1920s as a hunting 'cottage' for a Philadelphia industrialist, is the centerpiece of the well-manicured Currituck Heritage Park in the village of Corolla. Tours take about 45 minutes and are self-guided. Visitors can learn about the history of the property and explore its art-nouveau ornamentation – including Tiffany glass sconces, a Victorian safe, and a Steinway & Sons grand piano. Tour times may vary in winter (November to March).

Alligator River National Wildlife Refuge WILDLIFE RESERVE

(Map p260; ☎252-473-1131; www.fws.gov/refuge/alligator_river; Milltail Rd, East Lake) FREE Although not strictly on an Outer Banks island (it's part of the mainland), this 154,000-acre wildlife

Coastal North Carolina Highlights

1 Olympus Dive Center (p273) Diving the waters of the Crystal Coast, home to more than 2000 sunken ships.

2 Fort Macon State Park (p273) Stepping back in time inside this remarkable five-sided fort built in 1834, with 26 vaulted rooms, plus 360-degree views from its roof.

3 PinPoint (p280) Trying true Southern-style farm-to-table cooking at this fine-dining Wilmington restaurant.

4 Sea Monkey Hostel & Kite School (p271) Zooming across the water propelled by wind energy with the friendly instructors from Ocracoke.

5 Eduardo's Taco Stand (p271) Inhaling the best Mexican food on North Carolina's coast at this unassuming Ocracoke food truck.

6 Mill Whistle Brewing (p277) Joining the locals in this hidden Beaufort brewery.

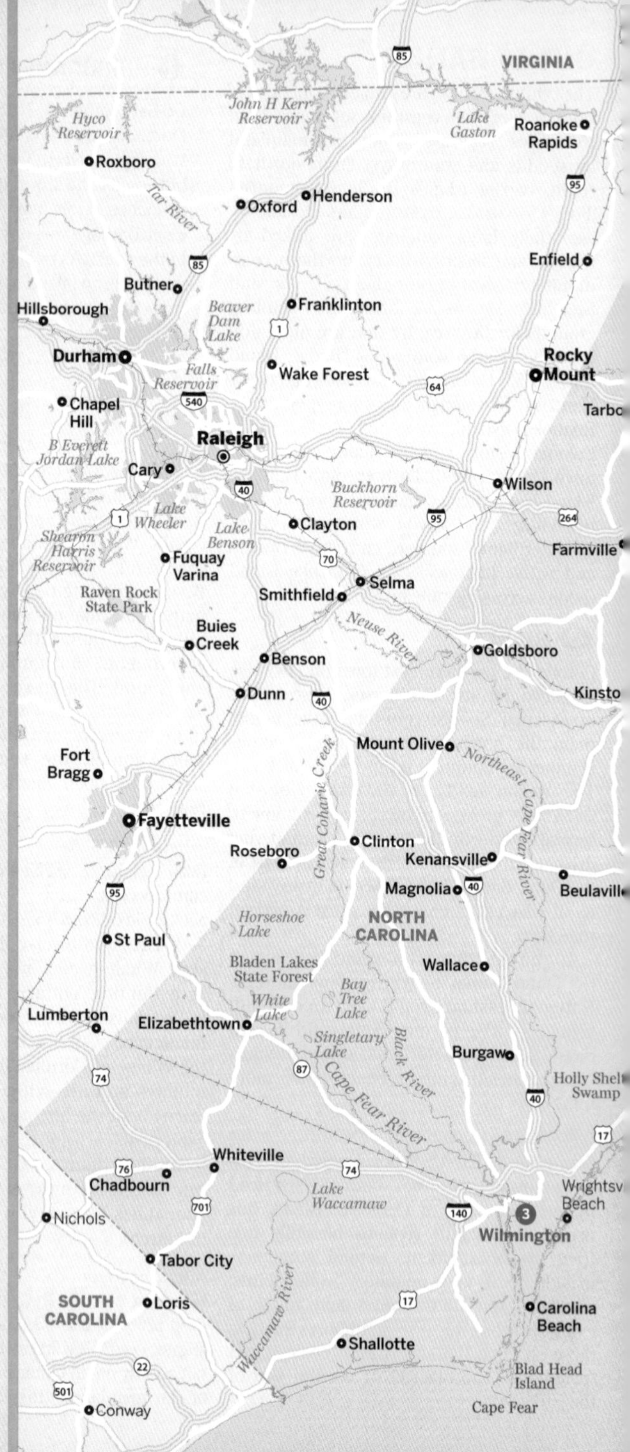

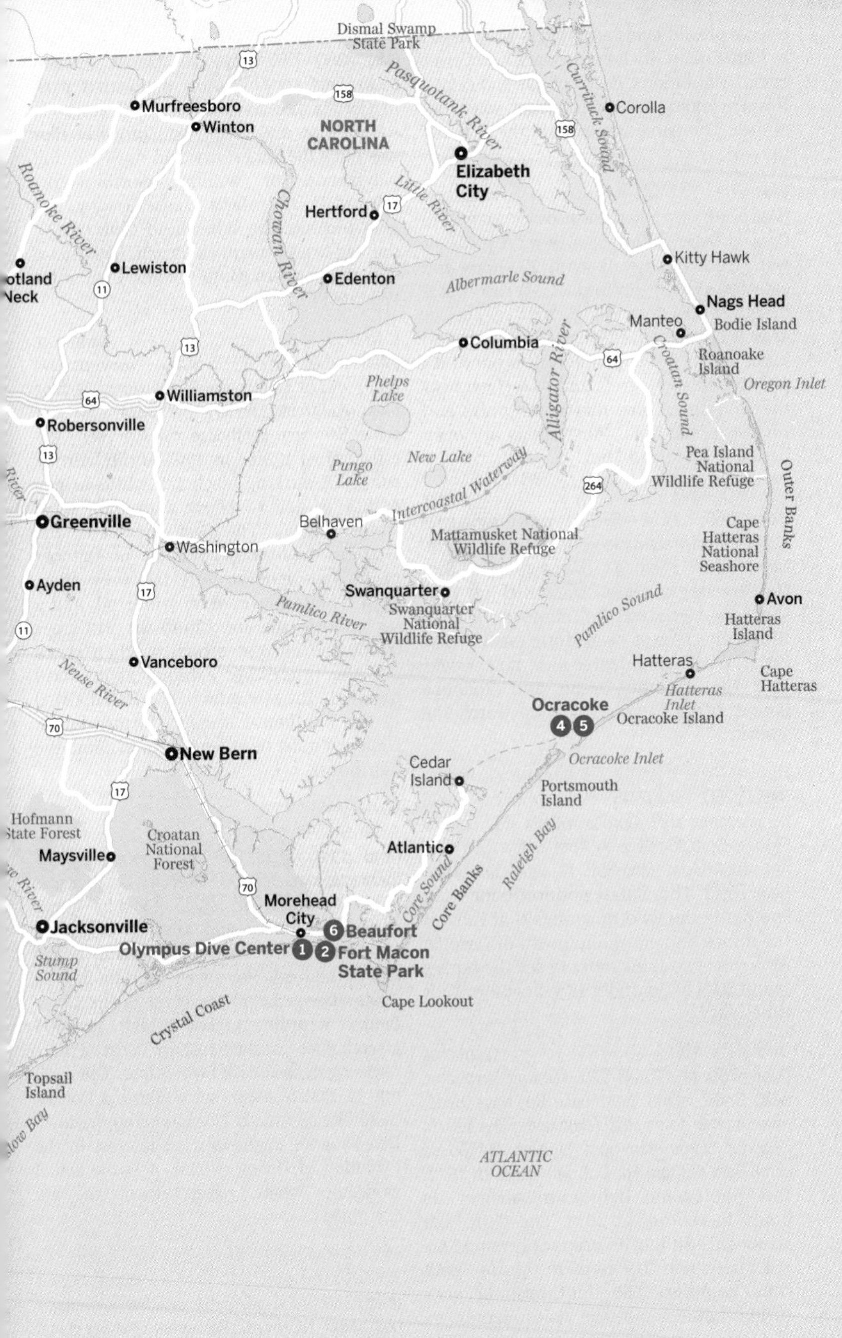

Dismal Swamp State Park
Murfreesboro
Winton
NORTH CAROLINA
Pasquotank River
Currituck Sound
Corolla
Elizabeth City
Hertford
Little River
Roanoke River
Chowan River
Lewiston
Edenton
Albermarle Sound
Kitty Hawk
Nags Head
Bodie Island
Manteo
Columbia
Alligator River
Croatan Sound
Roanoake Island
Oregon Inlet
Williamston
Robersonville
Phelps Lake
Pungo Lake
New Lake
Intercoastal Waterway
Pea Island National Wildlife Refuge
Outer Banks
Greenville
Washington
Belhaven
Mattamusket National Wildlife Refuge
Cape Hatteras National Seashore
Ayden
Swanquarter
Swanquarter National Wildlife Refuge
Pamlico River
Pamlico Sound
Avon
Hatteras Island
Vanceboro
Neuse River
Hatteras
Cape Hatteras
Hatteras Inlet
Ocracoke
4
5
Ocracoke Island
Ocracoke Inlet
New Bern
Cedar Island
Portsmouth Island
Hofmann State Forest
Croatan National Forest
Maysville
Atlantic
Raleigh Bay
Core Sound
Core Banks
Morehead City
Jacksonville
6
Beaufort
Olympus Dive Center
1
2
Fort Macon State Park
Stump Sound
Cape Lookout
Crystal Coast
Topsail Island
ATLANTIC OCEAN
0
100 km
0
50 miles

reserve of wild lands and waters is managed by Dare County. It's home to black bears, river otters, wild turkeys, deer, bobcats and eagles. If you're hoping to see an alligator, you're out of luck. The name comes from the shape of the park.

Waterfront Shops & Boardwalk WATERFRONT

(Map p260; www.waterfrontshopsduck.com; 1240 Duck Rd, Duck; ⌚10am-5pm; P 👪) A pleasant waterfront boardwalk with 27 shops and eateries dotted around it. Peruse local design shops, do a Village Yoga session, or grab a bottle of locally produced olive oil here. When fewer people are around, it's possible to spot egrets and waterfowl near the short pier, plus martins, ospreys and turtles in the area. Most shops are open between 10am and 5pm.

Jockey's Ridge State Park STATE PARK

(Map p260; ☎252-441-7132; www.ncparks.gov/jockeys-ridge-state-park; 300 W Carolista Dr, Nags Head; ⌚8am-9pm May-Aug, varies Sep-Mar depending on sunset) FREE Kick off your shoes for a leg-stretching climb up Jockey's Ridge, the largest sand dune on the East Coast. With a 360-degree view that sweeps over the Atlantic Ocean and Roanoke Sound, it's a gorgeous spot to watch the sunset.

Corolla Wild Horse Fund Museum MUSEUM

(Map p260; ☎252-453-8002; www.corollawildhorses.com; 1129 Corolla Village Rd, Corolla; ⌚10am-5pm Mon-Fri, to 4pm Sat & Sun Oct-Apr, 10am-4pm Mon-Sat, to 2pm Sun May-Sep) FREE This small nonprofit museum spotlights the wild mustangs that inhabit the dunes and shoreline north of Corolla. Also runs two-hour tours to see the horses (adult $45, child under 13 years $20). Tour times vary.

Bodie Island Lighthouse LIGHTHOUSE

(Map p260; ☎252-441-5711; www.nps.gov/caha; 8210 Bodie Island Lighthouse Rd, Nags Head; museum free, tours adult/child under 11yr $10/5; ⌚visitor center 9am-5pm Jan-Dec, lighthouse climb 9am-4:30pm Apr-Oct; 👪) Built in 1872, this photogenic lighthouse opened its doors to visitors in 2013. The 170ft-high structure still has its original Fresnel lens – a rarity. It is 219 steps to the top, with nine landings. The lighthouse keeper's former home is now the visitor center.

Historic Corolla Park PARK

(Map p260; 1160 Village Lane, Corolla; ⌚dawn-dusk) This very pleasant manicured park in Corolla preserves 39 acres of gorgeous sound-front and sound-side property that was once the waterfowl- and duck-hunting playground of wealthy Northeasterns Edward C. and Marie Louise Knight. The park includes the Whalehead Club (p255), the red-brick Currituck Beach Lighthouse and the modern Outer Banks Center for Wildlife Education.

Cape Hatteras Lighthouse LIGHTHOUSE

(Map p260; ☎252-475-9000; www.nps.gov/caha; 46379 Lighthouse Rd, Buxton; climbing tours adult/child under 12yr $8/4; ⌚visitor center 9am-5pm, lighthouse to 4:30pm early Apr-early Oct) At 193ft (or 198ft to the lighting rod), this striking black-and-white-striped edifice is one of North Carolina's most iconic images. The first version of the Hatteras Lighthouse was lit in October of 1803, a modest 90ft tall back then, with a lamp powered by whale oil, and a sandstone structure. Climb the 248 steps inside the current structure, then check out the interesting exhibits about local history in the **Museum of the Sea**, located in the lighthouse keeper's former home. Children must be at least 42in to climb the lighthouse.

Graveyard of the Atlantic Museum MUSEUM

(Map p260; ☎252-986-2995; www.graveyardoftheatlantic.com; 59200 Museum Dr, Hattaras; ⌚10am-4pm Mon-Sat) FREE Exhibits about shipwrecks, piracy and salvaged cargo are highlights at this maritime museum at the end of the road. There have been more than 2000 shipwrecks off the coast of the Outer Banks. According to one exhibit, in 2006 a container washed ashore near Frisco, releasing thousands of Doritos bags. One local told us that residents were enjoying Doritos casseroles for months! Donations appreciated. Dive fanatics might take an interest in the Evolution of Diving exhibit, plus the actual workshop where recent discoveries are examined.

Pea Island National Wildlife Refuge WILDLIFE RESERVE

(Map p260; ☎252-987-2394; www.fws.gov/refuge/pea_island; NC Hwy 12, Rodanthe; ⌚visitor center 9am-4pm, trails dawn-dusk) At the northern end of Hatteras Island, and named after the dune peas that grow in the sand, this 5834-acre (land portion only) reserve is a bird-watcher's heaven, with two nature trails (both are fully accessible to people with disabilities) and 13 miles of unspoiled beach for the 365 recorded species here. Viewer scopes inside the visitor center overlook an adjacent pond. Check the online calendar for details about guided bird walks, turtle talks and canoe tours.

Currituck Banks Maritime Forest Trail WILDLIFE RESERVE
(Map p260; ☎252-261-8891; btwn Ocean Trail & N Beach Access Rd; Ⓟ) A hidden 0.3-mile Boardwalk Trail (with disabled access) and a 0.75-mile Maritime Forest Trail snake through sections of the 950-acre Currituck Banks Reserve. These walks take visitors through various terrains – sand dunes, salt marsh and maritime swamp forest and onto a tranquil view of Currituck Sound. Look for owls, egrets, lizards, osprey and more. Wear mosquito repellent in the warmer months. Find it before you reach Corolla Beach (access by 4WD only); there's a small parking lot at the trailhead.

Frisco Native America Museum MUSEUM
(Map p260; ☎252-995-4440; http://nativeamericanmuseum.org; 53536 NC-12, Frisco; $5, family $15; ⏲10:30am-5pm Tue-Sun) Showcasing historic artifacts about the original inhabitants of the Outer Banks. Collectors' items come from all over the USA and include everything from masks and woven baskets to rare headdresses, instruments and tribal police badges.

Currituck Beach Lighthouse LIGHTHOUSE
(Map p260; www.currituckbeachlight.com; 1101 Corolla Village Rd, Corolla; adult/child under 8yr $10/free; ⏲9am-5pm late Mar-late Nov) You'll climb 220 steps to get to the top of this red-brick lighthouse, which is still in operation. The light from its Fresnal lens can be seen from 18 nautical miles. Cash or check only.

Outer Banks Center for Wildlife Education MUSEUM
(Map p260; ☎252-453-0221; 1160 Village Lane, Corolla; ⏲9am-5pm Mon-Fri; 👪) FREE This modern education center has an 8000-gallon aquarium and a life-size marsh diorama with a duck blind. Don't miss the 20-minute film about area history. Offers lots of kids' classes and activities.

Activities

The same strong wind that helped the Wright brothers launch their biplane, today propels windsurfers, sailboats and hang gliders. Other popular activities include kayaking, fishing, cycling, horse tours, stand-up paddleboarding, surfing and scuba diving. The coastal waters kick up between August and October, creating perfect conditions for bodysurfing.

Radikal Kiteboarding KITESURFING
(Map p260; ☎252-489-0451; www.radikalkiteboarding.com; 24202 NC Hwy 12, Rodanthe; 2-person lessons per hr $85, private lessons per hr $127.50; ⏲lesson times vary) Learn this extreme sport with this recommended local company owned by Ed Tack, who has more than a decade of experience teaching kiteboarding in the Outer Banks.

Village Yoga YOGA
(Map p260; ☎252-564-2219; https://duckvillageyoga.com; 1240 Duck Rd, Duck; drop-in classes $17) Practice your downward-facing dog next to the relaxing Atlantic Ocean inlet of Currituck Sound. Drop-in classes range from beginner to advanced and run all year round. Yogis wanting to feel the sand between their toes and hear the waves as they stretch can arrange sessions on the beach, with advance notice.

Natural Art Surf Shop SURFING
(Map p260; ☎252-995-5682; www.surfintheeye.com; 47331 NC Hwy 12, Buxton; surfboards/wetsuits/paddleboards per day $10/5/35; ⏲9am-8pm; 👪) Friendly surf shop offering board rentals and surf lessons. Stop in to rummage through the racks for beach gear and check the local surf report.

ROAD TRIP TIPS

Hwy 12, also called Virginia Dare Trail or 'the coast road,' runs close to the Atlantic for the length of the Outer Banks. Hwy 158/Croatan Hwy, usually called 'the Bypass,' begins just north of Kitty Hawk and merges with Hwy 64 as it crosses on to Roanoke Island. Locations are often given in terms of 'mile posts' (Mile or MP), beginning with Mile 0 at the foot of the Wright Memorial Bridge at Kitty Hawk.

Outer Banks

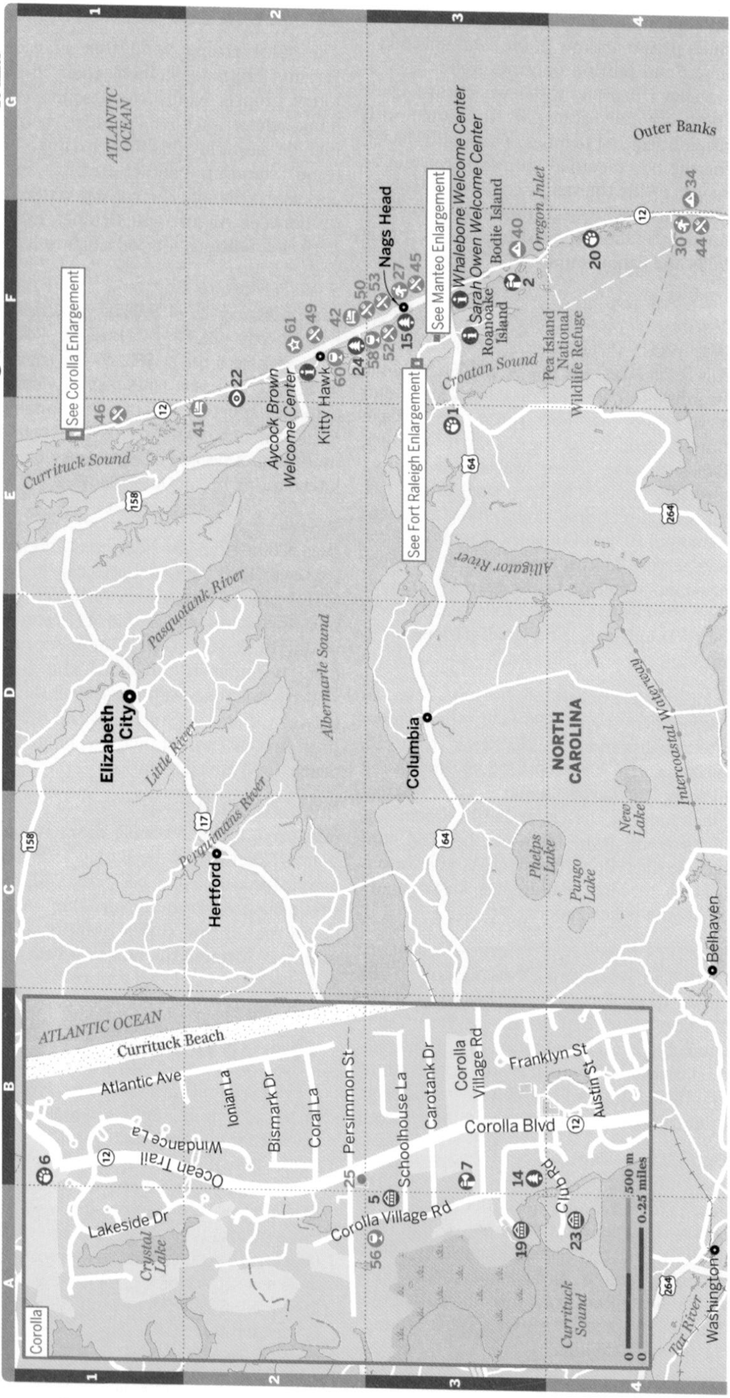

0 40 km
0 20 miles

Corolla
6
Lakeside Dr
Crystal Lake
Ocean Trail
Windance La
Atlantic Ave
Currituck Beach
ATLANTIC OCEAN
Ionian La
Bismark Dr
Coral La
25
Persimmon St
56
5
Corolla Village Rd
Schoolhouse La
Carotank Dr
7
Corolla Village Rd
Corolla Blvd
19
14
Franklyn St
Currituck Sound
23
Club Rd
Austin St
0 500 m
0 0.25 miles

Elizabeth City
Little River
Pasquotank River
Hertford
Perquimans River
Albermarle Sound
Columbia
Phelps Lake
Pungo Lake
NORTH CAROLINA
New Lake
Intercoastal Waterway
Alligator River
Tar River
Washington
Belhaven
Currituck Sound
See Corolla Enlargement
46
41
22
Aycock Brown Welcome Center
61
49
Kitty Hawk
60
42
24
50
58
53
52
Nags Head
27
15
45
See Fort Raleigh Enlargement
See Manteo Enlargement
1
Croatan Sound
Whalebone Welcome Center
Sarah Owen Welcome Center
Roanoake Island
Bodie Island
2
40
Oregon Inlet
Pea Island National Wildlife Refuge
20
30
34
44
ATLANTIC OCEAN
Outer Banks

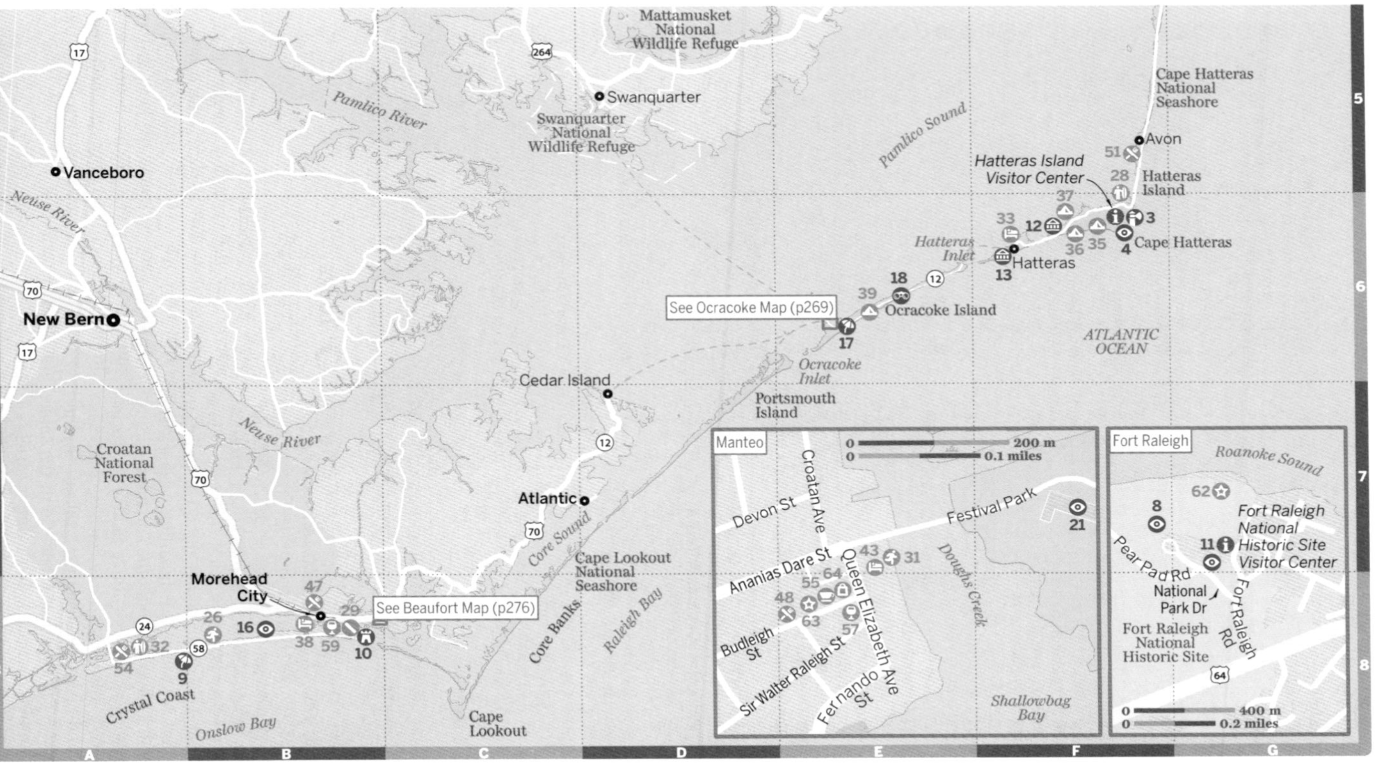

Mattamusket National Wildlife Refuge
Swanquarter
Swanquarter National Wildlife Refuge
Pamlico River
Vanceboro
Neuse River
New Bern
Pamlico Sound
Cape Hatteras National Seashore
Avon
Hatteras Island Visitor Center
Hatteras Island
Cape Hatteras
Hatteras Inlet
Hatteras
Ocracoke Island
See Ocracoke Map (p269)
ATLANTIC OCEAN
Ocracoke Inlet
Portsmouth Island
Cedar Island
Croatan National Forest
Atlantic
Core Sound
Cape Lookout National Seashore
Core Banks
Raleigh Bay
Morehead City
See Beaufort Map (p276)
Crystal Coast
Onslow Bay
Cape Lookout
Manteo
0 200 m
0 0.1 miles
Devon St
Croatan Ave
Festival Park
Ananias Dare St
Queen Elizabeth Ave
Doughs Creek
Budleigh St
Sir Walter Raleigh St
Fernando St
Shallowbag Bay
Fort Raleigh
Roanoke Sound
Fort Raleigh National Historic Site Visitor Center
Pear Pad Rd
National Park Dr
Fort Raleigh Rd
Fort Raleigh National Historic Site
0 400 m
0 0.2 miles

Outer Banks

Sights

1 Alligator River National Wildlife Refuge E3
2 Bodie Island Lighthouse F3
3 Cape Hatteras Lighthouse F6
4 Cape Hatteras National Seashore F6
5 Corolla Wild Horse Fund Museum A3
6 Currituck Banks Maritime Forest Trail B1
7 Currituck Beach Lighthouse B3
8 Elizabethan Gardens F7
9 Emerald Isle Beach A8
10 Fort Macon State Park B8
11 Fort Raleigh National Historic Site G7
12 Frisco Native America Museum F6
13 Graveyard of the Atlantic Museum F6
14 Historic Corolla Park B3
15 Jockey's Ridge State Park F3
16 North Carolina Aquarium B8
17 Ocracoke Beach E6
18 Ocracoke Pony Pen E6
19 Outer Banks Center for Wildlife Education A3
20 Pea Island National Wildlife Refuge F4
21 Roanoke Island Festival Park F7
22 Waterfront Shops & Boardwalk F2
23 Whalehead Club A4
24 Wright Brothers National Memorial F2

Activities, Courses & Tours

25 Corolla Outback Adventures B2
26 Island Water Sports Rentals B8
27 Kitty Hawk Kites F3
28 Natural Art Surf Shop F5
29 Olympus Dive Center B8
30 Radikal Kiteboarding F4
31 Sail Outer Banks E7
32 South Swell Surf Shop A8
Village Yoga .... (see 22)

Sleeping

33 Breakwater Inn F6
34 Cape Hatteras KOA Resort G4
35 Cape Point Campground F6
36 Frisco Campground F6
37 Frisco Woods Campground F6
38 Hampton Inn Morehead City B8
39 Ocracoke Campgrounds E6
40 Oregon Inlet Campground F3
41 Sanderling Resort & Spa E2
42 Shutters on the Banks F2
43 Tranquil House Inn E7

Eating

1587 Restaurant .... (see 43)
44 Atlantic Coast Cafe F4
45 Blue Moon Beach Grill F3
Blue Point .... (see 22)
Breakwater Restaurant .... (see 33)
46 Butcher Block E1
47 El's Drive-In B8
48 Hungry Pelican E8
49 John's Drive-In F2
50 Kill Devil Grill F3
51 Oceanas Bistro F5
52 Slice Pizzeria F3
53 Tortugas' Lie F3
54 Trading Post; Southern Food & Spirits A8

Drinking & Nightlife

55 Charis Coffee Company E8
Duck's Cottage .... (see 22)
56 Juice Jar A3
57 Lost Colony Brewery & Cafe E8
58 Outer Banks Brewing Station F3
59 Promised Land Market B8
60 Trio F2

Entertainment

61 Art's Place F2
62 Lost Colony Outdoor Drama G7
63 Ye Olde Pioneer Theatre E8

Shopping

64 Dare County Arts Council E8
Island Bookstore .... (see 56)

Kitty Hawk Kites ADVENTURE SPORTS

(Map p260; 252-441-6800; www.kittyhawk.com; 3933 S Croatan Hwy, Jockey's Ridge Crossing, Nags Head; bikes per day $15, kayaks per 2hr $39, SUP per hr/day $29/59; 9am-6pm) In business more than 30 years, Kitty Hawk Kites has several locations along the OBX coast. It offers beginners' kiteboarding lessons (five hours, $400) in Rodanthe and hang-gliding lessons at Jockey's Ridge State Park (from $109). Also rents out kayaks, sailboats, stand-up paddleboards, bikes, in-line skates (at Kitty Hawk Surf Co in the same shopping complex), and offers a variety of tours and courses.

Tours

Corolla Outback Adventures TOURS

(Map p260; 252-453-4484; www.corollaoutback.com; 1150 Ocean Trail, Corolla; 2hr tour adult/child under 13yr $50/25) Tour operator Jay Bender, whose family started Corolla's first guide service, knows his local history and his local horses. Tours bounce you down the beach and through the dunes to see the wild mustangs that roam the northern Outer Banks.

Sleeping

Crowds swarm the Outer Banks in high season (April to October), so reserve ahead. The area has few massive chain hotels, but hundreds of small motels, rental cottages and B&Bs; the visitor centers offer referrals.

The National Park Service runs four campgrounds on the islands, which feature cold-water showers and flush toilets. You'll enjoy close proximity to the coast at these campsites, but you won't find many trees for shade.

Cape Hatteras KOA Resort CAMPGROUND $
(Map p260; 252-987-2307; https://koa.com/campgrounds/cape-hatteras; 25094 NC Hwy 12, Rodanthe; tent sites with hookup & water from $64, RV sites with hookup from $64, 4-person cabins from $104;) Beachfront campground open all year, with lots of facilities (including a hot tub) and sites for RVs and tents, plus cabin accommodation. Kayak and paddleboard rental are available on-site. There's a cafe, a Wednesday outdoor cinema, and Monday-night bingo during high season (May to September). Tent and RV sites accommodate up to six people.

Frisco Woods Campground CAMPGROUND $
(Map p260; 252-995-5208; www.thefriscowoodscampground.com; 53124 NC Hwy 12, Frisco; tent sites without hookup & water $32-40, tent sites with hookup & water $40-54, 4-person cabin $55-85; Mar-Nov;) This family-friendly waterfront campsite is welcoming and tidy; the cabins are one of the best deals in the area, but book up quickly. Plenty of facilities on-site including a laundry, camp store, kayak rentals ($15 per hour) and dishwashing areas, and the campground allows portable barbecue use.

Cape Point Campground CAMPGROUND $
(Map p260; 252-465-9602; www.recreation.gov; 46700 Lighthouse Rd, Buxton; tent sites without hookup $20; Apr-late Nov) The largest campground on Cape Hatteras National Seashore with some 199 sites, plus four sets of restrooms and outdoor shower facilities.

Frisco Campground CAMPGROUND $
(Map p260; 252-995-5101; www.recreation.gov; 53415 Billy Mitchell Rd, Frisco; tent sites without hookup $28; Apr-late Nov) Near Cape Hatteras Lighthouse. Offers more than 120 sites with paved parking, a picnic table and a charcoal grill for cooking.

Oregon Inlet Campground CAMPGROUND $
(Map p260; 252-441-6246; www.recreation.gov; 12001 NC Hwy 12, Nags Head; tent sites $28, RV without hookup $28; Apr-late Nov) Near Bodie Island Lighthouse, Oregon Inlet is the northernmost campground on Cape Hatteras National Seashore. Facilities include more than 100 sites, plus flushing toilets and unheated showers.

Breakwater Inn MOTEL $$
(Map p260; 252-986-2565; www.breakwaterhatteras.com; 57896 NC Hwy 12, Hattaras; r/ste from $179/213, motel r from $117;) The end of the road doesn't look so bad at this three-story shingled inn. Rooms come with kitchenette and a private deck with views, and are some of the most affordable in the area. Want to make further savings? Try one of the older 'Fisherman's Quarters' rooms, with microwave and refrigerator. The inn is near the Hatteras–Ocracoke ferry landing.

Shutters on the Banks HOTEL $$
(Map p260; 252-441-5581; www.shuttersonthebanks.com; 405 S Virginia Dare Trail, Kill Devil Hills; r no ocean view/ocean view from $149/209, honeymoon ste from $499;) Centrally located in Kill Devil Hills, this welcoming 88-room beachfront hotel exudes a snappy, colorful style with pastel tones and beach art on the walls. The inviting rooms come with plantation windows and colorful art as well as flat-screen TV, refrigerator and microwave. Some rooms come with a full kitchen. Renovated 'Tower' rooms are even more inviting.

Sanderling Resort & Spa RESORT $$$
(Map p260; 855-412-7866; www.sanderling-resort.com; 1461 Duck Rd, Duck; r $279-459, ste from $519;) Remodeled rooms have given this posh place a stylish feel. Decor is impeccably tasteful, and the attached balconies are an inviting place to enjoy the ocean sounds and breezes. Plus, the resort offers sunrise yoga on the beach. Open year-round. Standard room deals from $119 in low season.

The property includes several restaurants and bars, and a spa offering luxe massage. Daily resort fee is $30 from mid-May to October, $15 from November to mid-May.

Eating

The main tourist strip on Bodie Island has the most restaurants and nightlife options. Many places are only open Memorial Day (last Monday in May) through early fall (September and October), or have reduced hours in the off-season (November to March). Obviously, seafood is what's for dinner.

Slice Pizzeria PIZZA $
(Map p260; ☎252-449-8888; www.slicepizzeriaobx.com; 710 S Croatan Hwy, Kill Devil Hills; slices from $2, 14in pizzas from $12.95, calzones from $11.95; ⏰11am-9pm; P📶🍴👪) Excellent budget option for a quick bite, with a few inside tables. This casual independent fast-food joint serves NYC- and Chicago-style pizza baked in a proper stone oven. The White Pizza comes with broccoli or spinach, with sliced tomatoes, garlic ricotta and mozzarella, while the Natural Gourmet has plum tomato sauce, fresh basil, olive oil and whole-milk mozzarella.

Off-season deals include two slices and a drink for $5.95 on Tuesdays, Wednesdays and Thursdays. Still hungry? Sides of buffalo wings, mozzarella sticks and onion rings will fill the gap. Takeout and delivery available.

Butcher Block SANDWICHES $
(Map p260; ☎252-453-3663; www.obxbutcherblock.com; Monterey Plaza, 807 Ocean Trail, Corolla; $7-9; ⏰10am-5pm Mon-Thu, to 6pm Sat & Sun) Located in a strip mall, you could easily miss this top spot for local barbecue-ready fresh meat and seafood, plus enormous freshly made sandwiches and craft beers to take out. There are two small tables in the store, if you must eat in. Closes when the season slows down in winter.

John's Drive-In SEAFOOD, ICE CREAM $
(Map p260; www.johnsdrivein.com; 3716 N Virginia Dare Trail, Kitty Hawk; mains $6-10, ice cream from $3.25; ⏰11am-5pm Thu-Tue May-Oct) A Kitty Hawk institution for perfectly fried boats (trays) of shrimp or crab cakes, to be eaten at outdoor picnic tables and washed down with one of many possible milkshake combinations – like M&M, peanut butter, Oreo, mint chocolate chip, pineapple and cherry, to name but a few. Some folks just come for a burger and some soft-serve ice cream. It closes down off season.

★ Kill Devil Grill SEAFOOD, AMERICAN $$
(Map p260; ☎252-449-8181; www.thekilldevilgrill.com; 2008 S Virginia Dare Trail, Kill Devil Hills; lunch $7-13, dinner $10-22; ⏰11:30am-9pm Tue-Thu, to 10pm Fri & Sat) Yowza, this place is good. It's also historic – the entrance is a 1939 dining car that's listed in the National Register of Historic Places. Pub grub and seafood arrive with tasty flair, and portions are generous. Check out the specials, and things like prime ribs or sea scallops, where the kitchen can really shine. Often closed between December and January.

★ Blue Moon Beach Grill SEAFOOD, SANDWICHES $$
(Map p260; ☎252-261-2583; www.bluemoonbeachgrill.com; 4104 S Virginia Dare Trail, Nags Head; mains $10-29; ⏰11:30am-9pm) Would it be wrong to write an ode to a side of french fries? Because Lord Almighty, the lightly spiced fries at this casual hot spot are the stuff of sonnets and monologues. And we haven't even mentioned the BLT with seared mahi-mahi, applewood bacon, local Currituck tomatoes and a jalapeño rémoulade for slathering.

Other choices include seafood sandwiches, burgers and voodoo pasta. The strip-mall view won't inspire poetry, but the friendly staff, come-as-you-are atmosphere and upbeat play list – Elvis's 'Jailhouse Rock' – will invigorate your spirit for sure.

Oceanas Bistro AMERICAN $$
(Map p260; ☎252-995-4991; www.oceanasbistro.com; 40774 NC Hwy 12, Avon; breakfast $4-15, lunch & dinner $5-27; ⏰8am-10pm Apr-Nov, 11am-9pm Dec-Mar; 📶) A good-time local's haunt open year-round, Oceanas' Bistro will win you over with friendly servers and a pretty damn excellent menu that includes outstanding crab-cakes or mahi-mahi sandwiches and some insanely good-looking 'grillers' (open-faced quesadillas, invented in-house) that come in veggie, blackened tuna, crab or Caribbean chicken. Eat at the bar to pair your meal with loads of local color.

Those with a sweet tooth should try one of the inventive desserts, such as coconut bomb cake filled with coconut cream and covered in coconut icing, or the peanut butter pie with a chocolate layer. In the off season, it's easily one of the best spots that opens south of Bodie Island.

Atlantic Coast Cafe SEAFOOD $$

(Map p260; ☎252-987-1200; http://atlanticcoastcafe.com; 25150 NC Hwy 12, Waves; breakfast $7-10, lunch & dinner mains $9-22; ⏰7am-9pm Apr-Oct; P ♿) Solid and reasonably priced place to stop on your way through the Outer Banks. The dining room is clean, with simple white walls, wooden tables and outdoor seating, and has a laid-back vibe. Order hearty seafood baskets with fried fish, shrimp, crab cakes and fries, or fresh fish tacos topped with salsa. Expect the cafe to be closed during winter.

Tortugas' Lie SEAFOOD $$

(Map p260; ☎252-441-7299; www.tortugaslie.com; 3014 S Virginia Dare Trail, Nags Head; lunch $5-20, dinner $8-23; ⏰11:30am-9:30pm Mon-Fri, to 10pm Sat & Sun) The interior isn't dressed to impress – surfboards, license plates – but who cares? The reliably good seafood, burritos and burgers go down well with the beer. Guy Fieri stopped by in 2012 and scrawled his signature on the wall. Fills up by 6:30pm.

Blue Point SEAFOOD $$$

(Map p260; ☎252-261-8090; www.thebluepoint.com; 1240 Duck Rd, Duck; big plates $27-39; ⏰11:30am-2:30pm & 5-9pm Tue-Sun) Cozy upmarket spot specializing in local seafood and farm-to-table produce. Grab one of the red booths for Currituck Sound views. The pan-fried jumbo crab cakes are a winner – they've been on the menu since the 1980s. There's a nice outdoor garden for waterside drinks, plus the Sunday brunch has live music and $5 Bloody Marys and mimosas.

Breakwater Restaurant SEAFOOD $$$

(Map p260; ☎252-986-2733; www.breakwaterhatteras.com; 57896 NC Hwy 12, Hattaras; mains $14-30; ⏰5-9pm Apr-Oct) This restaurant beside the sound has been serving food for nearly 30 years. Come here for steamed seafood, fresh fish and and big daddy crab cakes.

Drinking & Nightlife

Trio WINE BAR

(Map p260; ☎252-261-0277; https://triowinebeercheese.com; 3708 N Croatan Hwy, Kitty Hawk; cheese plates $7-21, tapas $6-18, toast & paninis $7-10, glass wine from $5; ⏰11am-9pm Sun-Wed, to 11pm Thu & Fri, 10am-11pm Sat) This simple but stylish wine and craft-beer bar is a welcome respite from OBX's typical fare. Select from 24 wines (in the self-service tasting bar) or 24 taps of local suds then complement your choice with housemade hummus, a cheese plate or various paninis and toast flavors. The retail store sells a wide selection of craft beer, wine, artisanal cheese and other gourmet products – perfect for picnic curating!

Duck's Cottage CAFE

(Map p260; ☎252-261-5510; www.duckscottage.com; 1240 Duck Rd, Duck; drinks from $2; ⏰7am-9pm Mon-Fri, to 6pm Sat & Sun, 7am-6pm low season) Set in a wooden building dating back to 1921, this atmospheric cubbyhole cafe and bookshop, formerly the Powder Ridge Gun Club, once had whalebones adorning the front. It's known locally as 'The Whalebone Club' and is a great place to find a corner seat, enjoy a coffee and peruse the eclectic collection. Open year-round, but hours can change at short notice.

Outer Banks Brewing Station MICROBREWERY

(Map p260; ☎252-449-2739; www.obbrewing.com; 600 S Croatan Hwy, Kill Devil Hills; beers $5.50, mains $8-$31; ⏰11:30am-10pm Mon-Thu & Sun, to 2am Fri & Sat; 📶) 🍃 This Kill Devil Hills microbrewery is powered by a 93ft wind turbine, the first such brewery in the USA. That means you'll be doing your part for global warming when you're downing your 'thankyousirmayIhaveanother' IPA or lemongrass wheat. The odd design is a modern interpretation of a turn-of-the-century lifesaving station; it also resembles a church.

It's also a great spot for food, so you can call it a night here (and throw down some of the housemade green sriracha on anything you order). Brewery tours take place on Wednesdays and Saturdays at 4:30pm ($8 per person including beer tasting and a free glass).

Juice Jar JUICE BAR

(Map p260; ☎252-453-0728; www.thejuicejarcorolla.com; 1130 Corolla Village Rd, Corolla; smoothies & juices from $8.50; ⏰8am-3pm) A healthy pick-me-up place serving smoothies, acai bowls and organic juices. Add nutritional shots like organic hemp, spirulina, maca, bee pollen or protein to your order for an extra $1. Drink your beverage on one of the wooden benches outside the Juice Jar's hut.

Entertainment

Art's Place LIVE MUSIC

(Map p260; ☎252-261-3233; www.artsplaceobx.com; 4624 N Virginia Dare Trail, Kitty Hawk; ⏲7am-9pm) You can't miss this colorfully painted haunt in Kitty Hawk, where tourists are 'sometimes tolerated.' This place prides itself on being a 'local secret' spot, and is a cozy place for chat, burgers and the like. Plus, there's a popular live jazz and open-mic night on Mondays and Wednesday from 7pm.

Shopping

Island Bookstore BOOKS

(Map p260; ☎252-453-2292; https://islandbooksobx.wordpress.com; 1130 Corolla Village Rd, Corolla; ⏲10am-5pm) Welcoming independent local bookstore chain, selling a good range of fiction, poetry, cooking and history books, plus a dedicated collection of Outer Banks photography, walking, nature and guidebooks. Look out for regular author signings.

Information

The best sources of information are at the main visitor centers, and there are plenty of them. Many smaller centers open seasonally. Also useful is www.outerbanks.org.

Aycock Brown Welcome Center (Outer Banks Visitor Bureau; Map p260; ☎877-629-4386; www.outerbanks.org; 5230 N Croatian Hwy, Kitty Hawk; ⏲8am-5pm Mon-Fri) On the bypass in Kitty Hawk; has maps and information.

Fort Raleigh National Historic Site Visitor Center (p267).

Hatteras Island Visitor Center (Map p260; ☎252-475-9000; www.nps.gov/caha; 46368 Lighthouse Rd, Buxton; ⏲9am-5pm) Beside Cape Hatteras Lighthouse.

Ocracoke Island Visitor Center (p273) Near the southern ferry dock.

Sarah Owen Welcome Center (Map p260; ☎877-629-4386; www.outerbanks.org; 1 Visitors Center Circle; ⏲9am-5pm) Just east of Virginia Dare Memorial Bridge on the Hwy 64 Bypass on Roanoke Island.

Whalebone Welcome Center (Map p260; ☎877-629-4386; www.outerbanks.org; 2 NC Hwy 12, Nags Head; ⏲8:30am-5pm Mar-Dec) At the intersection of Hwy 64 and Hwy 12 in Nags Head.

Getting There & Away

AIR

The closest commercial airports to the Outer Banks are **Norfolk International Airport** (NIA; ☎757-857-3351; www.norfolkairport.com; 2200 Norview Ave; 📶), 82 miles north, in Virginia or North Carolina's **Raleigh-Durham International Airport** (p370), 192 miles west. Manteo-based **Outer Banks Air Charters** (www.outerbanksaircharters.com) offers charter flights for up to five passengers from various US airports (Norfolk, Raleigh, Charlotte, Charleston, Baltimore and Washington Dulles are common routes) to any of the five Outer Banks airports.

CAR & MOTORCYCLE

If driving, try to avoid arriving or departing on weekends in summer, when traffic can be maddening. The **Outer Banks Visitors Bureau** (www.outerbanks.org) offers a comprehensive guide to driving to OBX, including tips and alternate routes to avoid spending your vacation stuck in your vehicle. In winter, the roads are empty.

FERRY

The **North Carolina Ferry System** (www.ncdot.gov/ferry) operates several routes, including the free one-hour Hatteras–Ocracoke car ferry, which fluctuates between hourly and half-hourly with 36 departures from 5am to midnight from Hatteras in high season; reservations aren't accepted. North Carolina ferries also run between Ocracoke and Cedar Islands (one way car/motorcycle $15/10, 2¼ hours) and between Ocracoke Island and Swan Quarter on the mainland ($15/10, 2¾ hours) every three hours or so; reservations are recommended in summer for these two routes. Pedestrians may use the ferries for $1 per one-way trip. Cyclists can use the ferries for $3 per one-way trip.

Getting Around

No public transportation exists to or on the Outer Banks.

Manteo

Wrapping around Shallowbag Bay, on the eastern side of Roanoke Island, the quaint waterfront area Manteo is a pleasant base from which to explore the Outer Banks. The easily walkable harbor has a village feel, and there are shops, cafes, restaurants and entertainment within a few blocks. Those looking to set sail around the nearby shores can launch from here (book via a local outfit), but the main draw near the harbor is the Roanoke Island Festival Park, a sprawling attraction where visitors can learn about the first English colonies on North American soil. In summer season (May to August), be sure to catch an atmospheric amphitheater performance by Lost Colony Outdoor Drama, which portrays the story of the colonists who arrived in Manteo in the 1580s (before the European settlers arrived at Plymouth Rock) then mysteriously disappeared.

Sights

History buffs can get their fill here in Manteo, with a number of attractions depicting the tales of the first European settlers in the area.

Roanoke Island Festival Park HISTORIC SITE

(Map p260; ☎252-47-1500; www.roanokeisland.com; 1 Festival Park; adult/child/under 2yr $10/7/free; ⏰9am-5pm Mar-Dec; 🅿👪) Go on a swashbuckling adventure at this 25-acre park, telling the story of the first English settlement attempt in 1585. Visitors can climb aboard a 16th-century sailing boat named *Elizabeth II*, where costumed role-playing sailors will answer questions about the vessel.

Meanwhile, a mock Native American town resembles what English explorers would have encountered when discovering these lands, and an early English site includes exhibits on the daily life of the soldiers and sailors who settled here. At the site's Adventure Museum learn about 400 years of the area's history and dress your kids up in historic garb.

Fort Raleigh National Historic Site HISTORIC SITE

(Map p260; ☎252-473-2111; www.nps.gov/fora; 1401 National Park Dr; ⏰grounds dawn-dusk) In the late 1580s, three decades before the Pilgrims landed at Plymouth Rock, a group of 116 British colonists disappeared without a trace from their Roanoke Island settlement. Were they killed off by drought? Did they run away with a Native American tribe? The fate of the 'Lost Colony' remains one of America's greatest mysteries. Explore their story in the visitor center (Lindsay Warren Vistor Center; Map p260; ☎252-475-9001; www.nps.gov/fora; 1401 National Park Dr; ⏰9am-5pm).

One of the site's star attractions is the beloved musical, Lost Colony Outdoor Drama (p268), staged between late May and August. The play, from Pulitzer Prize–winning North Carolina playwright Paul Green, dramatizes the fate of the colonists and celebrated its 80th anniversary in 2017. It plays at the Waterside Theater throughout summer. Other attractions include exhibits, artifacts, maps and a free 17-minute film to fuel the imagination, hosted at the visitor center. The 16th-century-style Elizabethan Gardens has a commanding statue of Queen Elizabeth I standing guard at the entrance.

TWO IF BY SEA

Manteo is a great place to get on the water, via a chartered sailing trip. **Sail Outer Banks** (Map p260; ☎252-473-2719; www.sailouterbanks.com; Manteo Waterfront Marina, 207 Queen Elizabeth Ave; $70; 👪🐾) is a private charter with licensed captains Dan and Katherine. On their classic 41ft Gulfstar, they offer sunset and day cruises. You can bring your dog onboard with advance notice, plus your own champagne. There's a minimum charge of $250 for up to six guests.

Elizabethan Gardens GARDENS

(Map p260; ☎252-473-3234; www.elizabethangardens.org; 1411 National Park Dr; adult/child 6-17yr $9/6; ⏰9am-6pm Apr-Sep, shorter hours Oct-Mar) The 16th-century-style Elizabethan Gardens include a Shakespearean herb garden and rows of beautifully manicured flower beds. Check online to see what's blooming. Closed in February.

Sleeping

There are half a dozen reasonable guesthouses and hotels in the area.

Tranquil House Inn INN $$

(Map p260; ☎252-473-1404; www.tranquilhouseinn.com; 405 Queen Elizabeth Ave; r $169-259) Situated at the harbor, with waterfront views, this inn is within an easy walk of the restaurants, cafes and attractions of Manteo. The 25 tastefully decorated rooms come in subtle colors, with crisp white linens, and some include four poster beds. Breakfast is included in room rates. Tuck into local seafood at the upscale 1587 Restaurant on site.

Eating

A small range of dining options includes casual cafes, a good coffee shop near the harbor and an upscale East Coast American restaurant, which uses local produce and homegrown herbs.

The Hungry Pelican CAFE $

(Map p260; ☎252-473-9303; http://thehungrypelican.com; 205 Budleigh St; small sandwiches from $4.25, large from $5.25; ⏲11am-7pm Mon-Fri, to 3pm Sat; 👪) Top spot for a sandwich to go, ahead of a cruise or hike. This cafe serves curb-sized creations like The Godfather – with hot Italian ham, salami, pepperoni and provolone cheese with salad, and hoagie sauce on ciabatta bread. Other menu items include heaped salads, hot soups and macaroni sides. There's a simple dining room, for those wanting to eat in.

1587 Restaurant AMERICAN $$$

(Map p260; ☎252-473-1587; www.1587.com; 405 Queen Elizabeth Ave; entrees $18-42; ⏲5-9pm Wed-Sun Mar-early Nov) Eat upscale, beautifully presented dishes in this waterside restaurant, hidden inside Tranquil House Inn. House chefs use herbs from the Inn's gardens, Atlantic seafood and locally sourced meat, fowl and veggies. Seared tuna steak comes piled high on a bed of kimchi shrimp fried rice, while the rack of lamb melts in the mouth. It's only open in high season.

Drinking & Nightlife

Most local restaurants sell local wine selections, and there's a good brewery by the harbor.

Charis Coffee Company CAFE

(Map p260; ☎252-423-3333; http://chariscoffeeco.com; 107 Budleigh St, Unit G; coffee from $2.20, bagels from $2.50; ⏲7am-5pm Mon-Fri, 8am-5pm Sat) In a sleek minimalist space with hardwood floors, grey soft furnishings and blackboard walls, this cafe is by far the coolest hangout spot in Manteo. Speciality drinks include a peppermint patty mocha and pumpkin spiced latte. Each month the owners donate 10% of profits to a worthy organization.

Lost Colony Brewery & Cafe BREWERY

(Map p260; ☎252-473-6666; http://lostcolonybrewery.com; 208 Queen Elizabeth Ave; ⏲11am-8pm Mon-Sat, until 4pm Sun) Classic American pub vibe and home-brewed beers make this a solid place to grab a pint after a day of sightseeing. On rotating taps, varieties include the Kitty Hawk Blonde, Stumpy Point Pale Ale and Nags Head IPA. The umbrella-shaded outdoor patio is a good spot when the weather is fine.

Entertainment

Lost Colony Outdoor Drama THEATER

(Map p260; ☎252-473-6000; www.thelostcolony.org; 1409 National Park Dr; adult/child from $20/10; ⏲7:45pm Mon-Sat) Staged between late May and August, this outdoor play, written by Pulitzer Prize–winning North Carolina playwright Paul Green, dramatizes the fate of 116 British colonists who disappeared without a trace from their Roanoke Island settlement in the late 1580s. It plays at the Waterside Theater throughout summer.

Ye Olde Pioneer Theatre THEATER

(Map p260; ☎252-473-2216; 113 Budleigh St; adult/child $7/2) Movies take place once a night at this atmospheric old theatre, dating back to 1918. Built in English Tudor–style, it remains the oldest family-owned theater in America. Phone ahead to check film listings. May be closed during off season.

Shopping

Dare County Arts Council ART

(Map p260; ☎252-473-5558; 300 Queen Elizabeth Ave; ⏲10am-6pm Mon-Fri, to 4pm Sat Apr-Oct, 10am-5pm Tue-Fri, noon-4pm Sat Nov-Mar) Inside the former Dare County Courthouse (built in 1904), this nonprofit gallery exhibits hundreds of paintings, jewelry and other local designs, inspired by the local area. Most items are up for sale.

Getting There & Away

Manteo is easily accessible by car. It is connected to the mainland via Hwy 64 (and the Virginia Dare Memorial Bridge) and to the rest of the Outer Banks via Hwy 158 (S Croatan Hwy) and Hwy 12 (North Carolina Hwy).

Ocracoke Island

Ocracoke Village is a funky little community that moves at a slower pace. With the exception of the village, the National Park Service owns the island. The older residents still speak in the 17th-century British dialect

Ocracoke

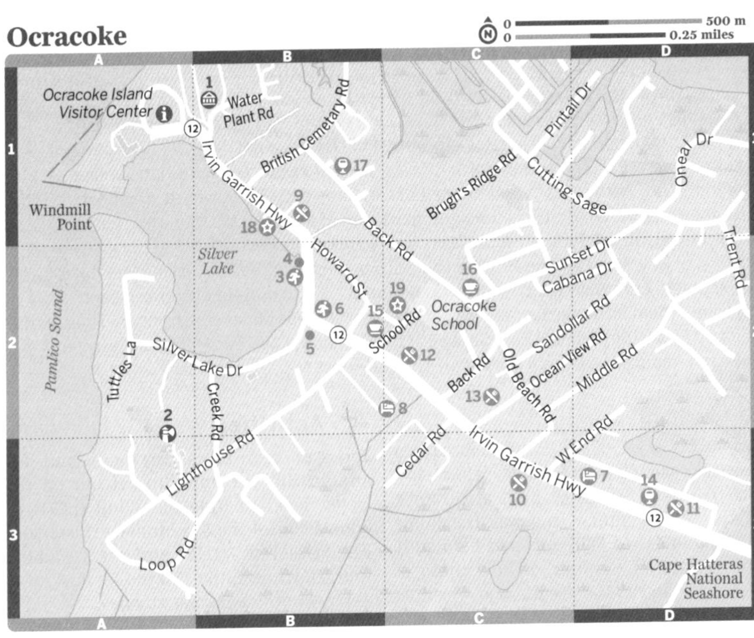

Ocracoke

Sights
1 David Williams House Museum ... B1
2 Ocracoke Lighthouse ... A2

Activities, Courses & Tours
3 Fish Tale ... B2
4 Portsmouth Island ATV Tours ... B2
5 Ride the Wind ... B2
6 Slushy Stand ... B2

Sleeping
7 Pam's Pelican B&B ... D3
8 Sea Monkey Hostel & Kite School ... C2

Eating
9 Dajio ... B1
10 Eduardo's Taco Stand ... C3
11 Howard's Pub ... D3
12 Ocracoke Bar & Grille ... C2
13 Pony Island Restaurant ... C2

Drinking & Nightlife
14 1718 Brewing Ocracoke ... D3
15 Magic Bean ... B2
16 Ocracoke Coffee ... C2
17 Zillie's Island Pantry ... B1

Entertainment
18 Coyote Music Den ... B1
19 Ocracoke Alive's Deepwater Theater ... C2

known as 'Hoi Toide' (p275). Edward Teach, aka Blackbeard the pirate, used to hide out in the area and was killed here in 1718. You can camp by Pony Pen, filled with the descendants of wild ponies abandoned by explorers hundreds of years ago, have a fish sandwich in a local pub, cycle around the village's narrow streets or nestle into holes in the sand dunes along 16 miles of coastline and catch some rays.

Sights

Ocracoke Beach BEACH

(Map p260; Irvin Garrish Hwy; P) Dolphins are commonly spotted on Ocracoke's gorgeous, undeveloped 16-mile stretch of sandy beach. Swimmers should be aware of rip currents. Find parking and toilet facilities at this access point on the right hand side of Irvin Garrish Hwy when traveling north out of town.

LOCAL KNOWLEDGE

OCRACOKE'S PENNED PONIES

Legend has it the Ocracoke Island 'wild' ponies are descended from feral Spanish mustangs abandoned by shipwrecked explorers in the 16th or 17th century, when it was common to unload livestock to lighten the load and get back out to sea after running aground. Known as 'banker' ponies, these horses are unique in the equine world – they harbor a different number of vertebrae and ribs as well as a distinct shape, posture, color, size and weight than those of other horses. But what's more fascinating about Ocracoke's ponies is they were eventually broken and tamed by a troop of Boy Scouts in the 1950s – you can see photos at the Pony Island Restaurant. They were eventually pastured in a 'pony pen' in 1959 to prevent overgrazing and protect them from the dangers of NC Hwy 12, which was under construction. They're cared for by the National Park Service at the Ocracoke Pony Pen (p270) at Pony Pen Beach. You can view them from an observation deck.

David Williams House Museum MUSEUM
(Map p269; ☎252-928-7375; https://ocracokepreservation.org; 49 Water Plant Rd; ⏲10am-4pm Mon-Fri, to 3pm Sat) FREE Built at the turn of the 20th century, this was the home of Captain David Williams and his family and is a good example of how those in Ocracoke lived 100 years ago. Visitors can wander around the rooms, filled with historic photography and furnishings – including everything from an old piano and tapestries to antique beds and outfits from the time. Practice your Ocracoke brogue in the room dedicated to the distinctive local dialect, which evolved due to Ocracoke's remoteness.

Ocracoke Pony Pen VIEWPOINT
(Map p260; www.nps.gov/caha; Irvin Garrish Hwy) From the National Park Service's observation deck, you can catch views of Ocracoke's formerly 'wild' ponies, which have been penned in here since the late 1950s and cared for by the NPS. The horses that remain in the herd are said to descend from feral Spanish mustangs abandoned by shipwrecked explorers in the 16th or 17th century. The pens are located 6 miles along Hwy 12 from the Ocracoke–Hatteras ferry landing.

Ocracoke Lighthouse LIGHTHOUSE
(Map p269; www.nps.gov/caha; Lighthouse Rd) Built in 1823, this is the oldest lighthouse still operating in North Carolina, though it cannot be climbed. The walls are 5ft thick and the non-rotating light at the top sits only 75ft above sea level. It can be seen as far as 14 miles away.

Activities

You can rent bikes on the island for around $10 per hour. To get out on the water, head to Ride the Wind (p271) or book a stay at the Sea Monkey Hostel and Kite School (p271). For a pleasant walking tour, download the **Ocracoke Navigator app** (www.ocracokenavigator.com).

Fish Tale FISHING
(Map p269; ☎252-928-3403, 252-921-0224; www.facebook.com/fishtalecharters; 410 Irvin Garrish Hwy; 1-4 person tours from $250, per additional person $25) Catch your dinner on this fishing charter with Captain John Ferrara, who has two decades of experience in these calm waters. No experience is necessary to be in with a chance of catching trout, flounder or red drum, bluefish and Spanish mackerel. All equipment is included on each trip – choose from two, four, six or eight hours.

Slushy Stand CYCLING
(Map p269; ☎252-928-1878; www.theslushystand.com; 473 Irvin Garrish Hwy; bikes per 1/24hr $10/19; ⏲7am-10pm) This drink, ice-cream and bagel shack rents out dozens of bikes on the main intersection in town. Helmets are included with all rentals. Bike trailers also available.

Tours

Portsmouth Island ATV Tours HISTORY
(Map p269; ☎252-928-4484; www.portsmouthislandatv.com; 396 Irvin Garrish Hwy; tours $90, max 6 people; ⏲2 trips per day 8am-noon & 1-5pm Apr-Oct) Runs two fascinating daily tours to the nearby island of Portsmouth, a 20-minute boat ride from Ocracoke, where you'll find an Outer Banks ghost town that was abandoned

in the 1970s. Guided ATV tours focus on shelling, bird-watching and swimming, in addition to the historic village.

Ride the Wind KAYAKING
(Map p269; ☎252-928-6311; www.surfocracoke.com; 486 Irvin Garrish Hwy; 2-2½hr kayaking tours adult/child under 13yr $39/18, group surf lessons from $75; ⊙10am-7pm Mon-Sat, to 6pm Sun) Want to get on the water? Take a kayaking tour with Ride the Wind. The sunset tours are easy on the arms, and the guides (we hear) are easy on the eyes. It also offers sunrise, midday yoga and tai chi tours, surf lessons and surfboard rental ($22 per day), bodyboards ($12 per day) skimboards ($19 per day), SUPs ($19 per hour) and kayaks ($14 per hour).

Sleeping

Many people come to Ocracoke on a day trip from Hatteras, but with its preserved culture and laid-back vibe, it's a nice place to spend a night or two. There are a handful of B&Bs, several motels, a park-service campground near the beach and rental cottages.

★ **Sea Monkey Hostel and Kite School** HOSTEL $
(Map p269; ☎540-223-2442; http://ocracokehostel.com; Wahab Village; r with shared/private bath from $37/93; P 🛜) Located on a side road in a residential house, this super-friendly hostel has four comfortable basic rooms, and is one of the most inexpensive options in town. Welcoming host Mike also teaches kiteboarding (group lessons from $75). Guests have use of the lounge area and kitchen facilities, plus the hostel's free bikes – the best way to get around town. Groups of up to eight people can rent out the whole house, if arranged in advance.

Ocracoke Campgrounds CAMPGROUND $
(Map p260; ☎877-444-6777, 252-928-6671; www.recreation.gov; 4352 Irvin Garrish Hwy; tent sites $28; ⊙Apr-late Nov; P 🐾) Good value for money for small groups, Ocracoke Campgrounds offers more than 100 sites on sand on the island. Flush toilets, drinking water, showers and grills are available. Electric hookups are not available. There's a maximum of six people per site.

Pam's Pelican B&B B&B $$
(Map p269; ☎252-928-1661; www.pamspelican.com; 1021 Irvin Garrish Hwy; r $175-200; P ❄ @ 🛜 🐾) This wildly popular B&B has just four rooms, reached via a series of colorful corridors, in a typical island home loaded with artsy knickknacks. Rates include use of bikes (and rides to the beach if you're so inclined) and there is sometimes live music streamed from the front-yard gazebo in high season. Guests have access to the 2nd-floor patio. Pam prefers pets to children, so bring Fido but board little Johnny with grandma. Lower rates can be bagged in low season (November to March).

Eating

Fresh crab, shrimp and scallops from the Pamlico Sound are the way to go on Ocracoke. You can find them at breakfast, lunch and dinner at numerous restaurants around the village. Or you can charter a boat and catch your own to barbecue.

★ **Eduardo's Taco Stand** MEXICAN $
(Map p269; ☎252-928-0234; www.facebook.com/amadowoch; 950 Irvin Garrish Hwy; mains $4-13; ⊙8am-9pm Mon-Sat Apr-Oct, 8am-3pm & 5-7pm Mon-Sat Nov-Mar; P 🌶) There's a long list of tacos, burritos and fresh and spicy salsas at this sensational taco stand. If you're over fried clams and crab cakes, dishes like prime rib-eye tacos with salsa *de xoconostle* (sour prickly pears) hit the spot, as do the fish with creamy chipotle apple slaw or poblano chowder with shrimp or clams. Full veggie menu, too. Get in line. Opening hours are approximate and depend on the number of customers.

Pony Island Restaurant BREAKFAST $
(Map p269; ☎252-928-5701; 51 Ocean View Rd; breakfast dishes $5-14; ⊙7:30-11:30am Apr-Oct) Filling local bellies with a wealth of American breakfast fare since 1959, this is a classic American family-style breakfast spot. Order pancakes, eggs any style and French toast. The biscuits and gravy, fish cakes and eggs, local crab and Swiss omelet and stacked English muffins are particularly good. It's all well done and a definitive gathering point for the townsfolk.

Take a gander at the photos on the walls, some of which document how local Boy Scouts broke the local wild ponies back in the day. Only open in high season.

Ocracoke Bar & Grille SEAFOOD $
(Map p269; ☎252-928-6227; www.ocracokebarandgrille.com; 621 Irvin Garrish Hwy; tacos from $3, seafood items from $6, entrees from $10; ⊙3-10pm Mon, Fri & Sat, 11am-10pm Wed & Thu,

noon-10pm Sun; P) A surf-themed bar and restaurant with ceiling and walls decorated with boards, and surf footage playing on screen all day. Try the Clam Box with 20 to 30 fresh clams of different sizes, served with green peppers and red onions. Wash it down with a Porky Mary – a take on the classic Bloody Mary, garnished with a slice of bacon. Other menu items include tacos, scallops, shrimps, oysters and fish sandwiches. Soak up the sun on the outside terrace.

Howard's Pub PUB FOOD **$**

(Map p269; 252-928-4441; www.howardspub.com; 1175 Irvin Garrish Hwy; munchies & burgers $9-15, mains $19-29; 11am-10pm late Mar-late Nov; P) A big old renovated wooden pub that's been an island tradition for beer and fried seafood since the 1850s. Good selection of local craft beer. Gluten-free dishes available. May stay open later on Friday and Saturday.

Dajio INTERNATIONAL **$$**

(Map p269; 252-928-7119; www.dajiorestaurant.com; 305 Irvin Garrish Hwy; dishes $9-28; 11am-9pm Apr-Oct; P) Menu items change seasonally at this eatery combining local art with local produce. Ingredients are sourced from both coastal famers and the restaurant's own garden. International flavors include Korean-style shrimp noodles and Cajun diver scallops, or pizza baked in a stone oven. Eat in the sleek dining room with hardwood floors and crisp white tablecloths, or on the open terrace.

Drinking & Nightlife

Ocracoke is a charming spot for a drink with locals. Aside from the pubs, many of the restaurants have bars and outdoor seating, and the island also has a brewery.

Zillie's Island Pantry WINE BAR

(Map p269; 252-928-9036; www.zillies.com; 538 Back Rd; wines $5-12, pints $5-8; 10:30am-8:30pm Apr-Oct;) Part gourmet-food shop (head here for beach-picnic provisions), part wine store, Zillie's is one of the classiest spots for a glass of wine ($21 by the glass) or a regional microbrew (eight taps). It sells more than 300 tipples, and on chillier days the fire-pit-warmed front porch is an enticing spot for a drink. Enquire about the regular wine-tasting evenings ($20 per person).

1718 Brewing Ocracoke BREWERY

(Map p269; 252-928-2337; www.facebook.com/1718brewingocracoke; 1129 Irvin Garrish Hwy; tasters from $2, pints from $6; 3-9pm Thu-Sat) Opened in 2017, this is one of the best additions to the island. Try the locally crafted stout and IPA, and tour the microbrewery to see how it's made. The interiors were designed from repurposed wood and metal.

Magic Bean COFFEE

(Map p269; 252-588-2440; www.magicbeanocracoke.com; 35 School Rd; coffee $1.75-4.75; 6am-6pm May-Aug, 7am-4pm Sep-Apr;) The antithesis of the slicker cafe experience on offer at Ocracoke Coffee, this colorful and artsy coffeehouse is open year-round and, according to born-and-raised owner Cait, 'a casual place for a gathering of strange people.' Think creative, liberal and open-minded. Smoothies and snacks too! Also rents rooms above (from $71 per night).

Ocracoke Coffee COFFEE

(Map p269; 252-928-7473; www.ocracokecoffee.com; 226 Back Rd; coffee $1.50-4.60; 7am-6pm Mon-Sat, 7am-1pm Sun late Mar-late Nov;) Locals and tourists converge at Ocracoke Coffee, home of the Grasshopper Latte (chocolate mint and toffee) and Island Smoothie (various flavors with a shot of coffee). Bites include acai bowls and bagels, and sometimes freshly made lavender honey scones and banana muffins.

Entertainment

Coyote Music Den LIVE MUSIC

(Map p269; 252-928-6874; www.coyotemusic.net; 288 Irvin Garrish Hwy; $12-15) This tiny live venue (or room) inside a clapboard waterside house offers a chance to hang out with real locals, and experience the island's homegrown folk, rock, blues and jazz. Throughout spring and summer, Coyote holds three ticketed events per week, check the website for details. The free open-mic Tuesdays run all year – just show up with an instrument (or a good voice) from 6:30pm.

Ocracoke Alive's Deepwater Theater THEATER

(Map p269; 252-921-0260; www.ocracokealive.org; 25 School Rd; from $15; performance times vary) Community theater showing amateur productions. Shows range from a comedic take on the story of Blackbeard (the pirate who took a liking to the island) to the Dingbatter's (foreigner's) Guide to Ocracoke. On Thursdays (during high season, approximately May to September) the local high-energy folk band Molasses Creek plays here.

Information

Ocracoke Island Visitor Center (Map p269; ☎252-475-9701; www.nps.gov/caha; 38 Irvin Garrish Hwy; ⏱9am-5pm) is near the southern ferry dock. There's limited info – park officials mostly deal with off-road vehicle permits, boat slips and commercial fishing licenses. There is a gift shop on-site.

Connectivity – especially mobile service – can be an issue in Ocracoke. Both coffeehouses, the gas station and some restaurants have wi-fi.

Getting There & Away

The village is at the southern end of 16-mile-long Ocracoke Island and is accessed from Hatteras via the free **Hatteras–Ocracoke ferry** (www.ncdot.gov/ferry; first come, first served). The ferry lands at the northeastern end of the island. Other options are via the $15 Cedar Island–Ocracoke or Swan Quarter–Ocracoke ferries (which land at the southern dock; reservations accepted). Pedestrians/cyclists can board the ferries for $1/3.

CRYSTAL COAST

The southern Outer Banks are collectively called the 'Crystal Coast.' Less rugged than the northern beaches, they include several historic coastal towns, sparsely populated islands and vacation-friendly beaches.

An industrial and commercial stretch of Hwy 70 goes through Morehead City, with plenty of chain hotels and restaurants. The Bogue Banks, across the Sound from Morehead City via the Atlantic Beach Causeway, have several well-trafficked beach communities – try Atlantic Beach if you like the smell of coconut suntan oil and doughnuts.

Just north, postcard-pretty Beaufort (bow-fort; p274), the third-oldest town in the state, has a charming boardwalk and lots of B&Bs. Blackbeard himself is said to have lived in the Hammock House off Front St. You can't go inside, but some claim you can still hear the screams of the pirate's murdered wife at night.

Sights

Fort Macon State Park FORT

(Map p260; ☎252-726-3775; www.ncparks.gov/fort-macon-state-park; 2303 E Fort Macon Rd, Atlantic Beach; ⏱9am-5:30pm; P) FREE This remarkable five-sided fort, with 26 vaulted rooms, is one of North Carolina's most visited attractions. Completed in 1834, it was the site of the Battle of Fort Macon fought in 1862. Exhibits inside the fort's walls and tunnels document the daily lives of soldiers stationed there. Constructed from brick and stone, the fort changed hands twice during the Civil War. Visitors can walk around the exterior and climb the stairs of the grassy structure for 360-degree views.

Guided tours run at 11am Monday to Friday. There are three trails around the park for visitors, ranging from half a mile to 3.5 miles. Choose from a beach walk or maritime forest walk, with the chance to see dolphins offshore and up to 302 bird species. Bring a picnic and use the outdoor grills, drinking water and picnic table facilities in the park.

Emerald Isle Beach BEACH

(Map p260; 2700 Emerald Dr, Emerald Isle; P) Emerald Isle's 12 miles of pristine beach has soft, golden sands and the green-blue waters the area is named after. The car park at the Eastern Regional Access point is the biggest area for beach access with 245 spaces, plus restrooms, picnic gazebos, showers and vending machines.

North Carolina Aquarium AQUARIUM

(Map p260; ☎252-247-4003; www.ncaquariums.com; 1 Roosevelt Blvd, Pine Knoll Shores; adult/child/under 2yr $11/9/free; ⏱9am-5pm; P) It's not the most impressive aquarium out there, and is a tad pricey, but offers a good option for small children or those wanting to explore the waters of North Carolina without getting wet. You can get up close to thousands of marine species, meet a stingray and white sea turtle, and come face to face with a shark. There's also an outdoor play area for the kids.

Activities

Olympus Dive Center DIVING

(Map p260; ☎252-726-9432; www.olympusdiving.com; 713 Shepard St, Morehead City; half-day dives from $70; ⏱9am-7pm Mon-Sat) Not only are North Carolina's warm, clear waters home to a variety of marine life, they're also home to more than 2000 sunken ships, which date back as far as 1526. This excellent dive outfit takes qualified divers to see them at depths of 60ft to 140ft (18m to 42m). Divers in this area make new discoveries every day.

South Swell Surf Shop SURFING

(Map p260; ☎252-354-7175; www.southswellsurfshop.com; 8204 Emerald Dr, Emerald Isle; half-day surfboards from $15; ⏰9am-9pm Sun-Thu, 9am-10pm Fri & Sat) A friendly local store offering surfboard rental and surf lessons, running seven days a week between July and September. Arrange well in advance for lessons out of high season.

Island Water Sports Rentals WATER SPORTS

(Map p260; ☎252-247-7303; www.h20sportsrentals.com; 1960 Salter Path Rd, Indian Beach; ⏰9am-6pm Apr-Sep) For the most fun you can have on the water, come here to rent equipment like pontoon boats ($300 per half-day), kayaks and paddleboards ($30 per hour), banana boats ($15 per 15 minutes) and jet skis ($60 per half-hour). Call ahead to book.

Sleeping & Eating

Chain hotels rule the roost in Morehead City and there are plenty of places to sleep in the Bogue Banks, but charming Beaufort is where you'll want to rest your weary head. Book ahead – there are not a lot of beds there.

Hampton Inn Morehead City HOTEL $$

(Map p260; ☎252-240-2300; www.hamptoninn3.hilton.com; 4035 Arendell St, Morehead City; r from $162; ❄@🛜🏊) Yep, it's part of a national chain, but the helpful staff and the views of Bogue Sound make this Hampton Inn a nice choice – plus it's in a convenient location near to Hwy 70, helpful for those driving the coast. Rates drop significantly on weeknights in summer.

El's Drive-In SEAFOOD $

(Map p260; www.elsdrivein.com; 3706 Arendell St, Morehead City; mains $1.60-14.25; ⏰10:30am-10pm Sun-Thu, to 11pm Fri & Sat) The food is brought right to your car at this old-school drive-in and legendary seafood spot, open since 1959. It serves fish fillets, po'boys and hot dogs. Our recommendation? The fried shrimp burger with ketchup and slaw plus a side of fries. Cash only.

> **BIG-SCREEN BEAUFORT**
>
> You might recognize Beaufort's historic downtown – scenes from the 2016 film adaptation of Nicholas Sparks' *The Choice* were filmed in town.

Trading Post; Southern Food & Spirits SOUTHERN US $

(Map p260; ☎252-424-8284; www.thetradingpostei.com; 8302 Emerald Dr, Emerald Isle; fish stew $6, mains from $12; ⏰7am-8pm Sun, Mon & Wed, 7am-9:30pm Thu & Sat, 7am-9pm Fri) Drop into this casual restaurant for the warming fish stew – it's just like Southern grandmothers would make it. Other Southern treats include chicken and waffles, shrimp and grits, and North Carolina barbecue sandwiches served with slaw and hush puppies.

Drinking & Nightlife

Promised Land Market BAR

(Map p260; ☎252-222-0422; www.facebook.com/promiselandmarket; 909b Arendell St, Morehead City; beer from $5, sandwiches & wraps $8-10; ⏰11am-10pm Mon & Tue, to 11pm Wed & Thu, to midnight Fri & Sat, 10:30am-9pm Sun; 🛜) Part craft beer, part wine and gourmet-provisions shop, this excellent newcomer is Morehead City's best time. Taps pour local and regional suds, and a dozen or so wines by the glass, both in the shop and large back bar. Drink with the town's trendy set, then chase drinks down with good sandwiches and wraps.

You can pick up a bottles of craft beer to take out too. Regular live events include open-mic nights.

Getting There & Away

American Airlines and Delta offer flights to **Coastal Carolina Regional Airport** (www.newbernairport.com), located 38 miles northwest of Beaufort in New Bern, from Charlotte and Atlanta, respectively.

Coming from the Outer Banks, the **North Carolina Ferry System** (www.ncdot.gov/ferry) operates ferries between Ocracoke Island and Cedar Island (one-way car/motorcycle $15/10, 2¼ hours) which is a 41-mile drive northeast of Morehead City. Check the website for up-to-date ferry departures.

Beaufort

☎252 / POP 13,500

Founded in 1709, North Carolina's third-oldest city is pretty as a postcard, perched alongside Taylor's Creek in the southern Outer Banks. A small town with big-time charm, Beaufort's mostly whitewashed and arctic blue–tinted historic homes occupy a 12-block area laid out in 1713. Now on the

National Register of Historic Places, the town seduces visitors with Queen Anne, Greek Revival and Gothic Revival architecture, plus a great legend. The infamous pirate Blackbeard ran aground here in 1718 on his ship the *Queen Anne's Revenge*. He's said to have lived in the Hammock House off Front St during his time here. Today, Beaufort is an endearing, white-picket-fence, moss-draped, live-oak-tree sort of spot with an adorable waterfront boardwalk perfect for a lazy afternoon wining and dining alfresco in the fresh sea air.

Sights

Old Burying Ground CEMETERY

(Map p276; Ann St; 9:30am-5pm) On the National Registry of Historic Places, this small but fascinating cemetery features the weathered tombstones of both Revolutionary and Civil War casualties and is well worth a stroll. Self-guided tour maps are supposed to be available inside the gates (not when we were there) and at the Beaufort Historic Site Welcome Center (p277).

Keep a lookout for the wooden plank in the back, denoted by the cryptic words: 'Little Girl Buried in Rum Keg.' A young girl from a family named Sloo was preserved in a barrel of rum when she died on a sea voyage back from England in the 1700s, an alternative to throwing her overboard. There is usually a pile of toys on her grave, left by visitors. You can still see the Sloo family house on Front St.

North Carolina Maritime Museum MUSEUM

(Map p276; 252-728-7317; https://ncmaritimemuseumbeaufort.com; 315 Front St; 9am-5pm Mon-Wed & Fri, 9am-8pm Thu, 10am-5pm Sat, noon-5pm Sun) FREE The pirate Blackbeard was a frequent visitor to the Beaufort area in the early 1700s. In 1996, the wreckage of his flagship, the *Queen Anne's Revenge*, was discovered at the bottom of Beaufort Inlet. You'll see plates, bottles and other artifacts from the ship in this small but engaging museum, which also spotlights the seafood industry as well as maritime rescue operations.

Tours

Hungry Town Tours FOOD & DRINK, HISTORY

(Map p276; 252-648-1011; www.hungrytowntours.com; 400 Front St; tours $20-75; booking center 10am-4pm) Local company holding recommended history- and culinary-focused walking and cruiser biking tours.

LOCAL KNOWLEDGE

'YOU'RE FROM OFF!'

Like Ocracoke Island, elder locals – mainly fishermen – in the Beaufort area speak in a 17th-century British brogue known as 'Hoi Toide' (their pronunciation of 'high tide'). If you hear someone say, 'You're from off!' that means you're not from around here, which in turn makes you a 'dingbatter.'

Island Express Ferry Service FERRY

(Map p276; 252-728-7433; www.islandexpressferryservices.com; 600 Front St; adult/child tours from $17/10; tour times vary, book ahead;) Offering various tours around the local area, including boat trips and heritage harbor tours. It's the only ferry service with official permission to drop passengers off at Cape Lookout Lighthouse and Shackleford Banks.

Sleeping

There aren't a lot of sleeping options in Beaufort – and that's the beauty of it. There are fewer than a handful of inns and historic B&Bs (150 beds or so in total) spread about the waterfront and several of the parallel residential streets.

★ **Inn on Turner** B&B $$

(Map p276; 919-271-6144; www.innonturner.com; 217 Turner St; r $200-250; P) Impeccably tasteful aqua-toned coastal contemporary decor – no gaudy antiques here – dominates this four-room B&B occupying an historic 1866 wooden cream-colored home two blocks back from the water. Innkeepers Kim and Jon are pillars of small-town Southern hospitality, despite not being from the South, and never having slept in a B&B before they opened this one in 2015. There is a lovely 2nd-floor porch dotted with rocking chairs on which to enjoy your morning java before the awesome gourmet breakfast, as well as a small garden. It has evening wine and appetizers and excellent dinners on request. Pretty perfect. Gay-friendly, and French is spoken, too!

Pecan Tree Inn B&B $$

(Map p276; 252-728-6733; https://pecantree.com; 116 Queen St; r $105-225) It was the first house in the town to have gas lighting, indoor plumbing and a telephone. Today, the six guest rooms are plush, but a little chintzy, all have private bathrooms, some have hot tubs. Have a light dinner – the breakfast is good and hearty.

Beaufort

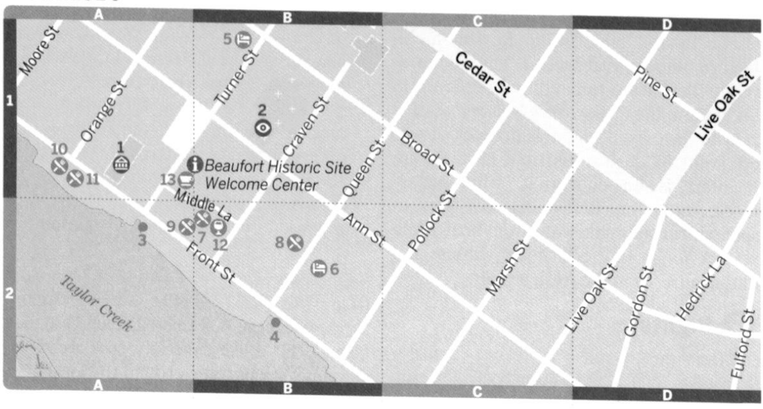

Beaufort

Sights
1 North Carolina Maritime Museum......... A1
2 Old Burying Ground......... B1

Activities, Courses & Tours
3 Hungry Town Tours......... A2
4 Island Express Ferry Service......... B2

Sleeping
5 Inn on Turner......... B1
6 Pecan Tree Inn......... B2

Eating
7 Aqua Restaurant......... B2
8 Beaufort Grocery......... B2
9 Clawson's 1905 Restaurant......... A2
10 Dank Burrito......... A1
11 Front Street Grill at Stillwater......... A1

Drinking & Nightlife
12 Backstreet Pub......... B2
13 Cru Wine Bar......... A1
14 Mill Whistle Brewing......... F2

It's a quintessential Beaufort experience, sleeping in this classic wooden property with its big Victorian porches. This site has always played a big part in the local community. In 1866 this was the location of the Franklin Masonic Lodge; it's also been used as a Sunday school, a teahouse and a doctor's office.

Eating

It's all about waterfront dining in Beaufort. Several good seafood restaurants line Front St with back porches overlooking Taylor's Creek.

★ Dank Burrito MEXICAN $
(Map p276; ☎252-838-9396; www.thedankburrito.com; 300 Front St; mains from $6.99; ⏲10:30am-9pm Apr-Oct, to 3pm Nov-Mar) Slightly out of place in olde Beaufort, Dank has graffitied walls and offbeat design features – including a retro (and playable) Ms Pac-Man arcade-game coffee table. Their homemade salsas, slaws and tacos are extremely good. Our favorite dish? The jerk chicken tacos with pineapple mango salsa and a dollop of the housemade hot sauce for good measure.

A success story, the owners started with a food truck and now occupy prime real estate, serving the best value eats on Front St.

Clawson's 1905 Restaurant GASTROPUB $$
(Map p276; ☎252-728-2133; www.clawsonsrestaurant.com/blog; 425 Front St; mains $11-23; ⏲11:30am-8:30pm Mon-Thu, 11:30am-9pm Fri & Sat) Paying tribute to former local business Clawson's Grocery & Bakery, this space was renovated in the 1970s, but you can still find hints of the past through photographs, old newspapers and various memorabilia inside. Enjoy a craft beer and classic American dishes like sirloin, meatloaf and baby back ribs, plus local seafood dishes.

Front Street Grill at Stillwater SEAFOOD $$
(Map p276; ☎252-728-4956; www.frontstreetgrillatstillwater.com; 300 Front St; mains $11-29; ⏲11:30am-9pm Tue-Thu & Sun, to 10pm Fri & Sat) The view reigns supreme at this inviting seafood spot overlooking Taylor's Creek. Nibble chili-lime shrimp tacos at lunch or seared backfin crab cakes at dinnertime. Enjoy people-watching at the small Rhum Bar.

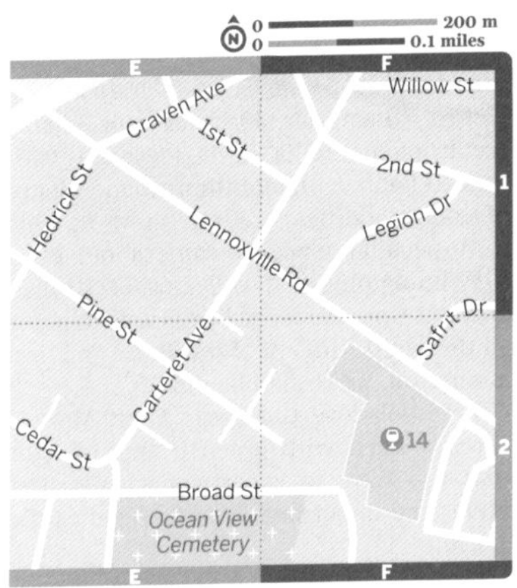

Aqua Restaurant SEAFOOD $$

(Map p276; 252-728-7777; http://aquaexperience.com/working; 114 Middle Lane; mains $12-28; 5:30pm-late Tue-Sat;) Just off Front St, Aqua is heavy on local produce and seafood, with some gluten-free, dairy-free and vegan options for good measure. The cast iron-seared crab cake comes with sweetcorn lima bean succotash, country ham and saffron lemon aioli, while the seared tuna has a Korean twist and is paired with pickled marinated vegetables. Wines $5 daily.

Beaufort Grocery MODERN AMERICAN $$$

(Map p276; 252-728-3899; www.beaufortgrocery.com; 117 Queen St; mains $25-42; 11:30am-2:30pm & 5:30-9:30pm Wed-Mon;) You'd never guess by the unassuming nature of the decor, but chef Charles Park is a James Beard winner and the food shines, whether that be smoked sea-salt tuna with chili yogurt, duck two ways with sweet-potato caramel or sage-wrapped chicken saltimbocca over tagliatelle. We didn't hear a bad thing about the place – and weren't disappointed.

Drinking & Nightlife

Any of the waterfront restaurants along Front St are as good for a drink as they are for food, or check out a couple of hidden local spots in the backstreets.

Backstreet Pub PUB

(Map p276; 252-728-7108; 124 Middle Lane; noon-2am Mon-Sat, from 5pm Sun) Behind Clawson's on Front St, you'll find this cozy cubbyhole hangout, housed in a historic bakery. The walls still contain the original brick ovens – only now they're covered with books and boaty memorabilia. The courtyard is the setting for many local events, including the annual Beaufort Music Festival and Hoot Nites, in which locals bring their instruments for a jam. Food trucks are hosted in the courtyard, too.

Mill Whistle Brewing MICROBREWERY

(Map p276; 252-342-6929; www.facebook.com/millwhistlebrewing; 1354 Lennoxville Rd; pints from $6; 3-9pm Fri, 2-9pm Sat Nov-Mar, 2-9pm Thu-Sun Apr-Oct) This one-barrel, hyperlocal brewery is as small as a commercial brewery can get. Just 31 gallons per batch of their 23 beers, which are brewed with solar-sterilized water, are produced. Everything is tasty, but their entry-level sours such as Low Toide are excellent and won't twist your tongue in a knot.

A friendly couple owns the place (he brews, she serves from the eight taps) and run the whole shebang on the site of the 100-year-old Safrit Lumber Mill (the original mill whistle hangs in the tiny taproom and a replica still blows). Most folks arrive on foot or bike.

Cru Wine Bar COFFEE, WINE BAR

(Map p276; 252-728-3066; www.thecruwinebar.com; 120 Turner St; wines from $6-12, coffees from $1.75, sandwiches $6.50; 6:30am-midnight;) In a tiny town like Beaufort, it's a revelation that decent coffee could be found at 6:30am, but it's even more fantastic that the connected wine bar is one of the most sophisticated spots in town for a drink at 6:30pm! This triple-action bar, coffeehouse and bottle shop fills the need on both ends. Great espresso, 31 wines by the glass and a full bar. Live music on Fridays and Saturdays (from 8:30pm).

Information

Beaufort Historic Site Welcome Center (Map p276; www.beauforthistoricsite.org; 130 Turner St; 9:30am-5pm Mon-Sat) has walking-tour maps and info on Beaufort historic sites.

Getting There & Away

Coastal Carolina Regional Airport (www.newbernairport.com), located 38 miles northwest of Beaufort in New Bern, is the closest commercial airport. It's serviced by American Airlines and Delta flights from Charlotte and Atlanta, respectively. If traveling by car, Hwy 21 is your best route into town.

WILMINGTON

910 / POP 117,600

Wilmington is pretty darn fun, and it's worth carving out a day or two for a visit if you're driving the coast. This seaside charmer may not have the name recognition of Charleston and Savannah, but eastern North Carolina's largest city has historic neighborhoods, azalea-choked gardens and cute cafes aplenty. All that, plus reasonable hotel prices.

At night the historic riverfront downtown becomes the playground for local college students, craft-beer enthusiasts, tourists and the occasional Hollywood type – there are so many movie studios here the town has earned the nickname 'Wilmywood.' You saw *Dawson's Creek*, right?

Sights

Perhaps the city's most notable sight is Cape Fear River (about 8 miles from the beach). Running along the waterfront is the 1.7-mile **RiverWalk**, with water views and restaurants aplenty.

The downtown area is comprised of Wilmington's **National Register Historic District**, one of the largest in the state numbering 230 blocks. It's a beautiful collage of staunchly preserved Queen Anne and Bungalow/American arts-and-crafts homes. It's a must-see, especially along 3rd and Market Sts.

Nearby **Wrightsville Beach** is laid-back and filled with fried-fish joints. When the surf is up, you ride waves. Rent boards close to the pier.

Battleship North Carolina HISTORIC SITE

(Map p279; 910-399-9100; www.battleshipnc.com; 1 Battleship Rd; self-guided tours adult/child 6-11yr/under 5yr $14/6/free, full-guided tours adult/child under 5yr $17.50/free; 8am-5pm Sep-May, to 8pm Jun-Aug; P) Self-guided tours take you through the decks of this 45,000-ton megaship, which earned 15 battle stars in the Pacific theater in WWII before it was decommissioned in 1947. Sights include the bake shop and galley, the print shop, the engine room, the powder magazine and the communications center. Note that there are several steep stairways leading to lower decks. Take the Cape Fear Bridge from downtown to get here. Full guided tours run on Saturdays between 10am and 12:30pm.

Museum of the Bizarre MUSEUM

(Map p279; 910-399-2641; www.museumbizarre.com; 201 S Water St; adult/child under 3yr $3/free; 11am-6pm) Pickled specimens, occult memorabilia, a taxidermied two-headed lamb, a bigfoot imprint and plenty of other oddities are on show at this truly peculiar place. It came about after a Wilmington-based collector of strange artifacts was convinced by his wife to move all the weird stuff out of the house and into a museum. We're glad he did.

Kids will love the Laser Vault Maze – a room filled with green beams of light that you have to expertly navigate over, under and in-between in a race against the clock.

Airlie Gardens GARDENS

(910-798-7700; www.airliegardens.org; 300 Airlie Rd; adult/child 4-12yr $9/3; 9am-5pm Apr-Dec, 9am-5pm Tue-Sun Jan-Mar) In spring, wander past thousands of bright azaleas at this 67-acre wonderland, also home to bewitching formal flowerbeds, seasonal gardens, pine trees, lakes and trails. The Airlie Oak dates from 1545.

Activities & Tours

South End Surf Shop SURFING

(910-256-1118; www.southendsurf.com; 708 S Lumina Ave, Wrightsville Beach; surfboards/body boards per hour $10/5, lessons from $40; 9am-9pm Mon-Sat, to 7pm Sun) Only 20 minutes from Wilmington's center you can go surfing with this recommended outfit. It offers daily lessons and cheap board hire. Call ahead to book and check the surf. Hours vary in winter, depending on sunset.

Port City Brew Bus BREWERY

(910-679-6586; www.portcitybrewbus.com; tours $55-60) Runs a few different good-time brewery tours around Wilmington. Pick-up points vary.

Sleeping

There are numerous budget hotels on Market St, just north of downtown. Wilmington counts at least 10 historic B&Bs, several of which are listed on the National Register of Historic Places.

Stella Maris Hostel HOSTEL $

(Map p279; 910-833-8271; www.hostelstellamaris.com; 605 S Front St; dm/d/t $27/65/75; P@) This great hostel, located in a 1913 house, is a good-value getaway within

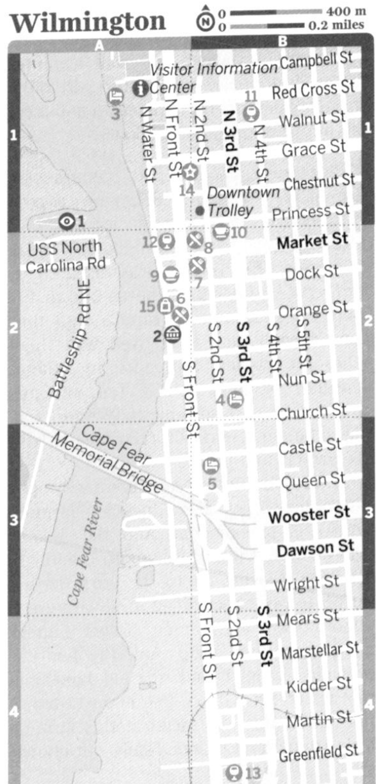

Wilmington

Sights

1 Battleship North Carolina A1
2 Museum of the Bizarre A2

Sleeping

3 Best Western Plus Coastline Inn A1
4 CW Worth House B2
5 Stella Maris Hostel B3

Eating

Dixie Grill .... (see 7)
Fork 'N' Cork .... (see 7)
6 Little Dipper A2
7 PinPoint B2
8 Shuckin' Shack Oyster Bar B2

Drinking & Nightlife

9 24 South Coffee House A2
10 Bespoke Coffee & Dry Goods B2
11 Flytrap Brewing B1
12 Front Street Brewery A2
13 Satellite Lounge B4

Entertainment

14 Dead Crow Comedy Room A1

Shopping

15 Old Wilmington City Market A2

walking distance of downtown. It's small – just two six-bed dorms (one mixed, one female) and one small private room with shared bathroom – and is mostly DIY (coded access, self check-in, staff not always in). There is a decent guest kitchen, a small common area and backyard hang space. Hardwood flooring throughout.

★ **CW Worth House** — B&B $$

(Map p279; ☎910-762-8562; www.worthhouse.com; 412 S 3rd St; r $160-200; ❄@☜) One of our favorite B&Bs in North Carolina, this turreted 1893 Queen Anne home is dotted with antiques and Victorian touches, but still manages to feel laid-back and cozy. Breakfasts are top-notch. The B&B is within a few blocks of downtown.

Best Western Plus Coastline Inn — HOTEL $$

(Map p279; ☎910-763-2800; www.bestwestern.com; 503 Nutt St; r $89-199, ste $129-279; ❄@☜🐾) We're not sure what we like best: the gorgeous views of the Cape Fear River, the wooden boardwalk or the short walk to downtown fun. Standard rooms aren't huge or too fancy, but every room has a river view. Pet fee is $20 per day and there's a set of bikes for rent. It's situated right next to the Wilmington Railroad Museum where there's a full-size steam engine.

Eating

You pay for the view at restaurants directly on the waterfront – and they can also be crowded and mediocre. Head a block or two inland for the best eats.

Dixie Grill — DINER $

(Map p279; ☎910-762-7280; https://thedixiegrillwilmington.wordpress.com; 116 Market St; breakfast mains $5-9, lunch mains $8.50-9.50; ⊙8am-3pm Mon-Sat, to 2pm Sun; ✎👪) A top breakfast spot in central Wilmington. This retro setting, with lime-green booths and a bar area for solo diners, serves apple-sage sausage patties, eggs all ways, and Southern classics including baked biscuits with onion gravy and all the trimmings. For lunch the menu is filled with burgers, sandwiches and salads.

Fork 'N' Cork BURGERS, SANDWICHES $
(Map p279; ☎910-228-5247; www.theforkncork.com; 122 Market St; mains $9-16; ⏱11am-11pm Mon-Thu, to midnight Fri & Sat, noon-10pm Sun; 📶) The kitchen's not afraid of kicky and decadent flavors at the hip Fork 'N' Cork, a former food truck that has cleaned up real nice. Juicy burgers such as the Hot Mess – with bacon, jalapeños, grilled onions, and blue and cheddar cheese – draw raves, as do the chicken, waffles, sandwiches and the day's mac 'n' cheese. Awesome fries!

Flaming Amy's Burrito Barn MEXICAN $
(☎910-799-2919; www.flamingamys.com; 4002 Oleander Dr, Carolina Beach; burritos $8; ⏱11am-10pm) The burritos are big and tasty at Flaming Amy's, a scrappy barn filled with kitschy decor from Elvis to Route 66. Burritos include the Philly Phatboy, the Thai Mee Up and the jalapeño-and-pepper-loaded Flaming Amy. Everyone in town is here or on the way.

★ **Little Dipper** CHEESE $$
(Map p279; ☎910-251-0433; www.littledipperfondue.com; 138 S Front St; fondue per person $18-29; ⏱5pm-late Tue-Sun Nov-May, 5pm-late Jun-Oct) Each table at this fun fondue restaurant comes with a burner at which to melt a pot of cheesy goodness. Choose from different combos – the classic cheddar and Emmental mix, or Italian cheeses (provolone, mozzarella and parmigiano) perhaps? Then order up a variety of dipping implements including meats, vegetables, bread and seafood. Save room for a chocolate fondue to finish.

Oceanic SEAFOOD $$
(☎910-256-5551; www.oceanicrestaurant.com; 703 S Lumina Ave, Wrightsville Beach; lunch mains $13-18, dinner mains $15-30; ⏱11am-10pm Mon-Thu, to 11pm Fri-Sun) This seafood restaurant on the pier ticks all the boxes for ambience, with simple outdoor and indoor seating with panoramic views of the coastline and Wrightsville Beach. Sunset dining doesn't get much better than this, and the food is pretty good too. Regional classics include crab cakes, shrimp and grits, Atlantic salmon, oysters and crab soup.

Shuckin' Shack Oyster Bar SEAFOOD $$
(Map p279; ☎910-833-8622; www.theshuckinshack.com; 127 N Front St; sandwiches from $8, mains $10-42; ⏱11am-10pm Sun-Thu, to midnight Fri & Sat) For an unpretentious local seafood and craft beer, it has to be this surf-themed bar-restaurant. Boards hang from the ceiling, sport plays on screens, there's surf rock on the speakers, and wall hangings (like an *Endless Summer* poster) add to the vibe. Satisfying menu items include lobster rolls and seared tuna salad bowls.

★ **PinPoint** SOUTHERN US $$$
(Map p279; ☎910-769-2972; www.pinpointrestaurant.com; 114 Market St; mains $22-35; ⏱5:30-9pm Mon-Thu, 10:30am-10pm Fri & Sat, to 9pm Sun; 📶) PinPoint was declared by *Southern Living* magazine as one of the South's best new restaurants – and they weren't lyin'! Chef Dean Neff was Hugh Acheson's kitchen compadre in Athens, Georgia's excellent Five & Ten, and he's sailing solo and shining in Wilmington, where he has a personal relationship with his farmers and fishers.

To start, the butter-bean hummus, topped with crunchy, pickled goodness and farmer's cheese, is phenomenal. And the oysters, wild-harvested from Masonboro Island, are delicious. Moving on to the crisp-smoked catfish (on celery-creamed grits with green tomato slaw and lemon brown butter), another culinary coup. And the flourless brownie caramel and roasted-dandelion-root ice cream? Gluten-free never tasted so fine! Of course, the menu at this farm-to-fork wonderland changes daily, but not the talent. Visit here now.

Drinking & Nightlife

It's not hard to find a fun place to drink in Wilmington. Use the wildly popular craft-beer app untappd.com to navigate this North Carolina brew town. Several local breweries make up the **Wilmington Ale Trail** (www.wilmingtonaletrail.com). Port City Brew Bus (p279) runs brewery tours.

★ **Satellite Lounge** BAR
(Map p279; ☎910-399-2796; www.facebook.com/satellitebarandlounge; 120 Greenfield St; ⏱4pm-2am Mon-Sat, 2pm-2am Sun; 📶) If you want to belly up to North Carolina's most stunning bar, you'll need to head in the opposite direction of Wilmington's historic downtown and into its up-and-coming warehousey South Front district. A gorgeously restored tavern highlights the space, which includes near-professional-level cornhole lanes, a fire pit and an outdoor cinema. It's also a bikers' favorite. Regular live music events, including bluegrass on Sunday night. Top spot.

The Workshop COFFEE
(☎910-679-8605; www.theworkshopwb.com; 86 Waynick Blvd, Wrightsville Beach; espresso drinks from $1.50; ⏰6:30am-4pm Mon-Sat, 7am-2pm Sun) For a cup o' Joe with bite, head to this small java house in Wrightsville Beach. The owners have combined their love of scuba diving, shark teeth and coffee. The groovy spot shows underwater footage on a big screen all day, and sells handmade jewelry crafted from recovered shark teeth and fossils, alongside espressos and toasted sandwiches. Smoothies, tea and cold brew with coconut water are also available.

24 South Coffee House COFFEE
(Map p279; www.24southcoffee.com; 24 S Front St; espressos from $1.60, smoothies $4.75; ⏰6:30am-6pm Mon-Fri, 7am-6pm Sat & Sun) Super-chilled atmosphere to enjoy a cup of coffee, with friendly baristas and unusual seats – like comfy armchairs and a church pew. Speciality drinks include a toasted almond mocha, gingerbread latte and funky monkey milkshake (banana, cold brew, peanut butter, honey and milk).

Bespoke Coffee & Dry Goods COFFEE
(Map p279; www.facebook.com/bespokecoffeenc; 202 Princess St; coffee $1.85-4.25; ⏰8am-7pm Mon-Sat, 9am-2pm Sun; 📶) Serving Durham's excellent Counter Culture Coffee, this hip coffeehouse is the most serious of many downtown java joints. In addition to caffeine, it dabbles in hipster dry goods such as denim, backpacks, shoes and candles.

Front Street Brewery MICROBREWERY
(Map p279; ☎910-251-1935; www.frontstreetbrewery.com; 9 N Front St; pints from $4; ⏰11:30am-midnight; 📶) It's only vaguely unusual that Wilmington's original brewery is North Carolina's biggest whisky bar! So, if beer isn't your thing, the 400+ bottles of brown liquor should have you covered. Not only that, this downtown brewery also serves pub grub (mains $8 to $17), which ought to come in handy after a few too many pints. Good times!

Flytrap Brewing MICROBREWERY
(Map p279; ☎910-769-2881; www.flytrapbrewing.com; 319 Walnut St; pints $5-6; ⏰3-10pm Mon-Thu, noon-midnight Fri & Sat, noon-10pm Sun; 📶) Located in a bright space in the Brooklyn Arts District just a short walk from Front St, Flytrap Brewing specializes in American-and Belgian-style ales among 12 taps. Look for food-truck fare and live music on weekend nights. The brewery is named for the Venus flytrap, the carnivorous plant whose only native habitat is within 60 miles of Wilmington.

☆ Entertainment

Dead Crow Comedy Room COMEDY
(Map p279; ☎910-399-1492; www.deadcrowcomedy.com; 265 N Front St; $15-18; ⏰from 7pm Tue-Thu, from 6pm Fri & Sat) Dark, cramped, underground and in the heart of downtown, just like a comedy club should be. Stop in for improv, open-mic nights and touring comedians, plus comedy bingo. Bar service and full menu available.

Shopping

Old Wilmington City Market MARKET
(Map p279; www.oldwilmingtoncitymarket.com; 119 S Water St; ⏰8am-6pm Sun-Thu, 10am-8pm Fri & Sat) Find local crafts, art and jewelry at stalls and in permanent shops under this impressive historic structure, with 14ft ceilings and a glass skylight. Market trading in this area dates back to the 1880s. Find it between Front St and Water St.

Information

Visitor information center (Map p279; ☎877-406-2356, 910-341-4030; www.wilmingtonandbeaches.com; 505 Nutt St; ⏰8:30am-5pm Mon-Fri, 9am-4pm Sat, 1-4pm Sun) In an 1800s freight warehouse; has a walking-tour map of downtown.

Getting There & Away

American Airlines and Delta Airlines serve **Wilmington International Airport** (ILM; ☎910-341-4125; www.flyilm.com; 1740 Airport Blvd) from Atlanta, Charlotte, New York and Philadelphia. It's 5 miles northeast of downtown. The **Greyhound** (☎910-791-8040; www.greyhound.com; 505 Cando St) station is an inconvenient 5 miles east of downtown.

Getting Around

The downtown area is easy to cover on foot, but a **free trolley** (Map p279; www.wavetransit.com/free-downtown-trolley-schedule; ⏰7:10am-8:50pm Mon-Fri, 10:30am-8:50pm Sat, 10:30am-5:30pm Sun) runs through the historic district from morning through evening.

North Carolina Mountains

Includes ➡

Best Places to Eat

- 12 Bones (p292)
- Bistro Roca (p286)
- Cúrate (p296)
- Buxton Hall (p293)

Best Places to Stay

- Sweet Peas Hostel (p291)
- Everett Hotel (p305)
- Lovill House Inn (p287)
- Bunn House (p292)

Why Go?

Towering along the skyline of western North Carolina, the mighty Appalachian Mountains hold several distinct subranges, among which the Great Smoky, Blue Ridge, Pisgah and Black Mountain ranges are especially dramatic. Carpeted in blue-green hemlock, pine and oak trees, logged a century ago but now preserved and protected, these cool hills are home to cougars, deer, black bears, wild turkeys and great horned owls. For adventurous travelers, the potential for hiking, camping, climbing and rafting expeditions is all but endless, while yet another photo opportunity lies around every bend.

The Cherokee who hunted on these forested slopes were later joined by 18th-century Scots-Irish immigrants looking for a better life. Lofty towns such as Blowing Rock enticed the sickly, lured by the fresh mountain air. Today, scenic drives, leafy trails and roaring rivers draw visitors from around the world.

When to Go

- May is the perfect month for hiking and cycling in the forests and mountains.
- Asheville's three-night Mountain Dance & Folk Festival in August showcases the very best traditional music.
- October is prime time for fall foliage; the mountains are ablaze with gold, orange and red.

HIGH COUNTRY

The northwestern corner of North Carolina, flanking the Blue Ridge Pkwyas it sets off across the state from Virginia, is known as High Country. Of the main towns, Boone is a lively college community that's home to Appalachian State University (ASU), while Blowing Rock and Banner Elk are quaint tourist centers near the winter ski areas.

Sights

Linville Falls WATERFALL

(828-765-1045; www.nps.gov/blri; Mile 316, Blue Ridge Pkwy, Linville; trails 24hr, visitor center 9am-5pm Apr-Oct;) FREE For a wonderful short hike, head up the hour-long Erwin's View Trail to spectacular Linville Falls. This moderate 1.6-mile round trip offers great close-up views of the Linville River as it sweeps over two separate falls. Climb the wooded hillside beyond for magnificent long-range panoramas back over the falls and, downstream, to where the river crashes a further 2000ft to enter the Linville Gorge Wilderness Area. Swimming is forbidden at the falls.

Grandfather Mountain MOUNTAIN

(828-733-4337; www.grandfather.com; Mile 305, Blue Ridge Pkwy, Linville; adult/child 4-12yr $20/9; 8am-7pm Jun-Aug, 9am-5pm Mon-Fri, 9am-6pm Sat & Sun Mar, 9am-6pm Apr, May, Sep & Oct, 9am-5pm Nov-Feb;) The highest of the Blue Ridge Mountains, Grandfather Mountain, looms north of the parkway 20 miles southwest of Blowing Rock. As a visitor destination, it's famous for the Mile High Swinging Bridge, the centerpiece of a private attraction that also includes hiking trails plus a small museum and wildlife reserve. Don't let a fear of heights scare you away; though the bridge is a mile above sea level, it spans a less fearsome chasm that's just 80ft deep.

Much of Grandfather Mountain – including its loftiest summit, Calloway Peak (5946ft), a strenuous 2.4-mile hike from the swinging bridge – belongs to Grandfather Mountain State Park (www.ncparks.gov). Its 12 miles of wilderness hiking trails can also be accessed for free at Mile 300 on the parkway.

Sleeping

Mast Farm Inn B&B $$

(828-963-5857; www.themastfarminn.com; 2543 Broadstone Rd, Valle Crucis; r/cottage from $169/299;) Featuring worn hardwood floors, claw-foot tubs, and handmade toffees on your bedside table, this restored farmhouse in the beautiful hamlet of Valle Crucis epitomizes rustic chic. Nine cabins and cottages are also available. Settle into the 1806 Loom House log cabin, fire up the wood-burning fireplace and never leave.

Shopping

Original Mast General Store SPORTS & OUTDOORS

(828-963-6511; www.mastgeneralstore.com; 3565 Hwy 194 S, Valle Crucis; 7am-6:30pm Mon-Sat, noon-6pm Sun;) The first of the many Mast general stores that dot the High Country, this rambling clapboard building still sells many of the same products that it did back in 1883. As well as bacon, axes and hard candy, though, you'll now find hiking shoes, lava lamps and French country hand towels.

Information

High Country Regional Welcome Center
(828-264-1299; www.highcountryhost.com; 6370 Hwy 321 S; 9am-5pm Mon-Sat, to 3pm Sun) Exceptionally friendly office, beside the highway between Blowing Rock and Boone, with full details on accommodations and outdoors outfitters.

Blowing Rock

828 / POP 1288

A stately and idyllic mountain village, tiny Blowing Rock beckons from its perch at 4000ft above sea level, the only full-service town directly on the Blue Ridge Pkwy. It's easy to be seduced by its postcard-perfect Main St, lined with antique shops, kitschy boutiques, potters, silversmiths, sweet shops, lively taverns and excellent restaurants. There are even a couple of bucolic, duck-filled lakes to drive home the storybook nature of it all. The only thing that spoils the illusion is the sheer difficulty of finding a place to park in high season.

Blowing Rock makes a homier base than nearby Boone, 8 miles north, for High Country attractions such as the Tweetsie Railroad (p286), North Carolina's only remaining fully functional steam-engine train, and Grandfather Mountain. As you drive in, pick up a historic downtown walking-tour map from the regional welcome center.

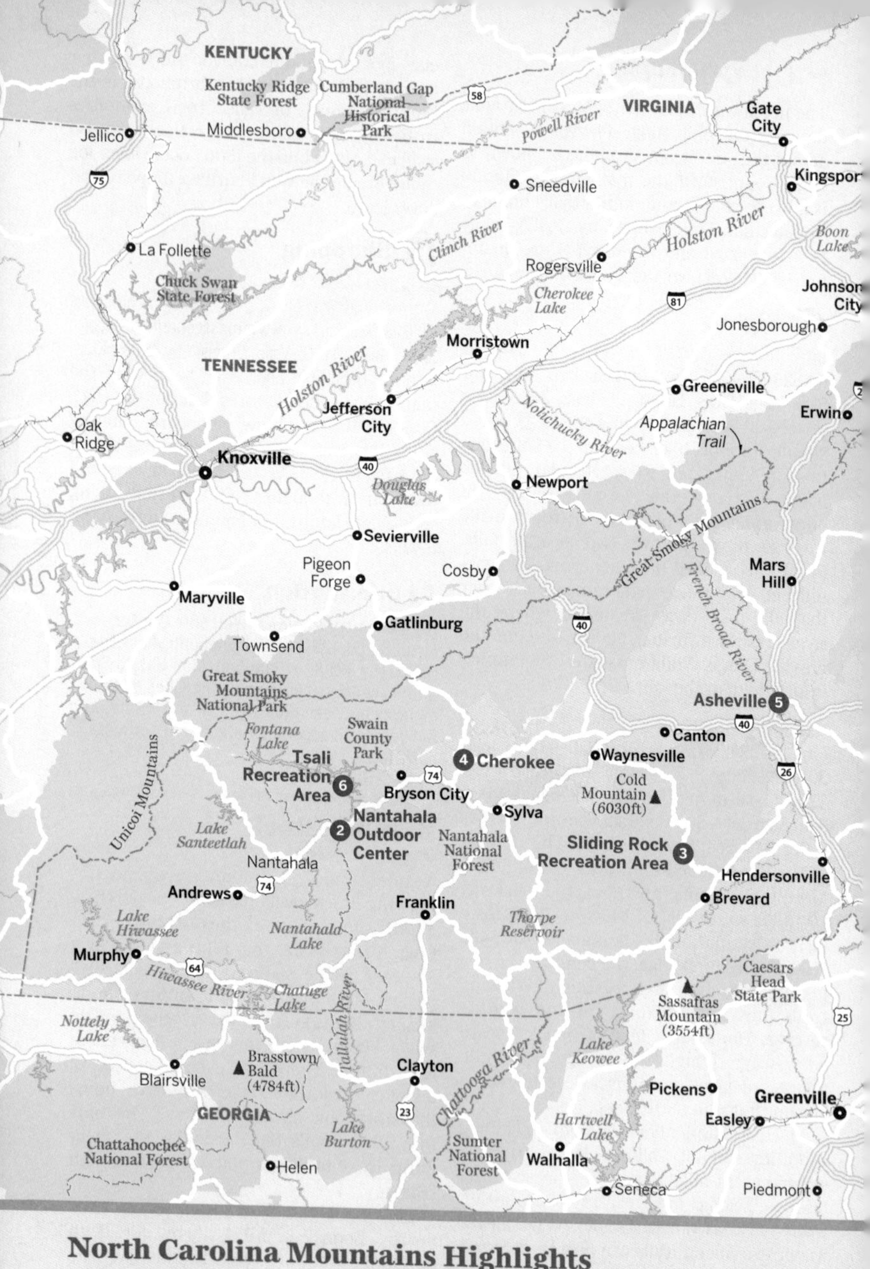

North Carolina Mountains Highlights

1 Blue Ridge Parkway (p306) Cruising the curves of America's most majestic mountain highway, at its finest in the fall.

2 Nantahala Outdoor Center (p299) Rafting the raging Nantahala River in North Carolina's wild western mountains.

3 Sliding Rock Recreation Area (p310) Slithering down slippery river rocks to splash into cooling mountain pools.

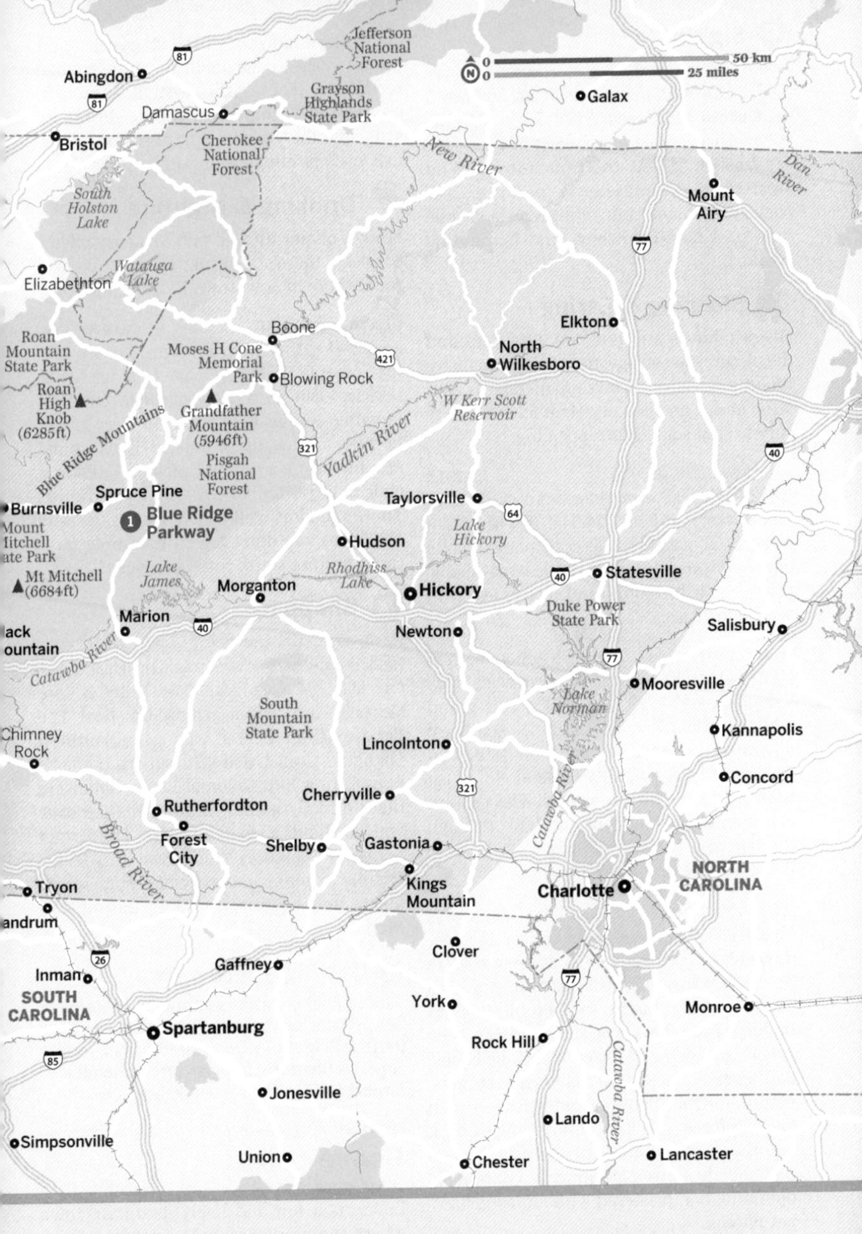

4 Museum of the Cherokee Indian (p302) Learning about the history and heritage of North Carolina's original Native American peoples in Cherokee.

5 Barbecue (p292) Munching melt-in-your-mouth meats, dripping in succulent sauces, at barbecue joints such as Asheville's 12 Bones.

6 Tsali Recreation Area (p312) Riding horses or bicycles through the rim-edge forests of a spectacular high-mountain lake.

Sights

Tweetsie Railroad AMUSEMENT PARK
(828-264-9061; www.tweetsie.com; 300 Tweetsie Railroad Lane; adult/child 3-12yr $45/30; 9am-6pm Jun-late Aug, Fri-Sun mid-Apr–May, late Aug-Oct;) At this much-loved Wild West–themed amusement park, a 1917 coal-fired steam train chugs on a 3-mile loop past heroic cowboys and marauding Indians.

Sleeping & Eating

Historic hotels and inns are dotted around the picturesque village, many with expansive mountain views. Browsing menus as you stroll along, and just off, Main St, and you're sure to spot something appealing.

Cliff Dwellers Inn MOTEL $
(828-414-9596; www.cliffdwellers.com; 116 Lakeview Terrace; r/apt from $124/144;) From its perch above town, this aptly named motel entices guests with good service, reasonable prices, stylish rooms and balconies with sweeping vistas.

Green Park Inn HISTORIC HOTEL $$
(828-414-9230; www.greenparkinn.com; 9239 Valley Blvd; r $94-299;) This grand white-clapboard hotel, 1 mile south of downtown, opened its doors in 1891, and was renovated in 2010 to hold 88 plush rooms and a grill restaurant. The eastern continental divide runs straight through the bar, and Margaret Mitchell stayed here while writing *Gone with the Wind*.

★ **Bistro Roca** AMERICAN $$
(828-295-4008; www.bistroroca.com; 143 Wonderland Trail; lunch mains $9-16, dinner mains $10-32; 11am-3pm & 5-10pm Wed-Mon;) This cozy, lodge-like bistro, in a Prohibition-era building just off Main St, serves upscale New American cuisine – lobster or pork-belly mac and cheese, kicked-up habanero burgers, mountain-trout banh mi sandwiches – with an emphasis on local everything. Check out the walls of the atmospheric Antlers Bar, North Carolina's longest continually operating bar, plastered with fantastic B&W pet photos.

Savannah's Oyster House SEAFOOD $$
(828-414-9354; www.savannahoysterhouse.com; 155 Sunset Dr; mains $10-32; 11am-9pm Tue-Thu & Sun, to 10pm Fri & Sat;) Get over the weirdness of finding a Low Country seafood place in the High Country – let alone the giant shark hanging in the stairwell – and there's much to like about this little cottage restaurant. There's the oysters, obviously, but also the sumptuous, cheesy shrimp 'n' grits, and the varied menu of seafood boils, fish 'n' chips and lobster potpie.

Drinking & Nightlife

From a quaint English pub to a cozy microbrewery, there's a drink waiting for you somewhere in downtown Blowing Rock.

Blowing Rock Ale House MICROBREWERY
(828-414-9254; www.blowingrockbrewing.com; 152 Sunset Dr; 11:30am-9pm Mon, Tue & Thu, 11:30am-10pm Fri & Sat, noon-9pm Sun;) Blowing Rock's first craft brewery offers 12 taps of locally produced suds (pints $5), including a popular pilsner, DIPA and chocolate porter, in a 1940s lodge house. There's food as well as five rooms upstairs ($175), so you don't have to stumble far – though those stairs could be tricky!

Shopping

Parkway Craft Center ARTS & CRAFTS
(828-295-7938; www.southernhighlandguild.org; Mile 294, Blue Ridge Pkwy, Moses H Cone Memorial Park; 9am-5pm mid-Mar–Nov) The Parkway Craft Center, where the Southern Highland Craft Guild sells superb crafts, is housed in a 1901 Colonial Revival mansion that's directly accessible from the parkway and also holds a small museum. The former home of Moses H Cone, who made his fortune in denim, it surveys an estate where hikers and equestrians share 25 miles of carriage roads.

Getting There & Away

Blowing Rock is 8 miles south of Boone via Hwy 321, or more like 25 miles if you detour along the Blue Ridge Pkwy. The nearest commercial airport is **Charlotte Douglas International Airport** (p370), 87 miles southeast.

Boone

828 / POP 18,834

Boone is a fun and lively mountain town where the predominantly youthful inhabitants – many of them students at bustling Appalachian State University – share a hankering for the outdoors. Renowned for its bluegrass musicians and Appalachian storytellers, the town is named after pioneer and explorer Daniel Boone, who often camped in the area. Downtown

DON'T MISS

LAP OF LUXURY

The largest privately owned home in the US, **Biltmore Estate** (☎800-411-3812; www.biltmore.com; 1 Approach Rd; adult/child 10-16yr $75/37.50; ⊙house 9am-4:30pm, with seasonal variations; P) was completed in 1895 for shipping and railroad heir George Washington Vanderbilt II, and modeled after three châteaux that he'd seen in France's Loire Valley. It's extraordinarily expensive to visit, but there's a lot to see; allow several hours to explore the entire 8000-acre estate. Self-guided tours of the house itself take in 39 points of interest, including our favorite, the two-lane bowling alley.

To hear the full story, pay $11 extra for an audio tour, or take the behind-the-scenes Upstairs Downstairs Tour ($20) or the more architecturally focused Rooftop Tour ($20). A 5-mile drive through the impeccably manicured estate, which also holds several cafes and two top-end hotels, leads to the winery and dairy farm in Antler Hill Village.

Boone features a fine assortment of low-rise brick-broad, Colonial Revival, art-deco and streamline-modern buildings. Those that line King St in particular now tend to hold house charming boutiques, cafes, and crafts galleries.

Every summer since 1952, local history has been presented in a dramatization called *Horn in the West*, performed in an outdoor amphitheater above town.

Sights

Foggy Mountain Gem Mine MINE

(☎828-963-4367; www.foggymountaingems.com; 4416 Hwy 105 S; buckets $30-325; ⊙10am-5pm; 👪) If you're traveling with kids or are a wannabe prospector yourself, stop 3 miles west of Boone to pan for semiprecious stones. Several gem-mining spots are located near the parkway, but this is a smaller operation, run by graduate gemologists who take their craft seriously. Buy rough stones by the bucketload – or even wheelbarrow-load! – and sift them in a flume line. For additional fees, they'll cut and mount your favorite finds.

Doc Watson Statue STATUE

(642 W King St) Bluegrass legend Doc Watson was born 10 miles east of Boone in 1923. He's commemorated by this bronze statue downtown, which depicts him seated and strumming his guitar.

Festivals & Events

Appalachian Summer Festival PERFORMING ARTS

(www.appsummer.org; ⊙Jul-early Aug) This prestigious month-long arts showcase, staged by Boone's Appalachian State University, uses venues all over campus, and centers on the Schaefer Center for the Performing Arts. Originally rooted in classical music, it now extends across theater, film, and the visual arts.

Sleeping

Accommodations in Boone traditionally consisted of standard chain hotels, but there is also Horton, downtown's first boutique hotel. You can also find the occasional historic B&B, rental farmhouse or cozy log cabin around town and in the surrounding countryside.

Hidden Valley Motel MOTEL $

(☎828-963-4372; www.hiddenvalleymotel.com; 8725 Hwy 105 S; r from $62; P 📶) A quintessential mom 'n' pop motel, set in delightful flower-filled gardens 8 miles southwest of town. The main house is bursting with vintage charm, while the eight guest rooms are cozy but plainer.

★**Lovill House Inn** B&B $$

(☎828-264-4204; www.lovillhouseinn.com; 404 Old Bristol Rd; r from $179; 📶) Boone's finest B&B is a splendid 19th-century farmhouse, a mile west of downtown and surrounded by woods. With its snug rooms, white clapboard walls, and wraparound porch decked out with rocking chairs, it's all wonderfully restful; the breakfast is worth getting up for, though.

Horton Hotel BOUTIQUE HOTEL $$

(☎828-832-8060; www.thehorton.com; 611 W King St; ❄📶) This ultra-central 15-room boutique hotel, in what was once a Studebaker showroom, adds a welcome dash of contemporary style to Boone's lodging options. Its open-air rooftop is a wonderful vantage point overlooking downtown.

WORTH A TRIP

MOUNT MITCHELL STATE PARK

A major decision awaits visitors to North Carolina's original state park, **Mount Mitchell State Park** (☎828-675-4611; www.ncparks.gov; 2388 Hwy 128; ⊙park 7am-10pm May-Aug, closes earlier Sep-Apr, office 8am-5pm Apr-Oct, closed Sat & Sun Nov-Mar; P) FREE. Will you drive up Mt Mitchell, at 6684ft the highest peak east of the Mississippi, or will you hike to the top? Make your mind up at the park office, which sits beside a steep 2.2-mile summit trail that typically takes around 1½ hours, one way.

Eating

Thanks largely to its many students, Boone holds the High Country's biggest concentration of restaurants. There's plenty of choice, ranging from Southern US to Latin American.

Wild Craft Eatery LATIN AMERICAN $
(☎828-262-5000; www.wildcrafteatery.com; 506 W King St; mains $11-14; ⊙11am-10pm Tue-Sun;) Colorful, quirky downtown cafe, with an outdoor deck on King St, and an emphasis on local ingredients. There's a definite Latin flavor to the menu, with tacos and tamales aplenty, but they also offer Thai noodles and shepherd's pie. Not everything's vegetarian, but most of the standout dishes are, including the Cuzco Cakes, made with smoked quinoa, Gouda and yams.

Melanie's Food Fantasy CAFE $
(☎828-263-0300; www.melaniesfoodfantasy.com; 664 W King St; breakfast mains $6-13, lunch & dinner mains $9-18; ⊙8:30am-2pm Sun-Wed, to 9pm Thu-Sat;) Students and hippie types gather at this farm-to-fork favorite – out on the patio, for much of the year – to gobble serious breakfast dishes (scrambles, eggs Benedict, omelets, pancakes) with a side of home fries. Later on, there's excellent creative Southern cuisine (chipotle-honey salmon and grits, blackened pimiento-cheese burger), with vegetarian options always available (tempeh, soysage etc).

Dan'l Boone Inn SOUTHERN US $$
(☎828-264-8657; www.danlbooneinn.com; 130 Hardin St; breakfast adult $12, child $5-9, lunch & dinner adult $19, child $6-12; ⊙11:30am-8:30pm Mon-Thu, from 8am Fri-Sun, dinner only Sat & Sun Nov-May;) Quantity is the name of the game at this restaurant, where the family-style meals are a Boone (sorry) for hungry hikers. Everyone pays the same price, and you can eat as much fried chicken and steak (lunch and dinner) or ham, sausage and bacon (breakfast) as you like. No credit cards.

Drinking & Nightlife

What with Boone being a university town, watering holes are not in short supply, including cheap student dives, microbreweries and mountain saloons.

Cardinal CRAFT BEER
(☎828-366-9600; www.thecardinalboone.com; 1711 Hwy 105; ⊙11am-midnight Mon-Thu, to 2am Fri & Sat, noon-midnight Sun;) Locals hunker down in this cozy, barn-like space, 2 miles south of downtown, for Boone's best range of local and regional craft beer (pints $5) – 12 taps in all, as well as $10 craft cocktails. You can also enjoy excellent, farm-driven burgers (beef, beet, bison, or game) and pinball or Skee-Ball.

Getting There & Away

The closest commercial airport to Boone is Charlotte Douglas International Airport (p370), 94 miles southeast.

ASHEVILLE

☎828 / POP 89,121

The undisputed 'capital' of the North Carolina mountains, Asheville is both a major tourist destination and one of the coolest small cities in the South. Cradled in a sweeping curve of the Blue Ridge Pkwy, it offers easy access to outdoor adventures of all kinds, while downtown's historic art-deco buildings hold stylish New Southern restaurants, decadent chocolate shops, and the homegrown microbreweries that explain the nickname 'Beer City.'

Despite rapid gentrification, Asheville remains recognizably an overgrown mountain town that holds tight to its traditional roots. It's also a rare liberal enclave in the conservative countryside, home to a sizable population of artists and hardcore hippies. Alternative Asheville life is largely lived in neighborhoods such as the waterfront River Arts District and, across the French Broad River, West Asheville. Remarkably enough, the French Broad River is the world's third-oldest river, its course laid before life on earth even began.

Sights

Downtown Asheville, which still looks much as it must have in the 1930s, is compact and easy to negotiate on foot. Apart perhaps from its breweries, the city's best-known attraction is the grandiose Biltmore Estate (p287), the largest privately owned home in the country. It luxuriates across a vast green expanse that stretches from Biltmore Village, 2.4 miles south of downtown.

Asheville Pinball Museum MUSEUM
(Map p290; ☎828-776-5671; http://ashevillepinball.com; 1 Battle Sq; adult/child 5-10yr $15/12; ⏰1-6pm Mon & Sun, 2-9pm Wed-Fri, noon-9pm Sat) A veritable time machine, this downtown treat transports gamers back to the much-lamented pinball arcades of yesteryear. With stock ranging from vintage cowboy-and-Indian games up to brand-new Game of Thrones editions, something is certain to flip your flippers. Your admission fee covers unlimited plays, though you may well have to wait your turn on popular machines.

Folk Art Center CULTURAL CENTER
(☎828-298-7928; www.southernhighlandguild.org; Mile 382, Blue Ridge Pkwy; ⏰9am-6pm Apr-Dec, to 5pm Jan-Mar; P) FREE Part gallery, part store, and wholly dedicated to Southern craftsmanship, the superb Folk Art Center stands directly off the Blue Ridge Pkwy, 6 miles east of downtown Asheville. Handcrafted Appalachian chairs hanging above its lobby make an impressive appetizer for the Southern Highland Craft Guild's permanent collection, a treasury of pottery, baskets, quilts and woodcarvings that's displayed on the 2nd floor.

Asheville Art Museum MUSEUM
(Map p290; ☎828-253-3227; www.ashevilleart.org; 2 S Pack Sq; $15 general admission, $13 adult discount, $10 student child age 6-17, under-6/military personnel free; ⏰Thu 11am-9pm, 11am-6pm Fri-Mon & Wed, closed Tue,) Reopened in 2019 after a huge transformation and expansion, this Asheville favorite is hope to permanent collection and short-term special exhibitions.

aSHEville Museum MUSEUM
(Map p290; ☎828-785-5722; www.ashevillemuseum.com; 35 Wall St; admission by donation, from $5; ⏰10am-10pm Sun-Thu, to 11pm Fri & Sat, shorter hours Nov-May) Who put the 'she' in Asheville? This dynamic downtown museum, where changing 'her-story' exhibits celebrate the achievements of women and girls the world over. There's an emphasis on local heroines such as Wilma Dykeman, whose 1955 book *The French Broad* decried the polluting of Asheville's principal river.

Thomas Wolfe Memorial HOUSE
(Map p290; ☎828-253-8304; www.wolfememorial.com; 52 N Market St; museum free, house tour adult/child 7-17yr $5/2; ⏰9am-5pm Tue-Sat) An incongruous survivor of old Asheville, this downtown clapboard structure was the childhood home of *Look Homeward, Angel* author Thomas Wolfe (1900–38). His autobiographical 1929 novel so offended locals that he didn't return to Asheville (which he fictionalized as 'Altamont') for eight years. Hourly tours, on the half-hour, enter the house itself.

Activities

Smoky Mountain Adventure Center OUTDOORS
(☎828-505-4446; www.smacasheville.com; 173 Amboy Rd; ⏰8am-8pm Mon, 8am-10pm Tue-Sat, 10am-8pm Sun) One-stop adventure shopping, across the French Broad River 3 miles southwest of downtown. On-site there's an indoor climbing wall, as well as yoga and tai-chi classes. They can also arrange bikes for the Blue Ridge Pkwy, inner tubes and paddleboards for the river, plus guided rock climbing, backpacking, day hiking, ice climbing and mountaineering trips.

Tours

BREW-ed BREWERY
(Map p290; ☎828-278-9255; www.brew-ed.com; adults $37-50, nondrinkers $20) Beer-focused historical walking tours, led by Cicerone-certified beer geeks and sampling two or three different downtown breweries, on Thursdays (5:30pm), Fridays (2pm), Saturdays (11:30am and 2pm) and Sundays (1pm).

Lazoom Tours BUS
(Map p290; ☎828-225-6932; www.lazoomtours.com; $23-29) For a hysterically historical tour of the city, hop on the purple bus, watch out for nuns on bikes – and bring your own booze. Weekend tours feature a live band and stop at breweries.

Asheville

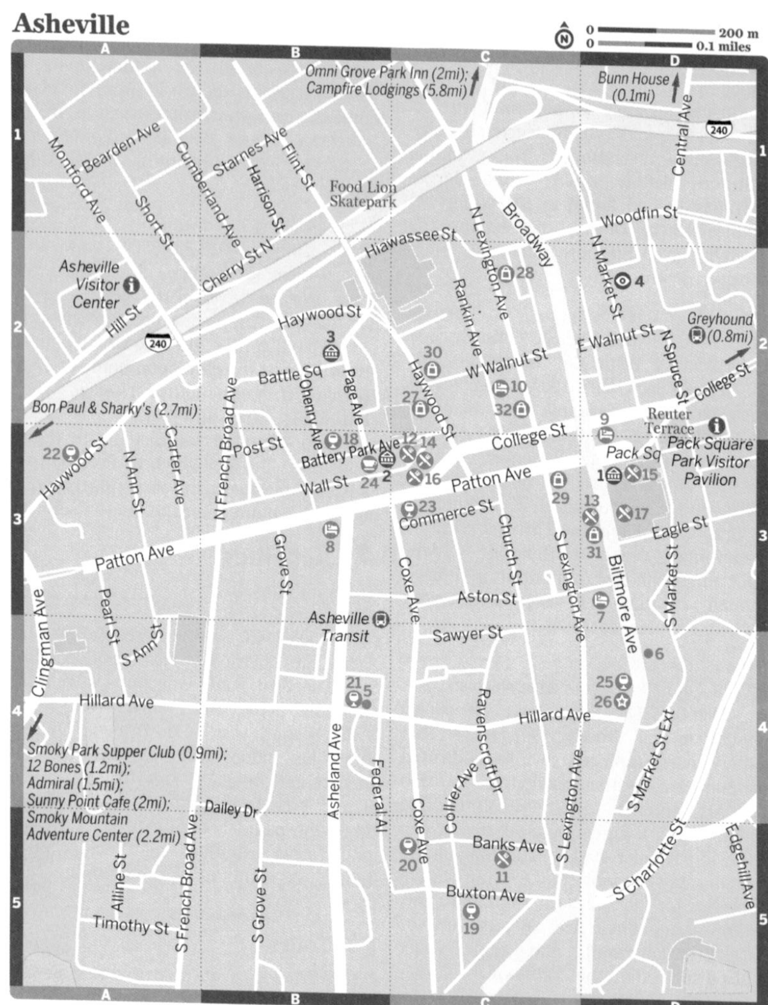

Festivals & Events

★ **Mountain Dance & Folk Festival** MUSIC

(828-258-6101; www.folkheritage.org; AB Tech/Mission Health Conference Center, 340 Victoria Rd; 1/3 nights $25/60; 1st Thu-Sat Aug;) North Carolina's premier showcase for old-time music, this three-day bonanza was founded as the first folk festival in the entire country by banjo and fiddle player Bascom Lamar Lansford in 1928.

Craft Fair of the Southern Highlands ART

(828-298-7928; www.southernhighlandguild.org; US Cellular Center, 87 Haywood St; 3rd weekends Jul & Oct) At these two three-day annual fairs, craft workers from all over the South gather to display and sell traditional and contemporary work in all media, including clay, metal, wood, glass and paper.

Sleeping

Asheville Bed & Breakfast Association ACCOMMODATION SERVICES

(828-250-0200; www.ashevillebba.com) Booking agents for a dozen local inns and B&Bs, from gingerbread cottages to alpine lodges.

Asheville

Sights
1 Asheville Art Museum D3
2 aSHEville Museum B3
3 Asheville Pinball Museum B2
4 Thomas Wolfe Memorial D2

Activities, Courses & Tours
5 BREW-ed B4
6 Lazoom Tours D4

Sleeping
7 Aloft Asheville Downtown D3
8 Downtown Inn & Suites B3
9 Hotel Arras D2
10 Sweet Peas Hostel C2

Eating
11 Buxton Hall C5
12 Chai Pani C3
13 Cúrate D3
14 Early Girl Eatery C3
15 French Broad Chocolate Lounge D3
16 Tupelo Honey C3
17 White Duck Taco Shop D3

Drinking & Nightlife
18 Battery Park Book Exchange & Champagne Bar B3
19 Burial C5
20 Funkatorium C5
21 Hi-Wire B4
22 O. Henry's A3
23 Thirsty Monk C3
24 Trade & Lore B3
25 Wicked Weed D4

Entertainment
26 Orange Peel Social Aid & Pleasure Club D4

Shopping
27 Chocolate Fetish C2
28 East Fork Pottery C2
29 Horse & Hero C3
30 Malaprop's Bookstore & Cafe C2
31 Mast General Store D3
32 Tops for Shoes C2

Hotel Arras HOTEL
(Map p290; www.mckibbon.com; 1 N Pack Sq) Pack Sq's BB&T tower, a 50-year-old modernist classic that's the tallest skyscraper in Asheville, is being revamped and overhauled to house this luxury hotel, with 360-degree mountain views from its upper floors.

★ **Sweet Peas Hostel** HOSTEL $
(Map p290; ☎828-285-8488; www.sweetpeashostel.com; 23 Rankin Ave; dm/pod $32/40, r without/with bath $75/105; ❄@☜) This spick-and-span, well-run, contemporary hostel occupies an unbeatable downtown location. The loft-like open-plan space, with its exposed brick walls, steel bunks and blond-wood sleeping 'pods', can get noisy, but at least there's a 10% discount at the Lexington Ave Brewery downstairs. They also warn you if an event coincides with your planned dates.

Downtown Inn & Suites MOTEL $
(Map p290; ☎828-254-9661; www.downtowninnandsuites.com; 120 Patton Ave; r $95; P☜) The Downtown Inn will only suit those who value location and price above amenities and peace. It's an old-style motel on a noisy street, with old-fashioned rooms, but they're reasonably sized and cozy, and you won't find a better price – or free parking, for that matter – elsewhere in the heart of downtown. Rates include a simple buffet breakfast.

Asheville Glamping TENTED CAMP $
(☎828-450-9745; www.ashevilleglamping.com; trailer/yurt/tipi/dome from $100/120/125/135, plus room-cleaning fee per stay $50; ☜) Friendly Joana runs three separate sites: two within 5 miles of downtown, the other 10 miles north towards Hot Springs. Each is peppered with a combination of glammed-up yurts, domes, tipis and vintage Airstream and Spartan trailers, some equipped with hot tubs, deluxe outdoor gas grills and prime Blue Ridge views. There's a minimum stay of two nights. You'll need to be self-sufficient, but for a certain kind of traveler this is a unique getaway.

Bon Paul & Sharky's HOSTEL $
(☎828-775-3283; www.bonpaulandsharkys.com; 816 Haywood Rd; tent sites per person $21.40, dm/r from $30/78, cottage $105; P@☜🐾) Bon Paul & Sharky's has been welcoming hostelers into this colorful West Asheville 1920 home, a $10 Uber ride from South Slope, for well over a decade. There's also a separate cottage, while campers in the garden share the bathrooms indoors. Plenty of good bars and restaurants lie within shouting distance (plus an organic market), or you can BYOB.

Campfire Lodgings CAMPGROUND $$
(☎828-658-8012; www.campfirelodgings.com; 116 Appalachian Village Rd; tent sites $35-40, RV sites $50-70, yurts $115-135, cabins $160; P❄☜) All yurts should have flat-screen TVs, don't

you think? Sleep like the world's most stylish Mongolian nomad in a furnished multi-room tent, half a mile up a wooded hillside on an unpaved but passable road, 6 miles north of town. Cabins and tent sites are also available. RV sites, higher up, enjoy stunning valley views and the only wi-fi access.

★**Bunn House** BOUTIQUE HOTEL **$$$**
(☎828-333-8700; www.bunnhouse.com; 15 Clayton St; d $249-424; P ❄ 🛜) The six rooms and suites in this meticulously restored 1905 home, in a residential neighborhood half a mile north of downtown, are awash with exposed brick and dark hardwoods. The small rooftop terrace boasts Blue Ridge vistas, while the heated bathroom floors and subway-tiled steam showers are glorious on chilly mountain mornings. There's no on-site reception – it's like having your own amazing studio apartment. Age 21 and over only.

Aloft Asheville Downtown HOTEL **$$$**
(Map p290; ☎828-232-2838; www.aloftasheville downtown.com; 51 Biltmore Ave; r from $289; P ❄ @ 🛜 ≋ 🐾) With a giant chalkboard in the lobby, groovy young staff, and an outdoor clothing store on the 1st floor, this place looks like the inner circle of hipster. The only thing missing is a wool-cap-wearing bearded guy drinking a hoppy microbrew – oh, wait, over there. We jest. Once settled, you'll find the staff knowledgeable and the rooms colorful and spacious.

Omni Grove Park Inn HISTORIC HOTEL **$$$**
(☎828-252-2711; www.omnihotels.com; 290 Macon Ave; r $149-419; P ❄ @ 🛜 ≋ 🐾) Commanding sweeping Blue Ridge views, this titanic Arts and Crafts–style stone lodge harks back to a bygone era of mountain glamor. Each of the 36ft-wide lobby fireplaces can hold a standing grown man, and has its own elevator to the chimney. Beyond the spectacular public spaces, though, the guest rooms can seem small by modern standards.

As well as a gargantuan underground spa, with stone pools and indoor waterfalls (day pass $90), the hotel has a golf course, indoor and outdoor tennis courts, and a 'base camp' for the Nantahala Outdoor Center (p299).

Eating

Asheville is a true foodie haven. Downtown and South Slope are bursting with enticing options, including simple (but oh-so-hip!) Southern-fried cafes, ethnic diners and elaborate Modern American and Appalachian kitchens. Farm-to-table is the rule; local, organic and sustainable are mantras. With more alternatives down in the River Arts District and over in West Asheville, you won't starve in these mountains.

★**12 Bones** BARBECUE **$**
(☎828-253-4499; www.12bones.com; 5 Foundy St; dishes $5.50-22.50; ⏲11am-4pm Mon-Fri) How good is the barbecue at 12 Bones?

TRAVEL WITH CHILDREN

Asheville is a family-friendly destination, bursting with opportunities for kids of all ages. The most fun you can have downtown has to be at the Asheville Pinball Museum (p289) – basically a vintage pinball arcade – though it's run a close second by the free **Splasheville** fountain that drenches unwary children in Pack Square Park each summer. Look out too for kids' activities at the new **Asheville Science Museum** (www.ashevillescience.org), located at 43 Patton Ave downtown.

There's plenty for kids to do out at the Biltmore Estate (p287), which, as well as its own farm and maze, offers activities including horse riding and a treasure hunt. They also cater to young fans of the fictional heroine Serafina, a mysterious girl said to have lived secretly in Biltmore House's basement.

Highlights in the surrounding mountains include a couple of scenic train rides, Tweetsie Railroad (p286) and the Great Smoky Mountains Railroad (p305). For active kids, you can't beat rafting at the Nantahala Outdoor Center (p299), cycling at the Tsali Recreation Area (p312), or simply slithering through a mountain stream at Sliding Rock (p310).

Chimney Rock (p299) makes a great day out for younger children; its 'Great Woodland Adventure' follows a trail leading to live local critters in the Animal Discovery Den.

Good enough to lure the vacationing Barack and Michelle Obama back to the River Arts District, a few years back. Expect a long wait, though, before you get to enjoy the slow-cooked, smoky and tender meats, or succulent sides from jalapeño-cheese grits to smoked potato salad.

The warehouse-like space is shared with an outlet of Wedge Brewing (p297); in-the-know regulars skip the line by picking up food from the take-out counter and carrying it around to the pub.

Chai Pani INDIAN $

(Map p290; ☎828-254-4003; www.chaipaniasheville.com; 22 Battery Park Ave; snacks $6.50-10, meals $12; ⏰11:30am-3:30pm & 5-9:30pm; 🖉) Literally 'tea and water,' *chai pani* refers more generally to inexpensive snacks. Hence the ever-changing array of irresistible street food at this popular, no-reservations downtown restaurant. Fill up on crunchy *bhel puri* – chickpea noodles and puffed rice – or live it larger with a lamb burger, fish roll, or chicken or vegetarian *thali*, a full meal on a metal tray.

★ **Buxton Hall** BARBECUE $

(Map p290; ☎828-232-7216; www.buxtonhall.com; 32 Banks Ave; mains $12-21; ⏰11:30am-3pm & 5:30-10pm; 📶) What happens when two James Beard–nominated chefs, Meherwan Irani and Elliott Moss, open a whole-hog barbecue joint in a cavernous former skating rink on the South Slope? You get the ridiculously good buttermilk-fried-chicken sandwich at Buxton Hall, that's what.

Sunny Point Cafe CAFE $

(☎828-252-0055; www.sunnypointcafe.com; 626 Haywood Rd; breakfast dishes $6-12, mains $10-19; ⏰8am-2:30pm Sun & Mon, to 9:30pm Tue-Sat) 🌿 Loved for its hearty homemade food, this bright West Asheville spot fills up each morning with solos, couples and ladies who breakfast; the little garden out front is the prime spot. Everything, waitstaff included, embraces the organic and fresh. The insanely good huevos rancheros, oozing feta cheese and chorizo sausage, should come with an instruction manual, while the biscuits are divine.

French Broad Chocolate Lounge DESSERTS $

(Map p290; ☎828-252-4181; www.frenchbroadchocolates.com; 10 S Pack Sq; desserts $2.75-7.50; ⏰11am-11pm Sun-Thu, to midnight Fri & Sat) Now happily ensconced in large, glossy premises beside Pack Sq Park, this beloved downtown chocolate shop hasn't lost its chocolate heart. Small-batch, locally produced organic chocolates, chunky chocolate brownies, chocolate-dipped ginger cookies, a sippable 'liquid truffle'…hey, where'd you go?

White Duck Taco Shop MEXICAN $

(Map p290; ☎828-232-9191; www.whiteducktacoshop.com; 12 Biltmore Ave; tacos $3.45-5.25; ⏰11:30am-9pm Mon-Sat, 10:30am-3pm Sun) The chalkboard menu at this downtown taco shop will give you fits. Every single one of these hefty soft tacos sounds like a must-have flavor bomb: spicy buffalo chicken with blue-cheese sauce, crispy pork belly, mole-roasted duck – even shrimp and grits! The margaritas are mighty fine too.

Early Girl Eatery CAFE $

(Map p290; ☎828-259-9292; www.earlygirleatery.com; 8 Wall St; mains $5-16; ⏰7:30am-3pm Mon-Wed, 7:30am-9pm Thu & Fri, 8am-9pm Sat & Sun) It's the all-day breakfast menu that draws the crowds to this downtown farm-to-table cafe, where the sunny dining room overlooks a small central square. Go for the house Benny, with tomato, spinach, avocado and poached eggs on grit cakes, or a grilled pimiento-cheese sandwich if it's past your breakfast time.

DON'T MISS

BEST OF ASHEVILLE

Asheville Pinball Museum (p289) Bumping the bumpers, pumping the plungers and flipping the flippers of vintage arcade games – what finer pleasures does life have to offer?

12 Bones (p292) Initiating your taste buds into the joys of North Carolina barbecue, down in the happening River Arts District.

Biltmore Estate (p287) Exploring America's largest private home – upstairs, downstairs and in my lady's chamber – then marveling at the vast estate that surrounds it.

Burial (p296) Brushing up on Belgian brews in Beer City's hippest microbrewery, on downtown's South Slope.

Sweet Peas Hostel (p291) Enjoying the futuristic style of downtown's best-value budget lodgings, perfectly poised to participate in the local nightlife.

THE BEST DAY TRIPS FROM ASHEVILLE

LINVILLE FALLS

A round trip to hike the forest trails at Linville Falls, with plenty of stops en route, is the perfect way to savor the splendors of the Blue Ridge Pkwy within a single day.

This moderate round trip offers great close-up views of the river as it sweeps over two separate falls, before you climb a wooded hillside to enjoy magnificent long-range panoramas in two directions. One looks back to the falls, the other faces downstream, where the river crashes a further 2000ft through a rocky gorge. (Swimming is forbidden at the falls.)

☆ Best Things to See & Do

Linville Falls A short (1.6 miles round-trip) hike along Erwin's View Trail will provide stunning views of two separate falls. (p283)

Linville Gorge Wilderness Area Check out one of the many hike options amid the 12,000 acres here.

Blue Ridge Parkway The best route from Asheville includes more than 20 miles of this legendary drive (p306).

☆ How to Get There

The only way to access this region is by car. From Asheville, take I-40 west to Hwy 221, the Blue Ridge Pkwy. The round trip is just over 100 miles.

CHEROKEE

Learn the tragic and extraordinary story of the Cherokee people at this otherwise unassuming town located near the southern approach to the Great Smoky Mountains National Park. Buy traditional crafts, and explore a pristine stretch of the Blue Ridge Pkwy. The town signifies the Qualla Boundary, an area that while not an official reservation, is tribal-owned land.

☆ Best Things to See/Do/Eat

Museum of the Cherokee Indian Most of the Cherokee tribe was violently removed from their home territory in these mountains in the 19th century, but their rich history is celebrated here. (p302)

Qualla Arts & Crafts Mutual This large cooperative gallery showcases and sells the area's best authentic Cherokee crafts. (p304)

Harrah's Cherokee Casino Surprise – this casino serves up Cherokee's best food, including a noodle bar and a pizzeria. (p304)

☆ How to Get There

Take I-40 west to Clyde to catch Hwy 74 west, the Great Smoky Mountains Expressway.

BREVARD

One of North Carolina's most beguiling small towns, and set amid spectacular scenery, Brevard makes a great base for mountain biking, hiking and swimming, with many different trails, swimming holes and hidden waterfalls. The scenery surrounding the town is also beautiful, and at its finest in the nearby Pisgah National Forest.

The town is also the home of the prestigious Brevard Music Center, which stages the acclaimed summer Brevard Music Festival.

☆ Best Things to See/Do/Eat

Hub If you're here to mountain bike, you'll want to stop in at the town's best bike shop for advice. (p311)

Sliding Rock Recreation Area Just outside of Brevard, this wild swimming area is a must-see. (p310)

Falls Landing North Carolina trout is a menu highlight at the city's favorite fine-dining restaurant. (p311)

☆ How to Get There

The fastest way here from Asheville is I-26 south to Hwy 280, but the more scenic option is to take I-40 west and connect to Hwy 276, part of the Blue Ridge Pkwy.

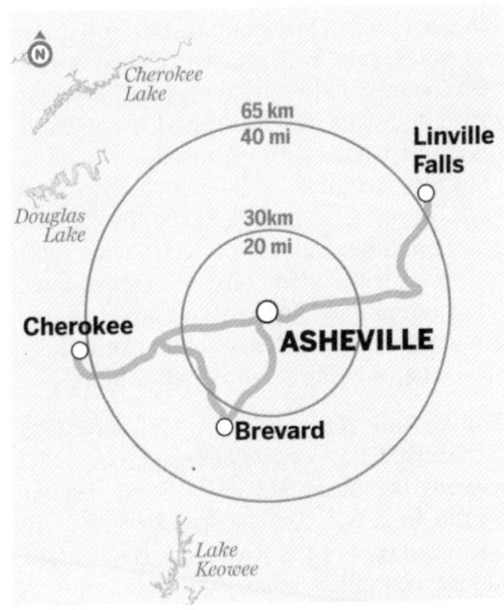

Asheville

Asheville is full of artsy charm, Southern food and top-notch craft beer. But the city is also beloved for its easy access to some of the best outdoor experiences in the North Carolina Mountains, many of which can be seen in a day.

★ **Cúrate** TAPAS $$

(Map p290; 828-239-2946; www.curatetapasbar.com; 13 Biltmore Ave; small plates $6-18; 11:30am-10:30pm Tue-Fri, from 10am Sat & Sun) Owned by hip Ashevillian chef Katie Button and her Catalan husband Félix, this convivial downtown hangout celebrates the simple charms and sensual flavors of Spanish tapas, while adding an occasional Southern twist. Standout dishes run long and wide: *pan con tomate* (grilled bread with tomato), lightly fried eggplant drizzled with honey and rosemary, and a knockout squid-ink 'paella' with vermicelli.

It also features a Barcelona-style *vermuteria* (vermouth bar). Savor the flavors, order another glass of Garnacha and converse with your dinner companions, not your phone. Reservations are a must, especially on weekends, but you can usually snag a bar seat fairly quickly after 9pm.

Smoky Park Supper Club AMERICAN $$

(828-350-0315; www.smokypark.com; 350 Riverside Dr; mains $13-36; 5-9pm Tue-Thu, 4-10pm Fri & Sat, 10:30am-9pm Sun;) An anchor of cool in the River Arts District, the largest container-constructed restaurant in the USA is more than the sum of its parts – 19 shipping containers to be exact. Choose between such wood-fired delights as garlic- and lemon-roasted half chicken, cast-iron-seared Carolina fish, or, for vegetarians, roasted local apples stuffed with kale, walnuts and smoked cheddar.

Tupelo Honey SOUTHERN US $$

(Map p290; 828-255-4863; www.tupelohoneycafe.com; 12 College St; brunch mains $6-17, lunch & dinner mains $9.50-30; 9am-9pm Sun-Thu, to 10pm Fri & Sat) The flagship downtown location of this Asheville-based chain is renowned for New Southern favorites, such as shrimp and grits with goat's cheese – even if the Tupelo-born Elvis himself would surely have gone for the fried-chicken BLT with apple-cider bacon! Brunches are superb, but no matter the meal, say yes to the biscuit. And add a drop of honey.

Admiral AMERICAN $$$

(828-252-2541; www.theadmiralasheville.com; 400 Haywood Rd; small plates $12-18, large plates $30-38; 5-10pm;) Set in a concrete bunker beside a car junkyard, this low-key West Asheville spot looks divey from the outside. It's inside, though, where the magic happens. One of the state's finest New American restaurants, the Admiral serves wildly creative dishes – saffron tagliatelle with lima beans, zucchini and basil pesto, for example – that taste divine.

Drinking & Nightlife

Asheville is the craft-beer capital of the South, only rivaled in quality and quantity across the entire USA by Portland's Oregon and Maine. The live music scene is extremely vibrant: you can find music nightly, with bluegrass and old-time aplenty but much more besides; and the Asheville Symphony Orchestra is very progressive, collaborating with hip-hop acts etc.

★ **Burial** MICROBREWERY

(Map p290; www.burialbeer.com; 40 Collier Ave; 2-10pm Mon-Thu, from noon Fri- Sun;) This ever-progressive brewery gives experimental batches of Belgian-leaning styles – farmhouse saisons, strong dubbels and tripels – a Southern kick in the pants, using local ingredients such as wildflower honey, chokeberries and juniper branches. Brewers in overalls, a menacing logo, and pitchfork-and-sickle tap and door handles add intrigue. It takes significant willpower to leave the outdoor patio. There's a decent food menu, too.

★ **Funkatorium** MICROBREWERY

(Map p290; 828-552-3203; www.wickedweedbrewing.com/locations/funkatorium; 147 Coxe Ave; 2-10pm Mon-Thu, noon-midnight Fri & Sat, 11am-10pm Sun;) If you need the funk, you gotta have that funk...and you'll find at it at the East Coast's first taproom dedicated to sour, wild ale, Brett and funky beer. For fans, it's pilgrimage-worthy. The rough-and-ready old world–style taproom holds more than 600 aging barrels, and rotating taps spit 8oz pours for the cause. Get funked up!

LGBTIQ+ ASHEVILLE

Downtown Asheville is home to North Carolina's oldest gay men's bar, O. Henry's, which has been open since 1976. The local LGBTIQ+ community celebrates **Blue Ridge Pride Festival** (www.blueridgepride.org) in downtown's Pack Square Park in late September or early October.

For event listings and community resources, visit www.gayashevillenc.com.

LOCAL KNOWLEDGE

BEER CITY, USA

If ever a city was transformed by the craft-beer movement, it's Asheville. A sleepy mountain city when its first brewery, Highland Brewing, opened in 1994, Asheville has become a true destination city for booze-bent hopheads. It now holds almost 30 breweries, catering to a population of around 90,000 locals; were it not for the half-million tourists who join them each year, that would be an lot of beer per person!

Inevitably, big-name national breweries have been flocking to Asheville too. Both New Belgium and Sierra Nevada, respectively from California and Colorado, have opened major brewing and taproom facilities here. Strolling from brewery to beerhouse in the pub-packed South Slope district – which, yes, slopes south from downtown – it's easy to see why Asheville has been nicknamed Beer City.

If you're ready to tackle the taps in Asheville, be sure to try a few of our favorite taprooms:

Burial Never mind its menacing logo; this friendly joint whips up some of Asheville's finest and most experimental Belgian-leaning styles (farmhouse saisons, strong dubbels and tripels).

Funkatorium Wicked Weed's all-sour taproom is a temple of tart and funk.

Wedge Brewing Our favorite microbrewery ambience – a festive, come-one, come-all outdoor space, rife with dogs, kids on tricycles, swooning couples and outdoorsy types.

Wicked Weed A former gas station turned craft-brew wonderland – with 58 taps!

★ Battery Park Book Exchange & Champagne Bar WINE BAR

(Map p290; ☎828-252-0020; www.batteryparkbookexchange.com; 1 Page Ave; ⊙11am-9pm Sun-Thu, to 10pm Fri & Sat) A charming champagne bar, sprawling through several opulent vintage-furnished rooms of a glorious old downtown shopping arcade, with every nook and cranny lined with shelves of neatly cataloged secondhand books covering every imaginable topic. Seriously, who could resist that as a combination? Other wines are also available, along with coffee, cakes, cheese and charcuterie.

Wedge Brewing MICROBREWERY

(☎828-505-2792; www.wedgebrewing.com; 37 Paynes Way; ⊙noon-10pm; 📶) Unlike the spit-shined, well-oiled breweries elsewhere in Asheville, the grungier Wedge in the River Arts District is happy to keep things edgy. The beers are excellent – especially the Iron Rail IPA – but it's the fairy-lit outdoor patio, packed with convivial locals and their dogs, that gives it a one-up on fellow taprooms. Food trucks nightly.

Wicked Weed MICROBREWERY

(Map p290; ☎828-575-9599; www.wickedweedbrewing.com; 91 Biltmore Ave; ⊙11:30am-11pm Mon-Thu, to 1am Fri & Sat, noon-11pm Sun; 📶) Henry VIII called hops 'a wicked and pernicious weed' that ruined the taste of beer. His subjects kept quaffing it anyway – just like the lively crowd in this former gas station, which overflows with hoppy brews. Equipped with 58 taps and a broad front patio, it's a big and breezy spot to chill.

Trade & Lore COFFEE

(Map p290; ☎828-424-7291; www.tradeandlore.com; 37 Wall St; ⊙8am-7pm Tue-Thu, to 10pm Fri-Mon; 📶) Deft baristas dole out serious java in this trendy downtown coffeehouse, drowning in industrial cool but leavened by occasional fits of vintage furniture. Espresso comes courtesy of a top-end La Marzocco machine, and there are four beer taps for lovers of another tipple.

Thirsty Monk CRAFT BEER

(Map p290; ☎828-254-5470; www.monkpub.com; 92 Patton Ave; ⊙4pm-midnight Mon-Thu, noon-1:30am Fri & Sat, noon-10pm Sun) This scruffy but lovable downtown pub nails a fine drinking trifecta. Downstairs you'll find 16 taps and nearly 200 bottles of Belgian ales; at street level, 20 taps of proprietary, North Carolina and regional craft beers; and on the roof, craft cocktails dating back before Prohibition.

O. Henry's GAY

(Map p290; ☎828-254-1891; www.ohenrysofasheville.com; 237 Haywood St; ⊙4pm-3am) Open since 1976, North Carolina's longest-standing gay men's bar is an Asheville institution, with 'Take the Cake' karaoke on Wednesdays – winners earn a fresh-baked cake – and drag at weekends. Its Underground dance bar, at the back, opens Friday and Saturday only.

Hi-Wire MICROBREWERY
(Map p290; ☎828-738-2448; www.hiwirebrewing.com; 197 Hilliard Ave; ⏲4-11pm Mon-Thu, 2pm-1am Fri, noon-1am Sat, 1-10pm Sun) Set in what used to be a mechanic's garage, this popular South Slope brewery offers a choice array of easy-drinking brews. Its taproom makes a mellow spot to hang with friends on a Saturday afternoon.

Westville Pub CRAFT BEER
(☎828-225-9782; www.westvillepub.com; 777 Haywood Rd; ⏲10:30am-2am) There's no better spot in West Asheville to bond with local 20- and 30-somethings, over a bottle or two of organic ale, than this veteran neighborhood bar.

Shopping

An afternoon spent strolling around downtown Asheville is a true delight, with unexpected shopping pleasures around every corner. Along its narrow streets, its century-old buildings hold an intriguing mixture of hip new boutiques and deeply traditional main-street stores.

Horse & Hero ARTS & CRAFTS
(Map p290; ☎828-505-2133; www.facebook.com/horseandhero; 124 Patton Ave; ⏲11am-7pm Sun-Thu, to 9pm Fri & Sat) For a taste of Asheville's contemporary creativity, and a distinctly psychedelic take on Appalachian art, drop into this groovy downtown gallery. As well as graphic design pieces and lithographs, it sells plenty of more affordable craftwork.

LOCAL KNOWLEDGE

JUICY JAMS

Asheville's premier live music venue, downtown's **Orange Peel Social Aid & Pleasure Club** (Map p290; ☎828-398-1837; www.theorangepeel.net; 101 Biltmore Ave; tickets $10-35; ⏲shows from 8pm) has been a showcase for big-name indie and punk bands since 2002. A warehouse-sized place, it seats – well, stands – a thousand-strong crowd.

Mast General Store SPORTS & OUTDOORS
(Map p290; ☎828-232-1883; www.mastgeneralstore.com; 15 Biltmore Ave; ⏲10am-6pm Mon-Thu, to 9pm Fri & Sat, noon-6pm Sun) This long-standing North Carolina favorite is great for outdoor gear, organic and natural cosmetics, provisions, candy, toys – you name it, much of it produced locally.

East Fork Pottery CERAMICS
(Map p290; ☎828-575-2150; www.eastforkpottery.com; 82 N Lexington Ave; ⏲11am-6pm Mon-Sat, noon-5pm Sun) Beautiful ceramic mugs and plates, made by a collective team of local ceramicists that includes Alex Matisse, the great-grandson of Henri himself. Their shop also sells a few of their favorite things, such as artisanal Japanese cutlery and nail clippers, and wonderful high-end handmade soaps.

Chocolate Fetish CHOCOLATE
(Map p290; ☎828-258-2353; www.chocolatefetish.com; 36 Haywood St; ⏲11am-7pm Mon-Thu, to 9pm Fri & Sat, noon-6pm Sun) With its silky truffles ($2.25) and sinfully good caramels, not to mention 20-minute tasting tours ($10), Chocolate Fetish deserves a flag on any chocolate addict's map. Our favorite is the Habanero Sea Salt, a caramel that hurts so good!

Tops for Shoes SHOES
(Map p290; www.topsforshoes.com; 27 N Lexington Ave; ⏲10am-6pm Mon-Sat, 1-5pm Sun) This may look like a run-of-the-mill, old-school shoe store, but venture inside – it's enormous, with an eye-catching assortment of hiking boots and hip footwear.

Malaprop's Bookstore & Cafe BOOKS
(Map p290; ☎828-254-6734; www.malaprops.com; 55 Haywood St; ⏲9am-9pm Mon-Sat, to 7pm Sun; 📶) Downtown's best-loved new bookstore is cherished locally for its expert staff, who maintain a carefully curated selection of regional fiction and nonfiction. The cappuccino and wi-fi are very welcome, too.

Information

Asheville's main **visitor center** (Map p290; ☎828-258-6129; www.exploreasheville.com; 36 Montford Ave; ⏲8:30am-5:30pm Mon-Fri, 9am-5pm Sat & Sun), alongside I-240 exit 4C, sells Biltmore Estate admission tickets at a $10 discount. Downtown holds a satelite **visitor pavilion** (Map p290; ☎828-258-6129; www.exploreasheville.com; 80 Court Pl; ⏲9am-5pm), with restrooms, beside Pack Square Park.

Getting There & Away

Asheville Regional Airport (AVL; ☎828-684-2226; www.flyavl.com; 61 Terminal Dr, Fletcher),16 miles south of Asheville, is served by a handful of nonstop flights, with destinations including Atlanta, Charlotte, Chicago and New York. **Greyhound** (☎828-253-8451; www.greyhound.com; 2 Tunnel Rd) is 1 mile northeast of downtown.

Getting Around

Although there's very little free parking downtown, public garages are free for the first hour and only cost $1 per hour thereafter. The handy Passport app (https://passportinc.com) facilitates paying for Asheville's parking meters and paid lots.

The 18 local bus routes run by Asheville Transit (ART) typically operate between 5:30am and 10:30pm Monday through Saturday, and shorter hours Sunday. Tickets cost $1, and there are free bike racks. Route S3 connects the **downtown ART station** (Map p290; ☎828-253-5691; www.ashevilletransit.com; 49 Coxe Ave; ⏰6am-9:30pm Mon-Fri, from 7am Sat, 8:30am-5.30pm Sun) with Asheville Regional Airport 10 times daily.

WESTERN NORTH CAROLINA

North Carolina's westernmost tip is blanketed in parkland and sprinkled with tiny mountain towns. The region is rich in Native American history. A large proportion of its Cherokee population was forced off their lands during the 1830s – by their erstwhile ally, Andrew Jackson – and marched to Oklahoma on the Trail of Tears, but many managed to hide in the remote mountains. Their descendants, now known as the Eastern Band of Cherokee Indians, live on the 56,000-acre Qualla Boundary territory, on the southern edge of Great Smoky Mountains National Park (p313).

Rolling across western North Carolina into the mountainous High Country, the contiguous Pisgah and Nantahala national forests hold more than a million acres of dense hardwood trees and windswept mountain balds, as well as some of the country's best white-water rapids – and sections of the Appalachian Trail.

It's the wilderness that's the true wonder of the west. Much of it is preserved in choice portions of Pisgah and Nantahala national forests, where adventurous visitors can launch themselves on hiking and cycling trails and rampaging rivers. Nantahala National Forest holds several recreational lakes and dozens of roaring waterfalls, while Pisgah highlights include the natural water slide at Sliding Rock (p310), the 3.2-mile round-trip hike to the summit of 5721ft Mt Pisgah, and the bubbling baths in the village of Hot Springs.

DON'T MISS

NATURAL WONDERS

The stupendous 315ft monolith known as **Chimney Rock** (☎800-277-9611; www.chimneyrockpark.com; Hwy 74A; adult/child 5-15yr $13/6; ⏰8:30am-7pm mid-Mar–Oct, 8:30am-6pm Nov, 10am-6pm Dec, 10am-6pm Fri-Tue Jan–mid-Mar; P) towers above the slender, forested valley of the Rocky Broad River, a gorgeous 28-mile drive southeast of Asheville. Protruding in naked splendor from soaring granite walls, its flat top bears the fluttering American flag. Climb there via the 499 steps of the Outcropping Trail, or, assuming it's been repaired by the time you read this, simply ride the elevator deep inside the rock.

Activities

★ **Nantahala Outdoor Center** RAFTING

(NOC; ☎828-366-7502, 828-785-5082; www.noc.com; 13077 Hwy 19 W; duckie rental per day $35, guided trips $50-200; ⏰8am-8pm Jun & Jul, reduced hours Aug-May) This huge and highly recommended outfitter specializes in wet 'n' wild rafting trips down the Nantahala River. Their 500-acre site, 14 miles southwest of Bryson City, also offers ziplining and mountain biking, and even has its own lodge, a hostel, a mostly year-round restaurant and a seasonal BBQ and beer joint (open May to October). The Appalachian Trail rolls across the property too.

Hot Springs Rafting Company RAFTING

(☎877-530-7238; www.hotspringsraftingco.com; 22 Hwy 25, Hot Springs; trips adult/child from $45/40; ⏰9am-6pm) Take a 4-mile, half-day guided trip down the French Broad River on class IIs and IIIs, or brave the 9-mile full-day trip with class IVs. To float at your own pace, rent a funyak (adult/child $35/30) or inner tube ($20) and hop in!

OUTDOOR ACTIVITIES IN THE NORTH CAROLINA MOUNTAINS

HIKE TO CHIMNEY ROCK

START CHIMNEY ROCK PARK
END CHIMNEY ROCK PARK
DURATION TWO TO FIVE HOURS
DISTANCE 3 TO 6 MILES
DIFFICULTY MODERATE

Whether you want to enjoy an easy family hike, or fancy a more demanding backcountry trail, it's hard to beat **Chimney Rock Park** (p299). While it's an easy day trip from Asheville – via a gorgeous 28-mile drive on Hwy 74A – the charming neighboring village of Chimney Rock means it's also an appealing overnight destination.

Chimney Rock itself is a stark 315ft monolith that juts from the soaring granite walls of Hickory Nut Gorge, a slender valley carved by the Rocky Broad River. Because it's a short distance under the crest, the rock is not immediately obvious from below. The park entrance is immediately across the river from the village; park in the meadow just inside.

From there, the Four Seasons Trail climbs through thick woods for three quarters of a mile, and meets the Hickory Nut Falls Trail atop a naked stone outcrop. Head right for a level half-mile to reach the foot of the 404ft Hickory Nut Falls, high above the river. This is Falls Creek, fed by natural springs atop the mountain. In the absence of direct sunlight, rare plant species flourish on its exposed slopes.

Now double back, and just beyond the trail junction you'll reach a stairway that ascends to the upper parking lot. The Outcropping Trail climbs from here via a further 499 steps to reach the flat top of Chimney Rock, surmounted by a fluttering American flag.

Thus far, you're likely to have shared the trails with a lot of fellow hikers. The crowds drop away, though, if you head 200ft higher still on the Exclamation Point Trail, a stiff 20-minute climb along yet more stairways and switchbacks, which passes some spec-tacular formations en route to a superb overlook. Beyond that, the recently reopened Skyline Trail heads into the backcountry, passing Peregrine's Point, from which views extend to Lake Lure, and crossing Falls Creek to reach the top of Hickory Nut Falls.

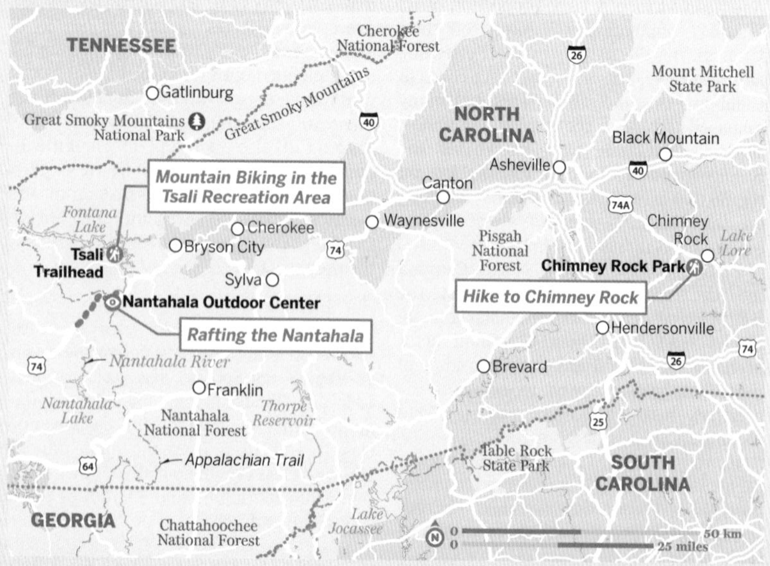

When it comes to attracting adventurous visitors, the mountains are North Carolina's trump card. Hikers and cyclists can enjoy trails to suit any level of expertise, while rafting operators offer expeditions on the wild rivers.

MOUNTAIN BIKING IN THE TSALI RECREATION AREA

START TSALI TRAILHEAD
END TSALI TRAILHEAD
DURATION HALF DAY
DISTANCE 12 TO 20 MILES
DIFFICULTY MODERATE

For a great day's mountain biking in superb scenery, head for the **Tsali Recreation Area** (p312), west of Bryson City. The pick of its four main trails – divided into two groups, each open to cyclists on alternate days – is the Left Loop, for its stimulating challenges, views and flexibility.

Head clockwise from the parking lot, and you soon drop down to the eastern shoreline of the Mouse Branch, a flooded former tributary. The trail now follows the very edge of the water; erosion has worn it to barely 1ft wide in places. It takes a couple of miles, and a few stream crossings, to reach the central waters of Lake Fontana, created in 1944 when the tallest dam in the eastern US blocked the Little Tennessee River. Next you start to climb higher up the bluff. Almost every Left Loop rider makes a brief detour at its far end, onto the Cliff Overlook Trail. This loops past an overlook perched a couple of hundred feet above the lake, with Great Smoky Mountains National Park looming on the far side.

Both the Left and Right Loops return to the trailhead via the 2.5-mile County Line Road, along the crest of a high ridge. If you're feeling really energetic, you can combine Tsali's two longest trails by returning via the Right Loop, for a total ride of 20 miles. Don't underestimate the extra effort – and climbing – this entails, though, and bear in mind that you'd be going against the Right Loop's usual anti-clockwise flow.

To reach the Tsali Trailhead, drive west from Bryson City on Hwy 74 for 9.6 miles, turn right onto NC 28, and then after another 3.4 miles turn right again onto Tsali Rd (SR 1286). The trailhead is signed on the right after 1.6 miles.

RAFTING THE NANTAHALA

START NANTAHALA OUTDOOR CENTER
END NANTAHALA OUTDOOR CENTER
DURATION HALF DAY
DISTANCE 8 MILES
DIFFICULTY MODERATE

As it heads towards its rendezvous with Lake Fontana, on a tumbling north-eastward course across North Carolina, the Nantahala River repeatedly rolls and tumbles through playful stretches of foaming, rocky white water. As such, it's renowned as one of the country's finest rivers for water-sport novices to get their first initiation into the world of rafting.

The **Nantahala Outdoor Center** (p299), 12 miles southwest of Bryson City, has been welcoming rafters since 1972. It's a large-scale operation these days, but with well-trained staff and years of experience, there's no better place for family groups to share an exhilarating, and drenching, white-water baptism.

The standard, three-hour guided trip sweeps eight-person groups on lurid yellow rafts through the dramatic Nantahala Gorge. The scenery is superb, with dense forest lining both banks of the broad, ever-frothing river. With a deft guide to handle any urgent changes of direction, there's no pressure to do more than minimal paddling. Tranquil interludes of gently floating downstream are punctuated by heady, swirling transitions through white-flecked class II rapids, before the pace inexorably picks up and the trip culminates with a white-knuckle dash through the class III Nantahala Falls.

If you're already confident of your skills, you can rent the one- or two-person inflatable kayaks known as 'ducks,' and make your own way down the river.

Trips end back at the NOC. There's a discount for taking another trip on the same day, or they can be combined with ziplining and mountain biking on-site.

Hot Springs Spa & Mineral Baths SPA
(828-622-7676; www.nchotsprings.com; 315 Bridge St, Hot Springs; mineral hot tubs from $25, massage $55-150; noon-10pm Mon-Thu, 10am-midnight Fri-Sun) Private outdoor riverfront hot tubs fed by natural springs that range from 102°F to 103°F, plus massage rooms and a fire pit for pre- or post-massage relaxation. Reserve ahead, even in off season.

Sleeping & Eating

Just north of Nantahala National Forest, quaint Bryson City, an ideal jumping-off point for outdoor adventures, harbors the best accommodations and dining options. You'll find historic and country inns, B&Bs, riverside cabins and larger, well-known chain hotels. Hot Springs holds a handful of historic B&Bs, simple motels and hiker-centric lodges and hostels, as well as a few local taverns serving decent pub grub, plus fine dining at Mountain Magnolia Inn.

Mountain Magnolia Inn INN $$
(828-622-3543; www.mountainmagnoliainn.com; 204 Lawson St, Hot Springs; r $140-250) Built in 1868, and featured in *This Old House, HGTV* and *Southern Living*, this upscale inn offers guests the chance to enjoy the health-giving properties of the springs, while its restaurant completes the experience with high-end, organic-driven cuisine (mains $26 to $34). Several rooms are in separate buildings, a considerable distance off-site.

Smoky Mountain Diner DINER $
(828-622-7571; 70 Lance Ave, Hot Springs; breakfast $2-16, mains $4-17; 6:30am-7:30pm Mon-Sat, to 2pm Sun) Beckoning hikers on the Appalachian Trail as it runs through town, this country diner will fuel you up for the day with a giant egg dish, then re-energize you with a burger, meatloaf or fried chicken when you return. Save room for pie.

Information

Hot Springs Welcome Center (828-622-9932; www.hotspringsnc.org; 106 Bridge St, Hot Springs; 10am-5pm) A friendly spot to get help with accommodation, dining and trail info, as well as wi-fi (Hot Springs is a dead zone for most cell-phone carriers).

Getting There & Away

Asheville Regional Airport (p299) serves western North Carolina.

Cherokee

828 / POP 2136

To most visitors, Cherokee is a typical and rather unlovely gateway town, guarding the southern approaches to Great Smoky Mountains National Park, and lined with tacky souvenir shops and fast-food joints, which culminate in the out-of-place spectacle of Harrah's Cherokee Casino.

To the Eastern Band of Cherokee Indians, however – the descendants of those Cherokee who managed to hide in the mountains rather than be expelled from their homeland along the Trail of Tears – this is the headquarters of the Qualla Boundary, an area of tribal-owned land that is not officially a reservation. As such, it holds a major historical museum and a fine traditional crafts gallery.

Sights

★ Museum of the Cherokee Indian MUSEUM
(828-497-3481; www.cherokeemuseum.org; 589 Tsali Blvd/Hwy 441, at Drama Rd; adult/child 6-12yr $11/7; 9am-7pm Jun-Aug, to 5pm Sep-May; P) This remarkable modern museum traces Cherokee history from their Paleo-Indian roots onwards. Its villain is the perfidious Andrew Jackson, who made his name fighting alongside the Cherokee, but, as president, condemned them to the heartbreak of the Trail of Tears. One fascinating section follows the progress through 18th-century London of a Cherokee delegation that sailed to England in 1762.

Sleeping & Eating

Cherokee holds plenty of motor inns and chain hotels. Roadside motels, log cabins and campgrounds also line the scenic, river-hugging Hwy 19 between Cherokee and Bryson City, 10 miles west.

As for food, it's easy to pick up the usual Great Smoky food – down-home cookin', skyscraper pancake stacks, fudge – in Cherokee. The best place to eat in town, though, has to be Harrah's Cherokee Casino (p304), where options include a buffet, a noodle bar and a pizzeria, along with Ruth's Chris Steakhouse, a high-end chain steakhouse that's the closest Cherokee comes to fine dining.

THE CHEROKEE AND THE TRAIL OF TEARS

Under the Treaty of Holston, signed with the United States in 1791, the Cherokee were guaranteed the right to remain in perpetuity in the mountainous regions of northern Georgia and western North Carolina. But within 50 years, they had been rounded up at bayonet point and moved west of the Mississippi, on the forced march remembered as the Trail of Tears.

According to the Cherokee, the villain of the piece was the man they called 'Sharp Knife,' President Andrew Jackson. At the Battle of Horseshoe Bend in 1814, Jackson fought alongside the Cherokee, against a rebellious Creek faction in Alabama. As president, however, he pushed through the Indian Removal Act of 1830, along with 94 separate removal treaties.

Under pressure to become 'civilized,' the Cherokee made huge efforts to adapt to the changing world, adopting Christianity, entering the economy as farmers and blacksmiths, and even holding black slaves. Increasing encroachment upon their lands by white settlers and prospectors, especially in Georgia after gold was discovered in 1828, should have prompted federal action against the states concerned, but Jackson declined to intervene.

The lack of an overall tribal government enabled a small group of Cherokee, the so-called 'Treaty Party,' to sign the Treaty of New Echota in 1835, ceding all Cherokee land east of Mississippi in return for $5 million and land in the west. Although more than 15,000 Cherokee petitioned Congress to be allowed to stay, the treaty was ratified in 1836, obliging them to leave within two years. The Treaty Party faction set off voluntarily, but the remainder stayed put.

In May 1838, 7000 federal troops swept through Cherokee territory, herding men, women and children into makeshift stockades. Some evaded capture, and became the ancestors of what's now the Eastern Band of Cherokee Indians. Of the rest, some traveled by rail and river to Chattanooga, where they met up with those who had walked and continued together, accompanied by a train of 645 wagons. Around 4000 died en route, and the final group reached Indian Territory, in what's now Oklahoma, in March 1839. Their reunion with the Treaty Party provoked bitter conflict, culminating in the execution of several Treaty Party leaders.

Andrew Jackson, meanwhile, had left the presidency. In his Farewell Address of 1837, he congratulated himself that 'the states which had so long been retarded in their development by the Indian tribes residing in the midst of them are at length relieved from the evil.'

Harrah's Cherokee Hotel CASINO HOTEL **$$**
(828-497-7777; www.caesars.com/harrahs-cherokee; 777 Casino Dr; r from $179;) While it's hardly rural or rustic, this enormous and ever-expanding casino resort holds more than 1000 high-quality hotel rooms, which are larger and more comfortable than anything else you'll find in Cherokee. It also offers indoor and outdoor pools, a spa, and a dozen restaurants.

Sassy Sunflowers BAKERY **$**
(828-497-2539; www.facebook.com/sassysunflowers; 1655 Acquoni Rd; sandwiches & salads $8-10; 9am-4pm Mon-Fri;) For a wholesome lunch or breakfast, stop for a sandwich and salad at the outdoor tables of this cheery roadside bakery-cafe. As well as turkey, chicken and prime rib, there are vegetarian choices such as their signature Sunflower Salad, with goat's cheese, apple, cranberries and sunflower seeds. It's south of the river, immediately outside Great Smoky Mountains National Park.

Drinking & Nightlife

As Cherokee falls within the Qualla Boundary, there are no bars or alcohol sales anywhere apart from the casino. The closest bars and craft breweries are in nearby Sylva and Bryson City.

Qualla Java Cafe COFFEE
(828-497-2882; www.quallajava.com; 938 Tsalagi Rd; 7am-5pm Mon-Fri, from 8am Sat, from 9am Sun;) This welcoming little Cherokee-owned coffee bar, conspicuous for its tower-ing pointed roof alongside the highway, is a good place to kick off the day.

ACCESSIBLE TRAVEL

The major attraction in Asheville, the Biltmore Estate (p287), is equipped with entrance ramps, and offers reduced admission charges for those who can't access the entire house. Sign-language interpreters are available with advance notice, and the on-site hotel offers accessible rooms.

As for the surrounding area, several viewpoints along the Blue Ridge Pkwy have picnic tables that are accessible via paved trails. At Grandfather Mountain (p283), there's wheelchair access, via elevator, to the Mile High Swinging Bridge. The adjoining Grandfather Mountain State Park is not wheelchair accessible, and neither is the waterfalls trail at Linville Falls, but Mount Mitchell State Park (p288) has a (short) paved trail to its Summit Tower, and a 4WD is available to take visitors to the Observation Deck. Assuming repairs to the elevator at Chimney Rock (p299) have been completed, visitors using wheelchairs can get almost to the top of the rock itself.

Both the scenic train ride on the Great Smoky Mountains Railroad, and the more child-oriented Tweetsie Railroad (p286), can accommodate wheelchairs. In Great Smoky Mountains National Park (p313), the excellent **Ocanaluftee Visitor Center** is fully accessible, while up at Clingmans Dome (p316) you can get great views from the parking area, although the ramp to the top of the observation tower is too steep for non-motorized wheelchairs.

Entertainment

Harrah's Cherokee Casino CASINO
(828-497-7777; www.caesars.com/harrahs-cherokee; 777 Casino Dr; 24hr;) As well as all the usual casino games, this high-rise complex holds a towering hotel block (p303), two swimming pools, a spa and restaurants of all kinds. There's also an impressive water-and-video display in the lobby.

Shopping

Qualla Arts & Crafts Mutual ARTS & CRAFTS
(828-497-3103; www.quallaartsandcrafts.com; 645 Tsali Blvd/Hwy 441, cnr Drama Rd; 9am-4:30pm, closed Sun Jan & Feb) To pick up authentic Cherokee craftwork, including basketry, stone carving and ceramics, head to this large cooperative gallery.

Information

Cherokee's nearest airport is Asheville Regional Airport (p299), 55 miles east.

Bryson City

828 / POP 1452

This tiny, charming mountain town straddling the Tuckasegee River is not only a cute little base for exploring Great Smoky Mountains National Park (p313), but an adventure destination in its own right. Handily poised for Nantahala National Forest, it's a great spot for water sports such as rafting and kayaking. You might remember it from Cormac McCarthy's 1979 novel, *Suttree* – the title character winds up here after wandering over the mountains from Gatlinburg.

Home to a smattering of good restaurants and breweries, Bryson City is also the starting point for the Great Smoky Mountains Railroad, which leaves from a historic depot downtown.

Activities

Class II and III white-water rafting on the Nantahala River, 12 miles west of Bryson City, draws more than 200,000 paddlers per year, while the Tuckasegee in town is a popular spot for fishing, paddleboarding and kayaking. The Deep Creek Recreation Area, 1.7 miles north of downtown, offers tubing and waterfalls.

Bryson City Bicycles CYCLING
(828-488-1988; www.brysoncitybicycles.com; 157 Everett St; mountain-bike rentals per 24hr from $40; 10am-6pm Tue-Sat) Quite apart from meeting all possible bike needs, including equipment sales, repairs and rentals, this friendly bike shop is worth its weight in saddlebags for the expert and freely given advice on local trail networks.

Road to Nowhere HIKING
(Lakeview Dr;) The so-called Road to Nowhere – officially, Lakeview Dr – leads northwest of Bryson City towards Great

Smoky Mountains National Park (p313). It was intended as a scenic drive, but only 6 miles were completed. For a quirky hike, park where the road ends, then keep on walking through the 1200ft tunnel beyond; alternative trails loop back in either 2.2 or 3.2 miles.

Tours

Great Smoky Mountains Railroad RAIL

(800-872-4681; www.gsmr.com; 226 Everett St; Nantahala Gorge trip adult/child 2-12yr from $58/34; schedules vary;) These scenic train excursions, lasting around four hours, follow two alternate routes – either east along the Tuckasegee River to Dillsboro, or southwest to the spectacular Nantahala Gorge. Up to four trains run daily on peak summer and fall weekends.

Sleeping & Eating

For such a small town, Bryson City is rich with lodging options. The Everett Hotel is the most pleasant spot to sleep, but there are mountain lodges and cabins, budget chain hotels and charming inns as well. The range of food options is limited but you'll find fresh trout at many local diners and one excellent bistro.

★ **Everett Hotel** BOUTIQUE HOTEL $$

(828-488-1976; www.theeveretthotel.com; 24 Everett St; r from $199; P) This nine-room boutique hotel occupies a century-old building that once housed western North Carolina's first bank. Beautiful pinewood hallways lead to rooms awash in a mineral-grey palette, with plantation shutters and wonderful dark-stained pinewood ceilings. A fire pit warms the scenic rooftop terrace. Rates include an à la carte breakfast in the excellent house bistro.

Fryemont Inn INN $$

(828-488-2159; www.fryemontinn.com; 245 Fryemont St; lodge/ste/cabin from $165/205/260; mid-Apr–late Nov; P) The views of the Smokies from this lofty bark-covered mountain lodge are unbeatable. Rooms lack TVs and air-con, but rates include breakfast and dinner in the on-site public restaurant (open 8am to 10am and 6pm to 8pm), which serves trout, steak and lamb.

The lodge itself closes in winter, as does its restaurant, but the cottage and balcony suites – the only areas with wi-fi reception – remain open.

Bistro at the Everett Hotel BISTRO $$

(828-488-1934; www.theeveretthotel.com; 16 Everett St; mains $18-35; 4:30-9pm Mon-Fri, 8:30am-3pm & 4:30-9pm Sat & Sun;) Big windows frame this classy downtown bar-restaurant, where the emphasis is on organic local ingredients, and there are local craft beers on tap. Typical dinner mains include meatloaf, mountain trout and scallops on goat's-cheese grits, while the weekend brunch menu features eggs Benedict and huevos rancheros.

Drinking & Nightlife

Bryson City is home to a couple of craft breweries, and there are a dozen or more en route between here and Asheville, 65 miles east.

Nantahala Brewing Company MICROBREWERY

(828-488-2337; www.nantahalabrewing.com; 61 Depot St; noon-11pm Sun-Thu, to midnight Fri & Sat May-Aug, reduced hours Sep-Apr;) In a massive repurposed WWII military Quonset hut, this Bryson City brewery (pints from $5) counts well over 30 taps in its main taproom. Standouts include the Dirty Girl Blonde Ale, Noon Day IPA, and assorted experimental versions using different hops or production methods.

Getting There & Away

Bryson City is 10 miles west of Cherokee. The closest airport is Asheville Regional Airport (p299), 70 miles east of town.

Pisgah National Forest

Pisgah National Forest extends across huge swathes of North Carolina's mountains, curling around Asheville in a convoluted but not quite joined-up circle. To the northeast it includes most of the Blue Ridge Pkwy between Blowing Rock and Asheville, extending almost to the summit of Mt Mitchell, while to the north it stretches via Hot Springs to the edge of the Smokies.

The section southwest of Asheville, known as the Pisgah Ranger District and incorporating parts of the original Biltmore Estate (p287), offers wonderful recreational opportunities. It's best approached by leaving the Blue Ridge Pkwy at Mile 412. Immediately north of here looms the forested bulk of Cold Mountain, immortalized in Charles Frazier's 1997

ROAD TRIP: BLUE RIDGE PARKWAY

This drive on America's favorite byway curves through the leafy Appalachians, swooping up the East Coast's highest peak and heading towards the Smokies, pausing at America's largest mansion.

1 Valle Crucis

How do you start a road trip through the mountains? With a good night's sleep and all the right gear, of course. You'll find both in Valle Crucis, a bucolic village 8 miles west of Boone.

After slumbering beneath sumptuous linens at the 200-year-old **Mast Farm Inn** (p283), ease into the day sipping coffee in a rocking chair on the former farmhouse's front porch.

Down the road lies the **Original Mast General Store** (p283). The first of the many Mast general stores that dot the High Country, this rambling clapboard building still sells many of the same products that it did back in 1883. As well as bacon, axes and hard candy, you'll now find hiking shoes, lava lamps and French country hand towels. The store's **Annex** (www.mastgeneralstore.com; ⏲10am-6pm Mon-Sat, from noon Sun), just south along Hwy 194, sells outdoor apparel and hiking gear.

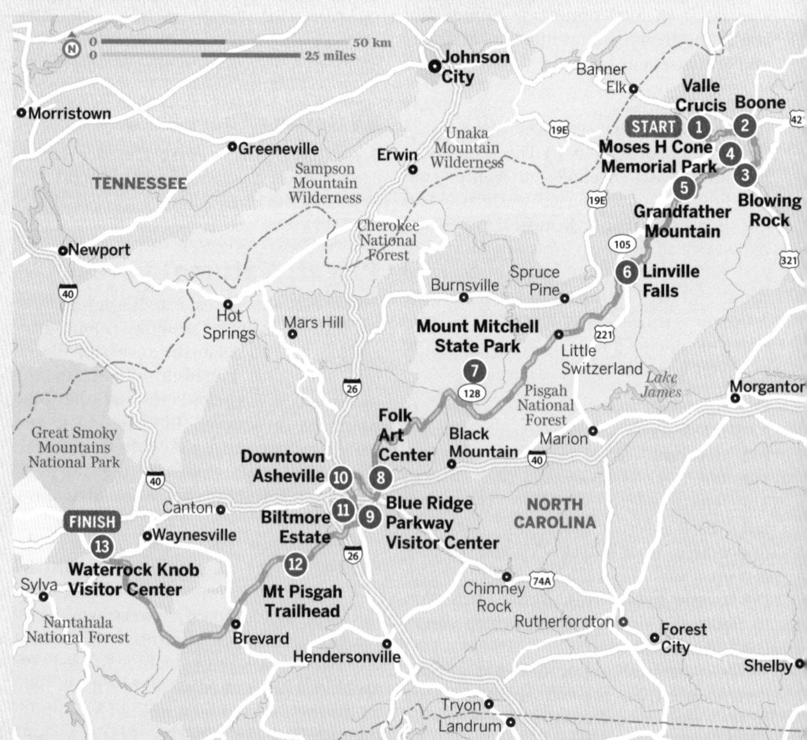

5 Days 210 miles / 338km

Great for... Outdoors; Families.

Best Time to Go May to October for leafy trees and seasonal attractions.

The Drive > Drive southeast on Hwy 194, also known as Broadstone Rd, through 3 miles of rural splendor, then turn left at Hwy 105.

2 Boone

If you're traveling with kids or are a wannabe prospector yourself, stop at **Foggy Mountain Gem Mine** (p287) to pan for semiprecious stones. Several gem-mining spots are located in these parts, but the graduate gemologists here take their craft a bit more seriously. Rough stones are sold by the bucketload, which you sift in a flume line. For additional fees, they'll cut and mount your favorite finds.

In downtown Boone, the bustling home of Appalachian State, you'll find quirky shopping and dining along **King St**, where **Melanie's Food Fantasy** (p288) is a good option for a hearty breakfast or tasty lunch. Keep an eye out for the bronze **statue** (p287) of bluegrass legend Doc Watson, born nearby in 1923 and depicted strumming a Gallagher guitar on a street corner.

The Drive > From King St, turn onto Hwy 321 just past the Dan'l Boone Inn restaurant. Drive 4 miles then turn right at the theme park.

3 Blowing Rock

The parkway runs just above the village of Blowing Rock, which sits at an elevation of 4000ft. On a cloudy morning, drive south on Hwy 321 to the top of the mountain to check out the cloud-capped views of surrounding peaks. The eastern continental divide runs through the bar at the **Green Park Inn** (p286), a grand white-clapboard hotel that opened in 1891. Author Margaret Mitchell stayed here while writing *Gone with the Wind*. For a memorable meal in a century-old lodge, call in at **Bistro Roca** (p286).

Riding the **Tweetsie Railroad** (p286), a 1917 coal-fired steam locomotive that chugs on a 3-mile loop past heroic cowboys and marauding Indians, is a rite of passage for every North Carolina child. It's the centerpiece of a theme park where Appalachian culture meets the Wild West, with midway rides, fudge shops and family-friendly shows to round out the fun.

The Drive > The entrance to the Blue Ridge Pkwy is near Blowing Rock, 2.3 miles south of the Tweetsie Railroad. Once on the parkway, drive north 2 miles.

4 Moses H Cone Memorial Park

Hikers and equestrians share 25 miles of carriage roads on the former estate of Moses H Cone, a philanthropist and conservationist who made his fortune in denim. Moses built a Colonial Revival mansion, Flat Top Manor, in 1901, which was given, along with the grounds, to the national park service in the 1950s. Directly accessible from the parkway at Mile 294, it now holds both a museum and the **Parkway Craft Center** (p286), where the Southern Highland Craft Guild sells superb Appalachian crafts at reasonable prices.

The Drive > Head south on the parkway, passing split rail fences, stone walls, streams and meadows. Just south of Mile 304, the parkway curves across the Linn Cove Viaduct, which, because of the fragility of the terrain, was the final section of the parkway to be completed, in 1987. Exit onto Hwy 221 at Mile 305, and drive 1 mile south.

5 Grandfather Mountain

The highest of the Blue Ridge Mountains, **Grandfather Mountain** (p283), looms north of the parkway 20 miles southwest of Blowing Rock. As a visitor destination, it's famous as the location of the Mile High Swinging Bridge, the focus of a privately owned attraction that also includes hiking trails plus a small museum and wildlife reserve. Don't let a fear of heights scare you away; though the bridge is a mile above sea level, and on gusty days you can hear its steel girders 'sing,' it spans a less fearsome chasm that's just 80ft deep.

Much of Grandfather Mountain – including its loftiest summit, Calloway Peak (5946ft), a strenuous 2.4-mile hike from the swinging bridge – is a Unesco Biosphere Reserve belonging to Grandfather Mountain State Park (www.ncparks.gov). Its 12 miles of wilderness hiking trails can also be accessed for free at Mile 300 on the parkway.

The Drive > Follow the parkway south and turn left just past Mile 316 to reach Linville Falls.

6 Linville Falls

If you only have time for a single parkway hike, an hour-long sojourn at spectacular **Linville Falls** (p283) makes a great option. Cross the Linville River from the parking lot, and head along Erwin's View Trail. This 1.6-mile round trip offers great views of the river as it cascades over two separate falls. Climb the wooded hillside to enjoy stunning long-range panoramas in two directions: back to the falls, the other downstream, where the river crashes into a rocky gorge.

The Drive > Drive south on the parkway and turn right, south of Mile 355, onto NC 128. Follow NC 128 into the park.

7 Mount Mitchell State Park

Be warned: a major decision awaits visitors to North Carolina's first-ever **state park** (p288). Will you drive up Mt Mitchell, at 6684ft the highest peak east of the Mississippi, or will you hike to the top? Make your mind up at the park office, which sits beside a steep 2.2-mile summit trail that typically takes around 1½ hours, one way.

Once up there, you'll see the grave of University of North Carolina professor Elisha Mitchell. He came here in 1857 to prove his previous estimate of the mountain's height, only to fall from a waterfall and die. A circular ramp leads to dramatic views over and beyond the surrounding Black Mountains.

The Drive > Return to the parkway and drive south to Mile 382. Look out for blooming rhododendrons during the last two weeks of June.

8 Folk Art Center

Part gallery, part store, and wholly dedicated to Southern craftsmanship, the superb **Folk Art Center** (p289) is 6 miles east of downtown Asheville. The handcrafted Appalachian chairs that hang above its lobby make an impressive appetizer for the permanent collection of the Southern Highland Craft Guild, a treasury of pottery, baskets, quilts and woodcarvings that's displayed on the 2nd floor. There are daily demonstrations by experts, and the Allanstand Craft Shop on the 1st floor sells high-quality traditional crafts.

The Drive > Turn right onto the parkway and drive south. Cross the Swannanoa River and I-40, then continue to Mile 384.

9 Blue Ridge Parkway Visitor Center

At the Blue Ridge Pkwy's helpful Asheville-area **visitor center** (☎828-348-3400; www.nps.gov/blri; Mile 384; ⏰9am-5pm), you can sit back and let the scenery come to you, courtesy of a big-screen movie that captures the beauty and wonder of 'America's favorite journey.' Park rangers at the front desk gladly advise on parkway hiking trails, and sliding the digital panel across the amazing 'I-Wall' map brings up details of regional sites and activities. A separate desk is stocked with brochures and coupons for Asheville's attractions.

The Drive > Drive north, backtracking over the interstate and river, and exit at Tunnel Rd, which is Hwy 70. Drive west to Hwy 240, and follow it west to the exits for downtown Asheville.

10 Downtown Asheville

The undisputed 'capital' of the North Carolina mountains, Asheville is both a major tourist destination and one of the coolest small cities in the South. Home to an invigorating mix of hipsters, hippies and hikers, and offering easy access to outdoor adventures of all kinds, it's also a rare liberal enclave in the conservative countryside.

Strolling between downtown's historic art-deco buildings, you'll encounter literary pilgrims celebrating the city's angsty famous son, and author of *Look Homeward, Angel,* at the **Thomas Wolfe Memorial** (p289); nostalgic gamers flipping the flippers at the **Pinball Museum** (p289); left-leaning intellectuals browsing at **Malaprop's Bookstore & Cafe** (p298); and design connoisseurs shopping for crafts in **Horse & Hero** (p298).

Head down the adjoining South Slope to find specialist microbreweries, such as spooky **Burial** (p296), which have earned Asheville the nickname 'Beer City,' or hit the River Arts District to enjoy barbecue emporium **12 Bones** (p292). Budget travelers looking to stay in Asheville should head for downtown's excellent **Sweet Peas Hostel** (p291).

TOP TIPS

➡ Driving the parkway is not so much a way to get from A to B – don't expect to get anywhere fast – as an experience to relish.

➡ The maximum speed limit is 45mph.

➡ Long stretches of the parkway close in winter, and may not reopen until March, while many visitor centers and campgrounds remain closed until May. Check the park-service website (www.nps.gov/blri) for more information.

➡ The North Carolina section of the parkway starts at Mile 216.9, between the Blue Ridge Mountain Center in Virginia and Cumberland Knob in North Carolina.

➡ There are 26 tunnels on the parkway in North Carolina, as opposed to just one in Virginia. Watch for signs to turn on your headlights.

➡ For more help with trip planning, check the websites of the Blue Ridge Parkway Association (www.blueridgeparkway.org) and the Blue Ridge National Heritage Area (www.blueridgeheritage.com).

The Drive > Follow Asheland Ave, which becomes McDowell St, south. After crossing the Swannanoa River, the entrance to the Biltmore Estate is on the right.

11 Biltmore Estate

The destination that put Asheville on the map, **Biltmore House** (p287), is the larg-est privately owned home in the US. Completed in 1895 for shipping and railroad heir George Washington Vanderbilt II, it was modeled after three châteaux that he'd seen in France's Loire Valley, and still belongs to his descendants. It's extraordinarily expensive to visit, but there's a lot to see; allow several hours to explore the entire 8000-acre Biltmore Estate. Self-guided tours of the house itself take in 39 points of interest, including our favorite, the two-lane bowling alley.

To hear the full story, pay $11 extra for an audio tour, or take the behind-the-scenes Upstairs Downstairs Tour ($20) or the more architecturally focused Rooftop Tour ($20). A 5-mile drive through the impeccably manicured estate, which also holds several cafes and two top-end hotels, leads to the winery and dairy farm in Antler Hill Village.

The Drive > Exit the grounds, then turn right onto Hwy 25 and continue for almost 3.5 miles to the parkway, and drive south.

12 Mt Pisgah Trail

To enjoy an hour or two of hiking that culminate in a panoramic view, pull into the parking lot beside the **Mt Pisgah** trailhead, just beyond Mile 407. The 1.6-mile trail (one way) climbs to the mountain's 5721ft summit, topped by a lofty TV tower. The going gets steep and rocky in its final stretches, but you'll be rewarded with views of the French Broad River Valley as well as **Cold Mountain**, made famous by Charles Frazier's eponymous novel. One mile south you can find a campground, a general store, a restaurant and an inn.

The Drive > The drive south passes the Graveyard Fields Overlook, where short trails lead to scenic waterfalls. From the 6047ft Richland Balsam Overlook at Mile 431.4 – the highest point on the parkway – continue south another 20 miles.

13 Waterrock Knob Visitor Center

This trip ends at the Waterrock Knob Visitor Center (Mile 451.2), which sits at an elevation of nearly 6000ft. With a four-state view, this scenic spot is a great place to see where you've been and to assess what lies ahead. Helpful signs identify the mountains along the far horizon.

book and the subsequent movie. Head south on Hwy 276, and en route to the delightful country town of Brevard, you'll pass several potential stop-offs as well as a helpful ranger station.

Sights

Sliding Rock Recreation Area WATERFALL

(828-885-7625; www.fs.usda.gov; Pisgah Hwy/Hwy 276; $2; staffed 9am-6pm late May-early Sep; P) For a totally exhilarating stop on a journey along the Blue Ridge Pkwy, stop off and strip down at Sliding Rock, 7 miles off the parkway. Propelled down this natural 60ft slide of smooth, gently sloping granite by 11,000 gallons of cool stream water per minute, bathers splash into a pool that's up to 8ft deep; swimming skills are essential. Time your visit if possible to avoid the noon-to-4pm crowds.

Lifeguards are present daily in summer, on weekends in fall. When they're not, changing rooms and restrooms are closed, and you should be very wary of entering the water.

Cradle of Forestry in America NATURE CENTER

(828-877-3130; www.cradleofforestry.com; 11250 Pisgah Hwy/Hwy 276; adult/child under 13yr $6/3; 9am-5pm early Apr–mid-Nov; P) The spot where scientific forestry management was first attempted in the US, financed by George Vanderbilt back in 1895, is now a showcase for the Forest Service.

Amid the original log cabins, 4 miles off the Blue Ridge Pkwy, a visitor center holds interactive exhibits targeted at children, including a scary simulation of a helicopter flying over a forest fire. Paved trails lead through the woods themselves.

Activities

While mountain biking and hiking are the most popular activities in the Pisgah Ranger District, rock climbing is also a big deal, especially on granite domes such as Looking Glass Rock. Several spectacular waterfalls in this ranger district can also be admired from roadside parking lots.

Hiking

Enjoyable and relatively straightforward trails lead to numerous spectacular waterfalls in the Pisgah Ranger District. Among the best are the Twin Falls, accessible on a 4-mile round-trip hike that starts 2.7 miles along Avery Creek Rd, a total of 5 miles up from the intersection of Hwy 276 and Hwy 64.

Mountain Biking

Mountain bike trails abound in the Pisgah Ranger District. The Black Mountain trailhead, immediately south of the ranger station, makes an ideal starting point, providing quick access to both the 4-mile Thrift Cove Loop and the 5-mile Sycamore Cove Loop.

Sleeping & Eating

As well as Forest Service campgrounds including Davidson River Campground, there are plenty of motels and B&Bs in nearby Brevard.

Lively little Brevard is the closest spot where you'll find restaurants to match every taste and budget, while food stores pepper the highway between Brevard and the village of Pisgah Forest, 3.5 miles northeast.

Information

For information and advice on the Pisgah Ranger District, call in at either the **ranger station** (828-877-3265; www.cfaia.org; 1600 Pisgah Hwy/Hwy 276; 9am-5pm mid-Apr–mid-Nov, 8:30am-4:30pm mid-Nov–mid-Apr) or Brevard's Hub, which also rents out bikes and outdoor equipment.

Getting There & Away

All three districts of Pisgah National Forest are readily accessible from, and connected by, the Blue Ridge Pkwy. For the Pisgah Ranger District, head south from the parkway at Mile 412.

Brevard

828 / POP 7822

One of those charming little mountain towns that set travelers daydreaming of putting down roots, Brevard is best known as the home of the prestigious Brevard Music Center. A summer school for music students, the center also stages the Brevard Music Festival.

Brevard is also the seat of the rather ominous-sounding Transylvania County, which more appealingly styles itself as 'Land of Waterfalls.' Visitors flock in year-round to enjoy the surrounding scenery, at its finest in the nearby Pisgah National Forest.

Activities

Brevard makes an ideal base for bikers and hikers, who come to explore the myriad trails, swimming holes and waterfalls hidden away in the slopes of the Pisgah Ranger District of Pisgah National Forest. For advice and equipment, including bike rental, call in at the Hub, at the foot of Hwy 276.

Hub MOUNTAIN BIKING
(828-884-8670; www.thehubpisgah.com; 11 Mama's Place, Pisgah Forest; bike rental per day from $40; 10am-6pm Mon-Fri, 9am-6pm Sat, 10am-5pm Sun) Even if you're traveling with all the right gear and equipment, and don't need to rent from the Hub's extensive array of bikes, be sure to call in at this excellent outfitters for advice and updates on the countless mountain and forest trails nearby. This being North Carolina, it also incorporates its own brewpub, the Pisgah Tavern.

Festivals & Events

Brevard Music Festival MUSIC
(828-862-2100; www.brevardmusic.org; Brevard Music Center, 349 Andante Lane; Jun–mid-Aug) The prestigious Brevard Music Center runs this summer-long festival, staging more than 80 concerts, ranging from classical and opera to bluegrass and movie music, in various venues around town.

Sleeping & Eating

Brevard offers accommodations to suit all budgets, including campgrounds in the adjoining public lands. For dining options, a wander down Brevard's simple downtown grid is sure to reveal something to tingle your taste buds.

Davidson River Campground CAMPGROUND $
(828-862-5960; www.recreation.gov; 1 Davidson River Circle, Pisgah Forest; tent sites $22-44) At the southern edge of the most spectacular stretch of Pisgah National Forest, 5 miles north of downtown Brevard, this riverside campground – tubing optional! – is better suited to tenters than RVs. The facilities are relatively basic, but the wooded setting is idyllic. Silence is requested, and insisted on, from 10pm to 7am.

Sunset Motel MOTEL $
(828-884-9106; http://thesunsetmotel.com; 523 S Broad St; r from $99; P) They don't make 'em like the Sunset Motel anymore, so if you've a penchant for vintage motor lodges, and you don't mind every last fixture and fitting looking like it came straight from the 1950s, you won't want to miss it. Choose from cabins, apartments and standard motel rooms, and don't worry – they've got wi-fi and 21st-century TVs too.

Red House Inn B&B $$
(828-884-9349; www.brevardbedandbreakfast.com; 266 W Probart St; r from $160; P) Built as a general store in 1851, the Red House went through various incarnations before becoming a B&B. Set in stately repose five minutes' walk from downtown, it offers superbly quiet, tastefully furnished en-suite rooms, plus full cooked breakfasts.

Falls Landing SEAFOOD $$
(828-884-2835; www.thefallslanding.com; 18 E Main St; dinner mains $15-28; 11:30am-3pm Mon, 11:30am-3pm & 5-9pm Tue-Sat) Brevard's favorite fine-dining restaurant works wonders with fish – the owner moved here from the Virgin Islands, and is as happy serving oysters or crab cakes as pan-frying fresh NC trout – but there's plenty more besides, including lamb chops and rib-eye. Burgers ($9) stay on the menu all day, joined by sandwiches at lunchtime.

Drinking & Nightlife

Brevard Brewing Co MICROBREWERY
(828-885-2101; www.brevard-brewing.com; 63 E Main St; 2-11pm Mon-Thu, noon-midnight Fri & Sat, 2-10pm Sun;) Though it's right in the heart of town, this small local brewery (pints from $3.50) always seems to have a peaceful, welcoming vibe. They specialize in German lagers and pilsners, but also make an American IPA, as well as seasonal variations including a coriander ale in fall. There's no food.

Getting There & Away

In the absence of public transportation, you'll almost certainly have to drive to Brevard. Ideally, make your way here on the Blue Ridge Pkwy, heading south on Hwy 276 from Mile 412.

Nantahala National Forest

The largest of North Carolina's four national forests, the Nantahala National Forest covers more than half a million acres of the state's westernmost portion, extending south from Great Smoky Mountains National Park all the way to the South Carolina and Georgia state lines.

The name Nantahala means 'Land of the Noonday Sun' in Cherokee, because only when the sun is at its highest can it penetrate all the way to the floor of the Nantahala Gorge. The gorge itself is in the forest's Nantahala Ranger District, which also holds the tallest waterfall east of the Mississippi. Very close to South Carolina, 26 miles southwest of Brevard, Whitewater Falls can be reached via a steep 1-mile hike from NC 281.

Sights

★Tsali Recreation Area FOREST

(828-479-6431; www.fs.usda.gov; Tsali Rd; 24hr; P) FREE The Tsali Recreation Area has been famed among mountain bikers for so long that local riders rather take it for granted. For out-of-state visitors, though, it offers a great combination of challenging but not over-technical trails, spectacular lake-and-mountain views, and convenient access. All the four main trails are categorized as moderate, incorporating waterfront stretches beside Fontana Lake plus significant climbs.

They're divided into two groups – the Mouse Branch and Thompson Loops, and the longer Left and Right Loops – each of which is reserved for bikers and horse riders on alternate days. The Left Loop is the toughest, with its steep ascents and narrow ledges, while novice riders can opt for a short 5-mile ride by tackling only a segment of the less demanding Right Loop. There are restrooms, showers and bike-washing facilities at the parking lot.

Activities

For outdoors enthusiasts, the most popular area of the forest is the Tsali Recreation Area, in the Cheoah Ranger District adjoining the southern edge of Great Smoky Mountains National Park.

Hiking

Every section of the Nantahala forest holds its fair share of hiking trails. To admire some magnificent – and all too rare – old-growth forest, head to the Joyce Kilmer Memorial Forest, 40 miles west of Bryson City. Easy loop-hikes lead past centuries-old tulip poplars, while the adjoining Slickrock Wilderness Area offers more demanding terrain for backpackers.

Note also that the legendary, long-distance Appalachian Trail (www.appalachiantrail.org) winds across both the Cheoah and Nantahala ranger districts.

Mountain Biking

Nantahala National Forest is famous for its mountain biking, with prime destinations including the Tsali Recreation Area, west of Bryson City, and the Jackrabbit Recreation Area, adjoining Lake Chatuge near Hayesville, 100 miles southwest of Asheville.

Sleeping

Both the Tsali and the Jackrabbit recreation areas offer lakeside campgrounds, while Bryson City makes a good overnight base for Tsali in particular.

Tsali Campground CAMPGROUND $

(828-479-6431; www.fs.usda.gov; Tsali Rd; tent sites $15; Apr-Oct; P) This forest-service campground holds around 40 tent sites, some beside a stream and some spreading across a meadow. It has showers and restrooms, but no electric or water hookups.

Eating

Visitors to Nantahala National Forest should bring their own food supplies; it has no stores or restaurants.

Getting There & Away

The Tsali Recreation Area is 15 miles west of Bryson City; follow Hwy 74 for 9.6 miles, turn right onto NC 28, and then turn right again onto Tsali Rd (SR 1286) after another 3.4 miles. Follow signs to trailheads and the campground.

Great Smoky Mountains National Park

Includes ➡

Best Views

- ➡ Clingmans Dome (p316)
- ➡ Charlies Bunion (p318)
- ➡ Gregory Bald (p330)
- ➡ Mt LeConte (p316)
- ➡ Newfound Gap (p315)

Best Places to Stay

- ➡ LeConte Lodge (p322)
- ➡ Deep Creek (p338)
- ➡ Elkmont (p323)
- ➡ Cades Cove Campground (p333)
- ➡ Balsam Mountain (p336)

Why Go?

Scenic drives and sun-dappled trails unfurl in the shadows of ancient peaks in this forested wonderland, where beauty, history and adventure collide.

Part of the vast Appalachian chain, the Smokies are among the oldest mountains on the planet. In spring, wildflowers bloom with colorful abandon while waterfalls tumble into gorgeous pools. Flame azaleas light up the high-elevation meadows in summer. Autumn dazzles with quilted hues of orange, burgundy and saffron blanketing mountain slopes. In winter, snow-covered fields and ice-fringed cascades create a serene retreat. This mesmerizing backdrop is a World Heritage site, harboring more biodiversity than any other national park in America. History abounds too. Early settlers built log cabins, one-room schoolhouses, stream-fed gristmills and single-steeple churches amid the fertile forest valleys. The park has preserved many of these historic structures. You can explore this beautiful place by foot, horseback or a pretty drive.

When to Go

- ➡ The park is open year-round, but summer and fall are the most popular seasons.
- ➡ Some facilities are closed late fall through early spring.
- ➡ Roads may be closed in winter due to inclement weather.

Great Smoky Mountains National Park Highlights

1. **Clingmans Dome** (p316) Enjoying panoramic views from the highest point in the park.
2. **Appalachian Trail** (p319) Hiking America's most fabled walk.
3. **Mt LeConte** (p316) Visiting the rustic lodge at the summit.
4. **Newfound Gap** (p315) Relaxing at a scenic viewpoint.
5. **Abrams Falls** (p330) Hiking to gorgeous cascades.
6. **Cades Cove** (p325) Watching wildlife, bicycling and exploring historic homesteads.
7. **Roaring Fork Motor Nature Trail** (p324) Braking for waterfalls and historic cabins.
8. **Gregory Bald** (p330) Picnicking on a mountaintop meadow.
9. **Cataloochee** (p334) Admiring elk and hiking to remote historic sites.

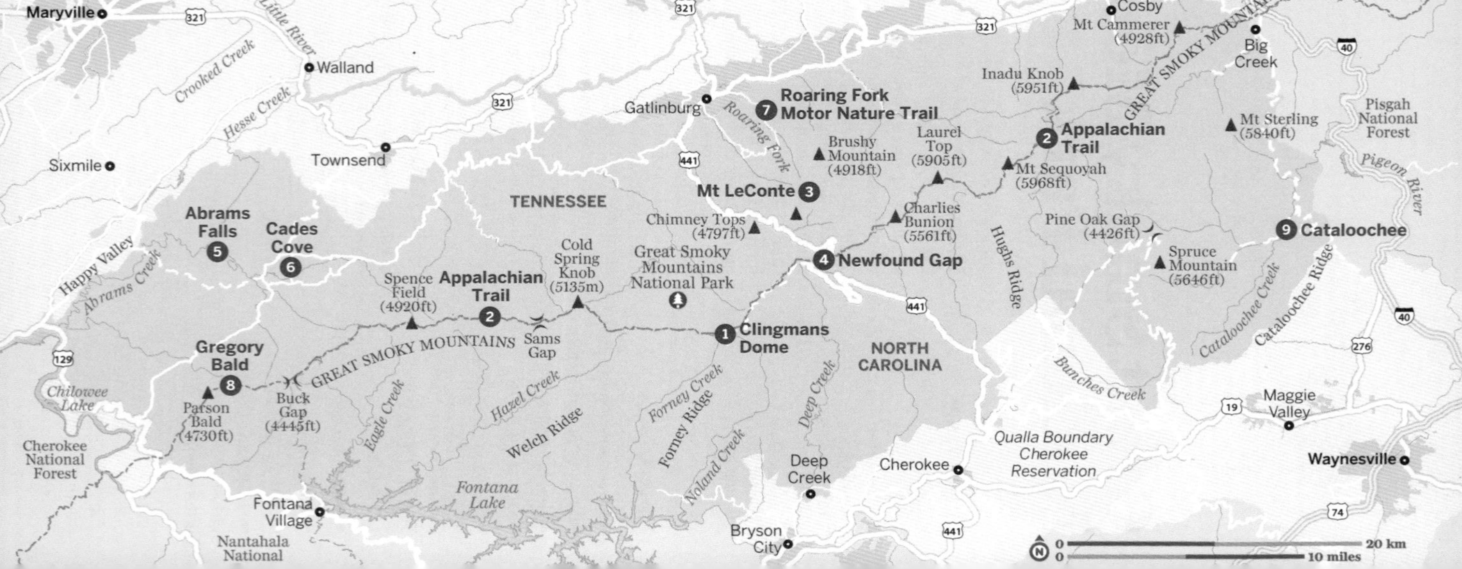

GREAT SMOKY MOUNTAINS NATIONAL PARK

The Smokies are packed with clifftop viewpoints, picturesque drives and forested trails that wind past rocky streams to thundering cascades. Early settlers left their mark in the fertile mountain valleys, and you can peer into the past by exploring the park's many log cabins, one-room schoolhouses and weatherboard churches.

Cades Cove and the northern part of the park (Tennessee) generally draw more visitors than Cataloochee and the southern half (North Carolina). Linking the two states is Newfound Gap Rd, which has a little of everything – views, hikes, historic buildings and even occasional wildlife viewing. Little River Rd joins Newfound Gap Rd at the Sugarlands Visitor Center.

This chapter divides the park into four sections: Newfound Gap Rd, Cades Cove, Cataloochee Valley and Balsam Mountain, and Fontana Dam and Western North Carolina.

Newfound Gap Road

Also known as Hwy 441, this 33-mile byway links Cherokee, NC, with Gatlinburg, TN. It is the only road within the park that crosses the mountains. Newfound Gap, a pretty mountain pass with a parking area, straddles the two states. Sights and activities along Little River Rd and the Roaring Fork Motor Nature Trail, both in Tennessee, are included here.

North Carolina

In North Carolina, most sights and activities along Newfound Gap Rd are clustered near the Oconaluftee Visitor Center, Smokemont Campground and Clingmans Dome.

★ **Newfound Gap** VIEWPOINT

(Map p320; Newfound Gap Rd) The lowest drivable pass through the Smoky Mountains is located here, at 5046ft. After the pass was discovered in 1872, a new road followed suit, eventually becoming today's Newfound Gap Rd. The site straddles two states and offers fantastic views to the north (Tennessee) and south (North Carolina). The rocky platform is where you'll find the **Rockefeller Memorial** (Map p320). It was on this spot on September 2, 1940 that President Franklin Roosevelt formally dedicated the park.

The Appalachian Trail travels right across Newfound Gap (you may see a few hungry hikers trying to hitch a ride up to Gatlinburg for a soft bed and a warm meal). This is also the starting point for the popular 8-mile (return) hike to Charlies Bunion (p317).

Mingus Mill HISTORIC BUILDING

(Map p320; Mingus Creek Trail, off Newfound Gap Rd, Cherokee; ⌚9am-5pm daily mid-Mar–mid-Nov, plus Thanksgiving weekend) FREE One of the park's most picturesque 19th-century buildings, the Mingus Mill is a turbine-powered mill that still grinds wheat and corn much as it has since its opening back in 1886. You're welcome to explore the multi-story structure, checking out its clever engineering mechanisms and walking the length of its 200ft-long flume that brings water from a stream to the mill's turbine. It's located about a mile north of the Oconaluftee Visitor Center (and 4 miles north of Cherokee).

There's usually a park employee on site who can share details on how the whole operation works. There's also a small stand near the entrance where you can purchase ground cornmeal (not milled on site, but still made the old-fashioned way).

Mountain Farm Museum MUSEUM

(Map p320; www.nps.gov/grsm; Newfound Gap Rd, Cherokee; ⌚9am-5pm daily mid-Mar–mid-Nov, plus Thanksgiving weekend) Adjacent to the Oconaluftee Visitor Center (p323), this excellent collection of historic buildings evokes life on a typical farmstead of the late 19th century. Together these structures paint a poignant picture of the mountain people who once eked out their sustenance from this rugged and isolated wilderness.

The wooden buildings are authentic, but were moved here from other parts of the national park in the 1950s. One of the first buildings you come to is the meat house, where a mountain farm's most valuable commodity (usually pork) was butchered, dried and smoked or salted for preservation.

Other structures are dedicated to apples (used for apple sauce, apple butter, cider, vinegar, apple pies and eaten raw), sorghum (used to make molasses) and corn (the most important crop on mountain farms, used for cornmeal and fresh corn, while its shucks were stuffed into mattresses and woven into chair seats, dolls, rugs and brooms). In the summer you can also see live hogs and chickens – a requisite stop for families with small children. A terrific time to visit is in mid-September for the Mountain Life Festival.

★Clingmans Dome VIEWPOINT

(off Clingmans Dome Rd; Map p320) 'On top of Old Smoky' is Clingmans Dome (elevation 6643ft), the park's highest peak. At the summit a steep, half-mile paved trail leads to an observation tower offering a 360-degree view of the Smokies and beyond. It can be cold and foggy up here, even when the sun is shining in Sugarlands, so bring a jacket. The tower resembles something of a flying saucer, with a gently curving ramp leading up to the top. Panels around the viewing platform indicate names of the surrounding peaks and distant places of interest.

As one of the must-see sights in the park, Clingmans Dome gets crowded, especially in the summer. Note that the 7-mile access road to Newfound Gap Rd is closed to vehicles from December through March. The viewpoint is open year-round, however, for those willing to hike in – take care on the trails, which can be icy even in April.

PARK INFORMATION

There is no entrance fee for **Great Smoky Mountains National Park** (Map p320; www.nps.gov/grsm). The park is open 24 hours a day, year-round. However, many secondary roads maintain seasonal closures, and only two of the park's campgrounds are open year-round. Backcountry campsites are open year-round, but some close periodically owing to bear activity.

Visitor centers are open year-round (closing only on Christmas Day), but the hours change seasonally. Other park sites, such as LeConte Lodge and the Mingus Mill, open seasonally (typically mid-March to mid-November).

Oconaluftee Visitor Center (p323)

Sugarlands Visitor Center (p323)

Clingmans Dome Visitor Station (p323)

Riding Stables

Sugarlands Riding Stables (p320)

Smokemont Riding Stables (p316)

Cades Cove Riding Stables (p332)

Activities

Oconaluftee River Trail HIKING

(Map p320; 👪) This flat, peaceful trail follows along the banks of the pretty Oconaluftee River. Go around dawn or dusk and you may see elk grazing in the fields. The 3-mile, round-trip walk begins just outside the Oconaluftee Visitor Center (p323). You can check out the historic buildings of the Mountain Farm Museum (p315) before setting off.

This is one of only two trails in the park that allows dogs, as long as they're on a leash (the other dog-friendly path is the Gatlinburg Trail, see p319). You can also ride a bike along the trail.

Kephart Prong Trail HIKING

(Map p320; off Newfound Gap Rd) This moderate 4.2-mile (round trip) hike takes you through thick forest to the ruins of an old Civilian Conservation Corps camp built during the Great Depression. It's located about 400yd from the trailhead. Further along, you'll have some fine views of the churning Kephart Prong and make several scenic crossings of the fern-dappled river on log bridges.

The trail ends near the Kephart Shelter, a popular backcountry site for backpackers. From here a left turn along the Sweat Heifer Creek trail goes 3.7 miles uphill to intersect with the Appalachian Trail. The trailhead is located along the park's main north–south road, about 7 miles north of the Oconaluftee Visitor Center.

Smokemont Riding Stables HORSEBACK RIDING

(Map p320; ☎828-497-2373; www.smokemontridingstable.com; 135 Smokemont Riding Stable Rd; 1/4hr ride $35/140, wagon ride $15; ⊙9am-5pm mid-Mar–Oct) Offers one- and four-hour horseback rides as well as waterfall and wagon rides.

Tennessee

Sights and activities along Little River Rd and the Roaring Fork Motor Nature Trail are easily accessed from Newfound Gap Rd and are included here.

Sights

★Mt LeConte MOUNTAIN

(Map p320) Mt LeConte (6593ft) is the park's third-highest peak and one of its most familiar sights, visible from practically

HIKING IN THE GREAT SMOKIES

Whether you have an irrepressible urge to climb a mountain or just want to get some fresh air, hiking in Great Smoky Mountains National Park is the single best way to experience the sublime beauty of this area. Even if you're only here for a short visit, be sure to include at least one hike in your itinerary. Trails range from flat, easy and short paths to longer, more strenuous endeavors. Many are excellent for families and there's even one wheelchair-accessible trail. No matter what your physical ability or endurance level, there's a hike out there for you.

Here are a few hiking essentials to consider before stepping onto the trail:

Weather Check the forecast before setting out. Always carry rain gear, just in case. Bring a winter hat, gloves and other warm-weather gear from October to March.

What to Pack Good hiking boots, walking stick (or hiking poles), rain jacket, high-energy snacks, water (2 quarts per person on long hikes).

Best Months for Hiking Mid-April to May for spring wildflowers, October for fall foliage, January and February for wintry landscapes.

Best Hiking Guide & Map *Hiking Trails of the Smokies* for a detailed overview of every trail in the park. *Great Smoky Mountains National Park Trails Illustrated Topographic Map* (by National Geographic) has a 1:70,000 scale.

every viewpoint. The only way to get to the top is on foot. It is accessible on five trails, which range from 5 to 8.9 miles in length. Near the summit, LeConte Lodge (p322) is the park's only non-camping lodging, but you better book ahead – reservations for the following year open on October 1, and are booked solid within 48 hours.

Reaching the summit (located 0.2 miles above the lodge) is a challenging goal, and it's well worth the effort. Aside from great views, you can stop in the office and lounge at LeConte Lodge to check out photos of cabin life dating back to the 1930s. A small shop sells T-shirts, socks, rain ponchos and other essentials, while you can pick up a sack lunch ($11), cookies ($1) or drink bottomless cups of coffee, hot chocolate or lemonade (all $4) at the restaurant.

Carlos C Campbell Overlook VIEWPOINT
(Map p320; Newfound Gap Rd) This scenic overlook provides a sweeping view of the various types of forests covering the slopes to the east. You'll see spruce-fir forest at the top, northern hardwood below, hemlock forest nestled in the valley and, just to the north, cove hardwood forest. You can also spy pine-oak forest and a small heath bald. A signpost helps show where to look to see the different forest features. The scene is at its most dramatic in autumn, when golds, reds and oranges blaze across the mountain.

The overlook is located about 2.5 miles south of the Sugarlands Visitor Center. Look for the small parking area to the left as you're driving south.

Elkmont Historic District HISTORIC SITE
(Map p320; off Little River Rd) Elkmont has much history hidden in its woodlands. Just south of the campground (crossing the bridge over Little River), you'll find a clubhouse and eclectically designed cabins dating back to the early 20th century when the area was a summer retreat for business leaders from Knoxville. One row of cabins, dubbed 'Daisy Town,' has a few dwellings you can wander through, and it's simple to imagine the easy summer living, clubhouse dances and concerts as you explore this abandoned settlement.

Metcalf Bottoms NATURAL FEATURE
(Map p320; off Little River Gorge Rd) A lovely spot for a picnic, with tables set up along the Little River. Afterwards you can dip your feet in the cool, rushing waters.

The Sinks WATERFALL
(Map p320) A requisite stop when driving Little River Rd is this series of cascades just off the road. Here, the Little River makes a sharp hairpin turn, with water rushing over boulders into deep pools. Although people do swim here, it's extremely dangerous (as is even wading) owing to strong currents and hidden underwater hazards. Drownings and serious injuries have occurred.

DON'T MISS

FIREFLY EVENT

Each year in late spring or early summer, parts of the national park light up with synchronous fireflies, a mesmerizing display where thousands of insects flash their lanterns (aka abdominal light organs) in perfect unison.

The event draws huge crowds of people to the Elkmont Campground, one of the best places in the Smokies to see it. Dates of the event change every year, but it can happen anytime between late May to late June.

Viewing dates are typically announced in April. All those who want to see the event must obtain a parking pass through a lottery system, and then take a shuttle to the site.

Since 2006 the park has limited access using the shuttle service, designed to reduce traffic and minimize impact on the unique fireflies. The service runs from the Sugarlands Visitor Center for eight days of predicted peak activity during the fireflies' two-week mating period.

The lottery typically opens for three days in late April. It's free to enter the lottery, which uses a randomized computer drawing to ensure fairness. Results are released 10 days after the drawing.

There will be a total of 1800 vehicle passes available, and applicants must apply for either a regular parking pass or large-vehicle parking pass and then can pick two dates to attend the event over the eight-day viewing period. The winners will be charged a $20 reservation fee, which will help cover the park's cost of organizing the logistics. You'll get a parking spot at the visitor center and take the shuttle ($2 per person) to see the event. The shuttle service is the only way that visitors can get there, except for registered campers staying at the Elkmont Campground. People cannot walk the Elkmont entrance road due to safety concerns.

To apply for the lottery, go to www.recreation.gov and search for 'Firefly Event.'

Activities

Hiking

Charlies Bunion HIKING

(Map p320; Newfound Gap, Newfound Gap Rd) This oddly named outcropping along the Appalachian Trail offers staggering views. The popular 8-mile (round trip) trail starts near the Rockefeller Memorial, which straddles North Carolina and Tennessee. After taking in the view, follow the rocky trail along the ridgeline, ascending 1000ft over the first 2.5 miles, then making a gentle descent before another brief uphill push to Charlies Bunion.

You'll arrive at the craggy promontory with its dazzling panorama sweeping from Mt LeConte eastward to the the jagged peaks of the Sawteeth Range. It's a great spot for a picnic, though be careful where you step, as some hikers have fallen to their deaths while scrambling around on the rock face.

The trailhead is at Newfound Gap, on the road of the same name, around 13 miles south of the Sugarlands Visitor Center.

Baskins Creek Trail HIKING

(Map p320) Near the start of the Roaring Fork Motor Nature Trail, you'll find this trail leading up to pretty Baskins Falls. The fascinating 5.6-mile (round trip) out-and-back hike draws a fraction of the number of visitors to more popular nearby sites such as Rainbow Falls and Grotto Falls. It's moderately strenuous, with a gain of about 1400ft over the course of the hike. Along the way, you'll spy white vein quartz, see fire-blackened tree trunks from the 2016 fires and have a few creek crossings.

Around mile 1.2, it's worthwhile taking the 400yd detour to the Baskins Creek Cemetery, with its weathered gravestones hidden in a mossy clearing. Another photogenic forest-fringed cemetery lies near the trail's end, which intersects a different stretch of the Roaring Fork Motor Nature Trail.

Grotto Falls HIKING

(Map p320) This moderate 2.6-mile round-trip hike passes through mature forests supporting old-growth hemlocks to one of Great Smoky's gorgeous waterfalls. The trailhead is on Roaring Fork Motor Nature Trail, 1.7 miles from the start of the one-way road. The parking area may fill up in summer, so get there early in the day.

You will be hiking along Trillium Gap Trail, one of the main arteries leading to the summit of Mt LeConte (p316), which is 6.6 miles from the parking area.

The well-maintained trail makes a moderate ascent all the way to the falls. There are a number of easy creek crossings along the way. You might encounter large black-and-white pileated woodpeckers, or hear their insistent drumming on the trunks of dead trees. During the spring you might see liverworts or silverbells in bloom or, on warm days, salamanders doing push-ups at the edge of a stream. Grotto Falls is a favorite subject for photographers. Here, Roaring Fork spills 20ft from an overhanging ledge as the trail passes behind a transparent wall of water – very cool.

Rainbow Falls

HIKING

(Map p320; off Cherokee Orchard Rd) Seeing these falls takes a bit of dedication (and lung power) – you must ascend 1600ft in a scant 2.7 miles. But oh, is it worth it. A long slog is finally rewarded by the sight of the misty Rainbow Falls, one of the park's prettiest and most delicate waterfalls. Rivulets of crystalline water spill over an 80ft bluff and then flow through a mossy boulder field in a succession of gentle cascades.

The entire trail is about 5.4 miles in length and takes about four hours (round trip) to hike. The trailhead is off Roaring Fork Motor Nature Trail.

Andrews Bald

HIKING

(Map p320; off Clingmans Dome Rd) A great hike to do while you're up visiting Clingmans Dome is this 3.6-mile (round trip) hike that starts near the visitor center. It's mostly downhill on the way there, making for an uphill slog on the return. When you reach the bald you'll be treated to some of the most spectacular views in the park.

Go early in the day (before 9am) to avoid the crowds. Although you can hike it any time of year, the road to Clingmans Dome closes in winter (December to March). Bring crampons if you come then.

Chimney Tops

HIKING

(Map p320) This hike is one of the park's most popular, thanks to its short length (3.5 miles round trip) and convenient location along Newfound Gap Rd. The view overlooking the twin peaks of Chimney Tops is striking. Unfortunately this was the flash point of the 2016 wildfires, and the last 400yd of the trail remain closed.

Much of a recent three-year, $750,000 trail renovation was spared from the fire, though the summit is badly damaged. Begin the uphill trek to the top after the trail crosses several streams, a rhododendron thicket and climbs through a mixed forest punctuated with giant yellow buckeye trees. After the first mile, the trail gets extremely steep, climbing up many steps before finally reaching a viewing platform with a splendid panorama.

Laurel Falls

HIKING

(Map p320; off Fighting Creek Gap Rd) With its close proximity to Gatlinburg and Elkmont Campground, this easy 2.6-mile round-trip waterfall hike has become so popular that the National Park Service has paved the entire length of the trail to head off the erosion caused by countless pairs of clomp-ing boots. The paved passage is wheel-chair accessible (with considerable assistance).

The trail to Laurel Falls climbs gently through a forest of oak and pine. At the top, Laurel Branch bursts from a grove of mountain laurel and falls nearly 50ft to collect in a pool that is ideal for soaking your weary gams. From here the water spills another 40ft to a second pool below. Plan on spending about 1½ hours on this hike.

APPALACHIAN TRAIL

The storied Appalachian Trail (AT) is an irresistible draw for many hikers. For some it's the only reason they come to Great Smoky. Around 71 of the AT's 2180 miles pass through the park, and many through-hikers consider these to be the highlight of the entire trail. For the most part, the trail follows the crest of the Great Smoky Mountains, shadowing the shared border between North Carolina and Tennessee.

An excellent time to make the hike is in September or October, when traffic on the trails has dissipated somewhat and autumn leaves are at their finest. In October, however, snow should be expected. Hikers on the AT sleep in backcountry shelters spaced 3 to 8 miles apart; reservations are required. During the summer, you'll likely need to make the necessary consecutive reservations well in advance.

Check out the Appalachian Trail Conservancy's website (www.appalachiantrail.org) for more information.

Great Smoky Mountains National Park

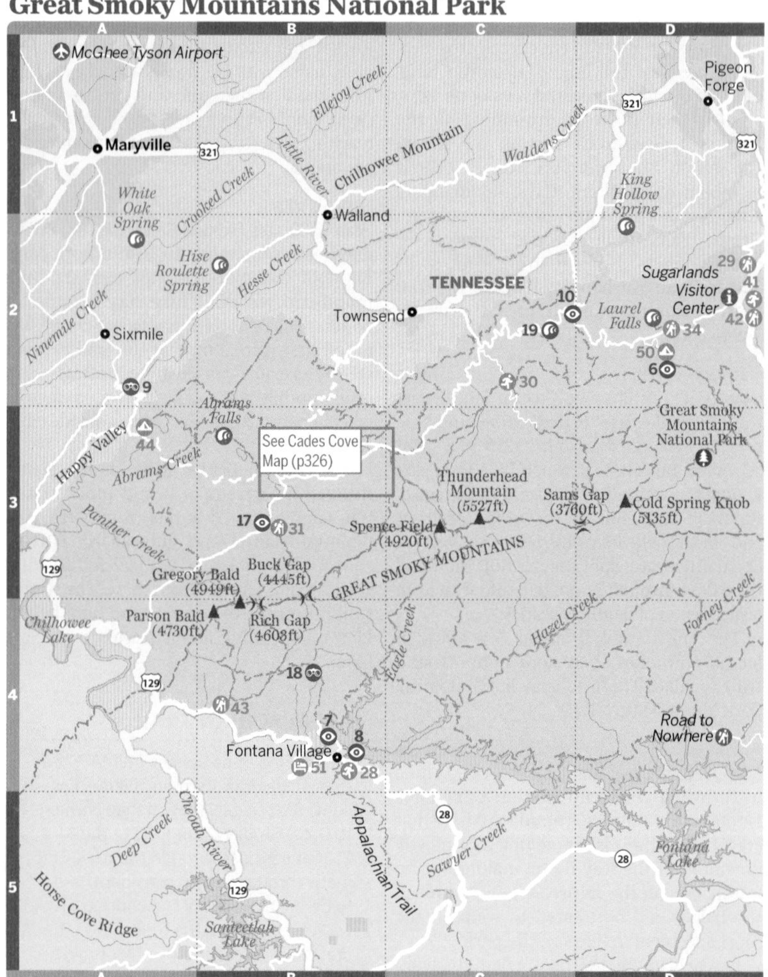

GREAT SMOKY MOUNTAINS NATIONAL PARK NEWFOUND GAP ROAD

Gatlinburg Trail HIKING
(Map p320; River Rd, off Hwy 441 S;) Although this 2-mile, one-way trail is completely within the national park, its northern trailhead borders downtown Gatlinburg, enticing folks into the woods and away from the Ripley's museums and pancake houses.

Pet and bike friendly, the easy trail parallels the West Prong of the Little Pigeon River and passes the ruins of old homesteads before ending at the Sugarlands Visitor Center.

Sugarlands Valley Nature Trail HIKING
(Map p320; off Newfound Gap Rd;) Less than a mile south of the Sugarlands Visitor Center, this easygoing half-mile loop is the park's only fully accessible nature trail. The paved, shaded path provides views of the West Prong of the Little Pigeon River, with rest stops along the way where you can contemplate the rushing waters against the forested backdrop.

Horseback Riding

Sugarlands Riding Stables HORSEBACK RIDING
(Map p320; 865-436-3535; www.sugarlandsridingstables.com; 1/2hr ride $35/70; 9am-4pm

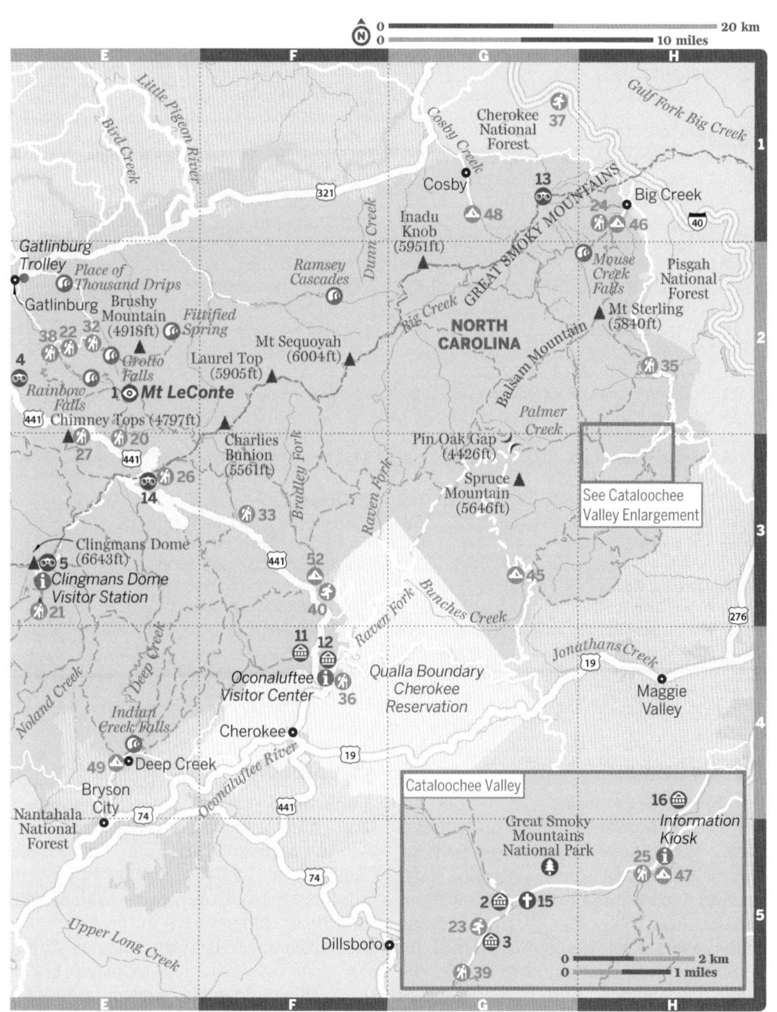

Mar-May & Sep-Nov, to 5pm Jun-Aug, closed Dec-Feb) Get out on horseback at the nearest stables to Gatlinburg.

Rafting

Rafting in the Smokies RAFTING

(Map p320; ☎800-776-7238; www.raftinginthesmokies.com; Hartford Rd; rafting trip $35-42, zipline $39; 👪) One of the highlights of a trip to the Smokies is heading out on a rafting adventure along the Pigeon River. This reputable outfitter runs two different trips: a 1½-hour, 5.5-mile-long whitewater adventure along the Upper Pigeon River (minimum age, eight), and a more easygoing two-hour paddle along the Lower Pigeon (ages three and up). Trips generally run Tuesday to Thursday and Saturday.

The locally owned operation has a lovely setting along the river, and offers other activities apart from rafting. Take the bouncy, 150ft suspension bridge over to the 10-acre island to reach the rock-climbing wall, ziplines and ropes course. There are also picnic tables, grills and a playground. A food truck is usually parked near the ticket booth. Go online or call to reserve a spot.

Great Smoky Mountains National Park

Top Sights
1 Mt LeConte E2

Sights
2 Beech Grove School G5
3 Caldwell House G5
4 Carlos C Campbell Overlook E2
5 Clingmans Dome E3
6 Elkmont Historic District D2
7 Fontana Dam B4
8 Fontana Lake B4
9 Look Rock Tower A2
10 Metcalf Bottoms C2
11 Mingus Mill F4
12 Mountain Farm Museum F4
13 Mt Cammerer Lookout Tower G1
14 Newfound Gap E3
15 Palmer Chapel G5
16 Palmer House H4
17 Parson Branch Road B3
Rockefeller Memorial .... (see 14)
18 Shuckstack Tower B4
19 The Sinks C2

Activities, Courses & Tours
20 Alum Cave Bluffs E3
21 Andrews Bald E3
22 Baskins Creek Trail E2
23 Big Cataloochee Valley G5
24 Big Creek Trail H1
25 Boogerman Loop Hike H5
26 Charlies Bunion E3
27 Chimney Tops E3
28 Fontana Marina B4
29 Gatlinburg Trail D2
30 Great Smoky Mountains Institute at Tremont C2
31 Gregory Bald B3
32 Grotto Falls E2
33 Kephart Prong Trail F3
34 Laurel Falls D2
35 Little Cataloochee Baptist Church H2
36 Oconaluftee River Trail F4
37 Rafting in the Smokies G1
38 Rainbow Falls E2
39 Rough Fork Trail to Woody Place G5
40 Smokemont Riding Stables F3
41 Sugarlands Riding Stables D2
42 Sugarlands Valley Nature Trail D2
43 Twentymile to Gregory Bald Loop B4

Sleeping
44 Abrams Creek Campground A3
45 Balsam Mountain G3
46 Big Creek Campground H1
47 Cataloochee Campground H5
48 Cosby Campground G1
49 Deep Creek E4
50 Elkmont D2
51 Fontana Village Resort B4
LeConte Lodge .... (see 1)
52 Smokemont F3

Courses

Great Smoky Mountains Institute at Tremont OUTDOORS
(Map p320; ☎865-448-6709; www.gsmit.org; Tremont Rd; overnight firefly camp $101, 3-day naturalist course $349, 4-day photography workshop from $668;) This learning center offers a wide range of courses for adults and kids. Among other things, you can go for a guided multi-day backpacking trip, attend a photography workshop, or take a naturalist class (dedicated to ecology, birds, plants, mammals, amphibians or developing interpretation and naturalist skills).

There are family camps (with hikes, crafts, swim time and music), discovery camps (for nine to 12 year olds) and wilderness backpacking trips for teens.

Overnight trips and multi-day camps include food and lodging. Located 4 miles southeast of Townsend, near the rushing Middle Prong of the Little River, the campus has classrooms and air-conditioned dorms, as well as cabin-style tents, for those staying on site.

Sleeping

Smokemont CAMPGROUND $
(Map p320; www.recreation.gov; Newfound Gap Rd; campsite $21-25) The Smokemont Campground's 142 sites are the only North Carolina campsites open year-round. As with most other campgrounds in the park, there isn't much space between sites. At 2200ft elevation, Smokemont is situated beside the rushing mountain stream of Bradley Fork, although no sites directly overlook the water. The campground is located just off Newfound Gap Rd, about 4 miles north of the Oconaluftee Visitor Center near the park's entrance by Cherokee, NC. This is a good base for hiking, with several trails leading off from the campground.

★**LeConte Lodge** CABIN $$
(Map p320; ☎865-429-5704; www.lecontelodge.com; cabins incl breakfast & dinner adult $148, child 4-12yr $85; ⊙mid-Mar–mid-Nov) The only non-camping accommodation in the park is LeConte Lodge. Though the only way to get to the lodge's rustic, electricity-free cabins is on five uphill hiking trails varying in length

from 5.5 miles (Alum Cave Trail; p328) to 8.9 miles (Trillium Gap Trail), it's so popular you need to reserve many months in advance.

Reservations for the lodge open on October 1 for the following season, and are booked solid within two days (the most desirable dates fill up within a few hours). However, it's well worth putting your name on a wait list, as openings often become available. If you score a spot, set out early to make the most of the experience. You can check out photos of past lodge life in the office and lounge, and climb to the very top of the mountain (a further 400yd beyond the cabins). After a hearty meal in the evening, you can sit in rocking chairs and watch the stars come out, or adjourn to the lounge for board games, guitar strumming and browsing old *National Geographic* magazines by lamplight.

Elkmont CAMPGROUND $

(Map p320; ☎865-436-1271; www.recreation.gov; Little River Rd; campsites $21-27; ⏲early Mar-late Nov) The park's largest campground is on Little River Rd, 5 miles west of the Sugarlands Visitor Center. Little River and Jakes Creek run through this wooded campground and the sound of rippling water adds tranquility. There are 200 tent and RV campsites and 20 walk-in sites. All are reservable beginning May 15. Like other campgrounds in the park, there are no showers, or electrical or water hookups. There are restrooms. Be sure to explore some of the historic sites while you're here. The campground occupies land that was once a logging village, and the abandoned resort cabins of Daisy Town are nearby.

Information

Clingmans Dome Visitor Station (Map p320; ☎865-436-1200; Clingmans Dome Rd; ⏲10am-6pm Apr-Oct, 9:30am-5pm Nov) At the trailhead to Clingmans Dome (p316), this small visitor center has two park rangers who can advise on park activities. There's also a bookstore and shop as well toilets.

Oconaluftee Visitor Center (Map p320; ☎828-497-1904; www.nps.gov/grsm; 1194 Newfound Gap Rd, North Cherokee, NC; ⏲8am-7pm Jun-Aug, to 6pm Apr, May, Sep & Oct, to 4:30pm Nov-Mar; 📶) At the park's southern entrance, near Cherokee, NC, this is the park's only LEED-certified visitor center. Its exhibits trace the cultural history of the region and provide fascinating insight into the indigenous people and the settlers who lived here before the park's establishment.

The shop is an excellent resource, with books, detailed maps, walking sticks, clothing items, souvenirs and activities for kids (puzzles, mini binoculars, junior ranger books). There's free wi-fi – useful for booking campsites if you show up to the park without reservations.

Sugarlands Visitor Center (Map p320; ☎865-436-1291; www.nps.gov/grsm; 107 Park Headquarters Rd; ⏲8am-7:30pm Jun-Aug, hours vary Sep-May; 📶) At the park's northern entrance near Gatlinburg, the Sugarlands Visitor Center has helpful park rangers on hand to advise on hiking trails and other activities. In back, you'll find displays on native plants and animals that you may later spot in the park. It's also worth attending a free screening of a 20-minute film on the park. There's a good shop and bookstore here.

Getting There & Away

The closest airports to the national park are **McGhee Tyson Airport** (Map p320; ☎865-342-3000; www.flyknoxville.com; 2055 Alcoa Hwy, Alcoa) near Knoxville (40 miles northwest of the Sugarlands Visitor Center) and Asheville Regional Airport (p299), 58 miles east of the Oconaluftee Visitor Center. Further afield you'll find **Chattanooga Metropolitan Airport** (CHA; ☎423-855-2202; www.chattairport.com; 1001 Airport Rd) 140 miles southwest of the park, Charlotte Douglas International Airport (p370) 170 miles east, and Hartsfield-Jackson International Airport (p370) in Atlanta (175 miles south of the park).

After you fly in, you'll need a car as there's no public transportation to the park. There's a wide variety of car-rental outfits at each of the airports.

Flights, cars and tours can be booked online at lonelyplanet.com/bookings.

Getting Around

CYCLING

Unfortunately, options are lacking for cyclists in the Smokies. There are no mountain-biking tracks in the park, and bikes are not allowed on most trails. The exception are three short, flat trails: the Gatlinburg Trail, the Oconaluftee River Trail and the lower Deep Creek Trail.

Cycling on the park roads is permitted but not recommended – even if you're a big fan of hills. The roads through the park are narrow, and with often heavy traffic to contend with, it's simply too dangerous to realistically consider.

One notable exception is the 11-mile Cades Cove Loop Rd (p325) , which is closed to motor vehicles from sunrise to 10am on Wednesday and Saturday mornings from early May until late September. Bikes are available for hire from the Cades Cove Campground store.

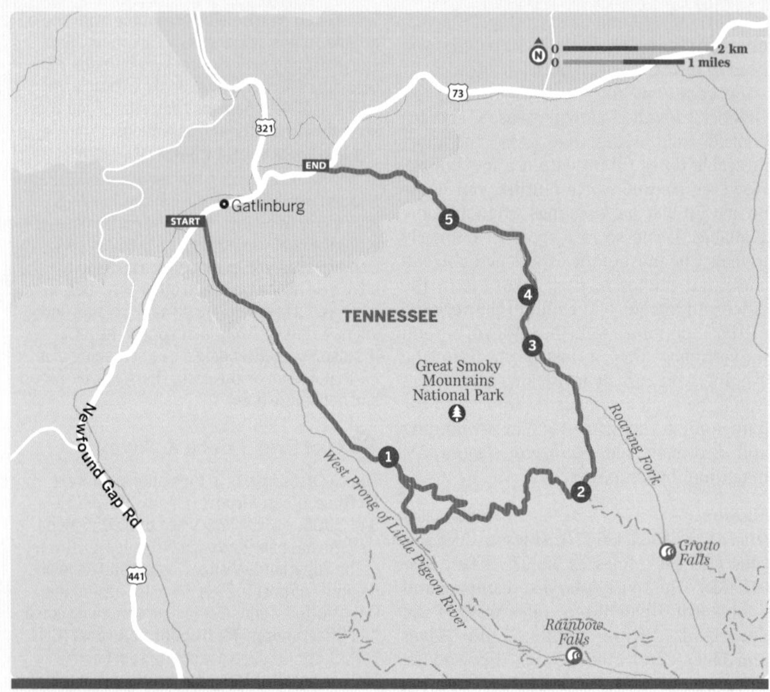

Scenic Drive
Roaring Fork Motor Nature Trail

START HISTORIC NATURE TRAIL RD, GATLINBURG
END ROARING FORK RD, GATLINBURG
LENGTH 8.5 MILES; ONE TO TWO HOURS

The Roaring Fork area is named for one of the park's biggest and most powerful mountain streams and is well loved for its waterfalls, glimpses of old-growth forest and its excellent selection of preserved cabins, gristmills and other historic structures. Don't let a thunderstorm ruin your day – this quick drive is at its best after a particularly hard rain. Keep in mind: the Roaring Fork Motor Nature Trail is open only from late March to late November.

The 5.5-mile road begins and ends near downtown Gatlinburg. From Hwy 441 turn onto Airport Rd at the eighth traffic light. Airport Rd becomes Cherokee Orchard Rd, and the Roaring Fork Motor Nature Trail begins 3 miles later.

The first stop is the 1 **Noah 'Bud' Ogle Nature Trail**, providing an enjoyable jaunt into a mountain farmstead and an ingenious wooden-flume plumbing apparatus.

Immediately after the Rainbow Falls Trail you can either turn around or continue on Roaring Fork Rd, a narrow, twisting one-way road. The road follows Roaring Fork, one of the park's most tempestuous and beautiful streams. It passes through an impressive stand of old-growth eastern hemlocks.

From the Trillium Gap Trail the delicate 2 **Grotto Falls** (p318) can be reached via an easy, short hike through a virgin hemlock forest.

Of historical interest is the hardscrabble cabin at the 3 **Home of Ephraim Bales** and the more comfortable 'saddlebag' house at the 4 **Alfred Reagan Place** (painted with 'all three colors that Sears and Roebuck had'). Reagan was a jack-of-all-trades who worked as a carpenter, blacksmith and storekeeper.

A wet-weather waterfall called 5 **Place of a Thousand Drips** provides a wonderful conclusion to your explorations before you return to Gatlinburg.

PUBLIC TRANSPORTATION

There's no public transportation within the park. A handful of shuttle companies offer private transport inside the park. The following outfits can take you to, or pick you up from, trailheads or transport you from lodging outside the park to in-park destinations. You'll need to reserve in advance.

A Walk in the Woods (☎865-436-8283; www.awalkinthewoods.com)

AAA Hiker Service (☎423-487-3112; www.aaahikerservice.com)

Smoky Mountain Guides (☎865-654-4545; www.smokymountainguides.com)

The **Gatlinburg Trolley** (Map p320; www.gatlinburgtrolley.org; ⏲generally 8:30am-midnight May-Oct, varies rest of year) serves downtown Gatlinburg and links to a few outlying areas. The trolley's tan line ($2) goes into the national park June through and October, with stops at the Sugarlands Visitor Center, Laurel Falls and Elkmont Campground.

Cades Cove

There's something about the morning light in Cades Cove (Map p326; www.nps.gov/grsm/planyourvisit/cadescove.htm; Cades Cove Loop Rd; P). With mountain-flanked meadows aglow under the golden rays, and deer, turkeys and black bears cavorting in the shimmering grasses, the scene is memorably enchanting. Unfortunately, with two million visitors exploring this valley every year, immersing yourself in that magic can be a challenge, particularly in summer and fall when bumper-to-bumper traffic jams the 11-mile loop road. The one-way road encircles land used as a hunting ground by the Cherokee before English, Scots-Irish and German settlers arrived in the 1820s. These determined newcomers built cabins and churches while clearing the valley's trees for farmland. Mills, forges and blacksmith shops soon followed, creating a thriving community. Today the creaky cabins, mossy spring houses, weathered barns and tidy cemeteries whisper the stories of the families who made this place their home. You'll hear them best if you arrive before 9am.

For Abrams Falls and Gregory Bald hikes, see Top Day Hikes on p328.

History

The first settlers – most of English, Scots-Irish and Welsh stock – arrived in the 1820s. By 1850 the valley's population had swelled to 70 households and 451 residents, later reaching a peak of 708. Today, thanks to the excellent preservation efforts of the National Park Service, you can still get a vivid sense of life in 19th-century Cades Cove through its surviving churches, gristmills and homesteads.

Sights

Cades Cove is the most visited area in the country's most visited national park. Because of traffic during peak season, it can take five hours to drive the 11-mile one-way loop road that links all of the sites – longer than it would take to walk!

There are more than 80 historic structures in the park. Those found along the Cades Cove Loop Rd, from cabins and churches to barns and a gristmill, were built in the 1800s. Look for them at the numbered stops along or near the loop. For details about these historic buildings, pick up the Cades Cove Tour booklet ($1) at the orientation shelter at the start of the loop or at the visitor center.

The loop road is open to car traffic from dawn to dusk, except on Wednesdays and Saturdays from early May through late September, when bicycles and hikers rule the road until 10am.

Lookrock Tower is west of Cades Cove and accessed from the Foothills Pkwy.

Cable Mill Historic Area HISTORIC SITE

(Map p326; Cades Cove Loop Rd; P) To get bread on the table, early residents of Cades Cove first had to mill their grains and corn. Above all other staples, corn was the most important. Every meal included food made from cornmeal, including corn bread, mush, hoecakes and spoon bread. Built in the early 1870s by John Cable, Cable Mill was once one of four or five water-powered gristmills to serve Cades Cove.

Powered by Mill Creek, the waters of which were routed into the mill via a 235ft-long flume, Cable Mill features a classic overshot waterwheel. The other historic buildings surrounding the mill were brought from other locations in the park to create a living history museum. There's a blacksmith shop, a barn, a smokehouse, a sorghum mill and a homestead, as well as the Cades Cove Visitor Center (p333) and shop – stop by to pick up a bag of corn ground on site.

Cades Cove

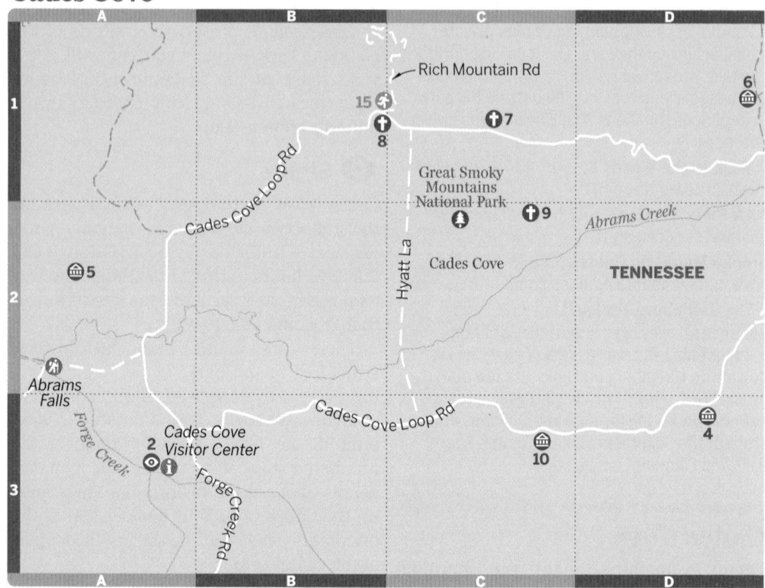

John Oliver Place HISTORIC BUILDING

(Map p326; Cades Cove Loop Rd; P) Built in the early 1820s, this rustic log cabin is the oldest in Cades Cove. Check out the stone chimney, made with mud mortar. The home was built by one of the cove's earliest settlers and remained in the family until the park was founded more than 100 years later.

Primitive Baptist Church CHURCH

(Map p326; Cades Cove Loop Rd; P) One of three rural churches that remain standing in Cades Cove, the 1887 Primitive Baptist Church is flanked by an atmospheric cemetery. Look out for the grave of Russell Gregory, 'murdered by North Carolina rebels' during the Civil War for being a Union sympathizer.

Methodist Church CHURCH

(Map p326; Cades Cove Loop Rd; P) Cades Cove's 1902 Methodist Church has a small but picturesque white steeple and includes gravestones on its lawn. It was built by blacksmith and carpenter JD McCampbell in 115 days for $115.

Note the two entrance/exit doors, which normally indicates that the church separated men and woman within the congregation, but that wasn't the case with the Methodist Church. It had simply borrowed building plans from a church that did separate its congregation, so two doors were built.

Missionary Baptist Church CHURCH

(Map p326; Cades Cove Loop Rd) The Missionary Baptist Church was formed in 1839 by former Primitive Baptist Church members who were kicked out for advocating missionary work. The building itself dates from 1915.

Elijah Oliver Place HISTORIC BUILDING

(Map p326; Cades Cove Loop Rd; P) The homestead farthest from the Cades Cove Loop Rd, this multi-building property sits at the end of a half-mile stroll through the woods. The cabin was the home of Elijah Wood, son of early settler John Oliver. Don't miss the springhouse and flume by the creek out back. The main house has a 'stranger room' for overnight guests.

Parson Branch Road AREA

(Map p320) This 8-mile-long road is permanently closed to motorized traffic, though it's open to mountain bikers and walkers, who can enjoy some serene forest views along its graveled length. Keep in mind, though, that the threat of falling trees is serious here. The road should definitely be avoided during high winds and after heavy rain, when loose soil can cause trunks to uproot themselves.

You'll go through rhododendron tunnels and pass over creek crossings as you wind

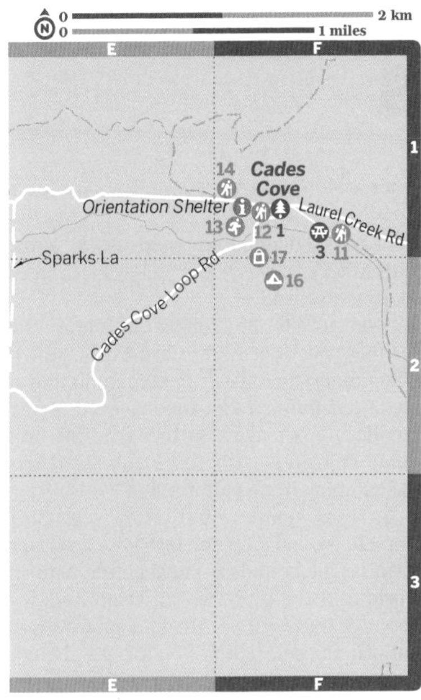

Cades Cove

Top Sights
1 Cades Cove........F1

Sights
2 Cable Mill Historic Area........A3
3 Cades Cove Picnic Area........F1
4 Carter Shields Cabin........D3
5 Elijah Oliver Place........A2
6 John Oliver Place........D1
7 Methodist Church........C1
8 Missionary Baptist Church........B1
9 Primitive Baptist Church........C2
10 Tipton Place........C3

Activities, Courses & Tours
11 Anthony Creek Trail........F1
12 Cades Cove Night Hike........F1
13 Cades Cove Riding Stables........F1
Cades Cove Trading........(see 17)
14 Rich Mountain Loop........F1
15 Rich Mountain Road........B1

Sleeping
16 Cades Cove Campground........F2

Shopping
17 Cades Cove Campground Store & Deli........F1

your way between Forge Creek Rd and Hwy 129 in the south. If you don't have a bike, you can hire one from Cades Cove Campground (p333) and make the trip down – a ride best undertaken when the Cades Cove Loop Rd is closed to cars (before 10am on Wednesday and Saturday, from May through September).

Tipton Place HISTORIC BUILDING
(Map p326; Cades Cove Loop Rd; P) The picturesque Tipton homestead was built by Mexican War veteran 'Colonel Hamp' Tipton in the early 1870s. The grounds include a spacious two-floor cabin, blacksmith and carpentry shops, and a replica cantilever barn.

Carter Shields Cabin HISTORIC BUILDING
(Map p326; Cades Cove Loop Rd; P) The last cabin on the loop road is arguably the most photogenic, tucked in a small grassy glade surrounded by the woods. Carter Shields, a Civil War veteran wounded in the Battle of Shiloh, lived here for 11 years in the early 1900s.

Cades Cove Picnic Area PICNIC AREA
(Map p326; off Cades Cove Loop Rd; P) Children enjoy splashing in the shallows of Abrams Creek at this woodsy picnic spot, where a number of tables are perched by the water. You'll find grills, restrooms, 81 picnic sites and the trailhead for the easy and family-friendly Anthony Creek Trail (p332).

Look Rock Tower VIEWPOINT
(Map p320; Foothills Pkwy) Located along the western section of the Foothills Pkwy (around Mile 7.3 if driving north from Chilhowee), this tower is reachable on an easy half-mile trail that starts just north of the parking area. From the top, you'll have 360-degree views of the Smoky Mountains to the west and the surrounding Tennessee River Valley to the east.

The tower is also used to study air quality in the region – you'll notice communication equipment and a control room (closed to the public) on top.

Activities

Numerous hiking trails crisscross the mountains surrounding Cades Cove, ribboning past creeks, rising over grassy meadows and bumping into historic cabins. Many of the hikes are strenuous half- and full-day adventures that climb to mountaintops, but a handful of family-friendly hikes teeter over log bridges and wander through groves of soaring trees. For Abrams Falls and Gregory Bald day hikes, see p330.

Cycling can be a challenge on the heavily trafficked loop road, but on Wednesday and

BEST DAY HIKES

ALUM CAVE BLUFFS

START/END ALUM CAVE BLUFFS PARKING AREA
DURATION 2½ TO 3½ HOURS ROUND TRIP
DISTANCE 4½ MILES
DIFFICULTY HARD
ELEVATION GAIN 2200FT

One of the 10 most popular trails in the Smoky Mountains, **Alum Cave Bluffs** (Map p320; off Newfound Gap Rd) often draws a crowd. It's a fantastic walk crossing log bridges, spying old-growth forest and enjoying fine views, though you should try to be on the trail before 9am to enjoy the scenery without the maddening crowds.

From the trailhead along Newfound Gap Rd, you quickly leave the sounds of traffic behind as you cross a stout bridge over a gurgling mountain stream (the Walker Camp Prong) and enter a wilderness of rosebay rhododendrons and thick ferns, with American beech and yellow birch trees soaring overhead.

Soon you'll be following along the rushing waters of Alum Cave Creek, which offers many fine places to stop and enjoy a bit of leisurely stream time (indeed, many families don't make it farther than the first mile). Enjoy this fairly flat, scenic stretch as the climbing begins after mile 1.1.

At that point you'll cross the Styx Branch, named after the mythological river forming the boundary between the natural world and the underworld. From here it's about 600yd to Arch Rock, a picturesque natural tunnel, which you'll pass though along carved stone steps leading up the steep slope.

The tough ascent continues, leading past old-growth hardwoods as it winds up Peregrine Peak (keep an eye out for the

Hiking the Alum Cave Bluffs

If you're seeking big views, old-growth forest, waterfalls or history on your walk in the woods, the park has a trail for you.

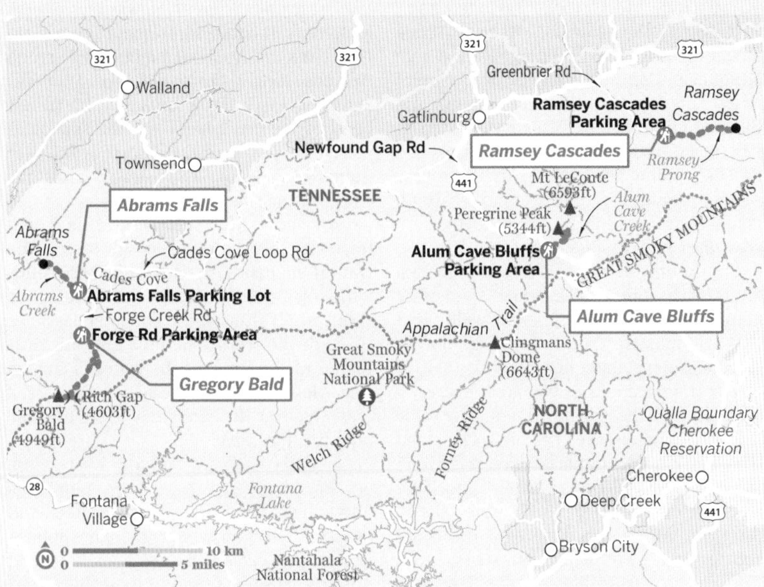

falcons for which the mountain is named). Around mile 1.8 you'll reach a heath bald where the views begin to open up, amid mountain laurel and sand myrtle. A bit further (around mile 2), you'll reach the aptly named Inspiration Point, offering even more impressive views of the forested valley below. Stop here to catch your breath before pressing on the final 600yd to Alum Cave Bluffs. Despite the name, this is not a cave but rather an 80ft-high concave cliff. It provides fine views and dry shelter when the rains arrive.

Though most people turn around here, you can press on to Mt LeConte, another 2.7 miles uphill, if you still have plenty of energy left. The terrain on this stretch is particularly challenging, as the trail passes over narrow rock ledges – steel cables bolted into the mountain provide useful handholds. At the summit, hot chocolate and other snacks await. Otherwise, it's an easy downhill descent back to your starting point.

RAMSEY CASCADES

START/END RAMSEY CASCADES PARKING AREA
DURATION 3 TO 4½ HOURS ROUND TRIP
DISTANCE 8 MILES
DIFFICULTY MODERATE TO HARD
ELEVATION GAIN 2280FT

The hike to Ramsey Cascades takes in some gorgeous forest scenery. Massive old-growth trees, boulder-filled streams and a forest floor sprinkled with wildflowers are among the highlights. The falls themselves are simply magnificent, with rushing white water spilling 100ft down rocky ledges. You'll have to work to enjoy the falls, however, as you ascend more than 2000ft over 4 miles.

The first part of the hike starts out with a fairly easy climb after a long bridge crossing over the rushing Middle Prong of the Little Pigeon River. The wide path initially follows the old road laid out by the logging company, though luckily they didn't get very far into the forest before the national park was created. Even here you'll find a few massive old-growth trees. A few benches are sprinkled along the first mile, where you can sit and contemplate the greenery.

Around mile 1.5, the path loops around a big circle filled with rhododendrons. Just below, the churning Ramsey Prong meets up with Middle Prong. Here a sign announces Ramsey Cascades as 2.5 miles away. This is where the trail narrows and the real climb begins. Watch your step as you make your way over the blackened roots spreading across the path. You'll pass a small stream cascading over moss-covered boulders around mile 2.1, then shortly after, cross over your first log bridge.

Continuing along, you'll pass through old-growth forest with some staggering giants. Around mile 2.6 you'll walk right past two massive tulip trees, with another even larger specimen just beyond.

The trail steepens as you grow nearer to the falls, with the last 400yd requiring some leg work to climb over the big rocks along the path. Finally, at mile 4.0, you've arrived. Take a break and congratulate yourself on reaching one of the prettiest waterfalls in the park. Afterwards, return to the trail's staring point by retracing your steps.

To reach the trailhead, take Hwy 321 for 6 miles east from Gatlinburg and turn right (south) down Greenbrier Rd. Parking for the trail is at the end of this road, 4.5 miles from the turnoff from the highway.

ABRAMS FALLS

START/END ABRAMS FALLS PARKING LOT
DURATION THREE TO FOUR HOURS
DISTANCE 5 MILES ROUND TRIP
DIFFICULTY MODERATE
ELEVATION GAIN LESS THAN 800FT

This hike is darn near perfect: a boisterous creek hugs much of the trail, log bridges keep things adventurous, wildflowers add color in spring, a horseshoe bend snakes into view halfway through and a photogenic waterfall crashes into a wide pool as the final reward. The only drawback is the crowds, which can be heavy. For solitude get to the trailhead before 9am.

Abrams Falls and Abrams Creek are named for Cherokee Chief Abram, who lived in a village near the mouth of the creek along the Tennessee River in the late 1700s. From the parking lot the trail enters the woods – filled with oaks, beeches and pines – and immediately crosses a bridge over Abrams Creek. A side trail to the right leads to the **Elijah Oliver Place** (p326), a half-mile north.

The main trail continues straight and level, tracking the creek. In warmer months look for rhododendron and mountain laurel blooms. At about 1 mile you'll ascend Arbutus Ridge. From the top, after the leaves have fallen, you can see the horseshoe bend of the creek below. In the spring, as you descend, you might observe wildflower hunters checking the steep sandstone slopes of the ridge for blooms.

From here, after another 1 mile, you'll hear the falls before you see them. The trail then drops to two creek crossings with log bridges. Before the trail bends right, you'll glimpse the crashing cascades through the trees. The falls are only 20ft high, but the force of the water is strong. The view and the sound of the creek crashing over the sandstone ledge into the pool is impressive.

Obey the signage and do NOT climb on the falls. There have been numerous drownings here. Rocks along the creek and near the falls can be surprisingly slippery. In fact, *Backpacker* magazine once named Abrams Falls one of the 10 most dangerous hikes in the US. But picnics and photos? All good.

The trailhead is at the end of the parking area between stops 10 and 11 on the Cades Cove Loop Rd. The turnoff to the parking area is about 5 miles from the start of the loop.

GREGORY BALD

START/END FORGE RD PARKING AREA
DURATION SIX TO SEVEN HOURS
DISTANCE 11 MILES ROUND TRIP
DIFFICULTY HARD
ELEVATION GAIN 3036FT

As you turn in a slow circle on the high grassy meadow known as **Gregory Bald** (Map p320; Forge Creek Rd, off Cades Cove Loop Rd), it's easy to appreciate Julie Andrews' joy in the *Sound of Music*. This may not be the Alps, but it's the next best thing in the southern Appalachians, with views of mountains and valleys stretching to the horizon in every direction. If you arrive

KURDISTAN/SHUTTERSTOCK ©

Abrams Falls

in mid- to late June, the orange, pink and fiery-red blooms of the flaming azaleas add one last dab of perfection.

The origins of the high-altitude balds in the park are uncertain. Some of these treeless meadows may have been cleared by early settlers for cattle grazing. Others say natural causes such as wildfires or high winds created small clearings, which were later expanded by cattle owners. Gregory Bald is named for Russell Gregory, a prominent Cades Cove resident whose cows grazed here in the mid-1800s. Today the park service maintains the balds, keeping them as broad, open spaces.

In the morning the Gregory Ridge Trail is disarmingly pleasant: birds are chirping, Forge Creek tumbles merrily beside you and sun-dappled leaves frame your views. At 2 miles the trail reaches backcountry campsite 12, a scenic spot in the shadows of towering old-growth trees. From here the fun ends and the climbing begins. The rock outcrop about 1300yd up from the campground provides your first bird's-eye view of Cades Cove to the north. The trail continues to climb, and climb, finally calling it quits at its junction with the Gregory Bald Trail in Rich Gap, 4.9 miles from the trailhead.

Take a breather here. The 1000yd final push on the Gregory Bald Trail is steep and punishing. Fortunately it's also short. On reaching the edge of the bald, walk right for broad views of Cades Cove then swing up the hill to the survey marker noting the altitude: 4949ft. You can return to the trail on the path through the azaleas, which typically bloom in mid- to late June. Blueberries appear in August.

From the Cades Cove Loop Rd, turn right onto Forge Creek Rd just beyond the Cades Cove Visitor Center parking lot. Follow Forge Creek Rd south just over 2 miles. Park at the small lot beside the trailhead sign for the Gregory Ridge Trail.

Saturday mornings from early May to late September cyclists can pedal with abandon because the park closes the road to motor vehicles until 10am.

Rich Mountain Loop HIKING

(Map p326; Cades Cove Loop Rd) This strenuous 8.5-mile loop passes the historic John Oliver Place (p326) before climbing to the ridgeline of Rich Mountain. From here the loop ribbons through the pines, serving up big views of Cades Cove and Townsend before a downward plunge. Additional highlights include creek crossings and wildlife sightings – potentially turkeys, deer and bears. Once the climb begins, you'll escape the crowds.

The loop is comprised of three trails: Rich Mountain Loop (3.4 miles), Indian Grave Gap (2.9 miles) and Crooked Arm Ridge (2.2 miles).

For the best views from atop the mountain, hike from late fall though early spring, when foliage does not block your sight lines. To avoid a steep and rocky climb up Indian Grave Gap Trail, hike the loop in a clockwise direction.

You can access the Rich Mountain Loop Trail from the parking lot at the orientation shelter at the start of the Cades Cove Loop Rd. At the western end of the lot, cross the road to the marked trailhead.

Cades Cove Night Hike HIKING

(Map p326; www.nps.giv/grsm; Cades Cove Loop Rd, orientation shelter; ⌚9-10:30pm Thu late Jun-early Aug) Bring a flashlight for this evening wildlife walk guided by a park ranger. Confirm the start time, which may change from year to year. This hike also depends on staffing, so you might not catch it on the park's online calendar in advance – check once arriving at Cades Cove.

Cades Cove Riding Stables HORSEBACK RIDING

(Map p326; ☎865-448-9009; www.cadescovestables.com; 10018 Campground Dr, Townsend; 1hr guided trail ride adult $35, child 2-12yr $25, carriage & hay rides adult $15, child 2-12yr $10; ⌚9am-4:30pm early Mar-Nov; 👪) Offers guided trail, carriage and hayrides near Cades Cove.

Cades Cove Trading CYCLING

(Map p326; ☎865-448-9034; www.cadescovetrading.com/bikes; adult per 1hr $7.50, child under 10yr $4.50; ⌚9am-9pm late May-Oct, to 5pm Mar-late May, Nov & last week of Dec, closed rest of the year) Rents cruisers and hybrid bicycles in a building beside the campground store. Opens at 6:30am on Wednesday and Saturday from late May through late September when the loop road is closed to automobile traffic until 10am – and is perfect for cycling!

Rich Mountain Road SCENIC DRIVE

(Map p326; off Cades Cove Loop Rd; ⌚early Apr–mid-Nov) For bird's-eye views of Cades Cove without a strenuous hike, turn right from the Cades Cove loop onto this gravel road across from the Missionary Baptist Church. Just know there's no turning back. Built in the 1920s, this 8-mile adventure takes a serpentine climb up and down Rich Mountain. After leaving the park, it ends in Tuckaleechee Cove to the north.

The road curves past modern mountain homes after leaving the park on the mountainside, when it also opens to two-way traffic. Townsend is 12 miles from the start.

Anthony Creek Trail HIKING

(Picnic Area to Bridges; Map p326; Cades Cove picnic area; 👪) After a picnic at Cades Cove picnic area, work off your lunch and wear out the kids with a creekside hike that rolls through hemlock forests, passes a horse camp and crosses Abrams and Anthony Creeks on several bridges. The trail is 3.6 miles one way, but younger kids will probably be ready to turn around after the fourth bridge at 1.6 miles.

The Anthony Creek Trail is well traveled because it links with the Russell Field and Bote Mountain Trails, which separately connect to the Appalachian Trail. The trailhead is at the back of the Cades Cove picnic area.

Sleeping

There is one developed campground in Cades Cove. A half-dozen backcountry camping locations (p335) can be found along trails in the surrounding mountains. Camping at a backcountry site requires a reservation and permit (www.nps.gov/grsm/planyourvisit/backcountry-camping.htm). The campground at Abrams Creek is west of Cades Cove and accessed from the Foothills Pkwy. The closest commercial lodgings are in Townsend, about 9 miles from Cades Cove.

Cades Cove Campground

CAMPGROUND $

(Map p326; 865-448-2472; www.recreation.gov; campsites $25) This woodsy campground with 159 sites is a great place to sleep if you want to get a jump on visiting Cades Cove. There's a store, drinking water and bathrooms, but no showers. There are 29 tent-only sites. Sites can be reserved in peak season – May 15 through October. The rest of the year, campsites are first-come, first served.

Reservations can be made up to six months in advance. Campsites are $21 during walk-in season. Follow all posted rules for camping in bear country.

Abrams Creek Campground

CAMPGROUND $

(Map p320; reservations 877-444-6777; www.recreation.gov; off Happy Valley Rd; campsites $17.50; late Apr-late Oct) This small, remote campground on the western edge of the park takes a bit of effort to get to, but you'll be well compensated for your journey. Just over half of the 16 sites face pretty Abrams Creek (book sites 01 through 09 for a waterfront view). The others are arranged along the edge of the woods.

You must book before you arrive; there's no pay-upon-arrival option – and no mobile service once you're at the campground.

The campground lies 7 miles north of Hwy 129 along Happy Valley Rd. Abrams Creek is a popular fishing spot and is also the starting point for some scenic trails, including the 5-mile (one way) Abrams Falls Trail (Map p326; Cades Cove Loop Rd).

Shopping

Cades Cove Campground Store & Deli

MARKET

(Map p326; 865-448-9034; www.cadescovetrading.com; 10035 Campground Dr; 9am-9pm late May-Oct, to 5pm Mar-May, Nov & late Dec) One-stop shopping for campers, hikers and day trippers, this compact souvenir shop and market sells T-shirts, hats, camping sundries, snacks, drinks, ibuprofen and firewood. Order burgers, sandwiches and hotdogs at the small deli counter, where you can also buy a soft-serve ice-cream cone after your hike. Also sells cups of coffee.

OFF THE BEATEN TRACK

COSBY & BIG CREEK

If you don't mind a short drive, you'll find fantastic hiking and camping (and fewer people) in the northeastern fringes of the park near Cosby, TN. A 1.2-mile round-trip hike leads to 360-degree views of ridges and valleys atop the Mt Cammerer Lookout Tower (Map p320). The Big Creek Trail (Map p320) follows a beautiful stream for 5.1 miles (one way), passing an inviting natural pool and waterfalls. The latter trail begins at the tent-only Big Creek Campground (Map p320; reservations 877-444-6777; www.recreation.gov; Big Creek Park Rd; tent sites $17.50; Apr-late Oct). The forested Cosby Campground (Map p320; www.recreation.gov; off Hwy 32; campsites $17.50; late Mar-late Oct) has more than 100 campsites but remains less chaotic than the campgrounds at Cades Cove and Smokemont.

Information

An open-air **orientation shelter** (Map p326; Cades Cove Loop Rd; 8am-5pm) borders the parking lot just before the start of the Cades Cove Loop Rd. Stop here for a free park guide. Copies of the *Cades Cove Tour* booklet ($1) are for sale if you are interested in the history of the buildings bordering the drive. A full-service **visitor center** (Map p326; 865-436-7318; www.nps.gov/grsm; Cades Cove Loop Rd; 9am-7pm Apr-Aug, closes earlier Sep-Mar) sits at stop 11, which is midway along the Cades Cove Loop Rd.

Getting There & Away

Cades Cove is 9 miles from the town of Townsend and 27 miles from Gatlinburg. From Pigeon Forge, also 27 miles away, it may be quicker to drive to Townsend and pick up Laurel River Rd off Hwy 73 rather than traveling through the park on Little River and Laurel River Rds.

Getting Around

Cades Cove Loop Rd is open to motor vehicles from sunrise to sunset. The road is closed to vehicle traffic until 10am on Wednesday and Saturday between early May and late September. This a great time for cyclists and pedestrians to travel the loop.

There are no park shuttles traveling the loop road.

WILDLIFE WATCHING

The wildlife watching is superb in the Smokies. Always keep your eyes peeled and try to move through the forest quietly for the best chance of seeing animals.

With over 1500 bears in the park, you may be lucky enough to spot one, though sightings are still rather rare. Good places to look for them are in the Cades Cove area, off Roaring Fork Motor Nature Trail, and on the way to Laurel Falls.

Elk are easier to find. These massive animals were reintroduced to the park less than 20 years ago, and are most commonly seen in the Cataloochee Valley and on the fields beside the Oconaluftee Visitor Center. Your best chance of seeing them is around dawn or dusk.

Owing to the diverse habitats, unique microclimates and varying elevations, the Smokies are a great place for bird-watching. More than 240 species have been found in the park. Late April and early May are peak migration in the Smokies, and the best time to spot birds.

The Smokies are one of the world's salamander capitals. Some 30 species are found in the park, including 24 species of lungless salamanders. True to name, these extraordinary creatures obtain oxygen not through their lungs, which they lack, but through the walls of blood vessels along their skin and mouths. You're best chance of seeing them is in and near mountain streams, sometimes hiding under rocks.

Other creatures you may see include wild turkeys, white-tailed deer, possums, raccoons, squirrels (both red and gray species), chipmunks, woodchucks, skunks and bats.

Nocturnal animals such as bobcats, coyotes, red foxes and gray foxes are rarely seen, but if you're out at night, be on the lookout!

Cataloochee Valley & Balsam Mountain

Tucked in a far-flung corner of the park, deep in the mountains of western North Carolina, Cataloochee feels untamed. It takes an edge-of-your-seat drive to get here, elk and turkey strut around like they own the place and stories of hermits and wild men give the woods a spooky edge. But it wasn't always so. In 1910 the community – comprising Big Cataloochee and Little Cataloochee – was the largest settlement in the Smokies, with 1251 citizens. Farming, apple production and tourism kept the economy buzzing right up until the late 1920s, when folks heard rumors that the park was moving in. Today historic buildings and lush meadows line Cataloochee Rd in Big Cataloochee Valley, which could double as a safari park with all the wildlife roaming between its 6000ft-high peaks. Over Noland Mountain lies Little Cataloochee Valley, where the sights can only be explored by foot or horseback.

Sights

There are a half-dozen historic buildings in Big Cataloochee Valley, all dating from the late 1800s and early 1900s. Most can be reached on a short drive along Cataloochee Rd. A handful of historic buildings line the Little Cataloochee Trail, which can only be traveled by foot or horseback. For more details, buy the *Day Hike & Auto Tour Cataloochee* booklet ($1.50) at a park visitor center, or get an overview at the information kiosk (p336).

Caldwell House HISTORIC BUILDING

(Map p320; Cataloochee Rd; P) With its weatherboarding, interior paneling and shingled gables, as well as its white exterior and jaunty blue trim, this frame house, built in 1906, seems almost of the modern era.

The L-shaped front porch is a pleasant place to soak up the history and the scenery, which includes a stream rippling out front, a photogenic barn and the sound of birds singing in the background.

Palmer Chapel CHURCH

(Map p320; Cataloochee Rd; P) No, this Methodist church isn't turning its back on Cataloochee Rd. Built in 1898 it faces the old road that once ran through the valley. Circuit-riding preachers visited the chapel one Sunday per month. Today the bright-white church hosts the annual **Cataloochee Reunion**, when old timers and the descendants of valley families gather to share memories and news. The reunion was held for the 80th time in 2017, and shows no signs of slowing down.

Beech Grove School HISTORIC BUILDING

(Map p320; Cataloochee Rd; P) This 1901 schoolhouse is the only one of three valley schoolhouses still standing. Inside you'll find rows of old desks and a blackboard. School was typically in session from November through January, with an extra two months tacked on if there was enough local funding.

Palmer House HISTORIC BUILDING

(Map p320; off Cataloochee Rd; P) The yellow Palmer House is a 'dog-trot' house, meaning it consists of two separate log cabins sitting side by side with a covered breezeway between them. The log cabins were later weatherboarded. Facing the house, the room on the left once served as the post office; today it holds a decrepit, but still interesting, collection of exhibits about the lives of the families who resided in Cataloochee.

Activities

Hikers who want to escape the crowds should head to Cataloochee, where lightly traveled trails pass isolated historic buildings and climb through quiet forests. Wildlife watching is also a draw, and you'll likely see elk and wild turkeys, and maybe the occasional bear.

Boogerman Loop Hike HIKING

(Map p320; Cataloochee Rd) Soaring old-growth trees, lonely stone walls and stories of a shy hermit lend a fairy-tale vibe to this 7.5-mile lasso loop that begins near Cataloochee Campground. The mature trees that mark this hike are here thanks to the hermit, Robert 'Boogerman' Palmer, who did not allow logging on his property. He requested the nickname in elementary school, we hear.

The hike begins with a creekside ramble on the Caldwell Fork Trail, open to hikers and horseback riders. After 1400yd the path intersects with the 4.1-mile Boogerman Trail, open only to hikers. From here, you'll climb through a forest wonderland, passing Eastern hemlocks, oaks, maples, tulip trees and white pines. The trail rises and falls, passing Palmer's old homestead (although we couldn't spot it) before a final long drop to a series of mossy stone walls – all that's left of abandoned homesteads. The trail rejoins the Caldwell Fork Trail for a 2.8-mile return.

After a storm, downed trees along the entire loop and washed-out footbridges on the Caldwell Fork Trail can turn this ramble into an epic adventure, so check the trail status with the camp host or read the signage at the trailhead after bad weather. On a couple of our creek crossings the fast-flowing water hit above the knee and could prove dangerous with younger kids. If you have a hiking pole, bring it.

Big Cataloochee Valley WILDLIFE WATCHING

(Map p320) Early morning and late evening are the best times to look for elk and wild turkey in Big Cataloochee. Two great spots for wildlife watching are the open fields beside Palmer Chapel (p334) and the mountain-flanked meadow behind the Caldwell House (p334) barn. On the way to the latter, you'll find a box of brochures about the local elk population.

Rough Fork Trail to Woody Place HIKING

(Map p320;) Families looking for an easy hike with a side of history should tackle this 2-mile out-and-back trail, which ribbons beneath white pines on an old road bed. Kids will enjoy scampering across the creek on foot logs. The house here began as a log cabin, which sheltered a family of 16 in the late 1860s. Frame additions were added in the early 1900s.

After the Civil War, two families merged *Brady Bunch* style in the home after widower Jonathan Woody married widow Mary Ann Caldwell. He moved into her log

BACKCOUNTRY CAMPSITES & SHELTERS

The national park has more than 80 backcountry campsites. It also has 15 shelters, most of which are located along the Appalachian Trail. The price to stay at either, including the permit, is $4 per person per night, with a maximum fee of $20. Permits are valid for up to seven nights. Sites have a capacity of anywhere from four people to 14. They can book up on weekends and throughout the busy summer months, so reserve well ahead. Reservations can be made up to 30 days in advance of the first night of your trip.

Keep in mind that some sites also accept horses, mules and other stock. Contact the **backcountry permit office** (865-436-1297; www.nps.gov/grsm/planyourvisit/backcountry-camping.htm; off Newfound Gap Rd; 8am-5pm) if you're planning to travel with your favorite llama.

cabin with his five children. Nine of her 12 children were still living there. Good times!

If you're hiking solo, never mind those rumors about the Wild Man of Cataloochee. We're pretty sure this legendary backwoodsman died in 2010, but what was that sound over there...?

Little Cataloochee Baptist Church HIKING
(Map p320; off Old NC 284) Built in 1889 this photogenic hilltop church in Little Cataloochee can only be reached on foot or horseback via the Little Cataloochee Trail, which stretches from Big Cataloochee to Old NC 284. The 4-mile, round-trip hike to the church from Old NC 284 passes the 1864 Hannah Cabin and the once-bustling community of Ola. Inside the church you'll find a pot-bellied stove and white wooden pews. There's a graveyard at the base of the hill.

If hiking to the church from Big Cataloochee Valley, you'll follow the Pretty Hollow Gap Trail to the Little Cataloochee Trail. If you backtrack to Big Cataloochee after reaching the church, it's about 8 miles round trip. To hike the entire Little Cataloochee Trail from Big Cataloochee Valley to Old NC 284 (just over 6 miles one way), consider leaving a car at the trailhead on Old NC 284 so you can shuttle back to your starting point instead of backtracking.

Sleeping

There is only one developed campground in Cataloochee. Backcountry site number 40 borders the Rough Fork Trail (p335) and requires a reservation and permit. Pretty Balsam Mountain Campground is a 35-mile drive from Cataloochee Valley.

Cataloochee Campground CAMPGROUND $
(Map p320; 877-444-6777; www.recreation.gov; Cataloochee Rd; campsites $25; late Mar-Oct) This remote campground in a forest of hemlock and white pine has spacious campsites arranged off a loop road. Six of the 27 sites lie along the excellent fishing waters of Cataloochee Creek. Reservations are mandatory year-round, and the campground fills up on summer evenings. The host has brochures and maps. Take exit 20 off I-40, go west on Hwy 276 to Cove Creek Rd and follow it to Cataloochee Rd.

Balsam Mountain CAMPGROUND $
(Map p320; www.recreation.gov; Heintooga Ridge Rd; campsites $25; mid-May–Oct) This small highlands campground is considered by many to be the park's most lovely, thanks to its privileged placement within an 'island' forest of red spruce and Fraser firs. Though the 46 campsites are somewhat small, the upside is that it discourages behemoth RVs from roosting (RVs up to 30ft are allowed). The campground is 8 miles from the Blue Ridge Pkwy via Heintooga Ridge Rd.

Information

An **information kiosk** (Map p320; Cataloochee Rd) Rd shares basic information about Cataloochee Valley and its wildlife. For specific questions about trails and sights, stop by the campground host's RV. The host's adjacent – but small – event tent doubles as a mini information center.

Getting There & Away

From I-40, take exit 20. Follow Hwy 276 for 350yd to Cove Creek Rd. Cove Creek Rd is paved for 5 miles then becomes gravel for 3 miles. If you pass the Bigfoot statue, you're headed the right way. Note that the unpaved section of the road is twisty and narrow. It can also be in bad shape – take it slow. You will then reach the paved Cataloochee Rd, also known as the Cataloochee Entrance Rd. Follow it 3 miles to the information kiosk and campground. Asheville, NC, is 40 miles east of Cataloochee Campground and the drive from the city takes about an hour.

Fontana Dam & Western North Carolina

Hiking, boating and paddling are top activities in the southwest corner of the park, where created Fontana Lake stretches for 29 miles along the park's southwest boundary. The Appalachian Trail (p319) rolls across the top of the dam. The AT trail shelter here has a view of the lake and is known fondly by hikers as the Fontana Hilton.

Sights

Fontana Dam DAM
(Map p320; off Fontana Dam Rd; visitor center 9am-7pm Apr-Aug, to 6pm Sep & Oct) Built in the early 1940s to provide power for America's industrial needs during WWII, Fontana is the tallest dam east of the Rockies. At 2365ft wide, it's an engineering marvel – and all the more impressive given it was completed in just three years. Water released from the 29-mile-long reservoir (an impoundment of the Tennessee River) plunges down a 480ft tunnel to spin three massive turbines, which in turn generate enough electricity to power 290,000 homes.

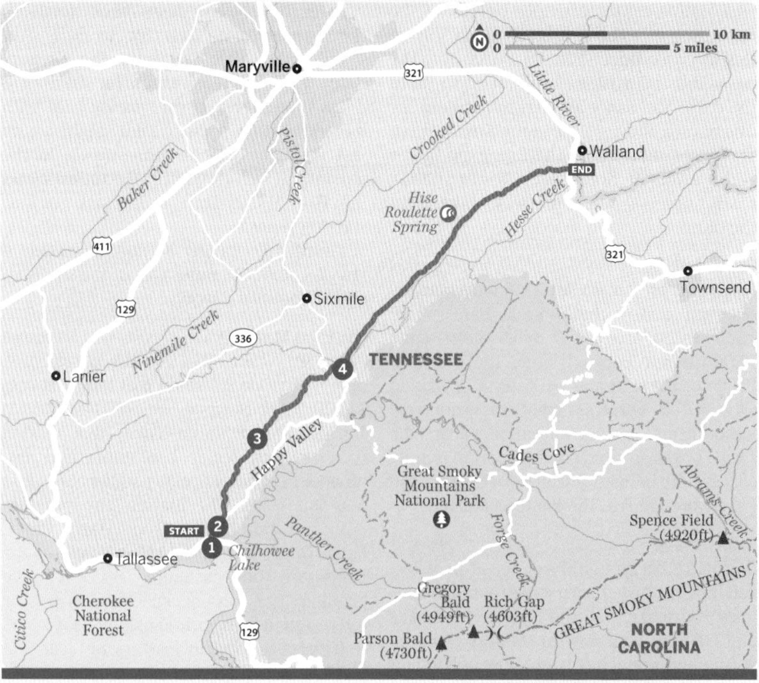

Scenic Drive
Foothills Parkway

START CHILHOWEE
END WALLAND
LENGTH 17 MILES; ONE HOUR

Running along the outer boundary of the national park, the Foothills Pkwy is a leafy motorway that offers spectacular views of the Smoky Mountains. Consisting of several separate, non-contiguous sections, the parkway is best known for its route between Chilhowee and Walland, on the Smokies' western edge. On this drive you'l enjoy staggering views across the rolling forests to the east as well as the fertile lands of the Tennessee River Valley and the distant Cumberland Mountains to the northwest. For the best lighting come early in the morning or late in the afternoon, when the mountain folds are bathed in a golden light.

Driving from south to north, the route starts near a picturesque stretch of **1 Chilhowee Lake**. The first stop is at the **2 vintage sign** about half a mile into the drive. After a few requisite photos of the arching market with its arching triangular backdrop, continue to the **3 first scenic overlook**, located around the 3.5-mile mark. The views sweep across the western expanse of the mountains. In springtime, you'll see every shade of green amid the thickly wooded layers covering the undulating ridges.

Continuing north, you'll pass several more overlooks, each offering slightly different perspectives of the mountain scene. Around 7.2 miles, stop at the unsigned lookout (number six, if you're counting) and walk to the viewing platform, which juts out of the valley and affords views of both the west and southwest. Afterwards, cross the road, and take the short but steep trail up to **4 Look Rock Tower** (p327). The half-mile walk leads to a lookout. Once you ascend the ramp to the top, you'll have mesmerizing 360-degree views. From here it's a 20 mile drive to end in Walland.

A visitor center provides details of the construction – the nearby Fontana Village Resort was once the barracks for the thousands of workers brought in to build the dam. You can walk across the dam for fine photos above – indeed the Appalachian Trail goes right along the top. Even better views await at Shuckstack Tower (p338), a strenuous, 4-mile (one way) hike from the dam.

Fontana Lake LAKE

(Map p320; off Fontana Rd) This long, narrow reservoir east of the Fontana Dam (p336) stretches for around 29 miles across some 10,000 acres. Located along the southern fringe of the national park, west of Bryson City, it's a gorgeous spot for canoeing, kayaking and fishing. You can hire gear, take scenic boat tours and get transport to remote corners of the lake (ideal for exploring the Lakeshore Trail) at the Fontana Marina.

Shuckstack Tower VIEWPOINT

(Map p320) It's an uphill slog to get here, but you'll be rewarded with jaw-dropping views once you make it to the historic fire tower and clamber your way to the top. From its 200ft perch you'll have fine views of Fontana Lake and the mountains beyond. It's located just off the Appalachian Trail, about 3.5 (tough uphill) miles from the Fontana Dam, in the southwest corner of the park. Take care climbing up the tower, as some rails are missing and there are loose wooden floorboards up top.

Activities

Twentymile to Gregory Bald Loop HIKING

(Map p320; Twentymile Ranger Station, Hwy 28) There aren't many loop hikes in the Smokies, so if you want a multi-day backpacking trip that doesn't involve a long shuttle ride at the end, you'll have to plan a DIY adventure. This 18.3-mile hike offers ample rewards, including a section along the Appalachian Trail, a climb up a vintage fire tower, and even more majestic views from a grassy bald atop Gregory Bald.

The hike starts at Twentymile Ranger Station in the southwest part of the park. You'll head along Twentymile Trail for 5 miles, which meets up with the Appalachian Trail. Before proceeding north, however, it's worth your while to take a 500yd detour south along the Appalachian Trail to six-story Shuckstack Tower with its mesmerizing views.

After the detour, head back north on the Appalachian Trail for a little over 4 miles and turn left onto the Gregory Bald Trail. You'll continue for another 3 miles then arrive at this grassy bald with its enchanting views. That night camp just past the bald at campsite 13. In the morning it's all downhill (6.8 miles) along the Wolf Ridge Trail, right back to your starting point.

Twentymile Ranger Station is located on Hwy 28, about 18 miles east of the southern end of Foothills Pkwy.

Fontana Marina BOATING

(Map p320; ☎828-498-2129; www.fontanavillage.com; off Fontana Rd; scenic boat tour adult/child $20/10, kayak or canoe hire per 1/4hr $10/25) Jutting over Fontana Lake, this marina runs 1½-hour scenic boat tours and also hires out canoes, kayaks, paddleboards and pontoon boats. The marina also provides boat transport to or from Hazel Creek, Eagle Creek and many other spots off the Lakeshore Trail – a handy service if you're heading out on backpacking trips, or interested in some prime fishing spots.

If fishing, you can load up on gear and tackle (plus drinks and snacks) at the store inside the marina. Fishing licenses are also available.

Sleeping

Deep Creek CAMPGROUND $

(Map p320; Deep Creek Rd; campsites $21; ⏲ late Mar-late Oct) Near Bryson City this medium-sized family campground with 92 sites offers a good variety of choices and splendid opportunities for hiking and bird-watching. Section C features creekside, tent-only sites; section D, a loop road through the woods, affords more privacy. The waters of Deep Creek give much joy to inner tubers and anglers (the park, however, discourages inner tubing here).

Fontana Village Resort LODGE $$

(Map p320; ☎828-498-2211; www.fontanavillage.com; 300 Woods Rd, Fontana Dam; d $150-250; 🏊) Near the national park's southern fringe, this old-school resort makes a fine base for a back-to-nature holiday, with miles of cycling and hiking trails right outside the door. Though the facilities are a bit dated, there are loads of activities on offer, including a swimming pool, mini-golf and a marina where you can hire watercraft (kayaks, pontoon boats).

Understand Georgia & the Carolinas

Rainbow Row (p170)

History

From the days of the Creek and the Cherokee, to the Conquistadors and Scots, German and English colonists, through the Revolutionary War and the Civil War to the Civil Rights era and beyond, Georgia and the Carolinas have accumulated centuries of stories.

Georgia

Native American culture in Georgia dates beyond pre-Columbian times, but the state began taking shape in the mid-1500s, when the Spanish arrived, followed by the English, who began the first colony at Savannah in 1733. Over its near 300-year history as a territory and state, Georgia has evolved from Old South stalwart to global vanguard, surviving the Civil War wounded but alive, prudently navigating the Civil Rights movement and embracing Hollywood, international business, hip-hop and tech along the way.

Colonization and Statehood

Spanish explorers first reached the coast of what is Georgia as early as 1513, when it's believed Juan Ponce de León arrived, preceding more certain visits by various Spaniards over the next three decades, including Hernando de Soto in 1540. A Spanish fort was established at St Catherines Island, a barrier island 20 miles south of Savannah, which was home to a Guale settlement – a Native American chiefdom of Mississippian culture.

Permanent English settlement began in 1732. Georgia was the 13th and last colony established by the British in North America. James Edward Oglethorpe and 114 colonists founded the colony of Georgia in Savannah with an altruistic Latin motto: *non sibi sed aliis* – not for self but for others. Although Georgia was intended as a buffer between the Spanish in Florida and an English colony in South Carolina, a St Simons Island battle in 1742 forced the Spanish to abandon all hope of local colonization, and English dominance in the region became firmly rooted.

TIMELINE

500m BCE

Ancient marine creatures inhabit the shallow sea margin that existed in today's Appalachian region. Their fossils are later found embedded in rocks along the Foothills Parkway and in other areas.

8000 BCE

Early nomadic people hunt game seasonally in the Smoky Mountains and on their periphery. Tools and projectiles made of chert (a non-local lithic stone) have been found.

1513

Spanish conquistadors, namely Juan Ponce de León, are believed to have landed in what is now Georgia. Spanish explorers continued surveying the area for three decades.

While an enduring myth says the original colony was founded by convicts, that's untrue – though hard liquor was originally banned, so it might have felt like prison to some. Also banned upon Georgia's initial founding was slavery. Following a few failed economic initiatives (silk production, among others), the slavery ban was lifted in 1750 and trustees turned the colony over to the king two years later. With labor virtually free, the colony began to grow at a rapid pace. By the time the Revolutionary War kicked off in 1775, enslaved people made up 50% of the population. Rice plantations sprung up along the coast, while small-scale farming and industry drove the more mountainous north, and agricultural cotton production fueled the lowlands.

The British captured Savannah in 1778, and later most of Georgia, but were driven out in 1782. Six years later, Georgia became the fourth state to ratify the US Constitution after Delaware, Pennsylvania and New Jersey. In 1793, Eli Whitney invented the cotton gin and the slavery-based plantation economy took off.

While today Georgia is the largest state east of the Mississippi River, it is considerably smaller than during its teething years when its territory initially extended westward all the way to the Mississippi River. Georgia was the last state to cede its western boundaries in the wake of the 1795 Yazoo land fraud (an audacious land scandal that remains one of the most egregious in US history). In 1802 the federal government purchased lands west of the Chattahoochee River in exchange for promises to settle contentious land claims and remove Native American lands from the state. Five years later, the Creek (Muscogee) tribe sold their land in Georgia.

The 19th Century & the Civil War

In 1828 gold was discovered in Dahlonega, sparking the first North American Gold Rush. The lust for wealth sped up the dispossession of the state's Cherokee population during the first half of the 19th century, culminating in their forced removal to Oklahoma along the 1838 Trail of Tears. The fifth state to secede from the Union, Georgia wasn't a big player at the beginning of the Civil War, but Atlanta's strategic position as a Confederate industrial, transportation and munitions center meant the war would eventually find its way to the state. After Union troops were defeated at Chickamauga, they invaded and defeated Atlanta, burning it to the ground in the process, before moving on to Savannah under the command of General William T Sherman, who intended to 'make Georgia howl' on his infamous and destructive 'March to the Sea.' On December 22, 1864, Sherman's famous telegram to President Abraham Lincoln was transmitted, presenting Savannah as a Christmas gift with guns, ammunition and cotton.

1584

Chartered by Elizabeth I, Sir Walter Raleigh sends an expedition to Roanoke Island. The following year, 100 colonists establish a settlement, and another 100 follow in 1587, but by 1590 all have vanished.

1670

England establishes the first successful colony in the Carolinas, naming it Charles Town after King Charles II. The first settlers are wealthy planters (and the people they enslaved) from a British colony in Barbados.

1680

Henry Woodward, known for venturing into the wilderness to befriend Native Americans, plants the region's first rice. It later becomes South Carolina's most important crop.

1715–17

Native American tribes attack South Carolina settlers, killing hundreds, in the Yamasee War. Charles Town survives thanks mainly to an unexpected ally: the Cherokee tribe.

After the war, Atlanta was quickly rebuilt, and cotton, weaving and the textile industry dominated the economy. In 1890 the first public institution of higher learning for African Americans was established in the state: Georgia State Industrial College for Colored Youth in Savannah, now known as Savannah State University. Manufacturing and trade grew through the early 20th century, including Dixie Crystals sugar refinery in Savannah. An ever-expanding agriculture sector began developing on the back of corn, fruit and tobacco, and post-WWII industrialization boosted city economies due to widespread farmworker migration to urban areas.

Modern-day Georgia

The wildly popular novel (and film) *Gone with the Wind;* the rise of Civil Rights icon Martin Luther King Jr (Atlanta eased through the Civil Rights movement compared to its neighbors, due not only to MLK's leadership but also to its somewhat more dominant African American culture); 1960s 'Georgia on my Mind,' a four-time Grammy Award–winning love song sung by Ray Charles; the rise of Jimmy Carter from a Plains, GA, peanut farmer to the US presidency; Ted Turner's Atlanta-based 24-hour Cable News Network (CNN); the capital's world-renowned hip-hop scene; and the 1996 Summer Olympic Games all elevated Georgia to national and international prominence through the 20th century.

In *Georgia Odyssey*, native Georgian historian James C. Cobb shoots down the myth that the state was founded by prison convicts: 'When I heard anyone repeat the outrageous falsehood that Georgians are descended from thieves and murderers, it made me so mad that I wanted to shoot him or at least take his wallet.'

Atlanta's rise as a global media and business center put it squarely under the world's spotlight and amends for the past began here sooner than other parts of the Old South. Georgia removed the Confederate battle flag from its state flag in 2001, a full decade before that conversation began elsewhere. In 2017, then Atlanta mayor Kasim Reed assembled a task force to decide the fate of Confederate symbols in the city and, in the years following, a number of monuments and memorials have been removed.

Today Georgia is thriving as a business and media hub and is in danger of overexposure – it is now the number-three overall production center for film and TV in the US. In 2021, Georgia garnered a record $4 billion in direct spending on some 366 productions made in the state that year. Tourism is the leading, billion-dollar industry in Savannah today. It remains a national leader in paper-pulp processing with International Paper Corporation (formerly Union Camp), and is home to Gulfstream Aerospace Corporation, one of the world's primary manufacturers of corporate aircraft. Georgia has become a major East Coast player in tech, both as a start-up epicenter in Atlanta and as a cybersecurity and data fortress in Augusta. It is home to one of the world's busiest airports

1733

The colony of Georgia was founded at Savannah by James Oglethorpe and a band of 114 self-supporting colonists who were given 50 acres each – a town lot, a small garden and a 45-acre farm.

1733

In July, 40 Sephardi Jews from Spain and Portugal settle in Savannah, the largest such group to arrive at a colony at that time.

1739

Creek leader Tomochichi dies and is buried in Percival (eventually renamed Wright) Sq in Savannah; Oglethorpe serves as one of his pall bearers.

1740

'Little London,' as the Charleston colony is now called, has the busiest port in North America, and it enjoys an economic boom, with wealthy planters raking in profits from indigo, rice and cotton (and slave labor).

(Hartsfield-Jackson Atlanta International Airport), the world's largest airline (Delta Airlines), the world's most important golf championship (the Masters) and the world's coolest and most ecofriendly new sports stadium (Mercedes-Benz Stadium). The Peach State is howling indeed.um (Mercedes-Benz Stadium). The Peach State is howling indeed.

North Carolina

The tides of history have flowed back and forth across North Carolina. For Native Americans, the fragile coastline fringed the periphery of their world; for European colonizers, it marked the point from which they steadily pushed the original inhabitants westwards. Once it became part of the United States, North Carolina's fortunes became entwined with the plantation South, and it eventually seceded to join the Confederacy. Since then, the state has continued to identify with the South, while industrializing and entering the global economy.

The Native Presence

Nomadic peoples are thought to have first reached what's now North Carolina around 15,000 BC. They hunted the continent's original 'megafauna' – mammoths, mastodons and the like – on the coastal plains, then much larger thanks to lower sea levels.

Life became more sedentary with the arrival of agriculture and pottery, from 1500 BC onwards, while sizable settlements appeared when the Mississippian culture spread through the region around AD 800. The Cherokee trace their roots to the Mound Builder site of Etowah, in modern Georgia. Dozens of other tribes were present when Hernando de Soto's bloodthirsty Spanish raiders passed through western North Carolina in 1540. Juan Pardo's party, who followed in 1566–67, hung around longer and probably brought smallpox with them.

Colonial Beginnings

The earliest European settlements, such as Sir Walter Raleigh's famous 'Lost Colony,' were precarious, vulnerable outposts. Scattered in isolation along the marginal, ever-shifting Atlantic shore, they were only able to survive on native sufferance. Raleigh's first expedition – he never came himself – reached Roanoke Island on July 4, 1584, while his second built a fort there the following summer, only to be evacuated by Sir Francis Drake in 1586. His third built a village in 1587, but it had disappeared entirely by 1590, having failed to become self-supporting or to be resupplied from England.

Civil Rights Sights & Tours

First Ebenezer Baptist Church (Atlanta)

Martin Luther King Jr Birthplace (Atlanta)

Civil Rights Tours Atlanta

International Civil Rights Center and Museum (Greensboro)

Ralph Mark Gilbert Civil Rights Museum (Savannah)

1742
The Battle of Bloody Marsh takes place in Savannah, where Oglethorpe and a group of Scot Highlanders thwart an invasion of St Simons Island by Spanish forces.

1757
Creek tribe signs the Treaty of Savannah, which cedes reservation land north of Savannah and St Catherines, Ossabaw and Sapelo islands to Georgia.

1765–83
More than 400 battles for independence take place in the region. Significant patriot victories occur at Fort Moultrie, Kings Mountain and Cowpens.

1770
Slave code is passed in Georgia, declaring children of slaves also slaves; slaves could be whipped for traveling without permission; and anyone teaching a slave to read and write would face fines.

The colony of Carolina was created in 1663, when King Charles II of England granted a charter to eight English noblemen known as the Lords Proprietors. It was divided into North and South in 1712. Ten years later, the Crown bought out seven proprietors, but the eighth, Lord Granville, refused to relinquish his control of the so-called Granville Tract, occupying the northern half of North Carolina, and the colony remained largely untamed and lawless.

As North Carolina lacked natural harbors like Charleston and Newport, European incursions tended to come via landward migration from north or south. The understandable hostility of the native inhabitants towards the freebooting adventurers who plundered the rich coastal plains for furs and slaves prompted the Tuscarora War (1711–13) and Yamasee War (1715–17). Native American defeat, coupled with a major smallpox epidemic in 1738–39, effectively cleared the way for large-scale European settlement. Great swathes of wetlands were drained to create huge plantations, especially along the Cape Fear River, and as tobacco and rice farming expanded, so too did the importation of slaves.

When the French and Indian War broke out in 1754, tribes including the Catawba and Cherokee initially sided with the British. By now, however, thanks to the opening of the Great Wagon Road from Pennsylvania to Georgia, Scots-Irish and German Moravian migrants were moving into the 'backcountry,' and clashes with native peoples swiftly escalated. At the end of the war in 1763, George II rejected tribal claims to their historic homelands while supposedly acknowledging Native American sovereignty over the lands beyond the mountains. During the Revolutionary War, British hopes that their Southern colonies might prove loyal to the Crown were soon dashed, and several important battles were fought hereabouts, especially around Charlotte.

THE ABSENTEE LORDS

Just because the colony of Carolina was founded by a group of English aristocrats – the so-called Lords Proprietors – in 1663, that doesn't mean it was actually English aristocrats who moved here. By and large, they stayed home in Europe and banked the proceeds. Instead, the earliest English colonists arrived from the prosperous, much smaller Caribbean colony of Barbados. Many were the younger sons of plantation owners, who didn't stand to inherit land there and came to North America to set up plantations of their own. The Carolina coast being too far north to grow sugar, as in Barbados, rice became the staple crop.

1775

The naturalist William Bartram becomes the first English speaker to explore the southern Appalachia region. He vividly documents the landscapes and people he encounters along the way.

1781

North Carolina's largest Revolutionary War battle is fought at Guilford Courthouse. With his soldiers outnumbered two to one, Britain's General Cornwallis wins a Pyrrhic victory that costs him a quarter of his army.

1793

Eli Whitney invents the cotton gin at Mulberry Plantation in South Carolina.

1838–39

Having been pushed westward by encroaching settlement, and spurned by their erstwhile ally President Jackson, some 14,000 Cherokee are forcibly expelled along the Trail of Tears. More than 4000 perish.

Independence & Civil War

With independence won, the new state of North Carolina shifted its capital (previously in Edenton and New Bern) to the neutral inland town of Raleigh. A sleepy enough agricultural backwater to be nicknamed the 'Rip Van Winkle State,' its fortunes were rooted in the cotton plantations of the east. Although the mountains held a small, free black population, some of whom even had the vote until 1835, a third of the state's one million inhabitants in 1860 were slaves.

Enthusiasm for the Civil War was far from universal, and North Carolina was among the last states to secede, only doing so in May 1861, a month after the attack on Fort Sumter. In total, though, it supplied more Confederate soldiers than any other state – around 125,000, of whom 40,000 died – while around 10,000 fought for the Union. At war's end, Wilmington was the last major Confederate port to fall.

John White sailed away from Roanoke in 1587, leaving behind 115 English colonists. When he returned in 1590, he found only a single word, 'Croatoan,' carved on a tree. The most persuasive explanation for their disappearance is that they sought refuge with Native Americans living inland, and rapidly dispersed.

Reconstruction & Civil Rights

During Reconstruction, the brief promise of black political participation swiftly receded in the face of Klan violence. The era came to a definitive end in 1898, when, in what historians consider a unique coup d'etat, white supremacists overthrew the 'Fusionist' city government of Wilmington, slaughtering at least 60 black citizens. The ensuing Jim Crow era of racial segregation lasted until the 1960s, when North Carolina's main contributions to the Civil Rights campaign were the emergence of the sit-in movement in Greensboro, and the formation of the influential Student Nonviolent Coordinating Committee (SNCC) in Raleigh.

Modern-day North Carolina

Meanwhile, entrepreneurs including RJ Reynolds in Winston-Salem and Washington Duke in Durham had made tobacco the mainstay of the state's economy, and industrial-scale textile manufacturing boomed too. Further west, large-scale logging operations cut down most of the magnificent old-growth forest during the early 1900s. In their wake, the Depression-era creation of Great Smoky Mountains National Park and the Blue Ridge Parkway kick-started the growth of recreational tourism. Charlotte, by now the largest city in the Carolinas, re-identified itself as a banking center later in the 20th century, while technology and medicine brought prosperity, and a population boom, to the Raleigh-Durham area.

1839

Present-day Atlanta was founded as Terminus, the end of the line for the Western and Atlantic Railroad. It would briefly become Marthasville in 1843–45 before its crowning as Atlanta.

1840s

A small group of 800 Cherokee are allowed to stay behind on their ancestral lands. This group and their descendants later purchase land that becomes known as the Qualla Boundary.

1854

The Coastal Hurricane of 1854 floods local rice and cotton plantations, affecting the port industry and shipping in the area.

1860–65

South Carolina is the first state to secede from the Union. After the first shots are fired at Fort Sumter, the Civil War decimates a generation.

South Carolina

South Carolina is one fiery state, as its contentious and bloody history rarely fails to demonstrate. Over the last 350 years, its settlers have squared off against natural disasters, Native American residents, the British, and – when the state became the first to secede from the Union in 1860 – countrymen to the north. Race relations may have improved since the days of slavery, but poverty, inequality and discrimination have proven difficult to eradicate. Occasionally these issues still flare up, with devastating consequences.

Early History

At least 29 tribes of Native Americans have lived in what is now South Carolina, and for centuries they hunted and gathered, fished, used tools, planted crops and traded with each other. When the British first showed up relations were friendly, but by 1715 they had deteriorated and the Yamasee War broke out. Hundreds of settlers were killed, but the British prevailed largely because the Cherokee Indians became their allies against other tribes. By the mid-1700s most of the smaller Native American tribes in South Carolina had disappeared, losing their land or perishing from disease brought by colonists. In the 1800s most of the Cherokee were forcibly removed during the Trail of Tears era.

Revolutionary Era

The colony of Carolina divided into two, North and South, in 1712. The colony of Georgia was established soon after as a buffer zone between the Carolinas and the Yamassee tribe in Florida.

The English founded their first Carolina colony in 1670, with settlers (and their slaves) pouring in from the royal outpost of Barbados. The new port city was named Charles Town after Charles II, and it had a distinctly Caribbean flavor. Because the colony was controlled by faraway leaders and interests, it remained locally lawless for several decades, attracting pirates, drifters and religious refugees. Fires, earthquakes and hurricanes often imperiled the settlement, but colonists rebuilt time and again, and many got rich off rice, cotton and indigo plantations (and off the backs of slaves). When Britain attempted to collect some of these spoils via taxation, the 13 colonies declared and eventually won their independence, which Great Britain formally recognized in 1783.

Civil War

West African slaves were brought over to turn the thick coastal swamps into rice paddies, and by 1860 more than half of the state's residents were slaves. When Abraham Lincoln was elected president without any support from pro-slavery states, and the nation's moral compass began to move toward abolition, South Carolina became the first state to secede from the Union. The first shots of the Civil War

1898

In what's later misleadingly known as the Wilmington Race Riot, the city's Republican government, elected with the support of black voters, is overthrown by a white mob that kills many prominent black citizens.

1934

George Gershwin starts hanging around in Folly Beach and James Island. Inspired by Gullah culture, he writes *Porgy and Bess*, the first great American opera.

1936

Margaret Mitchell's *Gone with the Wind* is published, an American historical epic romance set in Georgia. The film version, released in 1939, would go on to win eight Academy Awards.

1940

On September 2, President Franklin Roosevelt presides over the opening ceremony of Great Smoky Mountains National Park at Newfound Gap.

were fired by the Confederates on Fort Sumter in Charleston Harbor, and after four years of battle much of the state was left in ruins. The culture and language of South Carolina's West African slaves has been well-preserved by their Gullah descendants.

Modern-day South Carolina

Through the 1900s, South Carolina had remained a relatively poor agricultural state, trading in cotton and textiles, though its coastal tourism and shipping businesses thrived. In the 1900s the city of Charleston didn't have a lot of resources, which meant that development was minimal and buildings still standing were generally left alone and unrenovated. By the 1920s people were starting to recognize the value in keeping Charleston historic – in 1947, the Historic Charleston Foundation was created to purchase historic properties and resell them to preservationists, a major reason that the city is so well-preserved today. In more recent years the Palmetto State has garnered headlines because of its politicians, from Nikki Haley, the state's first female and first Indian American governor, to Congressman Joe Wilson, who yelled 'You lie!' during a speech by President Obama to Congress. In 2015, following the shooting of nine members of a historically black church for what appeared to be racially motivated reasons, the state legislature voted to remove the Confederate flag from the grounds of the state capitol, where it had flown since 1962.

The American rebels won the battle of Fort Moultrie in 1776 thanks to South Carolina's signature tree: British cannonballs were thwarted by spongy palmetto logs.

Great Smoky Mountains National Park

The story of the Smoky Mountains began in primordial times when clashing supersized continents created a chain of mountains that are today among the oldest on the planet. Humans have also left their mark on these ancient Appalachian landscapes. Nomadic tribes were the first to the area, followed by early settlers. In the 1900s lumber companies arrived, nearly wiping out the forests. Luckily, in the 1920s a few visionary locals fought for the park's creation, which finally became a reality in 1934.

Human Settlement

Indigenous people lived in the region of the Smoky Mountains since prehistoric times, leaving behind traces of their presence that are still being discovered by archaeologists. Among the finds are 10,000-year-old hunting projectiles used along likely animal migration paths. Ceramics from these early people date back to 700 BC, with primitive agricultural sites dating as far back as 1000 years ago.

When European settlers arrived in the 17th century, they encountered the Cherokee, who lived in settlements along the river valleys. The

1944

Primus E King, an African American man from Columbus, is turned away from voting in a Democratic primary. Defying death threats, he sues the county and wins – a pivotal battle in the struggle for voting rights.

1947

The Savannah Police Department integrates following efforts of Civil Rights leader Ralph Mark Gilbert, becoming the first in the South to hire African American officers.

1955

Eight local women save the 1820s-era Davenport House from destruction, resulting in the formation of the Historic Savannah Foundation.

1960

Civil Rights icon Martin Luther King Jr becomes co-pastor (with his father) of Ebenezer Baptist Church in Atlanta. 'Sit-ins' at citywide lunch counters began soon thereafter.

Smokies lay at the center of their vast territory, and they established seasonal hunting camps, as well as trails through the mountains that connected various settlements. Cades Cove likely once housed a permanent Cherokee village, called Tsiyahi or 'Place of the Otters,' which was located along the banks of Abrams Creek. The other permanent Cherokee settlement within today's park boundaries was Oconaluftee village, set along the river near the present-day Oconaluftee Visitor Center.

Spanish explorer Hernando de Soto was probably the first European to reach the Smokies, when he arrived in the southern Appalachian mountains in 1540. De Soto, who had earned notoriety for his successful invasion of present-day Peru and plunder of Incan riches, launched an expedition from the western panhandle of Florida in hopes of discovering gold in lands to the northeast. De Soto led an expedition of 600 men on a long, wandering journey from which only half of them would return. On their march west along the southern edge of the Smoky Mountains, the Spaniards stopped to camp alongside the Oconaluftee River. There they encountered Cherokee who were collecting mulberries – a delicacy the Spanish would write of extensively during their travels through the region. Although de Soto charted many lands never visited by Europeans, he never did find gold, and he died of a fever along the banks of the Mississippi River two years after setting out.

South Carolina hosted the first game of golf played in North America, according to George C Rogers Jr in *The Carolina Lowcountry, Birthplace of American Golf, 1786.*

Perhaps owing to de Soto's failed venture, the wilderness region remained largely unexplored by Europeans for the next two centuries. Then in 1775 the American naturalist and Quaker William Bartram spent several months in southern Appalachia during his four-year journey through the southeast. He became one of the first to accurately write about the region – both about its wildlife and its native people.

Toward the end of the 18th century, the first settlers began to appear in the region. The German immigrant John Jacob Mingus and his family were among the first Europeans to set up homesteads in the Oconaluftee River Valley when they arrived in 1798 (their descendants would remain in the region, and later set up the Mingus Mill). Over the next few decades, other homesteaders put down roots in Cades Cove and the Cataloochee Valley.

Life on the Appalachian frontier was a constant struggle for survival in the wilderness. Settlers cut down trees to build log cabins and fences (as well as provide much-needed heat for the bitterly cold winters). They toiled to clear land for farming (not an easy task with boulders often buried in the soil) and built farmhouses, corncribs and smokehouses. The land had rich soil and proved ideal for growing important crops such as corn, wheat, rye, oats, flax and sorghum. In the summer, farmers would hike their sheep or cattle up to the grassy mountain balds where the animals could freely graze. Hogs

1964

Louisa Walker, the last long-term resident of the Great Smoky Mountains National Park, dies. The homestead where she and her 10 sisters and brothers grew up in the 1800s passes to the national park.

1966

Savannah's Historic District is designated a National Historic Landmark.

1973

Maynard Jackson is elected the first black mayor of Atlanta (and any major Southern city for that matter). The 2017 documentary film *Maynard* explores his legacy.

1976

Former Georgia governor and peanut farmer James Earl 'Jimmy' Carter is elected the 39th president of the United States, one of only three one-term US presidents since WWII.

were left to forage in the thick forests of oak, hickory and chestnut trees surrounding their homes. Homesteaders had to be entirely self-sufficient, although hunting, fishing and trapping supplemented their income and provided goods for bartering, bringing in the likes of coffee, sugar and salt, which the settlers couldn't produce themselves.

Aside from the daily struggles of putting food on the table, there were also the ever-present threats around them: panthers and bears prowled in the forests, and packs of wolves sometimes devastated the pioneers' small herds. Although the settlers were generally on good terms with the Cherokee, renegade bands sometimes raided settlements, carrying off livestock and other goods. By 1819, however, the Cherokee largely disappeared from the area, having been forced to cede all of their lands in the Smoky Mountains in the 1819 Treaty of Calhoun. This formally opened up more areas to settlers.

As more settlers arrived, the growing collection of farmsteads turned into tiny villages, with the addition of blacksmith shops, gristmills, churches and later schoolhouses, post offices and dry-goods stores. Communities were tightly knit. Villagers knew each other well, and made a social event out of corn husking, preparing molasses and gathering chestnuts in autumn. They also helped out in times of need. When one settler died, the men would build a coffin, dig a grave and assist with the burial, while the women helped prepare the body. Everyone helped the family of the deceased, assisting around the farm, preparing meals and taking care of the small children. The men were also recruited to help build roads in the area, some of which followed old trails first created by Native Americans.

Creation of the National Park

While huge swaths of the forest were being felled by lumber companies, more and more locals were beginning to notice the devastation left by clear-cutting. In the early 1920s a few key figures from Knoxville, TN, and Asheville, NC, began to advocate for the conservation of the Smokies.

Ann Davis was one of the first to put forth the idea of creating a national park in the Smokies. After visiting several national parks out west in 1923, she and her husband, Willis Davis, worked tirelessly to recruit allies towards the goal of creating the park. She even entered politics, and in 1924 became the first woman elected in Knox County to serve in the Tennessee State House of Representatives.

David Carpenter Chapman, the president of a Knoxville drug company, was another outspoken early booster of the park's creation, and is credited with helping to make the park a reality. With his connections in business and politics, he was able to help secure funding for the park and overcome challenges along the way. One of the biggest

Reading the Past

Trail of Tears: the Rise & Fall of the Cherokee Nation by John Ehle

The Walker Sisters: Spirited Women of the Smokies by Bonnie Trentham Myers

Our Southern Highlanders by Horace Kephart

1981

Wayne Williams is arrested for the Atlanta Child Murders, the culmination of a paralyzing two years that saw 28 black children and adults killed. Williams was convicted, although doubts about his guilt linger.

1996

Atlanta hosts the Summer Olympic Games, becoming the third US city to do so behind St Louis and Los Angeles. A terrorist bombing kills two people and injures 111 others.

2005

Hartsfield–Jackson Atlanta International Airport becomes the world's busiest by passenger traffic, a title it has more or less kept since.

2012

Atlanta BeltLine Eastside Trail opens. This multi-use path is a repurposed 22-mile rail corridor and is one of the largest, most wide-ranging urban redevelopment programs underway in the US.

obstacles was negotiating with timber companies and private property owners to sell their land to the national park. This made the creation of the national park a unique challenge that boosters of western national parks never had to face – since out west, little of the land was privately owned, it was simply a matter of declaring the park's boundaries.

Negotiations began in 1925 and were complex – given there were more than 6000 property owners involved. In 1926 President Calvin Coolidge signed legislation creating Great Smoky Mountains National Park (along with two other national parks). Once signed it was up to the park boosters to secure the funds to purchase the 150,000 acres before the Department of the Interior would assume responsibility.

Then in 1927 the legislatures of Tennessee and North Carolina proffered $2 million each. This fell short of the estimated $10 million required, so park supporters campaigned for funds and received another $1 million from private individuals, groups, and even schoolchildren who sent in spare change they had collected going door to door. The funding still wasn't enough (the price of land had, not surprisingly, risen in the interim). That's when Arno Cammerer, acting director of the National Park Service, and David Carpenter Chapman approached the American financier John D Rockefeller Jr and secured a promise of $5 million in funding, which helped bring the final pieces of the puzzle together for the park's creation.

Even with cash in hand, purchases of the small farms and miscellaneous parcels (some of which had yet to be surveyed and appraised) was a cumbersome and lengthy process. Many landowners were reluctant to leave the only home they'd ever known, and some people – such as John Oliver of the Cades Cove community – fought the park commission through the Tennessee court system. But ultimately, he and others would lose their claim to the land. Some people, especially those who were elderly or too sick to move, were granted lifetime leases.

One group of sisters remained on their 1880s-era homestead well into the second half of the 20th century. Those who stayed had to give up traditional practices, such as hunting, trapping and cutting down timber, but they were allowed to farm and graze their sheep and cattle with special permits. The park viewed this relationship as beneficial, as farmers using the historic fields as pasture prevented reforestation and maintained their scenic, open views.

In 1930 the first superintendent of the park arrived, and he formally oversaw the first transfer of land – 158,876 acres deeded to the US government. At long last the Great Smoky Mountains National Park was a reality, though it wasn't until 1934 that the park was officially established. A few years later, in 1940, President Franklin Roosevelt dedicated the national park for the 'permanent enjoyment of the people' at the newly created Rockefeller Monument at Newfound Gap.

2015

White supremacist Dylann Roof fires on a prayer service at Emanuel African Methodist Episcopal Church in Charleston, killing nine people. He is later sentenced to serve nine life sentences without parole.

2016

Wildfires spread across the north of Great Smoky Mountains National Park. The fires kill 14 people, destroy more than 10,000 acres inside the Smokies and cause $500 million in damages.

2018

Hurricane Florence makes landfall at Wrightsville Beach in one of the costliest storms to hit the Carolinas. More than 50 people die and property damages top $17 billion.

2020

A historic turnout by Black voters in Georgia helps Joe Biden win the presidency. Two months later Democrats win both senate seats for the first time in two decades.

Music

Some of the USA's most famous songs and iconic musical genre have roots in the South – and musicians from Georgia and the Carolinas have made some serious contributions. From Tin Pan Alley to modern hip-hop, here are the tuneful highlights of this influential region.

Georgia

'Georgia on my Mind,' written by Hoagy Carmichael and Stuart Gorrell in 1930 but made world-famous by soul superstar Ray Charles 30 years later, is Georgia's official state song, but it barely scratches the vinyl of the state's rich and diverse musical history. Just an old sweet song it may be, but Georgia's sonic pedigree cannot be pigeonholed – it's all at once loud, proud, soulful, jangly, brash and downright *duurrty*.

The famous American rock band Hootie & the Blowfish formed in Columbia, SC, in 1986.

Soul, R&B, Jazz & the Blues

To discuss Georgian musical history, like discussing almost anything about Georgia, the contribution of the African Diaspora cannot be understated. In many cases, African American musical notes form the foundation from which a genre-busting potpourri of sound was eventually born. Case in point: Blind Willie McTell, a Piedmont blues and ragtime legend hailing from Thomson, wrote 'Statesboro Blues' in 1928, a song that would go on to become a signature blues-rock anthem for the Allman Brothers Band in the late '60s. The song sits at number nine on *Rolling Stone* magazine's list of the '100 Greatest Guitar Songs of All Time,' and Atlanta's most famous blues club takes its name from McTell.

From the 1930s to 1960s, the songs of Savannah's own Tin Pan Alley lyricist Johnny Mercer – some 1500 in total – were unstoppable radio juggernauts for a variety of artists (Frank Sinatra, Bing Crosby, Audrey Hepburn, Louis Armstrong), including such jazz, blues and swing smashes as 'Ac-Cent-Tchu-Ate the Positive,' 'Skylark,' 'Jeepers Creepers,' 'Blues in the Night' and 'Moon River.' Mercer won four Best Original Song Oscars and is considered one of the most prolific songwriters of all time.

In the 1950s and 1960s, world-renowned musicians Ray Charles, Otis Redding, James Brown and Little Richard defined soul and R&B, elevating Georgia to stratospheric status in the world of black music (a history that would later manifest itself in Atlanta's hip-hop scene) and, with the gospel-peppered boogie-woogie blues fusion of Brown and Richard, helped lay the foundation for rock and roll. To this day there are few names in soul/R&B as gigantic as this quartet of Georgia-born icons.

James Brown, 'Godfather of Soul', was born in Barnwell, SC, in 1933, and had been living in an estate on Beech Island (also in SC) when he died in 2006.

The dominance continued from there. Gladys Knight & the Pips' 1973 smash 'Midnight Train to Georgia' is probably the second-most-famous song ever written about the Peach State; and more contemporary Atlanta acts such as Usher and TLC were radio mainstays in the '90s and '00s (the latter remains the best-selling American girl group of all time and second worldwide to Britain's Spice Girls).

BLUIZ60/SHUTTERSTOCK ©

Top Wuxtry Records (p134), Athens

Bottom Breakdancers, Woodruff Park, Atlanta (p46)

Pop, Rock & Metal

While impressive rock, pop and metal acts hail from throughout Georgia – the Black Crowes, Collective Soul and Sevendust call the Atlanta area home and folksy-duo the Indigo Girls are from Decatur – no scene has been as groundbreaking as the college and alternative rock scene of Athens.

In the early '80s, when social misfit and politically active art-school student Michael Stipe and old-school record-shop employee Peter Buck struck up a vinyl-based friendship at Wuxtry Records in Georgia's most famous university town, Athens suddenly became the first – and biggest – college music scene in the country.

Nearly simultaneously, REM – and alternative rock itself – was born on the back of Stipe's mumbly, obscure lyrics, Buck's arpeggiated guitar and bassist Mike Mills' melodic backing vocals (the whole thing a curious yet eyebrow-raising musical enigma at the time). The B-52's, a quirky, new-wave five-piece fusing surf guitar and dance elements with party-favor lyrics about rock lobsters and private Idahos, burst to life after a drunken takedown of a shared flaming volcano cocktail. Of course, REM would go on to become the voice of a generation (or two), their fate as one of the most important bands in the history of music sealed. The B-52's remain a trademark, genre-busting post-punk pop-rock staple in our heads thanks to megahits such as 'Love Shack' and 'Roam.'

But Athens, an artsy and bohemian college town home to the University of Georgia, didn't stop there. Widespread Panic, Pylon, Drive-By Truckers, Vic Chesnutt, the Elephant 6 Collective (Neutral Milk Hotel, Elf Power, Olivia Tremor Control), Of Montreal, Bubba Sparxxx and Danger Mouse were all born or bred by Athens' diverse and legendary music scene, which continues today.

Savannah Songs

Moon River *(Johnny Mercer; 1961) About an inlet in Savannah, Mercer's hometown.*

West Savannah *(Outkast; 1998) Autobiographical homage by Big Boi (Antwan André Patton), who was born in Savannah.*

Hard-hearted Hannah *(1924) Tin Pan Alley tune about a local femme fatale; performed by several popular artists over the years.*

Country Grammar *(Nelly; 2000) Turn-of-the-century rap megahit drops a line about partaking in Savannah.*

Rap & Hip-Hop

American rap and hip-hop know no bounds but as the *New York Times* put it in 2009, Atlanta is the genre's 'center of gravity.' Born in the 1980s as a logical tributary of the electro-driven bass music coming out of Miami at the time and Bronx-style hip-hop imported by artists such as MC Shy D, the Atlanta scene began to garner widespread attention with intellectual acts such as Arrested Development (whose 1992 album *Tennessee* won a Grammy Award), kid rappers Kris Kross' catchy 'Jump' (also in 1992) and pop-forward Tag Team's 'Whoomp! (There It Is)' a year later.

But it would be a more eccentric style of Southern hip-hop that would eventually position Atlanta as the nucleus of something innovative, a middle-ground alternative to East Coast and West Coast rap styles. With the rise of LaFace Records and acts such as OutKast and Goodie Mob, Dirty South hip-hop emerged as its own regional style. OutKast's soul-minded marriage of rap with jazz, funk, psychedelia and techno on smash albums such as *Southernplayalisticadillacmuzik* (1994), *Stankonia* (2000) and *Speakerboxxx/The Love Below* (2003) shook up hip-hop and opened the floodgates. Between 2002 and 2004, Southern hip-hop hogged 60% of the hip-hop singles on US charts.

Ludacris and his four number-one albums followed in the mid-to-late '00s along with offshoot Dirty South genres like crunk, snap and trap, which characterize the scene today. Hotshot Atlanta producers such as Fatboi, Shawty Redd and Zaytoven have steered hip-hop smashes from hometown brethren including Young Jeezy, Gucci Mane, TI, Soulja Boy and Migos, giving Atlanta's hip-hop scene a second coming that shows no sign of vincibility. Migos' *Culture* was the 2017 rap album of the year by nearly everyone's count, its lurching lead single 'Bad and Boujee' (featuring Lil Uzi Vert) unlike any rap song to ever top the US charts.

Country

'The Devil Went down to Georgia,' composed by the Charlie Daniels Band in 1979, is quite easily the most epic ditty ever written about Georgia. Telling the sinister tale of a hotly contested, high-stakes fiddle battle between the devil and a local prodigy named Johnny, it's a countrified uptempo bluegrass anthem the likes of which just might be the best there's ever been. Daniels, a native North Carolinian, did Georgia a solid.

Elsewhere in country music, Georgia musicians can't boast the same immeasurable music-changing brilliance of other genres, but the state does deserve some historical credit and has produced a fair share of successful country acts. North Georgia was an early adopter of old-time string-band music and Atlanta was instrumental in the emergence of the 1920s so-called hillbilly music. Big-name country acts including Alan Jackson, Trisha Yearwood and Travis Tritt were mainstream country staples throughout the '90s and '00s. Today, the genre's continued evolution from grandpa's jangly, tear-in-his-beer front-porch cowboy ballads to far poppier crossover country-pop has produced Atlanta's Zac Brown Band as well as bits and pieces of Lady Antebellum, Florida Georgia Line and Lanco, all of whom have ties to Georgia. Jason Aldean, who was onstage headlining the Route 91 Harvest music festival during the 2017 Las Vegas shooting that left 58 people dead and 581 injured, is from Macon.

The Carolinas

Rooted in centuries of Appalachian tradition, the Carolinas owe their special place in the story of American music to their role in the emergence of bluegrass, the Piedmont blues and beach music, a 1950s version of R&B. On top of that, the states have also been home to some of America's greatest names in other musical forms, ranging from jazz to soul.

The Tar Heel State has been the birthplace of an amazing roster of musicians, including jazz legends Thelonious Monk and John Coltrane; soul and funk stars including Roberta Flack, Nina Simone, Clyde McPhatter, Ben E King and George Clinton; singer-songwriter Tori Amos; and country fiddler Charlie Daniels.

Appalachian Mountain Music

For the Carolinas' earliest colonists, living in isolation at the edge of the wilderness, music provided a precious link with their homelands in the British Isles. Traditions thus persisted in the New World long after they'd evolved or even disappeared back in Europe. English and Scottish settlers sang old ballads such as 'Barbara Allen' and 'Pretty Polly,' while Irish fiddlers played familiar reels from the old country. Other styles were present too; the German Moravians who founded Salem, for example, were passionate devotees of brass bands.

African slaves, and their African American descendants, also introduced their own traditions. Under slavery, black musicians were expected to play the popular music of the day as entertainment for social and public occasions. The banjo, which can be traced back to the stringed African kora, came to prominence at this time. After the Civil War, former slaves became professional entertainers, still catering primarily to white tastes. To mix things up further, white musicians increasingly adopted this 'minstrelsy' tradition, playing the banjo and, notoriously, performing in blackface.

Buskers, Asheville (p288)

Earliest Recordings

By the end of the 19th century, Appalachian music was a mélange of countless influences, with a distinctive sound of its own. Contemporary ballads were being written in the US, often in response to news stories such as train wrecks and mining disasters, and they remain staples of the local repertoire.

Musicians and folklorists alike began to realize the need to preserve Appalachian music in its authentic form. The most important early star was Bascom Lamar Lansford, a banjo and fiddle player from Mars Hill, western North Carolina, who established what's claimed to be the first folk festival, in Asheville, in 1928. Lansford died in 1973, but the Mountain Dance & Folk Festival is still going strong as it approaches its centenary.

Listening to early recordings today, there's little to distinguish between white and black musicians. It was the divergence of their favored instruments that created what we think of as separate genres. Blues musicians opted for guitars, country musicians for fiddles and amplification in general, and bluegrass players stayed acoustic, using a wide range of instruments.

The Piedmont Blues

The Piedmont blues, which evolved in Georgia and the Carolinas from the 1920s onwards, is characterized by nimble finger-picking on the guitar, with the thumb working through the bass line while the treble strings carry the melody. It's less raw and melancholic than the blues of the Mississippi Delta, with performers drawing on older banjo tunes, ragtime, and popular novelty songs, rather than chronicling their own experiences.

During the Depression, the still-booming tobacco warehouses of Winston-Salem and Durham were rare in offering dependable support for street musicians. Among them were Blind Boy Fuller, born just outside Charlotte around 1907, who coined the phrase 'keep on truckin',' and his teacher, Reverend Gary Davis, born in South Carolina in 1896 but based in Durham from the mid-1920s onwards. Davis, who was described by one contemporary as 'the playingest man I ever saw,' found renewed popularity during the folk revival of the 1960s, as did Elizabeth Cotten from Chapel Hill.

Bluegrass

Bluegrass, which evolved during the 1940s, took its name and direction from Kentucky-born bandleader Bill Monroe and His Bluegrass Boys. What Monroe characterized as a 'high lonesome sound' swiftly became identified with the quick-fire picking of his banjo player, Earl Scruggs, who wore picks on three fingers. Born near Boiling Springs, NC, in 1924, Scruggs played on Monroe's signature 1946 hit, 'Blue Moon of Kentucky.' Leaving the band soon afterwards, with fellow member Lester Flatt, he formed the award-winning duo Flatt and Scruggs, and passed away in 2014. And although none of that happened in South Carolina, the people of the Upcountry, who were ancestors of those who brought 'mountain music' over, certainly took to it.

Trumpet virtuoso John Birks Gillespie, aka Dizzy, was born in 1917 in Cheraw, SC. There's a park in the town dedicated to him, and a jazz festival is held in his honor every October.

Folks in the Appalachians are great appreciators of the piedmont blues, a blues style defined by its distinctive guitar finger-picking and gospel, country and ragtime influences, with roots throughout the South. Guitar virtuoso Reverend Gary Davis grew up in South Carolina and learned the piedmont blues from a blind guitarist here, and then taught the style to Blind Boy Fuller, who is thought of as the most influential piedmont blues musician of all time.

Scruggs' close contemporary, guitarist Arthel 'Doc' Watson, was born near Boone in 1923. He too was renowned for his deft picking, in this case flat-picking, playing fiddle tunes on his guitar with a pick held between thumb and forefinger. While he didn't restrict himself to bluegrass, and recast himself in the singer-songwriter mold during the 1960s, his repertoire remained rooted in traditional ballads. For around 20 years, he performed with his son Merle, who died in 1985. Doc himself died in 2012, but Merle Fest, which he set up in Wilkesboro to honor Merle's memory, continues to celebrate 'traditional plus' music each year.

Beach Music & the Carolina Shag

Around 1946 in North Myrtle Beach, vacationing college students (particularly frat boys and sorority girls) started getting wild on the dance floor, doing what would come to be known as 'the shag,' which was set to an evolving style of music that we now call beach music. It was edgy at the time because the South was still segregated, and the music was produced mainly by black artists, with stark similarities to what was then called 'race music' (later dubbed 'R&B'). The music is fast, with a 'blue shuffle' 4/4 rhythmic structure and a moderate or fast tempo. Popular groups included the Tams, the Drifters, the Catalinas, the Platters and the Embers, and in the 1950s their hits were getting serious jukebox time.

The shag was of course inextricably linked with the music, and it followed a 'one-and-two, three-and-four, five-six' pattern. There was a lot of stepping around, back and forth, shifting of weight side to side and staying in step with a partner. The shag is often referred to as 'the swing dance of the South' and to this day it's still seen at some

Southern weddings and Greek formals, and on a nightly basis at Fat Harold's Beach Club (p211) in North Myrtle Beach. Jimmy Buffett cites it as a major influence.

The Modern Era

Singer-songwriter James Taylor was born in Massachusetts, but grew up in Carrboro, outside Chapel Hill. He's best remembered in North Carolina for the song 'Carolina in My Mind,' now an unofficial anthem for both the University of North Carolina and the state as a whole. Chapel Hill has remained a musical hotbed, producing bands such as Southern Culture on the Skids, Superchunk, Squirrel Nut Zippers and Ben Folds Five.

In Pat Controy's novel *Beach Music*, a father introduces his daughter to beach music and the shag to get her more in touch with her Southern roots.

Perhaps the most intriguing North Carolinian music of recent years has been created by the Carolina Chocolate Drops, whose 2010 album *Genuine Negro Jig* won the Grammy for Best Traditional Folk Album. Playing stringed instruments including mandolins, ukuleles and banjos, and drawing on old-time songs from multiple genres, they've set about reclaiming the historical role of black performers in Appalachian music. During her acclaimed solo career, the band's central figure, Greensboro-born singer Rhiannon Giddens, has performed more overtly political material, written by herself as well as others, and won multiple awards.

South Carolina's biggest musical sensation of the 20th century was no doubt Hootie & the Blowfish. Their 1994 debut album, *Cracked Rear View,* has been certified platinum 21 times. In the 2000s, the state served up a few popular indie bands, including Band of Horses and Toro y Moi.

People & Culture

By the time Georgia and the Carolinas became part of the original 13 colonies, the region was already a potpourri of personality, with Scots-Irish, Salzburgers, Italians, Sephardic Jews, Moravians and Swiss among the bunch. Toss in the existing Native American cultures (Cherokee, Creek and Guale, among others) and African cultures (including the Coastal Gullah-Geechee societies), and you have an idea of the DNA of a modern citizen of this varied region. From the coastal Outer Banks to remote Appalachian villages, you can still hear echoes of the archaic accents of old Europe. And the region's demographics are continuing to change – today, almost 10% of residents are of Hispanic origin.

Native American Roots

In 1700, Native Americans still constituted half the population of Carolina. Pitting each tribe against the next, the European colonists provoked inter-tribal conflicts from which prisoners could be sold as slaves. To prevent escape or rescue, most such captives were carried to the West Indies, and swapped at a rate of two-for-one for African slaves.

Disease, wars and failed uprisings had such a swift impact that, by 1730, only one Native American was left for every 16 incomers. Modern North Carolina still holds a significant Native American population, however. Although most of the Cherokee were forcibly expelled along the Trail of Tears during the 1830s, many retreated deep into the mountains. Their descendants now own and occupy what's known as the Qualla Boundary – not technically a reservation – out west at the foot of the Smokies. Smaller groups include the Lumbee tribe, formerly known as the Croatans, in the southeast.

Cherokee Bloodline

For more than 2000 years, indigenous groups resided in the hills of what is now South Carolina's Upcountry. In the 1700s the Cherokee Nation was particularly strong in present day Oconee County and the Great Smoky Mountains, and tribe members lived in small villages set with sturdy wooden-frame houses, hunting and fishing and growing beans, corn and squash for sustenance.

When European settlers arrived, trading with the Cherokee was vital to economic development. A central trade route called the Cherokee Path ran from present-day Clemson to Charleston, and parts of it can still be hiked today. As the 1800s approached, though, treaties with the British and then the US continually reduced the size of the Cherokee homeland, and by 1816 it ceased to exist. Some of the Nation chose to stay anyway, adapting and intermingling (culturally, politically and romantically) with Scottish and Irish immigrants.

More than 10 million people call North Carolina home, of whom just under a quarter are black and less than 2% claim Native American ancestry.

Unfortunately, European contact spelled the beginning of the end for the mighty Cherokee nation. Introduced diseases such as smallpox – to which the Cherokee had no natural immunity – left a devastating swath across the continent. One such epidemic in 1738 killed as many as half the tribe. Conflicts flared with the encroaching settlers, and bloody warfare erupted numerous times over the 18th century. After big territorial losses in the late 1700s, the Cherokee went through a period of great change – spurred in part by George Washington, who sought to 'civilize the American Indians.' The Cherokee were encouraged to give up communal farming methods and instead settle in individual farmsteads.

The Cherokee organized a democratic national government, with a chief, vice-chief and 32 council members elected by members of the tribe. They drafted a constitution, with an executive, a legislative and a judicial branch, and ratified a code of law for the newly named Cherokee Nation. Modern farming methods, formal education and Christianity all made inroads into the nation, as mission schools, cotton plantations, gristmills and blacksmithing all opened on Cherokee lands.

One of the pivotal Cherokee figures of this time was Sequoyah, a silversmith and soldier. Although he could neither read nor speak English, Sequoyah became obsessed with the 'talking leaves,' and felt that was somehow key to white settlers' power. After working assiduously for nearly a decade, he invented a writing system for the Cherokee language, which he unveiled in 1821. Consisting of 86 characters, the Cherokee Syllabary became widely adopted by the tribe within a decade. Literacy spread quickly, and five years after the appearance of the syllabary, thousands of Cherokee could read and write – far surpassing the literacy rates of the white settlers around them. Sequoyah became something of a folk hero for the Cherokee, and his achievement is astonishing: it's the only recorded instance of one person single-handedly creating a system of writing.

Today there are still 27 known village sites where the Cherokee once lived, and in 2014 the Nation got its first and only museum, the Museum of the Cherokee in South Carolina (p217). The history of Native Americans is also on display in the Oconee Heritage Center in the same town.

Late Georgia writer and humorist Lewis Grizzard made a living on self-effacing Georgia jokes – and is worth a read for some hilarious insight into what makes a Georgian tick.

Scots

The largest contingent of early European immigrants came not from England, but from Scotland. Many were prompted to leave the newly formed United Kingdom by the defeat of Scottish rebellions in 1715 and 1745. Once in the region, they tended to stick together. Almost half were descended from Scottish Protestants who had attempted to colonize northern Ireland a generation earlier, only to be driven out by Catholic hostility and economic hardship. Known as the Scots-Irish – as opposed to the Irish themselves – they settled especially in the mountainous west, where they contributed many distinctive elements to what became Appalachian culture. Similarly, the Highlanders who gathered along the Cape Fear valley clung to their identity as a distinct cultural group.

If you're looking for visible signs of North Carolina's Hibernian heritage, head for the mountains – especially the rural villages around Linville, where the Grandfather Mountain area stages its own Highland Games every July.

English

Of the 18th-century arrivals from England, most were debtors or the poor, given a chance at a new life in exchange for providing a buffer between Carolina and Spanish Florida. Some were criminals. Sentenced to transportation rather than death, they were sold – for less than half the price of an African slave – to the plantation owners. In theory, they were indentured servants, due to be freed after around 14 years. Few survived that long, and even fewer subsequently prospered. English immigrants who came by choice mostly signed up for shorter periods of servitude, and many did indeed go on to acquire land and build independent lives.

Germans

German Protestants migrated to Georgia and the Carolinas en masse, to live and worship free from the chaos and persecution of their fragmented homeland. In the 1730s, persecuted Protestants from Salzburg were lured

ENGLISH GENTRY

If you're wandering around Charleston and start to feel like you're in Europe, but also kind of like you're in the Caribbean, there are reasons for that. Many of the first Caucasian settlers on the peninsula originally hailed from England, France, Spain, Germany and Switzerland. And the British folks who arrived first came via Barbados and brought with them their cultural backgrounds and architectural proclivities.

That was in the mid-1600s, but the family names of many of those original settlers are still commonplace in Charleston today, as are the customs and values that tended to be passed down through them. Being well educated was extremely important to the city's founders, along with being polite, well traveled, musically inclined and outspoken. Today those sensibilities are still palpable in the city, and if you're lucky enough to be invited for a wine and cheese hour with a born-and-bred Charlestonian, you can expect the conversation to be erudite, spirited and political.

to Savannah with the promise of free passage and 50 acres of land. The best-known, the Moravians, came by way of Pennsylvania, after Bishop August Gottlieb Spangenberg purchased the 100,000-acre Wachovia Tract from Lord Granville – the last of the Lords Proprietors – in 1753. The first Moravian settlement, Bethabara, was swiftly followed by Bethania in 1759, and in 1766 by Salem, which, as 'Old Salem,' can still be visited in Winston-Salem.

Gullah Culture

Starting in the 16th century, African slaves were transported from the region known as the Rice Coast (Sierra Leone, Senegal, Gambia and Angola) to a landscape of remote islands that was shockingly similar – swampy coastlines and tropical vegetation, plus hot, humid summers. These new African Americans were able to retain many of their homeland traditions after the fall of slavery and well into the 20th century. The resulting culture of Gullah (known as Geechee in Georgia) has its own language, an English-based Creole with many African words and sentence structures, and many traditions, including fantastic storytelling, art, music and crafts. The Gullah culture is celebrated annually with the energetic Gullah Festival (p206) in Beaufort and the Gullah GeeChee Festival in Savannah.

St Helena Island, to the east of Beaufort, has the highest concentration of Gullah people in South Carolina, and is the best place for a traveler to obtain an education on the culture (the Penn Center p208 has a museum that's a great starting place). You'll also notice plenty of Gullah restaurants around the island, and their menus are heavy with shrimp, fish, okra, rice, tomatoes and cabbage. Basically, Gullah cuisine consists of whatever the state's early African American residents could find, catch or grow. There's also a distinctly African influence in the cooking style.

Gullah Gullah Island, a children's television series that aired on Nickelodeon in the 1990s, was filmed on South Carolina's St Helena Island and was inspired by the Gullah people.

Gullah art has stood the test of time. In Beaufort and St Helena there are several folk art galleries with many brightly colored paintings influenced by the vibrance of similar works in West Africa. Sweetgrass baskets are another mainstay; these charming, coiled baskets are prevalent in Africa and are most easily procured on the streets and in the markets of Charleston. For a seriously entertaining Gullah experience, try to catch a storytelling session in Beaufort with Aunt Pearlie Sue (http://auntpearliesue.com). As is done in Africa, Gullah stories feature animals as characters, and involve changing one's voice and using animated facial expressions to tell tales of how small animals outsmart bigger ones.

Landscape & Environment

With a (mostly) wonderful climate, a diverse array of flora and fauna and acrophile- and thalassophile-pleasing geographic hallmarks that lend themselves to a wide array of spectacular state and national parks, Georgia and the Carolinas are a diverse playground. From the mountains in the north to the stunning Atlantic coastline, there's a little something for everyone.

Geology & Geography

Within their borders, Georgia and the Carolinas harbor a nicely dispersed and diverse selection of topographic variation. In the Blue Ridge and Appalachian Mountains, waterfalls are a dime a dozen. Rivers, pine forest and abundant farmland characterize the low-lying Piedmont plateau, which stretches from Virginia to northern Alabama. Further south, swampland, marshes and tidal rivers dominate the landscape across the Coastal Plain (the 438,000-acre Okefenokee Swamp near the Florida border is the largest freshwater wetland habitat in the USA).

The Mountains

Towering over 40,000ft in height at their time of formation nearly half a billion years ago, the Appalachians were once the tallest peaks on earth. Historically significant as an obstacle to migration and exploration, the Appalachian mountain range extends all the way from Canada to northeast Alabama. Within North Carolina, it's made up of several separate chains, of which the best known are the Great Smoky Mountains and the Blue Ridge Mountains. The highest summits are in the Black Mountains, a sub-range of the Blue Ridge that, despite being just 15 miles long, holds six of the tallest peaks in the eastern US, including the mightiest of all, the 6684ft Mount Mitchell. Around 300 million years ago, the Appalachians stood as tall as the Rockies, but even then the French Broad River managed to cross the entire range. The river now traverses modern Asheville as it flows north – one of only two US rivers to do so – to join the Tennessee River. In the highlands of North Georgia, waterfalls are ubiquitous, the result of the varied ridge and valley mountain ranges that traverse the top of the state.

As you move eastwards across North Carolina, you're moving from the very old to the very young. The Appalachian mountains are truly ancient, cut through by some of the planet's oldest rivers, whereas the shoreline is forever being reborn, a dynamic process that's most apparent in the ever-shifting barrier islands.

Industrial-scale logging in western North Carolina, early in the 20th century, did much to awaken conservationists, and prompted the creation of Great Smoky Mountains National Park and the Blue Ridge Parkway, along with several state parks. Little old-growth timber now survives – the finest is in the Joyce Kilmer Memorial Forest, 40 miles west of Bryson City – but the vast forests of the western mountains once more provide a magnificent spectacle. Sadly, the trees are still under threat, with insect infestation decimating the fir and hemlock, while air pollution and acid rain, largely from coal-fired power stations in the Midwest, wreak wider devastation. On a more encouraging note, wild elk were reintroduced to the mountains in 2001.

The Piedmont

Deriving its name from the French for 'foothills,' the Piedmont parallels the eastern flank of the Appalachians from New Jersey to Alabama, and essentially consists of eroded rock washed down from the mountains. In North Carolina, the Piedmont forms the state's central region, and is home to almost all its major cities, including Charlotte, Raleigh, Durham and Winston-Salem. Sloping from elevations of around 1500ft in the west to 300ft in the east, it's generally flat enough to count as a plateau. Its eastern edge, however, is delineated by a 'fall zone,' where rivers drop abruptly from harder sedimentary rocks down to the coastal plain. For early settlers, attempting to head west by water, that was a major impediment.

After the Civil War, the Piedmont became the powerhouse of the state's economy. Tobacco production boomed around Durham and Winston-Salem in particular, while conditions proved even more suitable for cotton. Both industries developed an infrastructure to process imported as well as homegrown raw materials, and by the 1920s the Carolina Piedmont had surpassed New England to become the largest textile manufacturing district in the US. While industrialization contributed to the urban sprawl that continues today, and banking and scientific research are major elements in the regional economy, agriculture – mainly small, individual farms – still dominates the Piedmont landscape.

South of the Piedmont in Georgia, the Black Belt – characterized by its sticky, black calcareous clay soil – stretches through South Georgia all the way to Texas.

The Coastal Plain

The coastal swamps and barrier islands of Georgia and the Carolinas, like much of the Southeast, are bogged down with thousands of years of layered peat. Sand and marine sediments canvas the region, the result of the Atlantic Ocean once covering this area before the last ice age.

The coastal plain has been so repeatedly reshaped that it's often hard to specify where the sea ends and the land begins. Its most distinctive characteristic is the beach-fringed string of barrier islands and peninsulas that shield it from the open sea, the northerly 200 miles of which are known as the Outer Banks. North of Cape Lookout, the islands tend to stand 4 or 5 miles offshore, though some are as much as 30 miles out. As they're not protected by reefs, they're vulnerable to endless reconfiguration by hurricanes. Wild mustangs still roam the Outer Banks, while the Atlantic here is rich in marine species from whales to manatees, thanks to the mingling of the warm waters of the Gulf Stream and the cooler Labrador Current. Sandy Myrtle Beach kicks off the South Carolina coastline, which continues for nearly 200 miles through estuaries and barrier islands such as Sullivan Island down to Hilton Head. Georgia's coast is somewhat less traveled but no less beautiful.

After he lost his job and his wife abandoned him, Horace Kephart (1862–1931) moved to the Smokies and reinvented himself as a naturalist and writer. He authored celebrated books about the Appalachian people and its landscapes, and was a major advocate for the creation of the Great Smoky Mountains National Park.

Sea levels have fluctuated enormously over the centuries. For most of human history they've been much lower, and the broad Albemarle and Pamlico Sounds bear witness to this being a drowned shoreline. On the other hand, the Sandhills in North Carolina's southwestern corner are the remains of ancient dunes deposited when levels were significantly higher.

Much of the coastal plain is fertile farming country – the valleys and estuaries especially held huge plantations in the 18th and 19th centuries. The low-lying areas closest to the ocean, known as the Tidewater, were originally wetlands, with ill-defined waterways threading through brackish marshes. Roughly half this region has been drained for agriculture since European settlement began. Much of what survives – including a small portion of the appetizingly named Great Dismal Swamp, which once extended from Chesapeake Bay to Albemarle Sound – is now protected within the national park system, as is Cumberland Island.

Climate

While none would be considered extreme beyond the hot and humid summers, Georgia and the Carolinas welcome four distinct seasons each year due to the varied landscapes and altitudes across the Southeast. Spring and fall are pleasant indeed, with seasonal blossoms in the mountains and Atlanta – check those dogwood trees every April – and a somewhat more fleeting spring in South Georgia and South Carolina that wraps up by the end of May. Winter is distinctly mild unless you are from the equator – temps hover around the cool but manageable 50°F mark everywhere except the mountains, and there is a blanketing of snow less than two days a year on average (though extremely rare, a blizzard will turns the region into a headless chicken once a decade or so).

Temperatures range from 52°F (11°C) in January to 90°F (32°C) in July. Things are a bit cooler in the mountains and a bit hotter in the coastal plains and South Georgia. But it's the humidity that's the real beast – the muggy air always makes things feel hotter and sweatier than the mercury indicates (although coastal breezes bring some relief along the shoreline).

Georgia is prone to tornadoes, though they are rarely serious or deadly, normally clocking in no higher than F1 (moderate damage). However, downtown Atlanta was hit with a rare tornado in 2008, killing one person (and injuring 30 others), and damaging the CNN Center, the Georgia World Congress Center and Philips Arena, among others. Due to the relatively short coastline, direct hurricane strikes in this region are rare (the last was Hurricane David in 1979), though tropical storms from waning hurricanes are fairly common, bringing heavy rains and strong winds.

> Spanish moss is draped over oak trees all over the city. It's not moss (it's a bromeliad), nor is it Spanish (it's native to the Americas). But French explorers thought it looked like the beards of the Spanish, hence the name.

Climate Change

It's no secret that Charleston has a flooding problem, and in recent years, two major storms have done considerable damage to the city and surrounding islands. Over on Folly Beach, the force of Hurricane Matthew's and then Irma's winds, which hit as tropical storms, eroded the beach beyond recognition, and countless homes have been wrecked due to tidal flooding. Savannah was also affected – Irma caused major flooding on River St. Scientists are predicting that by 2100 the sea level could rise by 3ft to 6ft, while at the same time storms will be strengthening. If you're thinking this could be a very big problem for the Lowcountry and the coastal regions of North Carolina and Georgia: gold star.

Scientists can't say for sure whether climate change would make this region wetter or drier, but temperatures are expected to rise. If the predictions prove accurate, by 2070 there will be an additional 30 days a year during which temperatures climb higher than 95°F (35°C). The city area has many residents that are skeptical of climate change, but the city isn't dragging its feet. It has adopted a sea-level-rise strategy for its different types of shoreline, assuming a 2.5ft rise in the next 50 years. Stormwater-drainage tunnels are one aspect of the plan; a new seawall protecting downtown is another. Perhaps most importantly, the plan dictates that evolving projections should be closely followed, and that the strategies be altered as necessary.

The non-coastal regions aren't out of harms way, either. Statewide, the agricultural, forestry and fishing industries are highly susceptible to changes in weather patterns. A warming climate could cause a litany of problems including drought, reductions in wetlands fish and shellfish, the proliferation of invasive species and forest diebacks. All of this could in turn threaten productivity, and it certainly wouldn't be good for wildlife species.

Flora & Fauna

Like most of the Southeast, Georgia and the Carolinas are home to a wide array of gorgeous and diverse plant and animal life, from color-bursting autumns valleys and fields of wildflowers to deceptively calm swamplands hiding lurking alligators. Floral and faunal diversity is a big draw for many visitors.

Flora

Towering maple, hickory, elm and poplar trees dominate the Appalachian forest, which has 130 tree types (compared with 85 in Europe). Fraser firs and red spruce appear at higher altitudes. In the Piedmont plateau, ash, black locust, wild cherry and American elm characterize the transition zone between northern and southern varieties, the latter of which is heavy with confers, pine and cedar. Along the coast, bald cypress, black gum and sweet gum trees yield to maritime oak, cedar and holly, with salt marsh and palmetto palms abundant in subtropical latitudes. Some of Georgia's most common flowering species include southern and Fraser magnolias, azaleas, mountain laurel, dogwood, redbud, rhododendron, wax myrtle and hydrangeas. Romantic Spanish moss dangles from live oak limbs along the coast, though it's not Spanish and it's not moss – it's a flowering plant related to the pineapple known as an epiphyte and rumor has it was named such due to its resemblance to a Spaniard's beard! Last but not least there's kudzu (kud-zoo), an unstoppable vine originally imported from Japan for ornamentation and erosion control. In the South, the long growing season allows it to grow as much as a foot per day, shrouding anything and everything in its path, choking growth and killing native species. Keep an eye out for it suffocating large swaths of highway-lined forest all over the region.

On August 27, 1893, a deadly hurricane that came to be known as the Sea Islands Hurricane struck near Savannah, with the storm's surge killing an estimated 1000 to 2000 people. It brought a 16ft storm surge that caused destruction along the coasts of Georgia and South Carolina and the offshore Sea Islands, with almost all the fatalities due to drowning.

Fauna

South Georgia's Okefenokee Swamp boasts more than 200 varieties of reptiles and amphibians – and the American alligator is everywhere along the coast, as are freshwater turtles (and water moccasins, though incidents are uncommon). Migratory birds, including dozens of duck species, herons, Canada geese, pelicans and egrets, ply the Atlantic Coast, one of four flyways on the North American continent. Flounder, drum, sea bass, mackerel, whiting and spot fish (along the coast) and bass, white perch, bream, sunfish and catfish (in the freshwater lakes) dominate the waters and local menus. In the forests, the white-tailed deer is by far the most common mammal, with raccoons, opossums, rabbits, squirrels and bats sharing the landscape. Black bears are found in the mountains, the Great Smoky Mountains National Park, along the Ocmulgee River drainage system in central Georgia and in the Okefenokee Swamp. Other common sights include feral hogs (Eurasian or Russian wild boar, free-ranging domestic hogs, and all manner of hybrids) all over the state; bottle-nosed dolphins off the Atlantic Coast and otters in Okefenokee. Elk were reintroduced to the region in 2001 and can frequently be spotted in Great Smoky Mountains National Park.

DARRYL BROOKS/SHUTTERSTOCK ©

Survival Guide

Savannah Belles Ferry (p371)

Directory A–Z

Accessible Travel

Major museums and blue-chip tourism sites have wheelchair-accessible entrances; the same goes for downtown hotels and restaurants. It may be harder to find accessible establishments at smaller businesses in residential neighborhoods.

The MARTA transit system is fully wheelchair accessible, and many sidewalks downtown are well kept; the situation deteriorates, again, in smaller residential areas. Check out http://wheelchairtravel.org/atlanta-ga for more information.

Download Lonely Planet's free Accessible Travel guides from http://lptravel.to/AccessibleTravel.

Accommodations

Atlanta and Savannah have the best variety of accommodations in Georgia. While Atlanta is flush with corporate and boutique hotels, Savannah has a ton of antique homes doubling as B&Bs. You'll find resort-style accommodations in the Golden Islands, and B&Bs and chain hotels throughout the state.

From the mountains to the sea, North Carolina has lodgings to suit everybody. You can sleep in early-1800s log cabins, boutique hotels, B&Bs with Smokies and Blue Ridge views, riverside campgrounds, and even a brewery or two, along the state's neatly 600 end-to-end miles from Cherokee County in the east to Rodanthe in the Outer Banks.

Dripping in history and coastal charm, South Carolina is home to an array of both historic and ocean-view sleeps. For the former, you'll be spoiled for choice in Charleston and Beaufort; for the latter, Myrtle Beach, Hilton Head and the islands flanking Charleston offer numerous options for crawling out of bed and on to the sand. With a few exceptions, chain hotels rule upstate.

Climate

Atlanta

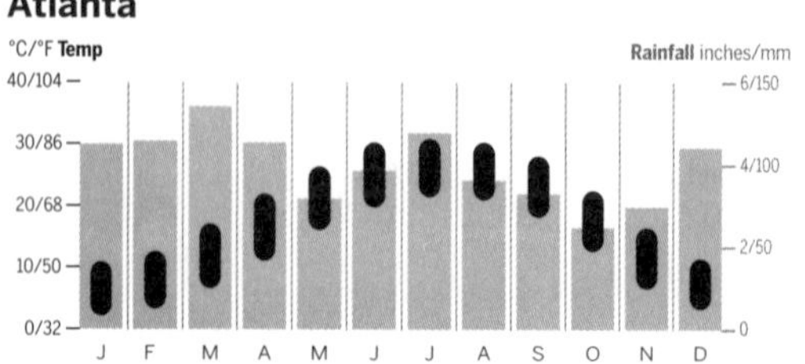

Embassies & Consulates

Embassies or consulates for Australia, Canada, France, Great Britain, Japan, Mexico and New Zealand can be found in Atlanta. Charlotte hosts consulates for France, Germany, Great Britain, Hungary and Mexico.

Electricity

Type A
120V/60Hz

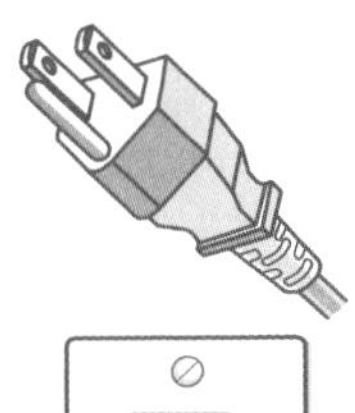

Type B
120V/60Hz

Food

The largest state in the Southeast has a deep well of homegrown dishes and immigrant recipes influencing its menus. Atlanta is one of the most exciting foodie destinations in the US, while Savannah and Athens have excellent haute Southern cuisine. Superb barbecue can be found across the state; seek out anything with peaches or pecans, two Georgia specialties.

Health

While the US offers some of the world's finest health care, it can get prohibitively expensive very quickly. Emergency rooms are required to treat all patients regardless of ability to pay, but clinics will require proof of insurance or immediate payment. It's essential to purchase health insurance if your home policy does not cover you for medical expenses abroad. Without it, the average cost for a basic visit at walk-in clinics is around $90, which is reasonable if that's all you need, but should your case be escalated with exams or hospitalization, your bill can soar into the thousands in no time. Don't take the risk.

BOOK YOUR STAY ONLINE

For more accommodations reviews by Lonely Planet authors, check out http://lonelyplanet.com/hotels/. You'll find independent reviews, as well as recommendations on the best places to stay. Best of all, you can book online.

Check the insurance section of the Lonely Planet website (lonelyplanet.com/travel-insurance) for more information. Find out in advance if your insurance plan will make payments directly to providers or reimburse you later for overseas expenses.

COVID-19

Non-US citizens are required to show proof of full vaccination from COVID-19 before entering the US. As of early 2022, all air passengers aged two or older, regardless of citizenship or vaccination status, must show a negative result of a COVID-19 viral test or documentation of recovery from COVID-19 before boarding a flight to the US.

For the most up-to-date information, see the Centers for Disease Control website (www.cdc.gov).

Insurance

Getting travel insurance to cover theft, loss and medical problems is recommended.

➡ Paying for your airline ticket or rental car with a credit card may provide limited travel accident insurance.

➡ If you already have private health insurance or a homeowner's or renter's policy, find out what those policies cover and only get supplemental insurance.

➡ If you have prepaid a large portion of your vacation, trip cancellation insurance may be a worthwhile expense.

➡ Some policies do not cover 'risky' activities such as motorcycling. Make sure the policy at least covers hospital stays and an emergency flight home.

Internet Access

Wireless internet access is readily available across much of this region. You can find networks in museums, public libraries, cafes, hotels and many restaurants and bars.

Free Public Wi-Fi

Atlanta Free wireless access in Piedmont Park.

Charleston Free wireless internet access in most city parks.

Savannah Free network 'surfsavannah' is available on River St, Bay St, Reynolds Sq, Ellis Sq, Franklin Sq, the South End of Forsyth Park and along Martin Luther King Blvd from Victory Dr to River St. Usage is limited to two hours per day.

SLEEPING PRICE RANGES

Prices are before taxes and tips for a double room in high season. In Atlanta, price ranges are $50 higher.

$ less than $150

$$ $150–250

$$$ more than $250

LGBTIQ+ Travelers

The South is a socially conservative region, but the major cities in Georgia and the Carolinas are welcoming to the LGBTIQ+ community and have vibrant cultural and nightlife scenes.

Atlanta (p83) has a noticeably active gay and lesbian population, including a massive annual Pride celebration in October. Check out the weekly *Peach ATL* (www.peachatl.com), monthly *Goliath Atlanta* (www.goliathatlanta.com) and www.gayatlanta.com.

The LGBTIQ+ community in Savannah is also quite visible. For useful information, check out Georgia's oldest LGBTIQ+ organization, **First City Network** (www.firstcitynetwork.org), which also has a dedicated **center** (www.savannahlgbtcenter.org) in Midtown. For a directory of a gay-friendly businesses, see **Gay Savannah** (www.gaysavannah.com).

The city of Charleston (p192) is very accepting of people from all different backgrounds and has a large and vibrant LGBTIQ+ community. **Beau Magazine** (https://beau-magazine.com) is a Charleston-based online resource that offers suggestions for LGBTIQ+-friendly businesses and events, and shares stories.

Money

ATMs are always within reach and credit/debit cards are accepted everywhere with very few exceptions – in fact, some places no longer accept cash.

Opening Hours

Standard hours are generally as follows.

Banks 9am–4pm Monday to Thursday, to 6pm Friday, some also 9am–noon Saturday

Bars 3pm–3am, from noon on Saturday

Businesses 9am–5pm Monday to Friday

Clubs 9pm–3am

Restaurants Breakfast 6am–11am, lunch and weekend brunch 11am to around 3pm, dinner 5pm–11pm.

Shops 10am to around 6pm weekdays, to around 8pm Saturday, 11am–6pm Sunday, if they're open at all.

Post

USPS has useful Atlanta branches at the CNN Center (190 Marietta St NW), Little Five Points (455 Moreland Ave NE) and Phoenix Station (41 Marietta St NW). In Savannah, there's a post office in the Historic District. Charleston's main post office is downtown. Find all USPS locations at www.usps.com.

Public Holidays

Major holidays and special events may mean many businesses are closed, or may attract crowds, making dining and accommodations reservations difficult.

New Year's Day January 1

Martin Luther King Jr Day Third Monday in January

Presidents' Day Third Monday in February

St Patrick's Day March 17

Easter March/April

Memorial Day Last Monday in May

Independence Day July 4

Labor Day First Monday in September

Halloween October 31

Thanksgiving Fourth Thursday in November

Christmas Day December 25

New Year's Eve December 31

Responsible Travel

➡ **Reduce your carbon footprint** Opt for trains and buses rather than planes if practical. Where possible, take public transportation and explore on foot or bicycle rather than rental car.

➡ **Reduce waste** Use a refillable water bottle rather than buying single-use plastic. Carry and use your own bag when making purchases.

➡ **Buy local** Shop at farmers markets, seek out locally owned restaurants and buy crafts straight from the source.

➡ **Avoid overtourism** Try to travel outside of peak season (generally June to August); visit major sights on weekdays rather than weekends. In state and national parks, skip the popular trails and look for quieter, less visited corners of the park.

➡ **Be kind** Southerners are generally polite to a fault. Be sure you give greetings when entering or leaving a business, and feel free to sprinkle your speech with 'ma'am' and 'sir' when talking with others.

Telephone

Phone numbers within the US consist of a three-digit area code followed by a seven-digit local number. To make an international call, dial 011 + country code +

EATING PRICE RANGES

The following price ranges refer to main course at dinner.

$ less than $15

$$ $15–25

$$$ more than $25

area code + number. When calling Canada, there is no need to use the 011.

Time

Eastern Standard Time (GMT/UTC minus five hours)

Toilets

- Public restrooms with toilets can be found in libraries, museums, malls and fast-food restaurants.
- In coffee shops and sit-down restaurants you may have to make a purchase to use the facilities.
- There are five Automatic Public Facilities (APF) around Atlanta: Atlanta City Hall, Piedmont Park, Woodruff Park, Fire Station No. 4 (309 Edgewood Ave) and Fire Station No 21 (3201 Roswell Rd). More are planned.
- There are very few public restroom facilities in Savannah. Find them at Ellis Sq, the Bryan St and Liberty St parking garages, the Visitor's Center on MLK Blvd and the River St Hospitality Center.

PASSES

Atlanta CityPASS (www.citypass.com, adult/child $76/61) gets you entry to the World of Coca-Cola, CNN Center, Georgia Aquarium, Zoo Atlanta or the Center for Civil & Human Rights and College Football Hall of Fame or Fernbank Museum of Natural History with a 37% discount. Buy online.

Savannah e-PASS (www.savannahepass.com/tourist) Mobile app that offers discounts on dining, shopping, entertainment, spas and tours with more than 300 merchants. $4.95 for three days.

Old Town Trolley Tours (www.trolleytours.com) Various hop-on, hop-off-style trolley-transport tour passes include discounted admission to many sights in Savannah. Pick from a range of themes and prices.

Tourist Information

Statewide tourism information is available through the Georgia Department of **Economic Development** (☎800-847-4842, www.exploregeorgia.org).

For information on camping and activities in state parks, contact **Georgia Department of National Resources** (☎800-864-7275, www.gastateparks.org).

Visas

Visitors from Canada, the UK, Australia, New Zealand, Japan and many EU countries don't need visas for stays shorter than 90 days. Citizens of other nations should check http://travel.state.gov.

Though most foreign visitors to the US need a visa, the Visa Waiver Program (VWP; www.dhs.gov/visa-waiver-program-requirements) allows citizens of 38 countries to enter the country for stays of 90 days or less without first obtaining a visa. Go to the website for a list of participating countries and detailed information.

US Department of State (www.travel.state.gov) Up-to-date visa and immigration information.

US Department of Homeland Security (www.dhs.gov) Clear details on requirements for travel to the US; follow the How Do I?/For Travelers/Visit the US links.

Electronic System for Travel (ESTA; https://esta.cbp.dhs.gov/esta) Visitors eligible for the VWP must apply for entry approval via ESTA. While it is recommended travelers apply at least 72 hours before travel, you may apply any time before boarding your flight and in most cases the process takes no more than half an hour.

Passports Your passport should be valid for at least another six months after you leave the US.

Volunteering

For a list of current and upcoming volunteer opportunities in Atlanta, visit Hands On Atlanta (www.handsonatlanta.org) and check its Projects Calendar. Options include mobile food distribution, community cleanups, gardening and reading to children. You'll also find volunteer opportunities through United We Serve (www.serve.gov). As with the rest of the US, Habitat for Humanity (www.atlantahabitat.org) operates in Atlanta, focusing on building affordable housing for those in need.

Spend some time giving back in Savannah by volunteering with a range of organizations. HandsOn Savannah, a service of the United Way of the Coastal Empire (www.unitedwayvolunteers.org), recruits and refers volunteers to nonprofit organizations in the area. Other options include helping with dolphin research with the **Dolphin Project** (☎912-657-3927; www.thedolphinproject.org), building and working retail for **Habitat for Humanity** (☎912-353-8122; www.habitatsavannah.com; 701 Martin Luther King Jr Blvd, ReStore; ⊙9am-5pm Tue-Sat), or helping the needy at the **Old Savannah City Mission** (☎ask for Connell Stiles 912-232-1979; www.oscm.org; 2414 Bull St; ⊙24hr). Check listings in the local newspaper, the *Savannah Morning News* (www.savannahnow.com) for more.

Transportation

GETTING THERE & AWAY

Atlanta serves as the main air hub not just for Georgia, but arguably, the entire South – **Hartsfield-Jackson International Airport** (ATL, Atlanta; ☎800-897-1910; www.atl.com) is the busiest airport in the world in overall passenger traffic. Amtrak train and Greyhound services connect major cities.

Air

Beyond the Atlanta airport, North Carolina's main gateways include **Charlotte Douglas International Airport** (CLT; ☎704-359-4013; www.cltairport.com; 5501 Josh Birmingham Pkwy) and **Raleigh-Durham International Airport** (RDU; ☎919-840-2123; www.rdu.com; 1000 Trade Dr, Morrisville). Smaller regional airports serve Asheville, Wilmington and, to a lesser extent, the southern Outer Banks and Crystal Coast.

South Carolina's three main gateways are **Charleston International Airport** (Map p196; ☎843-767-7009; www.chs-airport.com; 5500 International Blvd), **Greenville–Spartanburg International Airport** (☎864-877-7426; www.gspairport.com; 2000 GSP Dr, Greer) and **Myrtle Beach International Airport** (☎843-448-1580; www.flymyrtlebeach.com; 1100 Jetport Rd). Regional hubs include **Columbia Metropolitan Airport** (☎803-822-5000; www.columbiaairport.com; 3250 Airport Blvd) and **Savannah/Hilton Head International Airport** (☎912-964-0514; www.savannahairport.com; 400 Airways Ave), which is actually located in Georgia but is the major airport for the Hilton Head region.

DEPARTURE TAX

Departure tax is included in the price of a ticket.

Land

Major interstates connect Georgia and the Carolinas to the rest of the country, and there's bus service to most cities and towns via Greyhound. Amtrak provides train service to the region's major cities.

Bus

Greyhound (Map p98; ☎912-232-2135; www.greyhound.com; 610 W Oglethorpe Ave) provides bus service to Georgia and the Carolinas from hundreds of cities and towns. It's an affordable way of getting there, but also the most time-consuming.

CLIMATE CHANGE & TRAVEL

Every form of transportation that relies on carbon-based fuel generates CO2, the main cause of human-induced climate change. Modern travel is dependent on airplanes, which might use less fuel per kilometer per person than most cars but travel much greater distances. The altitude at which aircraft emit gases (including CO2) and particles also contributes to their climate change impact. Many websites offer 'carbon calculators' that allow people to estimate the carbon emissions generated by their journey and, for those who wish to do so, to offset the impact of the greenhouse gases emitted with contributions to portfolios of climate-friendly initiatives throughout the world. Lonely Planet offsets the carbon footprint of all staff and author travel.

MegaBus (www.us.megabus.com) has faster travel times but fewer stops. From Washington, DC, you can travel to Atlanta, Athens, Charlotte, Columbia, Durham or Fayetteville. Houston and Philadelphia also offer routes to Atlanta.

Car & Motorcycle

Major interstates including I-20, I-24, I-40, I-75, I-77, I-85 and I-95 will get you where you're going the fastest. Smaller state highways are typically more scenic.

Train

Atlanta's main **Amtrak** (www.amtrak.com/stations/atl; 1688 Peachtree St NW) station is just north of downtown. Trains depart from here to the Northeast Corridor and southern cities such as Birmingham and New Orleans.

Savannah's **Amtrak** (www.amtrak.com; 2611 Seaboard Coastline Dr) station is just a few miles west of the Historic District; trains run to Charleston, Jacksonville, and from there to points beyond.

Charleston's **Amtrak** (www.amtrak.com; 4565 Gaynor St) station is located in the north of the city.

Sea

Despite the miles of Atlantic Coast shoreline in Georgia and the Carolinas, boats and ferries are not a viable form of transportation to this region.

GETTING AROUND

Air

Other than flights to/from Atlanta, air travel between destinations in Georgia and the Carolinas is typically too expensive to be worthwhile (driving distances are short). Flights between regional airports are typically routed through Atlanta, adding additional travel time.

INTERSTATE INFO

The US Interstate Highway System as we know it today got underway in 1956 thanks to a federal act passed under President Eisenhower, and was built out over the next 30 years.

- North–south interstates were given odd numbers (I-65, I-75); east–west interstates are known by even numbers (I-20, I-24).
- Mile markers measure the distance between state borders and mark exits. They count up going north and east, and down if you are going south or west.
- Likewise, the interstates themselves are numbered from south to north and west to east.

Bicycle

The flat coastal regions in Georgia and the Carolinas are ideal for bicycling, and bike-shares are available in most major cities. That said, transportation by bicycle is not as common in the US; it's best to assume that drivers won't see you. Helmets are suggested but not required for adults.

Boat

Charleston Water Taxi (Map p174; ☎843-330-2989; www.charlestonwatertaxi.com; 10 Wharfside St; day pass adult/child $12/10; ⏰9am-8pm mid-Mar–mid-Nov, 10am-6pm Sat rest of the year) offers ferry service around Charleston Harbor, with stops at the aquarium, Patriot's Point in Mt Pleasant, the Charleston Harbor Marina (also in Mt Pleasant) and Waterfront Park. You can buy tickets online or on the boat.

There's also an app sort of like Uber, but for boats, called **HOBA** (www.hobarides.com). We're told it's a great way to get out on the water.

The free **Savannah Belles Ferry** (www.catchacat.org), designed in an old riverboat ferry style, connects downtown with Hutchinson Island across the Savannah River.

It has the following stops:

- River St at City Hall
- Waving Girl Landing at the Savannah Marriott Riverfront Hotel
- Hutchinson Island at the Savannah International Trade & Convention Center, near the Westin Savannah Harbor Resort & Spa

Bus

In Savannah, Chatham Area Transit (www.catchacat.org) operates local buses that run on bio-diesel, including a free shuttle (the dot) that makes its way around the Historic District and stops within a couple of blocks of nearly every major site.

The **MARTA** (Metro Atlanta Rapid Transit Authorit; www.itsmarta.com; single ride $2.50, 1-/3-/7-day pass $9/16/23.75; ⏰4:45am-1am Mon-Fri, 6am-1am Sat & Sun) (Metropolitan Atlanta Rapid Transit Authority) runs Atlanta's city bus system in Fulton, DeKalb and Clayton counties. You'll need to buy a reloadable silver Breeze Card ($2, valid three years) to ride. Download **MARTA On the Go** (www.itsmarta.com/marta-on-the-go.aspx) for schedules and real-time bus locations.

In Charleston, **CARTA** (☎843-724-7420; www.ridecarta.com) runs citywide buses; the one-way cash fare is $2. **DASH Trolley** (☎843-202-4410; www.charlestoncvb.com/blog/know-dash; ⊙times & schedules vary) has free streetcars that do three loop routes from the visitor center.

Car & Motorcycle

Your own wheels are the most convenient way to get around Georgia and the Carolinas.

Driver's Licenses

Georgia and the Carolinas recognize foreign drivers' licenses and do not require an International Driving Permit (IDP). However, an IDP, obtained in your home country, is recommended if your country of origin is a non-English-speaking one.

Some car-rental agencies require an IDP, so be sure to ask in advance.

Insurance

Liability insurance covers people and property that you might hit. For damage to the rental vehicle, a collision damage waiver is available for about $20 per day. Collision coverage on your vehicle at home may also cover damage to rental cars – check your policy before leaving home.

Some credit cards offer reimbursement coverage for collision damage if you rent the car with that credit card.

Most rental companies stipulate that damage a car sustains while driven on unpaved roads is not covered by the insurance they offer. Check with the agent when you make your reservation.

Parking

Parking is typically free or inexpensive in small towns and rural areas – many attractions will have private free lots for visitors. In cities like Atlanta, Savannah and Charleston though, parking can be more difficult to find and as much as $25 per day.

RULES OF THE ROAD

Throughout the US, cars drive on the right side of the road. Apart from that, road rules differ slightly from state to state, but all require the use of safety belts as well as the proper use of child safety seats for children under the age of five.

Speed limits vary. The maximum interstate speed limit in Georgia and the Carolinas is 70mph, although interstate speeds can drop to 55mph in urban areas. On two-lane highways, the speed limit is 55mph unless otherwise posted; on mountain roads it's 45mph unless otherwise posted. If you are pulled over by the police, do not get out of your car. Collect your license and other documents and wait for the officer to come to you.

Pay attention to livestock- or deer-crossing signs – tangle with a deer, cow or elk and you'll total your car in addition to killing the critter. You can incur stiff fines, jail time and other penalties if caught driving under the influence of alcohol.

Hitchhiking

Hitchhiking is not common or recommended in Georgia and the Carolinas.

Local Transportation

Atlanta is well served by the MARTA bus and rail system and a Downtown tram, but other cities in this region have very limited public transportation options.

Train

Amtrak connects major metro areas (Charlotte, Atlanta, Raleigh, Savannah and Charleston) and a few smaller towns.

Behind the Scenes

SEND US YOUR FEEDBACK

We love to hear from travelers – your comments keep us on our toes and help make our books better. Our well-traveled team reads every word on what you loved or loathed about this book. Although we cannot reply individually to your submissions, we always guarantee that your feedback goes straight to the appropriate authors, in time for the next edition. Each person who sends us information is thanked in the next edition.

Visit **lonelyplanet.com/contact** to submit your updates and suggestions or to ask for help. Our award-winning website also features inspirational travel stories and news.

Note: We may edit, reproduce and incorporate your comments in Lonely Planet products such as guidebooks, websites and digital products, so let us know if you are happy to have your name acknowledged. For a copy of our privacy policy visit **lonelyplanet.com/legal**.

WRITER THANKS

Amy C Balfour

Thank you to Tennessee locals Melissa Peeler and Lauren Batte for joining me on this adventure for a few days and sharing their expertise. Thanks also to Katie Lane, Teddy Colocotronis, Scooter Colocotronis, Stephanie Baker Jones, Chad Graddy, Jim Hester, Deborah Stacy Gebhardt, Jimmy Surface, Marjorie Joyce, Buck the Cataloochee camp host, the Cades Cove campfire and moonshine crew, and Lane and Beth Lastinger – Pilot Cove hosts extraordinaire. Many, many thanks to co-writer Regis St Louis and Destination Editor Trisha Ping.

Jade Bremner

Thanks to knowledgeable Destination Editor Trisha Ping for all her wisdom on the Southern States. Plus, the hardworking Georgia and North Carolina barbecue chefs for cooking all that mind-blowingly good smoky meat and sauce that fueled my entire trip around the South. Thanks to North Carolina locals Norm and Skye for their top tips and local advice. Last, but definitely not least, thanks to everyone working hard behind the scenes – Cheree Broughton, Dianne and Jane, Helen Elfer and Neill Coen.

Ashley Harrell

Thanks to Erin Morris for welcoming me to your state; Kourtnay King and Paul Haynes for taking me in and enabling me; Chandler Routman for getting me out of the house; Jason, Elizabeth, Iris and Loulou Ryan for being a great family; Patty Pascal for your unbridled enthusiasm; Halsey Perrin, Kim Jamieson and Ruta Fox for your help and expertise; and Chris Dorsel for still being amazing.

MaSovaida Morgan

Thank you to the lovely souls in Savannah and beyond who provided tips, guidance and feedback for this project. In particular, many thanks to Chad Faries and Emily Jones, Robert Firth, and Trisha Ping for bringing me on. Special thanks and love to Ny, Ty and Haj.

Kevin Raub

Thanks to my wife, Adriana Schmidt Raub, Trisha Ping and my fellow Georgian in crime, MaSovaida Morgan, and Jade Bremner. On the road, Jason and Jennifer Hatfield, David and Aynsley Corbett, Jeff Fenn, Sharon Crenshaw, Jerry Brown, Tobie Chandler, Teka Earnhardt, Jode Mull, David Junker, Travis Currie, Hannah Amick, Mary Reynolds, Jenny Odom, Mary Reynolds, Sarah Horten and Keaton Thurmond.

Regis St Louis

Many thanks to Trisha Ping for inviting me on board, and to Amy Balfour for sharing tips. I'm grateful for the insight shared by the many park rangers, backpackers and Appalachian Trail hikers I met along the way. Special thanks to my wife Cassandra and our daughters Magdalena and Genevieve, who joined me for frosty nights of camping and some magnificent hikes throughout the park.

Greg Ward

Thanks to the many wonderful people who helped me on the road, especially at Historic Stagville Plantation, Price's Chicken Coop, Bryson City Bicycles and the Orange County Visitor Center. Thanks too to my editor Trisha Ping for giving me this opportunity, and to my dear wife Sam for everything else.

ACKNOWLEDGEMENTS

Climate map data adapted from Peel MC, Finlayson BL & McMahon TA (2007) 'Updated World Map of the Köppen-Geiger Climate Classification', *Hydrology and Earth System Sciences*, 11, 1633–44.

Cover photograph: Macon, Georgia; historic downtown skyline at dusk, Sean Pavone/ Shutterstock©

THIS BOOK

This 3rd edition of Lonely Planet's *Georgia & the Carolinas* guidebook was researched and written by Amy C Balfour, Jade Bremner, Ashley Harrell, MaSovaida Morgan, Kevin Raub, Regis St Louis and Greg Ward. The previous edition was curated by Trisha Ping and Amy C Balfour, and researched and written by Amy C Balfour, Jade Bremner, Ashley Harrell, MaSovaida Morgan, Kevin Raub, Regis St Louis and Greg Ward.

This guidebook was produced by the following:

Destination Editor
Trisha Ping

Senior Product Editors
Grace Dobell, Vicky Smith

Product Editors
Kate Mathews, Rachel Rawling, Claire Rourke

Senior Cartographer
Alison Lyall

Book Designer
Fergal Condon, Mazzy Prinsep

Assisting Editors
James Bainbridge, Nigel Chin, Andrea Dobbin, Bruce Evans, Clare Healy, Alison Killilea, Helen Koehne, Kellie Langdon, Lou McGregor, Charlotte Orr, Gabrielle Stefanos

Assisting Cartographers
Anita Banh, Hunor Csutoros, Corey Hutchison, Julie Sheridan, Diana Von Holdt

Cover Researcher
Kat Marsh, Naomi Parker

Thanks to
Imogen Bannister, Piotr Czajkowski, Shona Gray, Clare Healy, Kate James, Alicia Johnson, Sonia Kapoor, Sandie Kestell, Chris Lee-Ack, Liam McGrellis, Martine Power, Kirsten Rawlings, Kathryn Rowan, Wibowo Rusli, Amanda Williamson

Index

Map Pages **000**
Photo Pages **000**

Map Pages **000**
Photo Pages **000**

N

O

P

Map Pages **000**
Photo Pages **000**

Map Legend

Sights

- Beach
- Bird Sanctuary
- Buddhist
- Castle/Palace
- Christian
- Confucian
- Hindu
- Islamic
- Jain
- Jewish
- Monument
- Museum/Gallery/Historic Building
- Ruin
- Shinto
- Sikh
- Taoist
- Winery/Vineyard
- Zoo/Wildlife Sanctuary
- Other Sight

Activities, Courses & Tours

- Bodysurfing
- Diving
- Canoeing/Kayaking
- Course/Tour
- Sento Hot Baths/Onsen
- Skiing
- Snorkeling
- Surfing
- Swimming/Pool
- Walking
- Windsurfing
- Other Activity

Sleeping

- Sleeping
- Camping
- Hut/Shelter

Eating

- Eating

Drinking & Nightlife

- Drinking & Nightlife
- Cafe

Entertainment

- Entertainment

Shopping

- Shopping

Information

- Bank
- Embassy/Consulate
- Hospital/Medical
- Internet
- Police
- Post Office
- Telephone
- Toilet
- Tourist Information
- Other Information

Geographic

- Beach
- Gate
- Hut/Shelter
- Lighthouse
- Lookout
- Mountain/Volcano
- Oasis
- Park
- Pass
- Picnic Area
- Waterfall

Population

- Capital (National)
- Capital (State/Province)
- City/Large Town
- Town/Village

Transport

- Airport
- BART station
- Border crossing
- Boston T station
- Bus
- Cable car/Funicular
- Cycling
- Ferry
- Metro/Muni station
- Monorail
- Parking
- Petrol station
- Subway/SkyTrain station
- Taxi
- Train station/Railway
- Tram
- Underground station
- Other Transport

Routes

- Tollway
- Freeway
- Primary
- Secondary
- Tertiary
- Lane
- Unsealed road
- Road under construction
- Plaza/Mall
- Steps
- Tunnel
- Pedestrian overpass
- Walking Tour
- Walking Tour detour
- Path/Walking Trail

Boundaries

- International
- State/Province
- Disputed
- Regional/Suburb
- Marine Park
- Cliff
- Wall

Hydrography

- River, Creek
- Intermittent River
- Canal
- Water
- Dry/Salt/Intermittent Lake
- Reef

Areas

- Airport/Runway
- Beach/Desert
- Cemetery (Christian)
- Cemetery (Other)
- Glacier
- Mudflat
- Park/Forest
- Sight (Building)
- Sportsground
- Swamp/Mangrove

Note: Not all symbols displayed above appear on the maps in this book

Kevin Raub

Atlanta; North Georgia; Augusta & South Georgia Atlanta native Kevin Raub started his career as a music journalist in New York, working for *Men's Journal* and *Rolling Stone* magazines. He ditched the rock 'n' roll lifestyle for travel writing and has written nearly 50 Lonely Planet guides, focused mainly on Brazil, Chile, Colombia, USA, India, the Caribbean and Portugal. Along the way, the self-confessed hophead is in constant search of wildly high IBUs in local beers. Follow him on Twitter and Instagram (@RaubOnTheRoad).

Regis St Louis

Great Smoky Mountains National Park Regis grew up in a small town in the American Midwest and he developed an early fascination with foreign dialects and world cultures. He spent his formative years learning Russian and a handful of Romance languages, which served him well on journeys across much of the globe. Regis has contributed to more than 50 Lonely Planet titles, covering destinations across six continents, from the mountains of Kamchatka to remote island villages in Melanesia. When not on the road he lives in New Orleans.

Greg Ward

Coastal North Carolina; North Carolina Mountains Since whetting his appetite for travel by following the hippie trail to India, and later living in northern Spain, Greg Ward has written guides to destinations all over the world. As well as covering the USA from the Southwest to Hawaii, he has ranged on recent assignments from Corsica to the Cotswolds, and Japan to Corfu. See his website, www.gregward.info, for his favorite photos and memories.

OUR STORY

A beat-up old car, a few dollars in the pocket and a sense of adventure. In 1972 that's all Tony and Maureen Wheeler needed for the trip of a lifetime – across Europe and Asia overland to Australia. It took several months, and at the end – broke but inspired – they sat at their kitchen table writing and stapling together their first travel guide, *Across Asia on the Cheap*. Within a week they'd sold 1500 copies. Lonely Planet was born.

Today, Lonely Planet has offices in the US, Ireland and China, with a network of over 2000 contributors in every corner of the globe. We share Tony's belief that 'a great guidebook should do three things: inform, educate and amuse'.

OUR WRITERS

Amy C Balfour

Great Smoky Mountains National Park Amy practiced law in Virginia before moving to Los Angeles to try to break in as a screenwriter. After a stint as a writer's assistant on *Law & Order*, she jumped into freelance writing, focusing on travel, food and the outdoors. She has hiked, biked and paddled across the United States and authored or coauthored numerous titles for Lonely Planet. She has also written for *Backpacker, Every Day with Rachael Ray, Lonely Planet Magazine, Redbook, Vegetarian Times* and *Women's Health*.

Jade Bremner

Augusta & South Georgia; Coastal North Carolina Jade has been a journalist for more than a decade. Wherever she goes she finds action sports to try, and it's no coincidence many of her favorite places have some of the best waves in the world. Jade has edited travel magazines and sections for *Time Out* and *Radio Times* and has contributed to *The Times*, CNN and *The Independent*. She feels privileged to share tales from this wonderful planet we call home and is always looking for the next adventure.

Ashley Harrell

Charleston & South Carolina After a brief stint selling day spa coupons door-to-door in South Florida, Ashley decided she'd rather be a writer. She went to journalism grad school, convinced a newspaper to hire her, and starting covering wildlife, crime and tourism, sometimes all in the same story. Fueling her zest for storytelling and the unknown, she traveled widely and moved often, from a tiny NYC apartment to a vast California ranch to a jungle cabin in Costa Rica, where she started writing for Lonely Planet.

MaSovaida Morgan

Savannah & Coastal Georgia MaSovaida is a Lonely Planet writer and multimedia storyteller whose wanderlust has taken her to more than 35 countries across six continents. Prior to freelancing, she was Lonely Planet's Destination Editor for South America for four years and worked as an editor for newspapers and NGOs in the Middle East and United Kingdom. Follow her on Instagram @MaSovaida.

Published by Lonely Planet Global Limited
CRN 554153
3rd edition – Jul 2022
ISBN 978 1 78868 092 9

10 9 8 7 6 5 4 3 2 1
Printed in China